John Steinbeck

Books by Jay Parini

Singing in Time (*poetry*)
Theodore Roethke: An American Romantic (*criticism*)
The Love Run (*novel*)
Anthracite Country (*poetry*)
The Patch Boys (*novel*)
An Invitation to Poetry (*textbook*)
Town Life (*poetry*)
The Last Station (*novel*)
Bay of Arrows (*novel*)

JAY PARINI

John Steinbeck
A Biography

HEINEMANN : LONDON

First published 1994
by William Heinemann Ltd
an imprint of Reed Consumer Books Ltd
Michelin House, 81 Fulham Road, London sw3 6rb
and Auckland, Melbourne, Singapore and Toronto

A CIP catalogue record for this book
is available at the British Library
ISBN 0 434 57492 9   Ma l001

Typeset by Deltatype Ltd, Ellesmere Port, Cheshire
Printed and bound
by Clays Ltd, St Ives PLC

For Leo and Verna Parini,
all my love

Contents

Illustrations

x John Steinbeck

Prologue

John Steinbeck was the last of that generation of American writers which included F. Scott Fitzgerald, Gertrude Stein, Ernest Hemingway and William Faulkner. When he died, in 1968, having won the Nobel Prize for Literature only a few years before, his fame was worldwide, though the future of his reputation as a novelist was by no means certain. A number of influential critics felt that his writing had declined since the publication of *The Grapes of Wrath*, in 1939, and they banished Steinbeck to the swollen ranks of the second-rate and half-forgotten. Blissfully unaware of these critics, readers from Cairo to Beijing continued to seek out his books in translation, while legions of American and British adolescents cut their literary teeth on books like *Of Mice and Men*, *The Pearl*, and *The Red Pony*. In the United States alone, some fifty thousand copies of *The Grapes of Wrath* are sold each year, while fresh adaptations of Steinbeck's more popular works frequently grace the stage and screen.

A biographer may, of course, approach a life and literary career from many different angles. What interests me is how this particular writer sustained the imaginative energy to create a shelf of books still worth reading several decades after his death. As the reader of this book will see, Steinbeck was a writer to the bone, possibly to the detriment of his development as, say, a father or husband. From his early days at Stanford University to the end of his life, he devoted himself to his craft with that burning fire which seems to be a critical feature of all substantial creative artists. Supported for more than a decade by his loving, if remote and disapproving, parents, Steinbeck focused on his books without having otherwise to earn a living (although he did take a succession of 'lowly' jobs that added a great deal to his experience of the world). Like so many middle-class American sons, he enjoyed a prolonged and productive adolescence made possible by his parents' income and good will.

The only son of John Ernst and Olive Steinbeck, he was both idealized and pampered by his three sisters and his puritanical, ambitious mother. His father, a failed businessman turned low-level public servant, withdrew from his son at an early age: a quiet act of sabotage that left Steinbeck emotionally stunted, unable to connect in later life to his own sons and tremendously shy with all but his closest friends. His complex, unhappy feelings about his father were never properly resolved. He also bore a resentment towards his mother, who often ridiculed his father in front of him, much to her son's chagrin. While instances of aggressive behaviour towards women (perhaps related to his relationship with his mother) rise to the surface here and there in his later life, Steinbeck overcame these impulses to a large degree. His third marriage, to Elaine Scott, was profoundly satisfying to him, and he sustained long and intimate friendships with several women, such as his lifelong agent, Elizabeth Otis, to whom he wrote some of his most revealing letters.

Having grown up with three sisters and a strong mother, Steinbeck was used to being taken care of by women, and he managed to re-create his childhood situation again and again. He also liked being a 'wild boy' in the vein of Huck Finn, and inevitably found some Tom Sawyerish friend to share his adventures. A succession of close male companions are part of the developing pattern of his life, and Steinbeck was adept at forming such connections. In particular, Steinbeck formed a remarkably productive friendship with Edward F. Ricketts, a feisty and brilliant marine biologist whom he met in Monterey in 1930. The story of this friendship, and Ricketts's influence on Steinbeck's fiction, is a crucial aspect of this study.

Steinbeck was a vivid correspondent, and I have drawn heavily on his copious letters (published and unpublished) to friends and relatives, attempting where possible to tell Steinbeck's story in his own grainy voice. I have also been blessed by the help of Elaine Steinbeck, the author's widow and literary executor, who was in touch with me throughout the writing of this book. Her affection for Steinbeck was for me a source of inspiration and awe. Mrs Steinbeck was also kind enough to put me in touch with dozens of people who knew and loved her husband and could explain aspects of his life and work in ways that deeply enriched my own views. These people are acknowledged in the Notes which appear at the end of the book, but among those who helped most were Steinbeck's second eldest sister, Beth Ainsworth, Burgess Meredith, Edward Albee, Terrence McNally, Robert Wallsten, Marjorie Benchley, John Fearnley, Tom Guinzburg, Gore Vidal, Allen Simmons, Elia Kazan, Judson Gregory, Elizabeth and James Wiltshire.

In rethinking Steinbeck, it has become clear to me that there is little point in ranking his publications, giving pride of place to work written in one decade over another. Nevertheless, one of my pleasures in research has been the opportunity to discover hidden treasures in Steinbeck's vast literary output, which includes not only novels but short stories, plays, screenplays, essays and reportage. Nearly everyone with an interest in American literature has read *The Grapes of Wrath*, *Tortilla Flat*, *Of Mice and Men*, and *East of Eden*, but Steinbeck's other work has long deserved closer attention. *In Dubious Battle* is by any reckoning a dazzling account of a Californian agricultural strike in the midst of the Depression. *Cannery Row* and *Sweet Thursday* – his post-*Tortilla Flat* portraits of Monterey – retain a small audience of

Steinbeck fans, but they warrant close rereading, as do several of his books which have virtually disappeared from public view. Chief among these are *The Pastures of Heaven*, a deeply affecting portrait of life in a bucolic farm community in the Salinas Valley during the early decades of this century; *The Long Valley*, a volume of remarkable stories set mainly in the Salinas region; and *The Log from the 'Sea of Cortez'*, his day-by-day account of a voyage in search of biological specimens which Steinbeck took with Ed Ricketts in 1940. Certain of Steinbeck's later novels, such as *The Wayward Bus* and *The Winter of Our Discontent*, have also been underestimated, even misread, by the critical establishment.

Steinbeck's dramatic writing and non-fiction have usually been ignored, although for decades he worked on the fringes of Broadway and Hollywood. While most of this writing does not compare with his major fiction, one must still account for the brilliance of *Viva Zapata!* (the Academy Award-winning film directed by Elia Kazan) and the nervous originality of a play like *Burning Bright*, one of his most idiosyncratically powerful works. His memorable non-fiction includes reports from the front during World War II, his periodical journalism for such magazines as *Saturday Evening Post* and *Collier's*, and a fair amount of travel writing: a vein that culminates in *Travels with Charley*, one of his most enduring books. Like many notable writers, Steinbeck was not bound by genre; he moved freely among various forms of writing. An argument could even be made that his finest writing occurs in his letters, which in 1975 were collected and edited by Elaine Steinbeck and Robert Wallsten in *Steinbeck: A Life in Letters*.

An interest in science sets him apart from other novelists of his generation. His fiction is rooted in a profound physical sense of the world, and he was attentive to its minutest operations. Under the influence of Ed Ricketts, he spent a great deal of time reading about and discussing scientific subjects and doing field research along the Monterey coastline.[1] He believed passionately that humankind had to fit within the larger community of living things, conscious of its 'organismal' place in the scheme of creation. Like Ricketts, he was careful not to assume that man was the measure of all things. On the other hand, he well understood the need to make a distinction between 'man' and other creatures, an aspect of his worldview which owed much to the traditions of humanism to which he was heir.

Steinbeck's work anticipates many current developments in thinking about the natural world, including bio-regionalism and the ecology movement. He was in some ways a founding father of modern ecological thinking, viewing all parts of nature as a united whole and recognizing that the existence of any single part is intricately dependent upon all other parts. He did not want to study man outside his natural setting, understanding that even the smallest of human interactions are, on some level, governed by the individual's place within his or her physical context. The underlying drive in all of Steinbeck's fiction (and much of the non-fiction) was to locate patterns, or *gestalten*, within apparently random circumstances.

He paid lip-service to what Ed Ricketts called 'non-teleological thinking' (i.e., thinking not directed towards some preordained goal or *telos*), but retained to an extent the old-fashioned religious idea that the universe had been created by a higher intelligence to some end or purpose. Indeed, Ricketts himself seems not to have understood very well the theological roots of his non-teleological thinking and admitted as much in an unpublished essay.[2] Ricketts wanted more than anything to get away from the heavy moralizing tendencies that afflicted even scientific research at the time, and (like Steinbeck) struggled to win the freedom to treat the universe as a phenomenon detached from universal purpose. While Ricketts preferred to concentrate on the marine life of the Pacific, avoiding large generalizations or philosophical speculation, Steinbeck found this detachment from a sense of *telos* exhilarating.

His fiction was energized by it, as in *The Grapes of Wrath*, where he sees the migrant wanderers as insects driven by huge external forces and adapting vigorously to the changing demands of their environment:

> The cars of the migrant people crawled out of the side roads on to the great cross-country highway, and they took the migrant way to the West. In the daylight they scuttled like bugs to the westward; and as the dark caught them, they clustered like bugs near to shelter and to water.

It is worth noting how Steinbeck describes the process of adaptation with eerie detachment, as if he really were talking about insects and not people. But the old humanist in him resurfaces, again and again, and it becomes more dominant in the later fiction. Referring in *The Grapes of Wrath* to the way families adapted as their lives evolved from single-family units on farms to a mass westward movement of migrants from the Dust Bowl states to California, he writes, 'Thus they changed their social life – changed as in the whole universe only man can change. They were not farm men any more, but migrant men.' The opening paragraph of Chapter 14 is even more aerial in its detachment, as humankind is again singled out for its unique adaptive powers:

> The last clear definite function of man – muscles aching to work, minds aching to create beyond the single need – this is man. To build a wall, to build a house, a dam, and in the wall and house and dam to put something of Manself, and to Manself take back something of the wall, the house, the dam; to take hard muscles from the lifting, to take the clear lines and form from conceiving. For man, unlike anything organic or inorganic in the universe, grows beyond his work, walks up the stairs of his concepts, emerges ahead of his accomplishments.

This is hardly an instance of non-teleological thinking; indeed, Steinbeck sounds more like George Eliot here, the classic meliorist in the tradition of nineteenth-century liberalism, believing firmly in the gradual moral, intellectual, artistic improvement of humankind:

> This you may say of man – when theories change and crash, when schools, philosophies, when narrow dark alleys of thought, national, religious, economic, grow and disintegrate, man reaches, stumbles forward, painfully, mistakenly sometimes. Having stepped forward, he may slip back, but only half a step, never the full step back.

Human beings, according to Steinbeck, are the one organism in the universe willing to 'suffer and die for a concept'. And 'this one quality is man, distinctive in the universe.' While his expression, here as elsewhere, suffers from a naive magniloquence, there is something deeply affecting about his simple faith in the power of the human species to stake out an intellectual and moral claim and to stand firmly behind it. His belief in human progress is heartening.

Steinbeck is one of the great writer-didacts, which means he was a perpetual student of humanity's ways and means. Like Emerson, the founder of what critic Harold Bloom has called 'the American religion', Steinbeck ransacked the natural world for signs of immortality. 'Man is the broken giant,' wrote Emerson, 'and in all his weakness both his body and his mind are invigorated by habits of conversation with nature.' Steinbeck cultivated these habits of conversation, rarely losing sight of his primary artistic goal: to dramatize the adaptive process of the human race, to locate the recurring patterns, and to find the *mythos* behind these patterns. He sought out individual stories from which he could generalize about the human species and its place in the natural world. He was, in Emerson's great phrase, an instance of *Man thinking*, a person whose thought was ongoing, exploratory, and always contingent, situated both temporally and spatially.

The matter of 'early' and 'late' Steinbeck is complex, and it has been simplified to the point of distortion by critics who argue too vehemently that he reached a pinnacle in the novels of the Thirties. He never wanted to continue writing in the mode of *The Grapes of Wrath*; that kind of realistic fiction no longer attracted him; it represented, he told his editor, 'a dead end for the novel'. His later novels, screenplays, plays, and non-fiction move in different directions, taking on new problems and solving them in ways appropriate to this later stage of his development. In some respects, his later writing is more complex, less naively realistic, more mature than the earlier work. Steinbeck was moving towards what might be called a mythopoetic view of the universe, and this view is reflected in the form and content of his later fiction.

When he received the Nobel Prize in 1962, the decision of the Swedish Academy was ridiculed in America by narrow academic critics and a handful of haughty journalists, who refused to believe that a writer with a popular following could be any good. This sad, rather pathetic, episode in Steinbeck's life is described in the final chapters of this biography; yet in his acceptance speech in Stockholm, he demonstrated his own quiet greatness, reflecting with a simple nobility of expression on his mission as a writer. Literature in his opinion was not written by the few for the few. From its beginnings in ancient times, it was created by writers who were 'not separate and exclusive', standing apart from the culture they wrote from and for. Instead, he suggested that the proper goal of the writer has always been to speak broadly, to a wide audience, on issues of deep concern. Steinbeck said: 'The ancient commission of the writer has not changed. He is charged with exposing our many grievous faults and failures, with dredging up to the light our dark and dangerous dreams for the purpose of improvement.'[3]

My purpose in writing this book has been to summon the honest spirit of John Steinbeck embodied in the man and his books. I have tried to make him live and breathe again, to invoke and animate the world he knew. I have lived with Steinbeck's work for several decades, first reading his novels in junior high school, but my encounter with the man began with the two biographies published before mine: Thomas Kiernan's *The Intricate Music: A Biography of John Steinbeck* (1979)[4] and Jackson J. Benson's *The True Adventures of John Steinbeck, Writer*.[5] Professor Benson's book, in particular, has proved invaluable. He interviewed many of the people who knew Steinbeck personally, and since the bulk of these are now dead, his work is an indispensable gift to all admirers of John Steinbeck and to all future biographers.

While researching and writing this book over the past four years, I have visited most of the places where Steinbeck lived – from California to Somerset in England. I have travelled in the path of the Joads from Oklahoma into California, visited farms in the Salinas Valley where George and Lennie might have bucked barley, sat in Steinbeck's various studies and looked out the windows he looked out, trying always to imagine the world as he would have seen it. I have listened for his voice in his published books – fiction, non-fiction, letters – and in a good deal of unpublished writing (the bulk of which is housed in the Green Library at Stanford University, where I was treated with unfailing courtesy). I have tried to resurrect that voice in its human and historical context, while not losing sight of the fact that biographies are necessarily partial, tinted if not tainted by language, and grounded in the biographer's subjectivities.

I have been lucky in my friends, and this book has benefited from the close reading of many eyes, including those of Elaine Steinbeck, Tom Weldon, Alan Peacock, Geri Thoma, Lee Richard Hayman and Devon Jersild. I have also benefited from the research help of Ryan Tranquilla, who unearthed all sorts of things I would have missed. Susan Shillinglaw, who heads the Steinbeck Research Center of the San Jose University Library, was remarkably generous with her time. I must also thank Mary Jean S. Gamble of the John Steinbeck Library in Salinas, and Ann Erickson, a dear friend, who helped me enormously on my various research trips to California.

A writer needs huge swatches of time, of course, to complete a book like this. I have been generously supported by Middlebury College over the years, and I am grateful to them. I also want to thank the John Simon Guggenheim Foundation for a fellowship in 1992–3 and Christ Church, Oxford, where I completed my work as Fowler Hamilton Research Fellow in 1993–4.

Jay Parini
Christ Church,
Oxford, 1994

I

The Fiction of Origins

'I remember the sorrow at not being
part of things in my childhood.'

Steinbeck, *Journal of a Novel*.

'I fancy that happy childhoods are usually forgotten,' mused
C. S. Lewis late in his life. He could never forget his, nor
could John Steinbeck, who scribbled in the margins of *The
Winter of Our Discontent*, his last novel, 'Why do I keep
dreaming of Central Avenue?'

It was on Central Avenue, the most fashionable residential
street in Salinas, California, that he was born in his parents'
high-ceilinged bedroom in their Victorian house on 27
February 1902, a year after President McKinley was shot by a
young anarchist in Buffalo, New York. Steinbeck lived there
for seventeen years, and what happened in those formative
years remained an inexhaustible source of nightmares, inspiration, daydreams, memories.

California was the setting for much of his fiction, a kind of
imperfect Eden which he lost and recovered periodically. In a
sense, Steinbeck never left home, though he wandered far
and wide, using New York City as a base during the last two
decades of his life. In particular, he returned to Pacific Grove,
on the outskirts of Monterey, at regular intervals. 'The house
in Pacific Grove, which had belonged to his parents, was a
touchstone,' his third wife, Elaine, recalls.[1] 'Whenever he
was troubled, or in need of a rest, he went back there. In his
early life, especially during his first marriage to Carol
Henning, it was probably the most important place for him.
He lived there for long periods. It stayed in his mind.'

Like most writers, Steinbeck searched his own life for stories he could make into fiction that would help him understand who he was and where he came from. But life is plotless, a random hail of facts and events that often lack a discernible pattern or arc of development. Against this confusing reality, or perhaps because of it, we tend to develop a personal *mythos*, a story about ourselves and the way our lives have been lived. Virginia Woolf's narrator in *The Waves* says: 'In order to make you understand, to give you my life, I must tell you a story.' In Woolf's sense, we are all makers of fiction in the original meaning of that word, from the Latin *fictio*, shaping. We create the story of our lives, selecting certain details from others to find order, to discover an aesthetically satisfying form without the chaos of experience.

The great bank of fiction, of course, is memory. Steinbeck was constantly revisiting his past, trying to conjure and revise it, hoping to isolate the pattern more distinctly. One of his later novels, *East of Eden*, began as a straightforward attempt to remember his past quite literally, to invoke the history of his family, and it tells us a lot about Steinbeck's sense of his origins. He intended to write a true historical account of his family's westward migration from New England to California which he could give to his sons, Thom and John, so that they could understand where they came from. As often happens with novelists, the manuscript quickly became a work of fiction; before long, it was seen by the author for what it was: a fiction of origins.

Steinbeck was a romantic at heart, and liked to see himself as someone who came from a long line of adventurers – men and women of solid stock and practical instincts who came from Europe to the New World, settled in the east, then travelled to California in search of Eden. As with Eden itself, there was a snake in the garden: the corrosive worm of evil that undermines each character's vision of Eden's perfection.

One often encounters a contradiction between Steinbeck's knowledge of his characters and his own self-knowledge. He remained to the end profoundly innocent, a believer in goodness and the American dream, and was perpetually stunned by the way things did not work out for him personally, in his first two marriages, with his sons, who drifted away from him, even with his books, which never seemed to satisfy the reviewers. He yearned for a simple life, without *angst* or human complication. One sees an image of himself crystallizing in the character of young Samuel Hamilton in *East of Eden*:

> He came to the Salinas Valley full-blown and hearty, full of inventions and energy. His eyes were very blue, and when he was tired one of them wandered outward a little. He was a big man but delicate in a way. In the dusty business of ranching he seemed always immaculate. His hands were clever. He was a good blacksmith and carpenter and woodcarver, and he could improvise anything with bits of wood and metal. He was forever inventing a new way of doing an old thing and doing it better and quicker. . . .

Steinbeck did not even trouble to disguise the family name, although he was writing 'fiction'. His mother was indeed a Hamilton, and Samuel was the name of his maternal grandfather, who came from Ballykelly in Northern Ireland, a man of solid Orange stock. Grandfather Hamilton, like his namesake in *East of Eden*, was a sun-burned, outgoing, muscular man with the gift of the gab; he migrated to the United States at the age of seventeen, where he married a shy young Irishwoman named Elizabeth Fagen. The wedding took place in New York City in the summer of 1849, and the couple followed Sam's eldest sister, who lived near San Jose, westward in 1871. The next year, Sam moved with Elizabeth to Salinas, where he became one of the original signatories of the Salinas city charter, thus establishing him as a town father, a fact that would figure rather prominently in his grandson's imagination.

Sam Hamilton did not stay in Salinas, however; it was too constricting. He was an outdoorsman by inclination, much taken with the image of himself as a frontiersman and pioneer. Preferring the rigours and adventures of home-steading to the more settled life of town dwellers, he and Elizabeth set themselves up on a large farm near King City, some sixty miles south of Salinas. Steinbeck spent a lot of time there as a child, often following in his grandfather's large bootsteps as he went about his daily chores; it was on the Hamilton farm that he learned so many of the practical things that stuck with him throughout his life. The routine of farm work – and the ethos of practicality that inevitably goes with it – hung brilliantly in his imagination and became an essential part of his way of being, even during the last decades in New York City when, as Elaine Steinbeck says, 'he was forever looking for a plot of ground to dig'. She adds: 'Like his Grandfather Hamilton, he was a practical man who liked to work with his hands: to fix things, carve wood, build a boat, hang a door.'[2]

The Hamilton farm became a vital part of his personal *mythos*, and it would reappear many times in his fiction, as in the Tiflin ranch in *The Red Pony*. The freshness and vividness of that novella derives in part from the sense of memory activated in some deep and satisfying way. Here is how Jody, the young protagonist of the story, views the farm:

> Then he turned and looked back on the ranch, on the low, whitewashed house girded with red geraniums, and on the long bunkhouse by the cypress tree where Billy Buck lived alone. Jody could see the great black kettle under the cypress tree. That was where the pigs were scalded. The sun was coming up over the ridge now, glaring on the whitewash of the houses and barns, making the wet grass blaze softly. Behind him, in the tall sagebrush, the birds

were scampering on the ground, making a great noise
among the dry leaves; the squirrels piped shrilly on the
side-hills.

Through his native ingenuity, Sam prospered despite the
notorious dryness of the soil in that region, and his youngest
daughter Olive (one of nine children) went to high school in
Salinas in preparation for a career in schoolteaching. In those
days, before the advent of mass higher education in the
United States, one didn't have to attend college to teach in a
simple one-room schoolhouse. (Indeed, only a tiny fraction
of the population made it through high school before the turn
of the century.) At seventeen, Olive qualified as a teacher
with the local education authority and eagerly took a position
in a small school near King City, not far from her parents'
farm, where she continued to live. She taught everything
from maths to history, and all ages were mixed in together.
'She had a sense of herself as an educated woman,' says
Elizabeth (Beth) Ainsworth, her second daughter. 'And she
wanted the same for her own children.'[3] She was also 'very
strict by nature. That was her personality; she had a strong
sense of what you should do and what you shouldn't.'
   Olive was fierce, ambitious, and somewhat puritanical.
She did not aspire to being a farm wife like her mother
(although her eldest daughter, Esther, would close the circle
and become a farmer's wife herself). Olive met John Ernst
Steinbeck in King City when she was twenty-four, and they
were married soon after. He was the manager of a flour mill, a
trade he had learned from his father, who had started a small
mill on his farm to add to the income derived from the dairy
and fruit products. Perhaps eager to get out from under the
long shadow of his father-in-law, Sam Hamilton, John Ernst
eventually took a managerial position in Salinas at the Sperry
Flour Mill.
   John Ernst and Olive set themselves up as members of

bourgeois society when they arrived in Salinas, rapidly acquiring the large house that would remain the family homestead until both of them died in the Thirties. Central Avenue was a prosperous street, wide and lined with long-necked, leafy elms; spacious gardens stretched out behind each dwelling, and white picket fences marked off one property from the next. The Steinbeck house was a two-storey gabled structure; its broad porches suggested that its occupants had, indeed, the leisure to sit on them in a rocker and watch the world go by. It radiated a solid, almost stolid, aura of respectability and privilege. Its gingerbread fringe and tall windows spoke of affluence and taste, and its elegant turrets reflected the fashion of the period. Its interior is still attractive, with large rooms and high ceilings. The entryway gives one pause, with its stately formality, and one looks ahead to the steep staircase. A formal dining room and elegant parlour make this a house where entertaining could be done with late-Victorian poise. There are numerous small bedrooms upstairs, and a huge cobwebbed attic; a back stairwell leads into the dark wood-panelled kitchen, which gives the house a feeling of space. Steinbeck's room at the top of the house was isolated, dark and spacious, with high ceilings and a grand view of the back gardens: a cosy place of retreat from the family. In all, the white house was as much a symbol as a residence; it radiated its inhabitants' class aspirations.

Steinbeck's paternal grandfather was John Adolph Grossteinbeck from Düsseldorf, a prosperous town with ancient roots. A cabinet-maker by profession, he was a Lutheran and deeply religious. He also had an adventurous streak greatly admired by his grandson, John Steinbeck, who liked to work with a portrait of fierce-looking John Adolph nearby. (John Adolph died before Steinbeck had a chance to know him.) In an extraordinary move that became a key part of the Steinbeck family *mythos*, John Adolph went to Jerusalem with his brother and his sister and her husband in 1852. Their bizarre idea was that they, pious German Christians, would convert the heathen Jews of Palestine – never mind that there were far more Arabs than Jews in the region. They would pursue their private crusade, attempting what so many well-financed and well-armed medieval kings and crusaders could not achieve. The journey took many weeks on horseback, and it was dangerous, but the small party arrived safely in the Holy Land. There John Adolph met Almira Dickson, the American niece of another missionary zealot, known throughout the region as Deacon Dickson. Almira would soon become his wife.

Some horrible misadventures lay ahead of these innocents in the primitive land of Palestine, then still part of the Ottoman empire. John Adolph's brother was attacked by Bedouin tribesmen and stabbed to death in the scuffle, and his sister-in-law was raped at knife-point. The missionaries were badly shaken and discouraged. Indeed, as one of his granddaughters said, 'This was traumatic. There was a sense of failure there.'[4] (Not surprisingly, one of Steinbeck's great themes was the ways in which quixotic adventures often end in disaster.) Seeing no future for themselves in Palestine, they retreated to New England, where Almira's family had long been established in a small town in Massachusetts. In a little shed behind his father-in-law's modest wood-frame house, John Adolph set up shop as a woodcarver (a skill his grandson would cultivate and pursue throughout his life).

Although life was good in Massachusetts, John Adolph soon found himself yearning for adventures. He eventually persuaded Almira (who was fiercely opposed to a further move) to pack their belongings and go with their six children to Florida. This was just before the outbreak of the Civil War, and it suggests once again that John Adolph had little in the way of political sense. He had no sooner moved everyone to

Florida than he was conscripted into the Confederate army. Feeling no special allegiance to the north or the south, he slipped out of uniform one night and deserted his company. Hiding in the woods by day, walking back roads by night, he eventually crossed the Mason-Dixon line, escaping back to New England. Almira and the children, through the generosity of a Confederate general, were allowed to follow: a miraculous piece of luck, given the situation. After the war, the family migrated again, this time for good.

In the winter of 1945, John Steinbeck came into this personal history in an unexpected way. He wrote to his editor and close friend, Pat Covici, 'My sister [Beth] gave me an olive wood box my father had left for me full of papers I didn't even know about. My grandfather's Civil War papers. His marriage license, his citizenship papers – last night we went over some of them. Passes for my grandmother to go through the Union lines signed by guerrilla officers. Deeds to property in Palestine and in Florida. A bill for a headstone for my grandfather's brother "murdered by the Bedowin" in Jaffa in 1853.'[5] Beth comments, 'John couldn't stop talking and thinking about it. It was as if he suddenly knew who he was . . . could lay his hands on his own history.' Perhaps he finally understood the origins of his own restless and quixotic nature.

John Adolph and his family now migrated to California, which had gained statehood in 1850, when it became the thirty-first state in the Union. Named after a mythical land of great bounty described in a sixteenth-century novel by Garcí Ordóñey de Montalvo, the appeal of this spacious and untouched paradise was irresistible to the imagination of John Adolph. Its economy, formerly based on the trading of hides and tallow and gold mining, had moved aggressively in the direction of agriculture by the time the Steinbeck family arrived in the Salinas Valley. Spending most of his savings, John Adolph purchased ten acres of farmland north of

Salinas, and set himself up as a dairy farmer. This meant acquiring a certain number of dairy cows and planting several acres with crops that could be turned into silage. He also planted some fruit trees, and once the main farm was in working order he established the flour mill that would interest his son, John Ernst, whose early career would depend on his boyhood experience of milling.

Unlike his father, John Ernst was not inclined to work with his hands for a living, although he had grown up on his parents' dairy farm. He lived his life in opposition to his father, who was rarely seen in a necktie. In many ways, John Ernst was a typical smalltown burgher of the period, a man who took seriously his place in the community and his role as *paterfamilias* within the big house, though he did not have the personal authority to carry off this role. 'He was very tentative about things,' says his daughter. 'He rarely raised his voice. Mother gave the orders.' John Ernst always wore 'fine suits and stiff collars, and he carried himself like a man of importance. It mattered to him what the neighbours thought about him.' One of his neighbours at the time observed: 'He was a fragile man, emotionally, not physically. He dressed like a dandy, and he was almost too fastidious. One rarely heard him raise his voice. He didn't socialize much with the rest of the town, although he was present at public functions.'[6] This buttoned-up, nervous and remote man had little on the surface in common with his father, although in his business dealings one detects the same restless, quixotic nature.

John Ernst had gone into flour milling because it was what he knew, but the business declined soon after he became manager of Sperry, largely because of a general downturn in the economy. He was set adrift in 1910, when Sperry collapsed altogether, partly due to John Ernst's lack of managerial competence. 'It was a hard blow to everyone,' says his daughter. 'Father did not know what he was going to do next or where the money would come from.' John Steinbeck was only eight years old at the time, and this family crisis affected him deeply. Like all boys of that age, he adored and depended on his father; it was therefore frightening to see the principal figure in his life come unmoored and – as soon happened – depressed. (John Ernst's depressive re-action to his crisis provided his son with an unfortunate model. A sensitive and impressionable boy, young Steinbeck was soon lost in daydreaming and depression.)

John Ernst would sit for hours without speaking in his brown wallpapered bedroom, the shades drawn and no lamps lit. His despair is understandable: for a burgher, position in the community is intimately tied to financial stability, and both were crucial to self-esteem. On some level, John Ernst never fully recovered his stability and confidence. Perhaps in reaction, Olive – who was in any event the more powerful of the two, possessed of great stamina and a strong drive to control herself and her family – assumed command. 'She could be very strict with father,' her second daughter recalls. 'Sloppiness or laziness were things she could not abide.' Indeed, Olive was often contemptuous of John Ernst, a situation which produced anger in her son, who could not bear to see his chief role model in a position where he could be ridiculed.[7]

For all his faults, John Ernst was careful with his money in the puritanical manner of most bourgeois gentlemen of the era, and he had saved a bit of capital over the years. He decided to try his hand at running a feed store in the wake of Sperry's crash, arguing that agriculture was a boom industry in California. The state was growing, and fresh immigrants from the east arrived every month to set up farms. The animals had to be fed.

What John Ernst had not counted on was the arrival of the internal combustion engine. Cars and tractors would replace horses, thus diminishing the need for another feed store in the Salinas area. On top of this, John Ernst did not have the entrepreneurial skills to make a new business work. The feed store collapsed before it ever got going, and the family savings were almost totally wiped out – an experience that frightened John Ernst for the rest of his life, making him a timid man who took few risks. Having only recently suffered the demise of Sperry, his sense of personal failure was now extreme, and he wondered how he would ever manage to support a wife and family: 'There was even talk of selling the house,' his daughter remembers, 'but that would have been too hard on everyone. I don't think we could have stood it.'

To the family's relief and surprise, the community in Salinas rallied around them; the Steinbecks had proved themselves decent, churchgoing citizens, and their neighbours were not about to let them sink. 'People pulled together in those days like they don't do now,' a former resident of Salinas recalls. 'I don't think it's easy to remember now, but everyone was a pioneer then; we realized that if one man fell, everyone would fall. You helped your neighbour. If his tractor broke, you loaned him yours. Your neighbour was a friend, often a relative. There was no sense of every man out for himself. That's what the cowboy pictures say, but it wasn't like that in the west then.'[8]

One of John Ernst's best friends was a fellow Mason, Charlie Pioda, who managed the Spreckels Sugar Plant, then the most established and successful business in the region. Charlie's wife, morever, was a close friend of Olive's (they were both members of the Order of the Eastern Star, a women's offshoot of the Masons, and they worked together for various local charities). Charlie got John Ernst an accounting position at the sugar plant, and this tided the Steinbecks over for a few years until the incumbent treasurer of Monterey County unexpectedly died in office. Charlie Pioda stepped in again, egged on by Olive; he pulled strings to get

John Ernst appointed to fill out the remainder of the man's term. John Ernst held this position for the rest of his working life (he died in 1936), and the job suited him well. While the salary was not huge, it was reliable, and the post carried some weight in the community. The Steinbeck family was, at least financially, on safe ground. They would never be wealthy, but they would never have to worry about their next meal either.

John Steinbeck was born at a good time for the country, which in 1902 was expanding and expansive. President Theodore Roosevelt brought to his presidency a flamboyance and optimism that rippled from coast to coast. Having been catapulted into office at the age of forty-three, he wanted above all else to widen the boundaries of the American empire. In style and substance, he embodied the charged, optimistic moment in the United States. As Woodrow Wilson, a young academic, said at the time: 'This is nothing short of a new social age, a new era of human relationships, a new stage-setting for the drama of life.' As the farthest western frontier, California had a special appeal. It was the Land of Milk and Honey, a place where anyone could go and begin life again. People moved steadily westward from all over the country, finding the landscape and climate 'like heaven only without the boring music', as Mark Twain said.

In the South there was Hollywood. The first film company opened in southern California in 1907, when William Selig shot *The Count of Monte Cristo* in a vacant field just outside Los Angeles (which had quickly become a magnet for ambitious sun-worshippers). In the central and northern part of the state, only San Francisco had attracted a large population. The countryside was mostly unspoiled agricultural land, or potential agricultural land. Salinas itself, which numbered some 2500 people in 1899, was a relatively small but prosperous town in the middle of nowhere, with one main street and several residential neighbourhoods. As farmers like Sam Hamilton moved in, it became the commercial centre of what Steinbeck called 'the long valley', a long and narrow strip of arable land. In spite of a sunny climate, farm failures were common at the time, largely owing to the inexperience of so many migrants to the region. One did not farm well here without a strategy, since the land was dry and lacked certain nutrients that would have made farming easy; it took know-how and experience to make a go of it.

In *East of Eden*, Steinbeck blames the economic problems of the region more on the land than on the people who worked it. Of the Salinas Valley, he writes: 'If the land had been any good the Hamiltons would have been rich people. But the acres were harsh and dry. There were no springs, and the crust of topsoil was so thin that the flinty bones stuck through. Even the sagebrush struggled to exist, and the oaks were dwarfed from lack of moisture. Even in reasonably good years there was so little feed that the cattle kept thin running about looking for enough to eat.' It was lucky for Steinbeck's parents that their natural inclination had led them away from farming.

One of the great problems for young Steinbeck was that his father had put up a thick wall between himself and his children. 'He was a distant sort of man,' his daughter says. 'I think mother was more important for John and the rest of us. She was the centre of the family.' Mary Graydon, a neighbour (who was slightly younger than Steinbeck) recalls, 'Mr Steinbeck stayed in the background. He didn't play with John or the girls. He seemed always in the shadows in the house, at the edge of things, lonely and depressed. I think John was very angry with him.' This anger makes sense: John Ernst did not shield him, even slightly, from the intense, even domineering, scrutiny of Olive. 'Mrs Steinbeck', says Graydon, 'was stern, even a little cold. She loved her son, but he was a little afraid of getting on the wrong side of her. He could never do anything right as far as she was concerned.'

Firm, and more than a little snobbish, Olive Steinbeck enjoyed her superior position in Salinas society as an educated woman from a respectable family. She was active in the community and she had lots of stamina. According to one native of the area, Olive 'never sat down. She was the head of every charity committee you could think of. She was always interested in cases of poverty or injustice, and she took these things personally. She thought of herself (and she was) one of those old-fashioned moral people.'⁹ One has to wonder if indeed this was not the source of John Steinbeck's own fierce, almost puritanical, code of morality, his urge to rectify wrongs, and his habit of identifying with the poor and needy. She clearly had high aspirations for her son, although it was often thought that she pushed him too hard in ways not appropriate for a boy of his temperament. 'Mrs Steinbeck was always despairing about her son, trying to get him to achieve more than he did,' said one neighbour. 'She saw his brilliance, and she recognized his abilities, but she found his misbehaviour, and his tendencies to be a loner, exasperating. It seemed to her that he should be doing better work in school and should be more obedient at home. She pushed him to join clubs and church organizations, but he wasn't very willing. And sometimes he would defy her and shout back. She often said that he would either go to the White House as president or go to jail.'¹⁰

One important feature of Steinbeck's character was his sense of himself as someone who never quite achieved enough. Every book he wrote felt to him like a failure, and he never thought he was going to be able to summon the energy and imagination to complete the project at hand. In his later years, the situation worsened, and in the end he found himself terrified of failure, unable to complete, for instance, his work on a translation of Sir Thomas Malory's *Morte*

D'Arthur. He reacted badly to criticism (and there was a lot of it) and was often plunged into dark moods that bordered on clinical depression. Alcohol was a vent which he often used to take his mind off his problems or alter his bleak moods. He was consistently self-castigating and harboured an anger towards women that seems to have had its origins in consistent resentment of Olive Steinbeck that mingled with genuine feelings of affection and admiration.

The most obvious fact of Steinbeck's childhood situation is that he was surrounded by women who took great pains over him: his mother, his two older sisters, Esther (born in 1892) and Beth (born in 1894), and his younger sister, Mary, three years his junior and therefore nearest to him in age. 'He was spoiled,' Beth says flatly.[11] 'Everyone took care of him. We were close to him, all of us, though he saw Mary more than the rest of us. John used to write to us constantly, long letters written in that small hand of his with several sheets of carbon paper so we would each have copies. They were like diaries. He never stopped writing letters and told us about the people he met and the places he travelled. He knew we wanted to know what he was doing, and that we thought of him as somebody special.'

The birth of John had been physically difficult for Olive, and her son's features had been distorted by the harshness of the delivery. By the age of three, however, he had 'come back to normal', as she put it. Olive called her son 'my little squirrel' through much of his childhood, while his older sisters, somewhat less affectionately called him 'muskrat' and 'mouse'. He did not enjoy any of these nicknames, and he became self-conscious about his looks: the bulbous nose and heavy brow; the long (and later craggy) face and massive ears that folded out like flaps; the swollen chest and long, spindly legs. To the end he retained a sense of himself as somebody unpleasant to look at, although he compensated in later years by adopting extraordinary clothes whenever he went out in public. Tom Guinzburg, a friend from this period, recalls, 'He was an amazing sight in old age: his big, rough face and massive ears, his floppy hat and satin cape, his blackthorn walking stick. Eyes turned to him when he walked into a room. People knew that here was somebody exceptional – or eccentric.'[12]

Steinbeck's earliest memory was of being taken by his father to see how the earthquake had damaged several buildings in the business district of Salinas, which was no more than ten minutes from his house on foot. Though a hundred miles south of San Francisco, Salinas was affected by the aftershocks of the famous earthquake of 1906, which struck at 5.13 a.m. on 18 April. It was among the biggest and most destructive earthquakes of this century, although it lasted only forty-eight seconds. In the city of San Francisco, whole buildings collapsed, killing over seven hundred people. The fires raged for days, and some two hundred and fifty thousand people were left homeless.

A former resident of Salinas recalls the effects on his town: 'The big department store on Main Street was toppled, and many buildings were pretty much knocked to smithereens. Windows were shattered in unlikely places, and the plaster was cracked in a lot of homes. I remember school was called off for a week because one of the supporting walls had caved in. But it wasn't anything like in San Francisco. We didn't really have much in the way of fire damage or actual deaths. I don't suppose a soul was hurt. Salinas was lucky, but all the preachers in the town accepted this as God's wink in their favour.'[13]

Two years later, in 1908, John Steinbeck enrolled at a primary school only a few blocks from Central Avenue. The school was commonly referred to as the 'baby school' by everyone in town. It was soon obvious to the teacher that her new charge was ahead of everyone else in reading and writing skills; this was largely because Olive, having been trained as a schoolteacher, focused attention on her only son, reading to him from a wide assortment of books at an early age and making him read aloud to her. (The family subscribed to a bountiful assortments of periodicals, including *Youth's Companion*, *National Geographic*, *Century Magazine*, *Saturday Evening Post*, and *Collier's*.) Steinbeck's reading included such classic books for children as *Alice in Wonderland* and *Tom Brown's Schooldays*. When he was older, he read some of the old standbys for boys: *Ivanhoe, Robin Hood*, and *Treasure Island*.

He was introduced to Malory's version of the Arthurian legend by Aunt Molly, his mother's bookish sister, when he was visiting her in the summer of 1912. He later recalled sitting under a tree, 'dazzled and swept up' by these powerful tales, which made a permanent impression on the young boy. The structure of these heroic stories would explicitly undergird many of his best novels, such as *Tortilla Flat* and *Cannery Row*, while aspects of the Camelot myth implicitly influenced almost everything he ever produced. (The Malorian quest for the 'good man' is crucial to his fiction, for instance. One also finds versions of Malory's idealized women cropping up regularly. Sir Lancelot's betrayal of his king was a pivotal image in Steinbeck's mind, and it informs a good deal of his work and, perhaps, his own life.) The extent to which Malory overwhelmed him is registered in the fact that he spent the last decade of his life obsessed by that work, even renting a cottage for a year in Somerset just to be near the supposed site of Camelot.

Another of Steinbeck's early (and somewhat painful) memories was of sitting with his mother in the parlour while she taught him to read. There was not, for him, a seamless transition from ignorance to knowledge, especially with Olive hovering beside him anxiously as he tried to make sense of the bewildering marks on the page that supposedly contained meaning. 'Trying to make those simple words on the page leap into my mouth and then to send them out as intelligible sounds my mother mouthed to me was so hard in the beginning,' he later recalled. 'It seemed like aeons before I was able to catch on.'[14] One can imagine the schoolteacher-mother coaching her nervous, frightened child, urging him on yet always disappointed by the results. This is the kind of childhood memory that sticks in the craw.

As a shy and shambling boy with jug ears and few social graces, Steinbeck was something of a loner outside the immediate family circle. He loved playing by himself in the woods, and he often simply stayed in his room to read books or magazines. His two closest friends were Max Wagner and Glenn Graves, both neighbours. Max was particularly close, and Steinbeck enjoyed hanging out at the Wagner house, where freshly baked raisin cookies were usually laid out on the kitchen table. Steinbeck was fortunate in some ways: Salinas offered, at least superficially, a small-town world of benevolent parents, concerned teachers and good neighbours. The violence which is now everywhere a part of American life was largely absent. There was neither radio nor television to distract him. And his family had sufficient money to see that the machinery of life was well oiled.

It is not, however, hard to imagine the devastating effect that John Ernst's financial troubles and subsequent emotional withdrawal would have had on Steinbeck. When the father of Herman Melville suffered the collapse of his business, his sensitive young son was deeply wounded, and the wound apparently festered throughout his life. Charles Dickens, of course, was dealt an extraordinary blow when his spendthrift father's fortunes crashed and young Charles was sent to the blacking factory; this was, unquestionably, a governing image in his life and work. Steinbeck's reaction was similar, if less open. His later anxiety about money and his general lack of compatibility with the world and its opinion of him suggest that he, too, never quite recovered from his father's commercial problems. That his father also withdrew emotionally and 'lived in the shadows' of the house must have added fuel to the fire.

The Steinbeck family regained its financial posture slowly but surely. Indeed, John Ernst was eventually able to buy a small cottage near Monterey that became a wonderful place of retreat for weekend excursions and summer holidays. This cottage, on Eleventh Street in Pacific Grove, assumed special importance for all the Steinbeck children and remains in the family to this day. It was profoundly associated in their minds with the family's recovery. Beth recalls, 'The place was always a lucky place for us. We used to go there for outings in our horse-drawn surrey. John and Mary, as babies, were bundled up and sat next to mother. It was a long trip in those days, over some rough country, but we loved it. Mother always packed a picnic basket, and we would stop by the roadside and spread out a blanket and eat. That's really one of my best memories of childhood. John and I often talked about those rides.'[15]

The bouldery and brilliant shoreline along the Monterey coast became a favourite haunt of young Steinbeck, who in *Travels with Charley*, his last book, recalled that he 'grew up on its shore, collected marine animals along the coast'. In *Tortilla Flat*, he offered a vivid sketch of the town and its setting: 'Monterey sits on the slope of a hill, with a blue bay below it and with a forest of tall dark pine trees at its back.' Famous in Steinbeck's day for sardine canneries, which crowded along the shore, Monterey became a setting for several of Steinbeck's best-known novels and stories, and it was for him a sacred place that he returned to in difficult periods throughout his life.

Not half a mile from the town, the coastline becomes one of the most spectacular in California, with its steep cliffs and jagged shoreline. Kelp and bladder-wrack swirl in brilliant colours in rockpools. Priestly gulls hang in the wind over brilliant stretches of blue-green water, and there are long strands of bone-white beach. Steinbeck fell in love with the smell of the sea, the wet rocks and kelp, the sharpness of iodine and the odour of washed, crumbling calcareous shells. He spent part of every summer on this coast until he left college, and he often had long weekends in the family cottage as a way of extricating himself from the occasionally oppressive academic and social atmosphere at Stanford. When he was first married, he moved into the Pacific Grove cottage with his new bride, Carol. Throughout his life the cottage remained a kind of home base, living warmly in his imagination, and the sea (it was the Atlantic in his later years that attracted him) continued to mean a great deal to him. 'Ever since he was a boy, he just loved to be near water,' Elaine Steinbeck says. 'There was just something in him that demanded this, which is why we eventually bought a house on Sag Harbor in Long Island. It reminded him of Pacific Grove and that coastline that had been so very important to him and his family.' In *Travels with Charley*, Steinbeck wrote that whenever he was near the sea he could feel 'an electric excitement . . . a kind of boisterous joy'.

Steinbeck matured later than many of his classmates in high school, retaining a beardless face and rather fluting voice until the age of fifteen, which seems to have contributed to his isolation. The feeling was exacerbated by the fact that he had skipped the fifth grade while at the 'baby school' and so arrived at Salinas High School in 1915 a year younger than most others in his class. From some reports, he did not involve himself to any great extent with his school, although a quick perusal of *El Galiban*, the high school yearbook, suggests that he was not exactly a wallflower. The high school was tiny, of course, which meant that everyone had to pitch in; Steinbeck was forced to play on the football and basketball teams and to work on the school yearbook and even act in plays when required. As Mary Graydon says, 'There was no way out of it. You had to get involved in everything, even if you were very shy like John Steinbeck.'

Since the United States was at war in Europe during his junior and senior years, a student training corps had been established, and Steinbeck was made a junior officer. (There are poignant photographs of him in an ill-fitting military uniform with a sad-sack look in his eyes.) He seems not to have distinguished himself at sport, but as associate editor of the yearbook he did command some respect; much to his surprise (and his mother's delight), he was elected president of his senior class – a remarkable achievement for a shy boy who had tried to avoid the limelight. Even if one takes into account the fact that Salinas High School was small, with scarcely a hundred students in the ninth through twelfth grades, Steinbeck was 'successful' in high school. Nevertheless, a man who was a year behind Steinbeck at Salinas High recalls: 'I don't think John stood out particularly through most of his years in high school . . . not till the very end, in fact. But everyone knew him and liked him. His sister, Mary, was more popular.' He adds, 'John was known as a writer even then. He would get you in a corner and spin a hell of a yarn. From what people said to me at the time, he wrote a good bit of the yearbook all by himself. It just didn't surprise any of us when he became famous for his books. It all made sense.'[16]

Steinbeck remained friendly with Max Wagner and Glenn Graves at Salinas High, though he had been pushed ahead of them. A new friend, an important one, was Bill Black, the best athlete and most admired boy in the school. Steinbeck was still thinking about him in 1938 when he mentions him in the journal he was keeping during the composition of *The Grapes of Wrath*: 'At that time, knowing little about the precocity of personality,' he writes, 'I should have said Bill

Black would have passed us all because I could not see that his very excellences were the rheostat of his mediocrity. Were I to look again and try to judge a future, I should pick a tortured child, frantic with uncertainties and unhappy in his limitations.' Steinbeck is describing himself here coldly and clearly; while to all outward appearances he was doing just fine, he felt deeply uncertain inside, even tortured about his prospects in the world that lay before him.

Most genuine writers are aware of their talents at an early age, and Steinbeck was no exception. His interest in writing and his obvious talents were recognized by himself and his teachers from his first year in high school onwards. In the ninth grade, his English composition teacher – one Ora M. Cupp – would read his essays aloud in admiring tones before the whole class, much to Steinbeck's chagrin. 'John said he wanted to crawl into himself and die when she did that,' a friend recalls. 'But he secretly liked it. Who wouldn't?'[17] Mrs Cupp seems to have taken a dim view of some aspects of her talented student. Like many shy people, he occasionally overcompensated and became 'loud or rude', as Mrs Cupp told Nelson Valjean, editor of the *Salinas Index-Journal*, in 1940, when the controversy over *The Grapes of Wrath* was raging throughout the country. 'I felt I sometimes caught him with his tongue in his cheek.'[18] In the same letter, she complained that 'no argument in the world would have made John hand in work if he decided not to,' and she categorized him as 'run of the mill college material'. Maybe so. But Mrs Cupp went too far, I think, in suggesting that his Depression-era books, where he 'sides' with the downtrodden of the nation, were written insincerely. 'These people were good copy,' she said. But the cynicism belonged to Mrs Cupp, not Steinbeck, who was the least cynical of modern writers.

Another teacher, Miss Hawkins, praised Steinbeck for his imagination and encouraged him to become a writer, but the most important boost came from a neighbour by the name of Lucille Hughes, one of his mother's best friends. She was herself an aspiring writer, and Steinbeck would cross the street to visit her once or twice a week, 'following her around and reading his stories to her'.[19] Mrs Hughes later recalled looking up and seeing Steinbeck framed in the window of his bedroom, the gaslight blazing behind him; he was bent over the pad on his lap with a pencil in hand, his lips pursed and 'his long hair falling forward'. It was a sight common to passers-by on Central Avenue. 'John was always up in that room,' his sister says, 'that was his hideaway.' Indeed, this seclusion might be seen as a metaphor: Steinbeck lived 'above' his family, aloof, dreaming, cut off, at times inaccessible. It was one place where Olive would not pursue him with demands, criticisms, accusations.

The pressure to become a respectable candidate for admission to a good college seems to have made itself felt in his junior year, when he succumbed to a flu in May 1918 that turned quickly into pneumonia. This was the same flu that had killed hundreds of thousands of Americans that year, and it was deeply feared. Steinbeck came home from school one day 'pale and dizzy' and collapsed in his bed, sending Olive into a frenzy.[20] His temperature shot up dangerously, and he was soon delirious. In those days, before the advent of antibiotics, there was every reason for panic. 'I went down and down,' Steinbeck later remembered, 'until the wingtips of angels brushed my eyes.' Dr Merganser, a local surgeon, was called in, and he turned the downstairs bedroom where Steinbeck's parents slept into a makeshift operating theatre. He opened the teenager's chest under ether, removing a rib to gain access to the infected lung, which was then drained of pleural pus. 'We thought surely he would die on us,' his sister says.[21] 'John looked horrible, horrible. We did everything we could for him. And then he had a relapse. It took a long time, but he was all right in the end. I must say, we were scared to death.' Despite this physically and emotionally traumatizing incident, Steinbeck recovered well enough to attend the last three weeks of school before the beginning of summer recess.

It is interesting to note that Steinbeck succumbed periodically to severe illnesses throughout his life. His lungs, in particular, remained a vulnerable spot, and he often collapsed for weeks at a time with coughs or racking colds. The psychological damage inflicted by this illness of 1918, which had brought him close to death and required such intrusive surgery, was also considerable. It seems to have given him a sense of himself as someone on the edge of life, reinforcing a vulnerability which had its psychological roots in his troubled relationship with his weak father. John Ernst was definitely a case of 'damaged goods', and his son could not expunge his imprint, carried over from father to son. Not surprisingly, in later life Steinbeck would often find himself physically ill when under severe psychological stress. The illness would, in effect, become the literal embodiment of a spiritual malaise, providing a focus for a hurt that might otherwise go unspoken for, unacknowledged.

Steinbeck's final year at Salinas High ended with a flourish that was marked by a major upturn in his grades, a clear sign that Olive's continuous pressure was paying dividends of a kind. The yearbook, for which he wrote an amusing little piece (reminiscent of H. L. Mencken, who was just coming into national prominence) about his 'English room', continued to be his main interest. He wrote, 'The English room, which is just down the hall from the office, is the sanctuary of Shakespeare, the temple of Milton and Byron, and the terror of Freshmen. English is a kind of high brow idea of the American language. A hard job is made of nothing at all and nothing at all is made of a hard job.'[22]

This is clever enough, for a highschooler, but few of Steinbeck's classmates thought he would become a famous writer. In the Class Prognostications, he was seen as a preacher in some distant city:

> The church of a far off city
> Came towering into view,
> Where John was preaching in solemn tones
> To many a well-filled pew.

To a degree, this precast of the future Steinbeck was not so far off the mark as it seems. His didacticism would become an integral part of his profile as a man and writer, and would infuse his best works with an edge of moral fervour that works brilliantly to create an aura one might call 'Steinbeckian'.

In June 1919 he was one of twenty-four graduates of Salinas High School for that year – the year after the Great War ended. It was expected that he would continue his studies. Esther and Beth had gone to Mills College, a first-rate institution in Oakland, several years before him. Indeed, Beth already had a graduate degree in business from a college in Boston: an achievement extremely rare for women in those days. (She would go on to have a successful business career in retailing, working for a large department store in San Francisco as a buyer and business manager.) Olive, of course, was education-minded, and she had told her son for as long as he could remember that he would one day attend college.

Steinbeck did not, however, want to go too far from home, and Stanford University seemed the obvious choice. It was easy to get to, and it was known to have high academic standards. Several of his classmates from Salinas High, including Bill Black, were going there, which must have made the decision easier as well. Furthermore, admission to a university was not even remotely as competitive then as it has become. Steinbeck applied with some trepidation but was immediately accepted for the following autumn term. His family and friends rejoiced. 'We were all delighted. Mother, especially, thought Stanford would force John to become more serious about his academic work, and that it would bring him out of his shell,' his sister recalls. As Toby Street, a Stanford classmate and close friend, later recalled, 'John left Salinas with a sigh of relief. I don't think it mattered where he was going. Anywhere was better than home.'

II

The Stanford Years

'Once in college I went flibbery geblut and got to going to
the library and reading what I wanted instead of what was
required. I got so far behind that I could not possibly catch
up.'

Steinbeck, *Journal of a Novel*

Steinbeck arrived in Palo Alto, at Stanford University – which
was then called Leland Stanford Junior University – in the
autumn term of 1919. He was seventeen years old, a mere
boy; but having spent the summer digging canals outside
Salinas, he was fit and strong, with a huge barrel chest and
labour-toughened hands. His long, dark hair was combed
back straight every morning, but by the middle of the day it
was unkempt; he shaved irregularly and balked at wearing a
tie on Sundays like most of his classmates. By all accounts, he
was a raw, ungainly, shy, and rather conceited young man
who thought he knew a great deal more than he actually did.
Since he had not worked especially hard in high school, he
was ill-prepared for the high academic standards that were
taken for granted at Stanford.

Having so recently dealt with the problems that follow
from the wrong choice of career, Steinbeck's father, John
Ernst, hoped that his son might want to study engineering or
something technical. But Steinbeck insisted that he was going
to be a writer, and his parents allowed him to register for a
general liberal arts curriculum. 'My parents knew John
wanted to be a writer,' his sister says, 'but they didn't know
how serious he was. He was dead serious, as we now know.
But there was no way to know that then.' On his entrance

card, he listed his career interests as teaching, journalism, and law.

College offered Steinbeck an unexpectedly rocky ride; indeed, he would attend the university off and on for the next six years, leaving without a degree of any kind, much to the chagrin of his parents and his own clear sense of disappointment. 'He often talked with anxiety about not having taken a degree,' his friend John Hersey recalls. 'He was self-conscious about it, and he said it had made his mother very upset. She would have liked him to go to law school and return to Salinas. In her mind there was something disreputable about being a writer.'[1] Steinbeck's official record was studded with reports of missed classes, botched courses, unexplained absences, withdrawals, readmissions, and what were then called 'cinch notices' or warnings that he was in danger of failing a course. He was rarely off academic probation.

Like so many gifted writers – F. Scott Fitzgerald, W. H. Auden and Robert Frost among the most prominent of them – Steinbeck could not accommodate himself to the academic grid and grind. Artists do not by nature advance along a preordained scale, and one cannot measure their success by grades or common academic standards. The question of whether or not Steinbeck 'succeeded' at Stanford is a moot one, at best. He was not a scholar, and he did not need a degree to pursue what interested him: writing. In the end, Stanford gave him plenty of time to read and think, to meet like-minded friends, and to develop as a writer. If his education could not be called 'systematic', there was still plenty of substance to the courses he took, and he spent the rest of his life following up interests in literature, history and science that were sparked during these years.

Olive Steinbeck did allow her son to choose his course of study, but she insisted that he return to Salinas to visit the family every weekend throughout his freshman year. As one friend later said, 'It was rather humiliating for him, but his mother said that he must report home like that and he did, though it made him angry as hell.'[2] To ensure that this happened, an arrangement was made with a friend of John Ernst's called Bernard Freire to pick up young John every Friday afternoon at Mountain View, a village south of Palo Alto. Freire worked for the Spreckles Sugar Company, and his job was to collect beet samples from the various ranches that supplied the company with produce. He would drive John back to Salinas in his pick-up, stopping for dinner at a truck stop in Gilroy. Once again, the long helping hand of Charlie Pioda can be seen outstretched.

Steinbeck's closest friend at Stanford was his freshman room-mate, George Mors, a level-headed young man who would later become an Army engineer. The two freshmen, who could not have been more unlike each other (Mors already had a military aura, and was disciplined about his studies), shared a room on the first floor of Encina Hall: a massive, five-storey sandstone building which threw a long shadow across the playing field beside it. The rooms that students lived in, then as now, were large, with lots of wood-panelling and heavy doors that stood in contrast to the bright stucco walls and amber tiled floors. There were two narrow beds in the room Steinbeck shared, a basin for washing, two oak desks, and a closet that both students had to share.

Encina Hall was one of many buildings on the Stanford campus which reflected the Spanish mission style of architecture, by now common throughout California. Influenced by Spanish and Mexican motifs (which in turn had been influenced by Moorish elements), the university was known for its elegantly sweeping Moorish arches, its lush courtyard gardens, its stucco and sandstone façades. There were tawny eucalyptus groves and cool stands of redwood trees; flowers bloomed throughout the year in bright succession. Stanford was, as it remains, one of the most spacious, carefully planned, and beautiful university settings in the country.

The rough-and-tumble side of male dormitory life appealed to Steinbeck, with its all-night bull sessions, the endless poker games, the bawdy jokes, and the generous supply of whiskey, gin, beer and wine. It was here, in 1919, that he began in earnest his long and troubled relationship with alcohol. Like so many American writers before and after him, booze was a constant factor in his life. And while he would never call himself an 'alcoholic', he did not go for extended periods without a drink of some kind. (This was common for people of Steinbeck's generation and class. Hard liquor, like tobacco and caffeine, were omnipresent props.) A man who suffered regular bouts of deep depression, he turned to alcohol as a mood-altering substance, a way of digging himself out of a trough which, of course, perpetually backfired and sent him deeper into the depths as soon as the temporary high had worn off.

Steinbeck wanted desperately to break free from parental bounds, and by mid-year he was refusing to visit his parents every weekend, much to their consternation. He cultivated a sense of himself as a libertine; indeed, he seems to have made a conscious point of straying from the narrow path his parents had laid down for him. Mors has recalled how, on those weekends when Steinbeck managed to elude the dutiful trips home to Salinas with Bernard Freire, he would escape into San Francisco to 'live it up'. In later life, Steinbeck remembered fondly those escapes into the big city: 'I was very broke and couldn't indulge in as much sweet-scented sin as I wished, but what I did manage to chisel in on was in San Francisco. Who needed Paris or the silken sewers of Rome when there were the Bush Street apartments and the Pleasure Domes of Van Ness Avenue?'

One of his classmates later said, 'I don't think John was as bad as he pretended, but he did live it up when he could. The drinking and visits to whorehouses – I doubt that he really did much of this – were just part of his story.'[3] It is not hard to imagine that a shy, imaginative boy like Steinbeck would go in for self-mythologizing. A writer invents himself first, then becomes his invention. Over the next decade, Steinbeck became something of the libertine he affected to be as a freshman at Stanford, but it always required large quantities of alcohol to pull off. This was not 'natural' to him; he was by nature more subdued. 'I think he was more comfortable in the library, reading,' says one friend. 'He found public occasions a strain. He once said, "You have to act when you go out. I play John Steinbeck. The problem is, I sometimes don't recognize him." '[4]

Although he certainly kicked up his heels, it seems unlikely that Steinbeck was as prodigally debauched as he later pretended. 'John loved to exaggerate, to romanticize, these things,' says Burgess Meredith, who would become a close friend in the late Thirties.[5] 'He thought of himself as a rake, I think, and he never tired of telling stories about his early days and what a bad fellow he was. I never did believe everything, and he really didn't expect you to. It was part of the fiction, and if you didn't accept that about him you could lump it.'

In those days (as today) athletes were by far the most admired students on campus, and Stanford was no exception. Football was king, and Steinbeck and George Mors went out for the freshman football team together. Steinbeck was big but not agile enough for collegiate athletics, and his training in football at Salinas High had been minimal. He did not make the team, and neither did Mors. As for other aspects of his social life, his shyness slowed its development. Mors later said that Steinbeck withdrew in the evenings to his room and spent much of his time with a stack of pulp novels and girlie magazines. Another friend said, 'He stayed in his room with the door locked on weekends, pretending he wasn't there. But the light would show under the door, and you knew he was in there. It was peculiar.'[6]

He limped through his first year at Stanford, getting two 'cinch notices' and missing many classes; while the subjects that he studied caught his interest, especially English composition and a literature course called 'Narration and Exposition', he generally found himself unable to keep up with the pace set by his instructors. In December, his parents were sent a letter by the Dean of Students, who warned them that their son was 'not working up to his potential'. This news, as might be expected, sent Olive Steinbeck through the roof. 'She wanted him to do so well,' his sister recalls, 'and she just couldn't believe it when he got into trouble with the deans. She guessed he would flunk out entirely, and it made her very angry.'

Steinbeck staggered through to the end of the academic year, and that summer John Ernst got his son and his son's roommate temporary jobs with a surveying unit working in the Santa Lucias, near Big Sur. Mors and Steinbeck were giddy with delight, imagining a summer of relative ease in the open countryside, but the work proved rougher than they expected. The young men were forced to lug heavy surveying equipment up steep hillsides through wiry brush and prickly scrub. The food was rotten, and – according to Steinbeck – there were rattlesnakes to sidestep and poison oak to avoid. The two college boys lasted only a few weeks, when they quit in frustration. John Ernst, who always hesitated to get into any kind of fight with his son and went out of his way to smooth things over, got them easier (and lower-paying) jobs as maintenance men at the Spreckles plant in Salinas.

Steinbeck's association with his father's old company, Spreckles, continued over the next few years, during summers and long drop-out periods. The sugar company had grown fairly large by 1920, and it owned or leased ranches all along the Salinas Valley from King City to Santa Clara; Steinbeck worked in different capacities on several of them. While cultivating beet for the sugar plant in Salinas was their major function, the ranches also raised beef cattle and, to feed the livestock, produced hay and alfalfa. Each ranch had a permanent staff, but during certain times of the year itinerant ranch-hands were hired. These were the 'bindlestiffs' who eventually became the subject of Steinbeck's *Of Mice and Men*: broken men who wandered the countryside looking for a bit of work on this or that farm. They would do anything – buck barley, feed the pigs, dig wells, harvest fruit or vegetables, mend fences.

Nothing was ever wasted on Steinbeck; he instinctively knew how to milk his experience for what it was worth in imaginative value. One can tie a huge number of characters, incidents and settings from his later fiction to early working experiences acquired during periods away from Stanford. The specific incident that sparked *Of Mice and Men* may have occurred during this time, as Steinbeck later suggested to an interviewer:

> I was a bindlestiff myself for quite a spell. I worked in the same country that the story is laid in. The characters are composites to a certain extent. Lennie was a real person. He's in an insane asylum in California right now. I worked alongside him for many weeks. He didn't kill a girl. He killed a ranch foreman. Got sore because the boss had fired his pal and stuck a pitchfork right through his stomach. I hate to tell you how many times. I saw him do it. We couldn't stop him until it was too late.[7]

While Steinbeck may have been indulging in a bit of role-playing for the interviewer here, the vividness of his fiction about people like George and Lennie may well be tied to his firsthand experience on these ranches. 'I think John preferred those jobs to studying,' his sister says. 'He always came home full of stories, and we would sit around the kitchen table and listen for hours. I didn't believe a lot of the stories, but I didn't care. They were good stories, and they were meant to be taken as such.'

Apart from the bindlestiffs, who were mostly Anglo-Saxon in origin, Steinbeck encountered workers who had flooded in from Mexico and the Philippines in search of wages. The Mexicans, in particular, caught the young man's fancy, and they would play a central role in *Tortilla Flat*, where he evoked a number of vivid Mexican characters, such as Sweets Ramirez, one of his most endearing creations. Indeed, Mexico itself would become a favourite place for him to visit, and he would set a novella, *The Pearl*, as well as the screenplay *Viva Zapata!*, in that country.

In the autumn of 1920 Steinbeck arrived in Palo Alto to try his luck once more. He roomed as before with George Mors, and under Mors's influence he signed up with the ROTC, an affiliation he would discontinue after one term: the regimentation went fiercely against his grain. By this time he was on academic probation and had several 'incompletes' to make up. 'I got so far behind that I could not possibly catch up,' he said later. But he plugged along for much of the term, attending classes sporadically and spending a good deal of time in the university library, where – according to his own confession – he read mostly books that were not on any professor's syllabus. He also worked furiously on his own stories, producing six of them (all juvenilia, which have been lost) in the autumn term alone.

Steinbeck saw, rather quickly, that he was not going to make it through the year. During the previous summer, when George had stayed as a guest with the Steinbeck family in Salinas, Mrs Steinbeck extracted from him a promise to keep a close watch on her son's academic progress and encourage him to stick with it. Reluctantly, George agreed. When he realized that his room-mate was sinking into

academic oblivion in about mid-November, he wrote a note
to Mrs Steinbeck saying that her son was in trouble. She
arrived on campus two days later, raging, and marched John
off to the Dean, who explained to both of them that John was
probably not going to make it. The mid-term reports from his
teachers were horrific. He was given a two-week probation-
ary lease on academic life, and Mrs Steinbeck went back to
Salinas in a state of fury, 'barely speaking to her son'.[8]

Steinbeck could not tolerate this pressure, and in late
November he decided to take matters into his own hands 'like
a man'. George Mors woke up one morning to find a self-
dramatizing note from his forlorn room-mate on his desk:
Gone to China. See you again sometime. The note ended with a
request for George to release his various animals – a canary, a
chipmunk and a turtle – from their captivity, much as he was
setting himself free from his. The rest of his things were to be
sent home to his sister, Mary, who was then and would
remain his closest sibling. He was not speaking to his mother.

Jack London was an immensely popular author at the time,
and Steinbeck entertained visions of sailing to the Far East
aboard a romantic freighter like his fellow Californian, who
chronicled these exotic travels in book after book. He took a
bus into San Francisco, carrying nothing but one small
suitcase, and found a cheap room in a flophouse on Market
Street. Somewhat dutifully, he went down to the waterfront
hiring halls to apply for jobs on eastbound vessels. Given his
lack of experience at sea and, perhaps more to the point, the
half-heartedness of his attempts, he did not get a job. The Far
East would have to wait for a few decades. Confused and
upset, he bummed around for a week or so, eventually taking
a job at Capwell's department store in Oakland, which was
hiring clerks for the Christmas rush.

The stint at Capwell's last only a couple of weeks, during
which time he stayed with a Stanford friend in Oakland by
the name of Robert Bennett, who has written a little pamphlet

detailing this period in Steinbeck's life. One of the chief anecdotes he recounts has to do with Steinbeck's visit to a Methodist church on Christmas day under the aegis of Bennett's parents, who were extremely pious. The preacher, a garrulous man, went on and on about the 'spiritual hunger' that was felt throughout the land. Steinbeck muttered under his breath that this was all a 'lot of crap'. With a moral fervour that seems in keeping with his later novels, he rose to his feet and shouted: 'Yes, you all look satisfied here, while outside the world begs for a crust of bread or a chance to earn it! Feed the body and the soul will take care of itself!'[9]

Where did this come from? One can assume, for a start, that this was not the first time Steinbeck encountered hypocrisy in a Christian church! Shyness and aggression are common bedfellows, and Steinbeck would throughout his life oscillate between them. The shyness certainly predominated, but this necessarily involved suppressing strong emotions at times. When these emotions leaped out, they occasionally did so dramatically: most of Steinbeck's close friends can recall having seen him behave aggressively or angrily at certain times. This behaviour, while hardly 'abnormal', may have had its origins in John Ernst's 'weakness'. It is a hard thing to see one's father fail and, perhaps even worse, to see him crumble beneath the failure. Steinbeck's shyness would have reminded him of this paternal weakness, and he might have attempted to overcome it with rage, with aggressive demonstrations of strength. One of his closest friends later recalled, 'John could be a firebrand at times. He could explode at public meetings like the English Club, a group of students and professors who met to read and discuss their writing once a month. John could be almost obnoxious there. Or in conversations in the dormitory. Most of the time he said nothing. Sometimes it wasn't easy to see what he might be angry about, but you stood aside till he cooled down, and you learned not to take his bad tempers personally.'[10]

Steinbeck was at this point in his life a moderately unstable young man in flight from the expectations of his parents, which he had internalized. He was in no state to return to Stanford for another bout of academic malaise. Indeed, it hardly mattered how he felt about resuming his academic course of study, since he had already been sent a letter saying that he was dismissed from the university until such time as he was willing to take his studies seriously. He needed time, and he knew it: time to dig his hands in the dirt, and time to get to know the bindlestiffs and other migratory workers whom he had come to admire. He had to let his body and mind mature to a point where he could re-enter college life with a reasonable hope of mastering his academic work. Much to his surprise, his parents (who had been frantic during the period his sisters called his 'disappearance') welcomed the prodigal son home with less censure than he expected; indeed, John Ernst once again went out of his way to find his son a job.

Steinbeck had returned to Salinas with his tail between his legs, still much more boy than man. His parents, aware that he was extremely fragile, said almost nothing to him about his 'failure', much to his surprise. They knew enough not to upset him, fearing another attempt to set out for China or somewhere equally exotic. It became clear to him at once that he could not live at home for long, so he took a job on one of the Spreckles ranches near Chualar, bunking with the men and serving as foreman to a gang of Mexican and Filipino migrant workers. They loaded heavy burlap sacks full of beets into trucks for transportation into Salinas: a gruelling job which left Steinbeck so exhausted at night that he could write nothing. His hands, he told his sister, were 'blistered' and his back was 'too sore to sleep'. After a dinner of 'gristle stew and potatoes', he sat with the men and listened to their stories, asking questions, probing for information. Four months of this were enough, and he quit one day without warning and returned to Central Avenue, taking up his old room – the lofty garret where he could sulk in darkness or read and write by a dim light until dawn.

After a brief rest, he found a series of jobs in the Salinas area that included a period of dredging a canal from Salinas to Castroville. This was hard manual labour, and Steinbeck was thrown once again into contact with the men who would become a passion for him and populate his later fiction. The difficulty of living with John Ernst and Olive soon began to outweigh the convenience of free room and board. Living at home meant regression; it meant being under his mother's thumb and succumbing to old habits and patterns he had tried so hard to break away from when he first went to Stanford. Old feelings of anger and resentment surfaced, rather painfully. He noted to his sister, Beth, that his mother dominated every discussion while his father withdrew into the parlour to read the papers in angry silence as he smoked his pipe. Not surprisingly, Steinbeck moved out as abruptly as he had moved in.

During the immediate postwar years in the US, the number of unemployed men had swollen alarmingly, and Steinbeck soon found himself joining a muddy river of 'hobos' washing from ranch to ranch, from town to town, in search of wages. Though he scrambled just to make ends meet, he did not lose sight of his goal of becoming a writer; in the most unlikely circumstances he would take notes for possible short stories on scraps of paper. He would also pump those he met on the road for stories, true or untrue: stories were what interested him, what mattered to him. There is even a story, recounted by Benson, in which Steinbeck is said to have paid a hobo two dollars for *his* story, much in the way Jack London paid people he met for stories he could make over into fiction. (He once paid a small sum of money to a young man by the name of Sinclair Lewis, for instance, for several anecdotes.)

Reading through Steinbeck's fiction of the Thirties, one sees the effect of these wandering months, which in the course of the author's intermittent Stanford career amounted to well over a year on the road. *The Pastures of Heaven* and *The Long Valley*, for example, are full of incidents and characters encountered on the various ranches where he worked in 1922 and 1923. 'He always said he wasn't good at thinking things up,' a friend recalls. 'Those times when he stayed away from Stanford were crucial for him. They gave him a sense of how people operated, how they moved among each other, how they talked and what they wanted. The Mexicans from *Tortilla Flat* and *Cannery Row*, for instance, were often based on people he knew then. He worked beside them in the hayfields, bucked barley with them, and he slept with them in the bunkhouses. They shared the same food. They got drunk together.'[11]

Partly to satisfy his mother and partly because he knew that a writer should know as much as possible, Steinbeck re-applied for admission to Stanford in the winter of 1923, arguing that he was ready to apply himself seriously. To his delight, he was accepted. He felt sure he could do the work, and this time around things went better for him in all ways. He got in with a group who belonged to the English Club, which he would eventually dominate and which became his base of operations. And two members of this club became his closest friends for life: Webster 'Toby' Street and Carl Wilhelmson, both of whom were veterans of the Great War and mature in a way that Steinbeck, just back from his time in the wilderness of the working man, could appreciate. Street was a tough, tobacco-chewing, hard-drinking man who had lost two fingers in the war. Though he pursued a career in marine law, he also wrote an unproduced play in the late Twenties that became the basis for Steinbeck's second novel, *To a God Unknown*. Wilhelmson was a Finn with a strong accent who hoped to become a writer himself. He eventually published one novel, *Midsummernight*, in 1930. Its lack of critical or commercial success drove him from literature into business.

In an interview from 1947, Steinbeck remembered how Wilhelmson was a staunch defender of Sherwood Anderson's collection of linked stories, *Winesburg, Ohio*, which was considered by many readers 'a stirring and shocking book' when it first appeared in 1919. 'The few of us who liked it were back up against the wall,' Steinbeck said. 'I have a friend, Carl Wilhelmson, a Finn. When we were at school Carl had a rather thick accent. He liked the Anderson book. One day on the campus a whole group of students surrounded him and baited him about it. One girl was thoroughly angry – not putting on angry. She shouted at Carl, "What do you mean by liking that book? What is the purpose of that filth? What is the purpose of it?" Carl was excited, too. "What iss der purpose of art?" You could hear him a long way off.'[12]

Another crucial friend of this period was Carlton 'Dook' Sheffield, who would remain a close friend and faithful correspondent in later years. Sheffield and Steinbeck ran into each other at registration, and they recalled having met during Steinbeck's previous years at the university. At this time, he was rooming with an immature young man 'who put up pictures of naked ladies all over the walls'. Steinbeck said that he liked naked women, but he didn't want to stare at them all day; in short order, he talked the room-mate into switching, so that Dook and he could room together.

Sheffield, like Street and Wilhelmson, also hoped to become a writer, and he and Steinbeck would 'sit for hours in a little diner off campus arguing about writers like Sinclair Lewis and Sherwood Anderson and Upton Sinclair. John seemed to have read everything, and he thought about what he read and came into the English Club bursting with ideas. He could be shy in public, but when he got on to a subject that mattered to him, the shyness vanished.'[13] Like Steinbeck, Sheffield was a votary of two strong women in the English Department: Margery Bailey and Edith Mirrielees.

Professor Bailey, a Yale PhD whom students called a 'dragon', was legendary on the Stanford campus as a fiery lecturer on literary subjects. 'You never got in her way,' one of her former students recalled.[14] 'She ate students for breakfast. I don't think anyone dared go to her classes unprepared. She had this withering stare, and she gave very low grades – even to the best students.' Bailey would later become a good friend to Steinbeck. Professor Mirrielees was less fierce by a long shot. She taught a course in the writing of short stories – one of the first 'creative writing' courses taught in an American university. Steinbeck talked about her fondly in a letter from this period: 'Miss Mirrielees is very kind, she hates to hurt feelings. She says that she thinks my stuff ought to be published but she doesn't know where.'[15]

Mirrielees had already acquired a minor reputation, having published stories in periodicals such as *The Atlantic Monthly*. She would eventually become a fixture at the Bread Loaf School of English in Vermont as well as the Bread Loaf Writers' Conference, and her two anthologies of short fiction would become standard classroom texts in later decades. She also wrote a handbook for beginner writers of fiction which counts as one of the first of its kind. Her advice to young writers is still worth having:

> The 'lean, terse style' is one towards which most beginners can profitably struggle . . . For most stories and most writers, deliberate ornamentation needs much scrutiny before it is allowed a place in finished work. Phrases pushing up like mushrooms above the level of the narrative have a habit a turning out to be toadstools on later inspection. 'Take out whatever you particularly like' is hard counsel, but oftener than not is wise counsel as well.[16]

It's interesting that Steinbeck, in his later books, would succeed to the extent that he followed his old professor's advice. When he veered from the 'lean, terse style', as he did in certain passages in *East of Eden* and *The Winter of Our Discontent*, he risked trying his readers' patience and losing their sympathy. It was also a kind of overwriting that marred his first novel, *Cup of Gold*, which was influenced by the florid styles of James Branch Cabell (author of many popular books, including *Jürgen*) and Donn Byme (best known for a novel about Marco Polo). Whereas the stories of *The Pastures of Heaven* and *The Long Valley*, like the prose of *The Grapes of Wrath*, *Of Mice and Men* and *Tortilla Flat*, are lean, hard, diamond-bright.

A former student of Edith Mirrielees remembers her well: 'She was a classic spinster schoolmistress type of professor: her hair pulled back in a bun, her blouses white and neatly pressed, her skirts long and pleated. She had a prim manner, very exact, and exacting. And she made students rewrite and rewrite their papers, and it seemed as if nothing would ever satisfy her. But she was friendly and approachable. She would encourage you to stay after class and talk about your own writing.' The fact that she had once taught John Steinbeck was a subject she occasionally brought up in class. 'She once had us read a Steinbeck story in class, and she had amusing stories about him at Stanford. She said he was terrifically shy and often lazy but that he had an unshakable confidence in his work. He told her he would become a published writer one day, and she believed him. But she tried to curb his sentimental side. That was his Achilles heel, she said. It marred some of the books, such as the ending of *Of Mice and Men*. She wished he had left off the last couple of paragraphs.'[17]

Steinbeck had come back to Stanford with no thought of conforming to the usual academic standards. He intended to study what pleased him, hoping to improve his prospects as a writer of fiction. 'This bull-headed independence of his amazed the rest of us,' Sheffield recalled. 'He read whatever pleased him, and he followed his own schedule.' He was writing a lot now, and he sought an audience with an almost charming stubbornness. Dean Storey, an acquaintance who lived in the same dormitory, said that Steinbeck would come into his dormitory room at night, a gangly and unshaven boy with a crudely typed manuscript under his arm. He would take off his boots, plop in an old leather chair, and read aloud in his deep, scratchy voice. You didn't dare interrupt him, according to Storey, or Steinbeck would suck in his breath, fold the manuscript contemptuously and storm out of the room. A similar story is told by Elaine Steinbeck: 'John used to come into the room with something he had written and sit down and begin reading. Soon after we were married, I offered a comment during one of his pauses. He looked at me sternly and said, "Please don't. I don't want criticism. I want you to listen." '

A third professor who made an impact on the young writer was William Herbert Carruth, who taught a course on Verse Writing and Prosody. Dook Sheffield took this course with Steinbeck, and they loved it. Carruth was a kindly man who relished Steinbeck's joking manner. As a writing teacher, he stressed the use of imagery and the control of metaphor. As Robert Penn Warren once said, 'Poetry is the great schoolhouse of fiction', and Steinbeck spent some time in this figurative schoolhouse, mastering techniques that would serve him well in his later career as a novelist. A poem was due every class, and this enforced a kind of steadiness that every writer of fiction must acquire at some point: a willingness to write even when the Muse seems to have taken the day off. (Steinbeck occasionally wrote poetry, mostly light verse, throughout his life, though he never tried to publish it.)

The practice of daily writing became part of Steinbeck's life now; he allotted certain hours, usually in the morning, to this work, putting a good deal of stock in consistency. This was the one area of his life where discipline was maintained, and the mere fact that he could sit down and write on a regular basis seems to have boosted his confidence. Steinbeck forged a pattern of morning work that he would follow throughout his life, although in later years he often stayed at his desk for eight or nine hours at a stretch. His productivity at Stanford is registered in a letter to Carl Wilhelmson dating early in the spring of 1924:

> There have been six stories this quarter. I wonder if you remember the one about the machinist who made engines and felt a little omnipotent until his own machine pulled his arm from him. Then he cursed God and suffered retribution at the hands of God or thought he did. That has finally been done to my satisfaction. Of the others, one was perfectly rotten, two were fair, three were quite good. About the only thing that can be said for them is that they do not resemble anything which has ever been written.[18]

One sees here the odd, and very distinctive, combination of self-doubt and self-assertion that would mark his letters to friends about his work for years to come.

Two of the stories, perhaps the ones that Steinbeck considered 'quite good', were published in the February and June numbers of the *Stanford Spectactor* in 1924. These may be considered his first real publications. One of them, 'Fingers of Cloud', is a remarkable piece of work about a retarded teenage girl named Gertie, who strays from her parents' home and drifts aimlessly across the northern California countryside in search of something elusive. She stumbles into a bunkhouse on a ranch filled with crude Filipino migrant workers who speak in a dialect that Steinbeck had mastered well. The boss, a stock character by the name of Pedro, takes Gertie in and soon marries her. She is alternately coddled and beaten by Pedro, and at the end of the story she drifts away, having moved – or been pushed – from innocence to experience, a theme dear to Steinbeck at this point in his life. 'Fingers of Cloud' might well be considered a dry run for the stories of *The Pastures of Heaven* (1932), which it resembles in texture, tone and theme. Furthermore, the story represents the first of Steinbeck's numerous attempts to portray mentally or emotionally impaired people in a sympathetic way. (One can hardly help but assume that Steinbeck identified on some crucial level with his impaired characters; one piece of his composite self must have felt insufficient, incompetent, bewildered by the world's ferociously complex demands.)

One of the more interesting phases of Steinbeck's second major assault on the citadel of Stanford University was the summer course at the Hopkins Marine Station near Monterey, which he attended with his sister, Mary, in the summer of 1923. (Mary followed her older brother there – another sign of their strangely close bond.) This was a seminal moment in Steinbeck's intellectual progress, and his later fascination with ecology and the organismal nature of life have their beginnings in this course with Professor C. V. Taylor, who introduced him to the writings of John Elof Boodin and William Emerson Ritter, among others. Steinbeck was able to observe a large number of marine creatures in their natural habitat in Monterey Bay, which was already familiar to him from the many summers and weekends spent at the cottage in Pacific Grove.

This period at the Marine Station laid the basis for his lifelong interest in marine biology and prepared the way for his later friendship with Edward Ricketts. Unlike most other writers of this century, Steinbeck was at heart a scientist, and he viewed human beings as part of a group that had to be considered, ultimately, within a general ecological perspective. Some of his critics could not understand what he was doing and would criticize him for dealing, as Edmund Wilson said in an influential review of *The Grapes of Wrath*, 'either with the lower animals or with human beings so rudimentary that they are almost on the animal level'.[19] Wilson simply did not appreciate the originality of Steinbeck's 'ecological' perspective, which ran counter to the mainstream of modernist writing, where (as in Lawrence or Joyce) the individual is commonly celebrated for his or her separateness from the crowd.

Margery Bailey was on the faculty in Monterey that summer, teaching an English course, and Steinbeck came under her broad wing once again. Her fierceness attracted him, and the feeling seems to have been reciprocal; from her side, she seems to have appreciated Steinbeck's irreverence and innate, even arrogant, self-confidence with regard to his writing. Benson reports an incident that shows something of the flavour of their friendship: one evening Steinbeck appeared at her apartment clad in a T-shirt, and she noticed a long scar on his shoulder. When she asked him how he got it, he replied with an off-hand cool designed to create the maximum shock, 'A Mexican woman with whom I was copulating bit me.'[20]

One cannot know how much of Steinbeck's frequent braggings about 'copulations' during his Stanford years are to be believed but, even if we scale down his claims, there must have been some residue of truth. Like many men who consider themselves 'ugly', Steinbeck was dependent on women. He needed the reassurance that he was sufficiently attractive to win their hearts; as a result, he was never long without some romantic affiliation. One can safely assume that, apart from the whores he may have visited on Van Ness Avenue in San Francisco, there were other women in his life and that he acquired a good deal of carnal knowledge in addition to whatever else he may have learned during his college days.

The zigzag course Steinbeck had been following through the fields of higher learning continued, and he found this exhausting, as anyone might. Though his intentions were good, he could not withstand the continual hail of demands that are part of academic life. In frustration, he decided to back away from the campus once again, to make a tactical retreat. The autumn term was to be spent at home in Salinas with his parents, the idea being that he would use the time to finish 'incompletes' and read some of the books for future courses in advance of their being required by some demanding professor. He could also make a little money on the side, thus relieving some of the financial burden John Ernst was quietly shouldering.

Salinas, alas, was boring, and he found the atmosphere on Central Avenue stifling. There was only one high-school friend in the area with whom he shared any intimacy – Glenn Graves – so he and Steinbeck spent a great deal of time playing cards and hiking in the nearby hills. During the night, from eleven until seven, Steinbeck worked at Spreckles as a 'chemist', which wasn't as fancy as it sounds. 'Night work claims me,' he wrote in late September to Dook Sheffield, who was likewise taking the term off in southern California. 'My tremendous powers are now directed at the manufacture of sugar.' In the next sentence, his wit caught fire: 'Just on the face of it, one might conjecture that a disposition so exposed might take on saccharine qualities, and such is in reality the case. I was becoming so sweet that the tips of my fingers got sticky, thus interfering with my work. I assure you that it took tons . . . of citric acid to bring myself back to normal.'[21]

He returned to Stanford for the winter and spring terms, this time living alone in Encina Hall in a sunny room on the fifth floor that overlooked the dining hall. He missed Dook Sheffield, who was still off campus, but he had numerous other friends who would listen to him read aloud from his stories. Frank Fenton was among them, a reserved and intelligent young man who worked as an editor of the *Stanford Spectator*. (He later became president of San Francisco State University.) Fenton was, in effect, Steinbeck's first 'real' editor, since he published several stories by Steinbeck in the school paper over the course of the next two years.

'John was rather sullen most of the time,' another friend who was living in Encina Hall at the time recalls.[22] 'He used to sit in his room for long periods with the shades drawn. Then he would burst into my room and demand that I listen to a new story. He was full of jokes, but his readings were no joke. You had to listen. The thing is, you wanted to. The stories were damn good. John knew so much more than the rest of us, it seemed. He had firsthand experience of the things he wrote about, and he read novels by great French or English novelists when he wasn't writing his own stuff. I remember him reading a book of Turgenev's stories and shaking his head: "This is the way to write," he said. "It's the real thing." '

One gets some sense of Steinbeck's avidity in a letter to Mrs Edith Wagner, the mother of his old schoolfriend, Max:

> You asked me what I had been reading. Here is the last list which we brought from the library. *The Book of the Dead* from existing papyri, *Les Femmes Savantes* of Molière, which I had never read in French before, and a low detective tale labeled *L'Homme du Dent d'Or* by a man of whom I never heard, and who in the French fashion manages to get his murder accomplished in a bedroom; *La Barraca* of Ibañez, which is shorter and I think more effective than his others; some short stories by Katherine Fullerton Gerould, and she certainly is the master of her kind of short stories. I have just finished the autobiography of Casanova and *The Judge* by Rebecca West, which is a wonderful piece of writing. If you haven't read it you must, for it is one of the best things I have read in many a day. In a maniacal period this summer I went through Pushkin and Turgenev.[23]

An element of youthful hyperbole runs through this letter, but it is obvious that Steinbeck was eager to improve himself, to 'read around', to become an educated man. His taste, here as later, was wide-ranging and eclectic, although he would always favour good storytelling writers like Turgenev or West over more complex and modernist writers like Proust or Joyce.

When the spring term ended, Steinbeck returned to Salinas in a good mood. His grades were, on the whole, mediocre, but he was no longer on probation. Much to his surprise, he had received an A in a course on the short story from Professor Mirrielees, who by now had developed a strong friendship with him. He planned to spend as much of the summer as possible working on stories, though he wanted to earn money too. He decided to look for a summer job in the Monterey area so that he could live with Dook Sheffield at the cottage in Pacific Grove. The two of them scoured the region, looking for jobs in the canneries, on boats, in warehouses. Nothing came their way, and soon they retreated to Salinas, hoping for work in the Spreckles plant. But even Spreckles was suffering from a slight downturn in the middle of the supposedly 'roaring' Twenties. Charlie Pioda, as ever, came to the aid of young John and Dook, getting them jobs at a branch factory run by Spreckles at Manteca, a stiflingly hot town in the San Joaquin Valley near Modesto. 'That was the summer we sweat off every bit of adolescent fat that we'd ever managed to acquire,' Sheffield later said.[24]

By mid-August, the heat and hideous boredom of working in the sugar factory defeated Steinbeck and Sheffield, who quit one day at lunchtime and left immediately for San Francisco, where they blew their small savings in the jazz-filled speakeasies which had grown up all over the city since the advent of Prohibition. 'We spent all our time looking for girls,' Sheffield said, 'more or less in vain.' In September they headed south to Sheffield's family house in Long Beach, where they were warmly greeted. The rather fantastic plan now was that both Dook and John would write cheap adventure stories and sell them to pulp magazines; this money would finance their more serious efforts. None of the stories, alas, panned out. 'We had a fine old time, but we ended up even worse off financially than when we started,' Sheffield said. 'It turned out that pulp was harder to produce than either of us imagined.' Steinbeck eventually drifted back to Salinas for Christmas, after which he would make his final assault on the citadel of Stanford.

Steinbeck returned to Palo Alto for the last time in the winter and spring of 1925, fairly certain that this would be his final encounter with academe, which had never been a comfortable environment for him. In general, his final terms seem to have been his most 'successful', personally as well as academically. Dook Sheffield was back as well, and their friendship, which had been strengthened over the summer and autumn they had spent together, made everything bright for Steinbeck, who quickly re-established his connections with the English Club. Two further important friendships – this time with women – began right away. John Breck (whose real name was Elizabeth Anderson) and Kate Beswick became two of his closest friends, and the latter was probably a lover as well. We know little of Kate Beswick, who would play a more important part in his life a few years later; but John Breck's story is well known.

Breck was the feisty and brilliant daughter of a wealthy industrialist from the midwest; over the years, she called herself by several names, including John Barton and John Breck, the latter a pseudonym under which she wrote stories and newspaper columns for a local paper. She was a strong-looking, attractive, masculine woman, and when Steinbeck met her at the English Club, she was in her late thirties and divorced with two teenage daughters who gave her lots of trouble. Although she was not a Stanford student, Breck attended the English Club as a 'distinguished guest', having had several stories published in magazines. She lived in a tumbledown house with brown siding on Palo Alto Avenue. Behind the house, in a tackroom attached to a stables, Steinbeck camped out. Dormitory life was now something he wished to avoid at all costs, and he enjoyed the romance of living in a shack. He was not confined there but wandered freely into the Breck house whenever he felt like it, and he would sit for hours chatting with Polly Smith, the sassy elder daughter of John Breck. Polly, a bright teenager whom Steinbeck found irresistibly attractive, would tell him her problems late into the night as he sat, with avuncular decorum, on the edge of her bed. She had acquired an interest in jazz, and the house teemed with amateur musicians. This was, after all, the Jazz Age, and the sound of clarinets and saxophones could be heard drifting through the open windows of the Breck house at all hours. The whole scene was 'bohemian and decadent and unforgettable', as Steinbeck later put it. He was accepted as part of the furnishings of the household, and he loved it, as did Webster 'Toby' Street, Dook Sheffield, and Carl Wilhelmson, who were all now a constant part of the Steinbeck entourage.

Margery Bailey was also a good friend of Breck, and a frequent visitor at the house. She, Breck and Steinbeck would sit around in the late evenings and smoke cigarettes and drink bootleg gin while arguing the merits of Sinclair Lewis, James Branch Cabell, Willa Cather, or F. Scott Fitzgerald, who had recently made a name for himself as the leading spokesman for this generation. 'This was John's real university,' Dook Sheffield later said. 'Everything was up for discussion: music, books, politics. I think everyone was surprised by how knowledgeable John was. It would have surprised most of his professors.' One has to admire Steinbeck's gumption and originality in finding a group of older intellectuals who could act as mentors. In those days students did not normally fraternize with their teachers, so the relationship with Bailey in particular would have been extremely unorthodox.

Steinbeck's tackroom was dubbed 'The Sphincter' by Dook Sheffield, and it had the singular virtue of being dirt cheap: five dollars a month. Since there was no running water or plumbing of any kind out there, Steinbeck's ablutions and bodily functions had to occur elsewhere, usually in the Breck house. The Sphincter was infested with ants, pill bugs and spiders, but Steinbeck appears to have relished the sordidness. He had only three or four changes of underwear, and these were always hanging on a clothesline that stretched across the dimly lit room. The grove of pine trees just outside the building was often used as a latrine. One can't help but think of the grubby but wonderful little house in *Tortilla Flat*, which houses Danny, Big Joe, Pilon and their carefree friends.

Steinbeck's romantic streak was long and wide, and 'The Sphincter' was his version of the traditional writer's garret. He slept on an army surplus cot and wrote stories on his old-fashioned Corona typewriter, which he propped on an orange crate. For diversion, he made his own red wine in gallon jugs, which he had collected from a nearby grocer. The wine, according to one friend, was 'foul but strong'. Steinbeck nursed many a hangover in that dark little room, lighted by gas lamps and candles. 'I once visited him there,' his sister recalled many years later. 'It was disgusting. He said to me, "Whatever you do, don't tell mother." Mother would certainly have hated John Breck.'[25]

Breck was perhaps the first published fiction writer Steinbeck knew as a friend. As Sheffield said, 'Breck was the opposite of Mrs Steinbeck,' and it seems probable that Steinbeck liked her in part because she was everything his mother was not: unpuritanical, saucy, and anti-bourgeois.

There was the double bonus that Breck took him under her protective female wing, thus replicating a familiar situation. Steinbeck was taken seriously, protected and admired. Even better, there were no emotional demands on him in Breck's household. He could come and go as he pleased, say what he thought, and drink as much as he liked. Sheffield said, 'The worse John behaved, the better Breck liked him. It was odd.'

Breck had constructed a writing studio in a garden house behind the main dwelling, and Steinbeck spent a lot of time there with her, reading her stories and getting his own read and criticized. He was maturing, emotionally and artistically, and he sensed it. Breck's admiration and encouragement boosted his self-esteem. 'John seemed happy there,' Sheffield said. Perhaps for the first time ever, his depression lifted, and he could delight in his own accomplishments. Among his many projects of the season was a story about Henry Morgan, the legendary pirate, which would emerge several years later in drastically revised form as his first novel, *Cup of Gold*. That story, originally called 'A Lady in Infra-Red', was written in 'The Sphincter' and retyped by Polly Smith; it remains one of his best early efforts, though it was never published.[26]

One gets a good sense of Steinbeck's peculiarly high-spirited mood at this time in a letter to Carl Wilhelmson, which is worth quoting at length:

It is very long since I made up my mind that I would write to you 'to-night'. This arcadian existence of mine has made of 'to-night' a receptacle for all of those things which do not have to be done in the terrible 'now'.

I am practicing hermitry in [my shed, 'The Sphincter']. Of course I have some rugs on the floor, the wall has a deep color and there are a few pictures, and I have even gone so far as a blue valenced curtain. I am comfortable, too comfortable I suppose for my own good, or rather, for the good of my soul. The place is far enough out of town so

there is no noise, it is isolated enough so that any little
irregularities may be practiced without let, the atmosphere is
suitable for my belated work. Needless to say I received your
letter, which I enjoyed beyond the power of saying.

Perhaps your rackings will be less felt some time . . . Time is
kind. It seems to anaesthetize these smoking ambitions and
aspirations which seem so important now. Life becomes
living, the moon ceases to be a golden plate for the eating of
thin dreams and becomes simply green cheese. We go on
practicing the blue magic just as the Cyclops tells us we must.

Do you think I do not know of the blue magic? I was
instructed in it from the start. My earliest memories are of my
mother's telling me how men could become bright shining
creatures with great white wings and all through the chanting
of simple incantations. The spell took rather long to work,
however, and I went to other wonderful things which could
be done.

You know the Cyclops loves the blue magic. He learned it
from his father, and Cyclops is ever respectful of the ways of
his father. True he may wear odd neckties and eat with his left
hand and rail at his father because he gurgles soup, but you
will notice that he walks with his toes turned outward and he
practices the blue magic, and who taught him that?

These charms must be worked very carefully. You must get
the vowel sounds exactly right and then there are waggles of
the head and forward motions of the index finger. I have not
succeeded so far, but I will if I take enough care. It works:
Cyclops says it does. I have tried the charm for romantic love,
but always I have failed on the vowel sound or moved my
head out of turn, and the thing has failed. I think I will stop
that one for a while and learn the chant which will bring me
success first and then happiness. It is very simple, they tell
me, and needs only a little practice with the blue chant. I will
practice arduously.

There have been six short stories this quarter . . .[27]

Now as later, Steinbeck was obsessed by magic, by chants,
by knightly quests, by 'heroism'. Art, for him, was an

incantation that made wonderful things happen, that turned men into 'shining creatures with great white wings'. His interest in myth and legend, in medievalism and the arcana of magic, would continue to inform his work to the end, as would his essentially romantic nature, which existed in uneasy propinquity with his more cynical side.

In the same letter, Steinbeck wrote about John Breck's lack of talent and his own sense of himself as a writer: 'John Breck is well. She continues to write stories, and, Carl, she cannot write stories; her sentences are good and her construction and technique are good, and she has a good plot sense, but she cannot write stories. Isn't that funny? I suppose that many people say the same about me, but I don't care. Like the needle in Hans Andersen which imagined itself a scarf pin because it had a nob of sealing wax on its end, "I know what I am." The only trouble was that it wasn't, but the poor thing never found it out and that is all that matters.' Steinbeck would not have said this to John Breck herself. He needed her, and would not have put their friendship at risk.

Kate Beswick had become increasingly important too, although the exact nature of their relationship must be inferred from their later letters; these suggest considerable intimacy. My guess is that Beswick was in love with Steinbeck, but that he preferred to think of their connection as a close friendship. By his own admission to Wilhelmson, he was at the moment 'in love' with a woman by the name of Margaret Gemmell, a dark-eyed beauty who wore her black hair cut straight across her forehead. She met Steinbeck in a course on European Intellectual History that both were taking that spring. By coincidence, she had also recently joined the English Club, which Steinbeck continued to dominate with his readings and pronouncements. The relationship blossomed quickly, and would figure in Steinbeck's imagination for the next year or so.

The actual courtship with Gemmell was brief but intense,

and it involved several trips into San Francisco for dinner and excursions to a local swimming hole called Searsville Lake. (His finances could ill afford the dinners in San Francisco.) This was the first genuine 'girlfriend' Steinbeck had, and he seems to have relished the notion. The young couple would study together in the university library or walk hand in hand around the sprawling, tree-studded campus. The fact that Steinbeck planned to leave Stanford in a very short while must have enhanced the ardour of both, although there was never any talk of marriage, and there seems to have been no pretence that the relationship would 'go' anywhere. Steinbeck was not ready to settle down with anyone, and Gemmell was young. If he wrote to her after he left Stanford, as he must have done, the correspondence has been lost. In any case, the romance was not able to withstand separation, and its memory became simply another part of Steinbeck's complex emotional palimpsest.

'I think I have had all of the college I deserve, and so I must face the economic situation or run away from it after next quarter,' Steinbeck had written to Carl Wilhelmson early in the spring. And when June came, he knew that he was finished with Stanford. He had not passed enough courses to qualify for a degree, and it seems not to have mattered to him. His idea now was to get away, as far as possible. The fantasy of going to China seems to have died, and what 'far away' meant now was New York City, where he intended to go and try to make his way as a writer. Meanwhile, he needed cash for the journey, and he began looking around for temporary work.

As luck would have it, his friend Toby Street was about to marry a young woman named Frances Price, whose mother, a stout woman with a booming voice and cascades of blue-grey hair, demanded evidence of his reliability. At Street's suggestion, Mrs Price interviewed Steinbeck about his friend's worthiness for holy matrimony, and she was much taken with the shy young man from Salinas. A recent widow, she owned and managed a holiday resort lodge on Fallen Leaf Lake near Lake Tahoe in the High Sierras, and she was willing to hire the aspiring young writer to mend windows and repair broken toilets and, less onerously, to drive the lodge's spacious Pierce-Arrow each day into Tallac, a local village situated on Tahoe itself, where he would pick up guests, shop for odds and ends required by his maintenance duties, and get the mail.

Steinbeck took the job eagerly, leaving Stanford with few regrets. He wanted his freedom more than anything, and that included the freedom to think and write about what interested him rather than some authority figure in a tweed jacket or stiff woollen skirt. He wanted, in short, to begin his life.

III

In the Wilderness

'I know that *Cup of Gold* is a bad book, but on its shoulders
I shall climb to a good book.'

Steinbeck to Kate Beswick, 10 April 1928

Steinbeck's passage into 'real life' from Stanford was precarious, strewn with hazardous moments in which his own
self-destructive tendencies emerged in frightening ways. He
had never been on his own completely except for brief
periods, and even then he could always retreat to Salinas.
Now he wanted to break away as fully as possible, to become
a man and make his way in the world as a writer. Looking at
the years immediately following his departure from Stanford,
one sees a troubled young man who does not have easy
access to his emotions. He is shy, but he compensates for this
shyness by dominating his friends, even bullying them, in
letters and conversation. Aspiring to manliness, which he
defines in a particularly western, even macho manner, he
behaves crudely at times. Even his close friends, as we shall
see, find themselves baffled and afraid of him, detecting a
pent-up violence that breaks through to the surface on
horrible occasions.

Steinbeck's main idea, after leaving Stanford, was to go to
New York, where he would struggle towards greatness as a
writer. This was, after all, 1925, an *annus mirabilis* for
American fiction. *The Great Gatsby*, Scott Fitzgerald's masterpiece, had just appeared, as had Ernest Hemingway's first
(and finest) collection of stories, *In Our Time*. John Dos Passos
brought out *Manhattan Transfer*, an influential (and currently
underrated) work of experimental fiction.

The older generation was on the boil as well: Sinclair Lewis, still bathing in the glow of *Main Street*, delivered *Arrowsmith* to his editor. Sherwood Anderson published *Dark Laughter*, his most original novel; Willa Cather brought out *The Professor's House*, one of her most haunting fictions, while Theodore Dreiser's *An American Tragedy* swept the country with its bleak portrait of a nation torn apart by hypocritical morality. Fiction had become an heroic profession, an arena in which young people could make their mark.

For John Steinbeck, the imagined pot of gold lay at the east end of a vast transcontinental rainbow. In this he was not unusual. Greenwich Village in particular had recently acquired an almost magical shimmer, and a young man could easily believe that this city of publishers, concert halls and theatres could accommodate one more writer, singer or actor. 'Greenwich Village was just where everyone had to be, whether you came from the South, the Midwest, or the West,' says Robert Penn Warren.[1] He adds wryly: 'The only people who didn't want to be there in the Twenties were the people actually living there.'

To earn money for his eastward migration, Steinbeck joined Toby Street at Fallen Leaf Lake for what would prove to be a summer and autumn of relative bliss. The lodge was a two-storey building constructed in the rustic way of mountain resorts, with rough-hewn logs and small boulders. There were two dining halls, where meals were taken communally (cooked by Chinese chefs), and a cluster of cabins for the help (rigidly divided into male and female living quarters). Some of the staff, including Steinbeck, slept in tents erected on wooden platforms. A boathouse was built out over the lake itself, which was surrounded by tall Norwegian pines and fluttering aspens. Mount Tallac rose nearly ten thousand feet in the middle distance like a scene from a Japanese print, cool and calming.

The Tahoe area had yet to fall under the mercenary gaze of

developers, and it was breathtaking to behold in its nearly pristine state. The lake was vast and darkly blue, criss-crossed by the occasional steamer or sailboat. Its wild shoreline was broken here and there by a summer house, a camp or a rustic resort. The Tahoe Tavern on the northwest shore was a gathering spot for local teenagers and young families, and there were dances every weekend. Because summer was high season at Tahoe, there were plenty of young people around, many of them working as staff at the local resorts.

Steinbeck adored driving the lodge's white Pierce-Arrow into Tallac along the deeply grooved dirt road, which zigzagged downhill through a balsam fir wood. He delivered and picked up mail, ran errands, and collected guests of the lodge and their luggage from the local train station. Occasionally he would steal away for the afternoon with Toby Street, who had just married Mrs Price's daughter, Frances (John had been the best man at the wedding). They would go trout fishing in the headwaters of the nearby American River, casting flies they had tied themselves during long evenings by the fire. Steinbeck liked to socialize with the college girls hired to work in the dining hall or retreat to his tent to write by the light of a kerosene lantern. His battered Corona stood on a three-legged table, and his co-workers recalled that he would pound away late into the night, the clack of keys muffled slightly by the tent's musty canvas.

Mrs Price soon discovered that Steinbeck was good with his hands and liked to solve technical problems, and she enlisted him to work on the resort's makeshift hydro-electric system, which had been rigged up by her late husband, William Whitman Price, a surgeon with a penchant for mechanical devices. In essence, a fast-running mountain stream above the lodge turned a generator; by midsummer, the stream would invariably dry out, causing the lights at the lodge to flicker off. Steinbeck and Toby were commissioned to build a dam to regulate the flow of water over the turbines, a task which involved dynamiting through stretches of solid granite – a skill acquired by the young writer during his days as a dredger on the Salinas-Castroville canal. Their work also involved lifting boulders, something that Steinbeck, with his strong arms and broad back, was nicely cut out for. Toby Street later recalled, 'John was like a giant in those days, with muscular back and arms. He could work for long hours without seeming to notice. Mrs Price thought he was a gift from heaven.'[2]

When most of the guests left the lodge in September, Toby and John were kept on to complete the dam, which was coming along nicely. Frances, Toby's wife, returned with Mrs Price to San Francisco, which left the young men on their own. There was plenty of time now for relaxing, reading and writing, and the work on the dam was physical enough to keep them from getting restless. The project was finished in mid-November, just when the weather began to get cold. (Steinbeck, who enjoyed knowing about such things, explained to Street that it was dangerous to use dynamite in cold weather.)

Steinbeck now owned a Model-T Ford, an old and battered one acquired just before he came to Tahoe. With work on the dam completed, he and Toby set off for San Francisco on what proved a rather epic journey, with the car breaking down so often that Toby decided to abandon the Model-T and take a train. Steinbeck, of course, pressed on. The eventual goal of his journey was New York, but that was still a long way off, physically and emotionally. He drove first to Palo Alto, where he and Margaret Gemmell said their goodbyes, aware that this would probably mark the end of their affair. Then he left his car (which he referred to as a 'heap of bolts') with his parents in Salinas and returned by train to San Francisco, where he hopped a taxi to the waterfront – the same place where, a couple of years before, he had tried to get a berth on a freighter heading to the Far East. This time, however, he landed a job on a ship headed through the Panama Canal for New York City.

The *Katrina* was a small freighter whose motley crew were mostly non-English speakers. It plied its way slowly along the coastline of California, pushing eventually through the Panama Canal with a two-day layover in Panama City. This stop fascinated Steinbeck, whose recent story, 'A Lady in Infra-Red', was partially set in Panama. This same tiny Central American country would soon become a crucial setting in Steinbeck's first venture into novel-length fiction, *Cup of Gold*. His one friend on the journey to New York was an artist and illustrator named Mahlon Blaine, who was delighted to find an intelligent young man aboard heading to Manhattan to pursue a career in writing. Blaine was handed a couple of Steinbeck's stories in typescript to read, and he admired them greatly; he offered to lend the slightly younger man a hand when they disembarked in the big city, and Steinbeck took him up on this offer two or three months later. (Blaine would play an important role in getting *Cup of Gold* published several years later.)

Once the freighter made it safely through the Canal, it headed north through the Caribbean, docking in Havana for a few days of Cuban high life. Steinbeck had been given a hundred dollars in spending money by his father, and he now tossed much of it away in the local bars, drinking and whoring around an exotic capital already famous for its decadence.[3] 'It was John's idea that a writer should experience as much of the world as possible,' a friend said.[4] 'The Cuban whorehouses would have been part of all that. It fitted in with his conception of himself.' He arrived in New York a short while later with virtually nothing in his pockets: 'I crept ashore – frightened and cold and with a touch of panic in my stomach,' Steinbeck later recalled.

Writing about this period in 1935, Steinbeck (who would eventually settle in New York permanently) remarked, 'I guess I hate New York because I had a thin, lonely time of it there. And I remember too well the cockroaches under my wash basin and the impossibility of getting a job.'[5] He went immediately by subway to his sister Beth's house in Brooklyn, where she and her new husband rented a third-floor walk-up in Fort Greene Place. 'He arrived looking like a lost little boy,' his sister later said. It was nearly Christmas, and cold, and he wore the same heavy brown sweater each day and a dark naval overcoat picked up in a second-hand shop in lower Manhattan for a few dollars. Within a week, the little bit of money he had was gone, so he was forced to borrow from his brother-in-law. Eager to earn his keep, he scoured the city for employment, landing a job with the James Stewart Construction Company.

The work, however, was not appealing. The project was the building of Madison Square Garden on Eighth Avenue and 50th Street, and his job was to push heavy wheelbarrows of wet cement up a wooden ramp to where masons laid brick on perilous scaffolding. A year later, Steinbeck wrote to Kate Beswick: 'You see I had landed broke in New York. I was at the time wheeling cement within the structure of the new Madison Square Garden, working about fifteen to eighteen hours a day. You can imagine that when I got back to my little room in Brooklyn at night, I was tired.'[6] Rather dangerous as well as exhausting, the work was obviously unsuitable for an ambitious young man in search of a career in the world of letters. 'He couldn't even read the newspapers when he got home at night,' his sister says. 'I'd give him a sandwich, and he'd go straight to bed, where he'd sit with a pencil and try to write a few lines. But he knew it would never work. You couldn't do that kind of physical work and think at the same time.'[7]

The family came to the rescue, this time with a benevolent

hand from Uncle Joe Hamilton, his mother's brother, who worked for a Chicago advertising agency. A big, bluff man with a rosy face who wore three-piece suits with a gold watch chain looping across his stomach, he had been sent to New York on business; he treated his niece, her husband, and his young nephew to several expense account dinners. 'He was staying at the Commodore Hotel,' Beth remembers. 'That was one of the best hotels in those days. I think he may have even had a suite.' With avuncular concern, Joe Hamilton listened to his nephew lay out his vision of the future. He liked the boy's spirit and offered him job at once in his Chicago firm. Steinbeck adamantly refused to consider it. He wanted to write, and he believed that staying in New York mattered. Furthermore, advertising did not strike him as the obvious route to literary greatness.

Joe Hamilton accepted his nephew's reasoning and made a few quick calls to friends in the newspaper trade. Journalism was a proven breeding-ground for American writers, and Steinbeck knew this. So he was thrilled when he was offered a job after only a brief interview by the New York *American*, one of many brash and popular papers owned by William Randolph Hearst. The cub reporter was sent into the streets of Manhattan to find stories, and he did – after a fashion; his reporting style, however, was much too florid – full of metaphors and images – to satisfy his editors. He was dispatched to the Federal Court, where he was taken under the wing of a crew of experienced court reporters, whose job was to wring the fuss out of his prose. He later recalled: 'I worked for the *American* and was assigned to the Federal Court in the old Park Row post office where I perfected my bridge game and did some lousy reporting. I did, however, perfect a certain literary versatility.'[8] This was during Prohibition, of course, and the federal judges were (according to Steinbeck) willing to pass out confiscated whiskey to bored reporters. It was, he said, 'a happy place to work'.

Nudged by his sister, who was eager to have the little apartment to herself and her husband again, Steinbeck moved into a shabby room on the sixth floor of the ancient Parkwood Hotel off Gramercy Park, where Mahlon Blaine (from the *Katrina*) lived on the first floor in a somewhat grander room. The friendship blossomed, and the two young men explored the city by night with Ted Miller, another of Steinbeck's Stanford friends who had made it to the big city. This merry threesome would often eat dinners at local restaurants, such as the Astor or Ticino's, an Italian *trattoria* in Greenwich Village. It was at the latter that Steinbeck first met Mary Ardath, a showgirl in the *Greenwich Village Follies*.

She was the second woman he had fallen in love with. According to all accounts, Ardath was a beautiful if rather unsophisticated woman: slender-hipped, green-eyed, with blonde hair that she pulled back and tied with a ribbon. She was also ambitious, and the idea of marriage to a down-and-out reporter and would-be novelist did not appeal to her. She tried to get him to switch careers, suggesting business, but he just laughed at these efforts to shape his future. He'd had enough of that at home. Poor Mary Ardath did not know she was dealing with one of the stubbornest and most deter-mined men of letters to come down the road since Mark Twain.

The romance flared, brilliantly, then faded, all in a matter of weeks. Reports vary on who dropped whom, and the truth is probably somewhere in the middle. Although the young couple lived together briefly, the affair ended in May. Ardath married a banker soon afterwards, and that was clearly the kind of future she wanted for herself. Steinbeck was in any case not ready to marry, and he became uneasy when she tried to suggest in subtle ways that there was more happen-ing between them than there was. The affair ended as abruptly as it had begun, although Mary Ardath would appear quixotically on his doorstep in California some years later with children in tow, hoping to spark the romance once again.

Meanwhile, Steinbeck's work at the *American* continued haphazardly. He hung about the court and reported trials or, less frequently, wandered into Queens and Brooklyn, where he often got lost in search of stories and spent more time finding his way home than he did reporting. Before long, his superiors – who frequently had to cover for him – got fed up and fired him. 'It was a disappointment, more to us than to John,' says his sister, 'because it seemed as if nothing was ever going to work out for him. My parents were frantic, especially my mother. She thought he was going to come to no good.'

Steinbeck's first response to being fired, however, was elation. It was spring in New York, and he was young. The trees were in bloom, and daffodils poked out of little garden plots everywhere in the Village. The liberated young man raced back to his hotel and told Blaine that he was a free man at last. Now he could write the novel that had been forming for some time in his head. Buying a new ledger and a dozen pencils, he set himself up in his room to write, scribbling a dozen pages of *Cup of Gold*, the novel about Henry Morgan, the Elizabethan buccaneer. Alas, within a matter of days he realized that he was broke, and that jobs were few and far between. The Jazz Age was on, but you could not live by jazz alone.

Mahlon Blaine offered to help and sent some of Steinbeck's stories to an acquaintance, Guy Holt, who worked for the small publishing firm of Robert M. McBride & Company. Holt read the stories and liked them; he summoned the out-of-work author to his office for a little chat. 'If you can write a half dozen more stories of this quality,' he said, 'I'll publish a collection.' Steinbeck wandered into the streets dizzy with hope. It was the first signal from the 'real' world that he might be a writer after all. Returning to his room at the hotel, with its brown peeling wallpaper and cockroaches as big as grasshoppers, he solemnly drew a fresh sheet of paper from the middle drawer of the desk by the window overlooking Gramercy Park, now full of flowers, and began to write a new story. *Cup of Gold* would have to wait.

For several weeks he lived on cans of sardines and mouldy crackers, involved in a frenzy of creativity. He quickly wrote half a dozen stories, most of them with New York settings. The best of them, 'The White Sister of Fourteenth Street', is a cross between Damon Runyon and early Somerset Maugham, featuring a saucy female narrator named Elsie Grough, who was based loosely on Mary Ardath. (She also anticipates Curley's wife in *Of Mice and Men*, written more than a decade later.) Elsie spends her evenings at a seedy dance hall called Harmony Gardens, where she falls for an Italian called Angelo, who looks like one of her favourite movie stars. He solemnly invites her to an opera, *La Monica Bianca* (hence the title of the story); she goes with him, but is bored to death. Angelo, alas, is bowled over, even tearful with emotion. Coming out of the theatre, Elsie suddenly reveals her ignorance by telling Angelo that she has seen the opera before in a movie version starring Lillian Gish. This *faux pas* does it. When she looks up after powdering her nose, Angelo is gone.

Steinbeck had stumbled into the abortive relationship with Ardath. During this brief courtship he indeed took her to an opera, imagining that her interest in music went beyond night-club singing; he soon discovered the truth: Mary Ardath was no fan of Verdi. Nor was she sensitive to his own deepest needs: just as Olive Steinbeck had never seen her son for who he really was (or so he imagined), Mary Ardath thought he was someone else. The figure of the sensitive young man who is not understood by his parents or girlfriends reappears many times in Steinbeck's fiction – right up to *East of Eden*, where this theme is given its final and fullest treatment.

Perhaps the chief outlet for Steinbeck's pent-up emotions now, apart from his stories, was what might broadly be called his ambition. He was a fiercely ambitious young man, and he would never lose his drive. Nothing pleased him better than to see the pages of freshly written manuscript accumulate on his desk. His letters and diaries are obsessively concerned with his productivity, with the number of words and pages written.

With high hopes for publication fanned by Guy Holt, Steinbeck now retyped the entire manuscript again, making revisions as he worked. Not wishing to entrust his sacred accomplishment to the US Postal Service, he carried the packet to McBride & Company. Much to his horror, he was told that Guy Holt had left the publishing firm. Steinbeck was led into the office of another editor, who listened impatiently to Steinbeck's story. Did he have a contract? Well, no, he said. But he had considered Holt's conversation something of a commitment. The man laughed. And Steinbeck was shown the door, his manuscript tucked under his arm. McBride & Company did not even offer to read the stories.

Steinbeck was crushed. Dizzy with anger, he spent the night in a bar in Greenwich Village, drinking a bottle of wine and several glasses of brandy by himself. The next day he learned that Guy Holt had taken a job at another publishing house, John Day Company. At Ted Miller's urging, he paid Holt a nervous call at his new office, but he was quickly discouraged. John Day was struggling to make it as a publisher in a competitive market, Holt explained, and short stories didn't sell, especially if the author happened to be unknown. He suggested that the young man try to write a novel; a novel was something he might sell. Once his name was established, the prospects for bringing out a collection of stories would be somewhat better. Suppressing his rage, Steinbeck assured Holt that he was indeed writing a novel, and that he would be back.

*

Now the little problem of money had to be solved, and quickly. Steinbeck could not bear the idea of going back to manual labour, and he could not impose on Uncle Joe again to find him a job. Ted Miller, however, had some business with the Port Authority and was able to find Steinbeck a berth on a freighter similar to the one that had originally brought him through the Panama Canal to New York. This one was headed in the reverse direction, from New York to San Francisco, and Steinbeck could earn his passage by working as a steward, serving meals and clearing the dishes afterwards. He accepted at once, boasting of his experience as a waiter for a sorority at Stanford. As usual, he fitted in very well with the ship's crew, entertaining them with bawdy verses and writing letters for them to their girlfriends. His shyness always disappeared in a situation where he felt comfortable with those around him, and this was more likely to be when he was among people from the working class. His own middle-class upbringing and Stanford education gave him a cushion of support, a sense of superiority which allowed him to relax among his shipmates.

He was not happy about returning to California as 'a failure', as he told his sister. But New York was not what they said it was; indeed, it had been harder for him to find the time to write there than it had been in California. In the middle of June, he arrived in San Francisco, taking a train to Salinas for a reunion with his parents, who were glad to see him back from the east but anxious about his seeming lack of direction. John Ernst was still not convinced that his son could become enough of a writer to earn a living, and he once again tried to persuade him to move in a direction that might ensure financial security. 'You can always write on the side,' he said.[9] 'Very few writers actually try to support a family from their writing.' Steinbeck insisted that he was an exception and vowed to take no job that would get in the way of his goal. His recent experience with Guy Holt in New York had (rather curiously) buoyed him up. If only he could write a novel. . .

With less than fifty dollars to his name, Steinbeck set off for Palo Alto in his Model-T, which his father had tinkered with and 'improved'. He called first on Dook Sheffield, who was now working towards an MA in English Literature. Ruth, his wife, did not much like her husband's friend because she knew he had tried to discourage Dook from getting married. It was not that he objected to Ruth especially: the very idea of marriage terrified him, and he could not bear to see a close friend get himself into such a permanent arrangement. Even as Steinbeck stood in the doorway of the Sheffields' apartment he eyed her suspiciously. Dook, however, was unfazed and insisted that his old friend stay with them in their minuscule apartment. Not surprisingly, tensions developed quickly in such close quarters, and Steinbeck avoided the Sheffields almost entirely.

His Stanford itinerary included a call on Margaret Gemmell, who thought her old beau was thousands of miles away in New York City. She was startled to find him standing in her doorway one afternoon. 'Why aren't you in New York?' she asked with an unwelcoming frown. 'Because I'm here', he said, hurt. He and Margaret went for a long walk together across the campus, as they had in the past; Steinbeck hoped to blow on the embers and rekindle the flame, but it soon became clear to him that their relationship had dwindled into mere friendship; the romance was no longer there. Margaret did not even invite him back to her dormitory room for a cup of tea.

Shrugging off his disappointment, Steinbeck charged around Palo Alto visiting other friends, including John Breck and her daughter, Polly. After a few days, he left to join Toby Street again at Fallen Leaf Lake, where he knew he could always find work. Mrs Price had written to him fondly in

New York, and he had promised to come back to the lodge as soon as possible. Why not now? It was still, after all, early in the season, and the delights of the previous summer had never been far from his mind during the long hard year in Manhattan.

The Lake Tahoe region became his home for the next few years. Mrs Price was delighted to see Steinbeck again, and Toby Street was practically hopping up and down with delight. Even Frances Street, who had been cool towards him at times, seemed glad to see him.

'John never came back into town quietly,' Street later recalled, 'he was like a big storm, a whirlwind. You stopped whatever you were doing and you listened to his stories. He knew how to make you listen – it was the same talent that made him a great writer. And he took himself seriously. Even his jokes were serious: they had a point.' Mrs Price assigned her new charge to maintenance duties that included plumbing and carpentry, both of which Steinbeck liked doing. When he told her one evening that he wanted to stay in the Tahoe region for much of the year to work on a novel for a New York publisher, an idea dawned. 'I have just the right job for you,' she said.

She drove Steinbeck over to the summer home of her old friend, Alice Brigham, who was also a recent widow. Mrs Brigham's husband had been a surgeon in San Francisco, and she had lots of family money. The Brigham estate was on the south shore of Lake Tahoe, and it was unusually fine. The family property stretched all the way from the shore of the lake to the foothills of Mount Tallac itself. The main house was in the elegantly rustic style common to the region, with pine bark nailed to the exterior walls to give the necessary look. The place was huge, with a massive living room on the south side which boasted a floor-to-ceiling stone fireplace. Bedrooms and bathrooms went off in many directions. The ceilings were high, vaulted and cross-beamed with huge oak logs. Dr Brigham had left a decent library which contained the classics of English and American literature and history. 'Everything is here,' Steinbeck said, 'but a dictionary.'

During the high season, Mrs Brigham employed over half a dozen servants, including a cook and two Filipino house-boys. Steinbeck, as a friend of the Price family and bona fide member of the middle classes, was immediately hired as caretaker and warmly absorbed by the family at large. He was given the caretaker's lodge, an upscale version of 'The Sphincter' that nestled cosily in a stand of fir trees. He slept in one room in a narrow cot; an adjoining room became his 'study'. He propped his Corona on a small deal table and could look out the window to the smooth lawn that ran downhill to a cliff overlooking the lake, the dock, and a small flotilla of rowboats and sailboats.

When Mrs Brigham's family was gone for good by mid-October, Steinbeck had the place to himself: a mixed blessing, as it turned out. He was hardly prepared for the relentless solitude which descends on resort areas when the high season ends. Tahoe, in particular, acquired an almost ghostly remoteness in the off-season, with the few camps around the lake boarded up for the winter and all restaurants and most local shops closed. Apart from a few caretakers, the population in the Tahoe region dropped to nil, and Steinbeck was left, for the first time in his life, genuinely alone with himself.

He would stay in this cabin for two years, and one might look at it as the young writer's necessary retreat before a major advance; a period of psychological and spiritual retrenchment. It was a frightening period too: John Steinbeck was like a young buck, running wild, frightened, darting this way and that in search of a safe place to stand. His boyhood and adolescence were over, and he was conscious of the need to declare his manhood. He did not want to become another John Ernst, terrified of the world, bullied by women, nursing a quiet rage. His assets were a driving sense of his native capabilities, a strong physical body, and a clear mind that rather quickly seized the world by the horns. Yet he could not break free of old patterns. And he was still emotionally tied to his parents: Olive wrote to him constantly, and wanted him to 'make something of himself', as she frequently said. She would allude sarcastically to his failure at Stanford, always hinting that he might yet 'succeed' if he returned. But in his mid-twenties, Steinbeck felt a long way from Stanford. He was certainly not going to become a lawyer or businessman, as his mother hoped. Once, when his mother suggested that he might return to Salinas and try a job in government, Steinbeck exploded.[10] He was an artist, he told her. An artist does nothing else but create the objects – books, paintings, music – his inborn nature wills him to create. Like the young writer-hero of Joyce's *A Portrait of the Artist as a Young Man*, Steinbeck knew he had to cut himself off from his bourgeois origins, from his family, his religion, from everything that held him back. He had to seek the isolation necessary for cretive production. This was all terribly romantic, but it was in the air. Steinbeck breathed these modern fumes, and they inspired him to fare forward.

The physical isolation of Tahoe was just the approach he needed. He had tried the opposite tack the year before, in Manhattan, where the mass of humanity offered a gigantic distraction, and a million voices challenged his own. Now, by the shores of Tahoe, he had only the wind in the high fir trees to compete with the sound of his inner voice, and he had all the time in the world to discover his inner voice and let that voice emerge, feebly at first, then more strongly. One might compare these years to T. S. Eliot's retreat to a sanatorium in Switzerland in the early Twenties, where he wrote *The Waste Land*, with its majestic evocation of solitude:

In this decayed hole among the mountains
In the faint moonlight, the grass is singing
Over the tumbled graves, about the chapel
There is the empty chapel, only the wind's home.

Steinbeck felt the pressure to return to nature, to accept the burden of solitude that Thoreau, more than anyone, had conjured and explored. *Walden* was among the handful of books he always treasured. Indeed, he had been sent a fresh copy by Dook Sheffield, at Steinbeck's urgent request. He often reread the chapter called 'Solitude', underlining a passage where Thoreau wrestles memorably with the issue of being alone in a natural setting:

> I have never felt lonesome, or in the least oppressed, by a sense of solitude, but once, and that was a few weeks after I came to the woods, when, for an hour, I doubted if the near neighborhood of man was not essential to a serene and healthy life. To be alone was something unpleasant. But I was at the same time conscious of a slight insanity in my mood, and seemed to foresee my recovery. In the midst of a gentle rain while these thoughts prevailed, I was suddenly sensible of such sweet and beneficent society in Nature, in the very pattering of the drops, and in every sound and sight around my house, an infinite and unaccountable friendliness all at once like an atmosphere sustaining me, as made the fancied advantages of human neighborhood insignificant, and I have never thought of them since.[11]

Steinbeck discovered during this period of self-imposed isolation in the Tahoe region that his artistic nature was such that he could create only in solitude; indeed, whenever he listened too much to the voices that crowded around him, he became distracted, depressed, uncomfortable and artistically barren. His later life is marked by serial retreats which were creatively strategic. He would find his own private Walden Pond in various places: in the hills outside of Monterey, in Sag Harbor, in Somerset, on the island of Capri. And he would always do his best work in retreat, in self-imposed exile from society.

Steinbeck threw himself headlong into the physical labour that went along with the responsibilities of caretaking the Brigham place. There were pipes to drain, windows and doors to winterize, boats to haul in, caulk and store. The grounds required constant attention of the sort Steinbeck loved to offer, and he spent many pleasant hours pruning trees and mending fences. The Brighams told him to make full use of the main house, and he did; most nights he would build a fire in the stone hearth and work on his novel-in-progress while sitting in a big brown leather chair with a blanket around his knees. He also began working his way through Dr Brigham's library, reading dozens of novels by Dickens, Scott and Thackeray for the first time.

His own writing did not go well at first. Well into mid-winter, he found himself unable to write except in fits and starts. The novel, which he now referred to as *Cup of Gold*, was not breaking easily, and he turned once again to short fiction. One of these stories, 'The Gifts of Iban', is set in a mythic land. The hero, Iban, is an innocently lusty young man who falls in love with an equally innocent (and lusty) young woman, Cantha. Iban is an artist of sorts, a singer, and he uses his craft to seduce Cantha, who is then forced by her mother to marry him. In the end, Cantha is persuaded by her mother – a vile woman who shows no sympathy for her daughter's wishes or welfare – that Iban's 'gifts' of song are worthless. The dutiful Cantha abandons Iban.

The story may have been aimed directly at Dook Sheffield, since Cantha in her fickleness and lack of will seems modelled on Ruth, his wife; the fear of offending Dook (and getting himself into deeper hot water with Ruth) was so great that Steinbeck changed his name on the typescript to John Stern when he sent the story to a little magazine called *The Smoker's Companion*. To his astonishment, this periodical accepted and published his unlikely fantasy (indeed, the editor wrote asking if there were more stories where 'The Gifts of Iban' had come from). The young writer's first royalties (seven dollars) came from this story, which its author suspected was not much good. He did not even mention this publication to his mother, perhaps because he unconsciously identified Olive with Cantha: yet another woman who did not appreciate a young man's creativity, sensitivity and potential.[12]

Steinbeck's chief diversion at Tahoe, apart from writing and reading, was his twice-weekly trip to Camp Richardson to fetch the mail and stock up on canned food. On one of these journeys in late February he met Lloyd Shebley, an employee of the Department of Fish and Game Commission who, like Steinbeck's great friend of the next decade, Ed Ricketts, was a naturalist and a man with a scientific, not literary, cast of mind. Shebley, in his mid-twenties, had been sent to operate the local fish hatchery in Tallac, and he welcomed Steinbeck's company. Disembarking from the steamer with the dazed look of all new arrivals, he found Steinbeck offering to help him with his luggage. They proceeded to the Tallac Hatchery, which was locked up tight, and Steinbeck – always ready with a dramatic gesture – calmly drew a revolver from his parka and shot off the lock. As Shebley said later, 'I had no idea the man was carrying a gun. He scared the devil out of me. It was a while before I even felt safe in the man's company.'

Shebley could not understand Steinbeck's obsession with literature and his insistence that certain hours were sacred for writing. For his part, Steinbeck found it easy to comprehend his new friend's interest in marine life. Through March and April, he spent several afternoons a week with Shebley, studying the breeding habits of fish. He was fascinated by their migratory patterns, an interest that would affect his later fiction as he reapplied his knowledge of fish and other wildlife to the movement patterns of human beings.

Steinbeck passed Shebley a copy of John Elof Boodin's *Cosmic Evolution*, which had been published two years before and which his elder sister had sent him from New York at his request. 'Nothing happens by chance, and it is not by chance that organisms have developed eyes, ears, and other sense organs,' writes Boodin.[13] 'Our senses are creative adaptations to specific energy patterns of the cosmic environment.' Thus unfolds a five-hundred-page book of musings on the way life – lower and higher forms included – adapts creatively to the 'energy patterns of the cosmic environment'. Always, Boodin stresses the process of Darwinian adaptation: 'Life is a creative adaptation of the energies of matter under certain conditions – themselves the result of cosmic adaptation – to the energy structure of the cosmos.'

One wonders what Shebley, who was intelligent but not especially intellectual, made of his friend's enthusiasms. In any case, Shebley and Steinbeck became friends, and they would drop in on each other frequently. The drink of the day seems to have been homemade fig wine, although quantities of bootleg gin and whiskey were available; Shebley's main recollections of Steinbeck involved the bootleg drinks his friend was able to acquire in that remote part of the world.

Perhaps because of the lack of connection with his own father, Steinbeck grew dependent on relationships with certain types of 'manly' men – tough, practical men interested in 'subjects'. 'John didn't talk about feelings,' one later friend recalls. 'He would shrink in horror from that sort of conversation. He talked about things, technical things. He was interested in how the world worked, how machines worked, how airplanes flew or books were typeset.'[14] In a letter to Kate Beswick, his old Stanford friend who became a pen pal during the Tahoe years, he commented rather strangely on the complicated issue of man-to-man relations:

Now let me go into my mawkishness in dealing with man

and man. Nine out of ten women, seeing man and man *in the presence of women* have not the slightest idea what goes on between man and man when women are not present. They subscribe to the myth of continual dirty stories or business. Then, too, so much of the literature of the British male *is* a horrible tangle of taboos. American writers, imitating the manly Britons of the nineteenth and twentieth centuries, distort their men. . . . The American man is not afraid of his emotions.[15]

This does not ring true. Anyone who has read Hemingway will know that American men, as portrayed in his writing, are deeply afraid of their emotions. Steinbeck himself was afraid of his: with good reason. Beneath his usually smooth emotional surface a cauldron boiled, and the bubbles would sometimes rise to the top in terrifying ways that he wanted to deny.

The relationship with Shebley was never especially intimate. Shebley was indifferent to literary matters, and in other circumstances he and Steinbeck might not have become friends at all. Nevertheless, their friendship did continue, and in mid-April Shebley hired Steinbeck for a two-week stint which involved clearing logs from the nearby Taylor Creek, an important trout run in the region. The money came in handy, and Steinbeck needed the break from his novel, which was now moving swiftly. 'I'm writing anywhere from three to four thousand words a day,' he had recently written to Dook Sheffield. To Bob Cathcart, another old Stanford friend, he echoed the same information, although his fears about the book were bluntly expressed: 'I am pounding on a novel which I had hopes for. But it seems to belie them. I set out to do a thing no one has ever succeeded in doing. I should not be terribly livid if I fail. Perhaps I should succeed sometime. There is a good deal of very fine writing in the book and much that isn't.'[16]

*

Steinbeck may have been isolated in Tahoe, but he kept up a ferocious correspondence with old Stanford friends. Kate Beswick received many of his best letters about his own work, and one must wonder about their relationship. It seems clear that he felt extremely fond of her, and she apparently harboured some hope of reconnecting with Steinbeck, perhaps in a romantic way. But when he was living in New York, practically next door to her, he did not go to any great lengths to look her up. The relationship seems to have flowered in ink, as it were. From the loneliness of his cabin in Tahoe, he poured out self-centred letters that largely indicate the nature of his ambitions for himself at the time:

> I am still determined to do something very beautiful. You
> see I am still a foal. I have given up writing bad stories to
> write a bad novel, but always am creeping upward toward
> that beautiful thing.

*

> I have made no concessions and therefore I am almost
> completely alone. That is my boast and pride. It makes me
> feel clean and free.

*

> Now you see, Katherine, I am only a wood chopper,
> making just enough to live on and to get drunk on now and
> then.

*

> I know I can work for ten – twenty – even fifty years with
> no success if only I may creep upward toward what I want.
> I am proud of that.

*

And, Katherine, we will eliminate one thing. There shall be no
back patting between us. I hate that and suspect it. There shall
be no pride between us any more, nor vanity, nor silly
prudishness. We shall like each other for what we are and for
no other reason.[17]

Steinbeck sent her an early version of *Cup of Gold* in a rather
unkempt manuscript version, and she wrote back with some
praise and some well-intentioned but shrewd criticisms. He
responded, with shocking condescension: 'My faith in your
judgement has grown. If you had written to me that *Cup of
Gold* was the novel of the century, or if you had gushed about
it – it would have dwindled. But you pointed faults very
clearly, and my failure to concur with one of them doesn't
stop their being faults. . . . I really haven't the slightest idea
that it will be published.'

Steinbeck was deeply involved in his writing, but he was
not so obsessed that he couldn't think intelligently about
other writers. In one letter, for instance, written in April to
Bob Cathcart, he offered some perceptive (if mistaken)
reflections on George Bernard Shaw, who was at this time
one of the most esteemed playwrights in the English
language:

I first read *Caesar and Cleopatra* about seven or eight years
ago, and was so impressed that I immediately wrote a
sequel to it concerning Mark and his battle with the few and
carefully misunderstood principles Caesar had left with
Cleopatra. It was a failure. I was about seventeen at the
time. And as I shall never write another play, I bequeath the
idea to you.

Shaw occupies a peculiar place in the minds of reading
people. I have no doubt that a few generations will show
him up as a charlatan. He is an artist but he is never able to
be all artist and no charlatan. One could say of Hardy 'His
divine coincidences are at times absurd', knowing that it
didn't make the slightest difference what one said of Hardy,

either to the man or to his reputation. He was always the artist
and never the charlatan. His greatness bored him. But Shaw –
he feeds upon plaudit. He has been the self-advertiser always
and his advertising has been taken for greatness. Rather than
the greatest writer of the day, I should say he is the greatest
press agent. As soon as he is dead, as soon as his paragraphs
stop appearing in the newspapers . . . I think he will
disappear. And such a thought would be very galling to Shaw.
Please don't think I derogate his work. His work is fine, but it
is not as fine as is generally considered. It appeals to the very
young mind, such as my own when I was seventeen. His wit is
so dazzling that we never stop to consider that he has never
said anything very important. And you must admit, often his
wit is obvious and vulgar. He and Anatole France will be
buried together and will be forgotten together.[18]

From this early stage, one sees in Steinbeck a scepticism with
regard to style and wit. What matters is what gets said. Like
Tolstoy, who also had little regard for style *per se*, he preferred
literature that took a firm moral line and conveyed a message.

In late May, parts of the Brigham family began arriving,
and Steinbeck temporarily cleared out of Tahoe for the first
time since arriving the summer before. He drove to Salinas to
see his parents, who were beginning to lose patience with
their son. 'It looked as though he was never going to make
anything of himself,' says his sister, 'but mother and father
each had their own reasons for sticking by him.' One senses
that Steinbeck understood this. In *Cup of Gold* one finds the
shadows of autobiography sprawling beneath the main text,
as in this passage:

Young Henry was conscious, this night, that he had lived
on for fifteen tedious years without accomplishing any
single thing of importance. And had his mother known his
feeling, she would have said, 'He is growing.'

And his father would have repeated after her, 'Yes, the
boy is growing.' But neither would have understood what
the other meant.

When Steinbeck arrived in Salinas, Olive took the offensive immediately, charging her son with 'laziness and lack of direction'. What did he think he was doing? Was he going to throw his life away? The harangue continued for twenty minutes in the dark living room. John Ernst 'sat smoking his pipe and reading the newspaper'. Having said nothing, Steinbeck suddenly lost his temper and shouted back at his mother that it was none of her business what he was doing in Tahoe. Olive turned to John Ernst and said, 'Look at him! Tell him he must not talk to his mother like that!' John Ernst folded his paper and quietly left the house.[19] Having arrived only half an hour before, Steinbeck turned and left as well. He was not going to squander the emotional gains of his time in Tahoe. His new-found independence was too dear for that.

He drove on to Pacific Grove, where he spent several weeks, renewing his acquaintance with the Monterey coastline and the bars and diners along Cannery Row. He also paid a visit to Toby and Frances Street, who had moved to San Francisco. Street was now trying to become a playwright, and he showed Steinbeck the manuscript of a work-in-progress, 'The Green Lady'. Much taken by his friend's play, Steinbeck would absorb some of this material in his second novel, *To a God Unknown*.

Steinbeck returned to his job at the Brigham estate at the end of June. By now, his mind was fully on the novel, and he spent much of the summer in the tiny cottage at his Corona or crouching under a large shady tree by the cliff with a yellow legal pad on his lap. His duties on the estate were light, but he agreed to take on the job of tutoring Mrs Brigham's grandsons, Charles and Harold Ebright, who were nine and seven that summer. He also read books to six-year-old Catherine Kemp, another Brigham grandchild. Catherine recalled Steinbeck affectionately in later years: 'He was a very, very interesting, warm man who kept to himself, except for our friendship. We were very good friends and used to share things. I was attracted to him because I thought he was crazy.'[20] Steinbeck often accompanied the family on picnics to Cascade Lake (which was part of the Brigham estate); he also took long hikes with little Catherine in the woods, impressing her with his knowledge of the plants and trees.

He remained at the Brigham cottage throughout the autumn and winter, working furiously on the novel and very rarely entertaining friends. Carl Wilhelmson, who had paid him a visit the previous summer, returned in February and stayed for several weeks. 'Carl went away a few days ago,' Steinbeck wrote to Dook Sheffield at the end of the month.[21] 'His last words were, "I know I'm a hypochondriac but I can't help it. I must go some place else." ' Wilhelmson, who was an extremely nervous young man, seems to have provoked a similar response in Steinbeck, who was glad to get rid of him. 'I am alone again,' he told Dook, '[but] there is some relief on me. Perhaps I can get to work now.'

He mentioned in this same letter that he had been making extensive notes on how to turn Toby Street's play into a novel of his own; he also said he was 'finishing the Henry [Morgan] ms out of duty'. 'I have no hope of it any more,' he continued, somewhat disingenuously. 'I shall probably pack it in Limbo balls and place it among the lost hopes in the chest of the years. Good bye Henry. I thought you were heroic but you are only, as was said of you, a babbler of words and rather clumsy about it. . . .'

The truth is that Steinbeck worked furiously on revisions of *Cup of Gold* during the long cold winter of 1928. He was mostly alone, although he now had the good company of two friendly Airedales he had bought from a man in Pacific Grove and brought back with him. Drafts of chapters from the novel were sent to Toby Street, Carl Wilhelmson, and Kate Beswick, each of whom responded in detail; to his credit, he listened to their advice, revising his manuscript with their reactions in mind. As he explained to Beswick, he would sit alone in the wilderness cabin, snowbound, reading aloud from the text to gauge its sound: 'I find it necessary for the sake of the rhythms.'

In a confessional mood, he wrote to Kate Beswick about his drinking, which had now become problematic: 'I have just finished being drunk for three days, a horrible period wherein I hurled duty taunts at my spirit, called it a literary magpie . . . a charlatan and a sneak. But I am sober now and the ego reasserts itself. I know that *Cup of Gold* is a bad book, but on its shoulders I shall climb to a good book. Critics could hurt my feelings, but they couldn't kill this ego. Something there is in me which is more stronger than lust and nearly as strong as hunger.'[22] This is clearly the statement of a man in psychological trouble; self-doubts and depression would overwhelm him, and he would combat them with booze, which swept him into deeper darkness. He would eventually fight his way back to sobriety, but he would be left with hard feelings of guilt. The cycle spun on.

He wrote to Dook Sheffield at the same time in a less confessional mode, although an undercurrent of despair is apparent: 'I finished my novel and let it stand for a while, then read it over. And it was no good. The disappointment of that was bound to have some devastating, though probably momentary effect. You see, I thought it was going to be good. Even to the last page, I thought it was going to be good. And it is not.'[23] (One hears this note sounded throughout his career. He never felt that what he had just written was any good – yet a further legacy of the discouragement he received at home, in Salinas, where nothing he did was ever good enough.)

In March, a huge storm hit the Tahoe region, and the Brigham estate suffered considerable damage. The roof of the main house caved in above the library in the middle of the night with a loud crash, and Steinbeck's first thought was to rescue the books. Pulling on some Wellingtons over his pyjamas, throwing on his thick overcoat and furry hat, he pushed his way through the deep snow to the main house. Once inside, he lit kerosene lanterns and worked frantically through the night, brushing off the snow, then piling the books on long tables in dry linen sheets. Book by book, the library was saved. Mrs Brigham and her family were extremely grateful.

For over two weeks Steinbeck did not leave the Brigham estate. 'The county almost starved,' he wrote to Beswick, but he 'had lots of rice and potatoes and beans, so did not suffer.'[24] He worked hard throughout April and May, supervising a small crew of carpenters whose help he enlisted to repair storm damage. It was a tedious job, but as spring came there were compensations. 'I wish I could send you some of the flowers that are blooming in the meadow,' he wrote to Beswick in April, 'yellow violets and johnny jump-ups and shooting stars and jacks and fen lupins. You would love the meadows now.'[25]

In late April the manuscript of *Cup of Gold* was nervously sent off to Ted Miller, who had agreed to act informally as an agent for his old college friend. That same month, he wrote to Shebley, who was coming to Tahoe City to work at the new hatchery there; he wanted to know if there might be a summer job for him. Before long, Steinbeck was hired as an assistant. But before the work was to begin, in June, Steinbeck and his friend decided to take a trip into San Francisco. 'As I write I am becoming exciteder and exciteder,' he wrote to Beswick.[26] 'I am going out in about four days. I have been eight months here with no one about me. And I have been getting out the seven deadliest sins and refurbishing them. Have come to the conclusion that only lust and gluttony are worth a damn.' Whimsically, he added, 'I wish I were a Catholic. It would be nice to tabulate my delinquencies before a priest.'

The two young men travelled in Steinbeck's newly

purchased roadster, a 1915 Dodge convertible. One of his tasks was to report to Mrs Brigham about the house repairs and collect his last pay check, and he proceeded straight to her house. Suddenly flush with cash, he and his friend checked into a hotel and began prowling the streets of San Francisco like two musketeers. Shebley had written ahead to two women he knew only vaguely, but he managed to fix himself and Steinbeck up with dates, which meant that both of them felt the need to buy new clothes. At Roos Brothers, on Market Street, they bought fashionable tweed suits. (Steinbeck referred to this as his 'courting suit'.) The dates, alas, did not pan out; the women were shy, and the men were worse. A lot of money was 'wasted'. 'The vacation has taken every last cent I owned,' Steinbeck wrote to Beswick, adding boastfully and untruthfully, 'I only hope that I did not get rid of that parent sperm whose duty it is to create a new family.'[27]

After brief visits to Shebley's parents in Palo Alto and Steinbeck's in Salinas, the vacationers returned to their new jobs at the hatchery in Tahoe City. The arrangement Steinbeck had struck was that he would work for three months for $345: a considerable sum for him. He and Shebley would share a house adjacent to the fishery itself: a large stone-and-shingle structure which quickly became a tourist attraction as well as a centre for the production of trout for stocking the state's northern lakes and streams. Steinbeck's job was to feed the freshly hatched trout and, less often, to conduct tours of the hatchery. The work was not very time-consuming, and Steinbeck spent much of his stay greedily consuming a set of Zane Grey's westerns left to him by Bert West, the hatchery's main supervisor.

It was in mid-June that two sisters, Carol and Idell Henning of San Francisco, wandered into the hatchery for a tour. Carol, who was slightly younger than Steinbeck, had rich brown hair that she wore long. Tall and slender, she had a fetchingly wry manner which appealed at once to her eager guide. Idell watched with curiosity as her sister traded barbs with Steinbeck. 'My job is that of a midwife,' he told Carol, 'I'm a midwife to lady trout.' The Hennings stayed through much of the afternoon, and when they finally had to go Steinbeck asked if he and Shebley might take them out to dinner that night.

Shebley was pleased when he heard about the blind date his friend had arranged, and the two set off expectantly; the old Dodge, however, had two flat tyres, which delayed the suitors by at least an hour. They arrived with filthy faces and hands, and had to wash up in the Hennings' hotel room before taking them to a local restaurant for dinner, then on to a dancing pavilion, where John and Carol danced under a starry sky until midnight to the sounds of a four-piece jazz band. Lake Tahoe, visible from the terrace where they danced, glistened under a big moon.

The next week or so was dazzling for Steinbeck, who had fallen in love. He and Carol spent as much time together as possible during the rest of her stay, eating in restaurants or sitting by the lake. When Carol had to leave on 4 July, he was devastated. Rather irrationally, he felt rejected and angry. 'I'm in love – really in love,' he wrote at once to Kate Beswick, quite ignorant of how she might have received this news. He had not written to her for several months, and she replied that she was 'awfully relieved to know that nothing more catastrophic than a love affair is responsible for your silence'.[28] In the same letter, she told Steinbeck that she loved him too: 'And you must have gathered that my love for you is of a somewhat peculiar brand.'

One of the most horrible events of the summer occurred a short while after Carol and Idell had gone back to San Francisco.

With Carol gone, Steinbeck spiralled into a strange depression. He was having difficulty dealing with his strong feelings for Carol, and he may well have feared what lay ahead. Real intimacy with a woman was terrifying, and he could not handle it yet. He reacted violently now, drinking heavily and behaving in a manner that betrayed his psychological instability.

The climax of the downward spiral occured one sunny afternoon when Polly Smith (the daughter of John Breck) appeared at the hatchery, having heard from her mother that he was working there. She remembered fondly the times in Palo Alto when he would sit on the edge of her bed and listen to her problems. The casual intimacy that arose between them had never toppled over into sex, largely because Polly was so young. Steinbeck was startled to see her, and as before, he found her sassy manner and lithe, athletic body arousing. She was in her early twenties now, an adult, and fair sexual game. Steinbeck opened a bottle of bootleg gin and passed her a glass.

Polly had no interest in keeping up with Steinbeck, who was soon terribly drunk; several hours later, after making a pass which Polly firmly rebuffed, he seems to have gone crazy. He began screaming at her, then he dragged her to the top floor of his house and dangled her by the ankles from the second-storey window. Polly shrieked for help, begging him to bring her back into the room, and were it not for the intervention of Lloyd Shebley, Polly might easily have been killed. One can hardly overestimate the insanity of this particular act.

The fact that Steinbeck was drunk doesn't excuse him, although it helps to explain the madness. Doubtless many factors contributed to this behaviour, and one of them was Steinbeck's strong need at times to have his own way – especially with women. He was not someone to be rebuffed casually, and his dignity was offended by Polly Smith. (His letters to Beswick show that at this time he was becoming extremely paranoid about his looks. Polly's reaction to his advances may have triggered this hysterical reaction.) A latent streak of misogynism is also evident here, and this may be traced back to his anger towards his mother. While the retreat to Tahoe had worked, to some extent, in fostering a sense of independence, Steinbeck was by no means a 'mature' young man at this time. It is no wonder both Kate Beswick and Lloyd Shebley confessed to being 'frightened' of him. 'I want to talk to you about your fear (you say) of me,' Steinbeck replied in a letter to Beswick in disbelief. 'What's that fear? In what does it lie? I am a gentler person now than I have ever been in my life before.'[29]

Steinbeck was clearly a troubled young man that summer, with a rather shaky grasp of what constitutes civilized adult behaviour. He was frightened and shy, yet he maintained a clear inward picture of himself as someone special, someone destined for greatness. He could be easily and readily critical of his accomplishment in *Cup of Gold*, but he also defended himself and his talent vigorously. Like all artists, he yearned for attention; but unlike many, he was willing to hole up for years in a mountain cabin with little in the way of human contact to achieve his goal. His imagination was strong, as were his emotions; he was, at times, out of control. As a result, he often suppressed a great deal, pressing the lid down tightly most of the time. Alcohol offered one form of release, sex another. The release, when it came, was occasionally violent, and it often poured oil on a fire which in sobriety might have subsided of its own accord.

The incident with Polly Smith seems to have been resolved (or passed over) hurriedly. The next day Steinbeck, fiercely hungover, drove to her hotel, where he apologized profusely and invited her out to dinner. To his relief (and surprise), she accepted, putting on a new dress and behaving as though nothing had happened the night before. He blamed his behaviour on the alcohol, and Polly apparently forgave him, although one wonders about her willingness to have dinner with him in the wake of such an incident.

In the midst of this frenetic summer, Ted Miller wrote to say that he could not send such a messy manuscript to publishers. It was full of typing errors and blotted-out sentences. Whole paragraphs were circled and arrows drawn to show where they should go. Decent publishers would refuse to read it, Miller said, and he suggested that Steinbeck get someone to retype it properly. 'Publishers judge a book by its typing,' he said wryly. Kate Beswick, who was living only a few blocks from Miller in New York, was asked to retrieve the manuscript from Miller and retype it, and she did so without complaint. Once again, friends came to the rescue.

Meanwhile, in mid-August, Lloyd Shebley decided to quit his job with the Department of Fish and Game to try to become a movie actor. He was a good-looking fellow, and Paramount was filming in the Tahoe area. Someone had offered him a screen test, and he had jumped at the chance. Steinbeck thought this a wonderfully amusing turn of events and encouraged Shebley in his quixotic venture. This left Steinbeck alone with Bert West, the hatchery's supervisor, who thought the young man from Salinas was taking the Zane Grey novels he had borrowed earlier in the summer a bit too seriously. One night he found Steinbeck lounging in his bunk with a bottle of bootleg gin on the floor beside him and his revolver on his lap; he was shooting holes in the ceiling – just for fun. When Steinbeck 'borrowed' a new truck belonging to the hatchery and wrecked it, West had seen enough. John Steinbeck had to go. It was almost September, and the agreed three months were nearly up. Steinbeck packed quickly, then left in his Dodge for San Francisco, where he knew that Carol Henning eagerly awaited his arrival.

IV

The Young Buccaneer

'Long ago I determined that anyone who appraised the *Cup of Gold* for what it was should be entitled to a big kiss.'

Steinbeck to A. Grove Day, 5 December 1929

Steinbeck arrived in San Francisco in late September 1928 with no prospects, nothing but a few dollars in his pocket and Carol Henning's phone number. He had just spent a week in Pacific Grove, where he took long walks along the beaches and idled over the prospect of beginning his second novel, which was going be based on Toby Street's play, 'The Green Lady', which Street had himself abandoned. (That play had become something of an obsession for Steinbeck, who was attracted to its mythic qualities. He would put the story through many tortuous revisions before it would emerge as not his second but his third novel, *To a God Unknown*, in 1933.)

He settled into life in San Francisco with enthusiasm. The contrast with his recent period in the wilderness of the Lake Tahoe region could not have been more extreme, but he was ready now to begin what he called 'his tour of duty as an intellectual Bohemian'.[1] His first move was to call on Carl Wilhelmson, who had a small apartment in a rundown tenement near the harbour. As luck would have it, Carl was going to be gone for a while, and he agreed to let his friend stay there until he found work and could afford to rent his own place. This particular job search did not prove difficult, since Steinbeck's young sister, Mary, had recently married a man named Bill Dekker, whose family owned a large bag manufacturing company. Using his brother-in-law's influence, he quickly got a job loading sacks of hemp and wheeling them into a warehouse.

It was hard work, somewhat reminiscent of his days at Madison Square Garden. He wrote to Kate Beswick that he came home every night 'in an aura of the most complete exhaustion imaginable'.[2] This was a pity, since San Francisco, as he wrote to several friends, was 'succulently beautiful in the fall'. He told Kate that he could not possibly continue to work eight hours a day in the warehouse and write another novel. 'Just now,' he wrote, 'I want the time or rather the energy to write more than anything on earth.' He said somewhat ruefully that he would be twenty-seven in February, and it seemed that he was losing his will to write. 'I don't know where the energy will come from, but I must find it. When I can't write, I feel so empty.' This feeling was terrifying, and he resolved to write on a full-time basis as soon as possible.

Life was not all work and no play, of course; John Steinbeck was neither hermit nor saint. On weekends, he would rush out to North Beach with a few silver dollars in his pocket, taking Carol to dinner at one of the sawdust-floored restaurants along the waterfront, such as The Purple Dragon, where good, cheap food and decent California wine could be found in large quantities. He and Carol would take a streetcar ride to the beach and lie in the sand, dazed and drunk, until dawn. They often woke (like his characters in *Tortilla Flat*) just as the sun peeked over the eastern horizon, with a dry mouth and banging head. (Carol later complained that she had been troubled by Steinbeck's drinking and had reluctantly gone along with it on too many occasions.)

After a lot of searching, Carol had found a job at the *San Francisco Chronicle*, where she worked in the departments of advertising and circulation. The young couple spent long hours at work, six days a week, so there was not much time for carousing or even courting. Steinbeck moved out of

Wilhelmson's apartment in October into a tiny apartment of his own on Powell Street, not far away, and lived most of the time on 'sardines and buns and doughnuts and coffee'. He lived in two rooms on the third floor, with mice 'scratching all night in the walls and ceiling'. The wall-paper was peeling, and his bed was only a canvas cot, but he didn't mind; the solitude and even the squalor appealed to his sense of himself as a bohemian artist. 'He never minded being down-and-out,' his sister says, 'I think he actually liked it. Young writers were supposed to be poor.'

He worked most evenings on 'The Green Lady', a mystical tale about a young man's vain attempts to understand and control the natural world, and every new version became more and more autobiographical, drawing heavily on family legends about his grandparents, both the Hamiltons and the Steinbecks. Partly because this was his first book set in California, he rightly felt that he had stumbled on his real 'material' for the first time. The book began to gather momentum by early November, with Steinbeck writing by hand anywhere from five to eight pages a day. Carol and her sister, Idell, would visit him in his garret, and he would read aloud each chapter as he finished it.

Occasionally, Carol (who had developed a strong interest in left-wing politics) took Steinbeck to hushed meetings of a group of socialists she had recently met through a friend at the Chronicle. These 'socialists' enjoyed talking in alarming tones about 'the coming revolution', and passed around translations of the works of Marx and Lenin. Steinbeck's interest in socialism varied over the years, although he would never have used the term socialist to describe himself. His politics were, and remained, those of a standard New Deal democrat with a fierce admixture of western individualism and Yankee independence. Indeed, his rather cynical view of the socialist movement is made apparent in a ferocious story called 'The Raid' in The Long Valley, where he treats socialism as simply another form of religion, and thus delusional.

Progress on the novel suddenly slowed, coming to a complete halt in early December. Kate Beswick grew anxious about the tone of Steinbeck's letters as winter approached, and she actually wrote to offer him money. 'I don't want you starving,' she wrote, 'it will be bad for your book.' He was grateful for her concern, but turned down her offer. He did, however, resolve firmly to change the conditions of his life to make writing possible. The work in the warehouse was simply too exhausting, and it was damaging his ability to pursue difficult imaginative work. 'I can't do it any more,' he wrote to Beswick, and he quit. At the suggestion of his father, he moved into the family cottage in Pacific Grove, where he intended to stay put until 'The Lady' was finished. 'Father gave him $25 a month from now on – or more – until he didn't need it any more,' his sister says. 'It was considered an advance against prospective royalties.' Clearly, John Ernst had decided to support his son now, financially if not emotionally. 'They had a strange relationship,' his sister recalls. 'I don't think Mother was ever happy with any of this, but Father was determined to help John now in whatever way he could.' (John Ernst had apparently come to admire his son's independence and wanted to reward it.)

The move to Pacific Grove, which parallels the move to Tahoe in the wake of the disastrous year in New York City, was a smart one. Steinbeck's artistic instincts moved always towards self-preservation, and he found himself able to work remarkably well in the little house that had been part of his life for so long. The weather was perfect this time of year: cool and bright, with the sun streaming into the living room where Steinbeck worked at a large oak desk beneath a photograph of his grandfather, John Adolph (who would figure prominently in the novel itself, which centres on a Vermont farmer who moves to California in search of a better life). The typescript of the novel began to gather bulk, and he was pleased by what was happening. 'By God, something is happening in this book,' he wrote to Beswick with enthusiasm.

Carol came down on weekends, secretly. This was long before the sexual revolution of the Sixties made 'pre-marital sex' an archaic concept, and they seem to have enjoyed the illicit nature of their romance. One weekend, alas, Steinbeck's parents dropped in unexpectedly on him, causing a near disaster. It was a Sunday morning, and Carol was lying in bed beside him. Since Olive and John Ernst were nothing if not conventional, they would have been scandalized if they had caught the couple in bed together. Fortunately, John had locked the doors the night before, and the shades were tightly drawn. Carol had (just) enough time to dress and scramble out a back door while his parents rapped on the front windows and hollered for John, who eventually opened the door and pretended that he had been asleep and hadn't heard them.

The couple spent many idyllic weekends together in Pacific Grove, which they called their 'honeymoon cottage'. They went crabbing along the Monterey shoreline, played tennis in the local park, or grilled pork chops over hot coals in the back yard beneath a spreading oak tree. The subject of marriage was often raised by Carol, but again the self-preservational instinct of the artist won out. Steinbeck was not ready to pin himself down or saddle himself with family responsibilities. He was not even sure about his ability to play the role of husband: 'That woman is fairly lucky who has me for a lover,' he told Kate Beswick, somewhat disingenuously, 'but I would curse no woman with me for a husband.'[3]

An astonishing wire from Ted Miller came, unexpectedly, in mid-January to say that Robert M. McBride & Company had accepted *Cup of Gold* for publication late in the coming summer. This was, of course, the same company that had refused to look at his book of stories only a few years earlier. Indeed, seven other publishing houses had turned down the novel, but this didn't matter to Steinbeck. As he knew, it takes only one publisher to publish a novel, and he was mightily pleased, although Carol Henning and Carl Wilhelmson were both surprised by his lack of overt excitement. (This was, I suspect, his self-protective tendency manifesting itself again: if you don't care to win, it doesn't really matter if you lose.) He was offered an advance of $250, the first 'real' money he had earned from his pen. Furthermore, the book would be illustrated and designed by Mahlon Blaine, his old friend from the *Katrina* and the year in Manhattan. The idea was that, since Blaine already had acquired a solid reputation as an illustrator, the book clubs might be interested in acquiring *Cup of Gold*, thus boosting sales immeasurably. (This never happened; the book clubs turned it down.)

What, exactly, was this *Cup of Gold*?

On the simplest level, the subtitle of the book tells all: *A Life of Sir Henry Morgan, Buccaneer, with Occasional Reference to History* . . . On the other hand, the reader looking for a simple biography of the famous English pirate, or a straightforward account of his historical times, will be sorely disappointed. *Cup of Gold* is a peculiar book in most ways, and it often disappoints Steinbeck fans who are looking for an early version of *The Grapes of Wrath*. The simple yet dignified prose style he perfected in his great books of the Thirties is only occasionally glimpsed in *Cup of Gold*, where the young author often adopts a baroque style reminiscent of James Branch Cabell's *Jürgen* (which contains a chapter featuring Merlin the magician, a contemporary source for Steinbeck's Merlin in the novel). One also hears in the prose the odd, inflated style used by Donn Byme in *Blind Raftery*, the improbable story of an eighteenth-century Gaelic poet, and in *Messer Marco Polo*, which Steinbeck often cited as an influence. Another popular author of the day whom he admired was Joseph Hergesheimer, best remembered today for *Java Head*, though in his time he was at the top of the literary heap. (Sinclair Lewis, in an almost comically self-serving act of homage, covered himself by dedicating *Main Street* to *both* Cabell and Hergesheimer!)

The novel shifts among various styles uncertainly, ranging from the Cabell-Byme style – ornate, precious, convoluted, highly allusive – to a more naturalistic style that does actually foreshadow the prose of Steinbeck's Depression-era books. In the former mode, he is apt to write about 'the mad incongruity, the turgid stultiloquy of life' or lavish too many adjectives on some innocent phrase, as when Henry Morgan is said to 'struggle madly against the folding meshes of his dream' instead of simply 'fall asleep'. The sun is referred to as 'a white, fevered ulcer in the sky' and a few pirate ships going up a river become 'The long line of boats writhed up the river like a tremendous jointed snake'. One cringes and turns the page.

In later years Steinbeck's dialogue would be immensely natural and taut, but here it is often utterly improbable, as when Morgan's father says: 'I imagine great dishes of purple porridge, drenched with dragon's milk, sugared with a sweetness only to be envisioned.' Or, at a crucial scene late in the novel, when Henry cries, 'May God damn La Santa Roja for sowing the world with insanity. She has made cut-throats bay the moon like lovesick dogs. She is making me crazy with this vain desire. I must do something – anything – to lay the insistent haunting of this woman I have never seen. I must destroy the ghost. Ah, it is a foolish thing to dream of capturing the Cup of Gold. It would seem that my desire is death.' It is hard to believe that Steinbeck thought human beings ever talked like this.

There are, on the other hand, stretches of the novel where

Steinbeck writes beautifully, conjuring the Caribbean in a lush but evocative prose in keeping with his better work. Here, for instance, is how Morgan's passage into tropical waters is first described:

> Now they had sailed into a warm sea, and a warm wind drove them on. Henry and the cook would stand at the rail, watching the triangle fins of sharks cut back and forth across their wake waiting for refuse. They saw little brown clusters of weed go floating by, and the leisurely, straight-swimming pilot fish on the point of the prow. Once the cook pointed to the brown birds with long, slender wings following them; hanging, hovering, dipping, swaying, always flying, never resting.

The descriptions of the push into Panama, where Henry Morgan pursues his dream of capturing the 'cup of gold' to the literal ends of the earth, are reminiscent of Joseph Conrad's richly imagistic, detailed and lyrical prose. Typically, Steinbeck writes: 'A yellow dawn crept out of the little painted hills of Panama and grew bolder as it edged across the plain. The sun flashed up from behind a peak, and its golden rays sought for their city.' These sentences would not have seemed out of place in *Heart of Darkness* or *Nostromo*.

The story, set in the late seventeenth century, is as simple as the quasi-historical legend on which it was based. Steinbeck opens with an adolescent Henry Morgan at home in the hills of Wales, where he consults the mythical Merlin for advice about his future. He has a passionately held, almost mystical, desire to go off to the New World to pursue his dream of a career in the West Indies. Quite naturally, his parents are nervous about their son's ambitions, although they remain supportive of his dreams – a situation close to the literal reality of Olive and John Ernst Steinbeck and their son's literary ambitions. Henry's father, Old Robert, is quietly behind his son; he is described as a man whose 'smile was perplexity and a strange passive defiance'. His mother is down-to-earth, pragmatic, brusque. She loves her son and husband 'with a queer mixture of pity and contempt'.

Henry sails off to the Indies without even saying goodbye to his parents. But his dream of independence is dashed when he arrives in the New World only to find himself indentured to an English planter named James Flower. Flower, who turns out to be a kindly man, takes Henry to his bosom, teaching him to read various ancient languages. Henry, meanwhile, squirrels away enough coins to serve as a kind of nest egg for future adventures; he also falls in love with a strangely seductive young woman, Paulette, 'a pretty little golden animal', although he will not admit to her that he loves her. Eventually, Henry is made a free man by his mentor and sets off marauding around the Caribbean in high style. His drive and commanding personality mark him for success, and he soon becomes the greatest buccaneer of them all, eventually taking a small fleet of pirates into Panama, which he conquers; he also tries to win the hand of La Santa Roja, a legendary woman also known as the Red Saint of Panama. His quest for this virgin saint (who turns out to be married already) is foiled, and Henry Morgan sinks into 'a disease called mediocrity'. His symbolic quest for the 'cup of gold' is thus foiled as well.

Soon enough, Henry is called back to England to answer to charges of piracy; at heart a patriot, he obeys the king's command and returns only to discover that he has become a populist hero of sorts. Charles II realizes that there would be no point in punishing him; in a clever move, he decides to bestow a knighthood on Henry and make him governor of Jamaica. Thus, Sir Henry returns to the New World tropics with the ironic commission from his king to stop all piracy. In strict if unlikely obedience, Henry sentences two of his old comrades to death, but he pays for his lack of fidelity to his original vision by dying himself: a mysterious disease kills him, and he is visited by his past sins in a surreal, visionary form reminiscent of an Elizabethan masque.

Sources for this unlikely novel include John Exquemeling's *The Buccaneers of America* and other studies of Renaissance voyaging, which Steinbeck plundered greedily for information and anecdotes. He was clearly pulling from many places as he fashioned his tale, and he felt sufficiently free to add and subtract from the legend of Henry Morgan rather boldly, following the dictates of his imagination whenever necessary.

It should not, however, be surprising to find so many influences in a first novel. The young author was busily processing different voices, trying to discover a voice of his own, and it remains interesting to read this novel against the later work. One hears Steinbeck talking to himself when Merlin advises the young Henry, 'You will come to your greatness, and it may be in time you will be alone in your greatness. . . .' One hears him again when he muses on the complexity of women in this description of Henry Morgan's first love, Elizabeth, who becomes a symbol as powerful as the 'cup of gold' itself at the novel's conclusion: 'She was a thing of mystery. All girls and women hoarded something they never spoke of. His mother had terrific secrets about biscuits, and cried, sometimes, for no known reason. Another life went on inside of women – some women – ran parallel to their outward lives and yet never crossed them.' It could also be argued that Henry Morgan's visionary quest for the 'cup of gold' parallels Steinbeck's desire for artistic success; he may have feared his own strong drive towards wealth and fame. As early as 1936, when *Cup of Gold* was first reissued, it was seen as 'a sort of key to Steinbeck himself' by Lewis Gannett, who wrote an insightful preface to the novel.

Before the book appeared in print, Steinbeck wrote to Bob Cathcart, 'I think all first novels ought to be burned just as a matter of course. Some good ones might suffer, but so few that the practice would be justified anyway. I shall model a little model of mud and call it art. Then I shall erect an altar with horns. And on this pyre shall my brainchild go up in smoke while flags wave and bands play.'[4] In a sense, he was right about what he had written. *Cup of Gold* does not stand with his best work, or even with his middle-level work. But it remains invaluable for its anticipation of the writer who would emerge in the next decade. Much that a sympathetic reader finds to admire in the mature Steinbeck is present here in *ur* form: the kernel story of a voyage, or quest; the image of an idealistic young man whose dreams go sour and end in disillusion; the concept of an intimate relationship between human beings and their physical environment; the understanding of how power may be abused by those who have too much of it; the theme of conflict between the sexes. Read as a covert autobiography, *Cup of Gold* does offer 'a key' of sorts to John Steinbeck; one can detect his pent-up rage against the existing social order, his rebelliousness, his private war against a grandiose self, which he none the less covets and protects (Henry Morgan's tendencies to self-aggrandizement are recognized and chastized). A careful reader will also find signs of Steinbeck's abiding quest for experience of Eden combined with his high sense of moral purpose. Novels are, perhaps inevitably, autobiographical, and first novels are famously so. *Cup of Gold* is no exception.

Steinbeck remained in Pacific Grove, hermitlike, through the spring and summer (with many excursions into San Francisco or up to Palo Alto, where Dook Sheffield was finishing his MA); he worked hard each day on 'The Lady', as he called it, abandoning the original version in mid-July to begin the novel again as a totally new story which he would rename *To a God Unknown*. He believed himself on to a good thing now, and his letters were full of enthusiasm for writing in general, if not for this specific manuscript. 'The main thing just now with all of us is to get as many words on paper as possible and then to destroy the paper,' he wrote to Cathcart.

He also 'wasted' a good portion of each day in Monterey itself, wandering among the huge canneries, with their roofs of corrugated iron, watching the sardine boats coming into dock with tall barrels full of fish as the stench wafted through the air from the factories that ground fish heads and tails into fertilizer. He often had lunch in a diner called Maria's and talked to the *paisanos*, the whores, the cannery workers and fishermen. He bought cheap wine from a bootlegger called Mike who operated out of the back of a restaurant, and shared his bottles with the local winos, many of whom camped in abandoned houses or slept in makeshift shelters near the sea. This 'material' – the stuff of real life – fascinated Steinbeck, who would incorporate much of what he saw and heard and smelled and tasted in *Tortilla Flat*, *Cannery Row* and *Sweet Thursday*.

Money was short, as usual, and towards the end of the summer he resolved to go back to San Francisco to work for long enough to lay some cash aside so that he could return to his desk. This move might also be seen as part of the migratory pattern he had been evolving since leaving Stanford: his inner clock required a shift back to the city. There was Carol too, who must be reckoned with; she continued pressing him to think seriously about marriage (especially now that he was 'a success' as a writer, having had a novel accepted by a New York publisher). Furthermore, Steinbeck missed the swirl of people found only in big cities; solitude, for him, was essential as a part of his natural oscillation or recoil from the public world. This oscillation formed a dichotomy that would operate throughout his life (in his last years he shifted back and forth between New York City and Sag Harbor, Long Island).

He moved in with Carl Wilhelmson, sleeping on his friend's dilapidated sofa. The springs poked through the slip covers and made sound sleep nearly impossible, and the apartment was miserably cramped, but Wilhelmson was a good influence – hard-working and earnest about the craft of writing. Perhaps more so than Steinbeck, he had set out to educate himself on the subject of contemporary fiction, and the two young men spent long hours talking about the latest writers; Hemingway and Faulkner were high on Wilhelmson's list of favourites. He was intrepidly professional in a way that inspired Steinbeck; having published his first novel and had a second one accepted, his third was already making the rounds of publishers. His fourth novel was now underway. This vivid example of persistence was not lost on his ambitious friend, who had yet to master the art of consistency. (The irony, of course, is that Wilhelmson's star faded quickly in the Thirties, and his novels today are found only by chance in second-hand bookshops.)

Steinbeck obtained some relatively untaxing part-time work as a sales clerk in a department store and continued to work on *To a God Unknown*, sometimes writing as many as 3000 words in the evening after dinner. (He would brag about his word-count to Carl, who would respond, 'But what kind of words are they?') Steinbeck was painfully aware of the stylistic dead end that *Cup of Gold* represented and wrote to Grove Day, another old Stanford friend, 'I have not the slightest desire to step into Donn Byrne's shoes.' He also claimed to have 'outgrown Cabell'. What he hoped to write from now on was lean, muscular prose – not a copy of Hemingway's style exactly, but his own equivalent.

It was about this time, in the summer of 1929, that he first read Hemingway with any seriousness. By now, *In Our Time*, *The Torrents Of Spring*, and *The Sun Also Rises* were well known among the literati, although Steinbeck seems not to have read them carefully or indeed at all. Carol, however, had given him a copy of 'The Killers' in October, and he was stunned by the compression and originality of style found in this remarkable short story. He had for some months been working to restrain his tendency to write floridly, with an excess of rhetoric, and the effect of reading Hemingway was overwhelming. Like virtually everyone of his generation, Steinbeck was influenced by the cool, indirect style with its modernist emphasis on what Ezra Pound called 'the thing itself'. The languid moralizing still prevalent among writers of the older generation was swept away by Hemingway. Steinbeck now described his new book to Grove Day in Hemingway terms as 'a straightforward attempt to set down some characters in a situation and nothing else'.[5] This was his 'new method' in writing fiction, one that 'reduced a single idea to a single sentence' instead of letting the idea fill out a 'whole chapter' in the manner of James Branch Cabell, whose star was fading. The modernist revolution had caught up with John Steinbeck.

Not surprisingly, he was defensive about the influence of Hemingway, now and throughout his life. 'I have never never read Hemingway with the exception of "The Killers",' he anxiously told Grove Day, who questioned him about the influence of Hemingway on his new theories. But this was smoke blown to disguise the obvious: he owed a great deal to his great contemporary. In a more honest moment, he told Carol that he considered Hemingway 'the finest writer alive', and the proof of the pudding is in the eating. The great Depression-era novels of Steinbeck reflect the debt to Hemingway, whose mastery of style and elliptical approach to narrative were crucial to his 'new method'. In later years, when Hemingway's fame was vast, people would try to ingratiate themselves with Steinbeck by referring to Hemingway in deprecatory terms in front of him, says Robert Wallsten. 'I remember once a person denigrated Hemingway in his presence, hoping to win his favour. But John simply bit his lip and changed the subject abruptly. He would never disparage another writer in public – and especially not Hemingway.'

It seems clear from his letters that Steinbeck relished the

bohemian image of himself and Carl Wilhelmson hammering away at their novels together in Wilhelmson's cramped apartment. 'We have taken the ordinary number of beatings and I don't think there is much strength in either of us, and still we go on butting our heads against the English Novel,' he wrote to Grove Day.[6] These 'beatings' probably refer to the few reviews of *Cup of Gold*, which had been published to a resounding silence. What reviews did leak into print were dismissive. Somewhat surprisingly, given the book's non-reception, the sales were not disastrous. The 1500 copies printed by McBride & Company were nearly gone by Christmas, although this modest commercial success may have had more to do with Mahlon Blaine's garish dustjacket, which featured a cartoonish pirate in colourful, billowing pantaloons and high black boots, than with Steinbeck's story. (The jacket made the book appear more like a comic-strip version of *Treasure Island* than a serious work of adult fiction, much to Steinbeck's horror.)

Authors always complain about their publishers, no matter how well they are treated, and Steinbeck was no exception. He did, however, have good reason for resenting Robert M. McBride & Company. To begin with, the editor who had accepted the novel – a man named Stuart Rose – quit his job shortly before the novel appeared, leaving the young author without an advocate in the house. And there had obviously been nothing one could reasonably call a publishing strategy. 'The reason there have been no reviews is that no review copies were issued,' he told Kate Beswick with digust.[7] 'I did not even get a copy for my folks. Naturally I could not afford to buy it. I know nothing about publishing but what little I know about psychology would indicate that they did prac-tically everything wrong. There are orders placed two months ago that are unfilled. All of the department stores seem to have it but none of the book stores.' Worse, he heard from Ted Miller that in New York the novel was being shelved in book stores as a work of juvenile fiction, in part because of the ridiculous dustjacket.

In November, Steinbeck and Carol made it known to their respective families that they intended to get married at some unspecified future date. In general, Steinbeck's parents and sisters were pleased. 'Carol was very bright, just right for John,' his sister says. 'She used to do a lot of his typing, and he could talk over his work with her. But she was independent. You couldn't push her around.' Indeed, she seems to have been ideal for Steinbeck: a woman who was fiercely individual and spirited, who was none the less devoted to him in her own way; she spent hours typing and retyping versions of *To a God Unknown* without complaining, and did not hesitate to offer editorial suggestions. 'There wasn't a shy streak anywhere to be found in Carol,' Beth continues. 'That was a good thing, because John was shy.'

Another crucial side of Carol was her social conscience, which was highly developed. As banks collapsed, factories closed and farms and small businesses failed all around the country, she sympathized strongly with the poor, the down-and-out, and the dispossessed; instinct led her to protest all forms of injustice when she encountered them. 'I think she was John's conscience in those days . . . or she ignited his conscience,' a friend said.[8] 'She knew what was happening in the country. She read all the papers and magazines, and she wanted John to read them.' Carol obviously had a profound influence on the development of Steinbeck's thinking in the Thirties, and thus on the direction of his best-known fiction. The smouldering sense of outrage which gives *Of Mice and Men* and *The Grapes of Wrath* their quiet dignity and moral force is partly a testament to Carol's impact.

She seems to have had a maturing effect on Steinbeck, who had in any event come a long way by himself in the last few years. On 5 December, he sent Grove Day a perceptive letter about himself:

I don't care any more what people think of me. I'll tell you
how it happened. You will remember at Stanford that I
went about being different characters. I even developed a
theory that one had no personality in essence, that one was
a reflection of a mood plus the moods of other persons
present. I wasn't pretending to be something I wasn't. For
the moment I was truly the person I thought I was.

   Well, I went into the mountains and stayed two years. I
was snowed in eight months of the year and saw no one
except my two Airedales. There were millions of fir trees
and the snow was deep and it was very quiet. And there
was no one to pose for any more. You can't have a show
with no audience. Gradually all the poses slipped off and
when I came out of the hills I didn't have any poses any
more. It was rather sad, but it was far less trouble. I am
happier than I have ever been.[9]

In the same letter, he described his bride-to-be: 'I'm engaged
to a girl of whom I will say nothing at all because you will
eventually meet her and I think you will like her because she
has a mind as sharp and penetrating as your own.'
   The young couple packed their bags into Steinbeck's Buick,
which was rusting out from under them, and set off after
Christmas for Los Angeles, where they intended to get
married without fuss or family in a civil ceremony. Unlike the
rest of the country, which had just begun sinking into what
would be known as the Great Depression, their mood was
high as they left San Francisco on a cold, clear day and drove
south along El Camino Real, one of the most scenic highways
in America. (One not inconsiderable reason for their confidence was the fact that Steinbeck's father had promised the
couple $50 a month until their financial situation 'stabilized'.
In effect, John Ernst doubled his son's allowance.)
   Steinbeck was undaunted as the Buick began to cough and
splutter when they had gone barely thirty miles beyond the
San Francisco city limits; he was less happy when it ground to

a halt in San Jose, which (fortunately) was not far from where Carol's parents lived in a middle-class, suburban house. Carol's father, an undemonstrative man who sold real estate, rescued them. The Buick was apparently beyond repair and was sold the next day to a junk dealer, who hauled the rusty carcass away. Meanwhile, the young couple were stranded with the Hennings for ten days ('They didn't really like me,' Steinbeck later confessed to Dook Sheffield). After grazing the used-car lots of San Jose for three days they settled on a Marmon (a fancy touring car with elegant red leather seats) and set off for Los Angeles in high style. The Marmon, alas, was mechanically unsound, and Steinbeck spent much of the next two months tinkering with its differential before trading it in for a black 1922 Chevrolet, which despite its ugliness (they called it 'the bathtub') was reliable.

The couple moved in temporarily with Dook Sheffield, who had recently divorced Ruth and married a woman named Maryon; the newlyweds occupied a small cottage southeast of Los Angeles in the San Fernando Valley, near Occidental College, where Dook had just assumed a teaching appointment. He had acquired his MA in English from Stanford the summer before, and this job had fallen into his lap rather suddenly. One of the ideas floating in the air between Steinbeck and Sheffield was that Steinbeck might be hired as well, now that he was a published novelist. Nothing came of this, mostly because Steinbeck refused even to go into the college with Dook to meet his colleagues.

Maryon Sheffield was not hostile towards Steinbeck, as Ruth had been; but she was not especially glad to have a couple camping on her living-room floor. She suspected that Steinbeck, with his famous aversion to marriage, would stall and never actually marry Carol, whom she liked and wanted to see wed. So she forced the issue, and on 14 January, 1930, she and Dook 'kidnapped' the couple and hauled them off to the old courthouse in Glendale, where they were married in a ceremony that lasted less than ten minutes. There were no parents, no relatives, and no other friends in attendance. The wedding party celebrated by drinking a gallon of Dook's home-brewed beer.

It did not pass unnoticed that Steinbeck's parents had not been included in the wedding. John Ernst and Olive Steinbeck were 'upset that John didn't want them at his wedding', says his sister. 'They didn't mind the idea of the marriage, in principle. They thought that Carol would settle him down. But it was a slap in the face.' Once again, Steinbeck was asserting his independence from what he now realized was an unhealthy family of origin. While there remains a bit of adolescent gesturing in this act of parental rejection, it was a necessary move. He wanted to go forward into full manhood unfettered; as if that were possible.

A True Liking

'Eventually I shall be so good that I cannot be ignored.
These years are disciplinary for me.'

Steinbeck to Carl Wilhelmson, late 1930

A cosy life evolved in the south-eastern suburbs of Los
Angeles for John and Carol Steinbeck and their friends. To
celebrate the marriage, they bought a puppy – a Belgian
shepherd called Oz (for Ozymandias) – yet another in a long
line of Steinbeckian dogs (the most famous of whom would
be Charley, *agent provocateur* of *Travels with Charley*). Meanwhile, Dook and Maryon kicked the newlyweds out of their
house, forcing them to find a place of their own, which they
soon did: a 'shack', as they called it, which perched boldly on
a deserted hillside on El Roble Drive in nearby Eagle Rock, a
town south of Van Nuys on the way to Laguna Beach. They
rented this flimsy and defiantly insubstantial dwelling, a
fresh incarnation of 'The Sphincter' he had loved so much at
Stanford, for fifteen dollars a month. The crumbling stucco
building had 'a bedroom, a bathroom, kitchen and sleeping
porch'.[1]

Steinbeck and Dook worked hard on the place for a month,
repairing broken windows, fixing the plumbing (none of the
faucets seemed to work), and refinishing the oak floor in the
space that was to become a thirty-foot living room with an
imposing stone fireplace which needed pointing but otherwise seemed to work. The electric wiring was 'antique, circa
George Washington', Steinbeck reported, and he replaced it
himself. Carol made broadcloth curtains for the windows out
of a bolt of paisley sent to her by her mother, and personally

wallpapered and painted the rooms. Maryon found some used furniture in a warehouse in Van Nuys, and pretty soon the Steinbecks were in business.

'In this community we make beer, much beer, and it is both cheap and pleasant to induce a state of lassitude intershot with moments of unreal romance,' Steinbeck wrote to Ted Miller back east.[2] In addition to making beer and engaging in 'unreal romance', Carol and Maryon, along with various friends who had flocked to the region because of Steinbeck and Sheffield, decided to start a plastics business. A couple by the name of Ritch and Tal Lovejoy (whom Steinbeck had met in San Francisco) appeared on the scene, and they would become lifelong friends. Tal's self-consciously bohemian and extroverted sister, Xenia, had moved south only a few weeks after John and Carol Steinbeck, and she entered the picture too, possessed by an idea for starting up a business that Carol latched on to quickly. The concept was interesting: a new Swiss plastic had come on to the market that could be made into moulds and casts far superior to the plaster of Paris type already in use. Everyone was sure that the new product would be attractive to the movie industry and to department stores, which needed an endless supply of window dummies.

'The group used to meet every afternoon like they were corporate moguls,' a friend of the period remembers.[3] 'John himself wouldn't participate. I think he thought Carol was crazy, but he was going to humour her. It was all Dook's money, and he put in a lot of it, though he didn't get involved either. The group pretty soon figured out that the plastic stuff didn't work like it was supposed to, that it just crumbled in their hands. They wasted a lot of time on this thing but they seemed to have fun doing it so nobody cared. That was the attitude in those days: you had to have fun.' Mahlon Blaine turned up unexpectedly one day, and quickly joined the group as 'artistic director'. (He had come west to seek work as a set designer in Hollywood.) This rag-tag bunch of amateur entrepreneurs called itself, rather whimsically, the Faster Master Plaster Casters.

This period would, in retrospect, be thought of fondly by Steinbeck, although at the time it often seemed difficult. 'Remember the days when we were all living in Eagle Rock?' he would later ask. 'As starved and happy a group as ever robbed an orange grove. I can still remember the dinners of hamburger and stolen avocados.'[4] The house, radically transformed by elbow grease, was a pleasant dwelling. Steinbeck spent long, happy hours in the garden, planting trees, flowers and shrubbery. Often he sat back and simply enjoyed the fruits of labour, lounging in the bright sunshine with his 'jet black puppy, Oz' lying dazedly at his feet. Best of all, as he wrote to Ted Miller, 'I am getting work done, which makes me more happy than any of the other things.'

Steinbeck had two projects underway: the revision of *To a God Unknown*, which he hoped to complete soon, and a sequence of linked short stories which he tentatively called *Dissonant Symphony*. The stories, which were never finished, focused on families in northern California, and his idea was to analyse their problems, not as consequences of individual action – the traditional Greek view of human nature; rather, Steinbeck wanted to examine the ways that environmental issues, such as drought, affected his characters and the way their lives were played out. He had, indeed, begun to move in the philosophical and aesthetic direction that would culminate in *The Grapes of Wrath*, where individual destiny is viewed in the context of geopolitical pressures such as drought, famine and capitalist greed. The problem with *Dissonant Symphony*, however, was that Steinbeck could not imagine how to link the stories in a plausible and logical way. 'Everything I try seems so damned forced,' he wrote to Kate Beswick with palpable dissatisfaction.[5] 'I do want to manage this thing, a book of connected stories. But maybe it can't be done. Or maybe, that is, I can't figure out how it should be done.'

He was working well, however, as one can tell from a letter he wrote about his life to Carl Wilhelmson: 'Carol is a good influence on my work. I am putting in five hours every day on the rewriting of this one and in the evenings I have started another. I have the time and the energy and it gives me pleasure to work, and now I do not seem to have to fight as much reluctance to work as I used to have. The start comes much easier.'[6] He referred to the new book as 'a series of short stories or sketches loosely and foolishly tied together'.

In late April, thanks again to Carol's diligence, he finally had a freshly typed version of *To a God Unknown* (the title came from a Vedic hymn). He sent it immediately to Ted Miller, saying, 'If McBride should decide to take this, tell them that I want a short foreword in which some mention of Toby Street should be made.'[7] One sees, again, his strong sense of loyalty to his friends. Miller did as requested, but the novel was rejected by McBride in a matter of days. On 28 May, Steinbeck wrote back to Miller, 'Your news of McBrides came as a final touch to a week of disaster, a series of small and tragic incidents leading up to the death of our dog who died in convulsions which seemed to be the result of poison. The rejection was nothing as compared to that.'[8] He gives Miller a short list of potential publishers, citing the influence that various friends or acquaintances might have here or there. Lying through his teeth, he wrote, 'I am not discouraged at all.' His next letter to Miller registers a slight note of panic: 'I am twenty-eight years old now and I must have at least one book a year from now on if I can manage it.'[9] The inward motor was running; what Steinbeck needed now was to find the right gear. He did: nearly a book a year appeared between 1932 and 1950, an astonishing feat of productivity.

In all, 1930 was an anxious year for him, despite the initial happiness of the marriage, the warm circle of friends and the hospitable surroundings at Eagle Rock. His letters to friends toll a fretful bell again and again. Was he going anywhere as a writer? Would any publisher accept *To a God Unknown*? Would it be necessary for him to live off his father's monthly stipend for the rest of his life? 'It is discouraging, isn't it?' he wrote to Miller. 'Nobody seems to want my work.'[10] Part of the difficulty lay in the transition from one style and manner of writing to another. While Steinbeck clearly understood what had to be done, it was not easy to change his approach. But he undertook the process of re-education seriously, and this involved a programme of reading – or reading again with an eye to method – the classics. 'I have re-read Xenophon and Herodotus and Plutarch and Marcus Aurelius,' he wrote to Miller from Eagle Rock in mid-winter. He also mentioned having read Henry Fielding, whose clean, swift, and unpretentious style made a crisp impression. Defensively, he also alluded to the writer who was really 'teaching' him how to write all over again: 'I suppose I shall be imitating Hemingway . . .'

The stories of *Dissonant Symphony* crumbled in his hands, and wisely he abandoned the project.[11] These undeveloped and unrevised stories contain several elements that reappeared two years later in the wonderfully realized stories of *The Pastures of Heaven*, which remains one of Steinbeck's finest, if least recognized, achievements. Throughout the winter and early spring in Eagle Rock he seems to have been working simultaneously on the final revisions of *To a God Unknown*, on *Dissonant Symphony*, and on the first of the stories that would find their way into *The Pastures of Heaven*. Somehow, in the midst of a hugely social scene, he was getting his work done.

As it became more and more obvious that the Faster Master Plaster Casters would never get off the ground, the economic situation of the newlyweds worsened, fanning the flames of disaster. The fact that every publisher in New York seemed to loathe *To a God Unknown* did not help matters. The Steinbecks were now wholly and embarrassingly dependent on John Ernst, who was not himself in the best of economic shape (as Olive kept pointing out, much to her son's despair).[12] The prospects for changing this situation did not seem good, although Carol did get a loan of several hundred dollars from her father, which they used to pay some urgent bills. This continuing financial crisis agitated Steinbeck considerably: 'I feel like an adolescent sometimes,' he complained to Kate Beswick, 'but I have no choice, do I? I have to keep writing, and there is no way I can do hard physical labor and write good books at the same time. I've tried it, and it doesn't work.'[13]

In late spring, the owner of the house in Eagle Rock decided suddenly that his tenants had done such a good job of restoring the place that he would give it to his daughter as a wedding present. The Steinbecks were told to leave at the end of June. Although both of them protested, nothing could be done; they were renters, after all, and no lease had been signed. They packed their few belongings and moved, briefly, to a seedy but inexpensive house on the outskirts of Glendale, then into a large wood-frame house just north of Eagle Rock in a place called Tujunga.

The house in Tujunga was rambling and attractive, set on the edge of the Angeles National Forest. The garden behind it gave way to rolling fields of scrub pine and brush, and there were mountains rising in the distance. It was a lovely place for Steinbeck to snip, prune and plunge his hands in the earth, as he loved to do. But the place, according to Carol, was haunted. She described to her friends the experience of seeing dishes fly across the room, of watching pictures dislodge from the wall, of hearing doors snap shut or open without explanation. 'We can't live here because the place is haunted,' Steinbeck told Kate Beswick. 'It's too unsettling. I can't concentrate. Who can explain such things?' Carol, meanwhile, was panicky about their finances. 'She has tried to find secretarial jobs in Los Angeles, with no luck,' he explained. By August, they had come to the end of their tether.

The last refuge, as always, was the family cottage in Pacific Grove. On 22 August they packed the Chevy, which showed every sign of having found the secret of eternal life, and abandoned the ghost-ridden house in Tujunga with a sense of relief. After an emotional farewell breakfast with the Sheffields which included 'flapjacks, a side of bacon, black coffee, and beer', they headed north. Soon they were firmly established on 11th Street, and Carol immediately began job hunting. Within three days she had landed a position as 'secretary to the Secretary of the Chamber of Commerce of Monterey'. Steinbeck wrote to Ted Miller that he was blissfully happy to be back in the Monterey region. 'It is a grand place,' he wrote.[14] 'There are thirteen fish canneries here, and within a couple of years the new breakwater is going in which will bring a greatly increased population because it will become a deep water port and hundreds of big ships will stop here.' He realised as he wrote that he was beginning to sound like a brochure issued by the Chamber of Commerce. 'As a matter of fact,' he continued, 'I am very much emotionally tied up with the whole place. It has a soul which is lacking in the east.'

Steinbeck was able to settle happily into *The Pastures of Heaven* now. It was as though he felt his strength as a writer for the first time, and he was confident that he would succeed. 'I have uncovered an unbelievable store of energy in myself,' he told Carl Wilhelmson. 'Eventually I shall be so good that I cannot be ignored. These years are disciplinary for me.'[15] The use of the house in Pacific Grove offered the safety net that he needed at that time, though it took considerable gumption for him to keep going as a writer. Steinbeck believed in himself deeply; this was part of his genius: his innate self-confidence allowed him to move through difficult spots into clearer patches. Later in life, he recalled this period in an article in *Esquire*:

> The Depression was no financial shock to me. I didn't have any money to lose, but in common with millions I did dislike hunger and cold. I had two assets. My father owned a tiny three-room cottage in Pacific Grove in California, and he let me live in it without rent. That was the first safety. Pacific Grove is on the sea. That was the second. People in inland cities or in the closed and shuttered industrial cemeteries had greater problems than I. Given the sea a man must be very stupid to starve. That great reservoir of food is always available. I took a large part of my protein food from the ocean. Firewood to keep warm floated in on the beach daily, needing only handsaw and ax. A small garden of black soil came with the cottage. In northern California you can raise vegetables of some kind all year long. I never peeled a potato without planting the skins. Kale, lettuce, chard, turnips, carrots and onions rotated in the little garden. In the tide pools of the bay, mussels were available and crabs and abalones and that shiny kelp called sea lettuce. With a line and pole, blue cod, rock cod, perch, sea trout, and sculpin could be caught.[16]

Progress on *The Pastures of Heaven* continued, with Steinbeck working for at least five hours every morning. Afternoons were spent in the activities he describes: basic food-gathering. Once or twice Steinbeck socialized with a local writer (who wrote boys' adventure stories for magazines) by the name of John Calvin, and here he encountered for the first time a commercially minded group of writers who (as he soon learned) disgusted him. In a distressing letter to Carl Wilhelmson he said, 'We went to a party at John Calvin's in Carmel last week. These writers of juveniles are the Jews of literature. They seem to wring the English language, to squeeze pennies out of it. They don't even pretend that there is any dignity in craftsmanship. A conversation with them sounds like an afternoon spent with a pawnbroker.'[17]

It may seem hard to imagine that a person of Steinbeck's calibre would sink to anti-semitic remarks like this, but one too easily forgets that in the Twenties and Thirties anti-semitism was commonplace among intellectuals. T. S. Eliot and Ezra Pound, for instance, didn't trouble to hide their sentiments, even in their public writing. In 1933 Eliot delivered a series of lectures at the University of Virginia which were collected in a volume titled *After Strange Gods*, where he argues that 'race and religion combine to make any large number of freethinking Jews undesirable' in a Christian society. (Both poets later repudiated their earlier anti-semitism, Pound calling it 'a dirty suburban habit' that he fell into unthinkingly.) One doesn't forgive Steinbeck the remark, but one can understand it in the context of the era when it was made. (Later in life, it should be said, he argued vigorously against anti-semitism and refused to countenance prejudice of any kind.)

Steinbeck did, however, find himself attracted to the idea of making a quick dollar by his pen, a mercenary urge that was exacerbated by a round of dental treatment he could not avoid. In frustration, he temporarily put aside *The Pastures of Heaven* for two weeks and, in a frenzy of composition, wrote a 63,000-word mystery, *Murder at Full Moon*. Not wishing to contaminate the good name of Steinbeck, he chose a pseudonym: Peter Pym. He sent the book to Ted Miller with a warning that it would make him sick. 'And remember that it makes me a great deal sicker than it does you,' he added. The story was never published, but it did help Steinbeck to acquire a good New York agent, McIntosh & Otis, who would remain his agent to the end.

Steinbeck's sister notes that 'Carol and John were good together when they were poor. It was only when the money started coming in, and when John became more famous, that things really went sour.' Carol livened up the household with her jokes, her energetic conversation and her gregariousness; these traits were in special demand given that her shy husband also had a tendency to sink into melancholic silence and retreat to his writing table. When bills came in, and there was no money to pay them, Steinbeck sometimes retreated into bed at noon. Carol would bring him little gifts of chocolate or flowers and would sit on the bed and tease him. She believed, and she often said it, that they were 'magic people' and that money meant nothing. After all, wasn't most of America broke at the moment?

Carol also spent hours retyping his manuscripts, and this involved some heavy editing. Like Scott Fitzgerald, his contemporary, Steinbeck could neither spell nor punctuate. And he always needed someone to take the extra 's' off 'bus' or to change 'freindship' to 'friendship'. In the heat of composition he rarely bothered to put in commas in serial adjectives or to use the possessive apostrophe, and the difference between a colon and a semi-colon eluded him throughout his long writing career. Carol was fortunately a good technical editor, and she also had a gift for deleting phrases that merely puffed up her husband's prose: it was not for nothing that she strongly admired Hemingway. (She forced her husband to read *A Farewell to Arms*, which had come out the previous year and ridden high on the bestseller lists for many months.)

In November another business opportunity presented itself to Carol, who was still cringing from the failure of the Faster Master Plaster Casters. A woman friend was opening a small advertising agency in Monterey and wanted Carol to join her in partnership. The notion of leaving a 'real' job at the Chamber of Commerce may seem foolhardy in retrospect, but Monterey's economy was doing better than that of the country as a whole. The US Army had established a base nearby, and the sardine industry was booming; indeed, cans of sardines were a staple of Depression-era family diets, and the bay had yet to suffer the depletion that was looming. The fertilizer made from fish by-products was, furthermore, a growing industry, and Monterey was a centre of production, warehousing and marketing. Steinbeck urged his wife to take the risk, and she was aided in the decision by her father, who had been stepping in with small monetary gifts throughout the past year. He came through again, supplying a small 'stake' which Carol could bring to the agency.

It was also in the autumn of 1930 that Steinbeck, on one of his many visits to the dentist, met a man in the waiting room by the name of Edward F. Ricketts – certainly one of the most important meetings of his life. As Richard Astro remarks in his study of the friendship between Steinbeck and Ed Ricketts, 'No analysis of Steinbeck's world-view, his philosophy of life, can proceed without a careful study of the life, work, and ideas of this remarkable human being who was Steinbeck's closest personal and intellectual companion for nearly two decades.' Eventually, Ricketts would serve as the 'real' person behind a central character in six novels or novellas (*In Dubious Battle*, *The Grapes of Wrath*, *The Moon Is Down*, *Cannery Row*, *Burning Bright* and *Sweet Thursday*) and one story ('The Snake'). But, more importantly, Ricketts would bring to the surface and help crystallize thoughts about human nature and its relationship to the natural world which for Steinbeck had been inchoate for some time.

Ricketts was born in 1897 and raised on the north-west side of Chicago in a middle-class family much like Steinbeck's. He enrolled at the University of Chicago in 1919, and there he encountered a professor by the name of W. C. Allee, now considered one of America's first professional ecologists. A friend of Ricketts later said: 'We knew W. C. Allee from Ed's conversations, discovering later that many of his former students got a holy look in their eyes at the mention of his name, as Ed always did. Allee was one of those prophetic teachers who inspired his students to think in fresh ways about things. And he wasn't just a scientist. He was a philosopher, too, and a man of culture.'[18] Again like Steinbeck, Ricketts never gained a degree, although this did not stop him from pursuing a career in marine zoology. He moved to California in 1923, a year after leaving the University of Chicago, where he set up a biological supply house in Pacific Grove with his college roommate, A. E. Galigher. This company became Pacific Biologicals, a successful venture which Ed Ricketts owned in conjunction with Steinbeck at the time of his premature death in 1948. In the Thirties, however, Ricketts and his fledgling company were struggling.

'It's hard to imagine how poor everyone was,' says Allen Simmons, who worked for Ricketts in the lab for several years.[19] 'John pretty much lived off the land, scraping around for food. Ricketts didn't fare much better. They used to trade fish for vegetables. John, you know, had this crowded garden, where you never knew what you'd find from root crops to flowers. He always insisted on the flowers.' He describes the friendship between Steinbeck and Ricketts: 'John was big and awkward, very quiet, kind of brooding until he got a few drinks into him, then he would melt and begin telling jokes. His eyes would grow fiery, and he had a big laugh. Literature was about the only thing he never talked about.' Ricketts, by contrast, 'was easy in his way, very open. He talked a lot about his work. He loved all kinds of marine life, and you almost couldn't get him off the subject. He had masses of dark hair, really thick, and he was compact and tense. He and John sat in the lab for hours and hours, sometimes saying very little. They were almost like a married couple, the way they communicated. It was love. Yes, they loved each other. It wasn't sexual or anything, but it was physical. There was no need for them to justify anything to each other. They just understood and could count on each other for support.' Steinbeck, the slightly younger man, was 'almost a student of Ed's. Ed gave him books all the time, had him reading about biology, the ecology. They argued and discussed things. John was tough, and he didn't swallow everything; he had his own ideas.' It was the mechanical side of things that especially attracted Steinbeck: 'Ed was good in the lab, and John admired the technical side of all that. He was always peering over Ed's shoulder and offering suggestions, some of which Ed took badly. But they didn't fight. You would never see that.'

The biological supply company provided living samples of marine creatures to high schools, universities and medical research facilities, which meant that Ricketts got to do what he liked best: comb the waters of the Pacific or inland California rivers for exotic specimens. In his lab in Monterey, he pursued his own research on marine life and wrote scientific papers on the evolutionary process. He was, as Simmons puts it, 'the kind of person who would give you a lecture on anything at the drop of a hat', and the topic might be politics or world history or the solar system, depending on his mood of the moment.

Steinbeck admired the intellectual side of Ricketts, but he also saw him as 'a man's man' who knew how to hunt and fish, to repair cars, to drink large quantities of alcohol, and to make love to a woman. The fact that Ricketts was outgoing and talkative, even domineering, meant that Steinbeck mostly listened, although he did not necessarily swallow all he heard. The certainty of Ricketts's opinions contrasted with his own tentativeness around people he considered his intellectual or artistic equals. Still a young man, he was groping towards maturity as well as fighting through the

Cabell-like prose of *Cup of Gold* towards the clear, shimmering style that typifies *The Pastures of Heaven*.

Style in prose is not accidental or unrelated to the mind that generates it, and the muddy waters of Steinbeck's earlier fiction began to clear under the stern tutelage of Ricketts. He went into the lab at Pacific Biological almost every day, and he was patient, listening and watching. 'He would sit on a stool and watch his friend work, and sometimes he would join in, and after work, he and Ricketts would visit the local establishments,' Simmons recalls. Steinbeck admired the way Ricketts could shift his conversation from the nature of invertebrate creatures to the personality of this or that whore in one of the teeming brothels along the waterfront. He also admired the social side of Ricketts, especially his ability to move among fishermen and winos as easily as among scientists and business people.

Ever since childhood Steinbeck had witnessed the robust social life along Cannery Row, but he had always remained at a respectful distance. Now Ed Ricketts plunged him into the midst of these people and their daily lives. He talked to them, and (perhaps more importantly) he listened to their speech, becoming expert in sifting the various strands of their society; this sifting would pay off in the dialogue of *Tortila Flat*, *Cannery Row* and *Sweet Thursday*, where Steinbeck has easy access to a dazzling range of voices. At first, he wasn't altogether sure that he could use in his stories the people who lived and worked (or loafed) along Cannery Row, but Ricketts soon changed his mind about this, believing firmly that his new friend could make something important out of these characters. He often said that people and marine life were not so different except that the people could talk, and he encouraged Steinbeck to write about what he saw each day, and to show that human beings were subject to the same biological drives as fish or animals. He argued that the work of the novelist and the work of the marine ecologist were not, in essence, dissimilar, that each involved the observation and classification of types. Both were compelled to understand their interaction as well as their place in the overall web of creation.

Ricketts was an original, but originality does not occur *ex nihilo*. There is finally no such thing as a new idea, and Ricketts had been reading William Emerson Ritter and John Elof Boodin (whom Steinbeck knew and admired) as well as J.S. Haldane, who wrote in *Mechanism, Life, and Personality* that 'the living body and its physiological environment form an organic whole, the parts of which cannot be separated from one another'.[20] While this seems obvious enough, Haldane's thesis runs against the grain of centuries of humanistic thought where humankind was placed 'above' or 'outside' the physical universe and 'nature'. But, as Ritter argues in *The Natural History of Our Conduct*, 'the living body and its physiological environment form an organic whole, the parts of which cannot be understood in separation from one another.'[21]

Under the guidance of Ed Ricketts, Steinbeck wrote a brief, unpublished paper on the Ritter/Boodin/Haldane idea called 'Argument of Phalanx', which allows us to peek into his thinking during these formative years in Monterey.[22] 'We have thought of mankind always in terms of individual men,' he writes.

> We have tried to study men and movements of men by minute investigation of individual men-units. We might as reasonably try to understand the nature of a man by investigating the cells of his body. Perhaps if we observe the phalanx, knowing it is a new individual, not to be confused with the units which compose it, if we look back at the things it has done in an attempt to correlate and analyse its habits under various stimuli, we may in time come to know something of the phalanx, of its nature, of its drive and its ends, we may even be able to direct its movements where

now we have only great numbers of meaningless, unrelated
and destructive phenomena.

The term 'phalanx' is used by Steinbeck in a quasi-scientific
way here, and it would become extremely important to his
later fiction. The term refers to group behaviour of any kind;
the original term, which comes from a Latin word for
tortoise, refers to the Roman legions who raised their shields
above their heads in unison and appeared somewhat like
tortoises. Steinbeck's central thesis is that men in groups,
like all units made up of individual parts, appear to connect
to a larger spirit or will that exists somewhere beyond
individual response. The individual pieces of the whole, as
Ritter puts it, 'are so located and so functioning in relation to
each other as to contribute their proper share to the
structure of the whole'.

Steinbeck concludes, 'Man is a unit of the greater beasts,
the phalanx. The phalanx has pains, desires, hungers, and
strivings as different from those of the unit man's as man's
are different from the cells [of his own body].' The individual
relates to the large unit, or phalanx, via the subconscious:
'Within each unit-man, deep in him, in his subconscious,
there is a keying device with which he may become part of the
phalanx.' What's interesting is how closely this resembles the
Jungian distinction between the collective and personal
unconscious, which was only just becoming well known. The
individual, according to Carl Jung, is possessed of a set of
mythic symbols that relate to him or her alone; they are the
by-products of having a unique history. The sea, for instance,
may strike ominous chords in someone because he or she
nearly drowned in a seaside accident in childhood. But the
unconscious connects to the larger, inherited unconscious of
humankind through a massive body of shared myths and
symbols. So the sea, for instance, will inevitably summon a
number of archetypal associations. It will constitute an active
symbol, then, on two levels, personal and collective.

This fascination with the inevitable conflict between the individual *qua* individual and the individual as part of a larger social unit remained with Steinbeck all his life. As late as 1955, for instance, he wrote a short magazine article called 'Some Thoughts on Juvenile Delinquency', in which he concludes that 'man is a double thing – a group animal and at the same time an individual. And it occurs to me that he cannot successfully be the second until he has fulfilled the first.'[23] It is this double nature that pulls us two ways at once, that calls to us to take into account the most idiosyncratic of personal details (the personal unconscious) while simultaneously answering a larger call (from the collective unconscious) which we may hear but not understand.

One must not imagine that Steinbeck, except for a brief and probably necessary period, accepted without question every-thing Ricketts said. An argument could be made that he finally arrived at a view of humanity deeply in contrast to Ricketts. He remained, as perhaps all artists must, an individualist and a humanist, devoted to the perils and exhilarations of the self in the act of realization; he never mistook the behaviour of fish or animals for human behaviour. He understood that an analogy is just that: a comparison, not a proposition of identity. The notion of human beings acting in a group is similar but not identical to the notion of fish acting *as* a group. Every decision a person makes, conscious or unconscious, is the product of a complex series of internal and external negotiations, and Steinbeck explored these negotiations ruthlessly and patiently in his fiction.

In *The Red Pony*, for instance, there is Jody's grandfather's speech about the process of westward migration that has been such an integral part of his life (and the subject of so many Steinbeck novels): 'We carried life out here and set it down the way those ants carry eggs. And I was the leader. The westering was as big as God, and the slow steps that made the movement piled up and piled up until the continent was crossed.' This movement of 'westering' is likened to 'a whole bunch of people made into one big crawling beast'. Nevertheless, 'Every man wanted something for himself . . .' Without the unique drive of each individual, the group movement could not have taken place.

One sees these notions in *The Grapes of Wrath* too, where delicate negotiations occur between individuals and 'phalanx' units as the selfish and family-orientated Joads, tutored by ex-preacher Casy, come to realize that their involvement in the larger group migration is essential to their survival and, ultimately, to the survival of the race. Every man is out for himself at the beginning of the novel, but the spiritual progress of the Joads moves from personal to collective consciousness as the sparks of human connection go off, one by one, in each of the characters' hearts. Their individual responses to these sparks constitute the 'meaning' of the novel as a whole, and the result is an affirmation of human dignity which benefits not only the 'phalanx' but the individual. Everyone dies alone, Steinbeck seems to be saying, but the meaning of any single life is best understood and, more importantly, best *realized*, within the context of a community and its shared dreams and values.

Ricketts and Steinbeck would sit up late, discussing art, music, literature and philosophy as well as biology. What set Ricketts apart was his eclecticism: he loved classical music, especially Bach, Mozart and Gregorian chants, and he could talk about modern art with ease and delight; he read and studied philosophical works, such as Kant and Hegel, and he could quote Walt Whitman by the yard; he took the trouble to learn German so that he could read Goethe in the original. (Indeed, Goethe was his model, a man of seemingly universal interests and sympathies.) Steinbeck echoed this picture in 'About Ed Ricketts', a charming biographical essay which he used as a prefix to *The Log of the 'Sea of Cortez'*, which appeared in 1951: 'His mind had no horizons. He was interested in everything.'

Ricketts's devotion to what he called 'non-teleological thinking' was part of his attempt to see the world in rational terms. As human beings, we tend to regard the world within the context of cause and effect relations. If no cause presents itself, we often leapfrog this barrier and jump to supernatural conclusions. God becomes the ultimate fill-in-the-blank, the final response to questions that fail to present an adequate natural answer. This may be all right for theologians, but what the scientist required, according to Ricketts, was great patience and the ability to live without certainty. An answer to a very basic question may not present itself for centuries; indeed, the answer may never reveal itself. The scientist has to forgo easy gratification and keep looking for appropriate explanations of natural phenomena, even when the odds are distinctly against finding any 'answer'. (Ricketts seems to have enjoyed the anarchic possibility that no answers exist to many important questions.)

He referred to the type of thinking he advocated as 'is' thinking, arguing that it was what every scientist and artist had to cultivate. While human beings keep asking 'why', Ricketts thought it wisest to step around this question, feeling (like the early Wittgenstein) it was best to remain silent about things that could not be properly embodied in language. Acceptance was crucial to his thinking, as in Alexander Pope's famous line: 'Whatever is is best'. In some respects, Ricketts's philosophy was deeply anti-political, almost quietistic, and this seems to contradict the direction that Steinbeck's writing took in the Thirties. A firm distinction, in fact, must be drawn between Ricketts's worldview and Steinbeck's. From the outset, Steinbeck remained much less 'scientific' than his friend, and he never overcame a deep human need to find causes for the effects he witnessed around him. He did not hesitate to seek political solutions to problems, and he largely subscribed to traditional liberal-humanist notions of 'progress' – a word that appalled Ricketts, who found the notion sentimental and simplistic.

Ricketts was a complex and fascinating man, an intellectual who did not lose touch with everyday reality. While he may not have been as original or profound as Steinbeck imagined, he was a strong and charismatic thinker. Steinbeck quoted him to good effect in his warm biographical (almost eulogistic) essay. One gets a sense of the man's practical wisdom when he talks about children, for instance: 'Adults, in their dealing with children, are insane,' Ricketts is quoted as saying. 'And children know it, too. Adults lay down rules they would not think of following, speak truths they do not believe. And yet they expect children to obey the rules, believe the truths, and admire and respect their parents for this nonsense. Children must be very wise and secret to tolerate adults at all.'

One aspect of Ricketts that deeply fascinated Steinbeck was his friend's sex life. 'His life was saturated with sex and he was to a very great extent preoccupied with it,' Steinbeck writes in 'About Ed Ricketts'. 'He gave it a monumental amount of thought and time and analysis.' Lest we feel uncomfortable in having the subject raised, Steinbeck puts us at ease, 'It will be no violation to discuss this part of his life since he had absolutely no shyness about discussing it himself.' Ricketts's lover for many years was a woman named Toni Jackson, whom he did not marry. At least in the early Thirties marriage was far too boring for Ed Ricketts, who craved difficulty as well as novelty in all sexual relationships. Steinbeck lights on this perverseness when discussing the whorehouse located across the street from the lab at Pacific Biological, noting that his friend adored the madam in charge but did not patronize her establishment: 'His sex life was far too complicated for that.'

Complicated it was. Steinbeck recalls in his essay that
Ricketts pursued one young woman, a reputed virgin, for
months on end without results. 'He not only was interested
in a sexual sense [with the woman being a virgin], but he had
also an active interest in the psychic and physical structure of
virginity.' An instance of non-teleological thinking? 'If a girl
were unattached and without problems as well as willing,'
Steinbeck later remarks of Ricketts in general, 'his interest
was not large.' What he liked were women with 'a husband or
seven chilren or a difficulty with the law or some whimsical
neuroticism in the field of love'.

It does seem odd, in retrospect, that Steinbeck should
devote so many pages to Ricketts's sexuality in what is
otherwise a eulogistic essay. The two friends obviously spent
a lot of time discussing their mutual interest in women, an
activity that is hardly rare among male friends. Steinbeck's
final view of Ricketts's sexuality is rather touching: 'But for all
of Ed's pleasures and honesties there was a transcendent
sadness in his love – something he missed or wanted, a
searching that sometimes approached panic. I don't know
what it was he wanted that was never there, but I know he
always looked for it and never found it.'

One of Ricketts's greatest gifts to Steinbeck was an understanding of the nature and necessity of self-love. (This self-
love was not mere egotism; in some ways, it was its negation,
allowing the individual the freedom to listen to, and be
influenced by, others.) 'For a very long time I didn't like
myself,' Ricketts told Steinbeck. 'It was a very difficult time,
and very painful. I did not like myself for a number of
reasons, some of them valid and some of them pure fancy. I
would hate to have to go back to that. Then gradually I
discovered with surprise and pleasure that a number of
people did like me. And I thought, if they can like me, why
cannot I like myself?'

With wise candour, Steinbeck comments, 'Most people do

not like themselves at all. They distrust themselves, put on masks and pomposities. They quarrel and boast and pretend and are jealous because they do not like themselves. But mostly they do not even know themselves well enough to form a true liking.' One hears in these sentences the voice of the young man concerned about his awkward manner, his lack of good looks and social graces. His boastings and pretensions, his withdrawals, his fits of bad temper: all are buried in these cadences. But Steinbeck was slowly learning to accept himself for who he was, and Ed Ricketts seems to have played a huge part in bringing his friend towards this self-understanding. He had, indeed, formed the beginning of 'a true liking' for himself, perhaps through his 'liking' for Ricketts.

What these years in Pacific Grove under the tutelage of Ed Ricketts were partly about for Steinbeck was the process of coming to accept his faults as well as his virtues. Previously, he was both unsure of himself and full of postures in which he affected greater self-knowledge than a young man can usually claim. Adjusting to marriage with Carol and settling into a writing style and subjects which reflected his truest nature, he was on the verge of that self-love which leads, when properly understood, to genuine self-knowledge. His work, now firmly rooted in the California landscape and culture that he knew so well, became open and impressionable. He was almost ready to shift into the major phase of his career.

VI

The Heavenly Valley

'The new eye is being opened here in the west – the new seeing. It is probable that no one will know it for two hundred years.'

Steinbeck's unpublished journal, 1933

While still in Eagle Rock, Steinbeck had met a writer by the name of George Albee, who was trying to write a novel and had published a few stories in small magazines. They didn't spend much time together, but Steinbeck felt comfortable with the younger man, who admired him openly and sought his advice. When he moved back north, he continued to write to Albee, and these letters from the early Thirties contain some of his frankest comments about his life and writing. 'I'm having a devil of a time with my new book,' he wrote on 27 February, 1931.[1] 'Largeness of character is difficult.' The novel, endlessly under revision, was *To a God Unknown*. Steinbeck had begun to feel like Sisyphus with his rock.

In another letter to Albee, he repeated a familiar line from this period: 'I have been filled with a curious cloying despair.'[2] As if there were no contradiction in doing so, he added a postscript to his lament, 'Carol's business is growing nicely. She gets prettier all the time. I'm more in love with her than I ever was. Sometimes I waken in the night with the horrible feeling that she is gone. I shouldn't want to live if she were.' The contradiction that seems to exist here was real enough. On the one hand, Steinbeck felt good about his marriage; Carol took care of him, like his mother, typing his manuscripts, offering encouragement, cooking his food and doing his laundry. Steinbeck was free to write. On the other hand, he felt that he was conning her, that his work did not measure up to this treatment. And rather like Steinbeck's mother, Carol was often disapproving. She criticized his work harshly at times, and she insisted that he read this book or that one. He felt continually like a failure.

The rapidly deepening friendship with Ed Ricketts absorbed Steinbeck as the new year, 1931, began. Throughout the spring he would rise at seven, have a strong cup of coffee with Carol before she went off to her office, then go to his desk in the living room of the cottage, where he worked on the stories of *The Pastures of Heaven* and wrestled with *To a God Unknown*, which in one revised version was making the rounds of New York publishers under Ted Miller's auspices without success. *Dissonant Symphony* was now firmly lodged in a bottom drawer, where it would remain.

Steinbeck worked hard until the middle of the afternoon, at which point (usually about two or three) he would go outside to 'play in the garden', as he put it. At four he would walk up to the headquarters of Pacific Biological, where he hung around Ed Ricketts in the lab. Allen Simmons recalls, 'John would stroll in with his hands in the pockets of his khaki trousers, almost sheepish. He would pull up a stool behind Ed and sometimes he'd just sit there watching for a long time. The two of them would eventually begin talking, and John would say what problems he was having with his book. Ed would listen and give advice. You never knew where Ed was going to take the conversation, but he was in charge.' At five-thirty or six, the two of them would wander out on to the streets of Monterey, usually making their way to a bar, where they might sit drinking until seven or eight. Sometimes he would not roll home until midnight, thus provoking an argument with Carol.

Once Steinbeck took Ed Ricketts to the Corral de Tierra (the original for the title of *The Pastures of Heaven*), which was tucked in the pale hills between Salinas and Monterey.

Steinbeck's now deceased Aunt Molly (whom he had felt very close to) had lived there on a spacious ranch which he had often visited as a boy. As he drove along the valley, he began telling Ricketts stories connected with the region, stories he was in the process of transforming into some of his best fiction. 'This is really your real material,' Ricketts told his friend with excitement. 'It's like daylight hitting you in the face.'[3]

In April, Carl Wilhelmson dropped by for a visit. His third novel had now been accepted, and he fizzed with optimism. 'Carl goes from strength to strength,' Steinbeck wrote to Kate Beswick, generously, 'but I . . . I seem to go nowhere.'[4] To Ted Miller, in June, he wrote: 'I don't know how long I can hold out now. Universal rejections are bound to induce a kind of a mental state. . . .'[5] A few weeks later he wrote again to Miller, 'Rejection follows rejection. Haven't there even been encouraging letters? Perhaps an agent with a thorough knowledge of markets would see the mss. were not marketable at all and would return them on that ground. You see the haunting thought comes that perhaps I have been kidding myself all these years, myself and other people – that I have anything to say or no art in saying nothing. It is two years since I have received the slightest encouragement and that was short-lived.'[6]

Like so many artists before him, Steinbeck had to fight his way through a period of intense negative reaction to his work that inevitably compounded his tyrannical self-doubts. What is required during such periods is a firm place inside where one can stand: a point of balance. As long as that is available, there is always hope. And Steinbeck, for all his talk about rejection and despair, was clearly able to find such a place, to maintain his equilibrium and keep going. He knew that he had valuable things to say and that, one day, his technical resources would match his imaginative and sympathetic powers. For the moment, he had simply to hang on.

*

Ted Miller was himself overburdened at this time. His
marriage was on the rocks, and he was struggling to pursue a
legal career just as the Depression was getting underway. He
gratefully took up his friend's suggestion and turned the
manuscripts in his care over to the agent recommended by
Carl Wilhelmson, Mavis McIntosh of McIntosh & Otis, a
young firm with a growing reputation. McIntosh read the
work and responded warmly, agreeing at once to take
Steinbeck on. His relationship with this firm would last for
nearly forty years, and the person who would mostly work
with him at the agency – Elizabeth Otis – would become, as
Elaine Steinbeck says, 'his closest woman friend from the
mid-Thirties until his death'. (In later years both Otis and
McIntosh liked to brag about having 'discovered' Steinbeck.
McIntosh had the better claim.)

Steinbeck seized the day, quickly following up the submis-
sion of *To a God Unknown* and *Murder at Full Moon* with a letter
in which he discussed *The Pastures of Heaven*:

> There is, about twelve miles from Monterey, a valley in the
> hills called Corral de Tierra. Because I am using its people I
> have named it Las Pasturas del Cielo. The valley was for
> years known as the happy valley because of the unique
> harmony which existed among its twenty families. About
> ten years ago a new family moved in on one of the ranches.
> They were ordinary people, ill-educated but honest and as
> kindly as any. In fact, in their whole history I cannot find
> that they have committed a really malicious act nor an act
> which was not dictated by honorable expediency or
> out-and-out altruism. But about the Monroes there was a
> flavor of evil. Everyone they came in contact with was
> injured. Every place they went dissension sprang up. There
> have been two murders, a suicide, many quarrels and a
> great deal of unhappiness in the Pastures of Heaven, and all
> of these things can be traced directly to the influence of the
> Monroes. So much is true.

I am using the following method. The manuscript is made up of stories, each one complete in itself, having its rise, climax and ending. Each story deals with a family or an individual. They are tied together only by the common locality and by the contact with the Monroes. Some of the stories are very short and some as long as fifteen thousand words. I thought of combining them with that thirty-thousand word ms. called Dissonant Symphony to make one volume. I wonder whether you think this is a good plan. I think the plan at least falls very definitely in the aspects of American life category. I have finished several and am working on others steadily. They should be done by this fall.[7]

Mavis McIntosh received this news eagerly, but she dismissed the current version of *To a God Unknown* as 'disjointed and confusing'. She also felt that it was badly paced. *Murder at Full Moon*, however, she thought had some commercial value, and she asked Steinbeck to send her more work in this vein. His 'serious' work did interest her as well, she said, and she believed that he possessed 'a remarkable gift for describing characters and landscapes'. She encouraged him to work hard at *The Pastures of Heaven*, which she guessed would have a market if the characters were 'unusual and attractive'. 'Avoid unnecessary oddities', she said, and warned him to 'curb his tendencies to write quasipoetic and pseudo-philosophical passages'.

Steinbeck was unnerved but excited by her response. Now that he had his foot in the door, he intended to keep it there. McIntosh & Otis had done wonders for his friend, Carl Wilhelmson, and he thought the same might be done for him. Meanwhile, Carol's advertising agency crashed on the jagged rocks of the Depression, which had finally hit Monterey. Because local businesses were doing so poorly, they had no money to spend on ads, so Carol and her friend were forced to close their office and seek work elsewhere. To make matters worse, Mavis McIntosh was, as she suspected, unable to place *To a God Unknown*. The market for fiction by unknown writers was, she told him, 'extremely tight and unpredictable'.

Throughout the dreary autumn of 1931, Steinbeck hammered away at the stories of *The Pastures of Heaven*, convinced that this time, finally, he was on to something. The mood of these autumnal months was caught beautifully in a note to George Albee: 'It is a gray day with little dusty spurts of rain. A good day for inwardness.' He continued to analyse himself as a writer: 'Only I doubt that I have many guts of my own to look inward at. That is one of the great troubles with objective writing. A constant practice of it leaves one no material for introspection. If my characters are sad or happy I reflect their emotions. I have no personal nor definitive emotions of my own.'[8] It is worth noting that this theory of 'objective writing' seems very much in keeping with T. S. Eliot's theory of literary impersonality, a bedrock idea upon which literary modernism was built. In 'Tradition and the Original Talent', his ground-breaking essay from *The Sacred Wood* (1920); Eliot argues that in the process of writing the true artist makes 'a continual surrender of himself to something which is more valuable. The progress of an artist is a continual self-sacrifice, a continual extinction of personality.'[9] This parallels Steinbeck's sense of having 'no personal nor definitive emotions' of his own.

The week before Christmas, he finished the manuscript of *The Pastures of Heaven* and shipped it off to Mavis McIntosh. He and Carol celebrated over a bottle of 'genuine French wine', a luxury in California, which had so much of its own cheaper wine. Sharing this rare bottle were Toby Street and Grove Day, who dropped in for a brief visit to their old classmate. 'We got severely horned,' he told Kate Beswick, 'and ran crazily along the beach.' When Toby and Grove left, he and Carol drove down to San Jose for Christmas with

Carol's parents, who still distrusted their perpetually broke son-in-law. 'They still don't like me,' he complained to Beswick. 'I don't think they ever will.'[10]

Mavis McIntosh wrote in the New Year with the disappointing news that she didn't like *The Pastures of Heaven* very much. The form – linked stories centred on a specific geographical place – didn't hold her interest in the same way a novel might, she explained; she also noted that the market for short stories had dried up and suggested that he get back to writing novels. In spite of her personal lack of enthusiasm, she would send the manuscript around to a small group of editors she knew. Steinbeck, though dismayed, thanked her for her willingness to do so, adding that he continued to have a good feeling about the prospects for this book about 'aspects of California life'. To Ted Miller, on 16 February, he wrote, 'And so *The Pastures* has begun its snaggy way.'[11]

The way was not as snaggy as all that. On 27 February 1932 – which happened by serendipity to be Steinbeck's thirtieth birthday – a telegram arrived from Mavis McIntosh saying that Cape and Smith (an American off-shoot of the English firm of Jonathan Cape) had accepted *The Pastures of Heaven* within three days of having seen it. Steinbeck wrote to George Albee saying that 'they showed a nice enthusiasm and intend to feature it on their fall list'. He added, rather touchingly, 'I am very glad, more for my folks' sake than for my own. They love it so much. Dad's shoulders are straighter for it and mother beams. I am no longer a white elephant, you see. I am justified in the eyes of their neighbors.'[12]

Carol got some good news too. Almost simultaneously with Steinbeck's offer on *The Pastures of Heaven*, Ed Ricketts invited her to do some work for him in the lab at Pacific Biological. In addition to typing and bookkeeping, she would help with experiments and even go into the field on occasion. He could pay her $50 a month, which was an improvement on the previous situation. Steinbeck was generally pleased that Ricketts would have Carol aboard, but the situation was not without its little awkwardness. Ed Ricketts belonged to *him*; it worried him that Carol might somehow interfere with this friendship, which had ripened into an extraordinary thing.

The editor at Cape and Smith who had taken *The Pastures of Heaven* was Robert O. Ballou, formerly literary editor of the Chicago *Daily News*. He wrote a warm letter to Steinbeck, suggesting that he enter into a contractual arrangement for his next two books. Steinbeck remained wary, telling Ted Miller that Ballou 'seemed over-impressed with the book' and speculating that this was 'probably his method of dealing with clients'.[13] But he could hardly not be grateful that something had happened to encourage him, and he was thrilled by the prospect of making a little money.

Steinbeck's sister, Mary, left her husband behind in San Francisco one weekend and came to visit her brother, bringing with her the gift of a new pair of riding breeches (though Steinbeck was never much of an equestrian), and both went charging about the countryside on horseback. As ever, Steinbeck kept almost obsessively in touch with his family. 'I don't think he ever forgot to write,' says Beth, 'even when he was married and busy. He wanted us to know everything that was going on in his life. It was a strange thing with him, that tie.' Indeed, John Ernst and Olive were never too far in the background; they hovered, emotionally, in his mental closets, judging and assessing, putting their thumbs up or down. 'Mary was never judgemental', however. 'I think that's why John stayed so close to her. She accepted what he did as the big brother. She didn't question anything. It was simple affection.'

Steinbeck began rewriting *To a God Unknown*, hoping to interest Ballou in this project as well. The revisions were so drastic that he soon realized what he had in hand was really a new novel. 'I can use much of the material from the Unknown

God,' he wrote to Mavis McIntosh, 'but the result will be no rewritten version.'[14] To Kate Beswick he said, 'It's hardly the same book. Different feeling and rhythm, with some passages taken whole and others re-digested. I see what to do with the story now. It's going to be a good book after all.'[15]

One influence on the book, a new one, had just moved into the neighbourhood. Joseph Campbell, who later became a famous author of books about myth and a legendary professor at Sarah Lawrence College, was an unemployed young scholar who showed up in Monterey one evening. He was drawn there by Idell Henning, Carol's sister, who had met Campbell on her way back from Hawaii by steamer seven years before. Idell told Campbell that her sister had married a young man (Steinbeck was two years older than Campbell) whom she thought he would like to meet. 'Her sister had married a chap who wanted to write,' Campbell recalls, 'and I was wanting to write, and we might enjoy each other. So she brought me down and introduced me.'[16]

'Campbell walked in, one of the handsomest men I ever saw,' Simmons recalls, echoing an opinion common at the time. To the end of his long life, Joseph Campbell was an extremely good-looking man. 'His way of talking was so engaging. You had to listen to him. He and Carol immediately hit it off,' adds Simmons. They had met before, in 1925, but he now found her 'much more delightful than I remembered her to be. She had a way of twinkling when she smiled, and there was a frank straightforwardness about her. John, on the other hand, was inclined to be solemn.'

Campbell had studied at Columbia, had travelled in Europe and met Carl Jung, had absorbed everything from Indian scriptures, Native American folktales, and Buddhist texts to Joyce, Goethe, Mann, and Proust. His current obsession was Oswald Spengler, whom he preferred to read in the original German. In many respects he was the ultimate cosmopolite: a tall, dashingly athletic man of impeccable breeding (but little cash) and awesome erudition. His Jungian bent offered a fresh way of thinking about the world of myth and symbol, and he was deeply engaged at this point in exploring the idea of the unconscious. The comprehensive reading and hard thinking he was doing would lead, eventually, to the publication of *The Hero with a Thousand Faces*, an extremely influential book which cut across disciplinary boundaries. His later four-volume sequence, *The Masks of God*, remains a masterwork in the field of comparative mythology.

Campbell did not become really famous until the early Eighties, when Bill Moyers introduced him to a vast television audience in his series *The Power of Myth*. None the less, he was popular with college students many years before that. (As a student in the late Sixties, I was strongly attracted to Campbell's work and wrote to him with many questions. He invited me to visit him at his townhouse at Waverly Place in Greenwich Village, and I did so several times. He was a great teacher, and he loved to talk with students. I once asked him about Steinbeck, and he said that he learned more from Steinbeck than vice versa, although he acknowledged that the final version of *To a God Unknown* was affected by their conversations.)

Steinbeck introduced Campbell to Ed Ricketts and other friends, and Campbell immediately found Monterey irresistible. He decided to move there at once, and within a week (as Simmons says) he had 'settled into a little place called the Pumpkin Shell; and after a couple of months there I learned from John that there was a house right next to Ed's that was vacant, a smaller, cheaper house – because the one main thing was we didn't have any money. Nobody did. You lived on air.' The place next door to Ricketts's boarding house on Fourth Street was called Canary Cottage because of its bright yellow clapboard siding.

Campbell and Steinbeck took to one another strongly. 'I had a good impression of a serious and sturdy chap,' Campbell recalled in later years. 'He was just about my size, and a couple of people took us for brothers, actually. I remember once we went around to a butcher shop that John was used to patronizing, and when we went in, John introduced me, and the butcher said, "Is that your brother?" And John said, "There it is again." ' (Steinbeck did not, of course, have Campbell's regular features or good looks. It was the size alone that made people think they were related. Simmons recalls, 'John was actually self-conscious around Campbell, who was such a striking man. John was rather plain-looking but thought of himself as ugly.')

Steinbeck knew a good audience when he found one, and he would sit Campbell down by the fire in the evenings after dinner at the 11th Street cottage and read long passages from the latest version of *To a God Unknown* or newly minted short stories. Campbell listened intently and responded with admiration and, occasionally, criticism. Overall, he recognized and revered Steinbeck's genius. In his journal of the time, he noted: 'John has a fine, deep, living quality about his work which ought to ring the bell, I think – if his work is ever discovered.'[17]

'At last,' Campbell wrote in his journal, 'a world of my contemporaries.' Indeed, the social and intellectual life in Monterey was remarkably brisk for a small town. Ricketts, Campbell and the Steinbecks would grill steaks in the Steinbeck garden, then sit for hours under the stars talking about whatever they happened to be reading – stories by William Saroyan, a novel by Aldous Huxley, the poems of Robinson Jeffers (one of Steinbeck's lifelong affections, a taste inherited from his mother). Goethe's *Conversations with Eckermann* and Spengler's *Decline of the West* were Campbell's chief interests of the moment, and he insisted that everyone read them carefully. (Spengler's dark vision of history as an evolving myth appealed to Steinbeck's fundamentally romantic temperament.)

Campbell loved to ruminate on the differences between Freud and Jung, and Steinbeck listened closely as the young mythologist talked, realizing that if he could get certain kinds of archetypical imagery working for him in *To a God Unknown*, the book would gain immensely in power. He found that Jung, in particular, blended well with his own continuing study of Boodin and Ritter.

Campbell was 'unemployed', of course, though in a different sense from the *paisanos* and 'hoboes' who lived on the fringes of Monterey society. This was the height of the Depression, and most the country was unemployed, or under-employed. 'John tried to get Campbell to go out with him among the local winos and bums, but Campbell recoiled,' Simmons recalls. Doubtless Steinbeck found it amusing to embarrass the fastidious and well-bred scholar; he was, in any case, defiantly anti-snobbish by nature and felt extremely comfortable with the *paisanos*, listening to their stories, talking to them. He would go to the beach and sit beside a couple of winos all afternoon, taking in their tales – tales that would make their way into *Tortilla Flat*, *Cannery Row* and *Sweet Thursday*.

Campbell, in a later journal, describes meeting several of the prototypes of characters who would appear in Steinbeck's Monterey novels. One of these was 'Crazy Monte' Shortridge, as he was called; he became the Pirate in *Tortilla Flat*. '[Monte] invited me to lunch with him,' Campbell writes:

> I drove . . . to a house in Monterey where two strange women 'poets' talked about writing and served us soup. Shortridge had a dog and a guitar there. He performed with both and sang me some of his sea ballads. Then he invited me to read a pulp story he was writing about an old California bandit.
>
> We went out then to get in the truck; and behind an old

wooden house where Casey should have been, we met a
drunken Indian to whom Shortridge introduced me. An
entertaining succession of scenes ensued – Casey returned
from pitching horseshoes with a drunken gang of his own.
The Indian took Shortridge's hat and went down the road
for some wine, but came back with a bloody nose and no
wine. We piled the Indian and another swash into the back
of the truck, and they all then drove me home . . .

   I recall that Monte told me at that time of how he and his
boys would drive out in their trucks at night, cut down
some tree that they had spotted on somebody's property,
drive off with it and cut it up to be sold as firewood – John
in *Cannery Row* seems to have amalgamated Monte's crowd
with our own, and I'm sure that that is pretty much what he
did in *Tortilla Flat* as well, though with the accent there
more on Monte.

One hears, even in Campbell's recollection, the cadences of
Tortilla Flat – that antic, archly comic tone. And one begins to
see how Steinbeck's life was transformed into Steinbeck's art.

   The life was, at this time, fuelled by Ed Ricketts and his
eclectic society of whores, scientists, bums, winos and local
artists, to which were added Steinbeck's increasingly wide
circle of friends. Ricketts was a natural ringmaster, and he
held regular and rather wild parties in the lab. The Steinbecks
were always there, as was Campbell, who, according to many
accounts, would stand against the wall looking as though he
didn't approve but after a few drinks would join in. Among
the occasional guests were Toby and Peggy Street, Carl
Wilhelmson, Dook and Maryon Sheffield, Ritch and Tal
Lovejoy and her sister, Xenia (who was married at this time to
John Cage, the avant garde composer, and who also came to
these parties on occasion), Toni Jackson, George Albee, and
any number of Steinbeck's friends from distant parts.

   A new friend was a sculptor who lived near Monterey by
the name of Francis Whitaker, who worked in metal. He and

Steinbeck met that winter, and took to each other immediately. Whitaker took to dropping in at the 11th Street cottage in the late afternoons, when he knew Steinbeck was ready to stop writing. He was a committed socialist, and he urged Steinbeck to attend several meetings of the local socialist club. Steinbeck did so, but could never work up much in the way of enthusiasm for this movement. 'He used to tell amusing stories about the socialists of Monterey,' Simmons recalls. 'He thought Frank Whitaker was a lovely man but far too gullible. He used to say that only innocents or monsters turned to socialism.'

Steinbeck's life in the late winter and spring of 1932 was a roller-coaster of sorts, with marked highs and lows. The writing was going well, and his confidence was higher than it had ever been. He had a tight circle of supportive and creative friends. But a dark cloud would not go away: something was not right with the marriage. Carol, according to Campbell, was starved for attention. Worse, he himself was providing the kind of seductive attention that Carol craved. Writing anxiously in his journal, Campbell said, 'Before, when I had visited John and Carol, I had felt myself to be the visitor to a splendid little home. Now it is John who seems the outsider. He is like someone who simply captured the girl that I was meant to have married.'

Campbell's journal tells the whole story. He felt strongly attracted to Carol Steinbeck, and she responded in kind. Putting caution to one side, he resolved to 'taste life as it comes'. Drinking was the first taste; he imbibed heavily, as did everyone in Steinbeck's circle in Monterey. 'This being in love is the second,' he writes. 'I really do feel as though I were living. I can feel a pulsing inside me such as I thought was completely dead.' The tenor of their relationship is clearly revealed in the journal. One night, for instance, he went to visit her when he knew Steinbeck was not there:

I looked around for Carol, and then in a dark little room I
found a black shape on a bed. She was covered with a
blanket. She was lying on her side, her back to the wall, her
knees pulled up. I sat on the bed and kissed her temple and
her cheek. Then I pushed the blanket aside and quietly
kissed her mouth. I got up to go away, because there was a
chill that was making me tremble. Her voice called to me,
but I went out to the living room, where I stood over the
radiator. Then I went back to her.

'Joe,' she said weakly, 'you're cold.'

'Oh, that's all right. It's nothing,' I said.

I was sitting on the bed.

'Lie down; put the blanket over you. You're cold.'

'Oh, that's all right,' I said.

'Please, Joe. I won't seduce you!'

I lay down under the blanket.

'Was it wrong for you to kiss me?'

'No,' I said.

'Then kiss me again.'

I kissed her gently again and again.

'Do you realize that in all our lives, this is probably the
only hour we'll ever have together?'

'Kiss me just once, Joe. Crucify me with a kiss.'

I kissed her a long time. 'Jesus Christ!' she moaned. 'Jesus
Christ! Jesus Christ!'

'Before we only felt it,' I said. 'Now it is explicit.'

One doesn't know exactly how far this 'affair' between
Carol and Joseph Campbell finally went, but there is no doubt
(Campbell's journal makes this point only too explicit) that
the marriage was shaky. Steinbeck, who was a proud man,
was anguished by what he saw going on between his wife
and his friend, especially since (according to Tal Lovejoy),
'Carol and Joe were acting like a pair of sixteen-year-olds in
love – holding each other's hands – mooning dreamily into
each other's eyes.'

One time Campbell asked Carol if he and Steinbeck had, in

her view, much in common. 'So far as I can see,' she said quite vividly, 'you are like two faces of the one coin.' Campbell responded, 'And both of the faces are looking at you.' Aware that Campbell was extremely distressed by the way the situation had developed, Carol suggested (more whimsically than seriously) that they enter a suicide pact. 'That bottle of cyanide down at the lab', she said, 'is certainly a temptation. It would be so easy!'

This impossible and painful situation continued for months, until one night after dinner Campbell appeared at Steinbeck's door and asked to speak with him alone. They went into the garden and sat together beneath the spreading oak, where Campbell explained that he had been anguished by the relationship with Carol and its effects on his friendship with John. Upon hearing this, Steinbeck (according to Campbell) 'looked shot'. 'It's positively ridiculous even to think of my marrying Carol,' Campbell told him. 'The only question is, John, how I'm to withdraw from this mess with the least pain for her?' Steinbeck said, 'And what about yourself?' Campbell, with melodramatic self-disregard, said, 'To hell with myself. I guess I ought to be able to tell my emotions what to do.'

John explained that he and Ed Ricketts had been discussing the situation at some length, and that Ricketts had said (in Campbell's words) that 'whereas John and Carol had already made a beautiful go of marriage, it was only possible, but not probable, that Joe and Carol could manage the same thing. It was reasonable to conclude, therefore, that a change would be unwise.' Like true Enlightenment gentlemen, Steinbeck and Campbell shook hands on their agreement. Soon after, Campbell withdrew altogether from Monterey, fleeing to New York – far from this madding California crowd.

Carol's affair with Campbell, such as it was, sowed the seeds of their later break-up. Steinbeck was too much a romantic to swallow betrayal of this kind. It was one thing for

Lancelot to betray his king; for the queen to betray her husband was untenable. Steinbeck repressed the situation forcefully, attempting to put it as far from his mind as possible, but it lurked there, a cancer that would continue to spread in the system of their marriage. The trust was gone, and Steinbeck was unable to recover it.

With Campbell gone, however, he began writing furiously, often spending seven or eight hours a day at his desk. Carol was shaken and remorseful, typing and retyping her husband's manuscripts with renewed devotion. In March, disaster of another kind struck Steinbeck and his family. Beth's only son died suddenly and unexpectedly of an illness. She and her husband were living in Fresno at the time, and Steinbeck quickly drove over to be with her during the funeral and for a few days afterwards. The whole family convened at what was a wrenching time for all of them, especially since everyone knew that Olive Steinbeck was ailing. For many years she had been suffering from high blood pressure, and by now her arteries had become severely clogged. There were other pointers too: she kept losing her place in the middle of a sentence and even forgetting where she was.

When Steinbeck got back to Pacific Grove from Fresno, there was a letter waiting for him from Robert Ballou: because of the hard economic times, Cape and Smith were in danger of collapsing. Ballou had decided to take a job at another publishing house, and he hoped to take Steinbeck with him, on similar terms. The new firm was Brewer, Warren, and Putnam, a respectable publishing company. Steinbeck agreed to go with Ballou, though he was edgy about the changes, which would almost certainly result in delay in the publication of *The Pastures of Heaven*. Once again, when he thought he was in a safe and comfortable position with a publisher, something happened to jeopardize this security.

Steinbeck liked the idea of purifying himself once in a

while, and he did so now, gathering a pile of old manuscripts from a trunk – some sixty or seventy stories, he told George Albee in a letter – and burning them. 'It's exhilarating to get rid of old work,' Steinbeck told Kate Beswick. 'I am writing so well now that I don't want the old stories around anymore. They are terrible reminders of where I've come from.'[18] (The tradition of writers burning unwanted material is a long one. The poet Gerard Manley Hopkins once tried to burn everything he had written to cleanse himself of the vile habit of verse composition. Luckily, he had sent copies of the same poems to his friend Robert Bridges, who did not replicate the bonfire.)

Many of Steinbeck's best early stories seem to have survived this bonfire, including 'St Katy the Virgin', a satirical tale about the conversion of a fourteenth-century pig to Christian piety; in its original form the tale dated back to his Stanford days, and it eventually made its way into *The Long Valley*, where it sits uncomfortably beside the author's more realistic tales of California life. In tone and style, it prefigures *The Short Reign of Pippin IV*, a novelistic *jeu d'esprit* which Steinbeck published in 1957 to the bafflement of many critics, who could not tell where it was coming from.

The recasting of *To a God Unknown* was moving ahead swiftly. 'I'm getting about eight pages a day done,' he told Albee.[19] 'The book is nearly half finished and I am filled with excitement when I contemplate it. The plan is working so far and the pictures, as I see them at least, are sharp and deep. If I can go on I'll be finished in two months.' But he was also afraid that he was working too hard for the book to be any good: 'Sometimes I feel an incipient exhaustion,' he confessed. Throughout July, which was hot and sticky, he continued revising intensely. One night, drained of energy, he proposed to Carol that they move back to Los Angeles. He still looked back fondly on the early days of their marriage in southern California, and he hoped that he and Carol might recapture their original affection for each other. The strain over the Campbell affair had been hideous, and this change of scene seemed necessary.

He and Carol still had many friends in the Los Angeles area, including Dook Sheffield and George Albee, whose friendship with Steinbeck had been cemented by their ongoing correspondence. The bedraggled and shaken couple, still broke, landed once again on the doorstep of Dook and Maryon Sheffield; as before, the brilliant sunshine of southern California went to their heads. Only days after their arrival, Carol persuaded her bemused husband to bleach his hair – and it turned bright orange. Dook suggested that a day at the beach was the only remedy for orange hair, and Steinbeck's sister, Mary, who had turned up unexpectedly, was invited along.

The merry group set off, driving along Sunset Boulevard towards Santa Monica in Steinbeck's antiquated car. The radiator suddenly began to leak, and he once again resorted to his legendary technical inventiveness by pouring a bag of cornmeal into the radiator, having heard that this was a good way to plug a leak. As they continued along Sunset Boulevard in the boiling sun, the engine overheated. Braking quickly and pulling off the road, he opened the hood just as cornmeal began spouting in a hot geyser that splattered the windshield and Steinbeck as well. (The car made it to the beach, although Mary was so appalled by her brother's 'bohemian' manners that – very briefly – she wouldn't speak to him.)

Two weeks later more unexpected visitors arrived on the Sheffield doorstep: Ed Ricketts and Frank Whitaker. The Sheffields, ever courteous, invited them to sleep on the living-room rug as well. Soon everyone got to drinking Dook's homemade beer and, after a while, Steinbeck insisted that everyone pile into Ed's large Packard to pay a visit to his old friend and former illustrator, Mahlon Blaine, who had just moved into a new apartment in Hollywood. Whitaker went along for the ride but said he did not feel like socializing; instead, he stripped off his clothes to sunbathe in the nude on Ed's car, parked in a secluded lot. When they finally came out, Whitaker was found asleep on the car's blazing hood. Delightedly, Steinbeck and his friends drove away with poor Whitaker clinging pathetically to the hood itself.

Whitaker's comment, heard that evening back at the Sheffields, was, 'This is a wonderful place to visit, but God, I couldn't stand the pace down here.'[10] He was joking, but he hit on something worth noting. Steinbeck had a taste, like Scott Fitzgerald (his slightly older contemporary) for the 'mad' life. He and Carol were less grand but no less manic than Scott and Zelda when the drinking started. 'There was a wild streak in John,' recalls Burgess Meredith, 'and it would leap out of nowhere. Most of the time he was quiet, very sober and thoughtful. But you never knew when it would change. When he got going – usually after a few shots of whiskey or a quantity of beer – you couldn't keep him down.'

The Pastures of Heaven came out in November, and as far as Steinbeck or his friends could tell made no impact on the national consciousness. The reviews were insubstantial and scarce. One could almost say there was *no* critical response. This compelling book has, in truth, never been properly recognized as one of Steinbeck's considerable achievements as a writer, probably because it cannot be called 'a novel' and it doesn't really fit the category of 'a story collection'. It is difficult to categorize: as a form, it has much in common with *Winesburg, Ohio*, which remained one of Steinbeck's favourite books. Sherwood Anderson's comments on the shape of his own masterpiece may be usefully recalled when thinking about *The Pastures of Heaven*. 'I have even sometimes thought that the novel form does not fit an American writer,' Anderson said, 'that it is a new looseness; and in *Winesburg*, I have made my own form.'[21]

This 'new looseness' is apparent in Steinbeck's book, and it is, I think, essential to the success of the book, which is largely plotless. His linked stories offer a portrait of a social group as a case study of human behaviour *in relation to* a particular region, and they must be read as a whole to be appreciated. Steinbeck heard a few of these tales from his mother (who once taught in a rural valley in circumstances similar to that of Molly Morgan, one of the most interesting characters in this book) and his Aunt Molly, who of course lived in the Corral de Tierra. In general, the people of this valley were a peaceable unit who formed an old-fashioned organic community not unlike Thomas Hardy's fictional Wessex. The community was land-based, and each integer played a part in the larger function of the whole. 'They were ordinary people, ill-educated but honest and kindly as any,' Steinbeck had written to Mavis McIntosh.

His book charts the disarray caused by the admission of an element that should not be there: a family that had about them 'a flavor of evil'. Steinbeck elaborated: 'Everyone they came in contact with was injured. Every place they went dissension sprang up.' In a way, the evil that the Monroe family brings to the valley is not of their making; it is mysterious and inexplicable, but it would be a mistake to imagine that bad luck is seen by Steinbeck as an inevitable response to some kind of unethical behaviour. He is never that simple-minded, nor is he a religious writer in any traditional sense. If anything, his stories in this collection resemble what Hardy called 'satires of circumstance'. They are laden with ironies of one kind or another, as when the ancestral home of a character, John Whiteside, is destroyed by fire when Bert Monroe, only wanting to be helpful, offers to burn the brush around it to help the old man.

In true modernist fashion, Steinbeck does not explain his twists of plot or moralize abstractly. This or that happens, and there are patterns that might be visible to a God if He existed; but human beings, caught in the moil of circumstance, cannot see these patterns. The job of the writer, in this context, is to be godlike, poised above his or her creation and 'paring his fingernails' (as in Joyce's *Portrait of the Artist as a Young Man*). Always interested in the design of a work, Steinbeck traces a delicate pattern in the carpet here; the various parts of this eclectic community are fitted together to form an organic whole, with the land forming a crucial backdrop to the human drama.

The aura of place is crucial to *The Pastures of Heaven*. It is one of those imagined landscapes almost too idealized to be real. As G. K. Chesterton said, 'There is at the back of every artist's mind something like a pattern or type of architecture. The original quality in any man of imagination is imagery. It is a thing like the landscape of his dreams; the sort of world he would like to make or in which he would wish to wander; the strange flora and fauna of his own secret planet, the sort of thing he likes to think about. This general atmosphere, and pattern or structure of growth, governs all his creations, however varied.' This landscape for John Steinbeck, which amounts to a pattern or 'general atmosphere', is first glimpsed in this collection of stories.

It amounts to a kind of Eden in central California, a lush valley bounded by equally lush (or occasionally burnished) hillsides. The families who dwell in this bucolic landscape are few: twenty or so in the Pastures of Heaven. They are descendants of the original conquistadors who wrested the land from the native American people who lived there before them and to this day remain only partially absorbed. This world was founded on violence, and violence remains a natural part of its texture, one that Steinbeck never shrinks from.

But there is immense beauty here too. There are fruit trees in cultivation, fields of beans, peas and various root crops. Live oaks grow majestically. One of the glories of this book is

the rich display of natural imagery that provides a continuous
feast for the reader's eye. Steinbeck evokes the landscape in
language both poetic – in the best sense of that word – and
frugal. One is made aware of the fragility of all human
encampments in this valley, of the force of nature so much
stronger than any human construct. The second story begins,
for example, with a description of the Battle house, which has
stood vacant for five years:

> The weeds, with a holiday energy, free of fear of the hoe,
> grew as large as small trees. In the orchard the fruit trees
> were knotty and strong and tangled. They increased the
> quantity of their fruit, and diminished its size. The brambles
> grew about their roots and swallowed up the windfalls.

Like Hemingway, Steinbeck was attracted to the violence that
had long been part of his world. But violence is not seen as a
test for manhood; it is random, pervasive, and morally
irrelevant. (This may be seen as one aspect of the interest in
non-teleological thinking. The bad things that happen to
Steinbeck's characters seem in no way related to any specific
sins.) This is not to say that Steinbeck, like Ed Ricketts, did
not abhor of the use of force; he most certainly did. As he
notes in 'About Ed Ricketts', his friend 'hated pain inflicted
without good reason'. Nevertheless, when 'the infliction of
pain was necessary, he had little feeling about it'.

One story 'about' violence and its place in the world
concerns a character by the name of Raymond Banks, a
chicken farmer who is 'forty-five and very jolly' and much
admired for the quality of his poultry. He takes great trouble
to slaughter his chickens with the least amount of pain. A few
times a year Banks visits an old school friend who is a warden
in the federal penitentiary at San Quentin. He goes there to
serve as an official witness to public executions. Just as in the
slaughtering of chickens he is fascinated by 'the killing time',
so in these hangings he is much taken by 'the sharp keen air
of the whole proceeding'.

Bert Monroe's interest in hangings, by contrast, is rather morbid. He likes to conjure in his mind the scene of an execution, and he enjoys the shudder this image produces. As ever, the Monroe family represents bourgeois morality in its least attractive aspects, and Steinbeck's relentless and lifelong attack on the bourgeoisie is evident here. He was still wrestling inwardly with his parents, and struggling with the burgher mentality itself: its insufferable moralizing and fixed sense of what is valuable and what is not. It was the heavy weight of judgement he wanted to break free of, personally and in these stories. He was aware that beneath the bright surface of middle-class respectability there is always a darkness to be found, and this darkness was to Steinbeck hypocritical and insufferable.

When Bert Monroe tells Banks about the tortuous images he imagines in connection with public hangings, the innocent chicken farmer is stunned and disbelieving, even angry: 'If you think things like that you haven't any right to go up with me.' Steinbeck implicitly sides with Banks, who has what might be called a 'natural' interest in the drama of death. Monroe, through excessive refinement, has ruined even this basic instinct for himself, and one consequence of his action is that he destroys Banks's innocence by making him self-conscious about his experience and thus unable to enjoy it.

The Pastures of Heaven was Steinbeck's first sustained fiction written in response to the theories of Ritter and Boodin and mediated, to some extent, by Ed Ricketts. Evil, in Boodin's theorizing, is not entirely negative. The universe must have limits for creativity to occur, and evil – seen as one of the many 'problems' or 'failures' or 'impediments' that exist in the world – is 'inherent not in matter as such'. He explains, 'The mystics who have always made matter responsible for evil have forgotten that evil also means creative possibility.' Thus, the horrible things that happen to people in Steinbeck's book are regarded 'scientifically' as part of an evolving universe. As in Milton's *Paradise Lost*, evil is seen as a necessary agent of righteousness. Without the 'fortunate fall' (*felix culpa*) of Adam and Eve, the grand design of human redemption would have been unfathomable. (Boodin combines the scientific and religious concepts of evil in a sythesis Steinbeck found attractive.)

On a less abstract level, each of the ten principal stories in *The Pastures of Heaven* concerns on some level the way these prissy, bourgeois, interloping Monroes (the sort of people his mother, Olive, spent her life admiring and playing up to) tend to ruin the natural life around them: an environmental whole which includes people as well as flora and fauna. The real heroes of Steinbeck's book are people like Junius Maltby, an educated man from the upper-middle class who has nevertheless resisted the corruption of bourgeois life. Obsessed by his favourite authors, such as Robert Louis Stevenson (whose *Travels with a Donkey* offered a model for Steinbeck's *Travels with Charley*), he fails to look after his farm in the meticulous way that Bert Monroe does.

Instead, Maltby cultivates his relations with his son: 'They didn't make conversation; rather they let a seedling of thought sprout by itself, and then watched with wonder while it sent out branching limbs. They were surprised at the strange fruit their conversation bore, for they didn't direct their thinking, nor trellis nor trim it the way so many people do.' Steinbeck, the gardener, endlessly gravitates to organic metaphors; and these metaphors provide a key to his vision of the universe as an organic whole in which mind expands outwardly to incorporate matter, a point of view developed carefully in Boodin's *Cosmic Evolution*, which Steinbeck and Ricketts were debating lengthily at this time.

In conversation with T. B. Allen, a strong figure in *The Pastures of Heaven*, Bert Monroe says mournfully, 'I had a lot of bad luck,' and recounts instances of it from his recent past. Allen, in a prophetic moment, responds, 'Maybe your curse and the farm's curse have mated and gone into a gopher role like a pair of rattlesnakes. Maybe they'll be a lot of baby curses crawling around the Pastures first thing we know.' In the stories that follow, these baby curses multiply almost uncontrollably, bringing a plague of misfortune on this formerly peaceful valley. Each member of the hapless Monroe clan casts a dark shadow on someone outside the family circle. Jimmie Monroe, Bert's teenage son, plays a large part in the downfall of Edward 'Shark' Wicks, for instance, while Bert unwittingly becomes responsible for the institutionalizing of sweet but simple Tularecito (an early version of Lennie from *Of Mice and Men* or Johnny Bear in the story of that name in *The Long Valley*). In another story, Bert's foolishness sets in motion a train of events that leads Mrs Van Deventer to kill her mentally unstable daughter. Mrs Monroe sets out purposely to destroy the paradise Junius Maltby and his son occupy on their blissfully unkempt farm. Mae Monroe, the beautiful daughter, drives good-natured Pat Humbert half mad by leading him on emotionally without having any intention of allowing the relationship to deepen. And so forth, culminating in the destruction of John Whiteside's house as well as his dreams in the final major story.

The setting of these stories in a California valley prefigures those of *The Long Valley* and, later, *East of Eden*. Ever fascinated with the mythic dimensions of fiction, Steinbeck played in all this work with the Christian notion of 'fallen man'. This included, almost to the point of misogyny, 'fallen woman'. Louis Owens, a recent critic, notes that the valley settings of these books determines that the stories 'will take place in a fallen world and that the quest for the illusive and illusory Eden will be of central thematic significance'.[22] It follows that the women often get the blame for many of Eden's problems, as feminist critics have pointed out.[23] They must therefore be controlled as vigorously as possible, much as Edward 'Shark' Wicks guards his daughter's virginity with an obsessiveness beyond the call of duty, or Helen Van Deventer tries to protect the virginity of her deranged daughter, Hilda.

These tales of rural life remind one of Robert Frost's desperate New Englanders in poems like 'The Hill Wife' and 'Home Burial'; indeed, Frost was only a generation older than Steinbeck, and many of his best poems were appearing just as Steinbeck was writing *The Pastures of Heaven*. Much like Frost, Steinbeck had an interest in the ways that individuals act in response to external pressures: traditions, economics, regional specifics such as weather and terrain, social up-heavals. More so than Frost, however, Steinbeck was disposed to analyse the group or phalanx to see how individuals connected to the larger unit. He was interested, as an artist, in mediating between 'group man' and the individual.

In thinking about *The Pastures of Heaven*, one can make too much of the curse of the Monroes. In a broader sense, this book demonstrates Steinbeck's firm allegience to ordinary people who are trying to make an honest living and raise their families. While he never hesitates to show their flaws – their self-aggrandizing instincts, their shallowness, their tendency to suspect the worst in their neighbours – he treats everyone, including the Monroes, with that impulse towards generosity which is so crucial in his fiction. Having finished with the romantic idea of 'heroism' in *Cup of Gold*, he was now free to examine human beings in all their sad complexity.

The Pastures of Heaven remains a small masterpiece of American literature, one that has rarely been acknowledged as such or, for that matter, even read.

The Depression had by 1933 moved into its deepest phase. The stock market had reached it lowest point in history, and nearly two million men roamed the country looking for jobs or handouts. President Hoover, in his last year in office, had created the Reconstruction Finance Corporation (RFC) for the purpose of lending money to railroads, banks, agricultural agencies, industry, and commerce; but this relatively small gesture had failed to turn things around. (The RFC would pump $3.5 billion into banks and trust companies under President Roosevelt in just a few years.) 'The money was all appropriated for the top in the hopes it would trickle down to the needy,' quipped Will Rogers. But as unemployment figures went from 4.3 million in 1930 to over 12 million in 1933, there was no hope of 'trickle down'. The needy were needier than ever.

Steinbeck's finances in 1933 mirrored the state of the nation's. *The Pastures of Heaven* failed to sell a thousand copies, and there was no other money coming in from his writing. Poor old John Ernst was still coughing up $50 a month to support his artistic son and his wife, but the time when this stipend would end was looming. Prospects were grim all around, and Steinbeck wrote to Mavis McIntosh in desperation, asking if perhaps he couldn't take his potboiler (which had not found a publisher) and 'cut it up into a sequence of detective stories for pulp magazines'.[24] Any money was better than no money.

When a letter arrived from his father asking him to bring Carol home for Christmas in Salinas, Steinbeck wrote back that he didn't have a penny extra for travel. (His father, as ever, responded with cash, although by now there was deep resentment on both sides about Steinbeck's seemingly never-ending demand for financial support.) As the winter deepened, so did Steinbeck's fiscal crisis: 'Apparently we are heading for the rocks,' he wrote to Robert Ballou. Putting these thoughts aside for the holiday season, the Steinbecks travelled to Salinas. It was apparent to them both that Olive Steinbeck was failing rather badly; quite often she did not even respond to questions, and she had trouble speaking when she did. Although she insisted on doing the cooking,

Carol had to stand behind her helping, terrified that she might topple over at any moment. John Ernst looked on with horror; Olive had been the mainstay of his life, and he could not envisage an existence without her.

Steinbeck was devasted by the decline in his mother's health. She had always been so disapproving, and now she was going to die without witnessing his 'success'. She would leave this world thinking him a failure, a leech, a perpetual child. This galled him, and he plunged into a depression unleavened by the bright sunshine of southern California. Hoping to lift his spirits, he and Carol rented a shack near the ocean in Laguna Beach for two dollars a month. Unless he shook himself out of this bleak mood, he was never going to complete the revised version of *To a God Unknown*. At least he felt good about what he had done thus far, as he noted in his diary: 'The story has grown since I started it. From a novel about people, it has become a novel about the world.'[25] With considerable prescience, he says, 'The new eye is being opened here in the west – the new seeing. It is probable that no one will know it for two hundred years. It will be confused, analyzed, analogized, criticised, and none of our fine critics will know what is happening.'

Meanwhile, Robert Ballou's career was going through various nerve-racking transformations. He had left one sinking ship for another, and this time he had decided to take a more dangerous leap and form his own publishing house, Robert O. Ballou and Company. Still believing in Steinbeck, he assumed responsibility for the publication of *To a God Unknown* and told Steinbeck he would stick by him no matter what. Here was a publisher any writer would love to have, and Steinbeck knew how lucky he was. But he felt little sense of elation as spring approached.

'Well, March is nearly over – the month my mother dreaded so,' Steinbeck wrote in his journal a few years later.[26] 'Mother never drew a carefree breath in March.' Indeed, his mother fell seriously ill in mid-March. She became faint one day and was driven by her husband to the Salinas Valley Hospital, where she suffered a massive stroke that left her paralysed on the left side and unable to speak except in muffled tones. Steinbeck was summoned to Salinas, and he and Carol quickly pulled up stakes and moved into the family house to help. Beth, Esther and Mary were each too involved with their own families at this time to return to Salinas except for brief visits, so the brunt of the responsibilities fell on the only son, who dutifully spent every day at the hospital for several weeks.

The doctors explained to the family that Olive would never recover; the stroke had done too much permanent damage. They did, however, lay out the possibility that she might survive for several years in a state of near-paralysis. Hearing this, Steinbeck panicked. The thought of having to stay in Salinas and nurse his dying mother for several years was more than he could stand. Guilt, anger, remorse and sorrow rushed upon him, a tumble of feelings that would not cohere. As Beth recalls, 'John had complicated relations with Mother.' It was not simply that he felt that she had never given him the unconditional love a child must have; she had, in fact, loved him very much. Her obsessive concern for his education and moral development was, in part, an expression of love. But it was always a contingent love, which meant that her son never felt satisfied; whatever he accomplished, he could never really measure up in the way she would have liked. Something was missing.

One day, having sat beside his mother for many hours without speaking, Steinbeck told Carol that he believed his writing career was over, that he would never regain the strength to continue. As soon as he said this, he determined to fight it – he was not going to let Olive kill his dream. He started bringing his writing pad to the hospital every day, and sat beside his dozing mother with a pencil ready. One morning he began a story that became the first part of *The Red Pony*, a sequence of stories which became one of his most popular and enduring works. The return to Salinas had brought back his boyhood with a flush of feeling. He was pleased by what he had written, though he typically played down his achievement in a note to George Albee: 'Went to the hospital and got a few pages of the pony story done, although I suspect it is pretty rotten. But between bed pans and calling relatives I got some done. I shall hate to spoil it because it is really a fine story.'[27] In the same letter, he ventured that he would tackle the history of this part of central California one day: 'I think I would like to write the story of this whole valley, of all the little towns and all the farms and the ranches in the wilder hills. I can see how I would like to do it so that it would be the valley of the world.'

The pressure of his mother's illness was bad enough, but John Ernst was not well either; he was feeble and confused and seemed unable to accept the severity of Olive's condition. When she was brought home from the hospital, the scene at the house on Central Avenue became exceedingly grim. Once Mary stopped by with her young children, but the effect was bad on everyone. The noise made by the children 'was out of place in this house of gloom', Steinbeck said.[28] Carol was 'a saint' and did not desert her husband or his family; she worked tirelessly to make everyone as comfortable as possible, shopping for food and cooking meals, helping to supervise the nurses who came and went at appointed times.

He often retreated to the attic, where in sweltering heat he wrote stories about the Salinas Valley prompted by his father's senile ramblings. Like Charles Dickens, Anthony Trollope and other prolific novelists, he could write anywhere; he carried his interior world with him, and it did not especially matter where he happened to be sitting at the time – in a shack at Laguna Beach, in a lawn chair at Eagle Rock, at the old family desk in Pacific Grove, beside his mother's hospital bed in Salinas, in the attic of the house on Central Avenue. The compulsion to write could not be stifled by a mere change of circumstances. If John Ernst and Olive doubted their son's future, he did not. He would succeed in his own terms, in his own time.

During the agonizing period from March until his mother's death the following February, Steinbeck was perpetually on call. He and Carol occasionally retreated for brief periods to the cottage in Pacific Grove, where he would spend much of his time renewing his friendship with Ed Ricketts. Once or twice they brought John Ernst along too, since Olive's illness had begun to take a severe toll on him. Steinbeck's reading at the time was central to his fiction: Jung, Boodin, Ritter. His letters to friends are full of musings on these authors, attempts to work out his 'non-teleological' way of thinking, to formulate an 'organismal' theory of creation. During this period, when he lived so close to death, he wanted desperately to formulate a thesis that 'takes in all life, and for that part, all matter'.[29]

He wrote a fascinating letter to Albee which includes an exposition of his ideas:

> We know that with certain arrangements of atoms we might have what we would call a bar of iron. Certain other arrangements of atoms plus a mysterious principle make a living cell. Now the living cell is very sensitive to outside stimuli or tropisms. A further arrangement of cells and a very complex one may make a unit which we call a man. That has been our final unit. But there have been mysterious things which could not be explained if man is the final unit. He also arranges himself into larger units, which I have called the phalanx. The phalanx has its own memory – memory of the great tides when the moon was close, memory of starvations when the food of the world was exhausted. Memory of methods when numbers of his

units had to be destroyed for the good of the whole, memory of the history of itself.[30]

One hears in these cadences the mingling voices of Ricketts, Boodin, Ritter, Jung – perhaps even the voice of Joseph Campbell. Steinbeck was creating his own synthesis of these voices, and his fiction was deeply affected by the results. This is especially true of the final version of *To a God Unknown*, which had been accepted by Robert Ballou for publication after a tense period when it looked as though Ballou might go belly-up in the Depression.

Mavis McIntosh had sent *To a God Unknown* to half a dozen publishers when it seemed that Ballou was not going to be able to honour his commitment to the book. A positive response that would probably have led to an offer came from Simon & Schuster, making Ballou frantic. He begged Mavis McIntosh for a two-week reprieve to raise the capital he needed to publish the book, but she would probably have refused had not Steinbeck insisted on standing behind Ballou. He did, and the book was published in the autumn as promised. McIntosh & Otis 'are probably mad at me for turning down the comparatively sure ready money from Simon and Schuster', he wrote to Albee, 'but I can't help that'.[31] No one would say that John Steinbeck was anything but loyal.

The summer of 1933 was a crucible of sorts for Steinbeck. It was not only physically hot, with temperatures in Salinas soaring to record highs, but the house on Central Avenue was emotionally sweltering. Steinbeck sat for long hours beside his mother's bed, watching her toss and turn in a feverish sleep. In addition to the 'pony story' and other tales of California life that would make their way into *The Long Valley*, Steinbeck began to think about the stories of *paisano* life told to him by Sue Gregory, the Monterey high school teacher whom he had met through Ed Ricketts the previous year. Gregory, who was partly of Mexican descent, had been studying the poor Mexicans who lived on a flat in the hills above Monterey in a shantytown known, cynically, as Tortilla Flat.

Steinbeck began writing down some of Gregory's stories, and they seemed to revive in him a joy of storytelling he had not felt in some time. He wrote to Robert Ballou at the end of that terrible summer, 'My father collapsed a week ago under the six months' strain and very nearly landed in the same position as my mother. It was very close. Paradoxically, I have started another volume and it is going like wildfire. It is light and I think amusing but true, although no one who doesn't know *paisanos* would ever believe it. I don't care much whether it amounts to anything. I am enjoying it and I need something to help me over this last ditch. Our house is crumbling very rapidly and when it is gone there will be nothing left.'[32] The result of this 'wildfire' was *Tortilla Flat*, Steinbeck's first major critical and commercial success.

VII

The Sorrow of His House

'What an extension of self is this pen. Once it is in my hand – like a wand – I stop being the confused, turgid, ugly and gross person.'

Steinbeck to Toby Street, August 1934

The autumn of 1933 brought no joy for Steinbeck, even though *To a God Unknown* was published in November by Robert Ballou. Olive Steinbeck's health grew steadily worse, and she was unable to speak or move by October, when John Ernst collapsed from exhaustion one evening after dinner. The constant strain of seeing his wife in such a condition was, as his son noted, 'too much for the poor man'. At Carol's suggestion, Steinbeck decided to leave his mother in the care of nurses and retreat, with John Ernst in tow, to Pacific Grove.

Writing to Dook Sheffield from 11th Street, Steinbeck said, 'Half of the cell units of my mother's body have rebelled. . . . She, as a human unit, is deterred from functioning as she ordinarily did by a schism of a number of her cells.'[1] The seeming coldness of these remarks provided a cover for the hugely sentimental man behind this mask. There is pain behind each word. 'Science', it would seem, was useful in this way: Steinbeck could detach his feelings about the individual from the 'process' whereby the 'human unit' was 'undone'. He described his father's physical and mental condition to Robert Ballou in less brutal terms, resorting to interesting (if still rather mechanical) similes: 'He is like an engine that isn't moored tightly and that just shakes itself to pieces.'[2] John Ernst was now suffering from 'numbness and loss of eyesight' as well as mental instability. 'Death I can stand,' Steinbeck said, 'but not this slow torture wherein a good and a strong man tears off little shreds of himself and throws them away.'

Oddly enough, Steinbeck was, as a writer, fuelled by these misfortunes. It was as if rocks were being moved deep in his unconscious; he could see things clearly which had been buried for so long, and this obviously stimulated the writer's imagination. Stories – or ideas for stories – leaped to the bright light of consciousness. Carol, meanwhile, spent much of her time with her ailing father-in-law, for whom she had genuine affection, taking him out every morning so that her husband could write. And write he did, completing three-quarters of *Tortilla Flat* in just over a month. (The last quarter would take longer, but this seemed to the author like a book that 'wrote itself', as he told Carl Wilhelmson.)

John Ernst became ever more difficult to live with, wandering through the house at all hours of the night, playing the radio at full blast, getting himself locked in the bathroom, refusing to eat the food Carol had cooked. Steinbeck gritted his teeth and turned away from his father, much as he had turned away from him as a boy. He kept his mind fixed on *Tortilla Flat*, explaining to one correspondent that his new book was 'a very jolly one about Monterey *paisanos*. Its tone, I guess, is a direct rebellion against all the sorrow of our house.'[3] His attitude towards his work never wavered: 'As long as I can eat and write more books, that's all that I require.'

A new puppy was added to the household, an Irish terrier called Jodie, and Steinbeck spent many happy hours taking it for walks along the beach. Ed Ricketts was heavily involved now with Toni Jackson, and Steinbeck felt somewhat cut off from him. He did, however, still drop by the lab once or twice in the late afternoons. One friends recalls, 'John seemed awfully depressed, which I suppose was natural. His father was living with them, and he was quite ill. There was a lot of tension at home. And Carol couldn't find any work that appealed to her.' There was also the fact that 'John's novels just weren't getting the kind of reception he hoped for. The critics were deaf to them. He would sit on a stool and watch us work, saying nothing. Once in a while he and Ed got to talking about philosophy, but it wasn't the same as the year before. Some of the enthusiasm was missing.'[4]

To a God Unknown appeared in late November, and (once again) there were almost no reviews; the few that did appear lacked enthusiasm. Later critics, however, have found a good deal to admire in *To a God Unknown*, which for all its tortuous composition remains an engaging if at times melodramatic story. The novel examines the human need for ritual, the desire to look beyond empirical explanations of life's raw and tragic data. The story's hero is Joseph Wayne, the name Joseph being full of biblical resonance. This is the Joseph of the Old Testament, the patriarch and deft interpreter of dreams and mysteries, the man of the coat of many colours, the prophet of wildness as well as wilderness, the trickster, the clairvoyant.

Steinbeck's Joseph leads his 'tribe' out of the stony desert of Vermont's hill country into the lush valley of California's Nuestra Señora (the Jolon Valley in early drafts of the book). There are four brothers, three of whom are eventually married (including Joseph), and each brother represents a different spiritual and psychological orientation. Burton is a fierce Protestant, a New England puritan in the tradition of Jonathan Edwards. He abhors all kinds of frivolity, such as dancing and drinking, convinced that salvation hangs in the balance at every moment. (His God is the fierce Yahweh who would force Abraham to kill his son, not the gentle Elohim who clothes Adam and Eve in the Garden of Eden.) Burton is married, but he 'had embraced his wife four times. He had two children. Celibacy was a natural state for him.'

Thomas, another brother, is married to Rama. They live in an easy, almost pagan, relationship with nature. He has an intimate relationship with the animals on his farm, aware of exactly when a mare or cow will give birth. Indeed, his barn might be thought of as a literal version of his collective unconscious. His long-suffering wife 'understood Thomas, treated him as though he were an animal, kept him clean and fed and warm, and didn't often frighten him'. Both regard religion, in any form, as 'a kind of little trap'.

Joseph's youngest brother, Benjy, is a drunk who cannot maintain a relationship with a woman. He flits from occupation to occupation, causing trouble in the community and bringing shame on the sacred family name. Apart from alcohol, Benjy is mainly interested in raucous merriment of any kind. He has no religious views whatsoever and comes to a sad end when he is stabbed in the back making love to someone else's wife.

It is Joseph who rules the family by sheer force of personality. Though not the eldest son, he is the one who received the patriarchal blessing from his father before he left Vermont (in the Old Testament style, by placing his hand between his father's thighs). And it is Joseph who beckons the others west, and who consequently feels responsible for the terrible and destructive drought that overwhelms the valley. Like the mythical Fisher King, he believes himself to be the cause of the disaster, and he also imagines that he alone can save his people from their impending demise. (The echoes of Eliot's *The Waste Land* are strong throughout this novel.)

It soon becomes clear that Joseph has developed an almost Druidic relationship with the valley, with its 'interlacing boughs and twigs' and with 'the long green cavern cut by the river'. The valley's 'endless green aisles and alcoves' radiate for him with 'meanings as obscure and promising as the symbols of an ancient religion'. In a scene that feels lifted from Lawrence's *Women in Love* (Steinbeck was an adroit mimic of other writers, and he never hesitated to 'steal' a scene if he thought he could use it), Joseph hurls himself on to the ground: 'He flung himself face downward on the grass and pressed his cheek against the wet stems. His fingers gripped the wet grass and tore it out and gripped again. His thighs beat heavily on the earth.'

In the tradition of the wandering Odysseus, Joseph builds his house under the limb of an oak tree, which takes on pagan significance. The marriage bed and the rooted oak (a version of the World Tree of ancient myth) combine to form a powerful symbol of inheritance and authority. The symbol is further complicated in Steinbeck's novel by Joseph Wayne's belief that his father's spirit has entered the tree; he therefore begins a sequence of ritual practices which disturb his brothers. When the sacred oak is killed by one of the brothers, Joseph thinks his father's spirit has fled to a nearby stone, upon which he makes live sacrifices.

We are told that Joseph, the practitioner of pagan rituals and ancestor worship, 'did not think these things in his mind, but in his chest and in the corded muscles of his legs. It was the heritage of a race which for a million years had sucked at the breasts of the soil and cohabited with the earth.' This is the Jungian racial memory Joseph Campbell had talked to him about at length, something that goes beyond the personal unconscious and digs deeply into the collective unconscious.

The primitivism of Joseph's would-be connection with the land seems to contradict the patriarchal need to control the environment, as Dennis Prindle points out: 'Even after forsaking the religion of his fathers, Joseph remains the acknowledged leader and new patriarch of his family. His is a new covenant with the demands and deep mysteries of the land itself, but he is none the less the patriarch, the new Abraham of this new covenant. Religious tradition and patriarchal authority only seem to yield to a complete identification with an unmediated experience of nature.'[5] Thus, Joseph cries out, 'I am failing to protect the land,' upon seeing that the drought is getting worse and will soon drive his family from the new homeland. 'The duty of keeping life in my land is beyond my power,' he says. Again, one hears on echo of *The Waste Land*, a text that Steinbeck – like all writers of his generation – had virtually memorized:

> Here is no water but only rock
> Rock and no water and the sandy road
> The road winding above among the mountains
> Which are mountains of rock without water

Steinbeck's valley shakes with the 'dry sterile thunder without rain' that Eliot evokes.

Like Eliot, he had been reading James Frazer's *The Golden Bough* (another of Joseph Campbell's favourite books) and he was familiar with primitive vegetation myths and tales of the dying and reviving god.[6] One of these dying and reviving gods, of course, is Christ, and Steinbeck does not miss the opportunity to add substantially to the depth of his symbolism. When Elizabeth McGreggor marries Joseph, she sees him as a Christ figure: 'When she drew a picture of the Christ in her mind, He had the face, the youthful beard, the piercing puzzled eyes of Joseph, who stood beside her.' Others in the novel also see in Joseph the Christ-image. The novel, indeed, is seeded with imagery calculated to make the reader identify Joseph as a Christ type. (He is working in the barn one day for instance, when suddenly he 'moved into a shaft of light and spread his arms'.)

Joseph is an obsessive character who generates considerable destruction. After his child is born, he makes his poor wife climb on to the massive rock located in his field (by now, in his mind, a sacred place) in order to 'tame' it. She is not enthusiastic about his practice, since her own impulses do not run to these Druidic extremes. She slips and is instantly killed in the process; here, as elsewhere, the novel strains credibility, an early sign that Steinbeck has little interest in 'realism', *per se*. (That critical tag, where Steinbeck is concerned, has little meaning.) As soon as she dies, Joseph notices that rain has begun to fall – at the height of the dry season. Though he thinks nothing of this 'coincidence' at the time, a profound association is made in his unconscious between blood sacrifice and the rain.

As the land goes into a deep drought, it comes as no surprise that Joseph finally takes it upon himself to lay down his life for his people. In the melodramatic final chapter of the novel, he sacrifices himself on the same rock where Elizabeth died:

> He worked his way carefully up the steep sides until at last he lay in the deep soft moss on the rock's top. When he had rested a few minutes, he took out his knife again and carefully, gently opened the vessels of his wrist. The pain was sharp at first, but in a moment its sharpness dulled. He watched the bright blood cascading over the moss, and he heard the shouting of the wind around the grove. The sky was growing grey. And time passed and Joseph grew grey too. He lay on his side with his wrist outstretched and looked down the long black mountain range of his body. Then his body grew huge and light. It arose into the sky, and out of it came the streaking rain. 'I should have known,' he whispered. 'I am the rain.'

Steinbeck did not himself believe in Druidic practices, although there does at times seem a lack of irony in his presentation of Joseph Wayne. He does, however, cast Joseph's story in a sceptical light by establishing a pattern of chance occurrences which put in doubt any simple-minded cause-and-effect relations. From the outset, we are made aware (a seer called Romas tells us this in the novel) that these droughts are simply part of the region's broad weather pattern; they have come 'twice in the memory of old men', and the seer predicts another drought – the one that, indeed, does come. We are also told that on the 'other side of the mountain where it is always green' lives an old man who makes live sacrifices to produce moisture; Steinbeck notes, with irony, that the old man lives on the western slope of the coastal range, where fogs tend to linger, thus producing greenness. These are only two of many instances where natural causes exist quietly beside supernatural causes for events that seem mysterious, thus giving *To a God Unknown* an undertow of irony not always visible on the surface of the narrative.

To a God Unknown is not one of Steinbeck's better books, but it contains impressive moments of lyrical writing. The portrait of Joseph Wayne is complex, if not fully satisfying (we cannot, finally, regard his Druidic impulses as more than a fascinating aberration). The novel may be seen as Steinbeck's first major attempt to come to grips with his most essential material, with the landscape that lay at the back of his mind and formed an intimate part of his dream-life. It is also important for what it reveals about the author's developing interest in myth and symbol, in the role the unconscious plays in daily life. Overall, *To a God Unknown* anticipates his more successful later novels; in a curious way, it has much in common with *East of Eden*, where some of the same material is reconfigured in more successful ways.

One thing *To a God Unknown* did not do was add to Steinbeck's financial security. He noted that, thus far, he had earned only $870 for seven years of steady writing – roughly $125 a year. To their credit, both Robert Ballou and Mavis McIntosh continued to believe in ultimate prospects, assuring him that critical and financial success lay only a short distance ahead of him. For obvious reasons, Carol now was getting edgy, pointing out to her husband that his mother's illness was draining the family finances and that John Ernst's subsidy was soon going to disappear. John Ernst himself had slipped into a confused, melancholic state, and it was not unlikely that soon he would himself become a financial burden. One night, when both were unable to sleep, Carol began to tell her husband about her fears that both of his parents would soon be in their care. Where would the money come from to support them? Would they have to sell the Salinas home, and then the cottage in Pacific Grove? After that, what next? Would John Steinbeck have to abandon writing?

Steinbeck sat on the edge of the bed, listening to his wife's recital of woe. She was right, of course, and he knew it; with strange insensitivity to Carol's needs he maintained a quiet space inside himself where he could retreat; he had learned to ignore Carol and turn to his work, where he felt safe. In August he had written to Carl Wilhelmson:

> I work because I know it gives me pleasure to work. It is as simple as that, and I don't require any other reasons. I am losing a sense of self to a marked degree and that is a pleasant thing. A couple of years ago I realized that I was not the material of which great artists are made and that I was rather glad I wasn't. And since then I have been happier simply to do the work and to take the reward at the end of every day that is given for a day of honest work. I grow less complicated all the time and that is a joy to me. The forces that used to tug in various directions have all started to pull in one. I have a book to write. I think about it for a while and then I write it. There is nothing more. When it is done I have little interest in it. By the time one comes out I am usually tied up in another.[7]

This was exactly what happened as the soft California winter approached with raw, damp mornings and early sunsets. *To a God Unknown* came out, but it seems to have made little impact on its author, who was writing *Tortilla Flat* and more

short stories with California settings, such as 'The Chrysanthemums', a key story in *The Long Valley*. Steinbeck retreated
for long hours into his work, avoiding Carol, who had grown
bitterly restive; avoiding his father, who slumped in a chair in
the small living room of the 11th Street house. There were
frequent trips over to Salinas, where Olive had been re-
hospitalized and was not expected to live much longer.

Perhaps the high point of the long autumn of 1933 was the
publication in *North American Review* of two sections of 'The
Red Pony' in consecutive issues. Elizabeth Otis, who at this
point dealt mostly with Steinbeck's short fiction, had placed
the long story in this prestigious magazine after trying several
others without success. This was the era of the high-paying,
slick magazines: *Saturday Evening Post*, *McClure's*, *Collier's*,
and a dozen other periodicals like them played host to
Fitzgerald, Hemingway, Sinclair Lewis, and other 'name-
brand' writers. But it took a successful novel to crack that
market, and Steinbeck, despite three published novels, did
not yet fall into this category. He was nevertheless thrilled to
get his story into *North American Review*, where it would be
seen by a moderately large, intelligent readership. Even
better, he was paid $90 for it, enough to live on for two or
three months, if he and Carol were frugal.

In November, Carol found a part-time job with the
Emergency Relief Organization (ERO), which had been
established by President Roosevelt as a way of combating the
worst effects of the Depression. A high percentage of the
destitute families she began to work with were Mexican
immigrants, and their problems were brought home to
Steinbeck, who listened every night to his wife's horrific tales
of poverty and injustice. Perhaps in response to the harrow-
ing scenes she witnessed every day, Carol began writing
poetry, and she would read her poems aloud to her husband.
He thought she was highly talented and sent a manuscript of
her poems to Robert Ballou, hoping that he might have some

useful comments. The poems were never published, much to Carol's dismay.

In the meanwhile, William Alton DeWitt, managing editor of *North American Review*, asked Steinbeck for more work. Readers had written in to say that they liked 'The Red Pony', and DeWitt himself claimed to 'adore' it. Flattered, Steinbeck quickly assented, and three more stories – 'The Murder', 'The Raid' and 'The White Quail' – were bought and published in the magazine over the next fifteen months. These formed the core of *The Long Valley*, and they are superb work, if still less widely admired than they deserve to be.

By Christmas Steinbeck was back in Salinas. His mother had come home from the hospital, but she was growing weaker every day. 'John felt responsible for mother and father,' Steinbeck's sister recalls. 'He stayed close by during their last illnesses, but it was hard on him. He took everything very personally, and he felt like the whole burden was his.' Emma Torville was a young nurse who came for several hours each day to care for Olive, and she remembers that Steinbeck 'was very gloomy. He sat in his bedroom in a rocking chair with a writing pad on his lap and wouldn't answer questions when you asked him. I used to think there was something wrong with him.'[8]

To get away from the desperate scene at home, Steinbeck went for long walks around the town of Salinas and outlying areas; for the first time he noticed the old jalopies from Oklahoma stacked high with furniture and spilling over with ragged people en route to what they imagined was a new life in the west. This was the first trickle of Dust Bowl refugees to reach California, and Steinbeck immediately saw the glare of disappointment on their faces and was moved. These 'Okies' set up a shantytown outside Salinas which was soon called 'Little Oklahoma' by the locals, and Steinbeck once spent an afternoon visiting them and hearing their stories. 'There's a novel here somewhere,' he said to Carol later.[9] Little did he know what an amazing novel it would be and how it would change his life.

Steinbeck worked on *Tortilla Flat* with fierce concentration; it offered a way out of the nightmare of this 'house of sorrows', as he kept calling it. In February 1934 the situation with Olive worsened, and she died on the morning of 19 February. Steinbeck felt greater relief than sadness and quickly returned to Pacific Grove, taking his father with him. To George Albee, only a week after his mother's death, he wrote: 'Just now my father is with us. Every nerve I have is demanding that I be alone for a little while, even for a day, to make adjustments, but that has been impossible so far. I have to figure some things out. I don't even know what they are yet.'[10]

Tortilla Flat was done by the beginning of March, and Steinbeck sent it to Mavis McIntosh, who was not impressed. She wrote to him that, compared to his other work, it seemed 'trivial', and that 'its themes, whatever they are, are not very clear'. She wondered if he shouldn't put it aside for the time being and work on something more 'serious'. Frustrated and angry, Steinbeck tried to explain some things about this book, which was very dear to him:

> The book has a very definite theme. I thought it was clear enough. I have expected that the plan of the Arthurian cycle would be recognized, that my Gawaine and my Launcelot, my Arthur and Galahad would be recognized. Even the incident of the Sangreal in the search of the forest is not clear enough I guess. The form is that of the Malory version, the coming of Arthur and the mystic quality of owning a house, the forming of the round table, the adventure of the knights and finally, the mystic translation of Danny.[11]

Steinbeck was further disillusioned when Robert Ballou turned the book down precipitately, saying it was 'too slight' and that 'it didn't make sense'. Ballou was still reeling from the financial failures of both *The Pastures of Heaven* and *To a God Unknown*, and he was terrified of putting another Steinbeck title into circulation so quickly. 'Maybe I am not a novelist,' Steinbeck glumly told Ed Ricketts. He wondered, half-heartedly, if maybe he shouldn't switch careers and take up marine biology.

Ricketts urged him to stick with short stories for the time being, and he did so. Between March and August 1934 he went through one of his most productive periods, writing a fair number of the stories that would eventually appear in *The Long Valley*. One sees in this work his evolution from a writer of quasi-allegorical tales (occasionally with an archly comic tone) to a writer of work that might be described as 'social realism'. In August he would begin his first 'protest novel', *In Dubious Battle*, a chilling and vividly drawn study of the 'phalanx' and its power to corrupt or enhance individual moral choice.

His mood during the spring and summer was, at best, lugubrious. In his journal, in June, he wrote, 'There is too much work to get out. This Monday afternoon must be given to working out of this week's story and perhaps beginning it. . . . The bottom of my stomach is dropping out with accumulated loneliness – not loneliness that might be mended with company either. I think Carol is the same way. There's a haunted quality in her eyes. I'm not good company to her. I can't help her loneliness and she can't help mine.'[12] It seemed to Carol that they had begun to live separate lives together.

More public recognition came in August in the form of an O. Henry Award. 'The Murder', which had been published in *North American Review* earlier that year, was given the top prize. Steinbeck was thrilled, hoping, as he wrote to his old friend Toby Street, that 'maybe this O. Henry selection might create some interest in my stories'.[13] 'The Snake', 'Johnny Bear' and 'The Raid' were all written in quick succession. 'The pen feels good to my hand,' he wrote to Toby Street.

'Comfortable and comforting. What an extension of self is this pen. Once it is in my hand – like a wand – I stop being the confused, turgid, ugly and gross person. I am no longer the me I know.'

Even though Steinbeck had not been much of a journalist during his brief period in New York in 1925, he often (especially from the mid-Thirties onwards) approached the writing of fiction from what could be called a journalistic viewpoint. His Depression-era novels, in particular, possess that journalistic flavour and might be thought of as part reportage; one senses the 'research' behind them. Now he kept an eye out for potential material.

One day an occasional acquaintance by the name of Sis Reamer suggested to Steinbeck that he write about some fugitives from the law whom she knew slightly. The Cannery and Agricultural Workers' Industrial Union (C & AWIU) had recently moved into the central California area, spurred on by local Communist Party members, and they supplied leaders for strikes where they were needed. Two of these, Pat Chambers and Caroline Decker, had been arrested for illegal striking activity; they hid out in a town near Monterey called Seaside, where they were soon joined by a young Okie named Cicil McKiddy. Reamer took Steinbeck to their lair, a seedy boarding house, and he offered to pay them a small amount of money for the rights to their story; it was his intention to write a story in the voice of a Communist labour leader.

He became more and more involved with the situation of labourers and migrant workers in the Monterey area. McKiddy proved especially important to Steinbeck, since he had made the trek from Oklahoma's Dust Bowl only a year before and had already acquired some experience as a union organizer during a large cotton strike which had broken out in the Bakersfield area the previous autumn. More recently, McKiddy had been working as a publicist for the C & AWIU in the Monterey region, typing and printing pamphlets. He had been visibly a leader in the cotton strike and had gone into hiding when rumours began to circulate that a warrant for his arrest had been issued by local police in Monterey. More like a reporter or police detective than a novelist, Steinbeck prowled the region with a notebook in hand. He knew he was on to something.

When he wrote to Mavis McIntosh to say that he wanted to write this non-fiction narrative, she wrote back quickly to urge him to use this material as the basis for a new novel, saying that 'it could find a large audience'. (Among the numerous popular books about strikes was *The Octopus* by Frank Norris, a novel dramatizing the clash between ranchers and workers in California's San Joaquin Valley.) This would not be the last time Steinbeck would begin with an idea for a non-fiction book and realize, soon after beginning the research, that the material could work better in fictional form. Indeed, the same thing would happen with *The Grapes of Wrath*, which began as a series of newspaper articles.

He was quickly absorbed by this material, which provided a chance to test his theories about group behaviour in a large-scale setting. *Tortilla Flat*, which had yet to find a publisher, had been merely a warm-up; now he would really stretch his wings. The new novel, set in the California apple country, would centre on conflicts between groups of men who represented different 'classes' and ideologies. For the first time, Steinbeck would write about migrant workers and discover inside himself a peculiar empathy for them in their plight. He understood them, and – more importantly – he knew how to represent them in fiction.

Unknown to Steinbeck, some things were happening in the early winter of 1934 that would have a permanent effect on his publishing future. In Chicago, the owner of a small, literary bookstore, Ben Abramson, had become a Steinbeck fan, having encountered 'The Red Pony' in *North American Review*. He got his hands on copies of *The Pastures of Heaven* and *To a God Unknown* and fell in love with them. When 'The Murder' appeared in the April issue of *North American Review*, he became convinced that Steinbeck was the best new writer of his generation. By chance, a friend and former Chicago bookseller, Pascal Covici, wandered into Abramson's shop and listened as Abramson extolled the virtues of this un-discovered writer. Impressed, Covici (who was partner in a New York publishing house) bought a copy of *The Pastures of Heaven* and read it on the night train back to New York City.[14]

He was so impressed that he contacted McIntosh & Otis immediately to inquire about Steinbeck's contractual rights. Had Robert O. Ballou locked up the young author's future work? 'In fact, there are no contractual agreements,' Mavis McIntosh told Covici, who was delighted to hear this news and asked to see anything McIntosh had in hand. *Tortilla Flat*, which had been rejected by many houses thus far, was sent to him immediately; within three weeks he made an offer. Covici was, in fact, so enthusiastic that he offered to republish the previous books by Steinbeck which had gone out of print and to remain the publisher of all his future work – a startling and perhaps foolhardy thing for a publisher to tell anyone in the middle of the Great Depression.

So Steinbeck finally had a publisher for *Tortilla Flat*, a novel in which he had never lost faith despite its countless rejections. But he was wary of Pascal (Pat) Covici, whose firm (Covici–Friede) was as badly off as most other publishers during those terrible economic times. Mavis McIntosh, astonished by the sudden sale to Covici, warned the author that she had heard 'ominous rumors' about the impending collapse of the company, but Steinbeck had no choice but to run with Pat Covici; nobody else wanted *Tortilla Flat*, and the small advance against royalties promised by Covici was desperately needed. Plus, the option on the next novel as well as the interest in republishing past work proved irresistible. He would cross his fingers.

The work on the new novel, to be called *In Dubious Battle* (after a line in *Paradise Lost*), could hardly have been going better: 'I have used a small strike in an orchard valley as the symbol of man's eternal, bitter warfare with himself,' Steinbeck explained to George Albee:

> I'm not interested in strike as means of raising men's wages, and I'm not interested in ranting about justice and oppression, mere outcroppings which indicate the condition. But man hates something in himself. He has been able to defeat every natural obstacle, but himself he cannot win over unless he kills every individual. And this self-hate, which goes so closely in hand with self-love, is what I wrote about. The book is brutal.[15]

It gathered bulk swiftly: 'I'm too tired to be writing a letter. I've written thirty thousand words in the last eight days. I'll finish this letter later. I'm going for a walk down by the water.' By the end of January, only five months from the time he began writing *In Dubious Battle*, he was finished with the book, having written over a hundred and twenty thousand words in that period. This Dickensian pace of composition was typical of Steinbeck at the height of his powers. (*The Grapes of Wrath*, a much longer book, was written at similarly breakneck speed, as was *East of Eden*.)

Tortilla Flat, which had been scheduled for publication in May 1935, was in the pipeline now, going through copy-editing and proofing, and *In Dubious Battle* was complete in typescript by the end of February. Steinbeck continued to mull it over through March, crossing out phrases and rearranging scenes; shortly before sending the book off to Mavis McIntosh he said to her, 'I hardly expect you to like the book. I don't like it. It is terrible. But I hope when you finish it, in the disorder you will feel a terrible kind of order.'[16]

McIntosh reassured her nervous author that it was a good book and passed the manuscript to Covici–Friede, as planned. Meanwhile, Pat Covici had written to Steinbeck asking for publicity material for *Tortilla Flat* (the usual photograph and biographical blurb). In a gesture that startled even himself, Steinbeck refused to cooperate in any way. He asked McIntosh to have a talk with Covici and explain that he wanted publicity for the book but not for himself. 'Good writing comes out of an absence of ego,' he told her fiercely, adding that 'any procedure which is designed to make a writer ego-conscious is definitely detrimental to any future work.'

This is the core of Steinbeck's rocklike artistic firmness. He understood the need to put the work before the personality, a point clearly missed by so many writers in what has become the Age of Publicity. A genuine writer, a writer committed to bringing into being works of the highest order, must disappear behind (or into) his or her work. The rest is distraction, and dangerous.

The issue of publicity was quickly resolved, with Covici backing down, but more trouble lay ahead. Not two weeks after the manuscript of *In Dubious Battle* was submitted to Covici–Friede, a letter rejecting it appeared at the office of McIntosh & Otis. Once again it seemed that a rocky road to publication was to be Steinbeck's fate, with rejections and disappointments lying in wait. Apparently the manuscript had been given to Harry Black, an editor at Covici–Friede, while Pat Covici was out of town for a week. Black was a Marxist of some stripe and read the novel with distaste. 'The book is totally inaccurate,' he wrote to Mavis McIntosh. He also felt it would not sell a copy: 'It is sure to offend people on the right as well as the left.'

Black's letter was forwarded to Steinbeck, who confessed himself 'deeply shocked by the attitude of Covici'.[17] 'Answering the complaint that the ideology is incorrect,' he fumed, 'this is the silliest of criticism. There are as many communist systems as there are communists.' He was disgusted by 'cocktail circuit' communists like Black. With considerable perspective, he explained that it was useless to postulate 'an ideal communist' since communists, like all others, are human beings and therefore 'subject to the weaknesses of humans and to the greatness of humans'. The letter ends with a poignant summation of where Steinbeck found himself, psychologically, at that moment: 'I am so tired. I have worked for so long against opposition, first of my parents who wanted me to be a lawyer and then of publishers who want me to be anything but a writer, that I work well under opposition. If ever I had things my own way I would probably go dry.' He had been hoping to go to Mexico with Carol for a vacation, but that plan was scotched now. He was also wary of beginning his 'big book', what would be 'a very grave attempt to do a first-rate piece of work'. Here one detects the first, self-conscious glimmerings of the ambition to write a book on the scale of *The Grapes of Wrath*.

Meanwhile, as he fretted over the fate of *In Dubious Battle*, his father was caught up in his own last struggle. John Ernst had grown steadily weaker throughout February, and by March he was so ill that one of his daughters, Esther, took him to live with her in Watsonville, in a large, handsome Victorian house with her husband and children. 'John had done so much for mother during her illness,' recalls Beth, 'and now Esther felt it was her turn to do something.'

Elizabeth Otis now took over Steinbeck's career at the agency, and from March onwards she dealt with him instead of Mavis McIntosh. She and Steinbeck became friends rather quickly, and in the coming years he relied on her heavily for advice and encouragement. She not only admired his writing, but she liked the man, and she believed in his vision. Otis passed the manuscript to an editor she knew at Bobbs-Merrill, and he promptly accepted it. In the meantime, Pat Covici returned to the office and discovered what Harry Black had done to Steinbeck; he was enraged and reacted by firing Black on the spot. Then he wrote an apologetic letter to Steinbeck, asking for the novel back. Elizabeth Otis urged her client to mull it over and decide: he could move on to Bobbs-Merrill or return to Covici. Steinbeck, trusting his gut instincts, chose to remain with Pat Covici. This was the last time he would change editors.

In late May, John Ernst died peacefully in his sleep, and John and Carol hurried to Salinas to make the funeral arrangements. 'I should have preferred no service at all for Dad,' he wrote to his godmother, Elizabeth Bailey, in a passage reminiscent of the end of Sinclair Lewis's *Babbitt*, 'I can think of nothing for him so eloquent as silence. Poor silent man all his life. I feel very badly, not about his death, but about his life, for he told me only a few months ago that he had never done anything he wanted to do. Worst of all he hadn't done the work he wanted to do.'[18] This is a devastating commentary on the life of John Ernst Steinbeck, who – in his son's eyes – had been a Walter Mitty character, a feckless man who had never dared to live the life he could imagine or do the work he had hoped to accomplish. One hears, underneath Steinbeck's sad cadences, his own note of resolve. He would certainly do the work he planned to do. He would not be dragged down by the example of his father. He would do what *he* wanted, not what his parents or anyone else prescribed.

Tortilla Flat appeared five days after the death of John Ernst. Although Steinbeck didn't realize it at first, it was the turning point that he had been expecting for so long. From now on, he was no longer in the category of 'struggling writer'. He would never again (despite his frequent protestations to the contrary) lack for money, and he would never again lack the world's attention.

*

As if he knew that his life was going to take a good turn, Steinbeck went out and bought some lumber; this was a time to build. With help from a few friends, he converted the garage of Pacific Grove cottage into a small but comfortable workroom with a stove for heating and a desk for his faithful Corona. Here he could work without disturbing Carol. In a sense, this writing room symbolized his independence; now that both of his parents were dead, he was his own man. His fourth novel had been published, and the fifth accepted. There was, at least in his own mind, no doubt about the direction of his career.

Tortilla Flat was, and remains, an admirable book, one of Steinbeck's genuine achievements. In its preface, the author explains what the story will be: 'For Danny's house was not unlike the Round Table [of King Arthur], and Danny's friends were not unlike the knights of it. And this is the story of how that group came into being, of how it flourished and grew to be an organization beautiful and wise. This story deals with the adventures of Danny's friends, with the good they did, with their thoughts and their endeavors. In the end, this story tells how the talisman was lost and how the group disintegrated.' The chapter titles make the themes of each clear: 'How Danny, home from the wars, found himself an heir, and how he swore to protect the helpless' or 'How three sinful men, through contrition, attained peace. How Danny's friends swore comradeship'. As a lifelong admirer of the *Morte D'Arthur*, Steinbeck was forever trying to write stories that recreated the spirit of those mythic adventures, and he admired chivalry in all its aspects.

There was something wonderfully droll about the association of Danny and his *paisano* friends with the Round Table of King Arthur. In this manoeuvre, Steinbeck's especially American qualities shine through: his rooted belief in democratic values and in what has more recently been called the 'meritocracy'. One is a knight by order of one's inward self;

one cannot inherit this brand of nobility. Walt Whitman, the self-appointed genius of democracy, stands behind Steinbeck here, singing his 'Song of the Open Road' –

> From this hour I ordain myself loos'd of limits and imaginary
>   lines,
> Going where I list, my own master total and absolute,
> Listening to others, considering well what they say,
> Pausing, searching, receiving, contemplating,
> Gently, but with undeniable will, divesting myself of the holds
>   that would hold me.

Still, one must not read *Tortilla Flat* simply as Malory dressed in the white blouse and long beard of Whitman. Right from the start, with its mock-epic tone, Steinbeck's novel runs its own course; the adventures of Danny, Pilon, the Pirate, Jesus Maria, Big Joe Portagee, and all the others in this motley community, have their own splendid integrity. The book was not written to idealize these 'noble savages' or to amuse middle-class readers wanting to go slumming with a book about the lower orders; Steinbeck was hoping, as he wrote to his agents, to examine 'the strong but different philosophical-moral system' of these *paisanos*. As in his two previous novels, he was also interested in the idea of group behaviour, the phalanx.

In brief, Danny inherits two adjoining houses in the Tortilla Flat area of Monterey and soon finds himself sharing his good fortune with some of his wino friends. A group code, analogous to the code of King Arthur, comes into being, and individual behaviour is constantly tested and measured against the group code. One instance of this occurs when Danny and his buddies try to get the Pirate to live with them because he is 'rich'. They want to steal his money, which they have been combing the nearby forest to unearth, without success. When the Pirate agrees to live with them, he cleverly gives them his money for safe-keeping, realizing that the *paisanos* will not steal his money now; they, too, are aware that 'it was all over, all hope of diverting the money. . . . There was nothing in the world they could do about it. Their chance had come, and it had gone.' The sacred trust of friendship would, and must, hold. When, in a later chapter, Big Joe Portagee does pilfer some of the Pirate's treasure, his friends punish him with a brutality that is startling. A code is a code.

Steinbeck uses these loosely connected stories, an off-shoot of the form he had developed in *The Pastures of Heaven*, to satirize bourgeois morality once again. The most essential plank in the platform of bourgeois life is a belief in the sacredness of private property, and *Tortilla Flat* represents a huge send-up of this notion. One chapter focuses, for example, on Dolores 'Sweets' Ramirez, who owns a vacuum cleaner, a potent symbol of bourgeois respectability. She has 'climbed to the peak of the social scale of Tortilla Flat', Steinbeck tells us. Within the community, which mirrors the bourgeois world beyond it, she is known as 'that one with the sweeping-machine'. She is seen by passers-by as she is whisking it through her little cottage, 'pushing the cleaner back and forth'. And they envy her, although her manner is unfailingly dignified and gracious; indeed, 'she held her chin high as befitted one who had a sweeping-machine'. Alas, the house has no electricity, and even if it did the machine has no motor. Appearance is everything.

Danny and his friends, however chivalric as a group, belong to a larger and less heroic society. The bourgeois world looms nearby, and its cult of individualism is perpetually threatening to corrupt this merry band. The 'philosophic-moral system' that undergirds *paisano* life in this novel crumbles in the end, and Steinbeck's charming characters sink into 'a depressed lassitude from which only the riotous and fatal party awakens them', as he wrote to Mavis McIntosh. Steinbeck, in effect, brandishes the sword of satire to point up defects in American society, although he does not go so far as to suggest that the *paisano* way of life is in any way superior to that of the mainstream. *Tortilla Flat* has limited aims, and it cannot be called a 'political' novel in any real sense. The author's satirical tone is a device for maintaining an aesthetic distance from the *paisanos*, for gently poking fun at them while viewing them sympathetically.

Recent critics have tried to reconcile Steinbeck's benign, often whimsical, attitude to poverty in *Tortilla Flat* (and two subsequent novels in the same vein, *Cannery Row* and *Sweet Thursday*) with the harsher approach taken in his 'protest' novels of the late Thirties. Sylvia J. Cook, in a recent article, suggests that there is no real contradiction here: 'The poor are Steinbeck's heroes not because they have arrived at any superior knowledge or conduct but because they are open, irreverently, to the possibility that there is no moral knowledge at all. They are engaged in, but have not finally resolved, the enduring conflicts between the virtues of society and those of solitude, between an active and a contemplative life, between the lure of flesh and the lure of the spirit, between responsibility and freedom.'[19] What varies from book to book is the degree of choice involved in the poverty of certain characters; the less choice, the less Steinbeck is willing to write benignly about their state. The ideal state for a human being with regard to wealth is what Thoreau in the first chapter of *Walden* calls 'voluntary poverty'. Thoreau wrote: 'None can be an impartial or wise observer of human life but from the vantage ground of what we should call voluntary poverty,' a condition which presupposes an adequate supply of food, shelter, clothing, and fuel, for 'not till we have secured these are we prepared to entertain the true problems of life with freedom and a prospect of success.'

The critics liked *Tortilla Flat*, and so did Steinbeck's many readers. Although the author loathed publicity, he could not avoid it now. A profile of him appeared in the *San Francisco Chronicle*, the first of many. He cut an intriguing figure for journalists to discuss. Here was a man who wrote directly out of his firsthand experience of the Depression. It was a good story, and the setting was irresistible. Furthermore, the writer was obviously a born storyteller. Warm reviews appeared in the *New York Herald Tribune*, in the *Los Angeles Times* and *The New York Times*, a few of the many periodicals that reviewed it well and at length.

In mid-August, Pat Covici appeared in California with the first royalty cheque from the sales of *Tortilla Flat* for almost $300. He met the Steinbecks in San Francisco and returned with them to Pacific Grove for the weekend. Author and editor got along well, even though Covici was very different in style from Steinbeck. A dapper man of Italian extraction, he favoured expensive Italian suits and handmade shoes. His black Borsolino was tipped rakishly to one side, and he carried a brown leather briefcase. His neatly trimmed hair was greying at the sides, just enough to make him look, as he said, 'distinguished'. He professed great admiration for Steinbeck's work, and Steinbeck, though wary of glib praise, was grateful for the enthusiastic support of his publisher – something he had not always enjoyed in the past.

With the cheque from Covici, the Steinbecks revived their plan to visit Mexico and set off happily in mid-September in the Model-A Ford sedan inherited from John Ernst. They had recently become friendly with a book reviewer from San Francisco named Joseph Henry Jackson, and they planned to meet Jackson and his wife in Mexico City on their way to a town called Puebla, where they would stay for two or three months. As it happened, Mexico City itself was so appealing to the Steinbecks that they decided to stay there instead, taking an apartment just off the Pasco de la Reforma. One gets a sense of what their life was like there in letters to George Albee. 'The air down here has a feel,' Steinbeck wrote, 'you can feel its texture on your finger tips and on your lips. It is like water.'[20]

Mexico appealed to both Steinbecks, with its richly textured landscape and colonial architecture, its robustly open people, and the aura of an ancient, continuing culture that seemed to suffuse every object or social manifestation. 'Carol is having a marvelous time,' her husband reported. 'The people like her and she likes them. Wherever she goes, howls of laughter follow.' Carol was collecting little clay animals (a Mexican speciality) and she went into a market where they were sold and said, blithely, to the man behind the counter: '*Quiero un toro*' (I want a bull). The phrase also means 'I want a stud', and the people burst into giggles. Carol, befuddled, blundered on. She said that she wanted one with flowers painted on its stomach. The man said, 'Sure, I have a bull, but he has no flowers on his stomach.' The crowd roared now, and the story spilled through the entire market.

Auspicious news came in November. Paramount had bought the film rights to *Tortilla Flat* for a sum of four thousand dollars, four times the amount Steinbeck had made in all his years of writing. Covici also wired that the novel had reached the bottom rung of several bestseller lists. Steinbeck's years of poverty had come to an abrupt halt. But, always wary of these signs of outward success, Steinbeck wrote to Albee: 'I am not proud of this sale of *Tortilla* to the pictures, but we'll slap it into government bonds which are cashable, and forget about it.' He assured his friend that 'the old standard of living stays right where it has always been'.

After three and a hàlf months, the Steinbecks had had their fill of Mexico City, and they returned to Pacific Grove via New York, where they stayed just long enough for Steinbeck to sign the Paramount deal. They were home by the end of December with the movie contract signed and royalties flowing on the sale of the novel. With one-quarter of his parents' estate in hand now, Steinbeck felt reasonably secure about the future for the first time in his life. He could plan to set aside a few years to write the 'big book' if he chose to do so. He could live wherever he pleased.

Soon after settling down he heard from Joe Jackson that he had been awarded a prize for the best novel of 1935 from the Commonwealth Club of California. He was 'stunned and delighted', as he said, but he would not appear personally to accept the award; 'The whole early part of my life was poisoned with egotism,' he explained. 'A reverse egotism, of course, beginning with self-consciousness. And then gradually I began to lose it.' He noted that in the 'last few books' he had identified 'in a most real way with people who were not me'. He calls himself an unheroic person. Nevertheless, 'the work has been the means of making me feel that I am living richly, diversely, and, in a few cases and for a few moments, even heroically.' This vivid, self-understanding letter concludes: 'I hate to run away, but I feel that the whole future working life is tied up in this distinction between work and person. And while this whole argument may seem specious, I assure you it is heartfelt.'[21]

VIII

The Front Line of Poverty

'I shall never learn to conceive of money in larger
quantities than two dollars.'

Steinbeck to Elizabeth Otis, 27 January 1937

By the mid-Thirties the genteel tradition of American fiction
had moved over and made room for what might, for lack of a
better term, be called 'political' fiction. The muckraking and
semi-documentary novels of writers like Sherwood
Anderson, Upton Sinclair and Theodore Dreiser had
acquired a readership some years before. 'I am accepted by
working people everywhere as one of themselves and I am
proud of that fact,' Anderson had famously, if somewhat
fantastically, remarked. But the subject of politics was now
pushed to the front by the sharp economic and social
inequities of American life, and many younger writers began
to think of themselves as activists.

The Depression played a key role in this shift of consciousness. Magazines like the *New Masses* and *The New Republic*
called for 'author-fighters' and 'worker-correspondents' to
join the cause, which was conceived in rather conventional
Marxist terms as 'owners of the means of production' versus
'workers'. Novelists like Jack Conroy, himself a steelworker,
came into temporary vogue. Richard Wright, the black writer
who would later gain a lasting audience, began to find
readers. Henry Roth's vivid portrait of growing up on New
York's Lower East Side, *Call It Sleep*, appeared in 1934 and
was warmly praised and widely read. Michael Gold's novel,
Jews Without Money, attracted a small but sympathetic
audience, as did Edward Dahlberg's vividly polemical

Bottom Dogs. Another populist novel, one that anticipated Steinbeck's *In Dubious Battle*, was *Strike!* by Mary Heaton Vorse. The turn-of-the-century political novels of Frank Norris, as mentioned, were especially important for Steinbeck, who read them avidly.

A well-publicized organization of the day was the John Reed Club, which took as its slogan, 'Art Is a Class Weapon'. The idea was that paintings and novels and poems should be used to influence people, to change their minds and create class solidarity among the workers. Thirty 'cells' of this club had formed by 1935, and the New York chapter founded a literary magazine to promote its ideas called the *Partisan Review*. Its politics, similar to those of the first American Writers' Congress of 1935, were (roughly speaking) Stalinist, although followers of Leon Trotsky could be found scattered among the Stalinists. The surge towards radicalism peaked in the mid-Thirties, just when Steinbeck was writing *In Dubious Battle*, and it would slow down after the infamous Moscow show trials of 1937, when it became obvious that Stalin was a vicious totalitarian dictator. (The signing of the Soviet-Nazi pact in 1939 was, for most intellectual Marxists of the Thirties, the last straw, though some stragglers did not depart the ranks of the Communist Party until the 1956 invasion of Hungary.)

Covici–Friede brought out *In Dubious Battle* on 15 January 1936, and the response was predictably strong, building upon the interest in Steinbeck's work that had been growing in the aftermath of *Tortilla Flat*, which was still on many bestseller lists throughout the country. Reviewers generally liked the book, although many complained about Steinbeck's use of violence, a complaint that would surface frequently in critical responses to Steinbeck's work of the Thirties. 'It seems that violence in itself has an inherent fascination for Steinbeck,' wrote one critic in typical mode, 'that its appeal lies merely in the glitter of the knife, the tearing of the flesh, the hangings, shootings, mutilations with which his work is filled.'[1]

Another prominent dissenting voice was Mary McCarthy, who would go on to considerable fame herself as a novelist and critic; she was then a young Vassar graduate, and she reviewed the novel for *The Nation*, calling it 'academic, wooden, inert'.[2] She complained that the 'dramatic events take place for the most part off-stage and are reported, as in the Greek drama, by a breathless observer'. With a bravura found often in young reviewers, she passed resounding final judgement on the capacities of John Steinbeck: 'He may be a natural story-teller; but he is certainly no philosopher, sociologist, or strike technician.'

McCarthy's views notwithstanding, *In Dubious Battle* must be considered one of Steinbeck's early successes. Its violence is hardly exaggerated, as this account of a strike in the lettuce fields around Salinas suggests, attesting to the level of brutality commonplace in this era:

> In 1936 a strike by lettuce packing shed workers was crushed at a cost of around a quarter of a million dollars. Civil liberties, local government, and normal judicial processes were all suspended during the strike and Salinas was governed by a general staff directed by the Associated Farmers and the big lettuce growers and shippers. The local police were bossed by a reserve army officer imported for the job and at the height of the strike all male residents between 18 and 45 were mobilized under penalty of arrest, were deputized and armed. Beatings, tear gas attacks, wholesale arrests, threats to lynch San Francisco newspapermen if they didn't leave town, and machine guns and barbed wire all figured in the month-long struggle which finally broke the strike and destroyed the union.

'I remember that strike,' says Willard Stevens, whose father was a strike leader.[3] 'John Steinbeck met with my father and the others. He didn't say much, but he stood by the farmers.

He knew a senator in Washington and he said he was going to get the federal authorities involved. The way the police were acting made him mad.' Stevens adds, 'I remember how my father claimed the feds wouldn't do a damn thing for the strikers, that they were on the other side, in fact. He told Steinbeck they were the problem, not the solution.' In fact, Steinbeck was sceptical of both extremes and eager to create a balanced impression in his novel, although his sympathies lay with the strikers overall. Once again, his interest is focused on the phalanx or group man, and on how once the farmers get organized they seem to become a separate entity.

The influence of Ed Ricketts continues to make itself felt, with the character of Doc Burton in the novel directly representing Ricketts and his detached, non-teleological viewpoint. But Steinbeck's sympathies occasionally seem at odds with Doc's as the afternoon debates that took place in the lab at Pacific Biological in Monterey are played out in the context of this fictional narrative.

As a westerner, Steinbeck could not help but celebrate the rugged individual who stands apart from the masses. His early interest in Malory yielded a lifelong commitment to the notion of heroism. *In Dubious Battle* thus follows the political adventures of one man, Jim Nolan, who quite literally 'wakes up' and smells the bacon. He has been sitting in a chair, stupefied, for a long time as the novel opens. One of American literature's classic *isolatos*, he is a man without a past, having no family, no property, and no visible attachments. He abandons his few connections to the people in the boarding house where he lives and takes to the road, having made the firm decision to join 'the Party'. 'I feel dead,' he tells the recruiter who has talked him into joining. 'I thought I might get alive again.'[4]

What he gets, finally, is dead. But in the meantime there is a great deal of life to be had through his experience with the group. Nolan is sent on the road with Mac, an experienced

Party man, to organize strikers. They soon arrive in the Torgas Valley, where the task is to mobilize some migrant apple pickers. Nolan watches with amazement as Mac delivers a baby at a makeshift campsite where these 'crop tramps' are living like animals, hand to mouth. Mac has no right to deliver a baby, of course; he is not a doctor, but he sees this act as a way to enter into sympathy with the young woman's father-in-law, London, a leader among the migrants. He explains his rationale to Nolan:

> We've got to use whatever material comes to us. That was a lucky break. We simply had to take it. 'Course it was nice to help the girl, but hell, even if it killed her – we've got to use anything . . . With one night's work we've got the confidence of the men and the confidence of London. And more than that, we made the men work for themselves, in their own defense as a group. That's what we're here for anyway, to teach them to fight in a bunch. Raising wages isn't all we're after.

Steinbeck summons a sequence of minor characters on the side of the apple pickers: Al Anderson, the owner of a local diner; Dick, the 'bedroom radical' who has a unique ability to gather funds from local Party sympathizers; and London himself, whose good standing in the community is crucial to his general usefulness and influence. Mac teaches these men to get themselves 'elected' as strike leaders. (The fact that 'democracy' is being manipulated does not bother Mac, who is cavalier about ends and means. Nothing concerns him but getting the job done.)

The Torgas Valley Growers' Association gathers the bad guys under one rubric, and they are a spiteful bunch. They line up 'the authorities' behind them, including the banks, the courts, the police, and most of the respectable local citizenry. The Association is flush with money for bribes, and they don't hesitate to use this cash to oppose the migrant workers. A violent chain reaction begins when a sniper's bullet kills Joy, who has been a good friend to Mac and Jim. This gives Mac his martyr, and the conflict really gets underway. An orgy of recrimination and mob action occurs as the 'phalanx' spins out of control on both sides.

Jim Nolan is, as one might expect, lost in the sweep of events. When he shows signs of 'weakening', Mac (who is almost too heartless to believe) says, 'Don't you go liking people, Jim. We can't waste time liking people.' Near the end, when Nolan is torn to shreds by shotgun fire, Mac props the lifeless body near a strikers' camp as a symbol of martyrdom, a call-to-arms for another round of violence. Clearly, Steinbeck parts company with Mac here. The reader's sympathies inevitably lie with the poor strikers, the apple pickers, who are ruthlessly mistreated by everyone, but Steinbeck is careful not to idealize them; he also goes a long way not to idealize the Party organizers, who use methods of group manipulation that chill the reader's blood. The strikers are generally not so violent as their opponents, but that is probably a result of their lack of weapons and nothing else. They bite, kick, pound, stomp, screech and burn, flailing at the authorities who oppress them so cruelly.

The characters in this drama are locked, as the line from *Paradise Lost* suggests, 'In dubious battle on the plains of heaven'. Critics have drawn the appropriate parallels between Milton's epic and Steinbeck's novel, seeing the Party as Satan (red is the Devil's colour), with London serving as Beelzebub, Satan's right-hand man. Dick, the 'bedroom radical', is Belial, and so forth. The debates about how to proceed against 'the authorities' echo similar debates among the fallen angels of Milton's epic. Once again, Steinbeck has linked his plot to some earlier work of literature, a typical modernist ploy.

The Christ symbolism seen in *To a God Unknown* is present again in this novel, with Jim Nolan standing in as Jesus, the figure who appears from nowhere with a passion for the

outcast and downtrodden; he ultimately sacrifices himself –
quite literally – for the sake of 'his people'. Steinbeck
reinforces these associations in several ways: near the end of
Chapter 13 one hears roosters crowing; when Jim is suffering
from his wound, he asks for water; in the last chapter we are
told that Nolan's 'face was transfigured. A furious light of
energy seemed to shine from it.' And after Nolan's murder,
Mac says of him, 'This guy didn't want nothing for himself,'
emphasizing his Christlike nature.

Chivalry and heroism were never far from Steinbeck's
mind, and Warren French wisely detects the Arthurian
legend emerging once more, citing 'a remarkable psychological similarity between Jim Nolan, the central character of
the novel, and one of the principal knights of the Round
Table, Perceval or Parsifal as he is best known. . . .'[4] Nolan is
seen as 'a modern exemplar of the chivalric ideals of
adventurousness (he longs for action and is finally killed by
his impetuousness), selflessness, and chastity'.

Critics often like to dwell on mythic and textual sources, but
this hunting for allusions can take one down irrelevant
byeways. Like Joyce and Eliot and any number of other
writers, Steinbeck used myth to organize his ideas and
ground his work in archetypal patterns. The important point
is that Steinbeck summoned a reality that was fresh and
highly particularized, always trying to examine 'the group'
and its effects on the individual. While he did want to make
certain political points in this book, he could hardly be called
a crude ideologue. The novel moves beyond a study of social
unrest and the oppression of the poor to a study of what one
critic, Julian Hartt, has called 'eschatological man'.[5] Hartt
suggests that *In Dubious Battle* 'deals seriously with eschatological man. Eschatological man so imaged is a creature with a
terrible duality of motivations: violent resentment of the
social forces which have cheated him out of his rights; and

passionate attachment to a splendid vision of an age to come when the furious conflict generated by injustice will have been resolved forever into the peace of a classless community.'

One senses this duality of attachments in Steinbeck himself. He had a peculiar and noble sympathy for those who were cheated of their natural birthright and dignity. Injustice drove him wild; as his sister, Beth, says, 'Even as a child John sided with the underdog.' These 'radical' or, more precisely, 'liberal' sympathies bound him psychologically to the present struggle, whatever it might be; on the other hand, his philosophical and spiritual drive led him to posit a utopian moment, 'the peace of a classless community'. All progressive politics depend on this duality, and Steinbeck (in his most activist period) seems to have drawn great energies from this unusually generative 'conflict'.[6]

Having had good luck in selling *Tortilla Flat* to Paramount, Elizabeth Otis set to work to get a film offer for *In Dubious Battle*. Hollywood was not interested, but Otis soon struck a deal with Herman Shumlin, a Broadway producer, who contracted John O'Hara to adapt the novel for the stage. O'Hara was at this point a much admired writer of short stories for *The New Yorker* and other magazines, although he had very little experience in writing for the stage. Steinbeck reported to Otis: 'Now for the dramatic thing. John O'Hara stopped on his way to San Francisco. I do not know his work, but I liked him and his attitude. I think we could get along well. I do not believe in collaboration. If he will maintain the intention and theme of the book (and I am convinced that he will) I shall not interfere with him at all. He said he would come up in a month with some script to go over. I am pleased with him as the man to do the job.'[7]

O'Hara later recalled that visit to Pacific Grove, saying that Steinbeck 'had kept him up all night with talk of the phalanx'. During this encounter O'Hara firmly insisted that anybody with Steinbeck's gift for narrative and dialogue would be able to write plays and screenplays in his sleep. This conversation stimulated Steinbeck's interest in the theatre and set him thinking. He eagerly awaited the O'Hara script, but nothing came of the project. When several months passed with no word from O'Hara, Steinbeck in frustration sat down to try to write the play adaptation for Shumlin himself. This too came to nothing, although it did get him thinking about his next novel in terms of a play.

Meanwhile, the Steinbecks came back from Mexico and settled into the house on 11th Street in January 1936. The weather was drizzly and cold, and Carol's sinuses began to act up. For some time she had been eager to leave Pacific Grove, and now she argued that it was time to move somewhere consistently hot and dry. The old cottage was too small, she complained; now that they had some money – quite a lot of money by their standards – shouldn't they move into a bigger house? Should they not buy something of their own? (Ownership of the cottage had been divided among the children by John Ernst and Olive Steinbeck.)

Steinbeck was very ambivalent about his new financial situation. The memory of what it was like to live close to the poverty line persisted; indeed, it was but a few months before this period that he had wondered if he could make it through the year without taking a job that paid a salary. He was also afraid that if the money continued to roll in (as it would) he would lose something of himself, and that this would adversely affect his writing. A sense of writing from poverty felt like an essential aspect of his creativity, which was grounded in a defiance of his parents' bourgeois attitudes. 'The subject of money drove him kind of crazy,' Toby Street later recalled, 'and this was true even after money was no longer an issue, when he was in reality a wealthy man. He needed to think he was poor.'[8]

In April, Carol found a piece of land that ran along a

gorgeous canyon in a thickly wooded area some fifty miles north of Monterey, called Los Gatos. She convinced her husband to buy the two-acre parcel and to let her build a house there, something that would genuinely be theirs and not a hand-me-down from the Steinbeck family. She was also eager to get away from Ed Ricketts, who tended to monopolize her husband and to ignore her. (Doubtless the affair with Joseph Campbell was still troubling her, and the Monterey setting reminded her of him.) A local carpenter-contractor who had worked on previous occasions for Carol's father was hired to supervise the construction, and Carol stayed with a friend nearby to oversee the project. The architectural plans were almost entirely Carol's, although Steinbeck sketched in a version of the room that would be his study, a workroom not unlike the one in Pacific Grove. He wanted isolation, and he insisted on having a cot in the room because when he was working intensely he liked to sleep in the room where he wrote; this somehow bound him, emotionally, to the project. It may also have helped to erase the borders between 'reality' and 'fiction'. The world of the text became everything.

Because of its remoteness, the house in Los Gatos, known as 'the Biddle place' because of the land's previous owners, did not yet have access to electricity or telephone lines, and Steinbeck liked these 'deficiencies'. Although he was not yet besieged for interviews, he had experienced enough of this pressure to convince him that sanity lay in avoiding the press; at least he could be certain in Los Gatos that the phone would not ring. The remote setting also recalled the compound at Lake Tahoe where *Cup of Gold* had been written.

Back in Pacific Grove, Steinbeck continued working on a story originally intended for children that would soon turn into *Of Mice and Men*, his most popular novella. For some time the idea that he should be writing plays or screenplays had been floating through his head, and to one friend he said, 'Between us, I think the novel is painfully dead. I've never liked it. I'm going into training to write for the theater, which seems to be waking up. I have some ideas for a new dramatic form which I'm experimenting with.'⁹ He fiddled with this 'experimental' work for several months and had a substantial manuscript in hand when, in early May, his new puppy (a setter called Toby) decided that his master's book would make a good lunch. Steinbeck told Elizabeth Otis that the dog had 'made confetti of about half of my ms. book', leaving him with 'two months work to do over again'. With considerable optimism, he estimated that by the beginning of the summer his 'new little manuscript', which he called *Something That Happened*, would be ready for publication.

In early July, with the novel still unfinished, the Steinbecks moved their relatively few belongings to the new house. (In the reshuffle, Steinbeck found an early draft of 'The Red Pony' that he had panicked about having lost.) The Los Gatos place suited the Steinbecks very well, and Carol was relieved to have her husband all to herself, away from 'the boys at the lab', as she called them. She had shipped two trunks full of quaint art objects from Mexico City, and she filled the house with them now: painted vases, little clay animals, pieces of colourful woven fabric, ceremonial masks used by the Indians. (One night when the moon was full Steinbeck slipped out of bed and donned one of these masks and leaped about the house naked, frightening Carol and the dog. She begged him never to do that again, fearing that he would provoke some ancient Indian deity.)

Steinbeck felt extremely happy in his new study, and he got up at dawn every morning to write. As he approached the end of most books, he would grow impatient and excited, pressing to the finish and sleeping in the same room as the manuscript. Without the distraction of Ed Ricketts and his friends at Pacific Biological, he worked dawn to dusk. It was, for the moment, 'all work and no play', as he told his agent. In a ledger that he kept that summer, he wrote: 'For the moment the financial burdens have been removed. But it is not permanent. I was not made for success.'[10] When he got down to discussing his short novel, he was no more sanguine about its quality. 'It is an experiment and I don't know how successful. It is two-thirds done. There are problems in it, difficult of resolution. But the biggest problem is a resolution of will. The *rewards* of work are so sickening to me that I do more with the greatest reluctance. The mind and will must concentrate again and to a purpose.'

Every morning he settled at his oak desk in his small workroom with a view of the canyon, the manuscript spread before him, always fighting to 'find the beauty to put into it'. He had a strong sense of 'experimentation'. This story was something new for him: a simple human tale, very bold in outline. He was no longer concerned so much with the phalanx. This tale of two lost souls, George and Lennie, was daringly simple. *Too simple?* he wondered. 'The idea of building too carefully for an event seems to me to be doing that old human trick of reducing everything to its simplest design. Now the designs of lives are not so simple.'

It was a 'long, slow summer' in which the marriage seemed to be going well. Steinbeck was utterly absorbed as he moved through various drafts of the novel, and Carol seemed content to write poems and garden and work on the new house, which still needed a lot of attention. They were 'practically camping' that summer, she said; the hope was that by the autumn the house would be fixed up as she wanted it. Steinbeck's pleasure in it is apparent in a letter to George Albee: 'I have a little tiny room to work in. Just big enough for a bed and a desk and a gun rack and a little book case. I like to sleep in the room I work in. Just at present there is hammering going on. We are building on a guest room. We had none and really need one. It will have big glass doors and screens so that it will really be an outside porch when we want to open the doors. Dr McDoughal of Carnegie was up

1 The Steinbeck House, 132
Central, Salinas, California, in
which Steinbeck was born.

2 & 3 Steinbeck's parents, John Ernst Steinbeck and Olive Hamilton Steinbeck.

opposite
4 Mary and John on Jill, the 'red pony'. This picture was sent out as a postcard by the Steinbecks in 1907.

5 11th Street House, Pacific Grove, California; the house that belonged to Steinbeck's parents was a touchstone for him, according to Elaine Steinbeck.

Here we are. Mary, John & Jill – Salinas Aug 28 07

6 Carol Henning Steinbeck, Steinbeck's first wife. According to a friend she 'ignited his conscience'.

7 The Steinbeck ranch, Los Gatos, where John and Carol lived before the break-up of their marriage. He called this property 'the most beautiful place in the world'.

8 Edward F. Ricketts, who became a great friend during the thirties.

9 Steinbeck with Carl Sandburg, another important friend, in 1963.

10 Tom Collins, manager of
Kern County Migrant Camp,
with a resident, 1936. *The
Grapes of Wrath* is partially
dedicated 'to Tom — who
lived it'.

overleaf

12 Gwyn Conger Steinbeck, Steinbeck's second wife, prior to their marriage. Their interrupted affair was rekindled when Steinbeck by chance heard her sing on the radio and rushed to visit her.

11 A migrant family stops for roadside repairs in California, 1936.

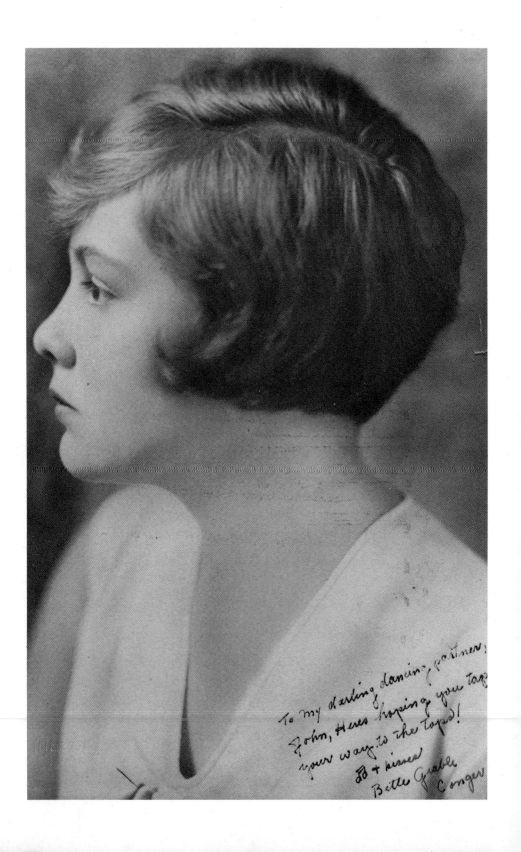

To My darling dancing partner,
John, Heres hoping you tap
your way to the tops!
Σ + kisses
Betty Grable
Conger

the other day and told us we have six varieties of oaks on the place besides manzanata, madrone and toyon. We're in a forest, you know.'[11] Steinbeck was happy, savouring the seclusion. His relationship with Carol had become less strained, and this seemed to him another by-product of the move from Pacific Grove. The fact that his novel was going well only enhanced his good feelings towards the place.

As noted in Chapter Two, the story had its origins in the author's experience of hoboes ('bindlestiffs') and migrant workers. In a startling interview that appeared on 5 December 1937, just after the play version of the story appeared on Broadway, he gave *The New York Times* a lurid account of having seen a man just like Lennie attack his foreman with a pitchfork. The man 'stuck a pitchfork right through his stomach', Steinbeck said with a straight face. One must take the general cautionary note of D. H. Lawrence to heart here, 'Trust the tale, not the teller.' The origin of a novel or story is necessarily obscure, buried in dreams, in sleights of thought, inklings, odd bits of overheard conversation. Steinbeck certainly had enough daily contact with men like George and Lennie in his youthful peregrinations and work-stints; he knew from experience how they thought, talked and felt. He may indeed have heard reports of a case similar to that of Lennie's. Or – perhaps the least likely possibility – he may indeed have witnessed a hobo sticking a pitchfork through his foreman's stomach.

Steinbeck was also a clever borrower of material from other writers. One hesitates to call him a 'plagiarist', as some critics have; literature is a tissue of allusions, and good writers invariably weave the notions, even phrases, of other texts into their text. They often suffer, in Harold Bloom's famous phrase, 'the anxiety of influence'. More often, they simply take what they need and, in so doing, transmogrify the material into their own. Scott Fitzgerald, no mean plagiarist himself, thought that Steinbeck had gone too far in *Of Mice and Men*. He wrote to Edmund Wilson about Steinbeck's dependence on Frank Norris:

> I'd like to put you on to something about Steinbeck. He is a
> rather cagey cribber. Most of us begin as imitators but it is
> something else for a man of his years and reputation to steal
> a whole scene as he did in 'Mice and Men'. I'm sending you
> a marked copy of Norris' 'McTeague' to show you what I
> mean. His debt to 'The Octopus' is also enormous and his
> balls, when he uses them, are usually clipped from
> Lawrence's 'Kangaroo'.[12]

In *McTeague*, there is a woman named Maria Macapa who has a relationship with a junk-dealer, Zerkow; Maria dreams of escaping from the hideous poverty of her surroundings much like Lennie; also like Lennie, she is often encouraged to recite her dream of the good life (although Zerkow torments her with this, whereas George has Lennie go through his litany of expectations just to make him feel better). The rhythms of their dialogue are deeply reminiscent of those in *Of Mice and Men*, but the similarities stop there.

The novel was finished by the second week in August and sent off to Elizabeth Otis, and Steinbeck entertained small hope that he would benefit materially from the book. 'I guess we'll have to pull in our horns financially,' he had written to George Albee, 'I don't expect the little book, *Of Mice and Men*, to make any money.' The reaction at the publisher was, as usual, mixed – Steinbeck had never yet written a book that everybody thought was going to do well – but Pat Covici claimed to like it and said he would bring it out 'early in the New Year'. Steinbeck sensed no real enthusiasm from Covici, although he was grateful that his editor was willing to stand behind him.

Covici had been standing firmly behind his new author, acquiring the rights to all of Steinbeck's earlier books (*Cup of Gold*, *The Pastures of Heaven* and *To a God Unknown*) and relaunching them in new editions with prefaces. Thus far, *Tortilla Flat* was by far the most commercially viable of Steinbeck's books, and it continued to sell steadily through the summer of 1936. The hostile reaction of some critics to *In Dubious Battle* had, unquestionably, depressed its sales, but it was none the less considered by Covici 'a moderate success'. The fact that Steinbeck appeared to be endlessly productive was heartening to Covici, who foresaw a long and continuing relationship between editor and author.

In mid-August, Steinbeck was visited by George West, a young editorial writer from the *San Francisco News* who had read and much admired *In Dubious Battle*. The bright-eyed journalist appealed to Steinbeck to write for his paper; much to his surprise, the novelist eagerly accepted a commission to write a sequence of pieces about the the situation of migrant farmers in California. The idea was that he should visit various regions of the state to witness firsthand the conditions under which these people lived and worked. West was especially interested in the success or failure of the camps set up by the federal government to aid the migrants, many of whom were undernourished and ill.

   Steinbeck always liked moving on to another project, especially one that would offer him a new kind of experience. He rushed out and bought an old bakery truck – a 'pie wagon' he called it – and transformed it into a version of the modern camper; it was fitted out with a cot, an ice box, a chest for storing clothes, and a trunk full of pots and plates. On 26 August he headed into San Francisco for a meeting with West and his colleagues to make sure that he understood the assignment exactly. He also visited the office of the Resettlement Administration, where he got a briefing about the federal programme in California to aid migrants; this was followed by a tour of the San Joaquin Valley led by the regional director of the organization, Eric H. Thomsen.

Thomsen drove Steinbeck down through the Central Valley, and they stopped at some of the camps along the way. He wanted the writer to see how different it was for families who had got help from the government and those who hadn't. The reality of the situation startled Steinbeck, who was unprepared for the starkness of what he saw: whole families lived in cardboard boxes or in large disused pipes; indeed, shelters were constructed from anything that came to hand – an old rug, some straw mats, cardboard, pieces of driftwood. Food was scarce and expensive, and people in some areas were reduced to eating rats and, it was rumoured, dogs. Babies were dying from lack of adequate nutrition or proper medical services. This was the front line of poverty in America, and Steinbeck was saddened and outraged.

He proceeded on his own after a certain point, stopping at some of the camps Thomsen had recommended, and everywhere he was stunned by the magnitude of the problem. The simple numbers were staggering; hundreds of thousands of families had arrived in California from the so-called Dust Bowl states of Oklahoma, Arkansas, Texas, and parts of Nebraska and Kansas. They were all called 'Okies' or 'Texicanos' by the Californians, whatever their state of origin, and they had all been rudely dispossessed, turned off the land their families had tilled for generations. In 1936 alone, almost ninety thousand Okies crossed the California border in search of jobs and a better life.

The Depression had combined with years of drought, land speculation and various wrongheaded agricultural practices to make survival in the Dust Bowl states impossible; the impoverished farms were being repossessed by banks and landowners. Another aspect of the problem was the drift toward 'agribusiness', which had begun in the Twenties; farming techniques were employed to maximize production, and one consequence of these techniques was that unexpectedly harsh winds blew away the topsoil in what were once fertile regions. The already precarious situation of farmers and sharecroppers in the southwest was miserably exacerbated.

The obvious place for migrants to go was California, with its extremely visible and successful agricultural industry, but they were sadly mistaken about their prospects. For a start, California's large-scale agriculture favoured the corporate farm: less than one-tenth of the farms generated over half the total produce in 1935. Absentee ownership was common, which meant that hired managers ran the farming operations. For many years these large farms had been encouraging the migration of badly paid foreign labourers; Chinese, Filipino, Mexican, and Japanese workers were commonplace, although the bulk were from nearby Mexico – a migratory trend that began in the first decade of the century and continues to this day. It was therefore not easy to filter a large new group of migrant workers into the system as it stood.

In a striking book published at the end of the Thirties titled *Factories in the Field*, Carey McWilliams described the change in the situation: 'In 1937 it became increasingly apparent that a basic change had taken place in the character of farm labor in California. Although the change had been taking place for some time, it was suddenly realized in 1937 that the bulk of the state's migratory workers were white Americans and that the foreign racial groups were no longer a dominant factor.'[13] The change had, in fact, begun about 1933, when the Depression had reached its lowest point. In 1925, only a small percentage of the agricultural labourers on large California farms were drawn from the white population, but the Commission of Immigration and Housing estimated in 1934 that roughly fifty per cent of the labour-camp population was native white American, with about one-third being Mexican and the rest from the relatively small Filipino, Japanese, and Chinese communities. This demographic shift naturally created huge problems of adjustment.

One of the many consequences of this influx of white American citizens accustomed to the working of democracy was that protests about low wages and poor working conditions were inevitable. As long as 'foreigners' were being exploited, the press was not going to say a word, but when 'regular' white Americans were being treated like dirt, herded into unsanitary camps, left to starve or work for starvation wages, a protest movement was bound to occur sooner or later. By 1935 Route 66, the major highway from Oklahoma to California's Central Valley, was clogged with jalopies, even though jobs were extremely scarce at the end of the journey. In his newspaper articles, Steinbeck describes in the starkest terms the mayhem that resulted:

> Thousands of them are crossing the borders in ancient rattling automobiles, destitute and hungry and homeless, ready to accept any pay so that they may eat and feed their children. And this is a new thing in migrant labor, for the foreign workers were usually imported without their children and everything that remains of their old life with them.
>
> They arrive in California usually having used up every resource to get here, even to the selling of the poor blankets and utensils and tools on the way to buy gasoline. They arrive bewildered and beaten and usually in a state of semi-starvation, with only one necessity to face immediately, and that is to find work at any wage in order that the family may eat.[14]

Most of the farms in the Central Valley were owned by corporations or wealthy farmers who operated multiple ranches, and their crops of fruits and vegetables had for many years been harvested by semi-skilled Mexicans or poor locals who did not mind earning ludicrous wages. The sudden surplus of labour led inexorably to grotesque living conditions and, ultimately, to violence as tens of thousands of Okies prowled the valley in competition for a handful of jobs.

The makeshift camps that arose on the outskirts of farms were filthy and overcrowded, and the migrants were hungry.

The local people reacted badly to this invasion, as Steinbeck explained: 'The hatred of the stranger occurs in the whole range of human history, from the most primitive village farm to our own highly organized industrial farming. The migrants are hated for the following reasons: that they are ignorant and dirty people, that they are carriers of disease, that they increase the necessity for police and the tax bill for schooling in a community, and that if they are allowed to organize they can, simply by refusing to work, wipe out the season's crops.'

Police attempted, without much luck, to turn the migrants back at the California border or, at least, to discourage them from continuing on. It was therefore miserable for the Okies, who were mainly self-respecting citizens from the Bible Belt who did not appreciate being called lazy and immoral. In addition to verbal abuse, they were preyed on by local vigilante groups and harassed by the police. That a war of sorts should break out was inevitable, although Americans beyond the California borders were not aware of the full extent of the trouble, another reason why Steinbeck found his assignment from the *San Francisco News* well worth the effort. Like so many writers of this era, he considered it part of a writer's responsibility to bear witness, to address a social crisis with the hope of effecting some kind of change.

The only relief for migrants came in the form of government camps, the brainchild of Paul S. Taylor, who worked for the California Department of Rural Rehabilitation. Beginning in 1935, these 'sanitary camps', as they were called, spread slowly along the Central Valley. Unfortunately, there was considerable opposition in Washington to this programme (tax revenues were obviously insufficient to meet the demand for services), and the original idea of creating twenty-five 'demonstration' camps was reduced to fifteen. There were three 'mobile camps' as well, which could be moved around to deal with emergency situations.

David Wyatt has suggested that 'Steinbeck's journalistic assignments drew him ever deeper into the fate of his culture, and especially toward those who had been discarded by it'.[15] And there is no doubt that the author's eyes were opened even wider by his journey through the Central Valley in August 1936. He went to the Gridley Camp, which was just outside the state capital of Sacramento. The manager of that camp liked Steinbeck and told him to be careful as he proceeded south: his picture had been circulating, or so he was told. Travelling in the baker's van, Steinbeck proceeded slowly, dropping by Salinas to see how the situation had developed in the small migrant city which had grown up on the outskirts of his boyhood home. 'It's a rotten and depressing situation here,' he wrote to Toby Street, 'this isn't the place I knew as a boy.' He stopped at several camps along the San Joaquin Valley, always blending in with the Okies to 'interview' them, attempting as best he could to find out what was really going on.

The federally funded camps were meant as examples or blueprints that could be emulated by the owners of large farms, who were encouraged to set up similar facilities on their own land. Almost none of the farmers agreed to follow suit, so the programme cannot be said to have served the purpose for which it was intended. On the other hand, the few camps that were funded did save many lives and gave the Okies who were lucky enough to land in them a chance to make a new beginning. Even more crucially, the camps became first-aid centres for people in the midst of a massive health crisis.

One of the original camp managers was Tom Collins, who would become Steinbeck's good friend as well as a figure in his imagination. *The Grapes of Wrath* is partially dedicated 'to Tom – who lived it'. And Tom did. He was head of the Arvin

Sanitary Camp, known by its denizens as 'Weedpatch'. It was easily one of the most successful operations in the programme, and Steinbeck was impressed by what he stumbled on. He later recalled meeting Collins:

> The first time I saw Tom Collins it was evening, and it was raining. I drove into the migrant camp, the wheels of my car throwing muddy water. The lines of sodden, dripping tents stretched away from me in the darkness. The temporary office was crowded with damp men and women, just standing under a roof, and sitting at a littered table was Tom Collins, a little man in a damp, frayed, white suit. The crowding people looked at him all the time. Just stood and looked at him. He had a small moustache, his graying, black hair stood up on his head like the quills of a frightened porcupine, and his large, dark eyes, tired beyond sleepiness, the kind of tired that won't let you sleep even if you have time and a bed.[16]

Two thousand people crammed into this camp's temporary shelter, and many were suffering from such contagious diseases as measles and mumps, even pneumonia and tuberculosis. 'You had children too weak to stand,' recalls one survivor of this camp.[17] 'They tried to put those with sickness in separate sheds, but it didn't work. There was influenza, typhoid, all kinds of things. Old people would just sit and stare, and a lot of them died more of sadness than anything else. The younger people were mostly full of anger. They were downright mad. Somebody had kicked them off their land back home, and here they were, with no work, nothing to look forward to. Riots broke out here and there, but they weren't so hard to squash because nobody felt good. You couldn't fight back if you didn't feel good. That was the secret the bosses and police had, and they knew they'd win.'

Collins had been raised a strict Catholic, and he trained for the priesthood for a brief while. As one friend later recalled, 'There was always about Tom something of the missionary.

He had that predatory look in his eye, a way of smiling when you talked. You knew he had your better interests at heart.'[18] Collins taught school in Alaska and Guam, then founded a school for juvenile delinquents in San Francisco. After moving to Los Angeles when his school failed, he took a job with the FTS (Federal Transient Service), founded by the Roosevelt administration to deal with the homeless. In 1935, he moved to the Resettlement Administration and became the first manager of a Sanitary Camp, where his success was legendary and unique, largely because of his instincts for democratic organization. He gave the residents the authority to govern their own daily lives in the camp, refusing to adopt a paternalistic attitude that could have backfired on him; a committee of residents was formed at Weedpatch and put in charge of making rules for the camp and enforcing them. 'There was a spirit in these camps,' says one former resident of Weedpatch.[19] 'It was people looking after people.'

Steinbeck spent a week in Weedpatch, following Collins around on his daily chores, interviewing residents, watching and listening, mingling. He took sheaves of notes each night in his 'pie wagon'. Sherm Eastom was head of the governing committee at Weedpatch, and his family (according to Dewey Russell, who succeeded Collins as camp manager) was said to have provided a model for the Joads in *The Grapes of Wrath*. One must, however, be wary of saying definitely that anybody was a 'source' for any given character; characters in fiction are always composites.

Steinbeck left Weedpatch in his bakery truck with a briefcase stuffed full of reports given to him by Collins. These reports, which Collins sent to headquarters in Washington twice a month, bristled with wry observations about camp life, with invaluable statistics, personal histories (including health records) of camp residents and other kinds of information which would be of use to Steinbeck in writing his articles for the *News* and, later, in composing *The Grapes of Wrath*. A born enthnographer, Collins also recorded camp songs and observations on Okie dialects which naturally fascinated Steinbeck.[20] The reports were a gold mine for a writer, and he knew it. He drove home to Los Gatos excited and resolved to do something to help the migrants and their cause.

On the way home he stopped again in Salinas and was horrified by the deterioration in the situation. The lettuce strike had led to violent behaviour from both sides. Even the local burghers, the sort of people his father and mother had known well and identified with, had become hostile, and some of them formed vigilante groups to attack the 'Red revolutionaries' who they believed were exciting docile migrant workers to violence. One resident of Salinas remembers that 'a group of maybe two dozen men, local merchants and members of the Rotary, went marching out there to the camp outside town with clubs and rifle butts. They wanted to bash some heads in. Everybody was so mad. But they did solve the problem. The troublemakers were put in a barn under armed guard, and the kingpins were sent away. Nobody was allowed to walk the streets after dark for over a month. The police just stayed out of it.'[21]

Steinbeck wrote immediately to Collins when he finally got home: 'I want to thank you for one of the very fine experiences of a life. But I think you know exactly how I feel about it. I hope I can be of some kind of help. On the other hand I don't want to be presumptuous. In the articles I shall be very careful to try to do some good and no harm.'[22] A cheque accompanied the letter, and Steinbeck suggested that the money be used by the migrants for raising livestock. He also promised to get in touch with some people who might send books that could be used by the camp's children, whose education was being seriously neglected in these hideous circumstances.

Huddled in his small study overlooking the woods, Steinbeck wrote in short order a general piece on the migrant situation for *The Nation* called 'The Harvest Gypsies' and completed the articles commissioned by the *San Francisco News*. The seven parts of the series took up in turn different aspects of the crisis: the origin of the problem, the contrast between California's older breed of migrant workers and the Dust Bowl migrants, the living conditions as he found them in squatters' camps, and so forth. His approach was judicious and balanced, although a polemical tone underlies it. A feeling of compassion was obvious throughout, and he made no bones about demanding justice. At the same time he began editing some of the camp reports, hoping to make a book of them. 'I'm working hard on another book that isn't mine at all,' he explained to George Albee. 'I'm only editing it, but it is a fine thing. A complete social study made of the weekly reports from a migrant camp.'[23] This was another of those projects that, for one reason or another, came to nothing.

Steinbeck returned to Weedpatch at the end of September, stopping in Salinas on the way back to track the progress of the crisis in his home town. He wrote to Elizabeth Otis, 'I just returned yesterday from the strike area of Salinas, and from my migrants in Bakersfield. This thing is dangerous. Maybe it will be patched up for a while, but I look for the lid to blow off in a few weeks.'[24] It was very painful to him to witness the destruction, he said, of 'that dear little town where I was born'.

The publication of the 'little book', as he often called *Of Mice and Men*, was scheduled for winter 1937. As usual, there were mixed reactions before publication. Herman Shumlin, the producer who had optioned *In Dubious Battle*, disliked it and refused to consider a play adaptation. Several of Pat Covici's colleagues shared these reservations about the book, although Covici himself remained loyal. The tide turned with some good news in January 1938: the Book-of-the-Month

Club had chosen *Of Mice and Men* as a main selection, thus guaranteeing a large audience and, of course, a substantial sale. Steinbeck told Elizabeth Otis that he found the news 'gratifying but also . . . frightening'.[25]

The Steinbecks took advantage of their new financial ease, adding some good pieces of furniture to their house as well as a homemade gramophone which Toby Street helped Steinbeck to assemble. Although isolated, the house in Los Gatos became a magnet for interesting people. As usual, Toby Street, Carl Wilhelmson, and Grove Day could be counted on as visitors. George Albee turned up for a weekend with his wife. The reviewer Joseph Henry Jackson came by several times in the winter of 1937. Tom Collins paid a call. Ed Ricketts stopped by on many occasions, as did Steinbeck's younger sister, Mary, who never liked to go for too long without seeing her brother. New friends entered the picture too, including Martin and Elsie Ray, who owned a local winery.

Judson Gregory was a local potter, and he went to several parties in the Steinbeck house off Greenwood Lane. He recalls that 'everybody drank a lot, mostly cheap local wine. John was the ringmaster, dominating the conversation, which was usually about politics. He thought the country was coming apart, and that if something wasn't done fast a revolution would break out. He didn't want that. He was no Communist, like all the papers said; he supported Roosevelt. His wife, Carol, disagreed with him on a lot of things, and some cold currents went back and forth between them. Sometimes John got out of line and raised his voice or slapped the wall with his hand, and you could see that Carol hated it. I once left a party angry about something John had said and she followed me to the gate and said not to mind him, that he was upset about his book that was coming out. She protected him and kind of mocked him in public at the same time. It was peculiar.'[26]

Of Mice and Men, the upsetting book in question, appeared in early February 1937. The public response was swift and gratifying, taking Steinbeck's publishers and the author himself by huge surprise. By the middle of February, the book had sold 117,000 copies. 'That's a hell of a lot of books,' Steinbeck wrote to Pat Covici on 28 February, rubbing it in. He was justified in doing so; the book was flying out of the stores, and the press had begun to swarm around Steinbeck, desperate for interviews.

The reviews were mostly respectful, even complimentary, although *Time* sneered at the little novel, calling it a 'fairy tale'. Writing in *The Nation*, Mark Van Doren embodied the negative reaction to the book: 'All but one of the persons in Mr Steinbeck's extremely brief novel are subhuman if the range of the word human is understood to coincide with the range thus far established by fiction.'[27] Ralph Thompson's review in *The New York Times* (27 February) was more typical, calling the book 'completely disarming'. Another critic, Harry Hansen, went so far as to nominate the novel 'the finest bit of prose fiction of this decade'.

Steinbeck's story of two wandering 'bindlestiffs', George and Lennie, has become a permanent fixture of American literature. The book's subject is the nature of innocence, and it is explored with extraordinary compassion and skill. The semi-retarded Lennie and his guardian, George Milton, are men with a fragile dream of owning land and settling down into a paradisial future. 'Guys like us, that work on ranches, are the loneliest guys in the world. They got no family. They don't belong no place,' George tells his friend, who can barely understand him. 'With us it ain't like that. We got a future. We got somebody to talk to that gives a damn about us. . . . An' why? Because I got you to look after me, and you got me to look after you, and that's why.'

Bound by their dream of settling down together on land they can farm, George and Lennie walk together into their inevitably dim future. On the farm where the story takes place, Steinbeck's odd couple meet Candy, an ageing farm-hand who grieves over his toothless, rheumatic dog, which is finally shot because it smells up the bunkhouse. They brush against the evil son of the boss, Curley, and Curley's wife, the seductive and stupid woman who is accidentally murdered by Lennie at the climax of the story. Other fine characters include Slim, a 'jerkline skinner' who has 'Godlike eyes' that fasten on to a man so firmly he can't think of anything else, and Crooks, a proudly benevolent stable buck with a hunched back who, because of his black skin, is shunned by the rest.

Ed Ricketts had told Steinbeck that he should not be waylaid by what 'could' or 'should' happen but by what 'did'. It is therefore interesting that Steinbeck originally called the book 'Something That Happened'. (Ricketts, in fact, suggested the change in title.) The author remains detached throughout, blaming no one for the fact that, in Robert Burns's words, 'the best laid schemes o' mice an' men gang aft a'gley'. Antonia Seixas has noted that 'the hardest task a writer can set himself is to tell a story of "something that happened" without explaining "why" – and make it con-vincing and moving'.[29] This, indeed, is what Steinbeck accomplishes in this brief, compelling novella (or novelette, as short novels were often called in the Thirties).

We do, however, get something like moral reflection from Slim, the most intelligent character in the story. He is a man 'whose ear heard more than was said to him', and he listens to George tell of the dream he shares with Lennie with rueful detachment. He alone realizes that the dream will necessarily fail; the economies of their situation will not allow for success. It is Slim, whom Steinbeck calls the 'prince of the ranch', who tells George in the final poignant scene that he had to act directly in response to Lennie's unfortunate killing of Curley's wife. 'You hadda, George', he tells him in the end, after George has killed his best friend humanely to save him from being lynched, 'you hadda.' That Slim is controlling the action is signalled by his invitation to George at the end to come and have a drink with him: 'Come on, George. Me an' you'll go in an' get a drink.' George agrees and is led up to the highway by Slim.

The novella showed a side of American life that most people had never experienced directly, and Steinbeck's plain style struck readers then, as it still does, as true and memorable. As simple narrative, *Of Mice and Men* demonstrates once again the raw storytelling power Steinbeck could summon, and the final scene, which teeters on the brink of sentimentality, seems both inevitable and deeply tragic. One grieves, with George, for Lennie.

But there are many other layers in this book. For a start, it can be read as sharp protest; the mere fact that Steinbeck describes so concretely the situation of bindlestiffs in California was a political act in the charged atmosphere of the late Thirties. The author's urgency, his anger at the way men like George and Lennie were being treated, is felt on every page. One might also find various allegorical strands in the text; its mythlike simplicity invites this kind of interpretation. Finally, as the fruit of Steinbeck's inquiry into 'non-teleological thinking', *Of Mice and Men* may be considered an accomplished piece of speculative fiction, as Peter Lisca has pointed out.[29]

The fact that *Of Mice and Men* was conceived as a play in novella form made it easily convertible for the stage, and it was not long before Steinbeck was engaged by George S. Kaufman, the Broadway playwright and director, to produce a version for the footlights. (Sam H. Harris, who was much revered on Broadway, was enlisted as producer, thus ensuring a first-class production.) Kaufman wrote to encourage Steinbeck, telling him that his novel 'drops almost naturally into play form and no one knows that better than you'.[30] He added, 'It is only the second act that seems to me to need fresh invention. You have the two natural scenes for it – bunkhouse and the negro's room, but I think the girl should come into both these scenes, and that the fight between Lennie and Curley, which will climax Act 2, must be over the girl. I think the girl should have a scene with Lennie *before* the scene in which he kills her. The girl, I think, should be drawn more fully: she is the motivating force of the whole thing and should loom larger.' (The fact that she was never even given a name shows that Steinbeck did not intend her to play a large part in the story. As Kaufman wished, her role was greatly expanded for the play and, later, for the film.)

Meanwhile, *Of Mice and Men* leaped on to the bestseller lists. Letters to Steinbeck poured in from strangers and friends alike, as did requests for interviews, readings, public appearances and autographs. To his chagrin, Steinbeck was often forced to travel several miles to the nearest telephone to respond to urgent requests of one kind or another, most of which proved mere annoyances. Once, a tourist turned up at his front gate with her little daughter in tow, and when she saw Steinbeck she cried, 'Dance for the man, darling! Dance!' To Elizabeth Otis, the frustrated Steinbeck wrote, 'This ballyhoo is driving me nuts.'[31]

For some time the Steinbecks had been hoping to visit Europe, and they had now both the money and a good reason to get out of the country. They boarded a freighter called *The Sagebrush* from San Francisco to the East Coast on 23 March, via the Panama Canal, thus replicating the journey he had made more than a decade before. The ship docked in Philadelphia, and the Steinbecks took a train into New York's Pennsylvania Station, where they were met by Pat Covici, eager to waylay his newly famous author for a couple of weeks.

Against his wishes, Steinbeck attended a dinner that very night in honour of Thomas Mann, then a famous refugee from the Nazis. Steinbeck protested that he didn't have a suit or necktie, but his worries were brushed aside by Covici. The banquet was held at a large New York hotel, and Steinbeck suffered through most of it. Near the end, he rushed out into the hotel bar, where he ordered a double brandy-and-soda. When Covici came to retrieve him, he muttered into his drink, 'I can't believe grown men will stand up and say such ridiculous things in public.'

He found himself in a bind that would become only too familiar. His growing reputation had turned him, suddenly, into a public person, but his shyness and essential disbelief in publicity and 'society' tugged him in the opposite direction. 'He was never happy at parties,' Elaine Steinbeck says. 'Never in his life. And he always detested public events. He would much rather stay home and read, or write, or talk to friends. Publicity always depressed him.' Covici, alas, insisted that Steinbeck give a press conference before he left for Europe, and he reluctantly consented. Reporters and photographers swarmed the offices of Covici–Friede, and the shy author was pictured in the national press the next day (in a photograph that became widely known) sitting behind a desk with a bottle of brandy beside him. Given the emphasis on alcohol in *Tortilla Flat*, it's not surprising that the public soon began to associate Steinbeck and drinking. It was an association he would never shake.

Apparently there was a lot of drinking during the two and a half weeks in New York. Steinbeck, when drunk, would become sullen, but Carol became loud and boisterous under the influence. Like Zelda Fitzgerald, she would do crazy things that embarrassed her husband. One night, for instance, she stormed out of the hotel after a drunken fight. Steinbeck went after her, but lost her in the crowd. When she didn't return, he grew frantic and began to search hospitals and police stations. Not finding her, he called Covici and others, who joined the search. Carol was nowhere to be found. When she turned up the next morning, dishevelled but unhurt, Steinbeck was beside himself with anger. This was just another in a mounting collection of grievances against Carol – most of them unjustified – which Steinbeck harboured. He was extremely conventional in many ways (a true son of John Ernst and Olive Steinbeck), and he did not like the idea that his wife was running around the city drunk; perhaps even worse, he could not tolerate any public embarrassment. 'That wild side of Carol', his sister says, 'was too much for John. I think she frightened him. He never knew what she might do next.'

Rather chastened, the Steinbecks boarded the SS *Drottning-holm* in late May, bound for Sweden. Their cabin was, much to their dismay, at the bottom of the ship, so there were no windows; it was also 'cramped and musty', and one could hear the engine clanging. But the prospect of a long sea voyage and a European vacation was infinitely appealing to them both just then. Steinbeck wanted to get as far away from the public din as possible, and Carol was eager to escape the trauma of her experience in New York. 'This escape ought to be good for us,' he wrote aboard ship to Pat Covici. 'I need to get away from being John Steinbeck for a little while.'

Writing the Big Book

'If only I could do this book properly it would be one of the really fine books and a truly American book.'

Steinbeck's journal for *The Grapes of Wrath*

Like so many American writers before him from Washington Irving and Mark Twain to Hemingway and Fitzgerald, Steinbeck was drawn to Europe. This was especially true in the later years, when he had plenty of money for travel. England, in particular, attracted him as the source of his beloved Arthurian legends, and London became, as Elaine Steinbeck recalls, 'almost a kind of second home'. This time, however, in his first transatlantic venture, he and Carol confined themselves to Scandinavia and the Soviet Union, partly as a consequence of the ship they happened to catch. After a week's journey in which very little was said about this mutual conflict in New York, they landed in the Swedish port of Göteborg in early June 1937.

After a few quiet days in a small village on the outskirts of Stockholm, they went by train to Copenhagen, where Steinbeck insisted on paying a visit to Elsinore, the castle used as a setting for *Hamlet*. (They attended an English production of the play at the castle that evening which Steinbeck found 'eerie and inspiring'.) Always an eager observer of society, he wrote to Pat Covici to say that the business people in Denmark all admired Hitler and wanted fascism to triumph but that the intellectuals were all Communists. He did not, himself, like either extreme.

The Steinbecks were still reeling from the New York fiasco, but they had formed a truce. They remained cool towards each other but polite and respectful. Fortunately, the novelty of European travel distracted them from the problems which had beset their marriage, and they were able to get their minds off themselves. After sampling 'every restaurant in Denmark', they returned by train to Stockholm, where they called on the sculptor and painter Bo Beskow, whom they had met with Pat Covici on their way back from Mexico City the year before. Beskow was a big, florid Swede who entertained them splendidly, introducing them to a circle of painters and writers whom Steinbeck found exceedingly congenial. When they moved on to Helsinki a week later, Steinbeck missed Stockholm. Helsinki was, by contrast, 'a sad, pleasureless city'.

They crossed the border into Soviet Russia in the first week of July, heading straight for Leningrad, with its grand, pinkish-purple buildings and wide streets. After visiting the Winter Palace and the Hermitage, where Carol found the French Impressionist paintings 'amazingly fine and fiercely colorful', they took a night train to Moscow. What Steinbeck made of that ancient city, which had become the capital of Soviet Russia, can be deduced from a passage in *A Russian Journal*, the book he published in 1948 with Robert Capa, the photographer. 'I had been there in 1936,' he wrote (mistakenly, it was 1937), 'and the changes since then were tremendous. In the first place the city was much cleaner than it had been. The streets were washed and paved, where they had been muddy and dirty. And the building in the eleven years was enormous. Hundreds of tall new apartment houses, new bridges over the Moscow River, the streets widened, the statues every place. Whole sections of the narrow, dirty districts of the old Moscow had disappeared, and in their place were new living quarters and new public buildings.'[1]

Steinbeck had hoped for some time to write about the Soviet Union, perhaps in fictional form, but he found the lack of individual freedom in that country a far cry from the wild west of his childhood. His ideas of the phalanx were complicated by what he saw; no consciousness of the group was possible, he thought, without a firm sense of individual identity, and the Russian people seemed to have lost all sign of this. It was the dialectic of self versus the group, after all, which informed *In Dubious Battle* and would, very soon, provide the essential tension in *The Grapes of Wrath*. In early August, as he and Carol sailed back to New York on a small freighter, Steinbeck put the idea for a book about Russia on the back burner, where it remained for a decade.

In New York, an expensive limited edition of *The Red Pony* had just been published by Pat Covici, and it was selling well – much to Steinbeck's surprise. Meanwhile, the script for *Of Mice and Men* awaited his immediate attention, and various people were chomping at the bit. Annie Laurie Williams, Steinbeck's theatrical and movie agent, corralled her wayward author and took him, with Carol, to her country house in Connecticut, where she sat him down to work; the idea was that he would quickly make the short novel over into an actable script. This was somewhat optimistic, however; even a novel written in the form of a play cannot be performed as is, and Steinbeck was unfamiliar with the play format. Williams, on the other hand, knew a lot about the theatre and was able, with difficulty, to help Steinbeck recast his story with appropriate notations for exits, entrances and set changes. Before long, they had something like a working script. It was typed by Carol on Williams's typewriter and sent off to George Kaufman, who was pleased by what they had done but aware that a good deal of work was still required. He met with Steinbeck in New York, talked over the script's problems with him, and offered some general ideas for revision which seemed, to the author, shrewd. Since the theatre was already booked for late November, there was no time to waste, so Kaufman suggested that they all retire to his farmhouse in Bucks County, Pennsylvania, for a brief but intensive period of rewriting. Kaufman later said that he found Steinbeck 'difficult because resistant to ideas for revision', but he pushed his author hard, getting a 'good, unusual script' out of him.

'It's damn good,' Steinbeck boasted to George Albee, unable to contain his enthusiasm. He had a final meeting about the production back in New York at the Music Box Theater, where the play was scheduled to open on 23 November, with Sam Harris as producer and Donald Oenslager as set designer. At the end of the meeting, Steinbeck stood, looming over the table somewhat ominously, and announced that he was off to California the next day. 'My work is done,' he said. Kaufman was startled and upset by this news, pointing out that further revisions might be necessary once the rehearsals got underway, but Steinbeck, always determined to control his own life, refused to listen to his objections, saying that his agents could deal with anything further that needed attention.

The Steinbecks were by now, after a summer in Europe and this intense period in New York, getting along. 'They went hot and cold with each other in the year or so before everything fell apart,' says a friend of Carol's, 'but travelling was always good for them. They had to pull together, and they did. They needed the commotion, the friends, the activity. It was only when they were home alone that everything went to hell.'[2] They bought a car in New York, a candy-red Chevrolet, and started for California via Washington DC, where the Farm Security Administration had its headquarters. Steinbeck met with Dr Will Alexander, the deputy administrator of the FSA, explaining that he hoped to write a book in the form of a novel about the situation of the Dust Bowl migrant workers. He explained that he wanted it to be realistic, showing exactly how these people lived, and, at Steinbeck's request, Tom Collins was assigned to work with him for a few weeks. After a day or two of sightseeing the Steinbecks drove straight to Chicago from Washington: an exhausting two-day journey in muggy, late summer weather. They spent a few days with John's uncle Joe Hamilton and had dinner with the bookseller Ben Abramson, who had first introduced Pat Covici to Steinbeck's work. The plan was to travel west along Route 66, retracing the path that so many thousands of migrants from the Dust Bowl had taken.

Jackson Benson reports a conversation with Carol in which she insisted that Steinbeck made no 'conscious effort to do any research for his book along the way' to California.[3] They key word here is 'conscious' – writers of fiction rarely work that way. Steinbeck would have been driving along Route 66 with ears and eyes wide open. Even today, 66 is visually stunning, with long stretches of deserted highway, a distant view of the violet mountains, patches of wild forest and a string of small, ramshackle towns. Except for the addition of some fast food restaurants and hotel chains, the highway has changed very little. One could easily read *The Grapes of Wrath* and drive Route 66 today with a full sense of recognition. Chapter 15, for instance, opens with a vivid evocation of the roadside stands (whose names have, of course, changed):

> Along 66 the hamburger stands – Al & Susy's Place – Carl's Lunch – Joe & Minnie – Will's Eats. Board-and-bat shacks. Two gasoline pumps in front, a screen door, a long bar, stools, and a foot rail. Near the door three slot machines, showing through glass the wealth of nickles three bars will bring. And beside them, the nickel phonograph with records piled up like pies, ready to swing out to the turntable and play dance music.
>
> . . . .
>
> Cars whisking by on 66.[4]

It was, of course, Steinbeck's eye for details like these that makes *The Grapes of Wrath* a stunning book.

Once back in Los Gatos, he began making plans to return to the 'sanitary camps'. He readied the 'pie wagon' and set off in mid-October, driving east to Stockton and north through Sacramento to Marysville. The magnet in Marysville, where he stopped overnight, was Dook Sheffield, who had moved from Los Angeles to this sleepy town, where he was working on the local newspaper as a reporter. Sheffield's prospects for an academic career seemed bleak now, since colleges and universities were not hiring and he did not have a doctorate. As expected, he found Sheffield in a state of gloom, unhappy in Marysville and anxious about his future; disconcertingly for Steinbeck, Sheffield seemed wary of his old friend, who had become a celebrity almost overnight.

This struck a raw nerve because Steinbeck was himself feeling awkward about his success. In a misguided moment of generosity, he offered to pay Dook's way through graduate school. 'Go anywhere you want,' he told Sheffield. 'Go to Oxford, if you like. I'll pay for everything! You won't have to worry about a penny!' Sheffield, quite naturally, shrank from his friend and refused even to contemplate the offer; this was shoving failure down his throat. A cooling-off period in the friendship followed, much to Steinbeck's dismay; he could not bear to think that he had hurt his best friend. Without joy, he set off the next morning for the FSA camp in Gridley, where Tom Collins was currently in charge.

The plan was that he and Collins would travel together for about three weeks, and that he would take extensive notes for his novel along the way, interviewing as many migrant workers as he could. He would also pick Collins's brain for stories. Steinbeck later claimed that he and Collins went all the way to Oklahoma and that they retraced the route along 66 followed by the Joad family in the novel, but there is no truth to this. The novelist often indulged in what Huck Finn called 'stretchers': white lies that enhanced his credibility in one way or another. This is perfectly understandable;

Steinbeck was a man with a strong sense of his own worth, but this self-knowledge was complicated by doubts about his intelligence, his public manner and his looks. His shyness seems to have added to the complicated mix; Steinbeck needed to dramatize himself to the world in certain ways, partly to explain to himself who he really was. He saw himself as a man of great daring and drive, and where the reality failed to measure up to the conception, he relied on invention, the most treasured arrow in his personal quiver. If he said he had gone to Oklahoma, he had gone to Oklahoma. Before long, he almost believed his own story.

The actual journey took place strictly within the California borders, and it involved visits to camps along Highway 99 from Gridley down through Stockton, Fresno, Arvin, Barstow, Needles and Brawley. Steinbeck listened closely as Tom Collins pointed things out, asking questions and taking extensive notes. (The travellers stopped over one night in Watsonville to visit with Esther on her beautiful farm.) By 7 November he was back in Los Gatos, where Carol had arranged a surprise welcome-home party with Toby Street as the honoured guest. In view of the disastrous meeting with Dook Sheffield in Marysville, the reunion with Street was welcome. It meant a lot now to stay in touch with old friends, with the people who knew him before he became famous. One friend recalls: 'John came back from that trip looking tired, like he'd marched on foot all the way from Oklahoma. He was subdued. Everybody – especially Carol – was excited about what he was doing and everything that was happening with his book and play, but John sure wasn't. I never saw him so down.'[5]

Meanwhile, rehearsals were underway in New York at the Music Box Theater. *Of Mice and Men* opened on 23 November, with Wallace Ford as George, Broderick Crawford as Lennie and Clare Luce as Curley's wife. One could not have hoped for a better cast, as the critics noted. Stark Young, one of the leading theatre critics of the day, wrote intriguingly about the production in *The New Republic*:

> How one might describe 'Of Mice and Men' as we get it at the Music Box I do not know; I have never seen a play quite like it, have no previous acquaintance with the nature of its suspenses, or with the curious artistic satisfaction that its development affords. But from that last point its quality derives, I am sure of that. That is to say you never quite recognize or believe the characters or the active moments; the speech is not compelling as an actual, sharp recording out of life; the locale is not borne in on you as exactly literal, as inevitable realism, an indisputable entity. But the whole of it seems to come off right in its own kind. It remains artifice, theatre, a work of art; but it loses nothing by it.[6]

Young appreciated the stylized quality of the melodrama and understood that Steinbeck was not attempting anything like 'realism'. What he had created, in both the novel and play versions, was a type of morality play. George and Lennie are symbolic figures in realist coveralls; we watch them, fascinated, moved, and frustrated, as they dance towards a climax that is inevitable (and unlikely) in the manner of Greek tragedy. The dream of owning a little piece of California real estate was always fantastic for these men. And Lennie, with his terrible strength and weak brain, was a bomb waiting to go off. The story is just 'something that happened', as the original title of the novel implied, something horrifying and emotionally true, however unreal.

Audiences responded well, as one might expect, and the play ran for 207 performances, making it a hit by any standard. George Kaufman was pleased by this success, even thrilled, but he continued to feel upset that Steinbeck had walked out on the rehearsals; he was also hurt by the author's refusal to attend the opening night (indeed, by his refusal even to see the New York production). Kaufman's misgivings

about Steinbeck were exacerbated by a false rumour that
Steinbeck had referred to him as 'a wiseacre New York Jew'.
He nursed this grudge for many years, and he and Steinbeck
never worked together again.[7]

Steinbeck in fact sent Kaufman an affable, congratulatory
letter, saying that 'as the reviews come in it becomes more
and more apparent that you have done a great job. I knew
you would. . . . It seems that for two hours you made your
play far more real than its audience and only the play
existed.'[8] It does seem strange, however, that Steinbeck did
not attend the opening night of his first play on Broadway.
This is among the first appearances of a syndrome that would
later affect him badly: a tendency to withdraw from any
outward 'success', as if to confirm his mother's opinion that
he would never amount to anything. There was something
oddly self-destructive here that remained in conflict with that
side of him propelling him forward in the profession, that
genuinely ambitious side which surfaces in the letters. He
both wanted and feared success; he sought it and when it
appeared he did his best to kill it.

One of many results of the success with *Of Mice and Men*
was that Jack Kirkland, who had fashioned a huge Broadway
hit from Erskine Caldwell's *Tobacco Road*, asked for the rights
to *Tortilla Flat*. He saw its obvious theatrical potential, and
Steinbeck agreed to let him see what he could do. Kirkland
quickly produced his script adaptation and sent it to Steinbeck, who realized at once that it would never work. This was
Tobacco Road set in Monterey, and Kirkland had no appreciation of *paisano* speech patterns. He suggested changes and
told his agent that 'the play is not going to have any sound of
authenticity'. Kirkland politely accepted the author's criticisms, but was unable or unwilling to make the necessary
revisions, and the play (which Carol attended soon after
Christmas) fell to earth with a thud. 'It was, says Carol, the
worst thing she ever saw. The lines were bad, but the

directing and casting were even worse. The thing closed after four performances, thank God,' Steinbeck wrote to Joe and Charlotte Jackson.[9]

The failure of *Tortilla Flat* on Broadway did nothing to quash the rising popularity of John Steinbeck. Myron Selznick, the producer, tried to get him to go to Hollywood to work for him, and even Zeppo Marx called with an offer. 'The dogs of Hollywood are loose,' he complained to Elizabeth Otis. Even worse, letters poured in from destitute people asking for handouts. 'I get sadder and sadder,' he wrote in one letter.[10] 'The requests and demands for money pour in. It is perfectly awful.' One poor man wrote from Illinois to say that his son needed an operation that would cost a hundred dollars. 'You got luck and I got no luck,' the man said. (Carol wanted him to send this man the money, but Steinbeck refused. He argued that it was impossible to choose among the various good candidates for his charity.) One day, a letter arrived from a peculiar young woman he had known briefly when he was still living in Salinas; she claimed that she was pregnant with his child. This was utterly fantastic, and nothing came of her lawsuit, but Steinbeck was deeply agitated by the episode, which seemed to point towards a future of claims and calamities resulting from his 'luck'.

Indeed, Steinbeck was suddenly blessed by the goddess Fortuna. *Tortilla Flat* continued to sell in book stores across the country, as did *Of Mice and Men*. The Broadway play drew full houses every night, and rights to it had been sold in England and Scandinavia. An American road tour was in the planning stages, and Warner Brothers was interested in acquiring the film rights because James Cagney had seen the play and thought he might want to play George.

The annoying side effects of success continued, too. Not only was Dook Sheffield barely speaking to Steinbeck, but now George Albee had turned sour. According to Albee's brother, Richard, it was pure jealousy on George's part that caused the problems. Steinbeck wrote to George with remarkable frankness: 'This has been a difficult and unpleasant time. There has been nothing good about it. In this time my friends have rallied around, all except you. Every time there has been a possibility of putting a bad construction on anything I have done, you have put such a construction.'[11] Near the close of the letter, he said, 'I'd like to be friends with you, George, but I can't if I have to wear a mail shirt the whole time. . . . I've needed help and trust and the benefit of the doubt, because I've tried to beat the system which destroys every writer, and from you have come only wounds and kicks in the face.'

Perhaps the worst consequence of his success was Carol's growing resentment of her husband's career, which seemed to underscore her own lack of accomplishment. What did she have to show after several years of marriage? No books of her own, no children. One friends recalls: 'Carol and John had been so good together before his books started selling. Now John was worried about money and intrusions, and he was frantic about the sudden demands. Carol seemed to resent his successes. Everything revolved around him, and she thought she deserved some attention herself. They quarrelled constantly. It was no fun being around them.'[12] There was also, of course, the Campbell affair, and Steinbeck's sense of having been betrayed by the person he loved.

As usual, he escaped his problems by burying himself in work. He was hard at *The Grapes of Wrath* by mid-winter 1938, taking occasional field trips to the sanitary camps, where conditions seemed only to worsen. In the interior valleys, he noted to Elizabeth Otis, 'five thousand families were starving to death.' What appalled him was that local bankers and businessmen, the class of people he in a sense came from, did everything they could to thwart the migrants, hoping to drive them back to the Dust Bowl. He decided to write about the crisis in the local papers as a way of getting back at those who were doing the damage. 'Shame and a hatred of publicity will do the job to the miserable local bankers,' he told Otis, full of just indignation. 'The death of children by starvation in our valleys is simply staggering.' (One article did eventually come out in a local paper.)

There was a huge flood in the Visalia region, with lightning flickering along the valley and rain falling slantwise for weeks on end. Migrant families found themselves sleeping in wet blankets, with water pouring through the thin cloth of battered tents. Children ran in the rain, got chilled, caught pneumonia and died for lack of medicine and dry clothes or bedding. Food was scarce, and frantic fathers hunted the dumps for rats, dogs and cats, which were duly cooked over smouldering fires. Those who still had working automobiles found themselves stranded at the roadside, their wheels sunk in mud, their carburettors soaked. The FSA worked day and night to bring relief in the form of food and medicine to these desperate people, but the amount barely scratched the surface of the problem.

On 14 February, Steinbeck joined Tom Collins for two weeks of work at the Weedpatch camp. The old pie truck couldn't make it through the waterlogged road to the camp, where the ridges were two and three feet deep in places, so he set out with Collins on foot, walking through the night to get to the camp. Once there, though chilled and splattered and racked with a deep cough, Steinbeck worked frantically to help the sick and dying for two days without sleep, often dragging half-starved people under trees for shelter from the rain, which was unabated. Mud-caked, drenched and exhausted, Steinbeck continued day after day, driven to action by the pathetic conditions of the migrants, many of whom were too weak from hunger to walk even a few steps towards a meal.

He returned to Los Gatos for a few days at the end of the month, then headed straight back to Visalia. This time he went with a photographer and an assignment from *Life*. If he was going to be famous, he might as well put his fame to good use; now people would pay attention to his by-line. 'I break myself every time I go out because the argument that one person's effort can't really do anything doesn't seem to apply when you come to a bunch of starving children and you have a little money,' he wrote to Elizabeth Otis.[13] But a serious blow came when *Life* refused to print the article. It was, the editor explained, too 'liberal' for their taste. It was never kosher, then or now, to suggest that all is not well in America. Our national intentions are always good; our people are generous, the government exists to help the sick and the poor, the lame and the needy. And so forth. Steinbeck ran smack into the self-censorship of editors which has always been a crude fact of American journalism: you can say anything you want, they tell the writer, but you can't say it here.

Just before leaving for the first trip to Visalia, Steinbeck had met Pare Lorentz, the documentary film-maker who had stirred audiences with *The Plow That Broke the Plains*, a beautifully paced and starkly filmed portrait of the Dust Bowl crisis and its origins. That film, like *The Grapes of Wrath*, followed the path of the migrants from Oklahoma to California, lingering over the harsh details: the driving wind and sand, the beleaguered migrants in crowded jalopies, the filthy roadside camps, the violence and meanness and rawness of daily life on the road and the great disappointment that awaited each pilgrim to Eden. As might have been expected, the film's 'liberal' viewpoint attracted fire from conservative legislators in Washington, who complained that federal money had been used to support this piece of 'naked propaganda', as one report called it.

Now Lorentz offered to help Steinbeck get his articles about the Visalia disaster into print, and he wrote to several editors about their extraordinary value. But the articles were turned down everywhere; the material was just too threatening, and editors backed away. It was disillusioning for Steinbeck; nevertheless, he was grateful to Lorentz for his support, and a warm friendship developed between the two men that would last for many years. Lorentz wisely felt that Steinbeck should not sit back and simply wait for the best offers to roll in; he should try to find film-makers sympathetic to his views and persuade them to adapt his material. With this in mind, he invited Steinbeck to Hollywood, and this time he went. He was introduced to King Vidor and Lewis Milestone, two well-known figures in the industry; the latter would prove a vital connection between Steinbeck and Hollywood.

While in Hollywood, he spoke on the phone to Jimmy Cagney about playing the role of Mac in a possible production of *In Dubious Battle*, and he was called again by Myron Selznick, who still imagined he could talk this newly famous writer into working for him. As before, Steinbeck remained wary of movie people, appreciating that the film world was a vortex which had swallowed many writers before him, including Fitzgerald and Faulkner. As he told Otis outright in a letter of 3 March 1938: 'I don't want to work in Hollywood.'

Back in Los Gatos, he was visited by Helen Hosmer of the Simon J. Lubin Society of San Francisco. She had met Steinbeck before, and he apparently liked her; she convinced him to allow her to reprint his articles from the *San Francisco News* in the form of a pamphlet which could be sold to raise money for the neediest of the migrant workers. Enthusiastic about this project, Steinbeck quickly added a fresh epilogue to the seven pieces already written – a vivid piece called 'Starvation Under the Orange Trees'. The epilogue ends with these ringing questions: 'Is it possible that this state is so stupid, so vicious and so greedy that it cannot feed and clothe the men and women who help to make it the richest area in the world? Must the hunger become anger and the anger fury before anything will be done?'

As usual, Steinbeck had difficulty staying with one project. 'L'Affaire Lettuceberg' – a novella that could be considered a dry run for *The Grapes of Wrath* – was finished by late April, amounting to just over sixty thousand words, but he suspected that it was no good. It was not the 'big book' he wanted to write. 'Not once in the writing of it have I felt the curious warm pleasure that comes when work is going well,' he wrote to Elizabeth Otis. And Carol agreed. She read it carefully over a long weekend, then came into his study with a glum expression on her face and said, 'Burn it.' He had apparently taken a satirical approach in that story, ridiculing the bankers and businessmen and anti-labour forces which combined against the interests of the migrant workers; the total impression made by the book was disconcerting. Steinbeck was not as his best as satirist (as a later work such as *The Short Reign of Pippin IV* demonstrates clearly). Taking Carol's advice, Steinbeck gathered the manuscript into a heap in the garden beyond his study and burned it, even though Pat Covici desperately wanted (sight unseen) to publish it.

He began again in mid-May, taking out a fresh ledger. The new work was, as yet, untitled, but Steinbeck had a vision of what he wanted to do; he would write a book on an epic scale that was politically engaged. As we can tell from the diaries he kept while writing this novel – an invaluable document that has since been published as *Working Days: The Journal of The Grapes of Wrath* – Steinbeck suddenly understood the structure and style of the book looming inchoate before him. He knew already that it would alternate chapters of exposition and narrative, following the trail of one particular family on its westward journey towards a better life in California. The diaries also suggest that Steinbeck had the novel's astonishing final image – the tableau where Rose of Sharon gives her breast to a starving man – right from the start. This was the culminating image towards which the entire, massive narrative flowed, slowly but inexorably.

A moment may come when a writer is suddenly prepared, emotionally and artistically, to accomplish a major phase of his or her work. This moment came for John Steinbeck in the late spring of 1938. He was ready, and he knew it. This is clear from what he wrote at the time about his friend, Louis Paul, who had just published a novel called *The Wrong World*:

> But the sureness of touch, the characters that move about,
> the speech that sounds like speaking, the fact that it
> happens, that one is never conscious of how a thing is said
> but only of what is said. I know the why and how of that.
> It's the millions of words written, all the short stories, even
> the ones that weren't any good. Without the millions of
> words written it is impossible to write a book like this. And
> by the same token – those millions of words are a guarantee
> that the last half will not falter for a moment.[14]

Steinbeck, though writing about Louis Paul, was describing his own situation as well. The millions of words he had written in the past decade were his preparation for writing *The Grapes of Wrath*. He was ready.

The entire 200,000 words were written, mostly, within an intense six-month period, a literary sprint that began in late May and ended in early December. Steinbeck stayed in Los Gatos during this time, leaving home only when absolutely necessary. He remained in his writing room each day until he completed his daily quota of composition, averaging about 2000 words. Beginning the novel at a slow pace, he gained speed as he went on. To set a mood for himself, he quite often played classical music in the background on his phonograph: Tchaikovsky's *Swan Lake* and Stravinsky's *Symphony of Psalms* were two favourite pieces. In writing *The Grapes of Wrath*, he worked, he said, 'in a musical technique', trying 'to use the forms and the mathematics of music rather than those of prose'.[15] The book is 'symphonic', he maintained, 'in composition, in movement, in tone and in scope'.

The second entry, for 31 May 1938, sets the tone for the diary that accrued alongside the novel:

> Here is the diary of a book and it will be interesting to see how it works out. I have tried to keep diaries before but they don't work out because of the necessity to be honest. In matters where there is no definite truth, I gravitate toward the opposite. Sometimes where there is definite truth, I am revolted by its smugness and do the same. In this, however, I shall try simply to keep the record of working days and the amount done in each and the success (as far as I can know it) of the day. Just now the work goes well. It is nearly the first of June. That means I have seven months to do this book and I should like to take them but I imagine five will be the limit. I have never taken long actually to do the writing. I want this one to be leisurely though. That is one of the reasons for the diary.

June of 1938 was a fine time for Steinbeck, with brilliant blue skies seeming to mirror his creative mood. Carol was his gatekeeper, fending off unwanted visitors. As usual, there were guests: Margery Bailey came down from Stanford to visit her old student; Broderick Crawford, who had played in *Of Mice and Men* on Broadway, dropped in for a weekend. Dook Sheffield, though still somewhat hurt, paid a call. Tom Collins, Frank Fenton, Toby Street, and the Lovejoys (Ritch and Tal) turned up at various times. Ed Ricketts, of course, was never far from view, and Steinbeck made regular visits into Monterey to see him. (Indeed, Steinbeck became a 'silent partner' now in Pacific Biological, which had been in financial trouble until he rescued it once and for all.)

One of the great annoyances of the summer was that Los Gatos had become excessively popular, and people started building houses all around the Steinbecks, destroying their sense of peace. Hammers stung the air. 'This place is getting built up and we have to move,' Steinbeck wrote in a panic to Elizabeth Otis in July. He and Carol began looking for a place deeper in the country, with enough land so that nobody could crowd them out again.

Work on the novel progressed with astonishing speed. Steinbeck's diary is full of exhortations to himself about work and discipline – pep talks, in effect. The entry for Monday, 13 June, is typical; the night before, he and Carol had gone over to the house of their friend Martin Ray, a vintner, and his wife; he had drunk far too much of his friend's champagne. Guilt swelled inside him as he entered his study the next morning:

> Now a new week starts and unpropitiously for me. Last night up to Rays' and drank a great deal of champagne. I pulled my punches pretty well but I am not in the dead sober state I could wish. However, I will try to go to work. Don't have to because I have a day caught up. All sorts of things might happen in the course of this book, but I must not be weak. This must be done. The failure of will even for one day has a devastating effect on the whole, far more important than just the loss of time and wordage. The whole physical basis of the novel is discipline of the writer, of his material, of the language. And sadly enough, if any of the discipline is gone, all of it suffers. And this slight fuzziness of mine may be a break in the discipline. I don't know yet. But right now I intend to find out.

Indeed, that day proved 'a bust', and the next day Steinbeck was frantic to make up for the loss. 'Well, I got it done,' he notes at the end of the Tuesday work session. On Wednesday, he reports to himself that 'the unity feeling is back', a sign that all would be well. On and on the diary unfolds, and one sees the oscillations that were part of the book's composition. Throughout, there is the feeling expressed on Saturday, 18 June: 'If only I could do this book properly it would be one of the really fine books and a truly American book.'

Beth, his sister, visited for a few days near the end of June. She recalls that 'John had never been so concentrated. You almost couldn't talk to him. I remember running through some family stories and he sat there at dinner looking through me. He didn't see me. His mind was on his book.' Another visitor confirms, 'It was almost as if there were a séance in the next room where John was working. John just kept writing and writing. Everyone in the town knew that something was going on, and they kind of stayed away. When John was outside, working in the garden, you didn't disturb him. It was part of the work. He was somewhere else, not where you saw him.'[16]

The first main section of the novel was finished on 30 June. In his diary, Steinbeck says, 'I felt very small and inadequate and incapable but I grew again to love the story which is so much greater than I am. To love and admire the people who are so much stronger and purer and braver than I am.' Steinbeck had come to see the story as something more real than life itself. Ma Joad, Tom, Casy – they were living people in his head. And when they didn't seem to be 'living', he admonished himself: 'Make them live.' On 6 July, he writes, 'My people must be more than people. They must be an over-essence of people.' The next day, he fell into despair about his ability to conjure lifelike creatures, but he quotes Carol to himself: 'Carol says, stay with the detail.' This was marvellous advice, and it worked. The details are what make *The Grapes of Wrath* as good as it is.

By 15 July, sixty-eight pages were written, roughly 70,000 words. He had planned to be halfway through the book by the first of August, so he was more or less on target. On 18 July, he broke for the day and attended a rodeo in Salinas: 'Drank lots of whiskey and had a fair time. Empty feeling, empty show.' This 'terrible feeling of lostness and loneliness' continued for a few weeks, even though he kept writing. On 8 August, he says, 'Well the work has pretty much gone to hell. Might just as well take it in stride.' The euphoria of June had passed, and Steinbeck entered what felt like a dark time.

Meanwhile, Pat Covici wanted to publish a book of Steinbeck's stories. By now there were well over a dozen strong stories, most of them published between 1933 and 1937 in *North American Review*, *Harpers*, *Colliers*, and elsewhere. It was a good idea, and Covici needed a strong seller to rescue his failing company. But it would take more than a single Steinbeck title to rescue Covici–Friede, which evaporated into thin air in June. *Time* reported the failure of the company on 29 August: 'Owing somewhere around $170,000, the ten-year-old publishing company of Covici-Friede last week was taken over by its printers, J. J. Little & Ives, who alone were in for a reported $103,000. Main asset of interest to creditors was Novelist John Steinbeck, ex-laborer and reporter whose tender tale of proletarian brutality, *Of Mice and Men*, had netted Covici–Friede about $35,000. How much Steinbeck was considered to be worth by his publishers was disclosed last week when his contract was sold for $15,000 to Viking Press.'

Pat Covici, too, was rescued by Harold Guinzburg, who headed Viking Press, one of New York's strongest and most venerable publishers. Covici had taken Steinbeck's collection of stories, *The Long Valley*, with him. In his diary of 9 August, Steinbeck records 'a new era' in his writing life ushered in by his signing the contract with Viking, which would remain his publisher to the end, although he was not feeling in an especially good mood just now. In mid-August, when the heat had become unbearable and the humidity was stifling, he marks his glum feelings: 'Demoralization complete and seemingly unbeatable.'

In spite of this depression, he and Carol finalized a deal on

14 August for this ranch on fifty acres some five miles north of
Los Gatos, which he bought for $10,000. A friend recalls, 'It
was a wonderful country place, with great views and such an
aura of calm. John loved the privacy there and the chance to
have a really massive garden. There was a big pond, and
woods you could hike in. Carol had a swimming pool added.
The setting was unusual and special.'[17] Steinbeck called this
property 'the most beautiful place in the world' and feared
that it was 'too good and too beautiful for me'. When exactly
they would move to the new house was not clear, but the
move was now possible. He could, if he chose, get away from
the noisy neighbourhood of Los Gatos.

'I'm not a writer. I've been fooling myself and other
people,' he notes on 16 August. Nevertheless, he determined
'to plod. Plod as the people are plodding.' On 23 August, he
curses his own limitations, which now loomed in ridiculously
exaggerated fashion: 'I shouldn't be thinking about getting
done. Should be thinking only of the story and, by God, I
will. I can't let future interfere with the hardest, most
complete work of my life. I simply can't. Always I have been
weak. Vacillating and miserable. I wish I wouldn't. I wish I
weren't. I'm so lazy, so damned lazy.' This self-admonition
was followed, the next day, with 'My nerves are going fast.'
Two days later, he complains, 'My work is no good, I think –
I'm desperately upset about it. Have no discipline any more.'
But he was determined, nevertheless, to make a good book.
'This one must be good. Very good.'

A new friend entered his life, unbidden, one hot day in
August. Steinbeck was writing in a deck chair in his garden
when a black limousine pulled up to his gate. A uniformed
chauffeur stepped out and opened the door for his employer,
a small, fine-boned man with grey curly hair and a cane. As
the man approached, Steinbeck sat forward with astonishment, recognizing the distinctive face of Charlie Chaplin,
America's first Hollywood megastar. The comedian, who

had read and admired Steinbeck's most recent work, lived in nearby Pebble Beach in a multi-million dollar compound; he thought it would be nice to meet the man who'd written the books, so he simply set off for Los Gatos without ever calling first: a king does not require a calling card. Steinbeck was baffled but pleased by the visit, and he quickly asked Carol to open a bottle of wine. They sat chatting in the sun for two hours, exchanging stories, and he and Carol would soon become part of Chaplin's circle, attending lavish parties at the great man's estate.

What with buying the new ranch, with Pat Covici's ups and downs (some of which necessarily affected Steinbeck) and, as usual, with the endless visitors, inquiries, requests, demands and genuine needs that had to be filled, he found himself writing his most important book under ludicrous pressure. 'Was ever a book written under greater difficulty?' he asks himself on 1 September. In spite of everything, he reports on 2 September, 'time goes on and the manuscript crawls on. And after a long time it will be done.'

The Long Valley appeared in September, when Steinbeck was just past the mid-point in writing *The Grapes of Wrath*. And while it did not sell quite on the same scale as *Tortilla Flat* or *Of Mice and Men*, it made it on to the bestseller lists, an unusual thing, then and now, for a volume of stories. It also received strong notices from the reviewers. Annie Laurie Williams wrote on September 23, '*The Long Valley* is getting marvelous press.'[18] Stanley Young, writing in *The New York Times Book Review* (25 September, 1938) predicted that Steinbeck would 'become a genuinely great American writer'. The next day, in *The New Yorker*, Clifton Fadiman called the book 'a remarkable collection by a writer who has so far neither repeated himself nor allowed himself a single careless sentence'.

The opening story, 'The Chrysanthemums', sets the tone for the book. It is a brilliant piece of writing, perhaps the best story Steinbeck ever wrote. We follow a brief period in the life of a woman, Elisa Allen, who is married to a dull but well-intentioned farmer. Steinbeck writes: 'The high grey-flannel fog of winter closed off the Salinas Valley from the sky and from all the rest of the world.' As in much of his fiction, this story opens with a personified landscape, a *passage moralisé* in which the weather and geographical setting are deeply symbolic, gesturing in the direction of the story's ultimate meaning. Here the claustrophobic world of Elisa Allen is signalled by the claustrophobic clouds pressing in on the valley. This frustrated woman will never break free.

The story concerns the way Elisa's dreams are manipulated by a passing rogue, a man who repairs household goods. Steinbeck's fiction is full of men like this one: there is Mac, for instance, from *In Dubious Battle*, who will do anything to win the migrant workers' confidence. The repairman plays upon Elisa's feelings, pretending to sympathize with her love of flowers, which is extreme. Her passion for chrysanthemums symbolizes her intimacy with the rhythms of the natural world and represents her deepest feelings. Only a gardener, like Steinbeck, could have written about the process of gardening so eloquently:

> There was a little square sandy bed kept for rooting the chrysanthemums. With her trowel she turned the soil over and over, and smoothed it and patted it firm. Then she dug ten parallel trenches to receive the sets. Back at the chrysanthemum bed she pulled out the little crisp shoots, trimmed off the leaves of each one with her scissors and laid it on a small orderly pile.

Steinbeck understands the metaphor of gardening in a deeply symbolic way and uses this knowledge to make his point. Elisa is finally hurt by the repairman, who was merely toying with her, but she is not broken, as Charlotte Hadella notes: 'even though, in the end, she thinks of herself as a

Sorry I know this isn't his answer his but it couldn't be obvious

weak, old woman, the powerful imagery of the strong, new crop of chrysanthemums waiting for rain still dominates the story.'[19] She compares Elisa's disappointment to a kind of 'pruning – the clipping back of the romantic "shoots" of her imagination before they bud so that her energy can feed a strong reality and produce large, healthy blooms'.

In other stories, the women hurt the men, as in 'The White Quail'. Protagonist Mary Teller is another fanatical gardener, and she seeks to create an unchanging world in her garden. She has married Harry Teller, a man who allows her the complete freedom to make her garden into an Edenlike enclosure, a prelapsarian paradise. She wants to keep out 'the world that wants to get in, all rough and tangled and unkempt'. But she is unable to recognize that her efforts to create this artificial world are misguided, linked to a neurotic desire to control what cannot be controlled. Mary identifies with a white quail – a sign of purity – that lives in her garden. This totemic animal is more symbolic than real, and when it is threatened by a cat she begs her husband to shoot it. He shoots the quail instead, murdering by proxy the wife who has gardened him out of her life. 'Oh, Lord, I'm so lonely,' he cries at the end. As Hadella says, this is 'a symbolic action by a character who is incapable of real action'. She underscores 'Mary's ability to dominate Harry so thoroughly that he is only capable of symbolic violence'.

It is the wife who is lonely in 'The Murder', a startling tale about another marriage on the rocks. Jelka and Jim live together without speaking or communicating. She is a Yugoslavian girl, the 'daughter of a heavy and patient farmer of Pine Canyon'. Steinbeck imagines the torture and indignity of their loneliness within marriage. And we are not surprised when Jelka takes a lover, her cousin, near the climax of the story. We are, however, stunned when Jim murders the man while he is sleeping with Jelka. The narrative spirals into further violence when he beats up his wife, thus establishing a form of 'communication' which is brutal but believable in the context of this story. 'The Murder' reads more like a morality tale than a realistic story, but it is written with extraordinary conviction and rings true.

'The Raid' is another story in which violence plays a key part, although Steinbeck's focus is on the psychological consequences of violence rather than on the violence itself. Dick and Root, the protagonists, are versions of Mac and Jim of *In Dubious Battle*. (They also bear a strong resemblance to Henry Fleming and Jim Conklin in Stephen Crane's *The Red Badge of Courage*, which was obviously a model for Steinbeck, who seems to have lifted whole passages from Crane.) Dick and Root belong to the Communist Party, and their job is to organize the workers in a small town. The action centres on Root's personal effort to overcome his fear of being thrashed by the anti-Party mob. Dick, the older man, is a seasoned veteran of the class war; 'If someone busts you,' he tells his neophyte colleague, 'it isn't him that's doing it, it's the System. And it isn't you he's busting. He's taking a crack at the Principle.' Steinbeck tells this story without taking sides, a considerable achievement in the mid-Thirties.

In the same way, the violence which generates narrative momentum in 'The Vigilante' occurs off-stage. Steinbeck focuses throughout on the psychological state of Mike, who has helped to lynch a black man and is stumbling home in the aftermath of this terrible act. Steinbeck examines the man's conscience indirectly through his conversations on the way home and, once home, through his encounter with his wife, who sees the look in Mike's eye and suspects that he has been unfaithful to her. He has, indeed, been unfaithful, but not in the way she imagines: 'He walked through the kitchen and went into the bathroom. A little mirror hung on the wall. Mike took off his hat and looked at his face. "By God, she was right," he thought. "That's just exactly how I do feel." '

In keeping with his interest in the phalanx, Steinbeck

explores Mike's relation to the mob; it appears that Mike has no sense of himself except in relation to the group. The story opens with the mob spirit beginning to dwindle in the wake of the lynching: 'A tired quiet settled on the people; some members of the mob began to sneak way into the darkness.' Consequently, 'Mike, knew it was over. He could feel the let-down in himself.' Once the group has disbanded, he is left without a centre, lost.

Peter Randall, the husband and respectable farmer at the centre of 'The Harness', is stifled by his marriage to Emma; she quite literally forces him to wear a special shoulder brace because of his weak posture. Though he occasionally escapes, usually once a year, to the whorehouses of San Francisco for 'relief', he is pathologically tied to his 'harness'. Painfully aware of his shortcomings, he says to a neighbour, 'A man ought to stand up straight. I am a sloucher.' Like Pat Humbert in *The Pastures of Heaven*, he cannot escape his destiny; the mark of the past cannot be erased. Even after Emma's death, Peter is bound to her, harnessed in a deeply neurotic fashion.

One shudders to count the number of husbands and wives in *The Long Valley* who live at each other's throats. Frustration is the chief emotion felt by these unhappy couples, who seem forcibly tied to the land rather than rooted in some organic sense; they are likewise bound to their histories and marriages. It is tempting to speculate about Steinbeck's own marriage and how its tension flowed into the writing of these stories. Carol was certainly present during their composition, and Steinbeck seems to have felt restrained by her, frus-trated, even 'harnessed' by her disapproval. Her affair with Joseph Campbell had seeded a jealousy and resentment that later bloomed into thorough disgust. On the other hand, the Campbell fling could not have happened if the marriage had been secure and comfortable. A rift had been widening over the years; by the time *The Long Valley* was published, there was little in the way of fresh life in the marriage. One observer says, 'She found him insolent, arrogant, selfish, and self-destructive. He found her petty, mean-spirited, and bad-tempered. If they had stayed together, they would have killed each other.'[20]

'The Snake' is a bizarre Freudian tale set in the labs of Pacific Biological and featuring a clone of Ed Ricketts called Dr Phillips. Since it makes fun of Phillips's fear of women and sexual frustration, I suspect the story was written as a private joke between Steinbeck and Ricketts, but it remains a psychologically gripping work with a subtly ironic twang. It features a mysterious woman with black hair who represents Eve – the woman who causes the fall of man. Dr Phillips is a freakish Adam, the 'pure' scientist trying to control the animal world in his makeshift and demented Eden of the lab. In the end, the dark forces (which the woman embodies) have their sway over the scientist, who seems himself to have created this dark woman; she represents his own duality, which he consciously denies. Steinbeck seems to be wagging a finger at Ed Ricketts, saying, 'Be careful, Ed. Good and evil, like reason and emotion, are two sides of the same coin. You can exclude one side only at your peril.'

The volume ends on a strong note with 'The Red Pony', one of Steinbeck's most enduring tales. (The final story in *The Long Valley* is called 'The Leader of the People', and it became Part IV of 'The Red Pony' when the tale was republished separately in book form by Viking in 1945.) 'The Red Pony' is really a brief, episodic novel in which Steinbeck traces the emotional development of a boy, Jody Tiflin, from the narrow self-concern typical of children to a more compassionate view of the world. In keeping with this development, the first story, 'The Gift', turns on the gift of a red pony, which signals Jody's movement towards responsibility. He is, however, totally dependent on his father, whom he obeys 'in everything without questions of any kind'. Trust is the central issue in the story, and Jody trusts Billy Buck, a farmhand, as well as his father. Billy promises to put the red pony in the barn if it rains, but he doesn't; the pony catches cold and eventually dies, running off into the field to collapse. Buzzards swarm over the carcass, and Jody, hysterical, manages to catch and kill one of them, staring at the bird with an 'impersonal and unafraid and detached' glare. The great and sad lesson Jody has learned is the fact of human fallibility, and his innocence is destroyed for ever.

'The Great Mountains' is the second story, a fierce tale of old age and its indignities. There is an old man on the Tiflin ranch whom Jody's father compares to a horse 'who ought to be shot'. But Jody strikes up a friendship with the old fellow, who radiates 'a nameless sorrow'. In the end, the old man goes off, like the red pony, to die by himself in the mountains. Jody's perspective has been widened once again: old age, like youth, has its tragic aspect.

The third story, 'The Promise', concerns a young colt which Jody's father has promised the boy as a replacement for the red pony. Jody's responsibilities here are specific: his father insists that he take one of the mares to be mated; he must pay the stud fee with money he has earned himself. Further, he is to tend the mare for nearly a year, during the pregnancy – an unbearably long period for a young boy, who feels 'reduced to peonage for the whole late spring and summer' as he waits for the horse, Nellie, to deliver her colt. When the time finally arrives, Nellie runs into trouble and has to be sacrificed for the sake of the colt. Jody gets what he wants in the end, a colt, but it comes with a huge sacrifice and another crucial lesson: old age must give way to youth.

Although 'The Leader of the People' was added later as a conclusion, it is centred on a visit from Mrs Tiflin's father, who originally led the family from the east to the west coast. The old man loves to recall his pioneering days, but Jody's father complains, 'He just goes on and on.' Mrs Tiflin tries to explain to her impatient husband, 'That was the big thing in father's life. He led a wagon train clear across the plains to the coast, and when it was finished, his life was done.' The problem was, the great trek came to an end, and the old man lost his function, which had a reality only in relation to the group. The old man, alas, hears his son-in-law complaining about him and is struck by the truth of what he hears. 'The crossing is finished,' he says. 'Maybe it should be forgotten, now it's done.' He sits on the porch alone, depressed. His grandson, Jody, feels very sorry for his grandfather and brings him a glass of lemonade. He is utterly empathetic, and in the discharge of these sympathies in this small act of kindness he moves beyond the self-concern apparent in 'The Promise'. Jody has matured.

'The Red Pony' is memorable for its simplicity and beauty. Steinbeck weds form and content so completely that one is never conscious of a 'moral'. The California landscape glistens in the background, giving the story its texture and depth of field. It is not surprising that this small book has become something that children are drawn to, generation after generation. Jody Tiflin's gradual emergence into maturity is traced with affection, reserve, clarity and compassion. In the process, Steinbeck writes forcefully about the painful transformations human beings must endure.

Although he paid only slight attention to the reviews and sales of *The Long Valley*, the argument has occasionally been made that Steinbeck's short stories are superior to his novels.[21] Even André Gide once said that Steinbeck wrote 'nothing more perfect, more accomplished, than certain of his short stories'. [22] As criticism, I find this a misguided attempt to overvalue one aspect of the writer's work at the expense of another. Steinbeck was certainly a capable and sometimes brilliant writer of short fiction, but after *The Long Valley* he seldom attempted to write in this genre again.

As the summer drew to a close, his mind was firmly on the

big novel which he christened with a name on 3 September: *The Grapes of Wrath*. The title, suggested by Carol, was perfect. She had taken it from a striking passage which she found in the manuscript itself:

> The people come with nets to fish for potatoes in the river, and the guards hold them back; they come in rattling cars to get the dumped oranges, but the kerosene is sprayed. And they stand still and watch the potatoes float by, listen to the screaming pigs being killed in a ditch and covered with quicklime, watch the mountains of oranges slop down to a putrefying ooze; and in the eyes of the hungry there is a growing wrath. In the souls of the people the grapes of wrath are filling and growing heavy, growing heavy for the vintage.

It was a relatively short sprint to the finish, although on some days Steinbeck managed only a page and on others he would write ten or twelve handwritten pages. The strain was terrible: 'I don't know whether it was just plain terror of the ending or not. My stomach went to pieces yesterday. May have been nerves,' he notes in the diary on 25 October. He was shivering and sick with some intestinal bug on 26 October, a Wednesday, when he wrote the last paragraphs, bringing his journey – and that of the Joads – to a close. The last sentence for that day's entry says it all: 'Finished this day – and I hope to God it's good.'

X

The Road to Canonization

'You say you are afraid of me. I'm afraid of myself. I mean
the creature that has been built up.'

Steinbeck to Dook Sheffield, January 1940

The Steinbecks had moved to the Biddle ranch outside Los
Gatos in October, camping in the old farmhouse on the
property while their new house was being built. The move
took place just as *The Grapes of Wrath* drew near to completion,
and it was at the Biddle ranch that Steinbeck finished his 'big
book'. Both he and Carol were exhausted by the effort, and
both succumbed to fierce bronchial colds; they nursed each
other through a rainy and emotionally wearing Christmas
season.

The new house and the new year, 1939, coincided; they
took possession of the house on a sunny but cool day in
January. Steinbeck was suffering the ill effects of his ferocious
period of creativity: 'I think I worked myself past the danger
point in that book. Broke out in a neuritis and only a basal
metabolism test showed the reason. Anyway I'm in bed and
can get some letters written for the first time in ages,' he
wrote to Pat Covici on New Year's Day, adding, 'It is beautiful
here. I can look out the window at the valley below. But I
want to get out and plant things.'[1]

Viking planned to bring out *The Grapes of Wrath* in late
March or early April, but there were some delicate problems
in the manuscript that had to be addressed. The main
objection concerned its language, which Pat Covici, Harold
Guinzburg and Marshall Best (a senior editor) considered
'rough' in places. The fear was that book stores might refuse

to stock a novel full of 'obscene' dialogue; the book might even be banned. Thus, Elizabeth Otis was dispatched to California to work with Steinbeck, who she knew would object sternly to any changes he suspected were being made for prudish or commercial reasons.

She arrived soon after the New Year and sat at a big desk in Steinbeck's new study while he lay, recuperating, on a couch. Each little change, he later recalled, felt like a blow. 'My whole system recoiled,' he said. As any decent novelist would, he had strong feelings about the rhythmical flow of the dialogue, insisting that if anything were dropped he must add something to maintain the rhythm. Otis meticulously extracted the four-letter words, putting in their place what-ever Steinbeck suggested; but she had difficulties in sending the telegram via Western Union. The operator was horrified; 'You are obviously not a Christian, madame!' the woman intoned. It took some fancy talking to convince her that what was being done was, indeed, an act of purification.

On 9 January, Pat Covici wrote that he and his colleagues at Viking had been 'emotionally exhausted after reading *The Grapes of Wrath*'. Marshall Best characterized the novel as 'the most important piece of fiction on our list'. This was, as Steinbeck saw it, 'just buttering up', a prelude to the request for revisions that Covici enclosed: 'We felt that we would not be good publishers if we failed to point out to you any weaknesses or faults that struck us.'[2] He explained that one of the weak spots was the ending:

> Your idea is to end the book on a great symbolic note, that
> life must go on and will go on with a greater love and
> sympathy and understanding for our fellowmen. Nobody
> could fail to be moved by the incident of Rose of Sharon
> giving her breast to the starving man, yet, taken as the
> finale of such a book with all its vastness and surge, it
> struck us on reflection as being all too abrupt. It seems to us
> that the last few pages need building up.

Covici also notes, in a curious postscript, that Marshall Best recalled a story by Guy de Maupassant where a woman offers her breast to a starving man on a train.

Steinbeck had about had it by now and responded testily on 16 January: 'I cannot change that ending.' He argued that the ending was 'casual' and that he could not build up the role of the stranger who is offered Rose of Sharon's breast; it is important that the 'Joads don't know him, don't care about him, have no ties to him.' After such an intense period of creative outburst, there was nothing left in him. Revision seemed impossible; furthermore, he believed his instincts in composition had been correct, and he would let the book stand as it was.

Good things continued to happen. The cross-country tour of the play, *Of Mice and Men*, was a success, and royalties poured in. Then, in mid-January, Steinbeck was elected to the National Institute of Arts and Letters, an honour which he accepted happily. More pleasant news came when Lewis Milestone, the director whom Pare Lorentz had recommended, acquired the film rights to *Of Mice and Men*. As Lorentz said, Steinbeck could not have found a better person; Milestone's *All Quiet on the Western Front* was already a classic, and he was a man of high intelligence and artistic integrity. Steinbeck could rest assured that his novella would be adapted with respect.

Charlie Chaplin, meanwhile, dropped by to relax on Steinbeck's ranch before shooting one of his best-known films, *The Great Dictator*. The two had become reasonably good friends in a brief time, and Steinbeck (at Chaplin's request) began to tinker with the shooting script of *The Great Dictator*, adding a few lines here and there. Chaplin suggested that he might want to write a book about the making of the film, and Steinbeck played along, but as soon as Chaplin left the idea was dropped. He was not about to waste his time on somebody else's film, even if that somebody else happened to be Charlie Chaplin.

One of the consequences of Steinbeck's growing fame was that a latent tendency towards paranoia occasionally rose to the surface; the truth was that Steinbeck had good reason to be paranoid. It seems difficult now to recall this, but there was great fear in the United States in the Thirties that a revolution might break out like the one which had taken place in Russia only two decades earlier. Franklin Roosevelt had played a crucial role in preventing such a turn of events, largely by creating a welfare state and giving people a feeling (or perhaps the illusion) that the government cared about what happened to them. But there was considerable anxiety in the middle and upper-middle classes about the possibility of revolution, even as late as 1939. With hindsight, we know that the war ended the Great Depression; in that last year of a terrible decade, however, it seemed all too possible that another ten years of economic chaos lay ahead.

Now, a month or so before the publication of *The Grapes of Wrath*, printed material began to circulate suggesting that John Steinbeck was a dangerous revolutionary. Steinbeck reported to his agent on 4 March that FBI agents had been investigating him. A friend of his, Jane Smith, ran a book store in Monterey, and she reported that two men who claimed affiliation with J. Edgar Hoover had appeared in her shop with inquiries about him. Had he ever talked about Communism? Who were his friends? What sort of books did he buy? Did he believe in the overthrow of the government of the United States by violent means? Their questions struck an ominous note.

Steinbeck also learned that the Associated Farmers intended to 'get him' in any manner they could, and that a right-wing group of northern California business people were supplying the names of 'known Communists and Red sympathizers' to the sheriff in each county and that his name had been duly entered as a Red revolutionary. Panicked by this, Steinbeck went to a lawyer to see what could be done, but there was apparently little defence against such charges. He was, however, warned to be careful about what he did, where he went, and with whom he associated. Trumped-up accusations, no matter how preposterous, could be dangerous. Dirty tricks had already landed dozens of migrant workers and their sympathizers in jail, and the possibility existed, however slight, that an attempt could be made on Steinbeck's life. He was frightened and began to live more cautiously.

The Grapes of Wrath arrived in the mail on 3 March, a month before its official release date, and Steinbeck was 'immensely pleased' by its look. 'The Battle Hymn of the Republic', at his insistence, appeared in the end papers. At 850 pages, *The Grapes of Wrath* was a hefty tome, intimidating in its size. Two weeks later, the first reviews began appearing, with a few reviewers disliking the philosophical chapters. 'Fortunately,' Steinbeck wrote to Pat Covici, 'I'm not writing for reviewers.'

On the whole, critics admired the book. Ecstatic praise issued from Edward Weeks in *The Atlantic Monthly* and John Chamberlain in *Harpers* – two extremely influential critics at the time. In *North American Review*, Charles Angoff wrote: 'With his latest novel, Mr Steinbeck at once joins the company of Hawthorne, Melville, Crane, and Norris, and easily leaps to the forefront of all his contemporaries. The book has all the earmarks of something momentous, monumental, and memorable.' Attacking in advance critics who might object to the novel's language and construction, Angoff added, 'The book has the proper faults: robust looseness and lack of narrative definiteness – faults such as can be found in the Bible, *Moby Dick*, *Don Quixote*, and *Jude the Obscure*. The greater artists almost never conform to the rules of their art as set down by those who do not practice it.'

Two influential reviews came from Clifton Fadiman in *The New Yorker* and Malcolm Cowley in *The New Republic*.

Fadiman began: 'If only a couple of million overcomfortable people can be brought to read it, John Steinbeck's *The Grapes of Wrath* may actually effect something like a revolution in their minds and hearts.' He compared the book favourably to Victor Hugo's *Les Misérables* and other great books of righteous indignation. Cowley, who resisted overpraising any book, wrote:

> I can't agree with those critics who say that *The Grapes of Wrath* is the greatest novel of the last ten years; for example, it doesn't rank with the best of Hemingway or Dos Passos. But it belongs very high in the category of the great angry books like *Uncle Tom's Cabin* that have roused a people to fight against intolerable wrongs.

More than half a century after its publication, *The Grapes of Wrath* remains one of the permanent fixtures of American literature.

The novel begins with Tom Joad's homecoming after being released from the Oklahoma State Penitentiary, where he has spent four years (of a seventeen-year sentence) for homicide. He hitches rides and, finally, walks home to Sallisaw, where he discovers that his family homestead has been strangely abandoned. The windows are all shattered, and even the well has been filled in. Muley Graves, a neighbour who has become somewhat deranged by recent events, stops to explain what has happened: the tenant farmers have all been evicted, 'tractored off', as he puts it.

The next day Tom rejoins his family just as his uncle has been ordered off his farm. Having no other visible choices, the whole family of Joads – twelve in all – heads for California in a broken-down jalopy. The rumour is that California offers good jobs and high wages, and that plenty of work is available for those willing to bend their backs. The Joads soon discover that the westering movement along Route 66 is epic in proportions, a modern version of the old wagon trains.

Everyone has the same idea and dream. The vast migration becomes a kind of reverse *Odyssey*, a journey away from home. Steinbeck writes:

> Highway 66 is the main migrant road. 66 – the long concrete path across the country, waving gently up and down on the map, from the Mississippi to Bakersfield – over the red lands and the gray lands, twisting up into the mountains, crossing the Divide and down into the bright and terrible desert, and across the desert to the mountains again, and into the rich California valleys.

The road runs through Oklahoma City towards Elk City and Texola, then across the Texas Panhandle through Amarillo, onwards through New Mexico and Albuquerque and Sante Fe, then down the Rio Grande into Arizona, where it crosses 'the broken sun-rotted mountains' of Arizona to the Colorado River. Across the river the state of California begins, with 66 continuing over the desert until Barstow, 'and more desert until at last the mountains rise up again, the good mountains, and 66 winds through them. Then suddenly a pass, and below, the beautiful valley, below orchards and vineyards and little houses, and in the distance a city. And, oh, my God, it's over.'

There are, alas, deaths along the way, and losses less definitive. Grampa Joad goes first. Then Gramma. The wearing out of a bearing in the engine becomes a tragedy of almost equal proportions, threatening the onward progress and the propelling dream of a better life. After a last hectic ride across the desert and up through the 'good mountains', the Joads cross the pass at Tehachapi and glimpse the promised land, like Canaan, shimmering in the distance:

> Al jammed on the brake and stopped in the middle of the road, and 'Jesus Christ! Look!' he said. The vineyards, the orchards, the great flat valley, green and beautiful, the trees set in rows, and the farm houses.

And Pa said, 'God Almighty!' The distant cities, the little
towns in the orchard land, and the morning sun, golden on
the valley. A car honked behind them. Al pulled to the side of
the road and parked.

'I want ta look at her.' The grain fields golden in the
morning, and the willow lines, the eucalyptus trees in rows.

Pa sighed, 'I never knowed they was anything like her.'

The second half of the novel is set in California, the paradisial
goal. Having reached their physical destination, the Joads
confront the dismal situation that greeted all migrants. For
the first time, they discover that they are Okies and not just
people in search of a livelihood; 'and that means you're
scum', they are told. 'We ain't foreign,' they say to each other
with horror-tinged voices. 'Seven generations back
Americans, and beyond that Irish, Scotch, English, German.
One of our folks was in the Revolution, an' they was lots of
our folks in the Civil War – both sides. Americans.'

Jim Casy, a preacher who has lost his faith in conventional
religion, had joined the Joads at the outset in Oklahoma, and
in the second half he becomes yet another of Steinbeck's
Christ figures. Like Jim Nolan of *In Dubious Battle*, he is
ultimately sacrificed, killed by vigilantes. The novel ends
with the controversial tableau in which Rose of Sharon,
whose baby has been born dead, offers her breast to save a
starving man's life. This simple act of charity is crucial,
symbolizing the humanity of these people. Misfortune has
both united and ennobled them.

The strongest character in the novel is Ma Joad, who holds
the family together throughout this ordeal. Tom Joad is the
'hero' only in the roughest scene (in the film version, starring
Henry Fonda, his role is enhanced to provide a suitable
vehicle for stardom). When he kills a man in the labour
skirmish in which Casy is murdered in Chapter 26, he must
flee. Before he does so, however, he and Ma have a long talk

about Casy's philosophy, a view of life that must be considered the ideological core of the book:

> 'He was a good man,' Ma said.
>
> Tom went on, 'He spouted out some Scripture once, an' it didn' soun' like no hell-fire Scripture. He tol' it twicet, an' I remember it. Says it's from the Preacher.'
>
> 'How's it go, Tom?'
>
> 'Goes, "Two are better than one, because they have a good reward for their labor. For if they fall, the one will lift up his fellow, but woe to him that is alone when he falleth, for he hath not another to help him up." That's part of her.'
>
> 'Go on,' Ma said. 'Go on, Tom.'
>
> 'Jus' a little bit more, "Again, if two lie together, then they have heat: but how can one be warm alone? And if one prevail against him, two shall withstand him, and a three-fold cord is not quickly broken." '

One can read this, obviously, in terms of traditional class solidarity, but Steinbeck's novel operates on many levels. He claimed to Pat Covici that the book had 'five layers', but he never said what they were. Critics have had a field day with this suggestion, tracing the literal, allegorical, moral and anagogical levels (a fourfold pattern popular in the Middle Ages as a form of interpretation). Like all significant works of art, *The Grapes of Wrath* contains many levels, although Steinbeck would probably have disliked thinking of these in hierarchical terms.

The literal and metaphor levels are intimately bound as the novel describes a literal and spiritual journey that is part journalism, part spiritual text. But these are not separate strands. *The Grapes of Wrath* must not be seen merely as a story about migrants from Oklahoma, nor should it be regarded as an allegorical tale about the endless pursuit of the American dream of a better life. It is also not a simple protest against 'man's inhumanity to man', as several critics have maintained. Rather, the novel tells the story of what Steinbeck calls 'Manself'. It is about the human quest for self-realization, as a group and as separate individuals. Chapter 14 contains a fascinating passage:

> This you may say of man – when theories change and crash, when schools, philosophies, when narrow dark alleys of thought, national, religious, economic, grow and disintegrate, man reaches, stumbles forward, painfully, mistakenly sometimes. Having stepped forward, he may slip back, but only half a step, never the full step back. This you may say and know it and know it. This you may know when the bombs plummet out of the black planes on the market place, when prisoners are stuck like pigs, when the crushed bodies drain filthily in the dust.

For all his interest in 'non-teleological thinking', Steinbeck's essential humanism shines through in passages like this. Richard Astro notes that the 'major portion of Steinbeck's world-view in *The Grapes of Wrath* emerges through the consciousness of Jim Casy'.[3] Casy, much like Doc Burton of *In Dubious Battle*, is another, if much less obvious, reincarnation of Ed Ricketts. Having abandoned the rigid humanism of post-Reformation Christianity, Casy moves increasingly towards an Emersonian vision in which man and nature are aligned. He is a visionary who breaks through to an understanding of the cosmic whole; like Tolstoy and Gandhi, he also comes to believe in the practical working out of his faith in deeds. His allegiance with the downtrodden is just part of his greater commitment to the Emersonian Oversoul, 'Maybe all men got one big soul ever'body's a part of,' he speculates. He knows this 'so deep down that it was true'.

The roots of Steinbeck's philosophy, only partially reflected by Casy, go deep into the American intellectual tradition. As Frederick Carpenter has noted, 'For the first time in history, *The Grapes of Wrath* brings together and makes real three skeins of American thought. It begins with the transcendental oversoul, Emerson's faith in the common man, and his Protestant self-reliance. To this it joins Whitman's religion of the love of all man and his mass democracy. And it combines these mystical and poetic ideas with the realistic philosophy of pragmatism and its emphasis on effective actions.' Jim Casy, the ex-preacher, 'translates American philosophy into words of one syllable, and the Joads translate it into action'.[4] A further strain of American thought present in Steinbeck's novel was the Jeffersonian. 'Because he had faith in the common man and thus gave his thinking a broad popular basis, Steinbeck was closer to Jeffersonianism than were the Southern Agrarians, who sought to resurrect not only an agricultural way of life but also the traditional cultural values of Europe,' argues Chester Eisinger. 'Steinbeck was concerned with democracy, and looked upon agrarianism as a way of life that would enable us to realize the full potentialities of the creed. Jefferson, of course, held the same.'[5]

One must not, of course, overlook the ongoing influence of Ed Ricketts, who was still a dominant figure in Steinbeck's life at the time of the novel's composition. In an article called 'A Spritual Morphology of Poetry', Ricketts (in one of his rare excursions into non-scientific writing) suggested that the basic message of all western literature was that 'all that lives is holy', quoting a line from William Blake. Casy, the ex-preacher who can't stop preaching, eventually concludes much the same thing.

Doc Burton could not act, but Casy can. He (like Tom, his protégé) has moved beyond non-teleological thinking towards the *telos* of political activism. He becomes a fighter 'for human rights and a twelve-hour day'. Like Christ, his last remark to his murderers is, 'You fellas don' know what you're doin'.' More than any other character in Steinbeck, Jim Casy unites the quest for a cosmic ideal with a gift for deeds. Casy wants to move from the 'I' to the 'we', and this is the progress defined by the Joad family, as symbolized by Rose of Sharon's final act of charity. The Joads, in effect, begin as a single family unit, selfish and self-contained. They move towards generosity and a feeling of belonging to a much larger unit, to humanity as a whole, that 'one big soul ever'body's a part of'.[6]

Ma Joad, 'the citadel of the family', regards the westering journey at the outset only in terms of the survival of this single unit. Her original hope is for 'one of them little houses' in California. She even threatens Pa Joad with a jack handle when she feels the family unit is being threatened. 'All we got is the family unbroke,' she says, 'I ain't gonna see us bust up.' Gradually, however, she shifts her viewpoint, expanding her consciousness to include the larger family of humankind. So when Rose of Sharon says 'Yes' to the prospect of suckling the dying man, Ma confirms her decision: 'I knowed you would. I knowed!'

The Grapes of Wrath has, if anything, suffered from critical indifference since its initial reception, although readers have continued to flock to its pages. It is not a cynical book, nor is it 'complicated' in the way of Faulkner's novels. Critics seem to prefer both cynicism and formal, if not stylistic, complication. There is, finally, something crude about Steinbeck's book; the same, I would argue, might be said of *War and Peace*. Steinbeck is, foremost, a storyteller; he is also a moralist who offers a bold statement in this novel. One thing is certain: the story makes a permanent impression on the reader, conjuring an indelible impression of an era, speaking nobly about humanity and its aspirations. For these and many other reasons, aesthetic and sociological, it continues to appeal to successive generations of readers.

Steinbeck cautioned Pat Covici about printing too many copies of the book, which he believed would attract a limited audience. Against this recommendation, *The Grapes of Wrath* appeared in a relatively large printing of 19,804 copies,

all bearing the yellow top-stain that marks the first edition.
This edition was quickly exhausted, and by 17 May the
number in print topped 83,000 copies. By the end of 1939,
over 430,000 books had been shipped – a staggering number,
then or now. Since then, the novel has never been out of print
or sold under 50,000 a year. (The number of translations and
books sold in non-English-speaking countries is also mind-
boggling.)

Steinbeck could hardly bear the publicity that followed, an
avalanche of attention beyond anything that had happened
to him before. Offers poured in from unimaginable sources.
A studio in Hollywood called, for instance, to offer him
$5,000 a week to write scripts. Carol took the phone from
John and shouted into it: 'What the hell would we do with
$5,000 a week. Don't bother us!' But Steinbeck *was* interested
in Hollywood, especially when it came to him through Pare
Lorentz. In mid-April, he joined Lorentz briefly in Chicago,
where the film-maker was working on a documentary about
the hazards of childbirth called *The Fight for Life*. Steinbeck
threw himself into the project, working for a month with the
crew (doing research and helping Lorentz with the script). 'I
never worked such long hours in my life,' he wrote to Pat
Covici.

He returned to the ranch via New York and Washington
DC, hoping to carve out a quiet space for himself, but this was
not possible. *The Grapes of Wrath* was big news everywhere,
and hundreds of letters from readers had been sent on by his
publisher. The news also came, through a phone call from
Elizabeth Otis, that the film rights had been sold for $75,000,
one of the highest prices then paid by Hollywood for a novel.

In the meantime Carol was raging. 'She could hardly bear
the clamour over John's books,' says a friend, 'and as soon as
John returned from travelling, they set on each other,
squabbling over little household details. The more money
John made, the more he resented spending it. He couldn't

handle the changes. He grew resentful and testy. Friends stopped coming by to see them.'[7] Carol also found it 'tedious to stay at home and act as a kind of screen for John', and she was not pleased when her husband, having been home only a week, announced that he could not stay on the ranch a minute longer. He wanted to spend the month of June in Hollywood. 'But you hate Hollywood!' she protested. 'It doesn't matter,' he said, 'I've got to go.'

In retrospect, it seems clear that Steinbeck was dizzied by his success as well as deeply unhappy in his marriage. He wasn't sure who he was or, for that matter, where he was. One of the problems that had developed between the Steinbecks involved the prospect of children: 'Carol had felt for some time that they should have a child, but Steinbeck was afraid that fatherhood would interfere with his writing.'[8] The situation intensified when, just after Christmas, Carol became pregnant. Steinbeck panicked, insisting that she get an abortion, and she finally agreed to this against her better judgement. Unfortunately, an infection developed in the uterine tubes which led, within months, to a complete hysterectomy, an utterly devastating operation for a woman of child-bearing age who wanted a child badly. Carol 'never got over the bitterness of this'.

Joseph Campbell heard about the abortion and its consequences and was deeply angered. In a late interview, he vented his rage about Steinbeck's treatment of Carol: 'I don't happen to have good feelings for men who stay with a wife through the tough years and then, when things begin coming in, they move to another wife.'[9] Indeed, Steinbeck must be severely castigated for his treatment of Carol, which borders on gross inhumanity. He seems not to have appreciated the massive efforts she made on his behalf: the sacrifices, the endless adjustments to meet his schedule, the willingness to type manuscripts on demand, the self-repression. Like many artists, Steinbeck was willing at times to sacrifice his family to pursue his work.

One must, however, try to understand what lay behind his hideous behaviour. He was a man who combined a deep sense of his own value with a peculiar vulnerability and lack of self-confidence; he could not, as nobody can, escape his past, and the accusing finger of Olive Steinbeck still wagged in his unconscious. One consequence of this was that he often mistrusted his talent and his ability to forge on. The diaries he kept during the composition of *The Grapes of Wrath* suggest more clearly than anything else that he was often plagued by crushing self-doubts, always sure that he might tumble off the slopes of Parnassus at any moment. Whatever got written was, in his mind, a wonder, a piece of luck, a gift from the gods. He often assumed that he was at the end of his career, and that terrible misfortune lay ahead. To defend against these feelings, he had to work harder and try harder than everybody else. When success finally came after so much defeat, as it did in the late Thirties, he suspected that it was transitory and braced himself to fight even harder.

He moved temporarily to Los Angeles on 8 June, taking a small furnished apartment near the house of his friend from Salinas, Max Wagner. He used Max's house as a mail drop-off, and largely kept out of sight. He did, however, meet several times with Lewis Milestone, who was now working on *Of Mice and Men* with a screenwriter named Eugene Solow. He also met Nunnally Johnson, who was doing the script for *The Grapes of Wrath*. It was quite a thing to have two major film adaptations underway at one time. 'I don't think any writer has ever been luckier,' says Gore Vidal. 'Steinbeck is one of those rare novelists who actually had a happy relation to Hollywood. His work adapted well, and it was treated with respect. He was lucky in the people who worked with his books, too. They knew what they were doing.'[10]

Max was trying to break into the movies as an actor, but had thus far only had bit parts. He spent a good deal of time with a friend, Gwendolyn Conger, who lived around the corner. She, too, was trying to get movie parts, with no greater success than Max. Gwyn [this is the spelling she preferred after 1941, when she abruptly stopped spelling her name Gwen] lived with her mother and grandmother, earning a little money now and then as a singer in local bars. She liked to read, and she was amazed to discover that Max had gone to school with John Steinbeck. Max soon introduced them.

Steinbeck was in bad shape that month, troubled by a bad back, an inflamed leg and raw nerves. He and Carol were barely speaking, and he was 'hiding out' from the publicity machine, the journalists who pursued him like Furies. He looked rather dimly on Max's efforts to introduce him to new people, but Gwyn Conger was not just anyone. The couple met for the first time one night when Max took his friend to Rick's, a nightclub where Gwyn was singing. He listened over a whiskey-and-soda, dazzled by her silky voice and long legs. Between shows, she came to Max's table and flirted with his guest. Steinbeck, still a shy man, said very little but listened to her attentively, his eyes fixed on her in a way that signalled interest. For her part, Gwyn was fascinated by this famous man whose books she had heard of. The way he looked at her spoke volumes.

Gwyn was only twenty, and Steinbeck was thirty-eight – a considerable difference in age. 'She had a mighty sharp tongue,' a friend of hers remembers.[11] 'She was pretty, too. Taller than most of us. With dirty blonde hair with a lovely curl. Everybody thought of her as the sexiest girl around, and that was her way with men. She played up to them. She teased them. It was a great act, but it worked. Men couldn't stay away from her. Her phone rang all the time.' Beth Ainsworth has another opinion of Gwyn: 'She was awful. You couldn't trust her one bit. I sure didn't. Nobody did, except John – and he learned the hard way about that girl.'

The relationship was not rushed. Steinbeck took several

trips to Los Angeles that summer and made a point of seeing Gwyn each time. They went out for dinner with Pare Lorentz, with Lewis Milestone, and with Frank Loesser, the Broadway composer. (Loesser, who wrote *Guys and Dolls*, would eventually move to New York and become a close friend to Steinbeck. He lived just around the corner from the apartment where John and Elaine Steinbeck eventually settled.) The marriage to Carol, however, still had a grip on him. Nobody in his family had ever been divorced before, and it would be a big step, one that he would take unwillingly. Divorce, in his mind, was a sign of failure.

When he returned to the ranch on 20 June, he found the situation as threatening as before. 'I got home three days ago,' he wrote to Dook Sheffield, 'and found about five hundred letters that had to be answered.'[12] He went on to describe the threats against him by the Associated Farmers, saying he would have to be 'a little careful not to go anywhere alone nor to do anything without witnesses'. He was afraid of a set-up. As he later wrote to another friend, 'You get alone in a hotel and a dame will come in, tear off her clothes, scratch her face and scream and you try to talk yourself out of that one.' Was this paranoia? 'I don't think so,' says a former editor of the *San Francisco News*.[13] 'Some pretty awful tricks were being played on anybody who came down on the side of the migrants. Feelings ran high. It was a tense time in California, and the FBI was the worst. Hoover's boys were all over the place, and they sided with the landowners.'

Another twist came in July. Steinbeck wrote to Elizabeth Otis: 'The vilification of me out here from the large landowners and bankers is pretty bad. The latest is a rumor started by them that the Okies hate me and have threatened to kill me for lying about them. This made all the papers. Tom Collins says that when his Okies read this smear they were so mad they wanted to burn something down.'[14] He added, 'Meanwhile the Associated Farmers keep up a steady stream of accusation that I am first a liar and second a communist. Their vilification has a quality of hysteria, too.'

In late July, Lewis Milestone and Eugene Solow arrived at the ranch with the script for *Of Mice and Men*. Steinbeck had agreed to help them with it, but he was still in poor health. His leg was swollen, his back felt weak and his energy level was extremely low. Benson quotes a revealing interview with Milestone about what happened during that visit:

> [Solow] read the whole script. [Steinbeck] sat up and said, 'It's fine. What do you want me to say?' I said, 'Come on. Don't get lazy now. It's nice to hear that you are pleased with the thing, but there is a little more than that, because there are a couple of things I did without you, and I want you to go through it very carefully and make sure it is your own.' He said, 'All right'. So he got up, and he sat at the desk, and I looked over his shoulder. He was going through the dialogue changing the punctuation, and then he would change an 'if', 'but', 'and', and whatnot, and before my very eyes the whole thing was being changed and became Steinbeck's writing.[15]

The actual shooting started a month or so later, in the San Fernando Valley, and Steinbeck visited the set. Lon Chaney Jr played Lennie, and Burgess Meredith was George. Meredith recalls, 'John came by the set often. He would stand to one side, watching. Everybody knew it was him, and it made them alert. He and I became friends during those visits. We just liked each other a lot. The friendship lasted until the very end of his life, although I didn't see much of him after he moved to New York and married Elaine Scott.'[16]

The script for *The Grapes of Wrath* was underway at the same time, and Steinbeck met several times with Nunnally Johnson. Johnson assured him that every effort would be made to stick to the spirit, if not the letter, of the novel. The fear, of course, was that Darryl F. Zanuck, the producer, would try to water down the political message. To his credit,

Zanuck did not. According to Johnson, making *The Grapes of Wrath* changed Zanuck's personal politics. After he visited several migrant camps, he was horrified by the harshness confronting him. Steinbeck and Johnson became good friends; indeed, when Johnson was later drafted to write a screenplay adaptation of *The Moon is Down*, Steinbeck's wartime novel, he consulted the author about his feelings. Was there any particular line he should take? Did he mind if he changed certain things? Steinbeck looked at him coolly and said, 'Tamper with it'.

Tom Collins, meanwhile, was hired as technical assistant on the film and received $15,000 for his efforts, a huge amount of money for him. A significant amount of shooting was done around the Weedpatch camp which Collins ran, and he advised the director on the dress, manner, habits, speech and culture of the migrants. He also served as a guide to locations of note in the Central Valley. This cooperation between Collins and the movie company doubtless contributed to the realistic, almost documentary, feel of the film, which ranks high in the annals of good Hollywood film adaptations.

While all these interesting things were happening to Steinbeck, the marriage continued to degenerate. 'I think the pressure was too much on him,' his sister recalls. 'He and Carol were fighting all the time.' A friend says, 'Whenever John was near Carol he started drinking heavily, and he would sink into a stupor, and she would scream at him. Or she would ignore him, which was worse. She became jealous of the people he was meeting, and he kept her away from his new life. He didn't share that life with her, so it was bound to drive her crazy.'[17] He and Carol travelled to Los Angeles together at the end of July, and her behaviour was, in her husband's view, erratic. The crisis moved to a head when Carol stormed out of a party at the humorist Robert

Benchley's house one night, embarrassing her husband in front of his new Hollywood friends. Steinbeck pursued her back to the hotel, where they had a catastrophic fight. 'Carol went hysterical in Los Angeles and pulled out,' he wrote to Elizabeth Otis.[18] 'I have no doubt that I am to blame for this. I have a very great sense of failure about it.' He was in bed for two weeks in the hotel room after she left, demoralized and depressed; as soon as he was on his feet, he took off for the cottage in Pacific Grove, always a place where he could find peace. It occurred to him on the drive north that something would have to give, that his life had to change.

Ed Ricketts came at once, and Steinbeck discussed the possibility of divorce for the first time with his friend. He felt too upset after their conversation to remain alone at the cottage and went home with Ed, who now lived in a set of rooms over the lab of Pacific Biological. The two friends did not talk. Ricketts played records: Stravinsky, Beethoven, Mozart. Steinbeck, according to one account, 'walked around the lab and watched everybody working but it was his body walking around. The mind and spirit were not there. We had never seen him like this. Ed was very patient, of course. That was his nature, especially with John.'[19]

After long meditation, Steinbeck decided he did not want to leave Carol after all; they had made it this far, and he believed that he still loved her. He drove back to the ranch, and a reconciliation took place; the reunited couple, wary of each other but trying to work things out, hopped into the car and headed north, driving through Oregon and Washington, just 'driving and stopping and sleeping', as he wrote in a postcard to Otis. The wilderness was (and remains) glorious in these states, and Steinbeck found it soothing to be close to nature. It was September now, and the air was crisp and cool. The skies were clear. There were no letters or phone calls to answer, no requests for speeches or autographs. They met up with John Cage and his wife, Xenia, in Seattle, and the foursome continued together into Canada. The atmosphere, according to Steinbeck, was one of 'false hilarity'.

When they got back to the Biddle ranch a couple of weeks later, they took a brief look at the mountainous stack of mail and immediately flew to Chicago. The holiday mood had been exhilarating; they had temporarily come together again – an oscillation cruelly suggesting that all might be well with their marriage after all. Not wanting the good period to end, they feared that if they settled down on the ranch they would have to face themselves, and their relationship, once again in a colder light. In Chicago they stayed in a 'small, quiet hotel near the lake', connecting with Uncle Joe several times for dinner. They also saw Pare Lorentz, who was still working on his documentary. Indeed, a flurry of socializing briefly distracted them from the problems of their marriage, although it was clear that soon they would have to deal with things.

Steinbeck often lulled himself into a condition of counterfeit calm. He 'suffered the delusion right to the end that everything between himself and Carol would be okay'.[20] He affected ease and goodwill in a letter to Otis in early October, when he and Carol were back on the ranch:

It's a beautiful morning and I am just sitting in it and enjoying it. Everything is ripe now, apples, pears, grapes, walnuts. Prunes and raisins are on the drying trays. The cellar smells of apples and wine. The berries are ripe and every bird in the country is here – slightly tipsy and very noisy. The frogs are singing about a rain coming but they can be wrong. It's nice.[21]

He added that Carol was 'well and rested' and noted with curious glee that The Grapes of Wrath had finally slipped into second place on the bestseller list: 'In a month it will be off the list and in six months I'll be forgotten.' This, of course, was merely an odd kind of wishful thinking.

Steinbeck now felt that he had done about all he could do with the novel as a form. 'I've worked the novel . . . as far as I can take it,' he told Dook Sheffield in a letter of 13 November. [22] He said that he 'never did think much of it', that is, the novel; it was 'a clumsy vehicle at best'. How odd this sounds in the mouth of the man who had just written *The Grapes of Wrath*. Instead of wanting to push on, to move from one peak to another, higher peak, he was bent on retreat. 'I think he disbelieved his own success,' says John Hersey. 'He somehow thought that anything he achieved was accidental.' Again, the son of John Ernst and Olive was resisting his own talents, refusing to wear the mantle of his achievement.

One of the many ironies of this period is that Steinbeck appears to have gone against his earlier notion that a writer must stay out of the limelight and avoid certain people. He was, or had been, a loner who preferred his oldest and truest friends: men like Dook Sheffield, Toby Street and Ed Ricketts. But sudden fame and wealth threw him into contact with people like Burgess Meredith, Charlie Chaplin, Spencer Tracy, Anthony Quinn and others. Quinn, who was a young actor then, recalls, 'Steinbeck was a great figure and we all wanted to know him. I remember meeting him at a restaurant in San Francisco. He had such wonderful authority, and people wanted to meet him and listen to him talk.'[23] Meredith adds, 'I think it was all too much for him, the money and the people, the rising expectations. He was not happy. He was, of course, admired. But he was suddenly in a very fast circle, and there was lots of drinking and craziness.' To his old friends, Steinbeck referred to these people as 'the swimming pool set', and claimed, disingenuously, that it was Carol's desire to associate with these 'fancy people' that led to the widening of their social circle. In truth, Steinbeck had temporarily succumbed to the temptations which, only a couple of years before, he had understood were fatal to a writer of his nature.

His financial picture was certainly rosy now: he paid over $40,000 in taxes to the Internal Revenue Service in 1940. Having purchased a major share of Pacific Biologicals, he hoped to become more intimately involved with Ed Ricketts's organization, financing and occasionally going on expeditions. It occurred to him that he might write about these trips in a literary way, adding to the genre of Charles Darwin's *The Voyage of the Beagle*, which had become one of his favourite books. This, perhaps, was the way out of writing novels. Soon enough he would publish his *Sea of Cortez* – based on his journey with Ed Ricketts – a book which anticipates the work of such writer/naturalists as John Hay, John McPhee and Bill McGibbon. (Steinbeck's more intimate *The Log from the 'Sea of Cortez'* would not appear until 1951, ten years after the original version.)

The drift back to Pacific Grove was, in part, a response to the madness of his new life, a way of fighting the publicity and pressure to socialize on a grand scale with people he did not, finally, admire. It involved a self-preservational instinct as well as a deep understanding of where his roots lay. He wanted, always, to stay within range of the ocean, and the coastline of Monterey wakened a productive nostalgia: he felt in touch with himself, or his earlier selves, there. What he seems to have wanted now, more than anything, was a sense of freedom, and freedom meant anonymity.

The Grapes of Wrath did not fade away, as he pretended to hope it might. It was the bestselling novel of 1939 and remained a strong seller into 1940 and, of course, beyond. Letters from enthusiastic readers seemed never to abate, nor did the anger the book aroused in certain quarters. A public luncheon was held at the Palace Hotel in San Francisco to denounce the novel and its author, and comments vilifying Steinbeck never ceased. 'I say to you, and to every honest, square-minded reader in America, that the painting Steinbeck made in his book is a lie, a black, infernal creation of a twisted, distorted mind,' railed Congressman Lyle Boren of Oklahoma.[24] The book was banned by school boards in New York, Illinois, California and elsewhere.

Among the more peculiar attacks on Steinbeck was the charge that he was Jewish and that his book was part of a larger Zionist plot. A minister named Reverend L. M. Birkhead, who chaired a group called the Friends of Democracy, wrote to inquire about his nationality. According to his letter, he and his organization were committed to combating 'pro-Nazi and anti-Semitic propaganda'. Steinbeck responded with anguish and forthrightness: 'I am answering your letter with a good deal of sadness. I am sad for a time when one must know a man's race before his work can be approved or disapproved. It does not seem important to me whether I am Jewish or not, and I know that a statement of mine is useless if an interested critic wishes to ride a preconceived thesis. I cannot see how *The Grapes of Wrath* can be Jewish propaganda, but then I have heard it called communist propaganda also.'[25]

While attacks came from all sides, there was strong support for Steinbeck in important places, including the White House. Eleanor Roosevelt thought highly of his book and said so repeatedly in public, and her opinion was widely reported in the press. Steinbeck wrote to thank her, saying 'I have been called a liar so constantly that sometimes I wonder whether I may not have dreamed the things I saw and heard in the period of my research.'[26]

The simultaneous production of the film versions of *The Grapes of Wrath* and *Of Mice and Men* strongly increased Steinbeck's national visibility and won for him countless supporters. He wrote to Otis to describe the trip he and Carol took to Hollywood in early December:

We went down in the afternoon and that evening saw *Grapes* at Twentieth-Century. Zanuck has more than kept his word. He has a hard, straight picture in which the actors are submerged so completely that it looks and feels like a documentary film and certainly it has a hard, truthful ring. No punches were pulled – in fact, with descriptive matter removed, it is a harsher thing than the book, by far. It seems unbelievable but it is true. The next afternoon we went to see *Mice* and it is a beautiful job. Here Milestone has done a curious lyrical thing. It hangs together and is underplayed. You will like it.[27]

The films were good. As George Bluestone points out in his excellent study, *Novels into Films*: 'Some deletions, additions, and alterations, to be sure, reflect in a general way the ordinary process of mutation from a linguistic to a visual medium.'[28] Milestone's *Of Mice and Men* is close to the book, closer than the Broadway version. 'It just came out so well. We were all surprised,' says Burgess Meredith. 'Everyone loved it.' It was 'just about as good as any picture has a right to be', according to Frank S. Nugent in his *New York Times* review of the film. Edmund Wilson had a more acerbic but no less interesting view of *The Grapes of Wrath* as a film:

> Since the people who control the movies will not go a step of the way to give the script writer a chance to do a serious script, the novelist seems, consciously or unconsciously, to be going part of the way to meet the producers. John Steinbeck, in *The Grapes of Wrath*, has certainly learned from the films – and not only from the documentary pictures of Pare Lorentz, but from the sentimental symbolism of Hollywood. The result was that *The Grapes of Wrath* went on the screen as easily as if it had been written in the studios, and was probably the only serious story on record that seemed equally effective as a film and as a book.[29]

The public success that Steinbeck seemed to be enjoying kept his private life off balance. Dook Sheffield, for instance, continued to feel that his friendship had been compromised by the swelling fame, and he wrote in January of 1940 to say that he actually felt afraid of his friend: 'The old easy relation isn't there. I find that I'm afraid of you – or what you've become.' Steinbeck understood what his friend was saying only too well; he replied in all seriousness, 'You say you are afraid of me. I'm afraid of myself. I mean the creature that has been built up.'

This 'creature' kept being built up by the press, the vast machine of publicity which caricatures writers and other artists and turns them into celebrities, de-fanging their work in the process. Steinbeck lost, at least temporarily, the ability to see himself clearly. The image flung at him by the world confused him, and he could not find himself in the wilderness of mirrors that replicated his image *ad nauseam*. His identity, or lack of it, frightened him. But the onslaught of publicity continued. When the Pulitzer Prizes were announced in May (just after Steinbeck had returned from his expedition to the Sea of Cortez with Ed Ricketts), he was awarded the fiction prize and smothered by 'an avalanche of interviewers'. The award for biography went to Carl Sandburg for his luminous *Abraham Lincoln: The War Years*, and the award in drama to Steinbeck's friend and California neighbour, William Saroyan, for *The Time of Your Life*. While Saroyan turned down the award, Steinbeck gave his prize money ($1000) to his friend, Ritch Lovejoy, to take time off from his job in Los Angeles and finish a novel he was working on.

Commenting on the prize to Joe Jackson, Steinbeck said, 'While in the past I have sometimes been dubious about Pulitzer choices I am pleased and flattered to be chosen in a year when Sandburg and Saroyan were chosen. It is good company.'[30] But he was, as might be expected, unsettled by the attention. Like all writers, he could not help but to welcome the approbation; it is always affirming to have one's work praised. On the other hand, he discovered that the fame which accompanies such a prize is both false and disquieting.

One part of him felt that he did not deserve the prize. He was not good enough. He would never be good enough.

For all these reservations and uncertainties, Steinbeck had indeed written his 'big book'. The results were impressive by any calculation. The public controversy did nothing to hurt the novel, as Otis and others constantly pointed out to him. Few books have ever been proclaimed 'a classic' so resoundingly and so close to their time of publication. *The Grapes of Wrath* was almost immediately accepted as a masterwork of American literature, and the enthusiastic popular response to Zanuck's film heaped further renown on the novel, which again soared to the top of the charts.

John Steinbeck had made it to the top of the mountain, even though he did not particularly like being there or trust his ability to breathe the air.

XI

A Very Personal War

'I have too a conviction that a new world is growing under
the old, the way a new fingernail grows under a bruised
one.'

Steinbeck to Dook Sheffield, 13 November 1939

From the late autumn of 1939 through the early summer of
1940, as the drum-roll of war began to throb in the ears of
Europe, Steinbeck plunged his head temporarily in the sand.
He did not want to think about war just now, nor did he feel
ready to face the consequences of his recent literary success.
He spent most of his time in the lab in Monterey with Ed
Ricketts, while Carol remained in Los Gatos, where she had
formed a large circle of friends; she did not look with
sympathy on her husband's sudden mania for zoological
research, but she understood that he needed this preoccupa-
tion as a way out of the turmoil he felt after publishing *The
Grapes of Wrath*. He had written to Elizabeth Otis that the
experience of publishing it had 'been a nightmare all in all',
and that his scientific work would be the ideal way to save
himself. It was not going to be a hobby; he was in earnest. 'I'm
ordering a lot of books to begin study,' he said.

His attitude is perfectly caught in a letter to Dook Sheffield:

It's funny, Dook. I know what in a vague way this work is
about. I mean I know its tone and texture and to an extent
its field and I find that I have no education. I have to go
back to school in a way. I'm completely without
mathematics and I have to learn something about abstract
mathematics. I have some biology but must have much
more and the twins bio-physics and bio-chemistry are
closed to me. So I have to go back and start over.[1]

The good news was that, having bought half of Pacific Biological, he had acquired 'equipment, a teacher, a library to work in'. The non-scientific world, as he saw it, was 'sick now'. For the moment, he wanted to avoid thinking about the dark cloud over Europe, the 'Stalinist, Hitlerite, Democrat, capitalist confusion'. World politics was a mere distraction from life's more essential issues, he said. 'So I'm going to those things which are relatively more lasting to find a new basic picture.' He was going back to nature, grounding his studies in the reality of the physical universe. With indomitable optimism, he pronounced: 'I have too a conviction that a new world is growing under the old, the way a new fingernail grows under a bruised one.'

He and Ed Ricketts planned to study the coastal waters near San Francisco, with the intention of writing an ecological guide to the region. They also began to make plans for a trip in early spring to Baja, California, to study the shoreline. The idea to go by land quickly gave way to a more elaborate journey by sea, an expedition that would lead to *Sea of Cortez: A Leisurely Journal of Travel and Research*. Steinbeck threw himself passionately into this planning, rushing up to Berkeley with Ricketts to buy an expensive but powerful microscope, for example. (His childlike enthusiasm for technical things remained prodigious.) 'My dream for some time in the future', he wrote to Otis, 'is a research scope with an oil immersion lens, but that costs about 600 dollars and I'm not getting it right now. The SKW will be fine for the trip. But that research model, Oh boy! Oh boy!'[2]

Through December and January he either worked with Ricketts on preparing for the Baja expedition or studied scientific books in his study in Los Gatos. An uneasy truce had formed between the Steinbecks, and they went about their business separately. Carol took piano lessons, wrote poetry, visited friends and cooked, while he read books about marine life, took notes, or worked in the garden. In a bizarre way, their marital situation mirrored that of the nation at large: black thunderheads crowded the horizon, but for the moment sunlight tunnelled through a narrow chink of blue sky immediately overhead. It was unreal, but the Steinbecks plugged away at their self-distracting tasks, hoping that the storm might blow over and leave them untouched.

By February it was clear that the Baja trip should be made by sea, mostly because the coastline they really wanted to get to was difficult of access by land. They now decided to 'take a purse seiner from Monterey and go all the way by boat'.[3] These impressive boats, used for sardine fishing, were anywhere from sixty to eighty feet long and required for operation a small crew of three or four men. Carol insisted suddenly (much to her husband's displeasure) that she be included on the trip; he agreed reluctantly, telling her that she would have to sleep alone in the wheelhouse.

Charting such a boat was expensive, so Steinbeck asked Elizabeth Otis to see if anybody would be interested in paying for a 'day-by-day account of what happens' on the journey in the form of a ship's log. It would be coolly descriptive, he warned her, 'Not fantastic adventure or anything like that. . . .' After considerable difficulty in hiring a boat, the trip began in the last week of March; they set off from Monterey on *Western Flyer*, owned and captained by Tony Berry, who had sailed in Mexican waters before. Their first stop was Loreto, a tiny Mexican village which sported a church built in 1535. The idea was to collect as many specimens of marine life as possible, to label and store them. 'We have thousands of specimens,' he wrote to Otis. 'And it will probably be several years before they are all identified.' In addition to this daily labour, they pursued 'adventures'. One night, for example, they travelled on muleback high into the mountains to hunt bighorn sheep. Ever ready for excitement, Carol loved all this, and Steinbeck felt good about the marriage, writing back to Dook Sheffield that she was 'a good sport'.

Meanwhile, the drums of war boomed across the Atlantic, with Hitler's armies marching in all directions, taking what they wanted – Austria, Poland, Belgium, one by one toppled under the weight of Nazi tanks. Only the most naive and optimistic of onlookers doubted that the entire world would soon be swept up in bloody conflict. For his part, Steinbeck told Otis that he 'didn't want to hear anything about all of this trouble in distant places'. The Mexican *paisanos* 'have never heard of Europe', he claimed, insisting that they were better off for this ignorance. 'This whole trip is doing what we had hoped it might,' he wrote, 'given us a world picture not dominated by Hitler and Moscow but something more vital and surviving than either.'[4]

In his introduction to the *Log from the 'Sea of Cortez'*, Steinbeck writes engagingly about the journey:

> We made a trip into the Gulf; sometimes we dignified it by calling it an expedition. Once it was called the Sea of Cortez, and that is a better-sounding and a more exciting name. We stopped in many little harbors and near barren coasts to collect and preserve the marine invertebrates of the littoral. One of the reasons we gave ourselves for this trip – and when we used this reason, we called the trip an expedition – was to observe the distribution of invertebrates, to see and record their kinds and numbers, how they lived together, what they ate, and how they reproduced. That plan was simple, straightforward, and only part of the truth. But we did tell the whole truth to ourselves.[5]

The larger goal of the trip was to 'build some kind of structure in modeled imitation of the observed reality'. With extraordinary candour, Steinbeck acknowledged the radically subjective nature of reality – or the reality that one can construct in language: 'We knew that what we would see and record and construct would be warped, as all knowledge patterns are warped, first, by the collective pressure and stream of our time and race, second by the thrust of our individual personalities.' Here Steinbeck is saying very little that contemporary theorists of language, history, and philosophy from Foucault and Derrida to Stanley Greenblatt and dozens of other post-structuralist thinkers haven't 'discovered'. Nevertheless, it's interesting that he was there ahead of them all, insisting on the tainted and contingent nature of truth.

Steinbeck's *Log* records not only the types and habitat of various invertebrates; there is present here a wealth of information about the natural landscape of the littoral, even the interior. There is also a wise and charming account of Mexican life as it contrasts with North American life. 'It is said so often and in such ignorance,' he writes, 'that Mexicans are contented, happy people. "They don't want anything." This, of course is not a description of the happiness of Mexicans, but of the unhappiness of the person who says it. For Americans, and probably all northern peoples, are all masses of wants growing out of inner insecurity. The great drive of our people stems from insecurity.'[6]

What the *Log* amounts to is wonderful travel writing mixed with acute (if pseudo-scientific) observation of the natural world. The details are neatly conjured: the lives of ghost shrimp, sponges, crabs, oysters, worms, urchins, snails and hundreds of other creatures are evoked. The journey lasted only a month or so, but was packed with visual and intellectual excitement. Steinbeck and Ricketts sat on the bridge every night under the stars, arguing about the nature of the universe and the way everything was mystically united in a single biosphere. Carol occasionally joined in, and the men were pleased to include her. It seemed, briefly, that the marriage of John and Carol Steinbeck would, after all, survive the tensions and rifts that had been developing over the past eight years.

On leaving Monterey on mid-March, Steinbeck had

ruefully noted the preparations that were underway for war. The US Navy had recently commandeered much of the harbour; warships of various kinds lay at anchor, being readied for action, as fighter planes zoomed overhead in formation like wild birds from hell. It was a darkly proleptic moment; the threat of war now absorbed the nation – just as Steinbeck and Ricketts were escaping into their fantasy of scientific exploration. This was the romantic Steinbeck, the author of *Cup of Gold*, the sailor-adventurer, the boy who envisioned himself as King Arthur as he played beside Max Wagner in the woods near Salinas. But Steinbeck knew, in his heart of hearts, that the end of an era was approaching: 'This little expedition had become tremendously important to us,' he wrote to a friend, 'and we felt a little as though we were dying.'

They headed back on 13 April, turning north at 3 a.m. under cobalt skies. They had come out of the Gulf and turned into the Pacific, which made an extraordinary contrast. The Gulf was the fantasy world, a place of 'work and sunshine and play'. The Pacific took hold of them ominously, 'the water took on a gray tone.' There were suddenly waves to buck. 'Now we plunged like a nervous horse, and no step could be taken without a steadying hand.' Steinbeck writes with muscular grace:

> The boat plunged and shook herself, and rivers of swirling water ran down the scuppers. Below in the hold, packed in jars, were thousands of little dead animals, but we did not think of them as trophies, as things cut off from the tide pools of the Gulf, but rather as drawings, incomplete and imperfect, of how it had been there. The real picture of how it had been there and how we had been there was in our minds, bright with sun and wet with sea water and blue or burned, and the whole crusted over with exploring thought. Here was no service to science, no naming of unknown animals, but rather – we simply liked it. We liked it very much.[7]

Back on the Biddle ranch at the end of April, Steinbeck pondered the future without enthusiasm. What would he do next? The success of *The Grapes of Wrath* had lifted him to a new level of expectation, both commercial and artistic, and Pat Covici wanted his prize author to seize the moment and build on the success of his most recent novel. But Steinbeck withdrew, clamlike, into a shell which Covici's arguments could not penetrate. The novel as a form 'was over' and 'no longer seemed of interest'. In truth, he was frightened by his own success and mistrustful of the clamour made by the press; he did not want to face the consequences of his own achievement – at least for now.

Sea of Cortez, co-authored with Ricketts, was not of great interest to Viking, who considered it a minor and eccentric book that would attract a limited audience. (More out of duty than real conviction, they published it in 1941.) But it mattered to Steinbeck, who imagined that his future work might well reflect his scientific interests. He wondered if, perhaps, it might even affect his fiction. But what fiction? *Tortilla Flat* had delighted him, and the idea of inventing further stories connected with Monterey struck him as a likely course; he began to collect the tales and anecdotes that would eventually find their way into *Cannery Row*. The possibility of working in the film industry, which he had once rejected vigorously, began to absorb him now as well, fuelled by an invitation from Pare Lorentz to write the narrative parts of *The Fight for Life*. Steinbeck did not accept Lorentz's invitation, but he began to think about making a documentary of his own. If Lorentz could do it, why couldn't he? Here might lie a way out of merely repeating himself as a novelist.

Unlike Faulkner and Fitzgerald, who wanted more from Hollywood than Hollywood wanted from them, Steinbeck was genuinely in demand by the film industry. His realistic storytelling was easily translatable to the screen, a fact that did not pass unnoticed in Tinsel Town, that great maw which consumes infinite amounts of narrative energy each year. Several well-known producers approached him about writing scripts for their studios, dangling vast dollar signs before his eyes; even Howard Hughes telephoned him, and they had dinner at Chasen's, an elegant restaurant in Los Angeles (although the dinner was interrupted by Max Wagner and Gwyn, who amused themselves by embarrassing their friend in front of the legendary Hughes). Another producer who suggested a project was Herbert Kline, who had in mind a film about a poor Mexican family caught up in a political revolution; this subject, he reasoned, would appeal to the author of *The Grapes of Wrath*, and he was right. Steinbeck agreed to work with him if the emphasis were shifted; instead of a revolution, the film should focus on the efforts to improve medical care in a Mexican village. This project eventually became a semi-fictive documentary called *The Forgotten Village*. With its forthright polemical edge, so obviously influenced by the work Steinbeck had done with Lorentz on *The Fight for Life*, it seemed to follow naturally from his concern for the welfare of the migrants in California.

Steinbeck took this work in deadly earnest, involving himself on every level of film-making; he became in effect a producer, largely because it was the one sure way of ensuring control of the project. While he and Herbert Kline both put up capital for the production costs, Steinbeck also persuaded Pat Covici and Harold Guinzburg to contribute to the financing (one wonders, alas, if they had much choice in the matter!). In all, the producers raised $35,000 – even then a low budget for a real documentary. But it was enough, and it meant that Steinbeck could begin on the project immediately.

He and Carol loved the idea of returning to Mexico so quickly after the Sea of Cortez expedition, and they set off via Los Angeles, stopping for a meeting with Lewis Milestone, who now hoped to follow *Of Mice and Men* (which had been hugely successful) with a film adaptation of *The Red Pony*. The Steinbecks attended a glitzy party at Milestone's Hollywood mansion on the eve of their departure for Mexico City. Waiters in black ties poured endless glasses of good champagne while a string quartet played by the kidney-shaped pool. Glasses tinkled, laughter erupted in giddy spurts, and 'everyone got drunk', as Steinbeck noted.[8] The guests of honour that night were Charlie Chaplin and Vladimir Horowitz, the pianist. Somewhat perversely, Steinbeck invited Max Wagner and Gwyn along, with Gwyn pretending to be Max's date; she was deeply curious about Carol and eyed her from a coy distance.

Steinbeck was living between two worlds now, dangerously; he seems to have almost wanted to bring disaster down on his head. But he pretended, to Carol, that all was well and headed off to Mexico City with her on an early-morning flight on PanAm. Mexico had always been, for both, a romantic destination.

Kline had rented for them a large Italianate villa with a lush, overgrown courtyard and a pool. While Carol sat in the garden under a palm tree and wrote poetry, Steinbeck made preparations for a scouting trip to the village of Pátzcuaro, where they meant to shoot the film. Ed Ricketts soon joined them (at Steinbeck's invitation), although the situation Ricketts found when he got there upset him. Steinbeck was overworked, anxious and exhausted, and previously covert tensions between him and Carol had erupted in an ugly way. 'It's a war between them,' Ricketts reported. He claimed to feel like 'the poor cousin', and decided not to stay. He was also unhappy about the fact that Steinbeck had so quickly put *Sea of Cortez* on the back burner and turned to *The Forgotten Village*, and his hostility manifested itself in his response to Steinbeck's script, which Steinbeck had dropped in his lap the day of his arrival. He wrote a little essay in the form of a rebuttal called 'Thesis and Materials for Script on Mexico', arguing that Steinbeck's emphasis on the need for 'change, acquisition, and progress' was wrong-headed.

In fact the thirty-six-page script never advocates unadulterated change in the direction of material or mechanical progress. The Mexican village is in the throes of primitive thinking; innocent people are dying here, the victims of microbes that live in and pollute their water. The villagers resist believing this, preferring to place their trust in the healing powers of the *curandera*, the local witch doctor. Steinbeck argues that rational progress must not supplant but join the mystical, shamanistic worldview of the villagers. He saw no contradiction between having clean water to drink and being in touch with primitive levels of consciousness.

The script was finished in mid-June, and Steinbeck's role came temporarily to an end. He planned to return to Mexico in the late autumn, when the filming was scheduled to begin. In the meantime, he and Carol flew on 22 June to Washington DC, where Steinbeck hoped to make contact with several government officials who might have some interest in the Mexican project. Uncle Joe Hamilton had been utilizing his publicity skills as an information officer for the WPA in the last few months and was able to introduce his nephew to several friends in high places.

In Mexico, Steinbeck saw that the Nazis had established an extremely efficient network for the release of propaganda. In a lavish gesture that reflects a rise in self-confidence after having won the Pulitzer as well as a sudden desire to involve himself with the war, he wrote directly to President Roosevelt from his hotel:

> For some time I have been making a little moving picture in
> Mexico. In this line I have covered a great deal of country
> and had conversations with many people of many factions.
>   In the light of this experience and against a background of
> the international situation, I am forced to the conclusion

that a crisis in the Western Hemisphere is imminent, and is to be met only by an immediate, controlled, considered, and directed method and policy.

It is probable that you have considered this situation in all its facets. However, if my observation can be of any use to you, I shall be very glad to speak with you for I am sure that this problem is one of the most important to be faced by the nation.[9]

Steinbeck slipped unexpectedly here into the kind of rhetoric that one might expect to hear in a high-school graduation speech: 'a crisis in the Western hemisphere is imminent', 'this problem is one of the most important to be faced by the nation'. Roosevelt must have smiled when he read this, having himself purveyed many phrases of the same order of generality and meaninglessness. James Rowe, Jr, an assistant to the President, sent Roosevelt a note saying that Steinbeck 'seems quite disturbed' by the situation but that he 'probably has no better information than any other sensitive and intelligent layman who has spent time in Mexico'. He added, in a scrawl, that Archibald MacLeish – the poet and, at that time, Chief Librarian of the Library of Congress – thought the President might enjoy meeting the author of *The Grapes of Wrath*, which had been one of his wife's favourite books. The President agreed, scheduling a twenty-minute meeting with Steinbeck.

At this meeting, which took place in the White House Oval Office, the author urged Roosevelt to set up a propaganda office which would make use of print and visual media, as well as radio, to unite the anti-fascist nations. He offered to use his own film crew to begin working on projects directed to this end. Roosevelt listened politely, thanked him for the visit and did not follow up any of the suggestions directly (although, of course, the US government was already adept at using Hollywood to its own ends and had been since the days of Woodrow Wilson, the first president to harness the terrifying power of Hollywood).

The Steinbecks returned to California by plane. After so much shuttling around, it felt good to be back on the ranch, which had been meticulously groomed in their absence by a Japanese houseboy by the name of Joe Higashi, who also cooked for them and screened telephone calls. Increasingly Steinbeck felt that his marriage was near the end of the line. Carol, he thought, was often petulant and domineering; she seemed to resent everything he did. Certainly the lack of a child weighed heavily on her mind, and she flushed with resentment whenever she recalled the abortion and its aftermath. Quite rightly, she blamed him for her sterility. The conflict between the Steinbecks mounted steadily through-out the summer, although very little in the way of open argument was noticed by friends.

Gwyn, meanwhile, had taken a singing job at a nightclub in San Francisco, where she was now staying with her mother. Quite by accident, Steinbeck heard her on the radio one night and was moved to tears. Unable to help himself, he drove to San Francisco to see her, and their affair rekindled. A few weekends later they met secretly in the cottage at Pacific Grove. 'There was a lot of sneaking around then,' a friend recalls. 'John seemed happy with Gwyn, and he was miserable with Carol. They used to go around San Francisco secretly, but a lot of people recognized him. It was a strange time for John, I think.'[10]

Steinbeck had met Carl Sandburg, the poet, a year before, referring to him in his journal as 'a good thinking man'. That summer he and Gwyn took Sandburg out for drinks one night to the Top of the Mark. In typical fashion, the poet wore an outlandishly wide and colourful tie, a white linen suit, and a brown fedora. His long white locks flowed over his collar. The waitress came up to Sandburg and said, 'Please, sir. Hats are not allowed in this restaurant.' Sandburg looked at her coolly and said, 'Quack, quack, quack, quack'. The waitress, rather startled, withdrew. Steinbeck so liked this response that he often responded in later years to unwelcome inquiries or comments with 'Quack, quack, quack, quack'.

With complete disregard now for Carol's feelings, he took Gwyn to Los Angeles on several occasions. He had a lot of business there, and the couple often dined with Pare Lorentz, Max Wagner, Robert Benchley, Charlie Chaplin and others. It was broadly noticed that Steinbeck had a new woman, but he seemed not to care. He began to drink heavily again, partly in response to his anxiety over the marriage, which was falling down around his ears. Even Gwyn began to object to his drinking. (He embarrassed her on the dance floor at a Hollywood party by toppling over her in the midst of a tango.)

Steinbeck sought distractions where he could find them. He wrote to Dook on 13 August to announce that he had taken up flying. The little airport at Palo Alto offered lessons, and he had signed up for a brief course. 'There's something so god damned remote and beautiful and detached about being way to hell and gone up on a little yellow leaf,' he said.[11] He viewed flying as 'not loneliness at all but just an escape into something delightful'. Clearly, the notion of being free, alone, and away from it all – of floating high above the ground – appealed to him just then. His life felt like a trap, and all he could think about was escape.

The war in Europe had now grown beyond the point where anyone could ignore it; suddenly a bold notion about how to defeat Germany seized Steinbeck, who probably welcomed the relief of thinking about something apart from his own marital conflicts. He wrote once again to Roosevelt, assuming that he would get a hearing:

Perhaps you have heard of Dr Melvyn Knisely, who has the chair of Anatomy at the University of Chicago. He is a

remarkable scientist and an old friend of mine. Discussing
with him the problem of the growing Nazi power and
possibilities for defense against it, he put forth an analysis
and a psychological weapon which seem to me so simple
and so effective, that I think it should be considered and
very soon. I would take it to someone less busy than you if I
knew one with imagination and resiliency enough to see its
possibilities.[12]

Roosevelt responded positively. 'Will you arrange for Steinbeck and Dr Knisely to come and see me on September 12th?'
he wrote to his assistant, General Watson. The idea was
indeed simple: to scatter large quantities of counterfeit
German money by air across Germany. This would confound
the economy by creating a vast oversupply of hard currency.
Roosevelt, according to Steinbeck, liked the idea, but the
Secretary of the Treasury, Henry Morgenthau, thought it
would not work. The idea was dropped, but Steinbeck had by
now had two meetings with President Roosevelt in a short
time. He was being taken seriously by the highest levels of
government: something very few writers can ever (or might
even care to) boast.

At home again, Steinbeck continued working on *Sea of
Cortez*, urged forward by Ed Ricketts, who was afraid that his
friend's commitment to the project was waning. Several
attractive film projects also competed for his attention,
including the film version of *Tortilla Flat*, which was still 'in
development', as studios say. (King Vidor had by now agreed
to direct and Spencer Tracy had signed on to play Danny.)
Herb Kline was supposedly still working on *The Forgotten
Village*, while *The Red Pony* continued to interest Lewis
Milestone, who was in serious discussion with financiers
about backing the project. Steinbeck also worked, briefly,
with Charlie Chaplin on the last scene of *The Great Dictator*.
'John had changed his mind about Hollywood,' says Burgess
Meredith. 'He liked being around actors, I think. And

directors. He knew a lot about films and making films. He wanted to see his work done well, and he had ideas about how they should be done.'

The Forgotten Village was dear to Steinbeck, and he was eager to see it through to completion, but Herb Kline was not very communicative. He failed to respond to several urgent letters and could not be reached by phone. Growing restless, Steinbeck decided to return to Mexico in late October to see if he could get the project moving again. (This time he decided to leave Carol at home, much to her disgruntlement.) On arrival in Mexico City, he learned that one of many problems Kline had encountered was finding appropriate light for shooting. 'Herb cannot learn that a Mexican answers what you want to hear,' Steinbeck wrote to Max Wagner on 1 November.[13] 'He asked if the October sky was clear and of course they said yes.' In spite of this, they were 'getting a picture on film – one of the first times a Mexican *pueblito* has been photographed. I hope it is good.' He ended this letter by asking his friend, 'Look after Gwyn a little, will you?' It was clear to him now that Gwyn, not Carol, was his future.

Steinbeck tried to help old friends when he could; it was among his most endearing traits. Max Wagner had been struggling for some time to make his way in Hollywood without much success, and Steinbeck rashly promised to get him the job of narrating *The Forgotten Village*. Kline, however, thought Wagner a bad idea; they needed a real star, he argued, suggesting Spencer Tracy. Reluctantly, Steinbeck agreed with him, and Kline asked Tracy, who was willing to do the job because of his admiration for Steinbeck. The only problem was that Tracy's current contract with MGM prevented his working for anyone else. Sadly, he declined the offer. Steinbeck was privately relieved and quickly (too quickly, as it turned out) offered Max the job.

No sooner had Steinbeck written to Max with the offer than Tracy called back to say he had worked out a deal with MGM.

he would do a picture for them that he didn't want to do (a new version of Robert Louis Stevenson's *Dr Jekyll and Mr Hyde*), and they would release him to do this narration. When Kline discovered that Steinbeck had already asked Max Wagner, he was furious. 'What?' he cried, 'you asked him without telling me?' Steinbeck apologized and wrote, tail between his legs, to tell Max the bad news. 'I value you as I value very few people in the world,' he explained to Max. 'When I called you *hermano*, I meant it in the most tremendous sense I know.'

The irony of all this was that MGM changed its mind just as Tracy began the narration and insisted that he drop the Mexican project. Steinbeck did not have the will to try for Max yet again. 'That's when John called me,' says Burgess Meredith, who quickly agreed to fill in for Tracy. Meredith was not quite the star Spencer Tracy was, but he was a reasonably popular actor who would certainly do a fine job. 'There was a lot of turmoil surrounding this picture,' Meredith adds. 'But it was a good little picture.'

Steinbeck returned home in mid-December. He was now both depressed and anxious, aware that his marriage to Carol had dwindled to the point of extinction, yet unable to summon the energy to break it off. He and Carol went together to Hollywood in the week before Christmas and were both overtaken by a flu that 'knocked them silly for three days with fevers and chills and coughing'. Driving back to the ranch through torrential rain, Steinbeck's flu turned into 'walking pneumonia'. Over the holidays, he became so weak he could barely lift himself from bed. 'John often got physically sick when he was down,' his sister recalls. 'Toward the end of the marriage to Carol, he was always sick. Everybody was worried about him.'

Steinbeck moved weakly, gloomily, into 1941. He occupied himself with small projects, including the preface to a novel by Tom Collins and some captions for a story in *Life* about Monterey. He met twice with Darryl Zanuck concerning the film version of *Tortilla Flat*, and he worked intermittently on *Sea of Cortez*; he also made notes about incidents in Monterey that would eventually become part of *Cannery Row*. But there was no sustained project before him. He was still exhausted in the wake of having published *The Grapes of Wrath*, and he could not imagine what his future work might look like.

Carol's physical condition seemed to decline along with his. 'She had a dreadful cough that wouldn't go away. Her head ached all the time. She looked awful,' a friend remembers.[14] One day when she was too weak to get out of bed, Steinbeck brought her a cup of tea and suggested that she take a vacation by herself – somewhere hot and dry because it had been raining non-stop that winter in California. He recommended New Mexico, saying that a desert climate was ideal for someone with her problems. She, however, had been thinking about a trip to Hawaii for several years, and when she mentioned this he quickly (perhaps too quickly) agreed she could go there: 'He told her not to think of the money, that money was no problem.'

Carol was scarcely out of the house before he got into his car and drove to Los Angeles to pick up Gwyn. They stole away to a cabin by the sea that belonged to his sister Esther. Huddled there with Gwyn, he set to work earnestly to finish *Sea of Cortez*, which had dragged on for much too long. The cabin was wonderfully secluded, surrounded by huge red-woods and strongly scented eucalyptus trees. It was cool, but Steinbeck got up early every morning and built a fire in the stone fireplace. All morning he worked in a chair by the fire, writing with a clipboard on his lap. Gwyn slept until midday; as soon as she was awake he would put away his work and devote himself to her. They took long walks together by the sea, picnicking among the dunes.

This was a strange, delicious and troubling time for

Steinbeck. He loved Gwyn, and he felt renewed by their relationship. But he still loved Carol, and he worried deeply about hurting her. Because he was by nature a moral man, he could not simply behave like a cad without feeling the pang of conscience. This blatant infidelity hurt him, especially in the light of Carol's abortion and sterility. Throughout the painful process of separation and divorce, he never felt comfortable with his actions or certain about what he was doing. 'I don't think he ever really resolved the marriage to Carol,' says his sister, Beth. 'John just drifted away from her, uncertain, wondering what to do next.'

He returned, with Gwyn, to the ranch, arousing suspicions all around. Joe, the houseboy, was horrified when his employer turned up with a woman who was clearly a lover. Then Carol wired to ask if she could stay another two weeks; she was feeling much better and enjoying herself in Hawaii. Steinbeck wired back immediately to say that she could stay a month longer if she liked. By all accounts, this was the first time Carol began to suspect that her husband was having an affair.

On 28 March, Carol arrived home. An evasiveness in her husband's voice and demeanour rang the alarm bells, and she pressed for an honest response from him: 'What the hell is going on, John? You're keeping something from me, aren't you?' Her husband, taken aback, said, 'Sit down. I'll tell you everything.' He did, more or less. In a letter to Mavis McIntosh, written two weeks later, he said,

This has been a hell of a time and I'm pretty shaky but at least I'll try to give you a small idea of what happened. My nerves cracked to pieces and I told Carol the whole thing, told her how deeply involved I was and how little was left. She said she wanted what was left and was going to fight. So there we are. All in the open, all above board. I'm staying with Carol as I must. I don't know what Gwyn will do nor does she. Just as badly tied there as ever – worse if anything.[15]

They decided to sell the ranch at once; the place housed too many bad memories for either of them to want to remain there. In mid-April, they returned to Pacific Grove, where Steinbeck had recently purchased a small house at 425 Eardley Street. ('The house on 11th Street was only a quarter his,' his sister explains, 'and he didn't want to presume that he could use it any time he wanted.') For the purposes of writing, Steinbeck could utilize an office connected to the lab at Pacific Biological. Carol, who was not on speaking terms with her husband, soon realized that she could not live there. On 28 April, a month after her return from Honolulu, she left for good. Steinbeck wrote to Elizabeth Otis, 'I've been very raddled and torn out by the roots. Nightmared, etc. In many ways I have more of a sense of peace than I have ever had and am working hard but I get the horrors pretty often.'[16] The only thing, he said, that saved him from going crazy was his work; he resolved 'not to try to think but to let the work go on'.

Steinbeck lived, off and on, at the lab, where Ed Ricketts soothed his friend's badly jangled nerves. From Ricketts's point of view, the separation was a good thing. Now Steinbeck would be free to focus his energies wholly on *Sea of Cortez*. The collaborative process was difficult for a man like Steinbeck, who was used to having sole control over everything he produced, and Pat Covici suggested delicately that perhaps his name should be connected to the narrative and Ricketts's name to the catalogue. 'I not only disapprove of your plan,' Steinbeck wrote back, 'but forbid it.' He knew, of course, that Ed Ricketts would have been horrified by this arrangement, and he was not going to risk offending his best friend, who was currently helping him through a personal crisis. Furthermore, Ricketts had made a genuine contribution to the book.

It is impossible to reconstruct exactly what part of *Sea of Cortez* belonged to Ricketts and what was Steinbeck's, although the correspondence of both suggests that Steinbeck did much of the final draft. From a memorandum sent to Pat Covici by the authors in tandem on 25 August, it appears that Ricketts had done a fair portion of the log-keeping and taken copious notes, and that Steinbeck worked from this material, substantially rewriting from Ricketts's notations. The final product was passed back and forth for comments and revisions. Inevitably, reviewers fixed on Steinbeck's contribution: 'There is more of the whole man, John Steinbeck, in *Sea of Cortez* than in any of his novels,' opined Lewis Gannett in the *New York Herald Tribune*. And, in some ways, he is correct; although this was meant to be a 'scientific' book, Steinbeck's personality shimmers through the prose. One hears his characteristic blend of charm and cussedness, as in the entry for 20 March:

> No doubt we were badly cheated in La Paz. Perhaps the boatmen cheated us and maybe we paid too much for supplies – it is very hard to know. And besides, we were so incredibly rich that we couldn't tell, and we had no instinct for knowing when we were cheated. Here we were rich, but in our own country it was not so. The very rich develop an instinct which tells them when they are cheated. We knew a rich man who owned several large office buildings. Once in reading his reports he found that two electric light bulbs had been stolen from one of the toilets in one of his office buildings. It hurt him; he brooded for weeks about it. 'Civilization is dying,' he said. 'Whom can you trust any more? This little theft is an indication that the whole people are morally rotten.'[17]

The book was finished and sent off to Viking by the end of July 1941. At Covici's suggestion, Steinbeck now turned to an unfinished piece of fiction titled 'God in the Pipes', which had been started in Mexico the year before, but he could not work up much enthusiasm for the story. His thoughts kept returning to his marital crisis the way one's tongue lingers over a cavity. He told Elizabeth Otis that he could not predict Carol's future behaviour: 'I know so well her basic violence and if she becomes vindictive you are quite right, anything may happen.'[18] Carol, meanwhile, had moved to New York, so there was at least the safety of distance between them.

The ranch was sold in early August, and Joe moved into the Monterey house to cook and clean for Steinbeck. Ed Ricketts's companion, Toni Jackson, became his secretary, taking dictation and typing his letters and manuscripts. There was always plenty of work to cling to. In late August, for instance, Lewis Milestone called to say that the financing for *The Red Pony* was in place and asked Steinbeck to do a treatment. Eager to take his mind off his troubles, Steinbeck agreed. Not losing a second, Milestone turned up in Monterey the next week, checking into a nearby boarding house so he could work on the script with Steinbeck as they had done a few years before with *Of Mice and Men*.

They had grown to trust each other, and now they worked smoothly, talking their way meticulously through each scene. The problems presented by *The Red Pony* were considerable. It was not, like *Of Mice and Men*, already a story in quasi-dramatic form. Consisting of linked but not necessarily related incidents, it lacked the unitary narrative progression essential for a screenplay to work. Milestone, who had limited time and a strict budget, kept Steinbeck's nose to the grindstone, hovering over his shoulder as he drafted dialogue and action. Toni Jackson stood by, ready to type (and often retype) the scenes as soon as they were finished.

Although Steinbeck seems to have been unaware of it, he was approaching a decision that would change his life for ever: to leave California. It was a decision that many of his friends, then and later, would view with great scepticism. 'It was a mistake,' Elia Kazan says flatly.[19] 'Steinbeck was a

Californian, never a New Yorker. It was a great error for him to leave the West Coast. That was the source of his inspiration. He was himself there. In New York, he was awkward, out of place. I think it hurt him as a writer.'

The decision to go east was prompted by Carol's decision to return to California. 'If I got out of the way, she would be able to come here and see her friends,' he told Elizabeth Otis, justifying what was supposed to be a temporary move to New York City with Gwyn (who had not yet been asked to go with him). Gwyn's dislike of Monterey also fitted into his decision to leave the landscape and culture that had inspired every one of his novels except *Cup of Gold*, and nearly all of his stories.

He drove to Los Angeles in early October to ask Gwyn to answer a few important questions. Did she love him? Would she leave California and move to New York City with him? Did she, indeed, want to marry him once the divorce from Carol became final? When Gwyn answered yes to all three, they went back to Monterey together. Gwyn, it seems, had never before lived in a house of her own and was supremely happy to be with her lover in his little town by the sea, however temporarily. Steinbeck thought they would stay there a few months or longer, but in mid-October he was summoned to Washington by the Roosevelt administration to consult with people who were setting up an agency designed to counter German propaganda.

In his original meeting with Roosevelt, Steinbeck had suggested that he might help with such activities, and Roosevelt called in his card. William 'Wild Bill' Donovan, a hero of World War I, had been tapped as Coordinator of Information to head the new agency, which soon evolved into the Office of Strategic Services. In a remarkable book about Steinbeck's work as a propagandist, Donald Coers describes Donovan as 'an open-minded and occasionally unorthodox administrator who, despite his political conservatism, was willing to use outré people and ideas if they suited his purposes'.[20] Several units were established, among them the Foreign Information Service (FIS), which Robert E. Sherwood, the Pulitzer Prize-winning playwright, was selected to head. Sherwood invited Steinbeck (and other writers, such as Thornton Wilder and Stephen Vincent Benét) to Washington to discuss the role of the FIS in combating Nazi propaganda.

Steinbeck never worked officially for the FIS; that is, he was never paid for his work. But he enjoyed saying that he wrote his next novel, *The Moon Is Down*, on assignment for this agency. What happened was that he met a number of refugees in Washington from various occupied nations and, with horror, listened to their stories. Their tales of secret organizations dedicated to resisting the Germans intrigued him, as they well might: the world they evoked was a dark one, full of turncoats and spies, double agents, collaborators and heroes of the Resistance. In a late essay Steinbeck meditated on the Occupation and those who dared to oppose it, 'Gradually I got to know a great deal about these secret armies and I devoted most of my energies in their direction.'[21]

Steinbeck stayed on the east coast. 'I had a farmhouse in Suffern, New York, and I wasn't using it. So I told John and Gwyn they could stay there,' explains Burgess Meredith. *The Moon Is Down* began to take shape quickly; like *Of Mice and Men*, it was written in play form, with the dialogue paramount. Gwyn took complete charge of the house, cooking, cleaning and doing the laundry, while Steinbeck worked intensely in a long, narrow room at the back of the house which overlooked an apple orchard. 'He always said he was very happy working there. His book just came along easily,' Meredith adds.

Steinbeck found himself having to go frequently into New York, where an office of the FIS had been established, and the Meredith farm was a good forty miles outside the city, in

Rockland County. Thus, on 16 November, he and Gwyn moved into a comfortable hotel on East 40th Street, the Bedford. Annie Laurie Williams lived there, and she arranged for her client to have a pleasant two-bedroom suite with a kitchenette. He liked being in Manhattan, despite the freezing weather, and seems to have enjoyed having many irons in the fire: the play version of *The Moon Is Down*, as yet untitled, *Sea of Cortez*, *The Forgotten Village*, and *The Red Pony*.

There was some difficulty now with *The Forgotten Village*; New York's Board of Censors had decided that the documentary was 'indecent' and promoted socialism. They refused to let it open, as planned, in New York City. Having put so much of himself into the project, Steinbeck was devastated. He issued a statement to the press, noting

> In the picture there is no nudity. No suggestiveness and no actual birth is shown. The indecent fact which seems to have upset the board is that childbirth is painful and in primitive communities where there is no medical care, not only painful but dangerous. The Mexican government is not upset about this film because it is trying with every resource at its command to remedy the situation.

Eleanor Roosevelt decided to intervene personally in the legal process, and a special hearing was held in early December. Doubtless because of the First Lady's efforts, the ban on *The Forgotten Village* was lifted. Steinbeck wrote to thank her, saying that the project was 'undertaken and carried out with considerable purity of motive'.

The US had been moving quickly towards commitment to the war in recent months. In July, Japan announced that it was assuming a protectorate of the whole of French Indochina. Roosevelt, almost immediately, received the armies of the Philippine Commonwealth into the US Army; he also began to urge Japan to evacuate Indochina (and China, which it had previously occupied). The Japanese response, led by General Tojo, who had recently been made Prime Minister, was belligerent. Tojo put several untenable demands before Roosevelt, who dismissed them as ludicrous. On 26 November 1941, the Japanese striking force of 6 aircraft carriers, 423 planes, 2 battleships, 2 heavy cruisers, and 11 destroyers gathered in the Kurile Islands in preparation for an attack on Pearl Harbor, which came on 7 December 1941 in a dawn strike. America was at war.

The day after the attack, Steinbeck wrote to Toby Street with his reactions: 'Last afternoon was the attack on Honolulu. Wasn't that a quick one? We'll take some pretty brutal losses for a while, I'm afraid, but I think the attack, whatever it may have gained from a tactical point of view, was a failure in that it solidified the country.'[22] It certainly focused Steinbeck's attention on the war, taking him outside himself for the first time in months. He was able to project his private wars on to the public screen, and the clash of Allied and Axis powers became a subterranean metaphor of sorts, a way of marshalling and reifying emotions. It was curiously exhilarating.

The FIS, however, did not like The Moon Is Down, the propagandistic play-novella. The story was set in a mid-sized American city under occupation by the Germans, and Robert Sherwood thought it would do nothing to help the war cause. He argued that 'postulating an American defeat might backfire and actually demoralize people' rather than inspire them to resistance. Dutifully, but without joy or agreement, Steinbeck withdrew the manuscript, saying he would probably revise it and resubmit it later. He complained to Elizabeth Otis that everything of late had been going sour, on both personal and literary fronts.

First, he had been forced by Viking to make changes in the final proofs of Sea of Cortez, and this had annoyed him considerably; then The Red Pony once again stalled for lack of funds (indeed, it would not be filmed until 1949). Out of the blue, Carol began hounding him with a variety of threats; indeed, she gave an embarrassing interview to the *New York World-Telegram* in which she claimed that her husband would eventually give up his 'paramour' for her. On top of everything, Gwyn found New York less exciting than she had thought and began to complain that she knew almost nobody there and that Steinbeck spent all day locked in his room, writing. When he went out for lunch with his publishers or agents, he did not take her. Steinbeck was unsure what to do to make her feel more comfortable. 'I think this was a very bad time for John,' his sister recalls, 'because he just wasn't able to make a move without someone criticizing him.'

Sea of Cortez appeared on 5 December in a modest edition of 7500 copies, and got reasonably good reviews. It did not, however, have anything like the sales that Steinbeck's previous work had enjoyed, largely because of its specialized nature. Reporters nevertheless flocked to the Bedford for interviews; it was a treat for them to have John Steinbeck right on their doorstep. For the most part, he disappointed them, locking himself in his hotel suite to work on a fresh version of *The Moon Is Down*. Taking into account Sherwood's negative response to the first draft, he now chose an anonymous coastal town in Europe for his setting. 'No one had yet written such an account of the experience of Nazi occupation,' writes Coers.[23] Steinbeck's friends in the Resistance 'were certain that his story would boost morale in their homelands'. Steinbeck later recalled, 'I placed the story in an unnamed country, cold and stern like Norway, cunning and implacable like Denmark, reasonable like France. The names of people in the book I made as international as I could. I did not even call the Germans Germans but simply invaders. I named the book "The Moon Is Down" from a line in *Macbeth* and sent it to press.'[24]

Using a method that was unusual for him, Steinbeck hired a court reporter, an overweight, 'very severe-looking' woman who wore boiled wool suits; she propped her typewriter on the dining-room table and clacked away as Steinbeck (in the manner of late Henry James) paced and dictated the manuscript, making revisions as he went along. Coers notes that as soon as Steinbeck 'discovered that she was making significant changes of her own – including leaving out entire passages', he fired her. He later found that she was a Nazi sympathizer and belonged to a group in New York actively trying to sway American opinion in Hitler's favour.

Steinbeck submitted the manuscript to Viking in mid-December, not long after the bombing of Pearl Harbor had made the subject all the more relevant, even urgent. As Christmas approached, he waited nervously for Pat Covici's response. In all, 1941 had been a bad year, probably the worst of his life. He had gone through a painful separation and had experienced rejections, both small and large, in his professional life. He could not fathom the future direction of his writing career. Worse, his life had become frenetic and confusing. He was a long way from the idyll of boyhood summers along the Monterey coast, and the chances of regaining that kind of peace seemed, for the moment, painfully remote.

XII

'The Genial Famous Man'

'I have been working madly at a book and Gwyn has been
working calmly at a baby and it looks as though it might
be a photo finish.'

Steinbeck to Toby Street, 4 July 1944

'After the war is done,' Steinbeck wrote to Toby Street on 12
January, 1942, 'I know what I want if my domestic difficulties
and my finances will permit it. I want about ten acres near the
ocean and near Monterey, and I want a shabby comfortable
house and room for animals, maybe a horse, and some dogs,
and I want some babies.'[1] Steinbeck was only forty, but he felt
old; his hair was beginning to streak with grey, and his face
had turned craggy. He had long suffered back pains and
other minor ailments. Like George and Lennie, his wandering bindlestiffs, he dreamed of settling down for good in
Monterey, the one place where he had always found peace.

He and Gwyn were living what he called 'a suitcase life',
moving here and there without a sense of purpose. Men of
forty were beyond the draft age, but the thought that he
might get personally involved in the war effort continued to
haunt Steinbeck. For the time being, he put aside the idea of
entering the conflict directly and planned to write books,
screenplays or stage plays that might help his country
indirectly. As we have seen, *The Moon Is Down* was written as
an unabashed piece of propaganda.

It is a simple book with a strong mythic underpinning.
Steinbeck described it in a letter to Street:

> The play? It's about a little town invaded. It has no
> generalities, no ideals, no speeches; it's just about the way

the people of a little town would feel if it were invaded. It isn't any country and there is no dialect and it's about how the invaders feel about it, too. It's one of the first sensible things to be written about these things and I don't know whether it is any good or not.[2]

This novel (and its stage version) is slight by any reckoning, an immediate reaction to the war by a writer who often wrote in response to a political or social crisis. Both the novel and the play divide neatly into eight sections, and what happens is identical in both: an unnamed democratic nation is invaded by troops from somewhere unspecified. The protagonist is the old mayor, Orden, who is led off to be executed at the end. His execution is foreshadowed by that of his townsman, a miner named Alexander Morden. (The juxtaposition of Morden/Orden is a bit much for the ear.) A kindly doctor, Dr Winter, acts as unofficial adviser to the mayor and a wise presence generally. Assorted servants bow in and out of the scene. The plot's antagonist is the town's secret collaborator, a popular storekeeper who betrays his countrymen.

On the side of the invaders, there is Colonel Lanser, the polite commander of the battalion (whom some critics of the book found too civilized to represent the Nazis in any serious way). There is also Major Hunter, an engineer; Captain Bentick, who is killed; and various minor but well-drawn others (two with Dickensian names, Prackle and Tonder). In general, the invaders are considerate and, at times, humane. The author almost appears to sympathize with them, treating them as human beings who happen to be invaders.

The plot consists mainly of the efforts of the town to resist being conquered as repressive measures increase. Mayor Orden, in a dramatic final scene, tells Lanser, 'Free men cannot start a war, but once it is started, they can fight on in defeat. Herd men . . . cannot do that, and so it is always the herd men who win battles and the free men who win wars.' That is the point of the story, baldly put. Lanser, perhaps in agreement with Orden, says, 'I will carry out my orders no matter what they are. . . .' Whatever its merits as a novel or play (and they are relatively few), *The Moon Is Down* struck a sympathetic chord throughout America and Britain; it was also popular in various European countries, mostly those under occupation. Indeed, a year and a half after the war ended, King Haakon VII of Norway saw fit to decorate Steinbeck for his contribution to the war effort.

Steinbeck remained in New York throughout the winter, awaiting the publication of the novel and working with a producer, Oscar Serlin, on a Broadway version of the story. (Herman Shumlin had bought the rights before the novel was published, but he turned them over to Serlin because he did not 'care for its politics'.) Serlin, best known for his production of *Life with Father*, correctly thought that Steinbeck's play would attract a large audience. (The play ran for only nine weeks on Broadway, but was immensely successful on the road and abroad, especially in London and Stockholm; rather surprisingly, it was nominated for 'Best Play' by the New York Drama Critics Award and came in second.)

The novel appeared in March, with pre-publication orders exceeding 85,000 copies. Taking Viking's breath away, the Book-of-the-Month Club ordered 200,000 copies for their membership. These numbers topped those of *The Grapes of Wrath* by two to one, an astonishing performance. As before, there was little in the way of critical agreement about the book. Reviewing it on 6 March, *The New York Times* praised Steinbeck's 'universality' and noted his 'exact perception of how a free people must react to an attempt to enforce slavery upon it'. The novel was called 'the most memorable fiction to have come out of this war'.[3] The first major negative response came from Clifton Fadiman (who had adored *The Grapes of Wrath*) in *The New Yorker*; he questioned the form of the story, which lay somewhere between a novel and a melodramatic play. The simplistic assumption in the story that good always triumphs over evil offended him; he argued that *The Moon Is Down* 'seduces us to rest on the oars of our own superiority'.

In *The New Republic*, James Thurber agreed with Fadiman, attacking the soft-headedness of the title; John Gunther, elsewhere, found the novel 'almost maddeningly fair-minded to the Germans'. So many letters, pro and con, poured into *The New Republic* that the editors decided to create a special section, printing a barrage of letters on both sides, some more credible than others. One European refugee wrote to protest that Steinbeck's Nazis were entirely too sympathetic. Others complained about the stereotypical characters. Fadiman, in a rare instance of returning to the scene of a review, wrote a second time in *The New Yorker* to say that he disapproved of the 'fairy-tale atmosphere' generated by Steinbeck in this novel.

Lewis Gannett, always one of Steinbeck's strong advocates, objected on 4 May to what he considered a programmatic attack on Steinbeck by *The New Republic* and other periodicals. He suggested, as Coers notes in his lively book, that men like Colonel Lanser were 'more dangerous than the undoubting Nazis'. This was because they were 'betrayers of intelligence'. *The New Republic* lost no time in responding, dismissing Gannett's complaints as 'triumphant and total nonsense'. They argued, somewhat tangentially, that Steinbeck did not have sufficient intimacy with Europe to justify this choice of setting. Furthermore, they found his characters stiff and unreal. 'The characters make admirable speeches,' they said, 'but they do not talk like human beings.'

The play opened on Broadway in the first week of April, starring Otto Bruger as Colonel Lanser and Ralph Morgan as Mayor Orden. As might be expected, the controversy continued, and many of the same criticisms recurred: Steinbeck was too easy on the Germans, too optimistic about the ultimate victory of the Allies, too moralistic, and so forth. 'I'm sending you the reviews,' he wrote to Toby Street, 'and as you will see they are almost uniformly bad.' Coers writes, 'Despite the general popular and commercial success of *The Moon Is Down* in the United States, and even though the number of critics who applauded the work was at the very least roughly equal to the number of those who denounced it, Steinbeck was stunned by the kinds of attacks spearheaded by Thurber and Fadiman.'[4] Bad reviews sting, and there was no way around this brute fact of the literary life.

Over a decade later, Steinbeck looked back ruefully on this period in an essay called 'My Short Novels':

> The war came on, and I wrote *The Moon Is Down* as a kind of celebration of the durability of democracy. I couldn't conceive that the book would be denounced. I had written of Germans as men, not supermen, and this was considered a very weak attitude to take. I couldn't make much sense out of this, and it seems absurd now that we know the Germans were men, and thus fallible, even defeatable. It was said that I didn't know anything about war, and this was perfectly true, though how Park Avenue commandos found me out I can't conceive.[5]

Steinbeck recalled later that he was 'violently, almost hysterically, attacked by several powerful critics as being defeatist, unreal, complacent and next door to treasonable'. He did not find these comments easy to swallow: 'I must admit that my feelings were hurt by these attacks because I had thought I was doing a good and a patriotic thing.' He did, however, have mixed feelings about the artistic success of the work in its play format. A feisty war correspondent, Quentin Reynolds, met Steinbeck in North Africa in 1943 and told Steinbeck bluntly that he had seen *The Moon Is Down* on Broadway and hated it. Steinbeck quickly replied, 'I never liked it. It didn't play well. No, it was a bad play.'[6]

As a piece of propaganda, the novel succeeded admirably. As Coers suggests, *The Moon Is Down* gave an emotional boost to many Europeans who were suffering brutally under the

Occupation; he details the vivid responses to the book in Norway, Denmark, France and elsewhere. To explain its powerful effect on readers at the time, he quotes Swiss professor Heinrich Straumann, who argues that it was Steinbeck's 'basic value of solidarity . . . connected with the traditional ideals of freedom, personal dignity, and local self- government' that made *The Moon Is Down* 'the most powerful piece of propaganda ever written to help a small democratic country to resist totalitarian aggression and occupation'. It passed through a stupendous seventy-six editions between 1945 and 1989, including translations into Korean, Urdu, Slovak, Persian and Burmese. Readers, obviously, needed this book long after the war had ended (doubtless because of the continuing reality of 'occupation' as a political situation throughout the world). It was devoured and appreciated.

Whatever its effectiveness as propaganda, *The Moon Is Down* does not succeed as a work of literature. Its characters are idealized and wooden, while the setting is too unspecific to make a definite impression. The novel does seem too much like a fairy tale, as Fadiman charged. Steinbeck's earlier fiction derived its power from the fact that he had given 'a local habitation and a name' to inchoate feelings which readers found in themselves. The specific settings, so perfectly realized, were the source of his uncanny power. For all time, John Steinbeck and California will remain identified in the minds of people who love American literature. Despite its obvious flaws, however, *The Moon Is Down* deserves recognition in the link-chain of Steinbeck's overall development as a writer, anticipating better work that was coming, such as the screenplay of *Viva Zapata!* It also marks an early stage of Steinbeck's experimentation with the parable as a literary form. In this sense, the novel looks forward to *The Wayward Bus* and *East of Eden*, where the parable is lifted to a much higher level of articulation.

*

Carol, meanwhile, stirred the pot by making strong demands
that had to be satisfied before the divorce could happen. Her
situation was unenviable, of course. Having stuck by Steinbeck
through the hard years of his apprenticeship, she now felt
cast off for a younger woman. Quite rightly, she wanted
some of the material benefits of his success to come her way,
arguing that he would never have got where he was without
her help in the apprentice years. Steinbeck, for his part, had
no inclination to behave dishonourably. 'I don't want to
chisel in any way from Carol,' he wrote to Toby Street.[7] 'I
want to give her everything I can.'

He and Gwyn began to find their suite at the Bedford
cramped, and in April they moved across the Hudson River to a
rambling house at Sneden's Landing, an upmarket neighbourhood where some of Steinbeck's friends later settled. (Among
his neighbours were Burl Ives, the folksinger, and Maxwell
Anderson, the playwright.) From there, some twelve miles
from Manhattan, he continued working for the FIS, writing
broadcasts which he sent to Washington by wire from a post
office in the nearby town of Nyack. This was unsatisfactory
work, however, and he kept his eyes open for something more
exciting. A war was on, after all, and it was passing him by.

The Moon Is Down continued to sell briskly; indeed, a
million copies were sold in its first year, as *Time* reported.[8]
This success prompted Twentieth Century-Fox to offer
$300,000 for the film rights (as compared to $75,000 for *The
Grapes of Wrath*) – an unprecedented sum. (The film eventually appeared in March 1943 with a script by Nunnally
Johnson. Irving Pichel was the director.) Steinbeck was
amazed and embarrassed that even his slightest productions
were capable of bringing in so much cash. Furthermore, he
knew that *The Moon Is Down* did not represent his best work
by any stretch of the imagination, and feelings of guilt and
inadequacy overwhelmed him.

In mid-May Gwyn left for the west coast to visit her mother, and Steinbeck stayed behind to work (in part because he could not stand Gwyn's mother, who disliked him as well). During her absence Steinbeck was asked to write a book about the selection and training of bomber crews; the idea was that he would travel from base to base, living with the men as they trained so that he could discover what their days were like. If the first book were successful, a second would follow that would describe the same men in combat. 'It's a tremendous job I've taken on and I have to do it well,' he told Gwyn in a letter.

In Washington, he was briefed by General 'Hap' Arnold and introduced to John Swope, the photographer who would accompany him on this project. The two of them would spend about a month at twenty airfields in many states. It was a challenging project, and he and Swope set out together almost immediately on a journey that took them from Texas up through Arizona and California, with stops in Florida and Illinois. Steinbeck flew on virtually every kind of plane the armed forces had in their command. He attended classes with the men, ate dinner with them, slept in their barracks. He found himself overwhelmed by their 'courage and good spirits and dedication'. The trip lasted through late June, and he was given until the first of August to complete the project: 'I'm dictating a book into the ediphone now,' he wrote to Street, describing this as his 'first experience in this kind of dictation'.[9] He discovered that he was able to dictate 4000 words a day and worried that he was going so fast that it would be no good when he was done.[10]

The text of *Bombs Away: The Story of a Bomber Team* was a remarkably efficient piece of journalism. Peter Lisca comments, 'The Air Force could not have chosen a better man for the job. Steinbeck's prose is straightforward, simple, but retains some of the effectiveness of the intercalary chapters in *The Grapes of Wrath. Bombs Away* had a wide sale and was bought by Hollywood for $250,000.'[11] Steinbeck, who was already feeling rich with the money paid to him for *The Moon Is Down*, turned over the money to the Air Forces Aid Society Trust Fund, believing that he should not profit from the war effort. He was asked to go to California to start work on the film, and he agreed; again, all this work was done without pay, and Steinbeck did not even receive travel expenses.

The book has received little attention, but some critics, such as Robert Morsberger, have argued for its literary value. Morsberger writes, 'Though written on assignment and under pressure, *Bombs Away* is by no means a piece of hackwork journalism. Perhaps Steinbeck's most neglected book today, and one of the few out of print, it is well worth reading and has a number of elements significant to Steinbeck studies. In particular, it is the most elaborate treatment of Steinbeck's so-called phalanx theory, his interest in what happens when people work together as a group.'[12] In a sense, *Bombs Away* develops in a particular way the generalized theme of allegiance to a group for the benefit of its individual members that was stressed in *The Grapes of Wrath*, although – despite Morsberger's arguments – it appears in an oversimplified form in this sound but superficial piece of propaganda.

In September 1942, he and Gwyn moved to Sherman Oaks, California, a lovely town in the San Fernando Valley, where he was going to see the film version into production. As with *The Forgotten Village*, however, he soon found his good intentions frustrated by a sequence of problems. The man who was supposed to work with him on the film was apparently in England, and chaos reigned at the studio. Nobody seemed to know much about Steinbeck or this particular project. In frustration, he tried to resurrect his old idea for a story about an American town invaded by the enemy (this time it was to be Japanese troops who landed, not the Germans), and he got the support of Twentieth Century-Fox and Nunnally Johnson, who thought it a brilliant idea.

Any such film required government clearance, and the war office still thought the idea was a poor one. They believed it would demoralize and frighten people on the home front rather than inspire them. Propaganda, after all, is the art of deception; one doesn't want to waken too many fears, however justified. To Steinbeck, it now seemed that anything he generated was slapped down quickly, and his nerves began to fray. From October through March, he languished in California, writing very little, getting nothing done on the film. Despite all indications to the contrary, he continued to nurse the hope that he might secure a commission in the armed forces as an intelligence officer.

Meanwhile, his own draft board in Monterey (Selective Service Board 119) began to contemplate drafting him as a foot soldier. General Arnold quickly wrote to them to say that Steinbeck was doing important work for the government and should be deferred, but the draft board refused to hear of this. *How could anybody who wrote such trash as* The Grapes of Wrath *be of service to the nation in time of war?* they wondered. Arnold's request was turned down. On the other hand, the draft board did not move to conscript Steinbeck, perhaps because of his age. Men over forty who were not doctors or specialists of some kind were largely exempt from conscription, although each draft board retained the flexibility to draft whom it pleased. It seems likely that Steinbeck's board merely wanted to remind him of their presence and power.

A minor project of this period was *A Medal for Benny*, a film Steinbeck co-authored with Max Wagner's brother, Jack, during the long Hollywood winter of 1942–3. The story was entirely Jack's, and Steinbeck agreed to work with his old friend from Salinas only if any money that came from the project went directly to Mrs Wagner, mother of Max and Jack, whom Steinbeck continued to admire and occasionally engage in correspondence. Steinbeck wrote to Toby Street, 'Jack Wagner and I wrote a movie in about three weeks – a kind of vicious comedy. I don't know who will make the film but every studio in town is bidding for it. It would make a pretty good picture, too.' The film was released (and promptly forgotten) in 1945.

Another project was the script for *Lifeboat*, a film about the victims of a U-boat sinking. While still in New York, Steinbeck had begun (but left unfinished) a story about a group of survivors in a lifeboat, drawn by the obvious potential for drama inherent in such a story; he also found the self-contained and existentially charged setting attractive. Another incident now fired his imagination: Eddie Rickenbacker, the legendary pilot, crashed in the Pacific; he and seven others spent nearly a month in a small, rubber raft in a hot, salty sea north of Samoa. When Twentieth Century-Fox asked him for another script idea, Steinbeck put this one forward. It was greeted enthusiastically by Kenneth MacGowan, who was head of development. The Maritime Commission had just asked MacGowan to do a film about the merchant marines, and he had already enlisted Alfred Hitchcock as director. Steinbeck's idea fitted right in with this projected film. Working with his usual speed, he finished the script in a month.

Soon after turning in the script, he and Gwyn moved back to New York, taking a light-filled apartment in the lower half of a brownstone on East 51st Street. The place had two big fireplaces and, much to Steinbeck's delight, a small garden at the back which he could use. Shortly after his arrival in March 1943 he wrote to Toby Street that he and Gwyn were going to New Orleans to get married. 'Gwyn is going next week, and I'll go down about the 27th if I can get a plane.'[13] Fortunately, the divorce came through on 19 March, in the nick of time. Steinbeck noted, 'I can't say there was any joy in that final decree. In fact, it snapped me back into all the bad times of the last years. The final failure of an association. But the association had no chance of succeeding from the very first. I can see that now. . . .'

He had for some time been trying to get himself appointed as a war correspondent for a big newspaper or news agency (he had approached Associated Press and Reuters without luck). In April, the *New York Herald Tribune* offered to hire him on the condition that he get the necessary clearances. Army Counterintelligence interviewed a number of people as part of their usual 'security check', and Steinbeck was painted as a dangerous radical by some. A bizarre right-wing group known as the American Legion Radical Research Bureau had compiled what they considered 'damaging' information on him, pointing out that he had contributed articles to several well-known 'red' publications, such as *Pacific Weekly*. Steinbeck was finally allowed to operate as a war correspondent, but his activities were strictly limited and closely watched.[14]

On a chill, foggy morning in New Orleans, John and Gwyn were married in the courtyard of Lyle Saxon's house in the Latin Quarter on 29 March 1943. No sooner had the ceremony started than a fine drizzle began; indeed, the bad weather might have been taken as an omen. Saxon, a writer who knew Steinbeck only slightly, was pleased to offer his house for the occasion, although only a few friends were present. Gwyn's mother, who had flown in from California, grimaced through the ceremony. And there were various disasters: to begin with, Gwyn lost her wedding ring the day before (and so the double-ring ceremony became a single-ring ceremony); then the minister arrived so drunk that he could barely stand on two legs to recite the liturgy; finally, the bakery failed to deliver the wedding cake on time.

When the cake *did* come, and the newlyweds were poised to cut it, two policmen appeared out of nowhere and claimed to have a warrant for Steinbeck's arrest. 'What can this mean?' Steinbeck said, choking out the words. The room fell silent. 'A young woman outside claims that you are the father of her child,' one of the policemen said. There were gasps all around. 'This is impossible,' Steinbeck said. 'What's her name?' Suddenly everyone broke into laughter; it was a practical joke, instigated by Paul de Kruif and Howard Hunter, who were serving as witnesses to the marriage. Steinbeck said, 'I need a drink.' As he later wrote to Nunnally Johnson, 'People cried and laughed and shouted and got drunk. Oh! It was a fine wedding.'

On arrival in New York, the honeymooners learned that Steinbeck had been granted the necessary clearances by the war department and would soon be going overseas. He was thrilled, but his new wife was not. 'How can you do this to me?' she asked, bursting into tears. Steinbeck was at a loss to know how to deal with her outburst; he had hoped that his new wife would sympathize with his desire to be part of the war. 'I think that was the first inkling that something was wrong,' his sister recalls. 'Gwyn thought she would be able to control him. But she couldn't. John didn't want to be controlled that way.' Gwyn tried everything she could think of to prevent her husband from going, but to no avail. His mind was made up, although he soon discovered, much to his chagrin, that he also had to gain clearance from Selective Service Board 119 in Monterey. The board was (as he said to Toby Street) 'doing its usual shit', and this extra round of negotiating held him up a further two months.

He was not able to leave until June, when he boarded a troopship to Britain. In his first dispatch from 'Somewhere in England', dated 20 June 1943, he wrote:

> The troops in their thousands sit on their equipment on the dock. It is evening, and the first of the dim-out lights come on. The men wear their helmets, which make them all look alike, make them look like long rows of mushrooms. Their rifles are leaning against their knees. They have no identity, no personality. The men are units in an army. The numbers chalked on their helmets are almost like the license numbers on robots. Equipment is piled neatly – bedding rolls and

half-shelters and barracks bags. Some of the men are armed
with Springfield or Enfield rifles from the First World War,
some with M-1s, or Garands, and some with the neat, light
clever little carbines everyone wants to have after the war for
hunting rifles.

Steinbeck's dispatches from this period were collected in
Once There Was a War and published in 1958. In the introduction to that volume, the author explains what it was like to
enter the war so late in the game: 'To this hard-bitten bunch of
professionals I arrived as a Johnny-come-lately, a sacred cow,
a kind of tourist. I think they felt that I was muscling in on
their hard-gained territory. When, however, they found that
I was not duplicating their work, was not reporting straight
news, they were very kind to me and went out of their way to
help me and to instruct me in the things I didn't know.'
Robert Capa, now a photographer in the war, gave Steinbeck
some pithy advice, 'Stay where you are. If they haven't hit
you, they haven't seen you.'

Steinbeck spent nearly five months in the European
theatre, reporting on whatever interested him (or happened
to fall his way) in England, North Africa and Italy. While
some of this reporting is workaday, there is memorable
writing throughout. He came, increasingly, to see himself as
a journalist and took pride in these dispatches, a few of which
(the last ones, dated in December from Italy but written much
earlier) aspire to the condition of art. Gore Vidal comments:
'The truth is that Steinbeck was really a journalist at heart. All
of his best work was journalism in that it was inspired by
daily events, by current circumstances. He didn't "invent"
things. He "found" them.'[15]

Steinbeck arrived in London in June. He was dazzled by an
architecture reflecting centuries of successful empire as well
as by the damage resulting from exhaustive bombing raids.
The fortitude of the British people, who went about their
daily business as though nothing were wrong, caught his

attention as he listened to 'hundreds of stories, and all of them with a little incident, a little thing that stays in your mind'. He retells many of them in his dispatches, such as the one about a little old lady selling lavender in the midst of a terrifying midnight raid: 'The city was rocking under the bombs and the light of burning buildings made it like day.' Against this holocaust, the woman's voice piped up, 'Lavender!' she said. 'Buy lavender for luck!'

Steinbeck's two months in England gratified him enormously. In addition to reporting on the war, Steinbeck amused himself with doing some research on the King Arthur legend, his boyhood obsession. He also had time to look up various friends in the army, such as Max Wagner, who was stationed there and waiting to be shipped across the Channel.

His approach to journalism was highly personal, not so far off what decades later would be called the New Journalism. Like Ernie Pyle, the much-admired correspondent who was killed late in the war when a bullet struck him between the eyes, Steinbeck stayed away from 'objective' reporting. The statistics issued daily by the Office of War Information did not concern him. He (like Pyle) lived with the troops, ate meals with them, walked the streets among them, travelled on the same ships as they did, sat on the edges of their bunks, talked and (mostly) listened. His 'columns' were like pieces of short stories, rich in dialogue and description, and each had a slight undertow of plot that pulled the reader effortlessly forward through a page or so of print.

In England, where *The Grapes of Wrath* had been a huge hit, Steinbeck was as famous as he was at home. Lord Beaverbrook, the press baron, eagerly published his columns in his mass-circulation *Daily Express*. Back home, the column appeared first in the *Herald Tribune* and was then syndicated to every state except Oklahoma, where Steinbeck was still *persona non grata*. Newspapers in Argentina, Chile, Bolivia and elsewhere published the columns in translation. *News-week* (on 5 July 1943) observed that Steinbeck's 'cold grey eyes didn't miss a trick, that with scarcely any note-taking he soaked up information like a sponge, wrote very fast on a portable typewriter, and became haywire if interrupted'.

Lewis Young, an American officer attached to the press corps in England, shepherded Steinbeck around various military bases, and he recalls, 'He had a good way with the men. Some of them hadn't heard of him, and he seemed to like that. The word seemed to get around fast, though, that he was a famous writer. A lot of the men had seen his movies, like *Grapes of Wrath*. He would ask them about their home towns, and he seemed to know somebody in every one-horse village. He didn't really talk so much himself. He was a listener. I think people appreciated that. He was there to find out what was going on, and he did. He was a fine man, and that showed through loud and clear.'[16]

A sense of suppressed emotion gives this wartime journalism its power and dignity; one constantly thinks that Steinbeck will spill over into sentimentality, but he rarely does. One of my favourite columns, for instance, is a tribute to Bob Hope, who tirelessly moved from base to base, from hospital bed to hospital bed, entertaining and cheering the troops. The column ends with a poignant scene in a ward full of wounded men. Frances Langford, hoarse from doing so many shows in a short time, sings 'As Time Goes By' at the request of a young man with a head wound who suddenly breaks into tears. Langford, stunned, finishes the song and leaves the ward in tears herself. Bob Hope steps forward, the whole ward listening breathlessly, and quips: 'Fellows, the folks at home are having a terrible time about eggs. They can't get any powdered eggs at all. They've got to get the old-fashioned kind that you break open.' Steinbeck comments, 'There's a man for you – there is really a man.'

In mid-August Steinbeck got the permission he had been

seeking to go to North Africa, recently conquered by the Allies. There was still heavy fighting in Sicily, and the infamous siege of Salerno lay just ahead. He shipped out (having had less than a day to pack) to Algiers, where he checked into a seedy hotel 'like a set from a Gorki play'. The walls were cracked and sweating, the bed was lice-ridden and hard. He quickly fell prey to diarrhoea, lice and heat stroke. But he didn't seem to mind. This was, after all, a war. He had come prepared for worse. He spent several miserable days in Algiers, adjusting to the hot climate, the rank discomfort everywhere, and the genuine threat of lethal German bombing raids. Disoriented at first and hit by an inexplicable fever, he recovered after a week in bed and began to pump out columns. The one dated 28 August 1943 begins:

> Algiers is a fantastic city now. Always a place of strange
> mixtures, it has been brought to a nightmarish mess by the
> influx of British and American troops and their equipment.
> Now jeeps and staff cars nudge their way among camels
> and horse-drawn cars. The sunshine is blindingly white on
> the white city, and when there is no breeze from the sea the
> heat is intense.

As for the difference between soldiers abroad and soldiers in training camps in the States or in England, he says with a kind of wise whimsicality, 'Here the qualities of the mess, the animosities with the sergeant, the price of wine are much more important than the world at war.'

The Italian front columns, which begin in late September and run through December (well after Steinbeck had gone back to New York) are by far his most vivid pieces of reportage. Covering the invasion of Italy by General Mark Clark's Fifth Army, his prose becomes more particularized, more genuinely poetic and unsentimental. In Salerno, for example, he describes seeing 'a small Italian girl in the street with her stomach blown out', one of the many horrors of a war-torn city, with its 'wreckage of houses, with torn beds hanging like shreds out of the spilled hole in a plaster wall'. There is the sharp smell of cordite in the air on top of the odour of 'the accumulated sweat of an army', Steinbeck writes,

> While the correspondent is writing for you of advances and retreats, his skin will be raw from the woolen clothes he has not taken off for three days, and his feet will be hot and dirty and swollen from not having taken off his shoes for days. He will itch from last night's mosquito bites and from today's sand-fly bites. Perhaps he will have a little sand-fly fever, so that his head pulses and a red rim comes into his vision. His head may ache from the heat and his eyes burn with the dust. The knee that was sprained when he leaped ashore will grow stiff and painful, but it is no wound and cannot be treated.

Steinbeck had chosen to attach himself to a special unit, and he made the trip to Italy on a small PT boat whose chief mission was to divert and confuse the enemy. He joined the main convoy off Salerno just in time for the big invasion, which afforded him his first real contact with battle, an experience many of his friends felt left him permanently affected. He spent a week in the middle of the fighting, then retreated to a troopship to write his columns (the ship was constantly under fire, so it was hardly a relief from battle). On 20 September he wrote to Gwyn: 'I'm gay today – maybe because I'm still alive but more I think because I've been as far away from you as I am going and now I'm starting back – slowly, perhaps, but always in that direction. And it makes me very happy. Because I've done the things I had to do and I don't think any inner compulsion will make me do them again.'[17] He described himself that day as wearing a 'ragged dirty khaki shirt and trousers, canvas rope soled shoes bought in an Italian town – no hat or cap, nothing but a helmet'.

The English, African and Italian columns were all written, as Steinbeck said later, 'under pressure and in tension'. He relied heavily on techniques long accepted (tacitly) as standard journalistic practice: 'I never admitted seeing anything myself. In describing a scene I invariably put it in the mouth of someone else. I forget why I did this. Perhaps I felt that it would be more believable if told by someone else.' His work, for security reasons and because of the unspoken conventions of reportage, is full of composite portraits and rearranged conversations. Steinbeck, a fiction writer, understood that *fictio* – the process of shaping – is crucial to all good writing. And he fashioned these shapely little vignettes from the billion-faceted mass of reality.

He worked on his columns for a while aboard the destroyer *Knight*, which housed the Special Operations Unit and where most journalists stayed and worked. Elaine Steinbeck comments, 'John had always told me that he and Douglas Fairbanks had sailed into Capri just as it was being liberated. I took this with a grain of salt. In January 1962, John and I went over to Capri from Rome and as we approached the hotel where we were to stay, the French couple who operated it ran out to greet John, shouting, "Libérateur! Libérateur!" ' Be this as it may, the ship was anchored off Capri, not far north of Salerno, with a dazzling view of the Amalfi coast, where the mountains press right up to the sea. British, American and Dutch ships huddled in the old harbour, and Steinbeck enjoyed a lively social life, hopping from ship to ship. While the American boats were determinably 'dry', the British were 'wet'. Steinbeck often socialized with Fairbanks, a high-ranking officer whom he had known from his Hollywood days, and with fellow-journalists Quentin Reynolds and Lionel Shapiro. Fairbanks, Steinbeck later recalled, was the life of the party, doing riotous impressions of Chaplin, Barrymore and Errol Flynn. And he had a fund of David Niven anecdotes so funny that the wardroom was often crippled with laughter. This was the lighter side of war.

Steinbeck headed back to London at the end of September, where he met Burgess Meredith, who had recently arrived in Britain to work on propaganda films. 'John wanted to get home now,' Meredith recalls. 'He was extremely tired. The work had become repetitious. He and I were working together on an army film. I loved his stories about Africa and Italy. He told them so damn well.' The *Herald Tribune* implored him to stay; his columns were terrifically popular. The Army, as might be expected, hoped he would stay to finish the script he was doing with Meredith. But Steinbeck, as ever, followed his own timetable. He had done what he had to do, and he had promised Gwyn that he would be home well before Christmas.

A rather fragile forty-one-year-old Steinbeck, with deep ridges in his leathery face and a slight limp (he had twisted his ankle on the voyage), disembarked from his troopship in New York on 15 October 1943, just as the first autumn chill had swept the city. The leaves in Central Park swirled in little tornadoes, and a light snow – the first of the season – blew against the windows of the apartment on the upper east side. 'The war shook him up,' says one friend.[18] 'He had seen some things that hurt him. This was clear from his eyes, which had a faraway look in them, a kind of vacancy that frightened all of us.' Steinbeck was plagued by burst eardrums from the Salerno landing and temporary losses of memory, which left him unsure where he was. He appeared to Gwyn and many others both depressed and anxious, and he agreed with their observations; he got one doctor to administer shots of male hormones and vitamins, a combination someone in Europe had recommended for 'nerves'. At night, he was weakened by fierce headaches and sweats.

Gwyn was also nervous and depressed; she could still

hardly believe that Steinbeck had taken off for the war right after their wedding. That her protests had been roundly ignored still galled her, and she had been left to languish in New York, relatively friendless and terrified that he might be killed. Now that he was back, thin and grey, riddled with ailments, she had to deal with his moodiness as well. She told Jackson Benson that for 'one solid year after he came back from the war he had no sense of humour at all. He had a chip on his shoulder the whole time. He was mean, he was sadistic, he was masochistic, he resented everything.'[19] His sister confirms this change of attitude: 'John wasn't himself when he got home. The humour was gone, the play knocked right out of him. The war changed him.'

He finished writing up his columns for the *Herald Tribune*, then began working on what was eventually to become *Cannery Row*, 'a funny little book' that he seems not yet to have taken seriously as a project. (Pat Covici had been urging him for some time now to write a novel set in Cannery Row along the lines of *Tortilla Flat*.) As winter approached, he began to speculate about the possibility of returning to Mexico. He had loved the brief time spent in La Paz on the Sea of Cortez trip and now thought he might do some research there that could lead, eventually, to a novel with a Mexican setting. (This project became *The Pearl*.) The form that still attracted him most was the play-novella, the genre he had used in *Of Mice and Men* and *The Moon Is Down*.

Lifeboat appeared in January, attracting lots of media attention, but Steinbeck was horrified by what he saw. He wrote to Twentieth Century-Fox in protest: 'While in many ways the film is excellent there are one or two complaints I would like to make. While it is certainly true that I wrote a script for *Lifeboat*, it is not true that in that script as in the film there were any slurs against organized labor nor was there a stock comedy Negro. On the contrary there was an intelligent and thoughtful seaman who knew realistically what he was about. And instead of the usual colored travesty of the half comic and half pathetic Negro there was a Negro of dignity, purpose and personality. Since this film occurs over my name, it is painful to me that these strange, sly obliquities should be ascribed to me.'[20] In a letter to his movie agent, Annie Laurie Williams, he called Hitchcock 'one of those incredible English middle class snobs who really and truly despise working people'. Steinbeck resolved to work on future projects only with producers and directors whom he knew he could trust.

In mid-January he and Gwyn left the bitterly cold winter in New York for Mexico, stopping in New Orleans to visit friends. Once south of the border, they travelled around by car at a leisurely pace in the bright winter sun and visited the ruins of Mitla and Monte Albán, near Oaxaca. They spent a week in a small hotel in Cuernavaca, high in the mountains, with its clear, crisp air. Because of rationing in the US, plenty of Americans were in Mexico on vacation, gorging themselves on things like steak. (Then, as now, Mexican prices seemed cheap to Americans.) For a few hours each day, Steinbeck sat by himself in the hotel room wherever he happened to be and worked; *The Pearl* had begun to take shape in his head, and he was now outlining the plot before beginning to write. He was reading, in Spanish, a book of Mexican folktales that he hoped would inspire him.

Once back in the States, in March, he put together (with the assistance of Lewis Milestone and other Hollywood connections) a deal in Mexico with partly Mexican financing for a movie version of *The Pearl*. As before, he would write the play version first, and this would be followed by a novella. Not having a suitable room at home, he accepted Pat Covici's offer of a little office at Viking, and he worked there on both *Cannery Row* and *The Pearl*. But he was not satisfied by his progress on either. He knew that neither of these books equalled *The Grapes of Wrath* in scope or ambition, and it depressed him that he had been unable to move from strength to strength.

Gwyn was now pregnant, the baby due in July, and Steinbeck did not want her to have the child in the city. He dreamed of returning to Monterey, and he often talked about buying an adobe house there and settling into domestic life in California. But Gwyn was a social person, and New York felt increasingly like home to her. Her circle of friends had widened in the period her husband was away in Europe, and she did not like his notion of a return to a small California town. (Steinbeck, who had been resistant to parties and socializing for much of his life thus far, had evolved into a social creature as well, although he was not especially aware of this.[21]) That spring, through Covici, he met John Hersey, then a young and promising writer, who recalls: 'John seemed to take pleasure in making friends and knowing people. I suspect he was secretly competitive with other writers, but he rarely showed it. He usually talked very little. Or he talked a lot, if the situation hit him a certain way. We met at "21", where he had his own table. The *maître d'* loved him, called him by name. People would come over to the table and introduce themselves, and he played the genial famous man. He seemed to get more and more comfortable in this role. It was as if he were finally accepting the consequences of his fame, which was genuine fame. Readers loved him. Even people who really didn't read books read Steinbeck.'[22]

One time Hersey and John O'Hara contrived to introduce Steinbeck to Hemingway. 'It was a disaster,' Hersey remembers. 'John had given O'Hara a walking stick, and Hemingway grabbed it and broke it over his own head and threw the pieces on to the ground, claiming it was a fake of some kind. Not the kind of wood O'Hara had supposedly boasted it was. Steinbeck had given that stick to O'Hara, and he was quite rightly horrified. He never liked Hemingway after that – not as a man. He understood the importance of the work, of course. Every writer did.' For the most part, as Hersey observes, 'Steinbeck was courteous to other writers, helpful, and polite about their work. He was a deeply generous man by nature.'

Throughout the spring and early summer he worked furiously on *Cannery Row*, while Gwyn – who became increasingly anxious as the pregnancy neared its term – sat drinking martinis under a broad pin oak in the garden of their townhouse on 51st Street. The lease on this place was falling due, and Steinbeck did not plan to renew it. He was desperate to get back to Monterey, which had been strongly on his mind as he worked on the novel, and Gwyn reluctantly agreed to go back with him after the baby was born. Meanwhile, in Europe, the Allies landed 326,000 troops in France for the major invasion of the war (6 June 1944), known as D-Day.

On 2 August, Thom was born. Steinbeck wired Max and Jack Wagner the same day: BOY NAMED THOM SIX POUNDS TEN OUNCES BOTH DOING SPLENDIDLY. By the middle of the month, Gwyn and the baby were home and healthy. Friends dropped by every day with presents, and to see Thom and his gloating (and exhausted) parents. 'This has been a busy and an exciting time,' he wrote happily to Toby Street. 'Thom seems to be a baby-shaped baby and I like him very much. . . . He just eats and sleeps and shits, but I can think of worse kids.'

He noted casually in a letter to Dook Sheffield in late September, 'I finished the book called *Cannery Row*. It will be out in January.' It was, he said, full of 'extensions of things we talked about years ago. Maybe we were sounder then. Certainly we were thinking more universally.'[23] He insisted that the 'crap' that he 'wrote overseas had a profoundly nauseating effect on me. Among other unpleasant things modern war is the most dishonest thing imaginable.' From

October through Christmas, he intended to work on the script for *The Pearl*. 'Within a year,' he continued, 'I want to get to work on a very large book I've been thinking about for the last two years and a half. Everything else is kind of marking time. Work is still fun and still work. It hasn't ever got any easier.'

It's interesting to contemplate Steinbeck's working methods. More than ever, he liked to have many projects circling in the air, like so many planes waiting for permission to land. The 'big book' was *East of Eden*, but it would not emerge for many years. In progress at this moment was *The Pearl*, as yet inchoate but existing in outline form. It would soon be written as a script, then a story. *Cannery Row*, now finished, would require some revision. This was a lot of material to keep in his head and heart, but Steinbeck seemed to know no other way of proceeding.

On 5 October, Steinbeck set off by car across the continent, a gruelling five-day drive. Gwyn and Thom flew. They were all reunited in Monterey, moving briefly into the 11th Street house (which happened to be empty) while Steinbeck scouted for another place for them to live. With the help of Toby Street, he was able to purchase an adobe house he had admired since boyhood: the so-called Soto House, dating from 1830. It was a landmark in town, with its large walled-in garden; even better, it was only four blocks from the sea. Steinbeck was prepared to set himself up in royal fashion.

The Soto House needed a lot of work, however, so he had to hire a large crew of carpenters, plasterers and plumbers. By chance, his old friend from Tahoe days, Lloyd Shebley, was in town, and he gladly hired him to work on the house. Meanwhile, it was delightful to have fallen back among his old friends: Ed Ricketts, Toni Jackson, Ritch and Tal Lovejoy, and others. Robinson Jeffers, the poet, dropped by to see him, as did his sisters, Mary, Esther and Beth. Beth recalls: 'It seemed that John had come home for good. He always wanted a house like that one, and now he had it.'

Ed Ricketts and Steinbeck took long walks together on the beach, renewing their friendship. 'Ed was just the right sort of person for John,' a friend recalls. 'He didn't try to one-up anybody. John respected him. They came from different angles toward the same centre.'[24] Steinbeck found that he and Ed could take up in conversation just where they had left off, as though neither time nor distance had intervened. He nervously asked Ricketts to read *Cannery Row*, in which he is overtly fictionalized as 'Doc'. Ricketts read it but did not bubble with enthusiasm. He said, 'It is written in kindness. Let it be published as it stands.'

Steinbeck did, however, get himself into a battle at this time with Ritch Lovejoy, to whom he had given his Pulitzer money. (It was Gwyn's well-known opinion that her husband quarrelled eventually with all his male friends, but this was patently not so.) The fight with Lovejoy centred on the fact that *Life* had recently asked Steinbeck to write a piece about Monterey that focused on Cannery Row. Somewhat irrationally (given his latest novel), Steinbeck thought this was a terrible idea, a form of exploitation. As soon as he turned it down, Lovejoy stepped in to accept the assignment. Steinbeck was furious, considering this a 'betrayal' of some kind. Their friendship was never resumed on quite the same footing, largely because Steinbeck possessed a firm sense of what was right and what was wrong and insisted that his closest friends – especially old friends who were beholden to him in any way – respect this.

Throughout the late autumn Steinbeck worked on *The Pearl* in the rustic woodshed behind his house: yet another working space reminiscent of 'The Sphincter' in Palo Alto. The shed was dark and unheated, so he bought a kerosene lantern for a combination of heat and light; it swayed from a hook overhead. When the writing did not go well, Steinbeck would put down his pencil and step into the garden, surrounded by a high redwood fence. Among his many landscaping projects was the planting of a row of Monterey cypress trees, which (as he explained to Pat Covici) were 'unique in the world except for one part of China'. He also occupied himself with the building of a patio, where he hoped to 'doze in the sun in future years into senility'.

Life was cosy in the new house, with a nurse helping out with baby Thom and the weather perfect – an astonishing row of brilliant, sunny days that lasted right into the dead of winter. Sometimes he and Gwyn went out with the sardine fleet, just to watch them work and get a feel of the coastline from the 'other' side. He bought Gwyn a Ford convertible so that she could learn to drive, and she took to it quickly; soon she was taking off by herself on day-trips into San Francisco to meet old friends. The baby was growing fast. In late January Steinbeck noted that 'Thom is fine and gay. Getting to be a kind of personable child. He has been very happy ever since his last tooth came through.'[25]

Cannery Row was published in January 1945, just as the Battle of the Bulge was drawing bloodily to a close and the Allied troops turned towards the Rhineland for the final assault. In some ways, the novel represents a retreat for Steinbeck, a way back to his old prewar life and times. The realities of contemporary life are largely absent from the book, which may be read on one level as Steinbeck's loving tribute to a place, Cannery Row, and to his friend, Ed Ricketts. One hesitates to call it a novel at all, unless one defers to E. M. Forster's default definition of the novel as a fictional prose narrative exceeding 40,000 words. Thirty-two short chapters comprise this book of related anecdotes, which begins with a brief prose poem by Steinbeck in which Cannery Row is invoked as 'a poem, a stink, a grating noise, a quality of light, a tone, a habit, a nostalgia, a dream'.

The setting is both a physical place and a mental condition, a place of 'tin and iron and rust and splintered wood, chipped pavement and weedy lots and junk heaps, sardine canneries of corrugated iron, honkey-tonks, restaurants and whore houses, and little crowded groceries, and laboratories and flophouses'. The first six chapters of the novel establish the place and its residents, including Doc, the Ed Ricketts figure; Dora Flood and her 'girls' at the Bear Flag whorehouse; Lee Chong, the grocer, and Mack and the boys – a group of charming winos and bums reminiscent of Danny and his friends in *Tortilla Flat*. There is a variety of settings, which appear like movie sets: the Palace Flophouse, the Bear Flag, the lab at Western Biologicals, the grocery, the waterfront and the streets of the town itself.

Steinbeck abandons the allegorical form of *Tortilla Flat*, however, preferring a looser, anecdotal structure. Once again, he focuses on a group of men who have in common 'no families, no money and no ambitions beyond food, drink, and contentment'. Sylvia Cook sensibly notes, 'Although Mack and the boys do not embrace the predominant values of their environment, they are not opposed vigorously either.'[26] Steinbeck himself writes, 'In the world ruled by tigers with ulcers, rutted by strictures bulls, scavenged by blind jackals, Mack and the boys dine delicately with the tigers, fondle the frantic heifers, and wrap up the crumbs to feed the seagulls of Cannery Row.' In a sense, this was how Steinbeck liked to idealize himself: he was a man living on the margins but participating fully, dining with tigers but managing to feed the seagulls too.

The novel is deepened by the parallel group of women who appear in this narrative, the prostitutes who work in Dora's brothel and lead 'decent' and 'virtuous' lives at the margins of society. These women are noticeably missing from the world of *Tortilla Flat*, where Danny and his friends are rather sexless and women appear only as props in the background. In *Cannery Row*, Dora Flood is a rich and vivid person, as are a host of minor characters, such as the party-loving Mary Talbot, who throws six birthday parties a year for her lugubrious husband, Tom. (It has often been suggested that Mary was based on Carol; like Carol, she is a woman of fantastic high spirits who types her husband's manuscripts.[27])

The last twenty-five chapters focus on two parties that Mack and the boys are planning for Doc, who needs to revive his sagging spirits. (Eight other parties are either partially evoked or alluded to in the course of the narrative.) The first party gets out of control before Doc ever gets there; the final one, which brings the novel to its climax, is a success; indeed, *Cannery Row* might be described as the anatomy of a good party. The narrative action oscillates between the partying and the work of collecting specimens for Western Biologicals.

The chief character in *Cannery Row* is Doc, whose face is 'half Christ and half satyr', and who is 'concupiscent as a rabbit and as gentle as hell'. He adores his scientific work, beer, women and Gregorian music. The degree to which Doc was based directly on Ricketts is revealed by Steinbeck's memoir of his friend in *The Log from the 'Sea of Cortez'*, with the lives of Doc and Ed Ricketts paralleling each other in most details. Rather self-consciously enigmatic, the novel's dedication reads, 'For Ed Ricketts who knows why or should'. While Doc is portrayed as a deeply sympathetic and friendly man, Steinbeck complicates the portrait: 'In spite of his friendliness and his friends, Doc was a lonely and set-apart man. Even in a group Doc seemed always alone.' Both his dedication to his work and his extreme and original intelligence isolate him from the rest of the community.

A pervasive melancholy suffuses this novel, which seems to argue on the surface that parties are what ward off loneliness. But in spite of the parties, Doc remains a lonely man. The novel ends on the morning after the big party, with Doc reading aloud to himself from 'Black Marigolds', a sentimental Sanskrit poem he had read the night before at the party. When he finished reciting, 'He wiped his eyes with the back of his hand. And the white rats scampered and scrambled in their cages. And behind the glass the rattle-snakes lay still and stared into space with their dusty frowning eyes.'

The critical reaction to *Cannery Row* was swift and often dismissive. Orville Prescott weighed in early on 2 January 1945, in *The New York Times*, arguing that 'ever since his triumph with *The Grapes of Wrath* Mr Steinbeck has been coasting.' He continued:

> This little tribute to a waterfront block in Monterey and its indecorous inhabitants has some of the Steinbeck mannerisms, much of the Steinbeck charm and simple felicity of expression, but it is as transparent as a cobweb. For all its 208 pages it is less substantial than a short story. There just isn't much here, no real characters, no 'story', no purpose. Instead, with considerable pointless vulgarity and occasional mildly humorous scenes, a series of loosely connected incidents is thrown casually together.

In similar vein, Margaret Marshall in *The Nation* (20 January) complained that the writing in the novel was 'factitiously simple, after the fashion of the moment; it is at the same time highflown and flyblown, cheap, fancy, and false.' Even worse, she said, 'If proof were needed that sentimentality and cruelty are two sides of the same coin, it may be found in this book. The unpleasant pleasure with which Steinbeck describes the killing of a mouse by a cat, the "murder" of a crab by an octopus, the sadism of a small boy toward a smaller boy, is disturbing, to say the least.' In a judicious piece in *The New York Times Book Review*, J. Donald Adams wrote,

> It seems to me that the book yields the most pleasure if it is read simply as a sort of gentle parable on the irony that so often attends the attempt to carry out good intentions. Read

in that light, the efforts of Mr Steinbeck's lovable bums to throw a party for Doc because he was such a 'nice fella' have a humor and tenderness that are genuine and warming. There are good things in *Cannery Row*, and the story of the frog hunt is Steinbeck at his humorous best. But I think it will leave most readers with the feeling that it falls curiously between the inconsequential and the pretentious.

The novel may well be considered an example of Steinbeck's non-teleological thinking translated into literary form. Malcolm Cowley once called it 'a very poisoned cream puff' that conceals in its smooth confection a lethal attack on contemporary American values. Certainly Mack and the boys represent the flotsam of society, cruelly treated and ignored. As Stanley Alexander has written, they are 'outcasts from a social world which has arrogantly and wrongfully denied its connections with and dependence upon nature'.[28] More so than in any previous book, Steinbeck here accepts Ed Ricketts's thesis that 'progress' is specious, that it represents the destruction of nature, and that it inevitably corrupts human nature as well. In *The Log from the 'Sea of Cortez'*, Ricketts is said to be thinking these thoughts, which seem apposite to Doc's attitudes:

> The things we admire in men, kindness and generosity, openness, honesty, understanding and feeling are the concomitants of failure in our system. And those traits we detest, sharpness, greed, acquisitiveness, meanness, egotisms, and self-interest are the traits of success. And while men admire the quality of the first, they love the produce of the second.[29]

Cannery Row is, indeed, a poisoned cream puff thrown at society beyond the town lines of Monterey. The tone of the book, generally, might be described as passive-aggressive. Steinbeck, writing at his most lyrical in places, indicts his country and its misguided valuations. Identifying with Doc,

he regards the wild conjuring of Mack and the boys as a
protest, a natural form of resistance. He identifies with and
implicitly endorses their anti-social behaviour, their ribaldry
and drunkenness, their irresponsibility and love of mayhem,
and he celebrates their natural warmth, piety and generosity.
While the novel may lack the bite of Steinbeck's very best
work, it remains one of his most readable novels, perhaps
because of its lively evocation of a community. Unlike many
of his contemporaries, Steinbeck understood that while
human beings must die alone, they live in concert with
others. The fleshly being of a community as a whole is
beautifully evoked here, in language at once 'honest' – in the
sense of seeming a genuine response to the subject at hand –
and 'poetic', in that Steinbeck's specific heightenings of the
prose add to its memorability.

XIII

An Uncertain Homecoming

'It seems to me that for the last few years I have been
working on bits and pieces of things without much
continuity and I want to get back to a long slow piece of
work.'

Steinbeck to Toby Street, 17 November 1947

Steinbeck had sent galleys of *Cannery Row* to Dook Sheffield,
who duly noted and complimented his friend's 'constantly
improving technical skill'. Dook also thought the critics
would say 'that the world marches on but Steinbeck wallows
at the same old trough'. He was eerily correct. The reviewers,
more than ever before, denounced Steinbeck for returning to
an old subject. He wrote defensively to Pat Covici about his
predicament:

> The first reviews seem to bear out Sheffield's thesis exactly.
> But there was something he forgot. There is a time in every
> writer's career when the critics are gunning for him to
> whittle him down. This is my stage for that. It has been
> since *The Grapes of Wrath*. I see it all the time. The criticism is
> good, but what saddens me is the active hatred of most of
> the writers and the pseudowriters around here. It will not
> be terribly long before we will be associating only with
> fishermen, which is the best thing of all. There is a deep
> and active jealousy out here that makes me very sad.[1]

In the same letter, he says, 'I'm still in a slump with *The Pearl*.
This has been a long slump.' On top of all this, Gwyn was
relentlessly sick and out of sorts, suffering from what her
doctors called 'exhaustion'. What should have been an idyllic
return to Eden was fast becoming a negative experience.

'People would cross the street rather than talk to John Steinbeck,' one native of Monterey recalls.[2] 'He never thought the people in Monterey would react that way, but they did. He gave the whole country a picture of the town that wasn't true. It wasn't all bums and flophouses and bad women. These were good people, and they didn't like it one bit when he published that book. Photographers landed on the place from all over. *Who does he think he is?* the local people were all saying.'

'The small fry of writers and some of the academic ones will always be gunning for you,' Pat Covici wrote back to comfort Steinbeck. 'Better start building a tougher protective skin around you. Poisonous javelins will be constantly coming your way.' In another letter, he lays it on a bit thick: 'I read *Cannery Row* over again. It's a good book, John. You poured a great deal of poetry into it. You give a good many reasons for living and for dying. And I am glad you were born and happy that you are alive.' One occasionally cringes to read Covici's pandering remarks to Steinbeck, whom he treated with kid gloves. He sensed a disturbing vulnerability at the core, and his reaction was constantly to praise him, to try to make him feel better about himself and his work. Steinbeck's real mood, however, was somewhat less fragile than Covici thought. He wrote to Jack and Max Wagner about the critical response to his novel:

> *Cannery Row* took a frightful pounding by the critics and they went too far. Annie Laurie phoned to say that her telephone rang all the time from studios wanting to buy it and what should she do. So I told her she was on her own – to sell or not to sell – whenever she was ready. She has a magnificent sense of timing for such things. And she knows what we want. A lot of money, control of the script. And this time I am going to ride herd on it. I'll act as consultant – for a consideration. I thought the adverse criticism would hurt the book, but she says quite the opposite. The sales are

tremendous and that's what interests the studios – not the critics.[3]

One hears a new, rather aggressive note in this letter. The negative reaction of the critics to *Cannery Row* seems to have lit a creative fire under Steinbeck, and he began to pour himself into *The Pearl* in mid-January. A draft was completed in just a few weeks, and he left for Mexico almost immediately, on 14 February. The film's director was to be Emilio Fernandez, a Mexican whom he had met the year before and found 'charming, and original'. The somewhat fanciful idea, promoted by Gwyn, was that she would do the musical arrangements, using Mexican folk themes for the score. Baby Thom was boarded, temporarily, in Berkeley with Beth and a nurse. In all, they spent a month in Mexico City while Steinbeck worked on an early version of the shooting script with Fernandez, who put them up in 'a moldy colonial hotel with slowly turning fans in a seedy palm court'. Gwyn pursued her research on Mexican music and drifted around the city by herself, often dropping into nightclubs to listen to the music. They flew back to San Francisco in mid-March to rescue Thom from his Aunt Beth, pausing briefly (at Beth's insistence) to have him baptized in an Episcopal church.

Pat Covici, meanwhile, was trying to persuade Steinbeck to edit a Viking Portable edition of Robert Louis Stevenson – a project that Steinbeck felt wary about, much as he admired Stevenson. Covici sent him the sumptuous Vailima Edition of Stevenson, hoping to tempt him, but it had the opposite effect. The prospect of reading so much Stevenson in one fell swoop terrified him; he claimed to have read nothing in recent months apart from the *Arabian Nights*, which he saw as the sourcebook for most Hollywood cowboy pictures (and he thought he should be able to mine plots from it for his own use, too). The Stevenson project dwindled and fell away and was, finally, edited by someone else.

From Berkeley, Gwyn took little Thom to see his grand-mother in Los Angeles, while Steinbeck (who would go to any length to avoid his mother-in-law) returned to the house in Monterey; there he spent a solid week drinking Scotch with Ed Ricketts. Things were getting to him now, and he could not sleep or work. The friendship with Ritch Lovejoy was in shambles, and this appears to have hurt Steinbeck more than he would admit. On top of this, the townspeople, more than ever, shunned him. He wrote to Pat Covici:

> You remember how happy I was to come back here. It really was a home coming. Well, there is no home coming nor any welcome. What there is is jealousy and hatred and the knife in the back. I'm beginning to think I made a mistake. I don't mind that but I'm not going to let a mistake ride me on through.[4]

He explained that even his old friends had rejected him, and this included nearly everyone except Ed Ricketts: 'Mostly with them it is what they consider success that gets in between. And the town and the region – that is the people of it – just pure poison.'

An element of paranoia may well have played into his change of attitude towards Monterey, but there were plenty of concrete indications of hostility. He was peremptorily refused office space by the landlords of several commercial buildings, for instance, without a word of explanation. Then the local gas board suddenly cut off his supply, claiming it was part of wartime rationing. A few weeks later he was denied permission to continue the repairs on his house that he had already begun, even though new homes were going up all around Monterey. 'I hate a feeling of persecution,' Steinbeck wrote to Covici, 'but I am just not welcome here.'

The idea of returning to live in New York lit his mind, and he asked both Pat Covici and Elizabeth Otis what they thought about this. Meanwhile, he returned alone by train to

Mexico to continue working on the film, stopping in Los Angeles to pick up Jack Wagner. (Gwyn and Thom followed a week later by plane; the rationale was that the baby could not tolerate a train journey.) They rented a villa in Cuernavaca with stupendous views and crisp white walls and a colourful tile floor. Three maids, a cook and several gardeners helped to ease their domestic life, while spring flowers were blooming everywhere. A large terrace and a pool added to the general ambience of luxury. Steinbeck rose every morning at six and went out into the garden, where he worked at a small table under a massive bougainvillaea, taking breaks throughout the day to swim or play with Thom. He finished rewriting the book version of *The Pearl* and sent it to Otis, who wrote back with great enthusiasm. Pat Covici, too, responded warmly, 'I just finished "La Perla" and I like it. . . . In this parable you say there are only black and white things and no in between, but what rich blacks and what dazzling whites.' Steinbeck was thrilled by their response, claiming great relief.

On the evening of 12 April Steinbeck heard on the radio that Franklin Roosevelt had died. He had loved the man, and this news hurled him – and the entire nation Roosevelt had nursed through the Great Depression and much of the Second World War – into a melancholic state. The bad news was tempered by the fact that the Allied armies were swiftly closing in on Germany. General Mark Clark's Fifth Army, which Steinbeck had encountered firsthand in southern Italy, had fought its way north to the Brenner Pass, where it met up with the Seventh Army, which had just picked its way through the Nazi stronghold of Austria. Generals Montgomery and Patton closed in from the east, racing through Germany, liberating towns and concentration camps along the way. Mussolini was captured and killed, then strung up like a side of beef, on 28 April. Two days later, Adolf Hitler turned a gun on his mistress, and then on himself, ending his dictatorship with more of a whimper than a bang. On 7 May, General Jodl surrendered, for Germany, to the Allied forces, and the war in Europe came to an end. Steinbeck celebrated the victory with a display of fireworks in his Mexican garden and by drinking, as he wrote to Dook Sheffield, 'a large quantity of Mexican beer'.

Throughout the long, hot summer of 1945 in Mexico, Steinbeck worked at the shooting script of *The Pearl* and on the synopsis for another script called 'The Wizard of Maine', which would never come to anything. He and Gwyn both suffered bouts of dysentery and were put on a rather peculiar diet of fruit and nuts by the local doctors. Steinbeck also began to make notes for *The Wayward Bus*, a novel that would appear two years later. In June, he was approached by a company called Pan-American Films about the idea of writing a screenplay based on the life and times of Emiliano Zapata, the Mexican revolutionary. He wrote to Annie Laurie Williams, 'Now there is no other story I would rather do.' He added, perhaps by way of caution, 'There are still men living and in power who helped to trick and murder Zapata.' The notion of working on Zapata was so enticing that he immediately began to draft an outline of the story. Gwyn, who had been taking Spanish lessons from a woman in the village, assisted him by doing research on Zapata in the archives of the National University. Steinbeck insisted that, if he were to continue working on this project, Pan-American Films had to secure an ironclad agreement with the Mexican government about their cooperation. He was afraid that, given Zapata's revolutionary attitudes, they would put up endless roadblocks. He did not want to risk undermining 'the things Zapata lived and died for'.

In spite of having so many projects on the boil, Steinbeck felt somewhat ill at ease. 'I seem to be waiting maybe for a design or a shadow or something to indicate a future,' he wrote to Covici in mid-July. He claimed to be 'heartily sick of this picture now', and he wanted to get down to writing *The*

Wayward Bus, which he hoped might become 'something like the *Don Quixote* of Mexico'. The book began, he said, as 'a funny little story', but it had grown in his mind into what he considered 'the most ambitious thing I have ever attempted'. He warned Covici that the book must not be tossed off idly: 'It isn't going to take a little time to write, but a long time, and I don't care, for my bus is something large in my mind. It is a cosmic bus holding sparks and back firing into the Milky Way turning the corner of Betelgeuse without a hand signal. And Juan Chicoy the driver is all the god the fathers you ever saw driving a six cylinder broken down, battered world through time and space.'[5]

In August, Gwyn (who continued to suffer from digestive ailments and wanted to see a good doctor) flew to New York with Thom. It was clear now to both of them that the return to Monterey had been a huge mistake, and that their future lay on the east coast. California was no longer the place Steinbeck remembered, and Monterey had spurned its most famous son. Even the friendship of Ed Ricketts could not lure Steinbeck back into permanent residence there; the 'real' and the 'imagined' Monterey were simply too far apart. So he commuted several times by plane between Mexico City and Manhattan, which would become his home from this time forward. There Gwyn had found a small, furnished apartment on the Upper East Side that would do until something more permanent arose.

The Pearl didn't go into production until September, just as the war in the Pacific came to a close with the Japanese surrender being signed on 15 August 1945, on the deck of the battleship *Missouri*, moored in Tokyo Bay. 'A new era is upon us,' General Douglas MacArthur intoned as the whole world listened with rapt attention. Steinbeck heard the speech in the kitchen of his new apartment in New York, and he did indeed see a new era dawning for himself. His parents were dead, his first marriage had dissolved in bitterness and mutual accusation, and his career had soared and dipped several times. California was history, part of his irretrievable past, a place he could find only his heart. California 'isn't my country anymore', he told Pat Covici. 'And it won't be until I am dead. It makes me very sad.'

In the middle of September Steinbeck bought two adjacent brownstones on East 78th Street, a secluded side street within easy reach of mid-town Manhattan and a short stroll to the green oasis of Central Park. The reason for buying two instead of one was that he and Gwyn could control who would rent the place next to them (and thus who would share the back garden, which was Steinbeck's chief interest in this property). The other house was also a solid investment: the war had depressed the price of real estate, and it was sure to climb in the postwar years as returning soldiers began to establish families. Both brownstones were in a poor state of repair because building materials were strictly rationed during the war, so they would need a lot of work to make them habitable, but Steinbeck was undaunted; he had done this kind of thing many times before.

Just before heading back to Mexico in October for the actual filming of *The Pearl*, Steinbeck learned that Gwyn was once again pregnant. She was not, however, happy that he had been planning to go without her, so he promised to send for her as soon as he saw where things stood. Meanwhile, work on the film got underway swiftly, much in contrast to the previous time in Mexico; Steinbeck moved into the same hotel that housed the rest of the movie company, and he, Jack Wagner and Fernandez worked from seven-thirty in the morning until late at night most days. Gwyn arrived, with Thom, in early November, hoping to have a genuine holiday with her family, but she soon discovered that her husband was preoccupied and busy. She reported to a friend that he 'looked haggard and old, like a man of sixty', and complained that he had little time for her; she felt 'excluded and unimportant', and after only three weeks she flew back to New York, disgruntled and resentful. This was the first visible tear in the fabric of her marriage.[6]

Steinbeck was not worried about Gwyn at all. The shooting went extremely well, and he got along nicely with Fernandez. In mid-December he felt confident that Fernandez could finish the project without him and left by car for New York, although his 1939 Dodge fell apart only one hundred kilometres outside Mexico City, and he was forced to hang around for three days while it was overhauled. He was travelling with his new houseboy, Victor, and a dog. The car was fixed rather tentatively, and as they proceeded north further problems with the car's temperamental heater erupted; indeed, as he wrote to Jack Wagner after arriving home, they 'nearly froze to death' along the way.

Steinbeck was welcomed back warmly by his friends, and it seemed clear that he had made the right choice about where to live. 'New York is a wonderful city,' he told Jack Wagner in January 1946, 'I'm glad to be putting down some kind of roots here. It is going to be the capital of the world. It isn't like the rest of the country – it's like a nation itself – more tolerant than the rest in a curious way. Littleness gets swallowed up here. All the viciousness that makes other cities vicious is sucked up and absorbed in New York. It is truly the great city of the world – an organism in itself – neither good nor bad but unique.'[7] The only curiosity was that Gwyn, who had lobbied so vociferously to move back to New York, was treating him coolly. He did not realize how upset she had been with his behaviour in Mexico, and she was unable to communicate her anger.[8]

Pat Covici realized that he didn't have a decent place to work and once again offered him a desk at Viking; he wanted to accept it, but Gwyn insisted on having her husband beside her. She was having a bad time with the pregnancy: her feet were swollen, she had dreadful morning sickness, and she felt dizzy much of the time. Feeling vaguely guilty about what had happened in Mexico between himself and Gwyn, Steinbeck agreed to work at home, writing much of *The Wayward Bus* at the kitchen table 'amid jampots and pieces of cold toast and stale coffee'. At one point, he threw out 'about 20,000 words' because it looked 'no good' to him. In truth, he was deeply anxious about the critical response to his last novel, and he wanted this one to be a good one.

In mid-March, several weeks before the contractor had really finished work on the brownstones, Steinbeck moved his family into their new home. He had carved out a large study for himself in the basement, hoping that being below ground would protect him from street noise and children. And he liked these new quarters, with their grey concrete walls and cement floors, the bulging pipes overhead, and the dim light. He had created for himself yet another incarnation of 'The Sphincter'. To furnish the room, he had bought some office furniture from the previous inhabitant: a cracked leather chair, a large oak desk, some wooden filing cabinets, and a standing lamp that 'drooped over his shoulder like a creature from Mars'. A long table for spreading his manuscripts was pushed up against one wall. No window beckoned him away from the project at hand (although there were a few 'slits' for light just below the ceiling on the street side). 'I don't need much air,' he told one interviewer, 'and a window kills me. I can find something to look at out any window.' An array of masks picked up in Mexico adorned one wall; on another was a gun rack and a couple of fishing poles and an old dagger – the Hemingway touch. 'I should get some work done here if I don't have to run upstairs too often to look at the garbage wagon,' he wrote to Toby Street.

The adjacent brownstone had been promised the previous autumn to an acquaintance named Charles Jackson, whom Steinbeck had met a couple of years before. Jackson was a writer, and Steinbeck liked him and his wife, but they suddenly pulled out of the deal, moving to the suburbs and leaving Steinbeck in the lurch. Hearing of his dilemma, the contractor put him in touch with Nathaniel and Marjorie Benchley, who were looking for a place to rent. 'It was a perfect match,' says Mrs Benchley.[9] 'John had been a good friend of my father-in-law, Robert Benchley. But he didn't know my husband, Bench. I was pregnant at the time, and Gwyn was pregnant, so it was really a good situation. We were all in the same boat.'

The two couples, soon happily ensconced in their newly renovated and twinned brownstones, became fast friends. 'We lived in each other's houses,' says Benchley. 'The boys – we each had two boys – roamed freely. The Steinbeck boys were in our house, the Benchley boys were in their house. We ate meals together. John and Bench would go off together after dinner to the local bar, which was just around the corner. They talked about everything, cooking up all kinds of projects. Once, for instance, they decided that we all had to have a swimming pool out back, and they concocted this above-ground thing. It was a big deal. Then one of the boys fell in and almost drowned, and that was it. We took it right down.' She remembers terrific parties at the Steinbeck place. 'Gwyn was very social, so they had frequent parties, and you would meet all sorts of people there – movie people, Broadway actors and directors, writers and journalists. Harold Ross, the editor of *The New Yorker*, was a regular guest. And John's publisher, Harold Guinzburg, and his editor, Pat Covici, were always there. You never knew who you'd run into. John seemed very much at ease with his fame at that time, as if he'd settled a few things with himself. He had plenty of money, of course, but that didn't matter. Nobody talked about it, and I don't think John ever thought about it much. He'd been looking for somewhere to settle down for many years, and I think he felt that he'd at last found the right place.'

Benchley was a writer for *Newsweek* when he first moved next door to Steinbeck, but he had always hoped to break free to write novels, biographies and children's books. 'John encouraged Bench to quit the job at *Newsweek*,' Marjorie Benchley recalls. 'He said to him, "Come on, you've got to do it." But it wasn't an easy thing to do if you had a family to support. And there wasn't so much money around then.' Benchley plugged away at *Newsweek* for some time, writing his fiction on the side. His first novel (published in 1950) was *Side Street*, a charming book that evokes family life on 78th Street explicitly. '*Side Street* tells exactly what our lives were like then,' says Mrs Benchley. 'The characters, the houses, the kids; it's all true, taken from life.' Benchley opens his novel:

> As you turn east off Lexington Avenue in New York, north of Sixtieth Street, there is a street like a small valley, blocked at one end by the Third Avenue Elevated and with its north wall rising slowly until it reaches the heights of the apartment buildings the next block up. The houses on this street are almost all four or five floors, made either of brownstone or brick, and they form a low bank, broken only by three apartment buildings, two on the north side and one on the south, near the Third Avenue end. In the morning and early afternoon, patches of sunlight brighten the sidewalks and parts of the street; later on, the block sinks into shadow and only the tops of the buildings reflect the yellow glare of the afternoon sun. Small sycamore trees grow at intervals from the sidewalk, and beyond them, on the south side of the Third Avenue corner, is a lighted awning that says, BAR LADIES ENTRANCE. It is the only lighted sign on the block.[10]

The protagonist of *Side Street* (who is obviously based on Steinbeck) is James Allen, 'a large man, although not fat', who has 'recently sold one of his plays to Hollywood'. In spite of this palpable good fortune, Allen seems nervous about taking on the responsibility of the two houses but genial in the role of landlord. 'This was John to a T,' says Marjorie Benchley. 'He was the perfect landlord, although he could be very nervous about it too. Bench liked to tease him, but it was all good-natured. They had fun together – like boys. They would drink, play games, think up schemes and adventures. There was a toy store around the corner, over on Third, and they used to love to stop in there. They brought home the most unlikely and unsuitable presents. It's all in *Side Street* – that light spirit.'

Steinbeck settled into urban life in a way he had never done previously. Gwyn was, as Benchley says, 'immensely social', and Steinbeck adapted himself to the new situation. He had always been interested in jazz, but now he had the opportunity to indulge that interest thoroughly; he and Gwyn would prowl the city on the weekends, looking for clubs. Their record collection grew exponentially as their tastes widened, and they often attended concerts. Steinbeck bought and read a small shelf of books about the history of jazz. Among his many new acquaintances was Eddie Condon, the jazz guitarist, who would come to the brownstone and sit in the study talking about American jazz, and Benchley and Steinbeck would often go down to Greenwich Village in the evenings to hear Condon play.

Steinbeck worked in fits and starts on *The Wayward Bus* throughout the spring, nervously awaiting the birth of his second child. Gwyn became 'extremely difficult as she grew more pregnant, demanding and whiny'.[11] The child arrived on 12 June 1946. It was a boy: John Steinbeck IV. The birth was difficult; Gwyn came home from the hospital exhausted and went straight to bed. For months, she remained in bed most of the day, suffering from a series of ailments: flu, allergies and mysterious fevers. Inexplicable pains ran up and down her legs, and she claimed difficulty walking. A nurse looked after the new baby who seemed robust despite his mother, while Thom had his own nanny to look after him. For his part, Steinbeck enjoyed the idea of being the father of two boys and settled rather easily into upper-middle class urban life. (For all his hatred of the bourgeoisie, this was after all the class he was born into; he felt comfortable in a large brownstone, with housekeepers, nurses, maids and nannies. He liked eating at '21' and attending opening nights of Broadway plays in black tie and top hat. The shyness that had plagued him in his younger years had been suppressed for the time being.)

The comedian Fred Allen was a leading figure on the radio in these years, and the Steinbecks would often go to his show and, afterwards, have dinner with Allen and his wife, who had become good friends (Allen was even made John Jr's godfather). The social swirl of New York exercised a strange fascination for the shy boy from Salinas. 'He loved all of this,' says Marjorie Benchley. 'I think he wanted this excitement. It wasn't just Gwyn. John pushed himself into wider and wider circles in the city, in the publishing and theatrical worlds.' But the situation was more complicated than it appeared on the surface; Steinbeck was using this robust social life to mask a deep sense of anxiety about his marriage.

Life with Gwyn began to degenerate quickly after she came back from the hospital with baby John. Steinbeck believed that her many illnesses were psychosomatic, and he grew sullen and unresponsive to her constant demands, glowering through meals and often lapsing into protracted periods when he barely said a word to her about anything. The birth of John certainly appears to have been oppressive to Gwyn, who still imagined a career for herself in the music world. She wanted to sing, to perform; now she felt compelled to stay at home with the boys. 'She was a bitter person,' says Benchley. 'She was lively and beautiful and intelligent, but she carried a grudge. The role of housewife and mother did not suit her, and John became very unhappy in the marriage. It was terrible to live next door and see the whole thing disintegrating before your eyes. There was nothing anyone could do.'

In spite of his domestic troubles, Steinbeck managed to write about 2400 words a day, and he was pleased by what he was doing. He told Nathaniel Benchley one night that he had settled on a new title: *Whan that Aprille*, taken from the prologue of *The Canterbury Tales*. Benchley winced, then suggested to his friend, gently, that this title would probably not work. 'Won't people find it rather . . . obscure?' he asked. He pointed out that the number of people who knew Chaucer had dwindled to a handful of college students. Steinbeck quickly abandoned the title.

Apart from a month-long trip to Mexico at the end of the summer to see the film of *The Pearl* brought to completion, Steinbeck remained at his desk in the basement of the brownstone. He had taken to dictating into a tape recorder because, he said, 'his secretary could never read his handwriting'. He had also heard from Pat Covici that Henry James used to dictate his novels to a typist, and he thought it worth trying a new method of composition. The book began to swell. 'I haven't any idea as to whether it is any good or not,' he wrote to Frank and Lynn Loesser. 'But the people in it are alive, so much so that sometimes they take a tack I didn't suspect they were going to.'

Having finished the novel, Steinbeck accepted an invitation from Otto Lindhardt, his Danish publisher, to visit Denmark. The memory of his visit to Copenhagen with Carol a decade before remained fresh, and he had long hoped to return. He and Gwyn threw themselves into a large *bon voyage* party, then sailed (leaving the boys behind with nurse and nanny) the next day on the SS *Drottningholm* for Sweden – exactly the same ship, by chance, that Steinbeck had sailed on with Carol. The journey took eight days, and they arrived refreshed and eager to travel. The next day they proceeded by train to Copenhagen, where Steinbeck received (as *Time* reported) 'a hero's welcome'. One Danish newspaper ran a headline, JOHN STEINBECK, ALL OF DENMARK IS AT YOUR FEET.

Steinbeck was pleased, claiming to feel 'like Lana Turner in Grand Central Station without any clothes on'. One of the crucial reasons for his celebrity here was that *The Moon Is Down* had played a substantial role in boosting the morale of those involved in the Resistance, and the Danes felt grateful to him; in fact, he still got letters from appreciative readers in that country. He made several public appearances and signed mounds of books. Seeing that Steinbeck was in Scandinavia from an article in a newspaper, the Norwegian king, Haakon VII, invited him to the palace and bestowed on him the Liberty Cross for his war efforts. (Steinbeck later gave this medal to one of his sons, who lost it; he went to considerable trouble to have it replaced, which suggests that the award mattered to him.)

A less gaudy but still enthusiastic reception awaited him in Norway, and finally, in Sweden, where he met with some former Resistance leaders, who told him how effectively his book had fired their confidence during the war's darkest hours. In Stockholm, his old friend Bo Beskow painted his portrait for the second time and introduced him to a wide circle of artists and writers. Much to Steinbeck's annoyance, Gwyn found the attention paid to her husband rather upsetting. 'People treat me like I'm invisible,' she complained repeatedly. 'I don't know why you brought me along just to humiliate me.'[12] She also began to worry about the boys. They had planned to move on to London, where Steinbeck had made arrangements to see his British publisher and go to some plays and concerts. Instead, they sailed home in late November.

In mid-December, Steinbeck wrote to thank Beskow for the photographs of the portrait that he had sent. In the course of this melancholy letter, he alluded to his marital difficulties, which seemed to intensify as Christmas approached.

'Relationships are very funny things,' he said. 'I've wondered what I would think if this one were over and I think I would only be glad that it had happened at all. I don't think I would rail at fortune, but then it is impossible to know what you would do in any given situation unless you have experienced it.'[13] He told Beskow openly that he was suffering from 'depression' and said he was taking 'some vitamins to see whether it could be a food deficiency'. One thing that was unquestionably affecting him was alcohol. 'John drank an awful lot. We all did in those days,' says Benchley, 'but I think this was exaggerated when John and Gwyn were having problems. It was, you know, his way of escaping from a situation that made him very unhappy.' The drink problem, the crisis in his marriage and his deep uncertainties about the value of *The Wayward Bus*, may all have contributed to what he called his 'depression'.

Christmas is a famously hard season for families, especially families in trouble. But the Christmas of 1946, for the Steinbecks, was inordinately full of tension and trauma. Somehow they pulled together despite the bad situation, and Steinbeck insisted on giving a huge party, inviting practically everyone he knew in the city – over fifty people. On Fifth Avenue he found a seven-foot Christmas tree which he set up proudly in the living room. Gwyn, pitching in, made several pots of oyster stew and various casseroles. Large smoked turkeys and hams were laid out on the table, with side dishes of cranberry sauce and coleslaw. Always happy in the role of *arbiter bibendi*, Steinbeck devoted himself to making 'the largest bowl of punch in the world'. Thom, old enough to toddle, was part of the domestic picture, while baby John slept soundly in his cradle. This party was, in effect, a kind of tableau: somewhat false, as such frozen images are. It was the last good Christmas for John and Gwyn as a couple.

Burgess Meredith and his new wife, the actress Paulette Goddard, had been there, and the week after the party

Meredith called on Steinbeck with an idea. 'I wanted him to write a play for me and for Paulette. The Abbey Theatre, in Dublin, had invited us to do something,' says Meredith. The play was to be called *The Last Joan* – it was all Meredith's idea, including the title – and the notion was that throughout the ages there will be people like Joan of Arc who respond to inner voices. This time Joan would speak out about the atom bomb and its threat to civilization. 'He was excited,' Meredith says, 'and thought he could do a lot with the idea.' However enthusiastic he may have seemed to Meredith, Steinbeck did not respond well to other people's suggestions when it came to choosing subjects. *The Last Joan* never got off the ground, although he did get a rather poor draft of it done by late winter.

A journalist, Robert van Gelder, whom Steinbeck had recently met at a party and liked, asked him for an interview in the New Year, and he consented. 'Ideas are like rabbits,' he told him. 'You get a couple, and learn how to handle them, and pretty soon you have a dozen.'[14] He talked freely about his working methods to van Gelder:

> An electric typewriter stands in the center of the small room, but Steinbeck says he uses it only to write letters. He writes his manuscripts at a large desk in a very small hand. There is evidence of the usual writers' greed for various kinds of papers – yellow pads, stenographers' notebooks and bound manuscript books.
>
> At one side of the desk is an electric machine that records sound upon narrowly grooved plastic discs. One disc takes fifteen minutes of dictation on each side. Steinbeck reads from his manuscript into this machine, then plays the record back to get the sound of what he has written. He makes corrections, reads the corrected version onto fresh discs and sends the discs to his secretary for typing. *The Wayward Bus* filled forty-eight sides, twelve hours of playing time.

To what extent Steinbeck was deceiving his interviewer can only be guessed. I suspect that he often did write the words first and record them later, for 'sound'. His manuscripts right up to the end suggest a powerful attraction to the written word and the paraphernalia of writing: pencils, pads, ledgers, erasers. He haunted stationery stores, ever on the lookout for the ideal notebook or some kind of exotic paper. Both Gwyn and his secretary, alas, maintained that he dictated his material straight on to the machine without having written a text by hand. In the long run, it does not really matter: Milton's *Paradise Lost*, the later novels of Henry James, and the short stories and poems of Jorge Luis Borges were all dictated by their authors with no loss of literary quality.

In mid-February, Gwyn's mother, Mrs Hueit, flew in from California to see her new grandson, making Steinbeck's life miserable for the duration. She claimed to dislike her son-in-law because of his well-known love for 'lower class' people, considering his books 'trash'.[15] Something of a snob herself, she hated the fact that he was known to associate with fishermen and winos in Monterey. His books were 'full of indecent language'. For his part, Steinbeck found her bossy and stupid, and he mostly avoided her by hiding in his study from after breakfast until bedtime. But there was trouble none the less; Mrs Hueit had brought with her a little terrier, and it fought incessantly with Steinbeck's beloved sheep dog, Willie. (The terrier did, alas, save the day once when it alerted everyone in the house to a fire that had broken out in the living room.) Steinbeck quarrelled openly with her at meals and referred to her, always, as 'Big Gwen' or 'Bird-eyes'. He was much relieved when, after two weeks, she went home.

That month Steinbeck turned forty-five, and *The Wayward Bus* appeared just after his birthday. (*The Pearl* was still not published, though it had been completed first.) Some reviewers, such as Bernard de Voto in the *New York Herald Tribune*, thought it a brilliant piece of writing, much less sentimental than his previous work, and a worthy successor to *The Grapes of Wrath*. De Voto praised 'the harsher, less involved treatment of the characters'. Other reviewers – perhaps the majority – complained that Steinbeck's characters were thin, unimagined and unlikable. A few considered the novel prurient; in *The New Yorker*, J. M. Lalley alluded to 'Steinbeck's priapic persuasion', and in *Commonweal* Frank O'Malley protested that 'Steinbeck's dreary, prurient pilgrimage has no real human or universal significance. It is nothing more than an unusually dismal bus ride – more dismal, depraved and meaningless than any man elsewhere has ever taken.' *Has ever taken?* These harsh words were mind-boggling and demoralizing for Steinbeck, who spent a dismal afternoon in his study going through the reviews, which Pat Covici had sent in a thick manilla packet in late February. 'I should never read the reviews, good or bad,' he wrote to Jack Wagner. 'They just confuse me because they cancel each other out and end up by meaning nothing.' To Mrs Maxwell Anderson he wrote, 'The trouble with Max and me is that we've been around too long. Critics get to resenting people if they don't die or go to pieces.'

The plot of *The Wayward Bus* is deceptively simple and linear: a dilapidated bus picks up passengers on a California route that Greyhound doesn't want to handle, an east-west county road between Rebel Corners and San Juan de la Cruz that 'winds through hills and a little desert and through farmland and mountains' until it hits the coastal highway. The driver and hero of the novel is Juan Chicoy, 'part Mexican and part Irish, perhaps fifty years old, with clear black eyes, a good head of hair, and a dark and handsome face'. His seventeen-year-old mechanic, Ed Carson, is called Pimples by those who know and despise him. Juan's wife, Alice, is 'a wide-hipped and sag-chested' woman who runs a lunchroom and service station. Norma is a waitress in the lunchroom.

On the journey that forms the spine of the novel, the passengers are few but representative of different classes and types. Mr and Mrs Elliott Pritchard are a bourgeois couple of the sort that Steinbeck detested, and their daughter, Mildred, is a spoiled college girl of a sort Steinbeck remembered from his Stanford days. (Her nattering, pretentious dialogue is unforgettable.) Ernest Horton is a seedy war veteran now employed as a salesman of bizarre gadgets. Camille Oaks (not her real name) is a stripper and whore. Van Brunt is an old man with a bad heart. Taken as a group, they represent a cross-section of the culture, and the fact that they have little in common is, indeed, the point: American society has lost its centre, and people talk as if on separate radio channels. There is no common language or shared vision of an ideal society; avarice and lechery motivate Steinbeck's selfish and self-deluding characters.

We learn early in the journey that there is a bridge over the San Ysidro River that may be washed out. Chicoy drives to the bridge, sees it washed out, takes an abandoned old stage-coach road instead, and purposely gets the bus stuck in the mud. He needs an excuse to abandon the bus, the route, his wife (who is drunk at home), and his life in general, and fantasizes about fleeing to Mexico, which represents freedom. Taking off for the wilds, he is pursued by the lustfully innocent Mildred Pritchard, who catches up and seduces him. While this sexual activity is underway, Mildred's father offers Camille (whom he finds attractive) a job in his business. She rejects him firmly, saying that he only wants to seduce her, and that the job offer is merely the first advance in that cause. She is right, but Pritchard is outraged; he reacts (rather oddly) by turning on his wife and raping her in the cave where they have taken shelter. Norma, who has quit her job in the lunchroom, fights off sexual advances from hot-blooded Pimples, while Van Brunt, unable to take all the commotion, suffers a well-deserved stroke. In the end, Juan Chicoy – having satisfied himself with Mildred – decides to resume his responsibilities, dig out the bus, and take the passengers, as planned, to San Juan de la Cruz, which appears as 'little lights twinkling with distance, lost and lonely in the night, remote and cold and winking, strung on chains'.

Most critics have read *The Wayward Bus* as some kind of allegory. Peter Lisca, in his standard reading of the novel in *The Wide World of John Steinbeck*, divided the characters into three groups: 'the damned, those in purgatory, and the saved or elect'. Juan Chicoy is seen as a Christ figure (J. C. are his initials). The journey is said to move from hell (Rebel Corners) through purgatory (the road) to heaven (San Juan de la Cruz). Read in these symbolic terms, the novel is surely a failure; Juan Chicoy must be considered a peculiar choice for a Christ figure. Rebel Corners certainly does not seem like hell; indeed, Steinbeck describes it as an intensely beautiful place. In the spring, he writes, 'there was no more lovely place in the world.' Nor can one imagine why San Juan de la Cruz should be considered heavenly; it's a dusty, one-horse town, an obscure stop on an unimportant route.

As seems to be the case with many good writers, Steinbeck's creative unconscious was smarter than his creative conscious. He talked about the book in allegorical and philosophical terms in letters, straining to make the symbolism work. But it just doesn't, at least not on the level that he would have liked. Why is Chicoy 'saved' and not Alice, his wife, or Louis (the first bus driver), or Norma, or Van Brunt? The cause of their iniquity is unclear. Overall, this is hardly a redemptive journey for anyone. Steinbeck has written a strikingly postmodern book with a plot that defies, even deconstructs, the old notion of plot and the rather stale symbolism of the redemptive journey. This bus is, indeed, wayward. Life is wayward. Our Christ figure is complex: a good man and a bad man, depending on the situation. The novel examines the infinitely complex relation between reality and the imagination, deconstructing our set notions of 'good' and 'evil' in a world where no identity is stable. Motives are concealed, then gloriously exposed in the end. It should also be noted that the women in this book – Mildred, Camille, Norma – are all strong; they 'develop' by moving into a consciousness of their repressed sexual identities. (Witness Camille's rebuff to Elliott Pritchard.)

The contrasting study of Juan and Elliott is another main subject implicitly examined by Steinbeck. On the surface, Juan is a typical macho male, caught up in his domineering role; he is called 'a fine, steady man' and 'a magnificent mechanic'. Hemingway would have liked to fish with him. 'His movements were sure even when he was not doing anything that required sureness.' He looks young and strong, despite his fifty years. The other side of Juan, neatly limned, is his gentleness; there is something curiously feminine about him, as if he embodies the opposite. His wife, Alice, notices this and finds this aspect of Juan distressing; why will he not resort to violence like other men? Is he a man in a woman's body? To her conventional mind, he appears weak, unmasculine. But he, it seems, understands (as the *Tao Te Ching* says) that 'the softest thing in the world overcomes the hardest thing in the world'.

Elliott, by contrast, is the type of man the world normally regards as successful and admires to extravagance: he is rich, strong, entrepreneurial, commanding. He is the sort of character that Steinbeck scorns in *Cannery Row*, 'All of our so-called successful men are sick men, with bad stomachs, and bad souls.' Once again, Steinbeck cannot resist attacking his own class – or the class he associates with John Ernst and Olive. We also learn that Pritchard had a 'radical' youth, which he has obviously betrayed. What he has become is a result of this betrayal: a man who does not understand fidelity or 'reality'. Juan, on the other hand, does understand these things. He is natural poet, a man in touch with the physical world, and though he is regarded by society as a 'failure', he succeeds admirably in his own terms. It is, I think, crucial that he does not abandon everything and flee to Mexico in the end. His goodness prohibits such a cynical novelistic turn. He must continue, get the bus back on track, and fulfil his responsibilities, however much he may be attracted to the allurements along the way. And when he sins with Mildred, he sins boldly.

Long before the feminist movement theorized and catalogued such things, Steinbeck understood (on a rather primitive level) the oppression of women. He is vicious in his satirizing of male behaviour, mocking the ritual stag parties that were (and remain) a part of American life, with their crude exploitations of the female body and their irrational disdain for 'otherness'. In talking about Pritchard, who likes stag parties, Steinbeck notes that he 'considered the young women who danced naked at stags depraved, but it would never have occurred to him that he who watched and applauded and paid the girls was in any way associated with depravity'. As ever, Steinbeck loved to gore the hypocrite.

While attacking sexual exploitation, Steinbeck remains an earthy and robust male writer who celebrates sexual urges, although he is far from prurient (as so many critics suggested). He treats Pimples Carson's high levels of testosterone, for example, with sympathy and acuteness: 'Pimples was loaded with the concupiscent juices of adolescence.' The boy's obsession with sex, however, can degenerate into 'deep and tearful sentiment' or 'a strong and musky religiosity'. Camille, the stripper (who is paradoxically the wisest of the women on this bus), has his number: 'Oh, he's all right,' she says of Pimples. 'He's just a little goaty. Most kids are like that. He'll get over it.'

Again, the portrayal of Camille is typical of the way Steinbeck loved to undermine easy assumptions. A casual reader, for example, might assume that Camille Oaks is a 'fallen' person, but a closer reading suggests that she is plucky and sensible. Highly intelligent, her sexual drive is less than one might imagine. Steinbeck comments, 'What she really wanted was a nice house in a nice town, two children, and a stairway to stand on. She would be nicely dressed and people would be coming to dinner.' (One might, of course, attack the stereotypically 'female' and 'bourgeois' aspects of her dream here as well as Steinbeck's rather boring sexism.[16])

Another complicating factor in *The Wayward Bus* is the degree to which each character embodies the dreams of another character, thus creating a peculiar mirror effect. Bernice Pritchard, for instance, has everything that Camille dreams of, but she is quietly miserable, prey to psychosomatic headaches, and a victim (like Mary Teller in Steinbeck's 'The White Quail') of her own fastidiousness, which has its roots in her class pretensions. This is all part of the complex thematic rope Steinbeck has twined for us. Every view is deconstructed, dismantled, exposed as fantasy. 'Reality' is, finally, the ultimate illusion, what Wallace Stevens would call 'the supreme fiction' but one that, for better or worse, seems necessary.

The Wayward Bus is a woefully misunderstood and neglected novel, much underrated by academic critics, who persist in reading it as failed allegory, thus diminishing its genuine originality as a novel that breaks through and dismantles the allegorical form, pushing towards a kind of symbolic realism. Much to Steinbeck's satisfaction, the novel enjoyed a substantial readership; the Book-of-the-Month Club sold 600,000 copies, and Viking unloaded another 150,000 in its first trade edition before publication, making it the author's most 'successful' book, commercially, to date. But Steinbeck wanted more than mere sales; he was deeply unsettled by the critics' lack of sympathy and understanding. Not an articulate critic of his own work, he did not (or could not) come to his own defence.

His marriage seemed to be unravelling faster than he could believe. As he worked through the winter of 1947 on the play about Joan of Arc for Burgess Meredith, he and Gwyn continued to argue about everything. 'It was a basic conflict in their natures,' says Marjorie Benchley, 'Gwyn didn't understand him, and he couldn't see eye to eye with her. It seemed like they couldn't agree on anything.' For days at a time, Steinbeck would avoid talking to his wife; he would sit in his basement study until late at night to avoid contact. And while their social life continued unabated, it was hollow. 'John and Gwyn had just lost the intimacy necessary for a marriage to work. You could see the sadness in John's eyes. He looked very old now: grey, haggard and exhausted.'

Steinbeck had been encouraging Nathaniel Benchley to quit his job at *Newsweek* and write full-time for over a year now, and Benchley had been spending more and more time on his own writing anyway. He had taken a room at the Bedford, where he wrote, and before long he was spending more time there than at the offices of the magazine. His superiors, not surprisingly, did not want a part-time reporter on a full-time salary, and he was fired. 'The day after Bench was fired,' his wife recalls, 'he and Steinbeck met in the bar at the Bedford and tied one on.' During this bout of drinking, Steinbeck confessed to Benchley that his marriage was a mess, a mistake, a wrong turn in his life. He knew that before long he would be separated, and it gave him great pain. 'It was the loss of the children that worried him most. That was just too awful to think about.'

In late February 1948, Gwyn left with Thom and John for California after she and her husband had a fight that lasted all night. Steinbeck sulked at home for a month, then flew to Los

Angeles, where he apologized and asked her forgiveness. Reluctantly, Gwyn agreed to return, with the boys, to New York. Burgess Meredith recalls, 'Things were bad between them. I could see it would never work out.'[17] One night, by chance, Meredith encountered the Steinbecks in the Plaza Oak Bar, rather drunk, and he sat down beside them. Suddenly Gwyn took off her wedding ring and put it on Meredith's finger. 'This is for you,' she said. 'You know what it means.' He didn't. Nor did Steinbeck, who was furious and began to scream at his friend, who had innocently stumbled on to the scene. 'I felt sorry for John,' Meredith says, 'he was a very unhappy man.'

The Last Joan, meanwhile, was a failure. Steinbeck tried several versions of it, then gave it up in a fit of frustration. 'The play is no good, and I have thrown it away and have so warned Buzzy Meredith,' Steinbeck wrote to Frank Loesser in Hollywood in April. Meredith says that 'John never really saw what the play was about. We dropped the idea, and there were no bad feelings.' This was just another of those abortive projects which are a natural part of any busy writer's life. Sometimes the wheel just doesn't turn, and it seems best to move on.

Frantic for a break from Gwyn, who was once again arguing with him about 'every little detail of domestic life', as he told Pat Covici, Steinbeck followed up a suggestion that he do some reporting from Europe for the *Herald Tribune*. One night, again in the bar of the Bedford, he ran into Robert Capa, the photographer whom he had met during the war in Europe, and Capa suggested that they go to Russia together to do a book. He would photograph the ordinary Russian at work or play, while Steinbeck wrote a diary-like text to accompany the pictures. The idea was that the Russia portrayed in the press was not the 'real' Russia. Ideology aside, the people of Russia were like you and me, argued Capa, who was 'one of the most charming men in the world'.[18] Steinbeck loved the idea, and he agreed, after a long conference with Gwyn, to go. Gwyn would accompany him to Paris; after a brief stay there, Steinbeck and Capa would proceed by themselves to the Soviet Union, and Gwyn would return to New York.

Born Andre Friedmann in Hungary, Robert Capa was a decade younger than Steinbeck. He had invented himself as 'Robert Capa', creating an identity (which included a complicated and fictitious past) for himself out of whole cloth. His girlfriend (and later his wife) – a remarkable woman named Gerta Taro – was also his agent, and she told potential clients that Friedmann was a famous and wealthy American photographer whose fees were three times what anyone else charged in Paris at the time (the Thirties). The trick worked, and clients flocked to 'Capa'. He became his own legend, photographing battle scenes close up during the Spanish Civil War, then in Europe during World War II. (Gerta Taro was killed during the Spanish Civil War.) A short man, with wiry black hair and dark, penetrating eyes, Capa was often unshaven and rarely bathed. He liked dirty leather jackets and heavy black boots. Although his manner was joking and light-hearted, he was in deadly earnest.

One balmy afternoon not long before Steinbeck was planning to leave for Europe, he fell through a weak railing on his balcony and crashed to the pavement below, breaking a kneecap and severely spraining one ankle; he spent several days in hospital, having had emergency surgery on the knee. (He had a terrible fight with the head nurse while in the hospital over whether or not he should have his pubic hair shaved for the knee operation. This was standard procedure in those days, but Steinbeck refused. The head surgeon sided with his famous patient, much to the nurse's consternation.) 'I'm very tired of the hospital,' he wrote to the Wagners the day after the operation, and he was home three days later, walking with a cane.

Steinbeck had hoped to leave Gwyn behind altogether, but

she insisted on accompanying him to Paris. They flew across the Atlantic in July, leaving the boys with their nanny. It pleasantly surprised Steinbeck that he was vastly popular in France: his suite at the Hôtel Lancaster was filled with flowers, bottles of champagne, chocolates. Photographers swarmed around him in the hotel lobby, and he and Gwyn could not eat a meal without a crush of autograph seekers. Far from pushing away these people, Steinbeck welcomed them; his reception here was in marked contrast to what he had suffered only a few months before in America with the reception of *The Wayward Bus*. 'If you think we haven't been going about eating and drinking things, you are very wrong,' he wrote to Elizabeth Otis. It so happened that a new French edition of *The Grapes of Wrath* had just been published, so there was a lot to celebrate. 'This is the first time I have ever played for so long a stretch,' he said in mid-July. 'And I can't take it.'

Gwyn returned home alone on 17 July, and four days later Capa and Steinbeck flew to Moscow. Nobody was waiting for them on arrival, even though they had wired ahead. It was rainy and cold, and they had to camp for several days with some foreign correspondents they had met by chance because hotel space was so scarce. (The fact that they had booked a room in advance made no difference.) It took them over a week to get permission to visit the Ukraine and Georgia, where they especially wanted to go.

It seems that Steinbeck liked Moscow despite the red tape that seemed to thwart their every move. He had, of course, visited the city ten years before, when he had found it filthy and boring. Now, with many new buildings on view, the streets clean, and the Russian people looking well-fed, he encountered an atmosphere of progress. He seems to have been strangely unaware of Stalin's atrocities, which had been widely rumoured if not documented by western journalists. (As later in his career, when he took Lyndon Johnson's side in the Vietnam War, he could be curiously naive about political realities and did whatever suited him best at the time.) Each morning in Moscow he would get up early and go for long walks around the city, returning to his hotel room before lunch to scribble notes in a ledger. At meals, he enjoyed drinking vodka in large quantities and consumed substantial amounts of caviar and brown bread. He wrote to Gwyn that he was 'having a terrific time'. Capa, however, was 'straining at the leash', he claimed. 'He has about 7000 exposures and he hasn't exposed any of them.' This was the beginning of the Cold War period, and one didn't casually take pictures in the Soviet Union. A permit was required, and it didn't come through until the end of the first week in August.

They flew to Kiev in an old C-47 transport plane, then began touring the Ukraine under the umbrella of the Intourist organization. They were treated to huge meals everywhere: 'There were fresh ripe tomatoes and cucumbers, there were little pickled fishes, there were bowls of caviar, and there was vodka. We had small fried fishes from the Dnieper, and beefsteaks, beautifully cooked with Ukrainian herbs. There was wine from Georgia, and Ukrainian sausages which are delicious,' he noted in *A Russian Journal*, published the following year. He writes:

> Our hosts had many questions they wanted to ask us. They
> wanted to know about America, about its size, about its
> crops, about its politics. And we began to realize that
> America is a very difficult country to explain. There are
> many things about it we don't understand ourselves. We
> explained our theory of government, where every part has
> another part to check it. We tried to explain our fear of
> dictatorship, our fear of leaders with too much power, so
> that our government is designed to keep anyone from
> getting too much power or, having got it, from keeping it.
> We agreed that this makes our country function more
> slowly, but that it certainly makes it function more surely.

He was startled that there was so much fear of the United States all around. 'Will the United States attack us? Will we have to defend our country again in one lifetime?' These were fair questions, given the massive postwar build-up in American military power. The Cold War had begun with a vengeance; indeed, the US had begun to create a vast, invisible government in the CIA that would conduct its own expensive and destructive foreign policy outside the glare of publicity. Steinbeck, of course, did not know this. He had, and would have until the end, an uncomplicated view of the United States and its foreign policy. It would take an actual visit to Vietnam to shake his conviction that US efforts in that region were less than noble.

In *A Russian Journal*, one winces slightly at Steinbeck's naiveté. The Ukrainians ask him, again and again, why the American newspapers 'speak constantly of attacking Russia'. He says,

> The old, old thing came up, that always comes up: 'Then why does your government not control these newspapers and these men who talk war?' And we had to explain again, as we had many times before, that we do not believe in controlling our press, that we think the truth usually wins, and that control simply drives bad things underground. In our country we prefer that these people talk themselves to death in public, and write themselves to death, rather than bottle them up to slip their poison secretly through the dark.

It's odd to think that Steinbeck, who had worked as a journalist at most stages of his writing life, did not understand that reporters in a market economy can push only so far with their criticisms; they must write within the boundaries of what the owners of their papers, who more often than not share interests with those in power, are prepared to publish. This is all part of what Walter Lippmann, the political analyst, famously called 'the manufacture of consent'. The United States is a consensual society; consent has to be 'produced'. But this kind of analysis, rarer then than now, would probably have dismayed Steinbeck.

On the other hand, his reportage stands up well as travel writing. He describes the landscapes of Russia beautifully, with a poet's eye for the concrete detail, conjuring the ancient Orthodox churches, the ballet in Moscow, the daily life of Russian peasants. He met a genuine cross-section of society, which included 'businesswomen, actresses, students', and he listened to what they told him and reported their views with candour. He roamed the stores, was entertained in Moscow by the leading writers of the moment: 'There were about thirty writers and officials of the Union there.' In the end, Steinbeck donned a lead shield to protect himself against his political critics, 'We know that this journal will not be satisfactory either to the ecclesiastical Left, nor the lumpen Right. The first will say it is anti-Russian, and the second that it is pro-Russian. Surely it is superficial, and how could it be otherwise? We have no conclusions to draw, except that Russian people are like all other people in the world. Some bad ones there are surely, but by far the greater number are very good.'

Steinbeck and Capa left Russia in mid-September, stopping in Prague and Budapest (Capa's birthplace) on their way home. Once back in New York, Steinbeck mentioned in a letter to Toby Street that he hoped to get the articles for the *Herald Tribune* and the book with Capa done by Christmas. Beyond that, he had more in his sights: 'I have a great deal of work to do this year,' he wrote, 'and I would like to get it all done by this summer because then I would like to stop everything to do a long novel that I have been working on the notes of for a long time. It seems to me that for the last few years I have been working on bits and pieces of things without much continuity and I want to get back to a long slow piece of work.'[19] As he settled down to work, he seemed very – perhaps overly – conscious that he had worked in 'bits and pieces' since writing *The Grapes of Wrath*. He wanted to do something 'big' again. This was a very American feeling, especially in the postwar decades. Hemingway wrote under the same pressure as others; Americans wanted, demanded, 'the great American novel'. 'The novel meant something then,' says Gore Vidal. 'Writers were heroes. It was thought that fiction could make a difference in the world.'

Steinbeck told Gwyn that he wanted to return to California soon to gather material for his 'big' novel, but she did not receive this news warmly. California had rejected them, she reminded him coolly; in any case, she preferred New York. He listened, nodding, but he grew quietly furious as he settled down to write up the Russian journey. It was obvious to him now that this marriage would never work, but he was frightened by the problems which would almost necessarily follow from yet another divorce. What about the boys? Where would he live? Would he survive another round of deep emotional turmoil? 'He was like a zombie,' one friend recalls. 'The Gwyn crisis about did him in.'[20]

XIV

A New Life

'I have a little life yet to lead. I'm pretty banged up. In fact I have been for quite a long time as you know. I've got to build back and at the same time I have a lot of work to do.'

Steinbeck to Toby Street, August 1948

While Steinbeck was in Russia, *The Pearl* was released by Viking to coincide with the release of the film version by RKO. By comparison with his earlier books and films, *The Pearl* in both incarnations went relatively unnoticed. The few critics who bothered to review the novella dismissed it as 'naive' and 'simplistic', and sales were mediocre, although in February Pat Covici (ever trying to buoy up his depressive author) wrote: 'I was surprised to learn that *The Pearl* sold over 2,000 copies in January. The book didn't move much during the holidays, as you know.'

Even Steinbeck's admirers have largely dismissed *The Pearl* as an unfortunate piece of melodrama. Warren French, for instance, calls the novella 'artistically inferior to most of Steinbeck's previous works' and wonders how such a careful artist could have let such a thing happen. To some extent this criticism is warranted, but something about the story commands attention. Like *The Wayward Bus*, it has been misread by critics startled by its allegorical superstructure. The plot has its origin in an anecdote in the *Log from the 'Sea of Cortez'*, where Steinbeck mentions an Indian boy from La Paz who 'found a pearl of great size'. The pearl is worth so much that the boy's future seems, to him, assured: he now will have the opportunity to be drunk as long as he wishes, 'to marry any one of a number of girls, and to make many more a little happy, too'. If he gets into trouble, he can buy sufficient masses at the church to squeeze him out of purgatory. When he takes the pearl to a broker in the town, he is offered far less than it is worth. Offended, he tries another, then another; all try to cheat him. Enraged, he takes the pearl to the beach, where he hides it under a stone, but he is soon attacked and nearly killed by greedy men looking to steal the precious object. In the end, he curses the pearl that has been the source of so much ill fortune, and hurls it back into the sea. 'He was a free man again' – at last.

Steinbeck creates a fisherman and his wife, Kino and Juana. This generic couple have a baby son, Coyotito, whom a scorpion bit at the beginning of the tale. When a doctor refuses to see the boy because his parents cannot afford his help, they go fishing for a pearl and find one: the greatest pearl in the world, as large as a seagull's egg. Alas, possession of such a valuable object goes to Kino's head, and he shows off by dressing in fancy clothes. As might be expected, he soon has enemies all over town. Hoping to unload the pearl for a great price, he takes it into La Paz, where buyers offer him much less than it is worth, which makes him very angry. In the final dramatic scene, he is pursued into the mountains by three men who want to steal the pearl, and in the scuffle that follows his son's head is shattered by a rifle shot into the cave where he hides with his mother. Kino, beside himself with grief and fury, becomes a murderer himself, and his life is ruined. In the last scene, Kino flings the pearl back into the sea.

Steinbeck's cinematic interests are evident in the arrangement of the story. He writes as the camera sees: objectively, coolly observing every angle. The town of La Paz is described in much the way it might be in a screenplay:

> The town lay on a broad estuary, its old yellowed plastered buildings hugging the beach. And on the beach the white

and blue canoes that came from Nayrit were drawn up, canoes
preserved for generations by a hard shell-like waterproof plate
whose making was a secret of the fishing people. They were
high and graceful canoes with curving bow and stern and a
braced section midships where a mast could be stepped to
carry a small lateen sail.

An atmosphere of unreality permeates the story, a mood
engendered by the light of the Gulf, which flickers on the
world as if it were a movie screen. Kino is Everyman, and his
journey is the classic hero's journey in search of fortune. He is
both protector and provider, and the doctor who refuses to
treat the child represents the vice of avarice; the trackers who
want to steal the pearl represent deceit. The scorpion that
originally bites the child is a symbol of evil or original sin.
And so forth. (The schematic nature of allegory is always
distasteful to critics raised in the tradition of realism: another
reason for the critical incomprehension that greeted *The
Pearl*.)

Unlike the characters in most folktales or allegorical stories,
Steinbeck's Kino and Juana have distinctive personalities and
cannot be seen simply as stock figures from the classic
repertoire of peasant types. Kino is sensitive, he has imagination, and he listens and responds to a strange inner music.
Juana is clear-eyed, sober, practical, and loving. (It is the
minor figures who are simplistic and justify the charge of
stereotyping that has often been levelled against Steinbeck's
characters.) The bright Mexican landscape is rendered
lyrically throughout, and it is not simply a mythic landscape.
Steinbeck's prose shimmers with hard, brightly particularized details which play against the dreamlike and
schematic plot. As in *The Wayward Bus*, Steinbeck was taking
away with one hand what he gave with the other. As Roy
Simmonds has pointed out, the novella has become a set-
piece of high-school literature courses and a perennial
favourite of young readers.[1] This is partly because Steinbeck

mediates between the allegorical dimensions implicit in the form and its realistic presentation; it is engagingly cinematic and complex beyond the reach of any simple allegorical reading.

But he was deeply conscious of having once again published a rather 'light' book. He wanted heft now, moral and physical bulk. It was time to settle into the big book about the Salinas Valley that had been on his mind for some years. On 2 January 1948, Steinbeck wrote to the editor of the *Salinas-Californian*, 'I am gathering material for a novel, the setting of which is to be the region between San Luis Obispo and Santa Cruz, particularly the Salinas valley; the time, between 1900 and the present.'[2] He wanted permission to look through the paper's files. 'I expect to be in Monterey soon after January 20th.' The editor cabled back: YOU ARE WELCOME TO SALINAS NEWSPAPER FILES.

Gwyn objected to this trip, but Steinbeck could not be dissuaded. He flew to Los Angeles, where he visited the Loessers, Max Wagner and other old friends; then, in a rented Buick, he set off for the Monterey region, where he planned once more to bathe in nostalgia. Because the 11th Street cottage was rented, he moved into a boarding house in nearby Casa Munras. Back home, Gwyn was working on a play with Nathaniel Benchley, *The Circus of Doctor Lao*. The idea had been Gwyn's, and Benchley thought he and she could make something of it. Burgess Meredith was consulted, and he thought he could get it produced. (He did, and it had a brief run in Chicago later that year.) Clearly, Gwyn had decided to move ahead on her own; she was not going to remain simply the wife of a famous writer.

More than ever before, Steinbeck involved himself in the film industry. After years of languishing in the wilderness for lack of proper funding, *The Red Pony* was finally being shot that winter by Lewis Milestone, and Steinbeck, who had written the script, dropped by to see how it was going. Burgess Meredith was making *Cannery Row* into a film, and Steinbeck was reviewing the script with him. (The film was released in the winter of 1949.) Meanwhile, he had been talked into forming a production company of his own with Harry S. White, Robert Capa and Phil Reisman, an executive with RKO. The company, christened World Video and incorporated that January, would package TV shows for this brand new market, which White had convinced Steinbeck was the medium of the future. Says Gore Vidal: 'I saw Steinbeck not longer after, and he told me that television drama was the thing to aim for. He understood the potential, the vast possible audience. Television spelled the end of the novel, and we all knew it.'

One shudders to see John Steinbeck taking such a wrong turn in his career. He was a man of the highest artistic integrity, and it always hurt him to associate with second-rate projects. In the past he had been extremely finicky about what he would and wouldn't do. Now, out of nowhere, he had decided to write for television and, of all things, to become a producer himself. He set up an office in Monterey and hired Toni Jackson, his old secretary, to work for him. At Harry White's suggestion, he began writing the script of a television show called, 'Paris: Cavalcade of Fashion'. This all suggests that Steinbeck had, temporarily, lost his direction. He was flailing.

White began to sign up writers, producers and actors and to commission projects right, left and centre. It was all rather insane; some sixty projects were put 'into development', that great entertainment burial ground. Steinbeck's name was a powerful attraction, and a wide range of well-known people agreed to work for World Video, including Elia Kazan and Burgess Meredith. Soon the entire pyramid would collapse, but for now it was both exciting and nerve-racking for Steinbeck, who had bitten off more than he could possibly chew. His one consolation was California itself. 'Have been going around the country getting reacquainted with trees and bushes,' he wrote to Annie Laurie Williams.[3] 'On a low tide I went collecting in the early morning.' Another day he wrote to her, 'Well, it is time for me to get out in the wind and look at the grass which is coming up on the hill. That's what I am out here for.' He wrote to Pat Covici, 'All goes well here. I am getting superb rest. The rain is over and the hills are turning green. I sleep about twelve hours every night and then go out and look at the bushes.' On 17 February, he wrote to Gwyn:

> Tuesday already. Again last night to bed at ten. Now quite early morning. Cloudy and likely to rain. This is the driest year anybody ever remembers. Yesterday was like a spring day. I went to Salinas and worked at the paper and then drove out toward the hills and found the old stage road which I haven't been over since I was about ten years old and we went to Hollister that way in the surrey. Went over to San Juan and do you know there were hundreds of places that I remembered? Kids do retain all right.[4]

He had certainly retained a bountiful amount, a trove of imagery and feelings deeply rooted in a particular landscape and culture; now his ambition was to recapture all this in language, to write a long novel that would both summon and sum up his California experience. The short novels, however good, had been too easily (and unfairly) dismissed by the critics, as Pat Covici kept reminding him. 'They assume you are not serious,' Covici argued, rather naively. Nevertheless, Steinbeck believed that he had to create something substantial, a book he could be proud of and one that would embody his familial past. It would be something he could pass on proudly to his sons. 'More and more I see that this book is the book and it has to be done by me,' he wrote to Gwyn. 'It may be my swan song, but it certainly will be the largest and most important work I have [done] or maybe will do.'[5]

One of the great pleasures of being near Monterey was the

propinquity of Ed Ricketts, who welcomed his old friend back to the lab and tried to persuade him to stay for good. They prowled the bars of Monterey together, dropping in on old friends, and did some collecting of marine samples along the coastline. Steinbeck suddenly began to question once again his move to New York, and he and Ricketts made plans for a trip in the coming summer to the Queen Charlotte Islands off the coast of British Columbia. Having done the southern reach of the Pacific coastline, they would now head north. He wrote giddily to Pat Covici about this expedition, suggesting (to Covici's evident dismay) that the whole thing could be paid for by an advance against royalties for another book along the lines of *Sea of Cortez*.

In late March, against his better judgement, he returned to his family in New York. For the past few years he had been plagued by varicose veins in his legs, and he decided it was time to have them removed. The operation, 'a bloody, gory mess', was done during the first week of April, and Steinbeck took a room at the Bedford to recover because he could not climb the steps of his brownstone. Gwyn, meanwhile, came down with a severe sinus infection and was hospitalized for treatment the day after Steinbeck got out of the hospital. Day by day, the conflict between them worsened. Steinbeck could think of nothing but escape, and now his health problems exacerbated his general decline of spirits. He was in a bleak mood already when, during the first week of May, he heard by telegram that Ed Ricketts had been involved in a car accident and lay near death. Ricketts had been crossing the railway tracks into Monterey when a train struck his old Packard and dragged him several hundred feet.

Steinbeck flew immediately to California, but it was too late. Ed Ricketts died just before he arrived, too late for the friends to exchange final words. The funeral was held a few days later in a small chapel that overlooked the bay, with over two hundred people in attendance, including a sizeable number of winos, whores, and bums, many of whom worshipped Ricketts as benefactor and friend. 'You couldn't get a seat in there,' a former resident of Monterey recalls.[6] 'They were crowded right up the aisle, all kinds of people. A lot of them had to stand outside.' Steinbeck, speechless with grief, sat in the front pew with Ricketts's family and stared ahead without expression throughout the ceremony. 'He could hardly move,' Dook Sheffield recalled. 'This was the worst thing that had ever happened to him.'

The day after the funeral Steinbeck went through Ricketts's personal files at the lab. Huge boxes full of letters, diaries, memorabilia and scientific data had to be sorted out. There were hundreds of phonograph records to dispense with, as well as books and manuscripts of unpublished articles. Some of the diaries and letters contained explicit references to love affairs Ricketts had had, and Steinbeck wisely burned them. He also burned his personal correspondence with Ricketts. This had been a deep, loving and intensely private friendship, and Steinbeck did not want the eyes of history peering in . A mysterious black safe sat in one corner, and none of the keys Ricketts had left behind seemed to work. Fearing something lay hidden inside that he should know about, Steinbeck called in a locksmith. Inside, Steinbeck found a note: 'What the hell did you expect to find in here? Here's a drink for your trouble.' A bottle of old Scotch was beside the note, the only other thing in the safe.

The one thing belonging to Ricketts which Steinbeck took for himself was the microscope he had purchased in Berkeley just before the Sea of Cortez expedition. Writing to Bo Beskow about the death a week later, he called his deceased friend 'the greatest man I have known and the best teacher'. He added, poignantly, 'It is going to take a long time to reorganize my thinking and my planning without him.'[7] Drained of emotion, he flew back to New York a few days

13 & 14 Steinbeck with Thom, his first child, at his christening and relaxing in the pool: 'He just eats and sleeps and shits, but I can think of worse kids.'

15 Burgess Meredith and
Lon Chaney Jnr in *Of Mice
and Men*, 1939. Meredith
became a close friend of
Steinbeck's.

16 Red Williams' gas station,
mentioned in *Cannery Row*,
1945.

opposite
17 John, Willie, Thom and
Gwyn in the pool at the
house in Cuernauaca during
the filming of *The Pearl*.

18 Steinbeck at the première
of *East of Eden* in 1956.

19 Steinbeck and Elaine at
the reception at the Swedish
publisher's after the Nobel
Ceremony. Steinbeck found
the Nobel hard to handle.

20 Steinbeck in Helsinki,
Finland, 1963, where one
morning he addressed an
auditorium of 900
booksellers

opposite
21 & 22 John and Elaine
Steinbeck arriving in
Moscow, *1963*, where
Steinbeck's work was very
well-known. Steinbeck raised
a few eyebrows there by
attempting to chase up his
royalties from Russian
translations of his book.

overleaf
24 Steinbeck's son, John IV,
meets president Lyndon
Johnson prior to his Vietnam
tour of duty, *1966*.

23 John and Elaine Steinbeck
in Eastern Europe. Steinbeck
was immensely popular in
this part of the world.

To John Steinbeck, Jr.
from his friend
Lyndon B. Johnson

after the funeral, wondering how he would survive without his friend.

When he arrived at the brownstone, so depressed that he 'could hardly walk', Gwyn greeted him with a cold stare. There were huge dark circles beneath her eyes and her hair was uncombed. 'What is it?' he asked. 'What's wrong?' 'I need to talk to you,' she said, taking him into the living room and pouring him a tall glass of Scotch. 'I want a divorce, John. There is no point in dragging this out.'[8] Steinbeck understood only too well why Gwyn should want a divorce, but he could hardly believe her timing. Did she not realize that his best friend in the world had just been killed? Had she not the slightest grain of human feeling or sensitivity? Dismayed, he packed several large suitcases, one full of various manuscripts in progress, kissed the bewildered children, and moved into a suite at the Bedford.

His mood grew bleaker every day. Soon he learned from a mutual friend that Gwyn planned to get as much of his money as possible, and this panicked him. In a letter to Toby Street in late May he said, 'In spite of what people generally consider, I do not have any money.'[9] This was hyperbole; Steinbeck had made vast amounts of money in the past decade. What he really meant was that his funds were not unlimited and that without his constant work they would soon be depleted. But money is often a metaphor. Steinbeck could feel the emotional ground shaking under him and was frightened by his own wild feelings of loss. Money meant security and comfort; for a writer, it meant time to work. He wrote candidly to Street:

I'm forty-six now and if I am going to be a writer I'd better god damned well get to it. I've piddled away a great deal of my time and I haven't an awful lot left. I don't think you can find anyone in my acquaintance to whom I have not loaned money and that is all right but now I need help in

the way of indulgence and support and I am asking for the
kind of support I have given to everyone else.

A few weeks later, he said to Bo Beskow, 'I am out of sadness
and into fierceness now.' Gwyn left for California in June,
taking the boys with her; she planned to spend the summer of
1948 with her mother. Steinbeck, who could not concentrate
enough to work on the big novel, turned his energies to the
Zapata project, egged on by Elia Kazan. 'I offered him the
movie,' Kazan recalls, 'and he was ready now, really
ready.'[10] He plunged into the work as if his life depended on
it, flying immediately to Cuernavaca, a place he always liked.
A note from Pat Covici awaited him at his hotel: 'I hope while
you are in Mexico that you will do some tall thinking and
wake up to yourself and your own peace of mind.' Throughout the summer, he travelled around Mexico in an old Ford he
bought in Cuernavaca, researching and making notes on the
life and times of Emiliano Zapata. The project absorbed him
totally.

He wrote to Gwyn several times about his travels, asking
her to tell Thom how much he missed him, but no replies
came. Gwyn had decided to cut him off completely, knowing
that to withhold news of the boys would amount to torture.
By August, Steinbeck could stand it no longer and drove to
Los Angeles, where he intended to confront Gwyn directly
about her tactics. He stayed with Frank Loesser, who found
him 'half mad with grief and depression'.[11] He waited
outside Gwyn's mother's house, confronting her as she left
one afternoon. Somewhat unconvincingly, he told her that
he still loved her and tried to persuade her to go back to New
York with him. Gwyn laughed at him and told him that what
she required now was a divorce; that way, she explained, he
would have legal access to the children. Despairing, Steinbeck returned to New York by himself. 'After over four years
of bitter unhappiness,' he wrote to Beskow in mid-August,
'Gwyn has decided that she wants a divorce, so that is that.'[12]

Steinbeck decided to let Gwyn take the children for the time being. What he needed was time to regroup, to find a solid footing. He told Beskow that he would 'go back to Monterey to try to get rested and to get the smell of my own country again'. But Monterey without Ed Ricketts was another thing altogether, and he couldn't imagine what he would do there. To Toby Street, in late August, he wrote, 'I have a little life yet to lead. I'm pretty banged up. In fact I have been for quite a long time as you know. I've got to build back and at the same time I have a lot of work to do.'[13] A week later, again to Beskow, he said, 'I have been thinking and thinking in circles, and it comes out the same.' This dark moment may well have been the nadir of the Steinbeck journey, a time when everything seemed to collapse around him and he could not see his way forward. He stopped eating regularly and lost weight; he could not sleep; his writing dried up completely.

What went wrong between John and Gwyn Steinbeck? 'Three years and more of treachery, consistent and careful, are not got over,' he told Pat Covici later in the year. Witnesses confirm Steinbeck's opinion of his wife. 'Gwyn was very deceitful,' Marjorie Benchley recalls, 'I never trusted her. Nobody did.' 'She wasn't equal to John,' says another friend. 'She would flirt with other men, too. He couldn't take it.'[14] Looking at it from Gwyn's point of view, Steinbeck was no model husband. He put his writing first, and he never tried to disguise the fact. 'For a woman of Gwyn's temperament, this was hard to take,' says Benchley. There was also the fact that Gwyn had lost the musical career she had treasured in California; that had been her dream, and she could not survive without it. Furthermore, she could not compete with her husband in the social arena; he had hundreds of famous friends, and many of them worshipped him. She felt jealous of these relationships, which seemed to affect her dealings with her husband. The substantial age difference between them may also have been an impediment to mutual understanding. One acquaintance suggests that 'neither Gwyn nor John entered the marriage with a clear view of the other. It was all projection. He wanted a beautiful young girl who would worship him and take care of him. She wanted a famous man who would help her career. She was blinded by his reputation, and she never saw the man. He had no idea who she was, ever.'[15]

'Yesterday we signed the separation agreement,' he told Street on 27 August, 'and as usual my wife gets about everything I have.'[16] He felt desperate for Monterey now, 'the cool coast', which for him symbolized peace of mind. 'This god damned climate drives me crazy,' he said of New York City in the same letter. 'The utter insanity of living in a place like this doesn't occur to the 9,000,000 people who inhabit New York. Except for visits I think I shall not be here any more as a resident.' Like a homing pigeon, he returned to the house on 11th Street in Pacific Grove in September, intent upon healing.

Looking back more than a decade later on 1948 and his return to his family cottage, he recalled: 'The little Pacific Grove house is many things to me, but its last patina is of the wild and violent heartbroken time after Gwyn, which stays with me like the memory of a nightmare. I don't think I will ever get over that.' The house was in utter disrepair from a bad set of tenants who had left without paying their rent, so he set to work to restore order, especially outside, where he pruned several big limbs off the trees to let more light into the garden; he felt an irresistible urge to grow more flowers and put in 'lots of geraniums and fuchsias'. He painted the trim around the windows and replaced several panes of broken glass. The chimney was blocked, but he cleared it so that he could have fires in the grate again: even in September, the nights were cool on the Monterey coast. His notebooks and journals, his books, his records, his best typewriter and dictating machine – all the tools of his trade were back in New York in what had become 'Gwyn's house'. But Steinbeck was not thinking about writing now. Through mid-October, he continued working on the house. Friends who visited him during this strange autumn remember him being grief-stricken, sullen and abstracted. Ed Ricketts's microscope was put into a glass case, enshrined in the living room as an altar.

The idea of returning to Mexico to work on Zapata suddenly swept him in late October, and he began to make plans to travel south. Mildred Lyman, who worked as an assistant to Elizabeth Otis, stopped by just before he took off on this trip, and she wrote back to Annie Laurie Williams, 'He is deeply disturbed and frightened about his work. If it doesn't go well in Mexico I honestly don't know what will happen. The fact that so much time has elapsed without his accomplishing anything to speak of worries him a great deal.' This judgement was clearly Steinbeck's; although he had accomplished a lot in the past few years, it didn't feel like anything. 'What John needs more than anything right now is discipline,' Lyman added. 'I'm afraid that he wanted to get to Mexico for reasons other than writing.'

He left in November, stopping briefly in Los Angeles to chat with Elia Kazan, who was going to direct the picture. Much to his surprise, Kazan decided to go with him. They flew into Mexico City, where they spent a few days before proceeding to Cuernavaca. Kazan was appalled by the condition in which he found Steinbeck, who understood very well the fragility of his situation. 'The sickness has been worse than I have been able to admit even to myself,' he wrote to Pat Covici. To bolster himself, he swore to Covici that he was tough in spirit and would emerge on the right side of the line when all was said and done: 'This is the worst season and I am still all right and it will get less bad.'

But it did not get 'less bad', at least not in Mexico. Travel only magnified his personal troubles. Unable to shake his depression, he was forced to return to Pacific Grove before he and Kazan got anywhere with Zapata. All he wanted was to curl up before a fire in the house where he had played as a small boy on weekends with his sister, Mary. 'My little house is now done and I am very glad to be in it,' he told Bo Beskow in a long and intimate letter written late in November.[17] He still had, as he called them, 'moments of rage', but he began to feel less miserable as the weeks turned into months. Gwyn had agreed that Thom and John could visit him the following summer for a couple of months, and that prospect cheered him greatly. He planned to take them for long walks along the beach, collecting specimens and teaching them about the natural world. He would instruct them in the use of his sacred microscope and the basic elements of fishing. 'We may even go camping in the mountains,' he told Beskow. Given the ages of the boys, these were rather fantastic propositions. Clearly, Steinbeck was erecting a kind of emotional scaffolding; the scaffolding would hold him up while the real work went on of rebuilding himself from the inside out.

He had collected enough material about Zapata to start writing, and he hoped to begin by December on the actual script. A real surge of creative energy overtook him, the first in a long time: 'I have so much work to do. As soon as my Zapata script is finished I shall get to the large book of my life – *The Salinas Valley*. I don't care how long it takes. It will be nearly three quarters of a million words or about twice as long as *The Grapes of Wrath*. And after that I have five plays to write. And after that I should like to do one more film – the life of Christ from the four Gospels – adding and subtracting nothing.' He was nothing if not ambitious . . .

Before writing the script, he decided to put together a long introduction as a way of sinking into the material, and this piece of writing is remarkable for its scope. Steinbeck had done his homework with a vengeance, probing every aspect of the Mexican Revolution. The screenplay was based on Edgcumb Pinchon's book, *Zapata, the Unconquerable*, and it would deal with the revolutionary period of 1910–19, culminating on the morning of 10 April 1919, when Zapata and his troops were ambushed by the government forces of Venustrano Carranza. Zapata himself was killed that day, effectively decapitating the movement, although the next year General Alvaro Obregon would overthrow Carranza, become President of Mexico, and make peace with the remaining Zapatistas, who were agrarian rebels in opposition to the power of wealthy landlords (closely connected to Mexico's corrupt President Porfirio Diaz, who had ruled the country as a paternalistic dictator for many decades). It was an excellent story for Steinbeck, and it seemed to follow naturally from his 'protest fiction' of the Thirties.

Steinbeck dug into libraries for material about Zapata, travelling often to Stanford to do research. He sought out people who had known the man or remembered the period. This work was 'oddly soothing', he told Covici, but he knew deep down that he was putting off the dreadful moment when he had to begin writing the script. 'This is just stalling,' he told Elizabeth Otis. As Christmas approached and his garden in Monterey turned brown, he grew more and more despairing; the idea of writing anything at all seemed impossible. This would be his first major holiday alone since he had separated from Gwyn and the boys, a situation he found 'intolerable'. He wrote to Toby Street that he was 'in mourning'.

In the midst of this depression, he received a letter from the American Academy of Arts and Letters informing him that he had been elected to its august body. William Faulkner, Mark Van Doren, and the painter Leon Kroll had also been elected to membership that year. 'Having been blackballed from everything from the Boy Scouts to the United States Army, this election is not only a great experience but for me a unique one,' he commented in his letter of acceptance.[18]

*

Hardly a letter that Steinbeck wrote in the late autumn or early winter of 1948 failed to allude to the fact that he was 'broke'. Gwyn had taken virtually everything, but Steinbeck was in no mood to fight her. 'She had the boys,' his sister says. 'That meant she had to have money, and John did not want them to suffer because of his mistakes.' Pat Covici grew increasingly worried about Steinbeck's financial plight; 'I know you are broke,' he wrote to him in December. He had checked his author's last royalty statement and 'couldn't believe it'. 'There is nothing to worry about,' he reassured him, 'only it is a shame to have pissed away two fortunes in so short a time.' This is certainly one way of looking at it: Steinbeck had tossed vast amounts of money down the drain. To demonstrate his faith in Steinbeck's future, Covici offered him an advance on *The Salinas Valley*, but he refused it bluntly. An advance, he said, was too much like a debt, and he didn't need more debts. In any case, he was putting *The Salinas Valley* on the back burner while he finished the Zapata script. He also had his eye on a sum to be paid out on the forthcoming release of *The Red Pony*.

Bo Beskow had become one of his most intimate correspondents in the past year, and the Swedish artist (who was deeply sensitive to Steinbeck's moods) invited him to Stockholm for the Christmas holiday. 'I should have gone to spend Christmas with you,' Steinbeck wrote on 28 December, 'but I am too broke.' He described his holiday as 'a lonely bad time' spent alone in Pacific Grove, nursing his wounds, fuming at Gwyn, and feeling that he was missing something 'rich and valuable' in the growth of his children; he deeply resented being 'cheated of it'. Each morning he built a fire in the stove, pulled up a chair and tried to work on the Zapata script, but his mind was frozen. Headaches, nausea and exhaustion plagued him. He missed the boys very much and wondered, seriously, if he should not give up writing.

The headaches got worse and worse; his doctor in Monterey suggested he get eyeglasses, and he did so in January. This dramatically reduced the headaches and eye strain, and Steinbeck responded by digging into some books that had been on his reading list for years, such as J. M. Doughty's *Travels in Arabia Deserta*, which he called 'the greatest secular prose in English'. Doughty, he said, 'makes the language a great stone with designs of metal and outcroppings of preciousness, emerald and diamond and obsidian. It is good to have here to see what can be done with the language. I do not think it was easy for him to write. No such sense of ease and flow ever came without great and tearing effort.'[19] Doughty's complex surfaces and deep musical recesses impressed him, offering a contrast to the Hemingway-type simplicity still in vogue among American writers in the late Forties, a simplicity not unlike Steinbeck's in *The Pearl*. He began to contemplate the possibilities of writing in a more ornate style: thoughts that would lead to passages in *East of Eden* which struck many reviewers as a descent into the swamp of purple prose.

Gwyn, meanwhile, was not cooperating with her husband at all. She refused to send the books he asked for, many of which had belonged to his father. 'Eventually he got back a lot of those books in a sneaky way,' Elaine Steinbeck recalls. 'He used to visit the boys wearing a big overcoat, and when Gwyn was out of the room he would stuff the books into his inside pockets. He got back most of the ones he really wanted. One thing he was always sure of: Gwyn would never notice they were gone.'[20] In February, he enlisted the help of Pat Covici in restocking his library with some classic works of poetry and fiction, what he called 'the tools of the trade'. (Gwyn, to give her credit, did return his big dictionary and the battered encyclopedia he had bought several years before in a second-hand book store in lower Manhattan.)

He worked throughout the late winter and spring on

Zapata, making another visit to Mexico in February: 'I need the country and the language in my eyes and ears,' he said. In April, he suddenly felt a compulsive need to see Thom and John and flew to New York for a week, staying at the Bedford. Gwyn, who was thoroughly unpredictable, turned a benevolent eye on this visit and he was allowed to see Thom and John each day, taking them to the Bronx zoo or out to lunch or for walks in Central Park. 'My boys were well and healthy,' he wrote to Beskow when he got back to Pacific Grove. 'I shall have them with me this summer and get to know them again.'[21]

The inward healing process had begun, and one senses an upbeat mood in many of Steinbeck's letters from the spring of 1949. He was writing again at last, having forged a regular working schedule: breakfast at 8.00, to his desk by 8.30. He wrote in the living room of the Pacific Grove cottage most days, working through lunch. In the afternoons, he walked on the beach or strolled along Cannery Row. He kept up his spirits, though he missed Ed Ricketts and the boys badly; the break-up with Gwyn still gnawed at him, and he told friends that he would never marry again, though gradually he did make his re-entry into the world of women. One of those he was seeing now was Paulette Goddard, whom he had first met when she was living with Charlie Chaplin; later she was married to his close friend, Burgess Meredith. Now she had separated from Meredith and was living alone in Los Angeles. They met at a party in Hollywood thrown by Lewis Milestone, and Goddard began flirting with Steinbeck. He responded in kind.

What must it have been like for John Steinbeck, the small town boy who considered himself ugly, to become the lover of a famous and beautiful movie star? He certainly seems to have enjoyed playing the game; his name appeared in all the gossip columns as 'Goddard's latest beau'. Max Wagner recalled his once having filled a trunk full of trinkets bought for petty cash at a five-and-dime store – part of a joke he was playing on Goddard, who adored jewellery. He also went out with Alice Johnson, whom he had known years before; Benson reports that Steinbeck would brag to her about how many women he was seeing. 'Why do you think I've painted my house stud red?' he supposedly asked, although much of this was just talk, the braggadocio of a teenager in his late forties. 'What John really wanted,' Toby Street said some years later, 'was a home, a steady place to work, a garden, and love.'

In April, he went to Hollywood to work on the Zapata script under the watchful eye of Darryl Zanuck, who gave him a huge office at his studio. Steinbeck set up shop there briefly, but he soon realized he couldn't work in such a space; a few days later he moved into a suite at the Beverly Hills Hotel, taking his lunch at midday amid the stars in the Polo Room. One afternoon Doris Johnson, wife of Nunnally Johnson, telephoned. 'What are you doing tonight?' she asked. He said, 'What do you have in mind?' She replied, 'Do you know Ava Gardner?' He didn't. 'Well, how would you like to have a date with her?' He told her there wasn't a man in the world who wouldn't want a date with Ava Gardner, so Doris told him to pick her up and bring her to dinner.

Not long before he was about to set off, Doris called back. 'I'm afraid Ava Gardner has a date already,' she said, 'but how about Ann Sothern? Do you know her?' He did not. 'Good. Bring Ann Sothern.' Ann Sothern was not quite Ava Gardner, but she was a famous and beautiful movie star none the less. Steinbeck took her to the dinner party happily and, sensing that she liked him, he bravely invited her to visit him in Monterey when she was next between pictures. Sothern agreed, and a few weeks later she called to say she was coming to visit over the Memorial Day weekend. 'May I bring a friend?' she asked. Reluctantly, Steinbeck consented. The friend was Elaine Steinbeck, his future wife.

'I'm afraid Ann Sothern has never quite forgiven me,' says
Elaine. 'We spent several days near John, staying at the Pine
Inn at Carmel. John took us around, showing us Ed Ricketts's
lab and the coast and, of course, his cottage in Pacific Grove.
He knew all the good restaurants, and the waiters all knew
him. We went over to Watsonville to meet his sister, Esther. It
was a little embarrassing, because it was pretty obvious that
he was interested in me, not Ann. The relationship just
worked . . . right from the start.' This was Steinbeck's view of
things too. A few days after Elaine and Ann left, he wrote to
Annie Laurie Williams, 'I kind of fell for the Scott girl. Who is
she – do you know?'

Elaine Anderson, now Scott, was tall, sharp-witted, and
outgoing. She had grown up in Fort Worth, Texas, the
daughter of an oilman, and studied drama production at the
University of Texas. There she met the actor Zachary Scott, a
native of Austin, whom she married. The young couple, with
their small daughter, Waverly, went to New York, Mecca of
the American theatre world. 'We were both hired by the
Westport Country Playhouse,' she explains. Scott, who was a
bright, articulate man with a strong interest in classical
theatre, eventually got leading roles in Broadway plays and
Hollywood films; Elaine worked her way up on the production side, eventually serving as stage manager of the original
Oklahoma! on Broadway.

With great reluctance Elaine had gone to Hollywood
during the war, when Zachary was offered a contract by
Warner Brothers that he could not refuse. They led a 'typical
Hollywood life . . . went to all the parties, knew the stars as
friends', but they gradually lost touch with each other, and by
the spring of 1949 the marriage was pretty well finished. 'We
just couldn't talk to each other any more,' Elaine says. 'It's
impossible to say what goes wrong between two people.
Zach and I just fell apart. Nothing seemed right any more.'
She emphasizes that her marriage to Scott 'definitely did not

crumble because of John. That just wasn't so. It was already over by the time John and I met.'

Steinbeck had by now finished an unwieldy draft of the Zapata script, so he had a good excuse for coming to Hollywood. While there, he saw a great deal of Elaine, introducing her to many of his oldest friends, such as Max and Jack Wagner. The veil of secrecy was in place: Steinbeck did not want Gwyn to know what he was doing, nor did Elaine feel comfortable with the fact that the marriage to Zachary Scott was finished. One senses caution on both sides. Although on the surface Steinbeck behaved like a man in love, he didn't want to risk anything. He had adopted what might be called a non-teleological approach to life, saying to John O'Hara in a letter of 8 June, 'For myself there are two things I cannot do without. Crudely stated they are work and women.' This, of course, is Freud's famous formula for happiness: work and love. To Beskow he said, 'I find that I am a very good lover but a lousy husband.'

Psychologists have placed so much emphasis on the early development of individuals that one would think growth stops after adolescence. A more truthful psychological profile of human development suggests that we are perpetually in a state of growth, or should be. Even death is simply one more turn of the spinning wheel. Steinbeck's intellectual growth had certainly not ceased; he had moved from the naive swashbuckling view of the individual in history represented by *Cup of Gold* through the grand 'social' novels of the Thirties, where his focus on the individual in relationship to the group dominated *In Dubious Battle* and *The Grapes of Wrath*. The mixture of Ricketts's speculations on non-teleological thinking with the holistic emphasis on the relations among all living creatures and their place in a complex biosphere had deepened Steinbeck's thought, enriching his subsequent work.

Now, with the death of Ricketts and the painful shift of personal circumstances, Steinbeck had been forced to confront himself again. He had to begin again, as if from scratch, and this was hard, deeply troubling, work. Out of this struggle came a new emphasis in his writing: a renewed interest in the individual in history, but not a naive view this time. The individual is seen in the later work (especially in *Viva Zapata!*, *East of Eden*, *Travels with Charley* and *The Winter of Our Discontent* – his major mature productions) as a separate integer within the larger context of the group and the environment as a whole. This vision lends a maturity that is missing from the more famous work of the Thirties. Writing, for Steinbeck, was and continued to be a process of self-discovery and personal growth.

He finished temporarily with the script of *Zapata* and began working on notes towards *East of Eden*. Meanwhile, the romance with Elaine blossomed; he sent her daily letters, and they talked frequently on the telephone. In midsummer, there was the long-anticipated visit of Thom and John, and Steinbeck found himself happy for the first time in several years. Elaine drove up to meet the children one weekend, and he wrote to her after she left: 'Kids had their enormousest day of play. They have dropped as though shot. Thom wanted to know where you had gone. I told him – home. "Isn't this home?" he asked. And of course he is right.'[22] With startling speed, Steinbeck had taken Elaine Scott to his heart; by midsummer, he already assumed that home was his house – for both of them.

He loved the days he spent with Thom and John, who seemed relieved to be away from their mother. His only regret was that their visit was to last for only two months. Father and sons walked the beaches, flew kites, picnicked, and played games. 'I am going to make my world-shaking macaroni for dinner and the kids are wild with joy because it means that there will be tomato sauce all over the kitchen and all over me. My dinners are not only food. They are decorations also,' he wrote to Elaine on 28 July.[23]

The letters to Elaine are often addressed to 'Belle Hamilton', a fictitious name which echoes his mother's family name. He found the secrecy romantic; love was much better if a little illicit. Furthermore, he was appropriating Elaine Scott by making her into a member of his family. He began to use her, in his letters, as a sounding-board, testing the waters of selfhood. In this, he is like the woman in an E. M. Forster novel who says, 'How do I know what I think till I see what I say?' On 2 August, for example, he launched into a fascinating if adolescent riff on his secret feelings of superiority, conceived in terms of the inferiority of those around him:

> I have so many things to say to you and I don't know what
> they are. But I will. One of them is that I am deeply tired of
> my inferiors. It seems to me that I have spent a good part of
> my life reassuring insecure people. And as with a bad
> tennis player, it ruins your game. What is this common
> touch that is supposed to be so goddamned desirable? The
> common touch is usually an inept, stupid, clumsy,
> unintelligent touch. It is only the uncommon touch that
> amounts to a damn.[24]

In a letter of 16 August, he ran through a ferocious and self-pitying chronicle of the miseries of his life in the past few years, ending with a fine upswing where he said, 'And the reason for telling you this dismal chronicle is that it is not true anymore. It is gone and the energy is washing back into me and I'm not dried up. And I feel wonderful.'[25]

The visit from Thom and John continued to go splendidly, with fishing trips and small expeditions into the hills near Los Gatos. Steinbeck had some fear of sending them back to New York in late August, as planned, because of an outbreak of polio in that city; he wrote to Gwyn, 'Naturally I should be very pleased if the boys didn't go back to the East until all the danger is over for this year.' The children did, in fact, stay with their father into mid-September. (The boys' nurse, a woman named Cathy, had been sent by Gwyn to make sure they were properly looked after. Steinbeck, as might be expected, associated her with Gwyn and deeply disliked her. She, for her part, reported back to Gwyn the sorts of things that went on, enraging her.)

With *Zapata* on hold, Steinbeck was quickly possessed by another idea for a little play-novella. He called it *Everyman*, regarding this as a working title. This meant, of course, that *East of Eden* would once again be postponed. (He also spent a little time discussing the script version of *The Wayward Bus* with Eugene Solow, who had adapted *Of Mice and Men* to the screen so efficiently.) '*Everyman* continues to grow in my mind. My Christ! it's a dramatic thing,' he wrote to Elaine on 11 October. 'Now it has beginning, middle and end and that's what three acts are and that's why there are three acts. The 5- act play is still three acts. And the form was imposed by the human mind, not by playwrights or critics. This doesn't mean that external reality has beginning, middle and end but simply that the human brain perceives it so.'[26]

Throughout the autumn of 1949 Elaine stayed in the marriage to Zachary Scott, however tenuously. She lived in Brentwood, near Hollywood, while Steinbeck remained in Pacific Grove, hard at work on his various projects. *Zapata* had grown into a strange, unfocused manuscript hundreds of pages long, and Zanuck had become impatient. He wanted a movie, and Elia Kazan stood by eager to direct. 'We had to hire somebody to cut the manuscript down, make it a playable script,' recalls Kazan. That person was Jules Buck, who had worked with Zanuck on other projects. Buck admired Steinbeck as a writer and seized this opportunity to work with him. He was, however, startled to discover that a large part of the manuscript was not in scenario form at all;

Steinbeck had effectively written a history of the Mexican Revolution and a psychoanalytical study of Zapata. Taking no pity on Buck, Zanuck commanded him to get a script out of Steinbeck in four weeks. It was a tall order, but the two men warmed to each other on first acquaintance. Buck moved into a hotel in Monterey, and every day he went to the Pacific Grove cottage to work. The very first day, Buck took firm control, scrolling a blank sheet of paper into Steinbeck's typewriter and typing ZAPATA in caps at the top of the page. 'Okay', he said to the amazed Steinbeck, 'now you give me the words.'

Steinbeck did. Often he would stop and insist on rewriting something, but for the most part he pressed on, and the screenplay unfolded seamlessly. Steinbeck would write a scene on his yellow pad in a tiny scrawl, then read it aloud into his Ediphone. Buck would type what he heard on the machine, making slight alterations as he went along. Sometimes Steinbeck would actually draw a picture of the set to block out the scene. The work went swiftly and brilliantly, beginning each morning at eight with an hour's break at midday. They finished work at six promptly, at which point a bottle of whiskey was produced from the cupboard. Working this way, the Buck/Steinbeck team produced twelve pages per day of script.

In mid-November, just as they were bringing the script to a close, Elaine called to say that she and Zachary had decided to get a divorce. 'All along,' Elaine remembers, 'John had said he didn't want to break up my marriage to Zach. That was the last thing he wanted on his conscience. He respected Zach and our marriage, and he didn't believe he should come between us. But if and when it happened, he said to me, he would be right there at my side.' Elaine came to Monterey in the midst of this crisis, staying at a small inn with Waverly; she and Steinbeck had a long talk about their future and they decided together that she would move back to New York once the divorce proceedings were over; he would follow as soon as possible. Zachary Scott, when he learned of these discussions, predicted that Steinbeck would walk out on Elaine as soon as she was free. 'That's his reputation,' Scott maintained. 'The man is unreliable.'

The divorce hearing was held in Malibu on 1 December, and Elaine moved to New York with Waverly and a maid immediately afterwards. A couple of weeks later Steinbeck and she rented separate apartments in a building on East 52nd Street. 'Waverly and I had a rather large apartment, and John lived above us in the penthouse,' says Elaine. Once again, Steinbeck was back in New York for Christmas Eve, and he celebrated with a 'good and noisy festival' that included his boys. Living in New York again meant he could be close to Thom and John, who were his major reason for moving there; he also liked the fact that so many friends, such as Pat Covici and the Benchleys, were nearby, and that Elaine was beside him. He wrote to Beskow on Christmas morning that 'for the first time in a very long time I am filled with hope'. The reasons for his enthusiasm were clear: 'I have a good girl now and work and energy again, so I guess I have healed over on the wounded places. I feel that I have much writing and much living to do yet and that I am ready to do it.'[27]

Exactly how Steinbeck conceived of his relationship with Elaine is evident in a letter to Beskow of 24 January 1950: 'Gwyn always seemed to need more of everything than she was getting. Elaine is very different. A Texan with a soft accent but not the usual boastful Texan – the kind that can take care of itself – not like American women. She doesn't want to be a man. But you will see. She radiates warmth.'[28] He believed that both Carol and Gwyn had been in competition with him, which he disliked. As a famous person, he was always noticed, and this had inevitably led to strains between husband and wife. 'Elaine is on *my* side, not against me,' he explained to Beskow. 'The result is that I am more relaxed than I have ever been.'

Elaine was neither shy nor unaccomplished, and she brought with her a world of theatrical associations that delighted Steinbeck, whom she introduced to people like Richard Rodgers and Oscar Hammerstein, Broadway's mightiest duo. 'Having worked in the theatre for so many years, I just knew everyone,' Elaine says. 'I knew actors and producers and production people. John was stagestruck. He always was. I think this is when he started getting the idea of putting more time into writing for the theatre himself.' The memory of his success with *Of Mice and Men* remained vivid, and he had done well throughout the world with *The Moon Is Down*. As the new year started, he began to focus on his play, which was called *In the Forest of the Night* until nearly the last minute, when he changed the title to *Burning Bright* (both titles are taken from 'The Tiger' by William Blake). Finishing a draft in one month, he polished the dialogue by reading it into his new Dictaphone.

Barely was the ink dry on the playscript than he was called to southern California for another conference on *Zapata* with Darryl Zanuck, who was chomping at the bit; he wanted the film to move ahead into production as soon as possible. The work he had done with Buck on the script was good, but it needed a little more attention, Zanuck explained. Steinbeck set to work quickly, adding and subtracting scenes. While in Los Angeles, he also had a long conference with Eugene Solow about *The Wayward Bus*, which was still being scripted. When he returned to New York, he and Kazan spent a further two months polishing the script. In March, Richard Rodgers called to say that he and Oscar Hammerstein wanted to buy the rights to *Burning Bright*, and that they intended to produce it in the autumn. Suddenly, doors seemed to be opening at every turn. 'This was a magical time for John,' Elaine recalls. 'Everything seemed fresh and good after some very dark years.'

Late in March, he and Elaine flew to Texas to meet the Anderson clan, some of whom were highly suspicious of Steinbeck, whose reputation in the gossip columns was less than savoury. Why was Elaine leaving Zachary, a fellow Texan whom they all knew and liked, for a man widely reputed to be a rake? They were saddened by the break-up of her thirteen-year marriage, and the situation was made worse because the Anderson clan and the Scott clan had become friends. Steinbeck strode anxiously into their living room in Fort Worth, and the family – who were equally panicked – stared at him blankly. 'I've never been so nervous in all my life,' he said, bluntly. This broke the ice, and everyone relaxed. With his fine eye for these things, Steinbeck picked out the ancient aunt who was the matriarch of the family and began to chat her up. 'John just singled her out, and they talked cattle and grass . . . that sort of thing. She liked him at once.' By the time the couple left, they had the blessings of the Anderson family.

Back in New York, Steinbeck went to work with Kazan on the Zapata script once again. Zanuck and Kazan had both liked the script he had written with Buck, and they thought the further revisions moved the story in the right direction, but they had numerous suggestions for pacing and character development. Showing monumental patience, Steinbeck sat down and applied himself once again to what must have seemed an interminable project. The work lasted a couple of weeks, then he turned to writing 'About Ed Ricketts', the memoir that would serve as an introduction to the new edition of Sea of Cortez that Viking intended to publish under the title The Log from the 'Sea of Cortez'.

Work breeds work, and as summer approached fresh ideas for theatrical work tumbled in Steinbeck's brain. He had long imagined that a stage version of Cannery Row might be successful, and he discussed this project with Elizabeth Otis and some of Elaine's friends. Everyone thought it a brilliant notion, and Steinbeck went so far as to lay out a sketch of the acts. To Frank Loesser, in late April, he wrote, 'I think that properly done, it will make a very good play.' Meanwhile, *Burning Bright* underwent final revisions.

That summer, he took Elaine, Waverly, Thom and John to a rented farmhouse in Rockland County, not far from where he once lived with Gwyn in Burgess Meredith's farmhouse. He also hired a Columbia University student as a tutor-cum-babysitter for the boys. ('The tutoring', Elaine recalls, 'was mainly in swimming and baseball, with maybe a little tennis on the side.') Steinbeck worked in a secluded study at the back of the house from eight-thirty until mid-afternoon, when he broke for the rest of the day to play with the children; in the evenings, he and Elaine entertained friends, grilling thick steaks outdoors and mixing strong martinis. Mary, who had not yet met Elaine, came from California to visit and liked her very much. 'It was an extremely easy summer,' Elaine says. 'That was really the first time we actually lived together in a house.'

The work Steinbeck was doing varied from revisions of *Burning Bright* for Rodgers and Hammerstein to taking yet a further lick at the Zapata script. 'It went on and on,' Kazan says, 'but it was finally a good script that worked on many levels.' One night, in late August, Elaine read the entire script aloud, and Steinbeck realized for the first time how good it was. At last, he said to her, it was done. He also finished his sketch of Ed Ricketts, sending it to Pat Covici in early September. Meanwhile, the play version of *Burning Bright* was scheduled to go into rehearsals on 5 September, and Steinbeck planned to move back into the city to be there.

He had certain misivings about it, since the novella had been turned down by several magazines and rejected by the book clubs. 'This is a highly moral story,' he explained to Toby Street, somewhat defensively, 'and they are afraid of it.'[29] He said he was desperately eager to be finished with it so he could move on to *The Salinas Valley*, which continued to haunt him. 'I think if I am not ready to write it now, I never will be. I am nearly fifty and I've been practicing for about 33 years.'

The producers and director were for good reasons sanguine about the play version of *Burning Bright*. The cast was extremely good, and Guthrie McClintic, the director, had a fine record on Broadway. Joe Mielziner, who designed the set, had outdone himself on *Burning Bright*. Furthermore, Steinbeck had always gone down well with audiences, even when the critics were hostile (as with *The Moon Is Down*). The play had two trial runs, first in New Haven, then in Boston, and almost immediately the trouble began to show. The second act, the producers discovered, seemed to lose energy, and people laughed at lines that were not meant to be funny. There was also confusion about the shift of settings from scene to scene. Frantic, Steinbeck rewrote the play on the spot, but to no avail. When the play opened on Broadway at the Broadhurst on 18 October, it was almost uniformly panned. 'The critics murdered us,' Steinbeck wrote to Eugene Solow. 'I don't know how long we can stay open but I would not think it would be long.'

What especially galled him, as he told Solow, was 'that it is really a good show and audiences like it'. The play was, and remains, a bold theatrical experiment with several flaws. As indicated by the original title, *Everyman*, it is a morality play and thus openly symbolic. The main character, the impotent Joe Saul, is Everyman, and his obsession with his blood line links him to earlier Steinbeck characters, such as Richard Whiteside in *The Pastures of Heaven* and Joseph Wayne in *To a God Unknown*. He progresses in the novel from a simplistic notion of bloodlines to a wider embrace of humanity. In the tradition of Ma Joad in *The Grapes of Wrath*, he comes to realize that 'it is the race, the species, that must go staggering on'.

The paternity of the child who is born in the final scene is not, ultimately, the issue. Instead, Steinbeck wants to suggest that we are all fathers and mothers of the world's children, and that for survival humanity must be regarded as a single family. Joe Saul is married to Mordeen, who suspects that he is sterile. She is an Earth Mother without a child, radiating affection for Joe Saul and Friend Ed (modelled on Ed Ricketts), the confidante of both Joe and Mordeen. Victor is Saul's partner, and their antagonism churns the plot. The time of the play is 'Anytime', designed to give *Burning Bright* a certain universality, although the literal setting changes from a circus to a country farmhouse to the tiny cabin of an old freighter in an unnamed harbour. The idea is that human character remains the same, however situations may change.

As one critic, Michael Willis, noted in a review of a West Coast revival of the play thirteen years later, in the *San Francisco Chronicle* (6 February 1963), the characters represent 'the ego, carnal, and conscience aspects of man's personality'. One contemporary reviewer of the novella, Alice Morris, noted in *The New York Times Book Review* (22 October 1950), that the characters were all legendary archetypes: Husband, Wife, Friend and Outsider. For audiences used to straightforward realistic drama, *Burning Bright* was incomprehensible; they could hardly believe this was the same man who had written *The Grapes of Wrath*.

Steinbeck was so upset by the critics' various misreadings of his play, which closed after thirteen performances (it was costing the producers $18,000 a performance), that he wrote a strident self-defence of it in the *Saturday Review* of 11 November 1950, called 'Critics, Critics Burning Bright'. He explained that he had tried to write the play in 'a kind of universal language not geared to the individual actors or their supposed crafts'. He wanted to move beyond the idiolect of the moment:

While I had eminent authority for this method from Aeschylus down through O'Neill, it was still problematical whether audiences used to the modern realistic theatre would accept such expression. This language did not intend to sound like ordinary speech, but rather by rhythm, sound, and image to give the clearest and best expression of what I wanted to say. The attempt was to lift the story to the parable expression of the morality plays. It is a method not without its great exponents. The test is whether it can be found acceptable in a modern book or play or whether an archaicness in its sound cuts if off. A number of critics both of book and play have become so enraged by the method that they have not looked beyond it at the subject matter.

The experiment is well-intentioned, but it often seems idiosyncratic to the point of absurdity. Steinbeck invented compound phrases (similar to the Old English use of kennings) such as 'wife-loss' and 'friend-right' and 'laughter-starving' which simply seem eccentric. Reviewing the book in *The Spectator*, the English critic L. A. G. Strong wrote, 'Have I, I wonder, the admirer-right to tell Mr Steinbeck that this trick has set me screaming silently in my reader-loss?' The dialogue of *Burning Bright* is stiffly formal, without the contractions necessary to make speech more palatable to the ear. Readers of the novella, in a similar vein, find it hard to swallow the endless repetition of characters' first and last names or the epithet 'Friend' always attached to Ed's name.

As impressionist theatre with ties to Brechtian Epic Theatre (as John Ditsky has pointed out),[30] it retains a certain eccentric power; Steinbeck's treatment of the sterility theme was daring, having modern theatrical links to Federico Garcia Lorca's *Yerma* and Eugene O'Neill's *Desire Under the Elms*. In spite of its linguistic oddities, the play attempts a lyric intensity rarely seen in American theatre. When it closed, Oscar Hammerstein commented to the press, 'We are very proud to have produced it because it's a play that should have been done. Few plays of that type are written or presented.'[31]

This was Steinbeck's third attempt at what he called the 'play-novelette', which still seems to me a sensible form to write in. In an introduction to *Burning Bright*, Steinbeck defended the form: 'In a sense it is a mistake to call it a new form. Rather it is a combination of many old forms. It is a play that is easy to read or a short novel that can be played simply by lifting out the dialogue.' He was right in thinking that plays are difficult to read, and that they are rarely read as literary texts except by professionals. The play-novelette (or play-novella) brings the theatrical text to the larger audience used to reading fiction. It also admits the writer more directly to the theatrical text, augmenting the play for the actors and director by making the author's intentions explicit. Steinbeck added: 'It is generally accepted that writers of regular fiction do not care, or are not able, to submit themselves to the discipline of the theater. They do not wish to keep the action within the boundaries of the proscenium arch; they do not wish to limit themselves to curtains and to scenes projected by dialogue alone.' Nevertheless, he argued, there was much to be gained in submitting to the 'disciplines of the theater'. 'You must be clear and concise. There can be no waste, no long discussion, no departure from a main theme, and little exposition.' A writer unwilling, or unable, to do this, such as Henry James, must necessarily fail in the theatre. Rightly, Steinbeck believed that such discipline could only be good for a writer of traditional fiction, and that the form of the play-novelette deserved wider use.

XV

'The Pleasure of Design and Some Despair'

'A good writer always works at the impossible.'

Steinbeck, *Journal of a Novel*

'We bought a brownstone at 206 East 72nd that would be our home for thirteen years,' says Elaine Steinbeck. 'It was a lovely place, with a piece of earth for John to dig his hands into out back, and large, sunny rooms.' The house would not be available until February 1951 so they were forced to spend another few months in separate apartments. To nobody's surprise, they had decided to get married just after Christmas. 'We are having a busy time,' Steinbeck wrote to Jack and Max Wagner back in Los Angeles. With all the arrangements going on, Steinbeck did no writing until February. 'He was still recovering from the response to *Burning Bright*,' says Elaine. 'That hit him very hard, though of course he never talked about it. He never said much about what anyone thought of his work.' This firm rejection by the critics had left him unexpectedly vulnerable and unready to begin *The Salinas Valley*, which he correctly assumed would require every ounce of emotional energy he could muster.

The wedding took place on 28 December at the Manhattan home of his publisher, Harold Guinzburg. 'It was a wonderful, festive thing,' Elaine remembers, 'with lots of our local friends present. Not too many people came from distant places, but most of the people we really wanted to be there were there.' Tom Guinzburg (Harold's son) adds, 'My sister played the organ: it was an extremely moving ceremony. Everyone felt happy for John. Everything had gone so badly with the previous marriage, but there was so much good feeling about Elaine.' After spending the night at the St Regis Hotel, the Steinbecks flew to Bermuda for a week of honeymooning. Elaine says, 'It had been a very cold winter in New York, with icy winds and more snow than usual, and we were just desperate for the sun.' They stayed at an old-fashioned seaside hotel, the Somerset; Steinbeck wrote back to Pat Covici: 'I haven't slept so much since I was a child – about 12 hours a day not counting naps which are pretty often. For two days we had a baby hurricane, but now it is warm and calm.'[1]

Steinbeck found himself in a contemplative mood, recollecting his life with an almost cinematic clarity. His dreams at night, he said, constituted 'a kind of autobiographical motion picture going way back and, curiously, in sequence'. In part generated by the clear demarcation in his life represented by his marriage to Elaine, his autobiographical meditations must also have been stimulated by the prospect of writing *The Salinas Valley*. He told Bo Beskow that it would be 'the longest and the most ambitious' project of his life as well as 'the best I have done'. Thoughts of the *Burning Bright* fiasco burned off in the bright Bermudan sunshine; Steinbeck felt a surge of creative energy as he boarded the plane for New York at the end of the week.

Before he could really begin *The Salinas Valley*, he had one more script conference to attend with Elia Kazan in Hollywood, and he seized the chance to pay a quick visit to Monterey which he hoped would put him in the right mood for the novel. Elaine went with him, and after the conference they drove north. Steinbeck felt uneasy about revisiting the site of so much 'prehistory', as he called it, but he was pleasantly surprised by what he found there. Ritch and Tal Lovejoy (two of his few remaining friends in the area) welcomed him warmly into their home; all hard feelings appeared to have vanished, and Elaine was taken into the circle. Steinbeck, according to his wife, 'was making peace with the Salinas Valley before actually settling in to write his book'.

Back in New York, he regarded the novel warily, like a marathon runner sizing up the track before the meet begins. Having been through the process of writing a novel many times, he knew that one must draw a deep breath, pace oneself, and proceed carefully. There will always be highs and lows, and one must build momentum during the highs to carry one through the hard days, when nothing comes or, worse, when something comes that is clearly useless. A novelist in the midst of writing a novel is like a pregnant woman: always taking care to eat and sleep well, to husband each ounce of energy, fearful that the outcome may be disappointing in some way.

The actual writing began when he and Elaine moved into the brownstone. Steinbeck decided to compose it by hand in large, blue-lined notebooks that Pat Covici had found for him. He would draft the novel on the right-hand page and scribble his thoughts to Covici on the left, creating a kind of private journal. These notes registered daily spasms of anxiety, self-doubts, self-encouragement and genuine exploration. Steinbeck kept in mind his original idea that *The Salinas Valley* should constitute a family history for the benefit of Thom and John, although he knew it was going to be a novel too, a blend of autobiographical fact and fictive imagination.

This early entry appears in *Journal of a Novel: The East of Eden Letters*, a volume published a year after the author's death, in 1969:

> I am choosing to write this book to my sons. They are little
> boys now and they will never know what they came from
> through me, unless I tell them. It is not written for them to
> read now but when they are grown and the pains and joys
> have tousled them a little. And if the book is addressed to
> them, it is for good reason. I want them to know how it

was, I want to tell them directly, and perhaps by speaking
directly to them I shall speak directly to other people.[2]

He plans to tell them 'one of the greatest, perhaps the
greatest story of all – the story of good and evil, of strength
and weakness, of love and hate, of beauty and weakness'.
Quickly realizing that such stark Manichean dichotomies are
false, he adds, 'I shall try to demonstrate to them how these
doubles are inseparable – how neither can exist without the
other and how out of their groupings creativeness is born.'
This lengthy note ends with one of his most inspiring
sentences: 'A good writer always works at the impossible.'
Few novelists, I suspect, have ever begun a work of fiction
with so much of a sense of awe, with so much mental, even
'spiritual' preparation, or with such visible ambition. Inevitably, this intentional front-loading was detrimental; the
novel seems, in many places, sanctimoniously full of
'meaning'. It might have succeeded more completely and
unambiguously if the author had not tried so appallingly
hard. One feels the strain in the muscles of his language as
well as in the attempt to cram so much into one comprehensive book.

Certainly his new working conditions were hospitable. 'I
have never had it so good and so comfortable,' he wrote in his
journal. 'He had a big room upstairs, with a drafting table and
a swivel chair,' Elaine recalls. This was a much better space to
write in than the previous brownstone (which now belonged
to Gwyn), where he was confined to the basement with tiny
slits of light just below the level of the ceiling. He kept a full
box of Mongol 480 #2 pencils on his desk (all supplied by Pat
Covici), and he would sharpen them meticulously every day
before beginning to write. The dependency on Covici during
the writing of this novel may seem idiosyncratic; he called
him constantly on the phone, and when Covici was away
from his desk he would grow frantic. He addressed him in his

journal five days a week, and he fully expected Covici to send paper and pencils, to do research for him, and to provide constant emotional support. Steinbeck would ship the manuscript in weekly instalments to his editor, who would have it typed by a Viking secretary and returned for corrections. Writing his own detailed criticisms of the novel in the margins, he would return them with the typed manuscript.

This rather laborious method of composition ran aground in mid-April, when Steinbeck objected to Covici's constant criticism. His ego was now too fragile for that: 'I hope you don't feel that I was short this morning on the phone, about the criticism. Right now, when I am only thinking ahead, it will do me no good. So write it all down and we'll go into it when the book is finished.'[3] Reading over Covici's letters to Steinbeck, one is embarrassed by his genial fulsomeness, however much Steinbeck wanted the praise. 'I had to hold his hand,' Covici later said to a friend. 'He seemed unable to do anything by himself.'[4] Having been bruised so badly by criticism of *The Wayward Bus* and *Burning Bright*, he felt extremely shaky. With part of himself, he was confident that he could pull off his 'big novel' and that it would be good, if not great. He did, indeed, write quickly, firmly, and without much hesitation, finishing a first draft of the entire novel between 1 February and the beginning of November. Without the constant attention of Pat Covici, it seems unlikely that he could have made such lightning progress.

One of the drawbacks to working so fervently was that Steinbeck did not have a lot of time to entertain Thom and John when they came to visit. But having them nearby meant that he could see them easily, and Gwyn increasingly let the boys visit him. Much of the work fell to Elaine, who was largely responsible for them (they were not after all her own sons) when they came to East 72nd Street or, in the summer of 1951, when they lived together on the island of Nantucket. 'A further problem,' a friend recalls, 'was that Gwyn spoke badly to the boys about Elaine and John. She made fun of them. She did everything she could to poison their view of things. This meant of course that they often misbehaved with John and Elaine – or were difficult.'[5]

Gwyn also demanded money – lots of money – for the boys, and Steinbeck did not begrudge these demands. He had the money, and plenty of it, but like his father, John Ernst, he suffered from a perpetual fear of financial ruin and decided to try to earn extra from incidental journalism. He persuaded his agents to find new outlets for brief essays on contemporary issues or opinion pieces on a range of subjects. Magazines such as *Life*, *Collier's*, and *Reader's Digest* had an inexhaustible appetite for such pieces, and since Steinbeck was a recognized name, they paid considerable sums for his pieces, sometimes as much as $2500 for a short article. Steinbeck found this kind of writing easy, and it offered (in addition to the cash) a welcome distraction from the gruelling work on *The Salinas Valley*.

Remembering the exhaustion, both physical and mental, that followed the publication of *The Grapes of Wrath*, Steinbeck took care to pace himself. With stunning accuracy, he predicted how long the writing would take. He usually got 800 words on to each handwritten page, and he completed two pages in his notebook each working day. As projected, he was a third of the way through the 200,000 plus words of the manuscript by 30 April. To get back in touch with the Salinas area, he subscribed to the local newspaper and probed, on the phone, the memories of his sisters Beth and Esther. 'He asked a lot of questions,' Beth recalls. 'He wanted to know everything, all the details. What was the name of that woman who helped mother with the washing or where did Grandfather Hamilton say he bought his wagon. All kinds of odd things. He liked to run through family history. He knew it pretty well, but it was important to say it again. To get it right.'

The Log from the 'Sea of Cortez' appeared in the spring of 1951, having been delayed by the fact that Steinbeck had claimed single authorship. Toby Street had been talking over this matter with the lawyers for the Ricketts estate, without success: they insisted on equal co-authorship. Finally, Steinbeck sent Pat Covici to Monterey to have a meeting with the lawyers and, more importantly, with Ed Ricketts's son, Ed Jr, who felt that his father deserved full co-authorship, as in the original edition. Steinbeck now believed that since most of the writing in its final form was his, the book belonged to him. Any guilt he might have felt about pushing Ed Ricketts to one side was assuaged by his long sketch, 'About Ed Ricketts', where he gives full credit to the man who inspired and directed the expedition. Under pressure, Ed Jr caved in, and *The Log from the 'Sea of Cortez'* was published under the name of John Steinbeck in a small edition of 7500 copies. (It received almost uniformly pleasant notices in the press, but nobody took it seriously as a scientific work. The sales, of course, were nothing like those of his fictional works.)

For many years the Benchleys had sung the praises of Nantucket, and that summer Steinbeck decided to take Elaine and the boys to the island for several months. They rented a two-storey, grey shingled house with a large Victorian porch on the beach in Siasconset. The palaver of seagulls and the crashing surf thrilled Steinbeck, and he loved the sea view, with a lighthouse gleaming in the middle distance. To go with the move, he bought a small sailboat, marking the beginning of what would become an abiding interest. Marjorie Benchley recalls, 'Elaine and I would take the children to the beach during the day while John stayed at home, writing. We had picnics, though, all of us together. John seemed very happy there. We all were.' He had set up a card table for writing in a spacious room overlooking the sea on the second floor, and he began to write each morning at eight-thirty sharp. He continued until early afternoon, when he joined Elaine and the children for swimming and games.

The title of the novel had always been tentative, a working title. Now he became thoroughly dissatisfied with it: *The Salinas Valley* was far too close to *The Long Valley*, his book of stories. He tried *My Valley*, but that seemed lacklustre. 'He was extremely frustrated about the title,' Elaine says. Pat Covici, too, kept pressing for a better title, noting that his previous ones had always been memorable. *East of Eden* came to him in early June when he sat down to write out the Cain and Abel story (*Gen.* 4:1–16) by hand. He had noted to Covici that 'the story changes with flashing lights when you write it down'.

The sailboat he had bought arrived (later than expected) in early July, and he reported to Elizabeth Otis that 'it handles like a dream'. He also noted that, with the swimming and exercise, he was getting strong and losing his stomach. He and Elaine had pretty much given up hard alcohol, except for Saturday nights. 'It is cool,' he went on, 'almost chilly here. It is such a wonderful place. We are falling in love with it. It is a nice quiet place but the air is filled with energy. Really a place to work as well as play.' As for the novel, he said that never had a book so intrigued him as *East of Eden*, 'I only hope other people can enjoy reading it as much as I am enjoying writing it.'

On 11 July, he commented in his journal, 'What a strange story it is and how it haunts one.' As the new title suggests, Steinbeck now envisioned reworking the story of Cain and Abel as he moved through several generations of the Trask family, with the biblical tale offering him a loom on which to weave his own text. This particular story struck him as a true account of the human condition, as in the moment when Cain offers to sacrifice himself, having slain his brother, and the Lord says: 'If thou doest well, shalt thou not be accepted: and if thou doest not well, sin lieth at the door. And unto thee shall be his desire, and thou shalt rule over him.' Steinbeck discovered a new translation wherein the Hebrew word *timshel* is rendered not 'shalt thou not' but 'thou mayest', thus giving man greater leeway for moral choice. 'Here is individual responsibility and the invention of conscience,' Steinbeck wrote to Pat Covici.[6] This Hebrew word took on vast importance in Steinbeck's head; indeed, the novel builds towards the final scene where the dying Adam says to his son, Cal, *'Timshel!'* only seconds before he dies, thus granting him the possibility of a moral life.

Covici wrote again and again, praising the novel, offering encouragement and odd bits of information, sending pencils. It was the greatest editorial performance of his life. In late July, he and his wife, Dorothy, visited the Steinbecks in Nantucket, and he was given his weekly supply of manuscript by hand. 'Pat would sit on the porch in a rocker, reading and making notes, and John would hover anxiously. Sometimes, after dinner, John would read from the book aloud,' Elaine recalls. 'But he didn't want criticism. He wanted an audience, and we all knew enough to say nothing. Criticism wouldn't have helped him anyway. At this stage he needed to work things through for himself.'

When Elaine's birthday arrived in August, Steinbeck surprised her by giving her a twenty-one gun salute with real naval cannons, a production designed to entertain the boys as well as Elaine. His birthday presents included a Dodgers baseball cap, a Swedish steel bow with a quiverful of arrows, and a Colt .22 pistol – all very unladylike, as he enjoyed pointing out to friends. He wrote to Elizabeth Otis on 16 August:

> The birthday is over and it was a humdinger and I think
> Elaine was happy with it. I am going to leave birthday
> telling to Elaine. I worked into Sunday and finished Book III
> so that now I have just one more book in this novel. And I

start it after a rest and a change which is good because it is different from the rest, in time, pace, and everything. I am still not bored with it. And I should be by this time. But it is, if anything, more alive to me than ever. And I feel a hugeness in my chest out of which I hope pigmies do not come. The last book will be between 70 and 80 thousand words or roughly two more months of work if I am lucky. So it is still on schedule even though I have tried to keep schedule out of it.[7]

Less than a month later, on 11 September, he wrote to Covici, 'Now the summer closes. We will get up at four in the morning on Sunday and tool our way homeward. And we have had our triumphs this summer in addition to the work. Thom has taken great jumps. Elaine almost despaired a number of times but at the end of the summer Thomas can read and do his arithmetic. He will start ahead of his class, and more important, he knows he can start. The block is gone. Catbird [his pet name for John] is the one who might have the trouble. He is so gifted in charm and cleverness and beauty that he will not have to go through the fire for a long time if ever. Poor Thom has it early and will have it long.'[8]

There had been a scare over the summer when Covici developed symptoms which suggested the possibility of a stroke. Remembering his mother's terrible last days, he had insisted that Covici see a surgeon of his acquaintance. Now Annie Laurie Williams fell ill. With his usual loyalty to a friend in need, Steinbeck dashed back to New York to visit her in the hospital, where to his great relief he found her recovering. One thing he did not want to lose was his support system: his editor, his agents, his friends, and Elaine – these were all crucial to him as he was moving into the home stretch on his novel.

On 16 November he wrote to Bo Beskow: 'I finished my book, a week ago. Just short of a thousand pages – 265,000 words. Much the longest and surely the most difficult work I have ever done. Now I am correcting and rewriting and that will take until Christmas.'[9] He had worked through late September into early November with a maniacal fury, pressing himself to his physical and emotional limits. 'It was just an obsessive thing,' Elaine Steinbeck says. 'He was focused on the novel completely, though it was only a short burst when you look back on it. I mean, that whole book was written so quickly. But it changed him. His life was different after *East of Eden*.' The difference was that, after nearly a decade of dissolution, emotional and artistic, Steinbeck felt he was putting himself together again, reweaving the strands, reconnecting to his deepest imagery and to the themes that most concerned him.

The complete manuscript was delivered to Pat Covici in a wooden box carved by Steinbeck out of a fine piece of mahogany during the summer on Nantucket. He enclosed a note which became the book's dedicatory page:

> Dear Pat –
> You came upon me carving some kind of little figure out of wood and you said, 'Why don't you make something for me?'
> 'I asked you what you wanted, and you said, 'A box.'
> 'What for?'
> 'To put things in.'
> 'What things?'
> 'Whatever you have,' you said.
> Well here's your box. Nearly everything I have is in it, and it is not full. Pain and excitement are in it, and feeling good or bad and evil thoughts and good thoughts – the pleasure of design and some despair and the indescribable joy of creation.
> And on top of all these are all the gratitude and love I have for you.
> And still the box is not full.

There were, as always, many revisions, though Steinbeck

(like most writers) disliked this stage intensely. The process of revision, he told Dook Sheffield, was like 'dressing a corpse for a real nice funeral'. It must be said, however, that Pat Covici was a light editor. My guess is that he was frightened that any but the most obvious suggestions would offend his favourite and most commercially successful author. And he could never forget how Steinbeck had stayed with him, in the late Thirties, when it really mattered. Covici's career was partly founded on his connection with John Steinbeck, and he was eager to maintain the smoothest of associations. But with *East of Eden* some drastic editing might have saved the author from some of the negative criticism that followed its publication.

'John was always very sensitive to criticism, and worried about it,' John Hersey says. 'He would write to magazines quite often, defending younger writers whose works got unfairly criticized. John O'Hara, in particular, was a good friend, and John would defend his works whenever he had a chance. He was a good friend to Arthur Miller as well. There were many younger writers whose work he liked a good deal, such as Joseph Heller and Saul Bellow.' Gore Vidal comments, 'Bellow was a great admirer of Steinbeck's work – even the later work, which many critics at the time dismissed. Saul was one of those responsible for Steinbeck's Nobel Prize. I can remember him going around telling everybody what an underrated writer Steinbeck was.'

After finishing the revisions of *East of Eden* in February 1952, Steinbeck decided that he and Elaine should go abroad for a while. He had been contacted by *Collier's*, and Elizabeth Otis negotiated an extremely lucrative contract with the magazine for him to serve as a roving European editor-at-large. The idea was not that he would do hardcore political reporting or serious reportage; his commission was for personal pieces not unlike those he had written during the war. He had a reputation for being able to talk to ordinary people, and he was asked to seek them out wherever his fancy led him; he would chat up waiters, artisans, blacksmiths, vintners; his job was to make everyday events interesting, to find human stories and bring them to life in his own way. Elaine, who had become adept with a camera, would take pictures to accompany the articles. In all, they would be gone for six months, returning in time for the autumn publication of *East of Eden*.

They left for Europe aboard a Genoese freighter in late March. 'We are anchored in Casablanca harbor, and we have just heard a donkey bray – the first land sound in 11 days,' Elaine wrote to Pat Covici. They entered the port at sunset with the city lights blazing and the sky full of stars. From Casablanca they continued to Algiers, where they attended a party thrown by a French general at a local palace with 'oceans of champagne, singing and dancing and fun'. A couple of days later they sailed from Algiers to Marseilles, where they hired a driver to take them into Spain. Their immediate destination was Seville, with its candy-striped cathedral and elegant town square lined with orange trees. 'Seville is *wonderful*,' Steinbeck wrote home. 'Spain excites me as I have rarely been excited.'

The Moorish architecture caught their fancy; they visited the Alhambra in Granada, and toured various well-known cathedrals. In Madrid, they lingered in the Prado, then moved on to Toledo to see more of the paintings of El Greco, which produced a vivid gut response in Steinbeck. He soon began to feel guilty about the fact that he had not yet written anything for *Collier's*, and he told Otis that he might write something about a famous bullfighter called Litri. Bullfights were, of course, 'Hemingway's material', as he said, but he thought he could put his own stamp on it by concentrating on the life story of one particular fighter. He and Elaine attended several bullfights in preparation for the article and did a considerable amount of background research on Litri, but the piece didn't get written until they left Spain and were on a train to Paris during the second week of May.

Steinbeck had heard from Elia Kazan while in Spain that he had testified before the infamous House Committee on Un-American Activities. Senator Joseph McCarthy, the fanatical anti-Communist, was hard at work in Washington pointing a finger at all sorts of innocent people; it had become a major crime to be involved in actions considered 'red' or 'un-American', and major careers in Hollywood and elsewhere were being ruined almost daily. (The great screenwriter, Dalton Trumbo, for example, was drummed out of the movie business for his left political leanings.) This was one of the blackest phases of modern American history, and Steinbeck, who was still unhappy about the way the anti-Communist right had accused him of being un-American after the publication of *The Grapes of Wrath*, sympathized with Kazan. Writing to Covici, he called Kazan 'a good and honest man' and said he hoped the 'Communists and the second-raters' would not now 'cut him to pieces'.[10]

Steinbeck must, I think, be faulted for supporting Kazan's decision to testify before the McCarthy Committee, but one can put this move down almost exclusively to friendship. The two men had grown close in the past couple of years, and Kazan had recently moved into a house near Steinbeck's on East 72nd Street. ('They were almost brothers,' Elaine says.) It is still difficult to imagine the author of *In Dubious Battle* and *The Grapes of Wrath* showing anything but hostility to McCarthy, a demagogue of the worst kind. However, Steinbeck also defended the playwright Lillian Hellmann's decision to oppose the committee. 'I understand both Hellmann and Kazan,' he wrote to Covici on 28 May from Paris.[11] 'Each one is right in different ways.' It should also be noted that when Arthur Miller was called to testify before the committee and refused, Steinbeck was a strong public voice in his defence.

At the end of May Steinbeck heard from Otis that *Collier's* had rejected his article on bullfighting, and he was furious, blaming their response on his attempt to write for what he imagined their audience to be. 'I do hate the feeling of a hot breath down my neck,' he told Otis.[12] 'There are two distinct crafts, writing and writing for someone. The second requires a kind of second sight with which I do not seem to be gifted. In writing you put down an idea or a story and then see whether anyone likes it, but in writing for someone you must first, during and after, keep an invisible editor sitting on the typewriter shaking an admonitory finger in your face. It is a special business and one I don't seem to learn very easily.'

The Steinbecks lived well as they travelled, staying in fine hotels and eating in the best restaurants. One of the immediate consequences of this good living was pressure on their pocketbooks. Although Steinbeck was never genuinely in trouble, he complained as usual about his finances to Otis on 27 May. Once again he wondered if she might not find some way of stirring the pot and generating more cash. He also mentioned that he had received the galleys of *East of Eden*, noting, 'It is better than I thought. Doesn't print make a difference?'

Fortunately, *Colliers* liked his second article and continued to like what he sent. Meanwhile, the Steinbecks enjoyed Paris, socializing for a few days with the Loessers before setting off through the French countryside for Switzerland in a new Citroën; they arrived in Geneva after a few days of leisurely touring and checked into a hotel overlooking the lake. Geneva 'was lovely and clear and clean', Steinbeck wrote to several friends, but he soon began to suffer from anxiety about Thom and John, experiencing 'the constant and never-changing sense of impending tragedy concerning the boys'.[13]

A couple of weeks later they were in Rome, having driven over the Simplon Pass, with stops in Milan, Florence, and

Venice. They stayed in a suite at the Hassler, a grand hotel at the top of the Spanish Steps. On the day of their arrival Elia Kazan telephoned to say that he had finished reading *East of Eden* and wanted to make it into a film. He would approach Darryl Zanuck first, but would not necessarily stop there. United Artists was another good option, and there was also the possibility that he could make it independently. *Viva Zapata!* had only just been released (starring Marlon Brando and Anthony Quinn), and had earned over three million dollars in less than a month. This commercial success augured well for the Steinbeck/Kazan association in the eyes of major studios.

Another good piece of news arrived from Pat Covici in late April: advance orders for *East of Eden* exceeded 100,000 copies, thus guaranteeing its status as a bestseller. There was a bit of bad news too – the Book-of-the-Month Club had rejected the novel. 'The doings of Katie in the whore house, I am afraid frightened them. Life still frightens them. Their attitude is bewildering to me,' Covici said by way of explanation.[14] Making lemonade from these lemons, Covici told Viking's sales representatives to explain to booksellers that they would now have exclusive rights to sell *East of Eden* without competition from the book club. This ploy worked, and a second large wave of orders for the novel rolled in.

One of the curiosities of Steinbeck's visit to Italy was an attack on him by a Communist newspaper, *L'Unita*. Like many periodicals of the Old Left, this one considered Steinbeck an ideological turncoat. He had once, they imagined, been a strong socialist and CP man who sympathized openly with the downtrodden and oppressed. They had seen him cavorting with Hollywood stars and, during the war, writing blatantly propagandistic books such as *Bombs Away* and *The Moon Is Down*. His *Russian Journal* was (rightly) considered naive. And now he was associated with Elia Kazan, who had testified before the McCarthy Committee.

In a real sense, Steinbeck *had* turned. One cannot imagine the writer of the Thirties living in luxurious hotels in Europe or seeking out the company of movie stars. On the other hand, he had grown away from his youthful self, as most people do. His sympathies still lay with ordinary people, as his journalism for *Collier's* and his novels showed right to the end. As far as politics went, he was, and continued to be, a New Deal Democrat with a fiercely independent streak. He never turned Communist because Communism was deeply anti-individualist and contradicted his philosophy of the individual, which came straight from Emerson's 'Self-Reliance', where the famous sentence appears upon which American individualism was founded: 'Trust thyself: every heart vibrates to that iron string.' Later in the same essay Emerson declares, 'Society everywhere is in conspiracy against the manhood of every one of its members.' Steinbeck did not want to join this conspiracy. Behind his brilliant fictional evocations of 'group man' lay a fundamental belief in the Emersonian Self.

The challenge for Steinbeck, ever since encountering Ed Ricketts and his non-teleological thinking, was to reconcile his essential belief in the individual with his awareness of the phalanx. Men and women were unique individuals, but they were also part of a larger context, participating in the various forms of group behaviour which create the complex drama of history. This pageant is partially determined by forces that exist outside the individual: the economy, the political sphere, environmental forces, and so on. In some ways his later view was the more complex one, taking into account both the phalanx and the individual, comprehending the influence of the larger movements while celebrating the individual moral choices that create an existential sense of (contingent) self-hood.

Before leaving Rome, Steinbeck dropped in on Ingrid Bergman, the movie star who had recently left her doctor husband in America to live with Roberto Rossellini, the flamboyant Italian film-maker. Steinbeck had been talking rather idly with Jules Buck about collaborating with him on another screenplay, and had hit upon trying a movie version of Ibsen's play, *The Vikings*. When he got to Paris, near the end of July, he wrote to Bergman to see if she might be interested in playing the female lead of a legendary woman named Hjordis. She replied rather archly, 'Thou art minded I play a woman mighty as Hjordis? Set thy hand to work . . .'[15]

Steinbeck did rough out a very crude screenplay based on *The Vikings* while in Paris, although nothing came of the project. One of the few mentions of it occurs in a letter to Dook Sheffield two months later from New York, where he called the Ibsen play 'a roaring melodrama, cluttered and verbose'. Praising his own adaptation, he says, 'Anyway – I shook out the clutter and I think it will make a good picture.'[16] While in Paris, the Steinbecks joined a movable feast, linking up with various friends, including Robert Capa and the director John Huston, who was filming *Moulin Rouge*. They celebrated Bastille Day with a big dinner in the Eiffel Tower restaurant (Capa took photographs of the fireworks from the dinner table). The evening ended, or failed to end, with a huge street party and dancing till dawn.

On 24 July they flew to London, staying at the Dorchester. Steinbeck met up with his new British agent (previously unknown to him), Graham Watson, who landed him assignments with several British newspapers and who would eventually get his *Collier's* articles published in Britain. Watson and his wife, Dorothy, became warm friends of both Steinbecks, and they often met for dinner on subsequent trips to London. 'We saw a lot of plays on that trip,' Elaine recalls. 'John was always crazy for the theatre. John Gielgud was starring in *Much Ado About Nothing*. That was the one we both loved best.'

In mid-August, they moved on to Ireland, where Steinbeck wanted to do a bit of genealogical research on his Hamilton ancestry. He wrote to Covici from Londonderry on 17 August:

> We just got here. We're on a hunt for the seat of the
> Hamiltons. The place they are supposed to have lived is not
> on any map no matter how large scaled but we have found
> a taxi driver who thinks he knows where it is and tomorrow
> we start out to try to find it. It should be a very interesting
> experience. I can't imagine any of them are still alive since
> the last I heard of them was fifteen years ago and there
> were then two old, old ladies and an old, old gentleman
> and they had none of them been married. However,
> whatever happens it will be a story to tell.[17]

The Steinbecks flew back to New York on the last day of August.

In September, as the publication of *East of Eden* loomed, he was in contemplative mood when he wrote to Dook Sheffield, 'Fifty is a good age. The hair recedes, the paunch grows a little, the face rarely inspected, looks the same to us but not to others. The little inabilities grow so gradually that we don't even know it. My hangovers are less bad maybe because I drink better liquor.'[18] The same letter contains an intriguing reference to Hemingway:

> Just read Hemingway's new book [*The Old Man and the Sea*].
> A very fine performance. I am so glad. The obscene joy with
> which people trampled him on the last one was disgusting.
> Now they are falling too far the other way almost in shame.
> The same thing is going to happen to me with my new
> book. It is the best work I've done but a lot of silly things
> are going to be said about it. Unthoughtful flattery is, if
> anything, more insulting than denunciation.

As noted, Steinbeck had come to dislike Hemingway

personally. He had grown increasingly sensitive to the charge, often heard, that he was 'a poor man's Hemingway', and it is true that there are many similarities. Both were born into 'genteel' families, and both had puritanical and overly protective mothers. Both valued courage and technical skill, and both began their careers as journalists and had covered World War II for American papers. The differences emerge in the fiction, where Steinbeck rejected the minimalism Hemingway made famous. It might be argued that Steinbeck is a more various writer than Hemingway, whose main achievement was the perfection of a style which in a sense became a substitute for life: a canny form of aestheticism. There was never anything 'realistic' about Hemingway, or anything 'political'. His politics boiled down to a crude Darwinism, and he was narrowly sexist. Steinbeck, on the other hand, confronted the political realities of the Thirties with a straightforwardness that remains startling. But whatever his private feelings about Hemingway, Steinbeck could not but sympathize with another writer who had suffered at the hands of critics as his own novel, *East of Eden*, approached its day of publication.

What happened with the reviews could hardly be called 'unthoughtful flattery'. They were often respectful, but few went overboard with praise. Orville Prescott's response, which appeared in the daily *New York Times* on 19 September, the day of publication, set the general tone for the reviews. The book, he wrote, 'is a quarter of a million words long. Clumsy in structure and defaced by excessive melodramatics and much cheap sensationalism though it is, *East of Eden* is a serious and on the whole successful effort to grapple with a major theme.' The following Sunday, *The New York Times Book Review* ran a positive front-page review by Mark Schorer, who called *East of Eden* 'probably the best of John Steinbeck's novels'. He elaborated: 'Mr Steinbeck's tightly constructed short novels, in fact, and even such longer works as *The Grapes of Wrath*, have given us no preparation for this amplitude of treatment that enables him now to develop, within this single work, not only a number of currents of story, but a number of different modes of tracing them.'

The negative reviews were led by Anthony West in *The New Yorker*'s review, 'California Moonshine' and Leo Gurko in *The Nation* (both 20 September). Gurko wrote, 'This is the longest and most ambitious of the six novels by Steinbeck since the appearance in 1939 of his masterpiece, *The Grapes of Wrath*. It shares the distinction with the other five of being unsatisfactory in one important aspect or another and raises anew the question of why Steinbeck's talent has declined so rapidly and so far.' Two days later, the anonymous reviewer in *Time* wrote, '*East of Eden* is a huge grab bag in which pointlessness and preposterous melodrama pop up as frequently as good storytelling and plausible conduct.'

Academic criticism has largely followed in the wake of the negative reviews. In *The Wide World of John Steinbeck*, Peter Lisca offers the most comprehensive case against Steinbeck's novel, pointing to stylistic, structural and thematic problems. Beginning with a scathing account of the author's occasionally baroque language, he argues that Steinbeck lost sight of his original intent: to tell the story of his maternal family, the Hamiltons. When the Trasks appear on the scene, in 1900, 'the importance of the Trask family grew' beyond the bounds of what fitted within the frame of the original conception. The result is an awkward, misshapen narrative, Lisca points out, dwelling on the confusion generated by the narrative 'I', who blends with the character 'John' and gets mixed in with the 'we' of the novel, who perform a role similar to that of a Greek chorus, affirming or commenting on the action and supplying a community viewpoint. Lisca also derides Steinbeck's attempt to write a modern version of the Cain and Abel story, especially the bifurcation of characters into those on the Cain side (Cyrus, Charles, Cathy, Caleb) and those on the Abel side (Adam, Aron and Abra).

These criticisms address some distinct failures in the writing, but after the lapse of several decades they seem beside the point. *East of Eden* is a 'loose baggy monster' (the phrase that Henry James used in describing *War and Peace*), a vast drawer into which Steinbeck stuffed, as he said, everything he knew. The prose is lyrical, warm and earthy, although certain passages represent a gaudy throwback to *Cup of Gold*. Despite its sprawl, its capacious lack of narrative direction, there is a narrowness of subject and theme that saves it from blowing apart. The Trask family, not the Hamiltons, become the focus after the opening chapters. *East of Eden* is finally their story, and it remains a shockingly believable tale of family pathology.

The novel kept changing under Steinbeck's hand as he wrote. He had been successful in *The Grapes of Wrath* with intercalary chapters, and he originally thought this novel would alternate between complementary narratives of the Hamilton and Trask families over three generations. But, as he wrote, the Trasks came to dominate the narrative, beginning with a Cain-Abel pairing in Adam and Charles Trask. The central character in Part One is clearly Adam, whose point of view controls the story as he survives the machinations of his evil father, Cyrus, and his ruthless brother, Charles.

There is 'history' in the voice of the novel from the outset, portending a visionary epic:

> The Salinas Valley is in Northern California. It is a long
> narrow swale between two ranges of mountains, and the
> Salinas River winds and twists up the center until it falls at
> last into Monterey Bay.

The narrator's voice emerges in the 'I' of the second paragraph:

> I remember my childhood names for grasses and secret
> flowers. I remember where a toad may live and what time

the birds awaken in the summer – and what trees and seasons smelled like – how people looked and walked and smelled even. The memory of odors is very rich.

In this mode Steinbeck conjures his maternal grandfather, Samuel Hamilton, who came from the east in 1870 and sired a large, happy family. The Hamilton story, never developed in detail, stands in contrast to the tragic family history of the Trasks. Samuel Hamilton is a classic Irish immigrant, and his eloquence is distinctly Celtic. His friend, Lee, is similarly eloquent, though he is a Chinese servant. (Lee has a philosophical bent and often speaks, it seems, for Steinbeck himself.)

The Trask family stories, with their conspicuous biblical parallels, are pursued with a vengeance in Parts Two and Three. Adam and Cathy give birth to twins, Aron and Caleb. Their mother, Cathy, shoots her husband in the shoulder as he tries to prevent her from leaving the family. She does leave, however, and winds up in a Salinas brothel, which she eventually owns. Adam, in the depths of depression, is saved by the godlike Samuel Hamilton, who has enough moral power to stir Adam back to life, encouraging him to accept his responsibility and raise the boys himself.

Part Four moves swiftly; indeed, this is the section Elia Kazan chose to focus on in his film adaptation of the novel. The narrative begins just before the outbreak of World War I and moves through the decision of the United States to enter the conflict. The father-son struggle between Adam and Caleb is robustly dramatized, as is the tension between the brothers. The section gathers speed as Steinbeck produces crisis after crisis: the revelation that Cathy is now a madam in a brothel crushes Aron and leads to Adam's stroke. In a grand finale, which Steinbeck called 'the most violently emotional scene' he had ever written, Cal receives a formal blessing from his father that releases him from his guilt and opens a future where moral choices become a real possibility.

Steinbeck did not manage to pull off what he had attempted, but the novel is affecting and probes the American psyche in ways only Steinbeck could have done. Adam Trask is, quite literally, the American Adam cast from Eden almost inadvertently. As in Milton's *Paradise Lost*, which stands behind *East of Eden* as a remote template, the founding father must deal with a 'sinful' woman. In Milton, of course, it is Eve who gets Adam kicked out of Eden, but it is also Eve who, in Book Ten of the epic, initiates the reconciliation with Adam which leads, ultimately, to their salvation. Steinbeck's greatest mistake in *East of Eden* is unquestionably the one-sided portrayal of Cathy. Why did she leave Adam and her newborn sons? Was there something to provoke such cruel behaviour? This is never made clear. Cathy seems to embody 'evil' almost abitrarily, much as Gwyn now did in Steinbeck's mind.

The story of Adam is, inevitably, about the fall of man. In this tragic story, it is always woman's fault that he falls. But surely Adam Trask is as much to blame as Cathy in *East of Eden*, just as Aron is as much to blame as Caleb for the calamity that befalls them? In some ways, this novel represents a final departure from Ed Ricketts's 'is' thinking and his non-teleological approach. Steinbeck also releases himself from his obsession with the phalanx, raising a hymn to individualism in the Emersonian vein. 'And this I believe,' Steinbeck writes in a passage that echoes in the reader's mind,

> That the free, exploring mind of the individual human is the
> most valuable thing in the world. And this I would fight for:
> the freedom of the mind to take any direction it wishes,
> undirected. And this I must fight against: any idea, religion
> or government which limits or destroys the individual. This
> is what I am and what I am about. I can understand why a
> system built on a pattern must try to destroy the free mind,
> for this is the one thing which can by inspection destroy

such a system. Surely I can understand this, and I hate it and I
will fight against it to preserve the one thing that separates us
from the uncreative beasts. If the glory can be killed, we are
lost.

While this many sound grandiloquent, it represents a
philosophically central rhetorical moment in *East of Eden*. If
The Grapes of Wrath may be read as a protest against the
rough-edged individualism that dominated the first few
decades of this century in America and led, perhaps necessarily, to the Great Depression, *East of Eden* may be read as a
counterpoint, a protest against the maniacal conformity of
the postwar years. Caleb Trask is a powerful creation,
complex and fully fleshed; he is, as Steinbeck noted in his
journal, 'the Everyman, the battleground between good and
evil, the most human of all, the sorry man'.

Steinbeck had moved, in his fiction, far beyond the simple
realism of the Thirties. While he had not been able to
command the allegorical mode as fully as he might have
liked, he was once again bravely experimenting, trying to
press the limits of the possible. His novel, which critic John
Timmerman places wisely within the tradition of what he
calls (lifting the phrase from Thomas Carlyle) 'supernatural
naturalism', is a tragic world from 'which God has
departed.'[19] Timmerman argues that it falls in the line of
novels of such writers as Stephen Crane and Theodore
Dreiser. Indeed, *East of Eden* is a bold, wildly ambitious, often
brilliant book that fails because it is nearly impossible to do
what Steinbeck had attempted here. Needless to say,
American literature would be poorer without it.

XVI

New Thinking About Writing

'I want to dump my technique, to tear it right down to the
ground and to start all over. I have been thinking of this a
lot. I think I have one answer, but I have not developed it
enough to put it down yet.'

Steinbeck to Elizabeth Otis, 17 September 1954

Almost immediately upon publication, *East of Eden* had
moved into number one position on most national bestseller
lists, including *The New York Times*. The amount of attention
this brought to Steinbeck unsettled him, as it usually did. He
was by nature a private man who did not enjoy being singled
out, and who distrusted all forms of outward praise. The real
standard in his life was the one raised by Olive Steinbeck, his
mother, and he would never satisfy her. Every outward
success was bracketed, equivocal and unearned. What was
given with one hand was taken away with another, as indeed
the critics only too willingly proved to him over and over.

Following the usual pattern in the wake of a major
publication, letters and phone calls began to deluge him.
Perhaps to distract himself, he joined the campaign for Adlai
Stevenson, who was challenging the popular Dwight D.
Eisenhower that year for the US Presidency. 'We felt very
strongly about Stevenson,' Elaine says. 'His ideas and politics
coincided with ours. John wrote speeches for him and
contributed ideas for speeches in later years. We later became
friends, but we didn't really know Adlai at first. Not in 1952.'
Stevenson was, indeed, a New Deal Democrat much like
Steinbeck; he was also a well-read, sensitive, intelligent man,
a rare bird in the context of American political life, where (as
in the cases of Harry S. Truman or Ronald Reagan) one often

succeeds by pretending to be 'just another guy'. Stevenson was definitely not just another guy, and his defeat in 1952 was taken in a curiously personal way by Steinbeck, who wrote to him shortly after the election:

> I hope you will have rest without sadness. The sadness is for us who have lost our chance for greatness when greatness is needed. The Republic will not crumble. But for a little while, please don't reread Thucydides. Republics have – and in just this way.
>
> It has been an honor to work for you – and a privilege. In some future, if you have the time and/or the inclination, I hope you can come to my house and settle back with a drink and – tell sad stories of the death of Kings.
>
> Thank God for the impeachment provisions.
>
> Yours in disappointment and in hope.[1]

There is something both naive and charming about this letter. Here was a man who believed that 'greatness' was still possible among politicians, and that a truly 'great' man would make the Republic well and whole again. (One continues to hear this sentiment every four years in the United States: if only a 'great man' would get elected, the vast interlocking bureaucracy that President Eisenhower dubbed 'the military-industrial complex' would begin to look human, compassionate, even rational.) One also notes the mildly ingratiating attitude of Steinbeck; he had met plenty of famous people, including movie stars and kings, but he especially liked the idea of knowing a presidential candidate. In later years, he would place immense stock in his connections with Lyndon Johnson.

One can only speculate about this need to attach himself to the high and mighty. It may have had its origins in John Ernst's lack of authority. The elder Steinbeck's weakness had been a huge embarrassment, and the way the community had been forced to rally around to save a member of the burgher class who could not take care of himself and his family like other men must have affected Steinbeck deeply, telling heavily in his relationships with Thom and John, neither of whom ever 'measured up' to their father's expectations. Steinbeck was perpetually seeking out a 'man's man' with real authority: Ed Ricketts, Adlai Stevenson, Lyndon Johnson. The chain is a long one, and none of them quite satisfied his needs.

As we have seen, Steinbeck often suffered from post-novel anxiety, a familiar syndrome among writers. And *East of Eden* had taken a lot out of him, although his suffering now was nothing like that which followed *The Grapes of Wrath*. He continued to go to his desk most days, writing pieces of journalism for magazines and trying to sketch out ideas for the musical version of *Cannery Row* which he and Frank Loesser had been discussing in an off-hand way for some time. By Christmas, it was obvious to him that this project would never work, and a new idea for a novel set in Monterey began to play in his mind: the blurred beginnings of *Sweet Thursday*. Writing to Dook Sheffield just before Christmas, he adopted a self-reflective tone:

> I had never expected to make a living at writing. Then when the money began to come in it kind of scared me. I didn't think I deserved it and besides it was a kind of bad luck. I gave a lot of it away – tried to spread it around. Maybe it was a kind of propitiation of the gods. It made me a lot of enemies. I was clumsy about it I guess but I didn't want power over anyone. Anyway that was the impulse. And it was wrong.[2]

The Steinbecks began 1953 in style with a trip to the Virgin Islands. 'John wanted to clear his head after *East of Eden*,' Elaine recalls. They had originally intended to go on this holiday with Steinbeck's lawyer, Arthur Farmer, who was dying of cancer, but Farmer died before the plan could be realized. The Steinbecks instead invited a new friend,

Barnaby Conrad (a writer who shared Elizabeth Otis as an agent) to go with them. When they arrived in St Thomas, however, Steinbeck was appalled to discover that the hotel did not overlook the water; on top of this, there were no good beaches around for swimming or fishing. So Elaine and Conrad went off in search of a better hotel, leaving Steinbeck to mope in his room. 'We had to go to the neighbouring island,' Elaine says, 'to St John, where we found some lovely beach houses at Caneel Bay.'

Frank Loesser wrote to Steinbeck in St John, urging him to continue with the idea of transposing *Cannery Row* to the stage. Loesser, of course, had considerable experience with musical drama, having written the songs for *Guys and Dolls* and other major productions. Steinbeck agreed to stick with the project, and when he returned to New York in February, sun-tanned and strong, he sat down with his Dictaphone and began to work again. But it was no good. With much chagrin, he told Ernest Martin and Cy Feuer, the producers who wanted to back the project, that he was not comfortable in writing in this form in the wake of the failure of *Burning Bright*. 'I think it was painful for him that his plays didn't do better,' says Terrence McNally. 'He loved everything to do with Broadway, with plays, and he seemed to enjoy the company of theatre people. He especially liked opening nights and would dress for them in a top hat and cape; it was the sense of occasion and spectacle.' Steinbeck decided to turn the material that would have been the new version of *Cannery Row* into a short novel: the form in which he felt most comfortable. He would begin the book after a visit to Nantucket with Thom and John during their school vacation in March. (Elaine decided to visit her family in Texas during the same period, thus giving her husband some time alone with his sons.)

The visit to Nantucket was a brief replay of the summer they had spent there so happily. Steinbeck once again found the island exhilarating, with its windswept beaches, rocky coastline and vast sky. He rented a Jeep so that he and the boys could run around the island at will, and devised wonderful entertainments for them. They collected driftwood and built fires on the beach and took long walks, sometimes scaling the rocky cliffs; they climbed the nearby lighthouse one day to meet the keeper and drove into town the next for a visit to the ice cream parlour. As usual, Steinbeck amused the boys with his cooking: corned beef hash, spaghetti and hamburgers were his main dishes, and the food had a way of scattering everywhere – on the walls, on everyone's clothes. With fatherly patience, he worked with the boys every day, making sure that whatever task they began (making their beds or sweeping the kitchen) they finished. In the evenings he sat them down before a log fire with mugs of hot chocolate while he read aloud from Stevenson's *The Black Arrow*, which had been among his own childhood favourites. This was, perhaps, his most successful attempt at fathering, one Thom and John would remember for years afterwards.

Having had an unusually good time with his sons, Steinbeck returned to New York in a fine mood, ready to begin in earnest on the novel, which he tentatively called *Bear Flag* after the cathouse at the centre of the story. Ernest Martin remained involved in the project, urging Steinbeck on. The idea was that he would write his novel in a form that could be swiftly adapted to the musical stage. By the time summer came, he was so involved in the little book that he decided not to go back to Nantucket with the boys as previously planned; instead, he would stay in New York to concentrate on his work. (Again, the strain between the demands of his craft and 'career' and the needs of his sons clashed, to the disadvantage of the children.)

It was hot and humid that summer, with temperatures soaring to 90°F most days. Steinbeck sat in his study without a shirt, a fan blowing on his back as he wrote, swooning himself back in memory to Monterey, to memories of Pacific Biological, Ed Ricketts, the friendly whores and bums who became his friends. He was trying to put the story of Doc and the boys into a form that would harmonize his needs as a writer of fiction with the peculiar demands of Broadway musical theatre, and this was not going to be easy. The two genres are, perhaps, mutually exclusive.

Much of the responsibility for the children fell on Elaine's shoulders, and one senses a mostly repressed undercurrent of resentment in her voice: 'I was busy with Thom and John and, of course, Waverly,' she says. 'Gwyn, as usual, caused as much trouble as she could manage. There was always some sort of crisis with Gwyn. She wanted to make everything as difficult as she could. There was just something wicked about this. But John was patient. He knew what she was like, and it was very important for him to have the boys with him for part of the year.'

By September, Steinbeck was fed up with New York and decided to rent a seaside house in Long Island, near Martin and Feuer, who spent their summers in the Hamptons. He found a large, shambling Victorian house in Sag Harbor, a picturesque fishing village that would become increasingly important to him in later life. The boys had gone back to Gwyn, and Elaine stayed behind in New York with Waverly for the first week. Steinbeck remained alone in the big house, writing to Elizabeth Otis about the delicious atmosphere of Sag Harbor at this time of year: 'The fall is coming quickly, a chill in the air and a hoarse wind blowing over the water. This is my favorite time and I couldn't be in a better place for it. I'll get my first draft of *Bear Flag* finished this week.'[3] Indeed, he was reluctant to finish his last two chapters; writing the book had brought back strong, emotion-drenched images of Ed Ricketts and his youth in Monterey. Writing about Mack and the boys, about Doc and the lab, about the Bear Flag and Lee

Chong's grocery and the canneries themselves, he was filled with nostalgia for a world lost for ever.

Oscar Hammerstein had taken the early part of *Bear Flag* to England with him; in general, he was keen on the idea for this musical. Feuer and Martin had only to convince Richard Rodgers that the project was a good one. 'I hope they will do it,' Steinbeck said to Otis, 'but I have my fingers crossed.' The thought of a successful Broadway musical in the heyday of the genre must have been incredibly satisfying to contemplate. And there could be no better team to write the score and script than Rodgers and Hammerstein, who were at the peak of their fame, having virtually reinvented the Broadway musical in a range of shows from *Oklahoma!* through *Carousel*, *South Pacific* and *The King and I*.

The book was finished in rough draft by late September and sent to Otis and Martin. Meanwhile, the Steinbecks returned to New York for what proved a difficult season. Depression overwhelmed him now, as it did whenever a project was completed, and this was a particularly difficult time in his career. That *East of Eden* had been panned by so many critics still nettled him, and his confidence was shallow. On top of this he was suffering considerable anxiety about the future of *Bear Flag* on Broadway. Was it good enough? Or the right sort of material for adaptation? Steinbeck harboured deep reservations, though it was too late to do much about them. The project seemed to have its own strange momentum.

Not willing to let any sleeping dog lie, Gwyn continued to make endless demands on her ex-husband. She demanded more money, and she complained about the way he 'ignored' the boys. On top of everything, Elaine was becoming restless: it was not easy to act as go-between and negotiate endlessly with Gwyn on her husband's behalf. Was this *her* responsibility?

The pressures mounted, and Steinbeck fell mysteriously ill

in mid-October. 'Looking back on this incident,' says Elaine, 'it was clearly the beginning of the illness that eventually led to his death. He had several of what we called little "episodes". John would lose the nimbleness in his fingers, would drop a cigarette for no reason or a cup. He'd suddenly stumble or get confused. These were essentially small, very small, strokes, although at the time we didn't really know what was the matter.' He spent ten days at the Lennox Hill Hospital, where tests were conducted to determine what was wrong with him. One day it occurred to Elaine that many of her husband's problems were more psychological than physical. 'He was really sick, I knew that, but he was also a hypochondriac in a way,' she recalls. 'I decided it was better not to baby him even if he was sick, and one day I came into his room and saw him sitting up in bed and laughing and looking extremely well, and I said, "John, let's take you home. There's nothing wrong with you." '

A certain amount of tension arose between the Steinbecks because she believed he was pampering himself; he of course resisted her attempts to talk him out of his sickness. But he soon acquiesced and went home. The next week he signed on with a psychologist, Gertrudis Brenner (a friend of Elizabeth Otis), who helped ease him through this period of anxiety and depression. 'Gertrudis helped John enormously,' Elaine says. 'He was very secretive about it, but I was glad he was seeing somebody.' Elaine notes that her husband 'had a strong tendency to depression. He wasn't a classic manic- depressive, but he was borderline. When he was writing, he could be immensely cheerful. When he wasn't, he could become impossibly glum.' Steinbeck did exhibit behavioural patterns often identified with manic-depression, such as the over-use of alcohol to counteract uncomfortable mood swings.

'It is a restless time for me between jobs,' Steinbeck explained to Dook Sheffield in November.[4] At one time he found that he could write himself through these slack periods by composing letters to friends; now, he told Dook, he found writing letters difficult. 'There is a vast difference between writing letters and answering letters,' he explained. There were still endless letters to respond to: requests for interviews, fan letters, business letters, but this sort of correspondence was unappealing. Awaiting word on the fate of *Bear Flag*, Steinbeck bided his time by writing short magazine pieces. No major projects loomed – a very odd situation for a compulsive writer like Steinbeck.

He and Elaine took a long winter vacation in the Caribbean, staying for the entire month of January 1954 at Caneel Bay on St John, a trip that would establish a yearly migratory pattern. 'This wasn't a fancy vacation spot in those days,' Elaine says. 'It was quite primitive; we were really cut off from the world.' During this month he spent much of his time in the water, snorkelling and diving with an aqualung. 'The sea is so beautiful here that it is heart-breaking,' he said. The company, too, was good: halfway through their stay on St John the economist John Kenneth Galbraith and his wife arrived. The Steinbecks and the Galbraiths had much in common: a love of sunshine and good food, an interest in liberal Democratic politics, and a pronounced distaste for Senator Joseph McCarthy and his House Committee on Un-American Activities. The couples would meet in late afternoon over cocktails for what Steinbeck called 'milking time', a period of gossip and good talk.

Plans for the musical picked up, and by the time Steinbeck left Caneel Bay he had a deal in hand with Oscar Hammerstein, who definitely wanted to write the book of the show. Richard Rodgers had agreed to write the music. The title shifted from *Bear Flag* to *At the Bear Flag Café* to *Sweet Thursday* (it would be called *Pipe Dream* in its final Broadway incarnation). Steinbeck suddenly had reason to be optimistic about his future on Broadway, although he found himself unable to settle down to work. As often happened in these situations, he decided to hit the road. Travel wakened the creative sap.

He and Elaine decided to go to Europe for several months, 'following the spring', as he said, as the season of greening proceeded northwards from the Mediterranean through Spain and France into Scandinavia. Their chief destination was Spain, which Steinbeck had found compelling on his last visit. 'I feel an affinity there,' Steinbeck wrote to Dook Sheffield, 'Mexico is a kind of fake Spain.' Steinbeck would drive himself this time, picking up a new Jaguar in Gibraltar. He had vaguely in mind the idea of writing a book that paralleled the travels of Don Quixote, and he planned to visit La Mancha and other places which had associations with Cervantes. From Seville, in mid-April, he wrote to Elizabeth Otis: 'Am rereading Cervantes. He lived here and was in prison here and the city has not greatly changed. The little square where we drink beer and eat shrimps he mentions many times. The prison where he served was about a block from the bull ring and his window looked out on the Tower of Gold, which is still there.'[5]

He delighted in the manners and eccentricities of the local people, especially the gypsies. Once, for example, he let a gypsy shine his shoes; the fellow managed, subtly, to rip off the heel of Steinbeck's left shoe, which he then offered to repair for a price. 'It was a good trick,' he wrote to Otis in admiration. When he ripped off the right heel, Steinbeck was less amused and gently scolded the man. 'In a way I love the gypsies,' he said. 'They are so uncompromisingly dishonest.'

He had applied for life insurance in New York before leaving on this trip and was stunned to receive a letter in Madrid saying that he had been turned down. The doctor who examined him had discovered an abnormally small heart, which meant it would have to work excessively hard to keep the author's large body going. Steinbeck was appalled by this news and determined to have the situation looked into more thoroughly by a specialist in Paris. 'It was on the trip to Paris that John had another of his episodes,' says Elaine. They were just entering Blois, in France, when he became flushed and weak. They quickly checked into the hotel, where he lay on the bed, his forehead speckled with perspiration. Within a short while, his eyes rolled back into his head and he became unconscious. 'It was terrifying,' says Elaine, 'but the hotel called a doctor, who arrived in a short while.' The doctor, and a young American man who was staying at the hotel, remained by Steinbeck's bedside all night. The next morning, the doctor examined him again and pronounced him well, attributing the symptoms to sun-stroke. In retrospect it seems clear that Steinbeck had experienced another small stroke, entering a pattern of intermittent ill health that would last until his death just over a decade later.

The French reading public continued to adore Steinbeck, as they still do. 'When you ask a Frenchman about American writers,' Graham Greene said, 'they invariably put Steinbeck at the top of the list. He has exerted a strong pull on the French mind. And they do not discriminate between the early and the late Steinbeck – that's just a critical fetish that seems quite inadequate in this case. They like all of it.'[6] A popular French weekly, *Figaro Littéraire*, learned that Steinbeck was in Paris and invited him to contribute short articles and opinion pieces to their pages, and he gladly accepted. Journalism was relatively easy for him, and allowed him to vent feelings in a way that brought an immediate response from readers. Throughout the summer he wrote a piece every week, turning himself into a reverse de Tocqueville, recording his impressions of Paris in charming, often witty, prose. 'I will offer you Paris,' he said in his first piece, 'perhaps not as it is, but as I see it.' And he did, much to their enjoyment.

The Steinbecks stayed first at the Hôtel Lancaster, then

moved into an elegant house on the Avenue de Marigny; this was next door to the Rothschilds and across the street from the French President, and came complete with housekeeper and cook. 'How's that for an address for a Salinas kid?' he wrote in boyish candour to Oscar Hammerstein. It was there that Steinbeck learned that his friend Robert Capa had been killed in Vietnam, having stepped on a land mine only days before he was scheduled to leave the country. 'This death was horrible for John,' says Elaine. 'Really horrible. He and Bob had grown close, and he took the death very hard. He got extremely depressed, and everyone felt worried about him.' One suspects that Steinbeck, in mourning Capa, was also mourning himself, having recently come face to face with his own mortality.

Despite his depression, life went on, with various friends, such as Pat and Dorothy Covici, passing through. Thom and John, who were now 'like small men with incredible bodies and quick wits', came to Paris as soon as the school year was over, creating a flurry of child-oriented excursions and activities. But Steinbeck felt extremely shaky in the wake of Capa's death and his own failing health. The heart problem now became a focus of his anxiety, and he was frantic about what lay in store for him. He also struggled consciously with his depression, corresponding about his problems with Gertrudis Brenner, who wrote him reassuring letters. Some relief came after he received the diagnosis of a well-known French cardiologist, who told him that, given his age and state of anxiety, he was a relatively healthy human being. Steinbeck begged Elizabeth Otis to excuse him for his continual grousing in his letters home, 'Get one flat tire and you want to throw the whole thing away'.

In the meantime, he was fêted by the Parisians, who were made aware of his continued residence in their beloved city by his articles in *Figaro*. The French Academy held an extremely formal dinner in his honour, and he was interviewed by streams of journalists and sought out by young French writers and literary scholars. Apart from writing, his daily life included playing with the boys, swimming and walking excursions in the countryside. The plan was that Gwyn, who was staying in Rome, would take the boys in August and return with them to New York in the autumn.

Steinbeck was blissfully out of the United States for the publication of *Sweet Thursday*, which Viking issued on 10 June 1954. It has often been said that reviewers hated the novel, but a survey of the notices suggests that the novel received, on balance, a favourable response, with many reviewers finding something to admire in it. On the negative side, *Time* (14 June) attacked the book as reading 'like stuff that has been salvaged from the wastebasket', and Ward More in *The Nation* (6 November) said that Steinbeck was no longer 'the poor man's Hemingway' but had become 'a slightly raffish Faith Baldwin'. On the other hand, the anonymous reviewer in the *Times Literary Supplement* (26 November) concluded that 'Mr Steinbeck's handling, deft and casual, gives the book very often a quality of inspired idiocy, a genuine hare-brained charm.' Edward Weeks in *The Atlantic Monthly* (August) described the novel as 'a postwar continuation of *Cannery Row*, every bit as juicy and relaxed as the original'. Harvey Curtis Webster in *Saturday Review* (12 June) thought the book 'better than *Cannery Row*', singling out for praise its 'uninhibited gusto'. As for the book's rather obvious faults (sentimentality, exaggeration), he said, 'Steinbeck is the most uneven excellent writer of our times.'

Sweet Thursday has often been seen as an attempt by Steinbeck to recapture the success of *Cannery Row* and *Tortilla Flat*. This impression is easily understandable, since the novel resurrects characters and places from the earlier fiction. Western Biological Laboratories, the Palace Flophouse, the

Bear Flag Restaurant, La Ida Café, Lee Chong's grocery, the abandoned boiler in the vacant lot that was formerly the residence of Mr and Mrs Sam Malloy – the props are all in place. But this novel is very different from its predecessors and may be seen as crucial to Steinbeck's developing *oeuvre* in the way it extends and complicates his shifting fictional portrait of Ed Ricketts. In the new novel, Doc has returned from the war to Cannery Row, after serving out his time as a sergeant. Irresponsible fishing practices have, alas, devastated the town of Monterey. Mack and the boys are still there, but Gay has been killed in the war and the inimitable Lee Chong has sailed off to the South Seas on a schooner. Dora Flood, the wonderful madam of the Bear Flag, has died in her sleep. Now Fauna, her older sister, has taken control of the business. All is not well in the enchanted village.

Doc, meanwhile, feels dislocated and depressed. Even science has ceased to thrill him. Mack and the boys decide that he 'needs a dame', and they come up with Suzy – a floozy of no discernible outward virtue but a heart of gold. Having turned up in town unexpectedly, she was magnanimously taken on by Fauna at the Bear Flag. The central plot of the novel concerns a matchmaking effort by Fauna in concert with Mack and the boys to yoke Suzy and Doc, an unlikely scenario which is nevertheless successful in the end. Like *Cannery Row*, *Sweet Thursday* builds towards a final party at which discordant elements of the plot are reconciled.

A cynical reading of the plotline would read: boy meets girl; girl and boy fall out with each other through simple misunderstandings; misunderstandings are cleared up; boy and girl live happily ever after. It's the stuff of musical comedy, quite literally and should be judged within these specific generic boundaries. 'You should think of my novels as musical comedies without the music,' P. G. Wodehouse once replied to his critics, who condemned his plots as 'weak-headed'. Readers never castigated the brilliant

Wodehouse for writing Wodehousian books, and one should not condemn Steinbeck for a book like this one. The question is, how successfully does he accomplish what he set out to do?

Like its predecessors, *Tortilla Flat* and *Cannery Row*, *Sweet Thursday* operates at several removes from the 'real' world. When V. S. Naipaul griped that Steinbeck had 'turned the Row into fairyland',[7] he missed the point. Steinbeck was not always writing realistic fiction; he was rarely writing such a thing. His imagination was puckish, and he worked by charm, incantation, invocation and philosophical musing. Nor was his vision static: one sees the image of Monterey and Doc shifting from book to book, for example. The clear-eyed, practical Doc Burrows of *In Dubious Battle* elides into the stuffy and naive Dr Phillips of 'The Snake', who becomes the wise Doctor Winter of *The Moon Is Down* and, of course, the protean Doc of *Cannery Row* and *Sweet Thursday*. As Peter Lisca has said, 'It is difficult not to see these changes in Doc's attitude toward life and toward his work as corresponding to shifts in Steinbeck's own attitude. The relationship of Doc and marine biology is just as significant and symbolic to Steinbeck as that of the bullfighter and the art of bullfighting or the fisherman and his fish is to Hemingway.'[8]

'Doc was changing in spite of himself,' Steinbeck writes in *Sweet Thursday*, 'in spite of himself, in spite of the prayers of his friends, in spite of his own knowledge.' He has been attacked by 'the worm of discontent'. He throws himself into his work, hoping to distract himself from the knowledge of his uneasiness with the world, hoping 'to smother the unease with weariness'. But this effort fails. 'And sometimes, starting to turn over a big rock in the Great Tide Pool – a rock under which he knew there would be a community of frantic animals – he would drop the rock back in place and stand, hands on hips, looking off to sea. . . .' Even as he peers into his microscope in the lab, a voice rises within him, crying,

'Lonesome! Lonesome! What good is it? Who benefits? Thought is the evasion of feeling.'

'We think by feeling. What is there to know?' asks Theodore Roethke, writing at the same time as Steinbeck. This distrust of the intellect was rampant among American writers in the Fifties, a time when fear of the atomic bomb loomed large and the Korean war seemed to portend an endless sequence of local wars bursting like blisters on the scab of the Cold War. On a more personal level, one can see that Steinbeck had placed considerable faith in Ed Ricketts, as in the theories of Boodin, Ritter, and others. Non-teleological thinking was fine; but here he was, a man with a bad heart who could suddenly see what looked disturbingly like a *telos*, an end to life. Perhaps Steinbeck realized that the only thing that survives, finally, is love: a romantic truth that undergirds *Sweet Thursday*, his most romantic novel.

At the end of the book Doc is saved emotionally by his union with Suzy, the ex-whore. Worldly success comes to him, too; he is awarded a research grant in recognition of his scientific achievements. But this is nothing compared to the satisfacton he finds in love. (It is tempting that Steinbeck's attitude was in part a response to the fact that he had finally found love himself, with Elaine.) Indeed, Doc postpones further biological research for the time being and settles back to enjoy his life with Suzy. As he idles away his time with her, his specimens die, impeding the progress of his scientific career. But he now seems genuinely relieved: 'He had worn thin the excuse of his lack of a proper microscope. When the last octopus died he leaped on this as his excuse . . . "you see, I can't go on without specimens, and I can't get any more until the spring tides." ' Life, it seems, is more than hard work and speculation. It involves commitment, which requires imagination and daring. This is the hard truth at the core of this charming, lyrical and somewhat cartoonlike novel.

*

The Steinbecks sadly packed Thom and John off to Rome and their mother on 1 September, making final preparations for leaving Paris themselves. 'Time in Paris is closing up now. Filled with the restlessness of ending things,' he wrote to Otis in a note filled with melancholy.[9] He and Elaine would travel to London a week later, and from there they too would go to Italy. This was in some ways a good period for Steinbeck: he was in love with Elaine, his health appeared to be improving, and *Sweet Thursday* had found a fair number of admirers among the critics; furthermore, the book was selling briskly, and would soon emerge as a Rodgers and Hammerstein musical on Broadway. The Eliza Kazan film of *East of Eden* (starring James Dean) had just been completed, and word was spreading that it was a masterpiece of film-making. Its success could hardly fail to increase Steinbeck's literary stock.

In London, staying in a suite at the Ritz, Steinbeck began to contemplate the art of fiction again, grappling with basic issues. He wrote a remarkable letter to Elizabeth Otis on 17 September:

> When a writer starts in very young, his problems apart from his story are those of technique, of words, of rhythms, of story methods, of transition, of characterization, of ways of creating effects. But after years of trial and error most of these things are solved and one gets what is called a style. It is then that a story conceived falls into place neatly and is written down having the indelible personal hallmark of the writer. This is thought to be an ideal situation. And the writer who is able to achieve this is thought to be very fortunate.
>
> I have only just arrived at a sense of horror about this technique. If I think of a story, it is bound automatically to fall into my own personal long struggle for technique. But the penalty is terrible. The tail of the kite is designed to hold and in many cases drags it to the earth. Having a technique,

is it not possible that the technique not only dictates how a
story is to be written but also what story is to be written? In
other words, style or technique may be a straitjacket which is
the destroyer of the writer. It does seem to be true that when it
becomes easy to write the writing is not likely to be any good.
Facility can be the greatest danger in the world. But is there
any alternative? Suppose I want to change my themes and my
approach. Will not my technique, which has become almost
unconscious, warp and drag me around to the old attitudes
and subtly force the new work to be the old?

I want to dump my technique, to tear it right down to the
ground and to start all over. I have been thinking of this a lot. I
think I have one answer, but I have not developed it enough to
put it down yet.

On the one hand, one detects in these sentiments a startling
lack of confidence in what he had thus far achieved as a
writer. A writer doesn't simply 'dump' a style, especially one
so highly developed as Steinbeck's, at this point in his career.
As usual, there is something of failed perfectionism in the
voice of this letter, which barely conceals an element of self-
contempt. On the other hand, how many writers of Steinbeck's achievement have ever been so willing to dismantle
everything, to attempt to begin again? Steinbeck was not
capable of doing what he wanted to do, and he understood
the threat of facility, wherein a writer develops a style of
writing that becomes a trap. T. S. Eliot makes a similar point
in the beautiful fifth section of 'East Coker'. 'So here I am,' he
says, in the middle of his career:

> Trying to learn to use words, and every attempt
> Is a wholly new start, and a different kind of failure
> Because one has only learnt to get the better of words
> For the thing one no longer has to say, or the way in which
> One is no longer disposed to say it. And so each venture
> Is a new beginning, a raid on the inarticulate
> With shabby equipment always deteriorating

> In the general mass of imprecision of feeling,
> Undisciplined squads of emotion.

Like Eliot, Steinbeck urgently felt the need to make a fresh start with the language, to pursue a 'raid on the inarticulate'. But how? The thought of writing plays nagged at him once again; he imagined a solution to his problem lay in the dramatic form. While in London, he and Elaine saw many new plays, and he wrote to Otis eagerly, 'I like the London theater so much. It is entirely different from ours. If I lived here I am sure I would want to be a playwright. Maybe I will want to anyway. Among other things I have thought it might be a good transition into the new thinking about writing.'[10] But this was not to be. Steinbeck had already travelled, with little success, the route of theatrical writing.

After two weeks in London, the Steinbecks ferried across the Channel to Brittany and began motoring south through France to Italy. They drove very slowly, staying in out-of-the-way villages, as Les Baux and Saint Paul de Vence then were. By October, they were in Rome, where a large cocktail party was held in Steinbeck's honour at the American embassy and followed by an elegant dinner party at the home of the American ambassador, Clare Booth Luce. It was in Rome that Steinbeck received word of Hemingway's Nobel Prize; he wrote to Otis that the news pleased him greatly, saying, 'He should have had it before this.'[11] Clearly, the hostile feelings about Hemingway that had bubbled up from time to time in the past had been suppressed for the dignity of the moment. Steinbeck was becoming what Yeats called 'a smiling public man', with all the necessary adjustments of opinion and tailoring of feelings.

At the end of October, in the company of John McKnight, the head of the United States Information Service in Rome, and his wife, the Steinbecks travelled to Athens for a week of sightseeing. 'We left our car in Bari,' Elaine recalls, 'and took a ferry to Athens, where we chartered a sailboat for two weeks in the Aegean. This was an extremely pleasant time for us all, very relaxed and not in any way elegant. We did our own cooking on the boat and went ashore for sightseeing.' Steinbeck, of course, knew a good deal about sailing and loved to be around boats and the sea, so he was in his element. They returned to Italy for a final week on the Amalfi coast.

It was a powerful experience to return to the beaches of Salerno, where he had witnessed the landing of American troops a decade earlier. 'It looks different,' he wrote to Pat Covici.[12] 'They have planted little pines where it was all shell holes and blood. But the place still had a kind of horrid charge for me like a remembered nightmare.' 'I never did write what I really thought of the war,' he added. 'It would have not been encouraging to those who had to fight it.' The Steinbecks drove north along the tortuous Amalfi coastline, with its cliffs bunched up against the stark blue sea. The lemons on the trees hung like globes, and there were wild flowers blooming on the steep hillsides. They stopped overnight in Positano and, finally, pushed on into the compulsively prodigal city of Naples, where they boarded the *Andrea Doria* to New York, arriving home just before Christmas.

In January 1955 William Faulkner was visiting New York and was taken by Jean Stein, a patron of the arts and good friend to many writers, to have dinner with the Steinbecks at their townhouse. Steinbeck did not usually want to meet other writers, but he admired Faulkner and felt a certain pang of curiosity. Faulkner, for his part, loathed other writers and most formal occasions. He swallowed half a bottle of whiskey before arriving, and the results were unpleasant, as might be expected. 'Faulkner was clearly drunk,' says Elaine, 'his eyes were wide and his cheeks bluff. He heaved himself into John's leather chair in the study, and just grunted and muttered unintelligible things the whole evening. John tried very hard to communicate, and I did, too, but he either couldn't or wouldn't engage in conversation. When I asked him about one of his books, he snapped at me that he didn't want to discuss his books. We had a dreadful time with him.' When Steinbeck met Faulkner some months later, at a literary function, the great Southerner said, 'I must have been pretty awful that night,' and Steinbeck agreed with him. 'You certainly were,' he said, with a wink that put things right between them.

In February, the Steinbecks bought a house at Sag Harbor, on Long Island, which would become their permanent summer home. 'We saw an ad in the papers for a house on a cove,' Elaine recalls, 'and a real estate agent took us to see it. John wasn't impressed, but he happened to see another house out the window, a little house surrounded by lawn, flower beds, and trees. It overlooked the water on a small peninsula of its own. John said, "That's the house I want." The broker said, "It isn't for sale." But John insisted. The real estate man inquired, just to please us, and it so happened that the house was for sale. The owner had only just decided to sell it.' The house came with two acres overlooking the cove. There were huge oak trees and a grassy point with a view westwards to the town of Sag Harbor itself, only a mile away. The property was right on the water, and it came with a boat dock. 'I think the place reminded John of Pacific Grove,' says Elaine. 'It had all the right smells, the sounds of seabirds, the water views. And there was a large plot of ground for John to garden.'

The house was utterly flimsy: a typical summer cottage that had grown by addition. It was not insulated, but there was a large fireplace in the main living area, which had a high vaulted ceiling reminiscent of various places Steinbeck had occupied in California. He began immediately to make plans for reconfiguring the living area to become a general-use room, complete with bookshelves and a dining room table. A screened-in porch would be turned into a tiny sitting room. 'What John liked was the fact that the house had possibilities. It had yet to be imagined,' says Elaine. 'The main thing about it was really the sea. John had been longing to live near water.'

Buying a new boat and beginning work on the new house occupied Steinbeck through much of the spring. Inwardly, he was casting about for a new direction, wondering how he might strip back to essentials and begin again as a writer, but nothing obvious occurred to him. Elizabeth Otis put him in touch with Norman Cousins, editor of *Saturday Review*, in April, thus beginning what would prove a long and happy relationship between Steinbeck and that magazine. The experience of writing for the Parisian *Figaro* had pleased him, and now he decided to try his hand at regular journalistic essays for Americans. *Saturday Review* provided a perfect home for Steinbeck, who shared the magazine's liberal political and social outlook. Christened 'Editor-at-large', he moved into irregular rotation with other editorial writers, taking up such issues as McCarthyism, the role of the United Nations, the problem of juvenile delinquency, and other topical subjects. John Hersey recalls, 'John was highly opinionated, but his opinions were thoughtful and clear. He apparently liked to write in the short, essayistic form, and the results were fine. There was a large and admiring readership for these opinion pieces.'[13]

That June the Steinbecks moved to Sag Harbor for their first summer in the new house. After weeks of intense looking, Steinbeck found a boat that he loved and would spend many days out on the water, fishing and exploring the coastline. On 5 July, he wrote to Toby Street:

This afternoon, we are taking our boat off Montauk Point to fish for blues. They are fine fighting fish and wonderful to eat and they are said to be running well right now. It is about a forty-five minute run in our boat, which will do thirty-four miles an hour if it has to. It is a sea skiff, lapstrake, twenty feet long and eight feet of beam and a hundred horse power Grey marine engine. I could cross the Atlantic in her if I could carry the gasoline. Has a convertible top like a car so that you can put it up when green water comes over the bow. Also it only draws eighteen inches so we can take it into little coves and very near the shore if only we watch the charts for rocks and depth. This is fabulous boating country and fishing country, too.[14]

This is Steinbeck in his 'man's man' persona, a role that reaches back to his boyhood in Salinas and one he would occasionally adopt throughout his life. Like Hemingway, he felt the need to make his masculinity an issue, though one often detects an element of posing in this role. (One has to wonder if the macho vein wasn't adopted in opposition to John Ernst's lack of orthodox manliness and his withdrawn nature.) On the other hand, Steinbeck was genuinely interested in the outdoors, in fishing and boating; these activities had been part of his life since boyhood, and the move to Sag Harbor brought him exquisitely into touch with a deep aspect of himself.

Most mornings, Steinbeck would try to write, but he was unable to work steadily, 'I don't seem to be able to get down to hard writing,' he told Elizabeth Otis. He mentioned to Toby Street that he had begun another play, although nothing seems to have come of this project. For the most part, he was content to enjoy his new house, his boat and his garden. He often wandered into the village for a cup of coffee with the locals or took long walks by himself along the coastline. In July, he and Elaine debated the pros and cons of her daughter Waverly's impending engagement (this particular one didn't come off), and Steinbeck wrote a wise letter to his step-daughter designed to make her think hard about what she was getting herself into. His basic advice is contained in one question: 'After the hay, (and believe me I am not knocking it, I love it) is the other person fun?' He described sex to her as 'a kind of war', praising the 'quiet time after' which is 'about the only time when a man and woman get together and become one thing'.[15]

The Steinbecks returned to New York at the end of September, tense but excited about the Broadway debut of *Pipe Dream*. Three days after the rehearsals began, Steinbeck wrote to Toby Street, 'The show is in rehearsal and Lord! it's a good show. Fine score and book and wonderful direction and cast.'[16] He noted coyly that there was a line in the play about the Webster F. Street Lay Away Plan – a warm private nod to his old friend Toby. *Pipe Dream* was a musical that should have worked, but it was evident from the rehearsals and try-out productions in New Haven and Boston that something was wrong with it as it stood. When the Boston critics slammed the production, Steinbeck wrote in panic to Oscar Hammerstein,

> What emerges now is an old-fashioned love story. And that is not good enough to people who have looked forward to this show based on you and me and Dick. When *Oklahoma* came out it violated every conventional rule of Musical Comedy. You were out on a limb. They loved it and were for you. *South Pacific* made a great jump. And even more you were ordered to go ahead. But Oscar, time has moved. The form has moved. You can't stand still. That's the price you have to pay for being Rodgers and Hammerstein.[17]

In this and other letters, Steinbeck poured out suggestions for improving the play. Ethan Mordden, in his book on the musicals of Rodgers and Hammerstein, asks the big question: what went wrong?

> Steinbeck, who remained close to [Rodgers and Hammerstein] throughout the process and after, thought their version of Cannery Row wasn't salty enough. There's

a famous line here: 'You've turned my prostitute into a visiting
nurse!' That is, Suzy's activities in the Bear Flag are glossed
over in favor of the Big Scene in which she cooks soup for Doc
after Hazel has broken his arm. . . . Steinbeck also felt that the
show lost the tender tragedy of a truly noble guy who is also a
loser and who is compromising some of his nobility – he
fervently and quite hopelessly believes – by marrying a
whore. This is not to mention an abused but spirited woman
who reluctantly mates with a man who will always resent her
past.[18]

The show was revised again and again, but Steinbeck's
suggestions were largely ignored. On 30 November, ready or
not, *Pipe Dream* opened on Broadway at the Schubert (the first
time Rodgers and Hammerstein had not opened either at the
Majestic or the St James). The play was tepidly received by
the critics, and even though advance ticket sales amounted to
over one million dollars, a record-breaking sum, it ran for
only a lacklustre 246 performances, surviving that long only
because it was a relatively inexpensive production, as these
shows went, and because of a recent innovation: theatre
parties. Whole blocks of tickets were sold wholesale, ensuring a minimum audience from Thursday through Sunday
nights. 'Thus *Pipe Dream* managed to see out its season,'
writes Mordden, 'from November 30, 1955, to the end of June
1956. But there was no joy in Mudville, and no tour. . . .
Today *Pipe Dream* is forgotten.'[19]

Steinbeck wrote to Elia Kazan a few days after the opening:
'Well, thank God that is over. We didn't get murdered but we
got nibbled pretty badly. I guess that was the coldest-assed
audience I ever saw. They dared us and we lost. Then the
notices said just exactly what I have been yelling about for six
weeks and I think were completely just. R. and H. thought
they could get away with it. And do you know, for the first
time in their history, they are going to make some cuts and
changes. The crazy thing is that I have written all the changes

weeks ago and have turned them in. I don't know whether they will ever look at them, but they are there.'[20] He added, 'What really is the trouble is that R. and H. seem to be attracted to my kind of writing and they are temperamentally incapable of doing it.'

Whatever the reasons for the failure of *Pipe Dream*, it brought to an end John Steinbeck's fascination with the theatre as a vehicle for his imagination. The play he had been working on petered out quickly, and he scuttled back to fiction once again, where he felt more comfortable. What he had in mind, vaguely, was a satirical novel about what would happen if an intellectual (in this case an astronomer) became king. Set in the near future, *The Short Reign of Pippin IV* would be one of Steinbeck's oddest productions. But it would open a clear path to his last two full-length books: *The Winter of our Discontent* and *Travels with Charley in Search of America*.

The Consolations of a Landscape

'A novel may be said to be the man who writes it.'

Steinbeck to Otis, 26 April 1957

Steinbeck's interest in sailing blossomed, and the sea became an escape for him, a place where the phones didn't ring and no literary expectations haunted him. In the wake of the disastrous debut of *Pipe Dream*, he really needed to get away as far as possible. Charting a forty-five-foot sloop (complete with captain and crew) with John Fearnley, who had been casting director for *Pipe Dream*, he and Elaine set off in high style and higher spirits for a leisurely tour of the Windward and Leeward Islands.

This giddy group of escapees all adopted Calypso names for the trip's duration: Steinbeck was Inside Straight, Elaine was Queen Radio, and Fearnley was Small Change. Steinbeck wrote a teasing poem for his wife for New Year 1956, which began:

> Old style Elaine in a time gone by,
> Got a red hot yen for a lukewarm guy,
> She sit up river in Astolat
> Singing the blues for Sir Launcelot.
> She love him good and she love him here,
> But he buzzing the Queen Bee Guinevere.[1]

He retained this hoaxing mood throughout the vacation. 'It was a fascinating thing to travel with Steinbeck,' John Fearnley remembers.[2] 'He seemed to know everything – and about things you wouldn't imagine.' Fearnley would get up before everyone else, at about six, and sit on the deck with a book in his lap as the sun came up. 'I remember that John's bearlike head would emerge soon thereafter, popping through the hatch. We wouldn't say anything to each other, but he would go to another part of the deck and lie back against a sailbag and read. He was reading a novel by John O'Hara. As soon as we could smell the bacon cooking for breakfast in the galley below, he would holler, "Well, good morning!" ' They fished and snorkelled and sun-bathed on the deck.

Entirely on impulse, they dropped anchor one day off the tiny island of Saba and went ashore as tourists; word spread quickly as they went through customs that John Steinbeck was on the island, and the governor suddenly appeared and invited them to his house for drinks. 'He gave us some terrible drink – warm apricot nectar. The governor's house was nothing to write home about. He was most interested in selling his wife's needlepoint,' Fearnley says. One of the amusing anecdotes of this visit concerned a hideous purple handkerchief, which Elaine bought because of its very hideousness from the wife of the governor who had paraded her wares in hopes of a sale. A year or so later, when John Fearnley was presented with a copy of a new Steinbeck book, he found the purple handkerchief pressed quietly between its pages. Not long after, he gave the Steinbecks a house plant with the same handkerchief tied coyly around the stem. The purple handkerchief was thus passed back and forth until, in the mid-Sixties, the Steinbecks were given a present by Lyndon Johnson which, alas, contained the purple handkerchief (Fearnley had persuaded Lady Bird Johnson's press secretary to keep the joke going). Fearnley says, 'I can remember when Elaine called and said, "Do you know who gave me that purple handkerchief tonight? The goddamned President of the United States!" '

By February, the Steinbecks were sun-tanned, relaxed and

back in their house in Sag Harbor, now fully winterized. The idea of returning to New York City seemed unappealing, even unimaginable. Steinbeck wanted solitude to dig into his 'experimental' novel, a project which never amounted to anything. Instead, he wrote a short story – one of the relatively few examples of work in this genre written after *The Long Valley* – called 'How Mr Hogan Robbed a Bank'. It appeared in the March issue of *The Atlantic Monthly* and may be seen as a dry run for *The Winter of Our Discontent*, his last novel, because it concerns the moral degradation of American society, a theme which now came to absorb him.

'The main book he started working on now', Elaine says, 'was *Pippin*. He came up with this idea when we were in France the year before. I think it grew out of all those pieces John wrote for the French newspapers.' This tart political fantasy is about the re-establishment of the Bourbon monarchy in France. It took him by storm, and by March he was working on it daily and with great relish. 'It started as a short story,' Elaine says, 'then expanded into a short novel. I can't remember when John seemed to be having so much fun with a book.' To Toby Street, he wrote on 20 March, 'I started out gaily on my novel and then, without warning, an idea happened that so charmed me that I couldn't shake it out. It seemed easier to write it than to lose it. It is the wrong length, the wrong subject, and everything else is wrong with it except that it is fun and I could not resist writing it. I must say I do have fun with my profession, if that's what it is. I get real cranky when too many things interfere with it.'³

Steinbeck loved the isolation of Sag Harbor, which was too far out of the city for casual visitors, and in the midst of a snowstorm which dumped two feet of snow on the region he found it spectacular. The storm 'was beautiful and violent', he wrote to Toby Street, and it reminded him of the wilderness cabin at Tahoe, where he'd had to fight his way through huge snowdrifts to rescue the owner's library. That isolation, in his twenties, had been a resource; now, in his fifties, it brought him back to himself. And this time, he had Elaine for friendship, comfort and love.

There was, as ever, a darker side to things. Steinbeck's already acute sense of his mortality deepened this spring, largely because so many friends were ill or dying. Fred Allen, the comedian (and his younger son's godfather), died unexpectedly, and then his old friend Ritch Lovejoy underwent a serious brain operation, with almost no chance of recovery. 'We are getting to the age when the obit pages have a great deal of news,' he said to Toby Street. In the meantime, he was mentally preparing himself for the political conventions in Chicago and San Francisco, where he would assume the role of reporter for a syndicate of thirty-four newspapers. His current view of journalism was expressed in a letter to John McKnight:

> What can I say about journalism? It has the greatest virtue and the greatest evil. It is the first thing the dictator controls. It is the mother of literature and the perpetrator of crap. In many cases it is the only history we have and yet it is the tool of the worst men. But over a long period of time and because it is the product of so many men, it is perhaps the purest thing we have. Honesty has a way of creeping in even when it was not intended.[4]

Steinbeck was becoming less and less enamoured of the literary life, *per se*, and the posing typical of so many writers of his generation. In a letter of 16 May, 1956, he commented on a recent interview that Nobel-laureate William Faulkner gave to the press, saying that it turned his stomach. 'When those old writing boys get to talking about The Artist, meaning themselves, I want to leave the profession,' he said, 'I don't know whether the Nobel Prize does it or not, but if it does, thank God I have not been so honored.'[5]

Each day the Pippin manuscript grew and grew. He wasn't

sure of its literary value, but he found it very droll. By the end of April, a first draft was finished and sent to Elizabeth Otis for comment. 'The basic structure is there,' he explained to her, 'but it needs warming and softening and sharpening and, horrors, lengthening.'[6] The idea was that he would finish revising the novel before August, when he would plunge headlong into the political conventions. 'I want to have Pippin behind me,' he said.

The Steinbecks visited Louisville in April, having been invited south by Mark Ethridge, publisher of the *Courier-Journal*, whom he and Elaine had met on their most recent transatlantic crossing. The *Courier-Journal* would, in effect, sponsor him at the conventions and distribute his pieces to their syndicate. Ethridge, a Southern aristocrat and dandy who favoured white suits, panama hats and Cuban cigars – was throwing a Kentucky Derby party at his plantation house, which looked like a stage set from *Gone with the Wind*. The Steinbecks found themselves involved in a sequence of parties, with a great deal more drinking than was good for either of them. This was unfortunate, because both had given up their before-dinner cocktails in February. Steinbeck now felt, sensibly, that excessive drinking brought on the depressions which continued to plague him, and he planned to limit his drinking to weekends. He was also concerned about his heart. 'We began to substitute tea for alcohol before dinner,' Elaine recalls, 'and this worked very well for us. We only drank on Saturday nights, and even then we didn't drink as much as we used to do.'

Alicia Patterson Guggenheim and her husband, Harry, were among the many well-heeled guests at the Ethridge bash, and the beginnings of a friendship were made. The Guggenheims were the publishers of *Newsday*, the Long Island newspaper (which Steinbeck read on a regular basis when staying at Sag Harbor). 'John took immediately to Alicia,' Elaine recalls. 'They became the best of friends.' This friendship would lead to Steinbeck's involvement with that paper during the Vietnam War, when he served as a regular columnist.

The summer was devoted to finishing *Pippin* and, as in the past, to entertaining Thom and John, who moved to Sag Harbor for the season. Another distraction, one that irritated Steinbeck and caused a certain amount of tension between himself and Elaine, was Waverly's upcoming wedding to a man named Frank Skinner, whom she had met only recently. His attitude to the marriage is apparent in a letter to his English agent, Graham Watson: 'Our daughter is getting married on July fourteenth, and this astonishing occasion is being produced only a little less splendidly than Billy Rose's Aquacade. You can't imagine how many clothes you have to put on a girl when the sole purpose is to get them off.'[7]

Because of the wedding, Elaine had to spend a considerable amount of time in New York. Steinbeck, rather selfishly, resented it whenever her attention moved away from him; he was also petulant when Thom and John interrupted his work, as children will do. Here was a residue of the spoiled child of Olive and John Ernst Steinbeck, the only boy who lived in a family of women and expected adoration or, at least, attention. Throughout his later life he went through periods when, as in Salinas, he expected everyone's attention, and it upset him when it was not given.

He normally worked in the tiny second bedroom of the main house or in a garden shed when the weather permitted, but this summer he moved anxiously from place to place, trying to find a quiet spot to write in. Sometimes he wrote in his car or on his boat. (He bought a cabin cruiser in July for the express purpose of sailing out into the cove, dropping anchor, and writing in a place where nobody could interrupt him.) These were not the ideal circumstances for finishing *Pippin*; only through rigorous self-discipline did he manage to write despite the distractions. 'One of John's most useful personal traits was an unusual dedication to his work,' recalls Robert Wallsten. 'He could block out the rest of the world and really focus on whatever work lay before him.'

The wedding turned out to be more fun than Steinbeck had imagined. '[It] was very pretty,' he wrote to a friend, 'the bride truly radiant, the groom handsome and properly frightened, the reception a gala of the youth and gallantry and beauty of Texas and Manhattan. I think I handled myself with the proper mixture of gruffness and tears – a regular Lionel Barrymore. Seemed to me that Elaine was prettier than the bride.'[8] It's interesting that Steinbeck saw himself as 'acting', putting on masks of gruffness and sentimentality. One must not go too far in analysing such a glib reference, but a gulf does seem to have existed between the private man and the public man, a subtle estrangement from the 'real' world that probably began in Salinas, when to remove himself from Olive's watchful gaze he retreated to the attic bedroom, where he entered the world of his own fantasy. His sense of detachment from the public sphere would certainly have been exaggerated by alcohol.

On 10 August, the Steinbecks flew to Chicago for the Democratic National Convention. To make life easier for himself, he had hired a gopher: someone to run errands, stalk interviews, acquire gossip and check details. It was at a small political dinner party in Chicago that the Steinbecks met Adlai Stevenson in person for the first time. 'We became friends right off,' Elaine says, 'and we saw a lot of Adlai in the years that followed. John agreed to write speeches for people in the campaign as a way of contributing – he was one of a few writers who really wanted to help Adlai.'

Steinbeck loved being in the thick of fast-moving events, and he scurried around the convention floor, doing more legwork than he thought he would. Charles Whitaker, who worked for Syndicated Newspaper Editors at the time, says,

'Steinbeck was like a cub reporter: enthusiastic, tentative, eager to please us. He threw himself into this reporting in a way that surprised everyone. The pieces he wrote were anecdotal, full of wry observations. There wasn't much political analysis, but Steinbeck wasn't that kind of commentator. He was a novelist, so he made little short stories out of what he saw, and he saw a lot.'[9] Whitaker adds, 'What rather surprised me was how vulnerable he was. He kept saying, "I don't know if this is any good or not." Of course it was, I would tell him. It was amazingly good.'

The Democratic Convention was more exciting than the Republican, largely because the outcome was less certain. Adlai Stevenson did win in the end, but there was serious opposition. The major challenge came from Governor Averell Harriman, who had the support of former President Harry S. Truman, while a minor challenger was the youthful and witty Senator John Fitzgerald Kennedy of Massachusetts. Truman accurately predicted that Stevenson, if nominated, would take fewer than the nine states he had carried in 1952. But Stevenson did win the nomination, and selected Estes Kefauver as his running mate.

The Republican Convention took place a week later in San Francisco. As expected, Eisenhower and Nixon were nominated on the first ballot, which left nothing for the political pundits to write about. Whitaker recalls 'that John was a little relieved that he didn't have to bother with political intrigue among the Republicans. Instead, he wrote about the city itself, and the mix of people, the sights and smells. He was a wonderful observer of group behavior, too.' As ever, his interest in the phalanx rose to the surface. His last article was filed on 23 August, with a note to Mark Ethridge and James S. Pope (the publishers) saying, 'I have had fun, some of which I hope communicated. And I'm very tired because regardless of the irresponsibility of the copy, I have missed very little and have stood still for every nuance of these fantastic rituals of complexity. I'm pretty sure I shall not want to see another one.'[10]

San Francisco was close to home for Steinbeck, and he drove to Watsonville to see Esther before the convention was officially over. 'Esther had such a very beautiful farm,' Beth Ainsworth says, 'with fruit trees and rolling hills. The farmhouse was very old-fashioned. Esther had settled into being a farm wife, and John always liked to visit there. It reminded him of his Grandfather Hamilton's place, I think.' From Watsonville, they drove in their rented car to Pacific Grove. It was several years since he had seen the old family cottage on 11th Street, and Steinbeck was moved, although it shocked him to see that Monterey was such a different place now; Ed Ricketts was gone, the canneries were almost all closed, and the tourist industry had replaced what had recently been a genuine organic community. The Steinbecks did not stay long; they drove back to San Francisco, then flew to Hollywood for a brief sojourn that confirmed their distaste for the place. From there, they went to Texas to visit Elaine's family. Leaving his wife behind, Steinbeck continued on to New York, where he picked up Thom and John from Gwyn and returned with them to Sag Harbor.

The chief project before him was *Pippin*. In truth, he felt disgruntled by Pat Covici's lack of enthusiasm for the book. 'I know that he simply wants me to write *The Grapes of Wrath* over and over,' he complained to Elizabeth Otis. Covici had tried to convince Steinbeck to write a sequel to *The Pastures of Heaven* that would show what had become of its characters several decades later, but Steinbeck was tired of rehashing California: for better or worse, he had left that state behind. The people who once lived in the Salinas Valley, in Monterey, and in the little valley where he had set *The Pastures of Heaven*, were all gone. A different kind of Californian had moved in, and he had lost touch with them. Nostalgia, as he well understood, was dangerous for a writer. He wanted to write about France now, or Sag Harbor, to conjure and seduce the realities that stared him in the face or thickened his imagination.

Among the many distractions that autumn was the presidential campaign, and Steinbeck had to live up to his promise to write some speeches. Alan Lerner called one day, asking that he write a speech for Kefauver, and Steinbeck agreed, drafting it overnight. Before long he was asked to write speeches for Stevenson himself, although by mid-October it was apparent that the Democrats were going nowhere fast. Wherever one looked, the familiar smile of Dwight D. Eisenhower gleamed from posters and campaign buttons: 'I Like Ike' was the slogan of the day. Furious, Steinbeck blamed the ineffectiveness of the Democrats on 'their failure to say things straight' and their refusal 'to name names or face issues'. He found Stevenson's refusal to dig in and fight depressing. 'I wish to God they would let me write one violent fighting speech,' he said in a note to Elizabeth Otis near the end of the campaign.[11]

With the election over and lost, Steinbeck turned to his novel again, adding final touches to *The Short Reign of Pippin IV*. To Otis, he pronounced himself satisfied. The fact that Pat Covici seemed uneasy and believed that the novel wouldn't sell appeared to bother him little. 'There's a great unease about it at Viking,' he told Otis, 'but there's an unease all over and maybe one thing transmits to another.'[12] In passing he mentioned that he had another project in mind: a retelling of the Knights of the Round Table legends; in effect, he wanted to rewrite Malory in modern English. 'This was something he wanted to do for many years,' says his sister. 'The legends, King Arthur – these had been part of him since childhood. Malory was his first real author.'[13]

In late November, Steinbeck joined a programme called 'People to People', which the Eisenhower administration had organized. The idea was that prominent people in the US should make contact with private and prominent people in countries behind what Winston Churchill had famously called the Iron Curtain. This was, after all, the height of the Cold War, and massive propaganda efforts were being launched from both sides. Steinbeck, somewhat reluctantly, joined the writers' committee of People to People, which (improbably) was chaired by William Faulkner. Other writers on the committee included Edna Ferber, William Carlos Williams, Donald Hall, Robert Hillyer and Saul Bellow. One issue Steinbeck particularly wanted to discuss was the failure of the US to aid refugees of the Russian invasion of Hungary. (He had in tow a Hungarian writer, George Tabori, who argued for an airlift of refugees to the United States.)

One of the few tangible results of this committee had nothing at all to do with the Cold War. Urged on by Donald Hall, they put together a proposal to free Ezra Pound, the poet, from his imprisonment in St Elizabeth's Hospital. (Pound had been convicted of treason for giving aid and support to the enemy while he lived in Italy during World War II. Instead of jail or execution, he was put into St Elizabeth's – a mental hospital – in Washington.) Steinbeck, rather surprisingly, argued against the idea of liberating Pound, believing it would anger the American public and render the committee useless. But William Faulkner insisted, and Pound was eventually released.

Throughout the winter, Steinbeck threw himself into research for the Malory project, taking huge pleasure in the task. 'Working on the Malory is a thing of great joy to me, like coming home,' he told his English editor, Alexander Frere of Heinemann.[14] He became an amateur historian, visiting the J. P. Morgan Library regularly to examine their collection of medieval manuscripts.

The Morgan Library has a very fine 11th century Launcelot in perfect condition. I was going over it one day and turned to the rubric of the first known owner dated 1221, the rubric a squiggle of very thick ink. I put a glass on it and there imbedded deep in the ink was the finest crab louse, *pfithira pulus*, I ever saw. He was perfectly preserved even to his little claws. I knew I would find him sooner or later because people of that period were deeply troubled with lice and other little beasties – hence the plagues. I called the curator over and showed him my find and he let out a cry of sorrow. 'I've looked at that rubric a thousand times,' he said. 'Why couldn't I have found him?'[15]

Reading through various books on Malory, Steinbeck hit on the notion that the Englishman may have gone to Italy as a mercenary soldier at one point in his career, and in a fanciful moment he decided to go to Italy to check this out. To help finance this quixotic expedition, he got his friends at the Louisville *Courier-Journal* to take on some travel pieces in the tradition of Mark Twain's *Innocents Abroad*. He promised nothing but 'lies, inaccuracies and whoppers'. How could the *Courier-Journal* resist?

Steinbeck's sister, Mary Dekker, was still very close to him, and she joined her brother and his wife aboard the *Saturnia* on 25 March, bound for Naples. It was a cold and wet crossing, and when they got to Italy the weather was no better. An Italian spring is not always something to be desired. Steinbeck was exhausted by the journey; in Naples, he wittily remarked to the press, 'Naples now had a ruin second only to Pompeii, namely me.' The threesome travelled to Florence, where the icy rain continued. 'We spent most of our time in bed, trying to stay warm and dry,' Elaine recalls. Three weeks later, they moved on to Rome, where Steinbeck was desperate for a crack at the Vatican Library. He wrote back to Otis that this was the most exciting place he ever saw, full of 'Manuscripts by the acre and all beautifully catalogued'.[16] He was greedily accumulating a large fund of Maloryana, and his enthusiasm for the project seemed to increase each day. On 26 April 1957, he wrote to Otis:

> Malory has been studied as a translator, as a soldier, as a rebel, as a religious, as an expert in courtesy, as nearly everything you can think of except one, and that is what he was – a novelist. The Morte is the first and one of the greatest of novels in the English language. And only a novelist could think it. A novelist not only puts down a story but he is the story. He is each one of the characters in a greater or a less degree. And because he is usually a moral man in intention and honest in his approach, he sets things down as truly as he can.[17]

'A novel may be said to be the man who writes it,' he continued, making a point that would seem to justify the art of biography. Most novelists deny the autobiographical element in their fiction, but Steinbeck argued in this letter to Otis that 'a novelist, perhaps unconsciously, identifies himself with one chief or central character in his novel'. He calls this character the 'self-character', claiming to know which in each of his novels was this person. 'Now it seems to me that Malory's self-character would be Launcelot,' he writes. 'All of the perfections he knew went into this character, all of the things of which he thought himself capable.' Steinbeck conceives of the autobiographical persona in a novel as an ideal projection, a goal of sorts, a dream of the moral self enacted on the page.

Meanwhile, back in the US, *The Short Reign of Pippin IV* was published to the usual flux of reviews, some finding it 'delightful', others preferring to bemoan the loss of the man who could once write *The Grapes of Wrath*. The reviews, Steinbeck complained to Otis, 'follow exactly the old pattern I am so used to, celebrating old books which the same people raised hell with when they were printed'.[18] Much to the surprise of Viking, the book sold well and was taken as a Main Selection of the Book-of-the-Month Club, which guaranteed a wide audience.

The book is a mixed bag. Set sometime in the not-too-distant future and subtitled *A Fabrication*, this political fantasy concerns the consequences of the restoration of monarchy in France. There is no plotline to speak of; rather, a loose assembly of episodes spoofs everything from current French politics to Texas millionaires to teenage girl novelists. This topicality almost necessarily limits the appeal of *Pippin* for later readers, though Steinbeck's high spirits remain appealing. Pippin Heristal, the amateur astronomer and 'codiscoverer of the Elysée comet', is a remarkably funny character who just happens to live in the exact house in Paris where the Steinbecks lived the year before: 'Number One Avenue de Marigny . . . above stables, very elegant with carved marble mangers.'[19] These seem appropriate quarters for the future saviour of his country, as it were. Descended from 'the holy blood of Charlemagne', he is called on to unite the forty-two squabbling factions that have failed to govern France.

Steinbeck's deep, even sentimental, romanticism is evident. Pippin is born of royal blood, and his house, we are told, 'was built as the Paris headquarters of the Knights of St John', a medieval order of Crusaders based in Malta and devoted to chivalrous acts, such as caring for the sick and homeless. For this reason, they were known as the Hospitallers, although their failure to live by their original moral principles led to their demise; in 1236 Pope Gregory IX threatened to excommunicate them. The point of all this is that Pippin is associated with a group whose original moral vision was severely eroded. That Pippin should now engage in the revitalization of his country is meant to suggest an era of moral rebirth, one founded on the ancient Christian principle of being one's brother's keeper.

For Pippin, ignorance is bliss; he hadn't realized into what a bad state his country had fallen. Desperate for advice on how to govern, he goes in search of his Uncle Charlie – Charles Martel, a dealer in 'unsigned paintings' and 'art and bric-a-brac'. Failing to get anything from this source, he tries his daughter's American boyfriend, Tod Johnson, son of the Egg King of Petaluma, California. He is described, with irony, as 'the ideal young man'. To help Pippin, he dreams up the idea of selling French titles to Texas oil millionaires. As usual, Steinbeck is wonderful when poking fun at his own countrymen. (The most amusing American in the novel is Willie Chitling, a Hollywood producer who 'built the entire bar in his ranch house at Palm Springs with the furniture, paneling, and thirteenth century altar from the chapel of the Chateau Vieilleculotte'.) Meanwhile, Pippin's tediously bourgeois wife, Marie, retreats into a relationship with her schoolfriend, Sister Hyacinthe, a former nude dancer who became a nun because her feet were killing her. Pippin's teenage daughter, Clotilde, is a novelist (she published her first book at fourteen, *Adieu Ma Vie*) in revolt 'against everything she could think of'.

The influence of musical comedy is again clear. *Pippin* is an even more fantastic satire than *Sweet Thursday*. Part meditation on the good life (a familiar Steinbeckian theme), part study of political and social corruption, the novel gestures in too many directions at once. There is, however, a serious undercurrent as Steinbeck attacks the decline of values which he believes is ruining both France and America. Pippin, a mock king, reminds his countrymen (and Steinbeck's readers) of this older way of thinking, clearly threatened by materialism and simplistic thinking in many forms. In the context of Steinbeck's developing *oeuvre*, *Pippin* is an important prelude to his strong last novel, *The Winter of Our Discontent*, in which the failure of public virtue predicates the dismantling of private virtue.

*

The Steinbecks went back to Florence in early May, where they ran into Robert Wallsten, an actor-turned-writer, in a café. 'Robert and I had known each other since the early Forties,' Elaine says. 'We had worked together on a production of Sheridan's *The Rivals*. He and John started their friendship in Florence.' Wallsten says, 'It was an extremely memorable meeting, partly because John gave me a rather curious present: a switchblade knife. I didn't know what to do with it!' Wallsten and his wife saw the Steinbecks regularly, 'We often went to the theatre or out to dinner, that sort of thing,' he says. 'John was simply the kindest, most charming man. He had a lovely sense of humour, and he played wonderful practical jokes. There was something about him very childlike at times, that freshness, a feeling that he was discovering the world every day.'[20]

Spring had burst forth with a vengeance, bathing Florence in a warm, yellowy light; flowers bloomed in every pot and garden, scenting the air. Steinbeck took long, meditative walks along the Arno, stopping to sit at outdoor cafés with a cup of foaming *cappuccino*. One thing heavily on his mind was the fact that Arthur Miller, a good friend, had been indicted by the government for refusing to testify before the House Committee on Un-American Activities. The situation was made all the more poignant by the fact that Miller's play, *The Crucible* (1953), had implicitly and devastatingly compared the activities of Joseph McCarthy's committee to the Salem witch hunts. Before he left for Europe, Steinbeck had written in Miller's defence for *Esquire*:

> If I were in Arthur Miller's shoes, I do not know what I
> would do, but I could wish, for myself and for my children,
> that I would be brave enough to fortify and defend my
> private morality as he has. I feel profoundly that our
> country is better served by individual courage and morals
> than by the safe and public patriotism which Dr Johnson
> called 'the last refuge of scoundrels'.[21]

A few days later, on 16 May, he elaborated on the Miller case in a letter to Pat Covici:

> I feel deeply that writers like me and actors and painters are in difficulty because of their own cowardice or perhaps failure to notice. When Artie [Arthur Miller] told me that not one writer had come to his defense, it gave me a lonely sorrow and a shame that I waited so long and it seemed to me also that if we had fought back from the beginning instead of running away, perhaps these things would not be happening now.[22]

That same month, he was invited by PEN, the international association of writers, to attend their Tokyo meeting the following September, and he accepted. This was in part to protest the fact that such an international conference of writers could never take place in the United States, where entry visas were often refused on the grounds of political beliefs or affiliations. (Graham Greene, for instance, was regularly turned down for entry into the States, as were such different kinds of writers as Iris Murdoch and Gabriel García Marquéz.) What kind of 'free' country was this? Steinbeck wondered to his friends, noting that Socrates would have been kept out of America for consorting with delinquents and Sappho for her homosexuality. Thomas Jefferson would probably not get into America were he living in this century. As John Hersey notes, 'A quality of naive optimism, of romanticism, existed in John. He could not accept the simple injustices that the world constantly throws in our faces. I suspect the ironies and harsh realities of American democracy upset him badly.'[23]

From Florence, the Steinbecks went to Rome, which in May was at the height of its glory. Brief articles poured from his pen for the *Courier-Journal* and *Saturday Review*, while Elaine took photographs to accompany a piece he intended for *Holiday*. Throughout this Italian visit Steinbeck remained in close touch with the United States Information Service (USIS), which helped him gain entry to various libraries. In late May, the embassy in Rome held a dinner for about fifty people in Steinbeck's honour. He made a vivid impression on a number of Italian writers, including the novelist Alberto Moravia, who said, 'We knew the work of John Steinbeck very well. Only Hemingway was better known of the current American writers. But Steinbeck seemed to us, somehow, more serious. He was political and philosophical. Hemingway was a writer of surfaces by comparison. I went to dinner with him at the embassy, and I was impressed. He was grave, but his eyes were very gentle. He had courage and dignity.'[24]

Steinbeck's sister, Mary, separated from her brother and sister-in-law to travel on her own. Elaine comments, 'We liked her very much, but she was something of an odd duck. Her husband had been shot down and killed in the war by friendly fire, and she was a little spooked by Italy, I think. John felt very close to her. She was intelligent and well-read but more conservative than John – and more conventional in a lot of ways. In later years she would often travel with us or visit us when we were abroad.'

They moved on to Stockholm, where Steinbeck met with Mikhail Sholokhov, who wrote *And Quiet Flows the Don* and *The Don Flows Down to the Sea*. Sholokhov was a slender, middle-aged man with thinning blond hair streaked with grey. He had a wide smile, with a gold tooth in front that gleamed eerily. A young man who acted as his secretary and interpreter accompanied him. Sholokhov assured Steinbeck that his books were greatly admired in Russia, even though his work was officially in disfavour because of the author's professed anti-Communism. This meant, in effect, that his books had to be circulated underground. As usual, Steinbeck visited his old friend Bo Beskow and sat for another portrait in oils. He also had a long, gregarious dinner with Dag Hammarskjöld, the writer and diplomat, whom he had met several times on previous trips to Sweden and in New York. The plan had previously been to sail back to the United States from Sweden, but Steinbeck now wanted to go to England to continue his research on Malory.

After a few days of theatre-going and socializing with old friends in London, the Steinbecks took a train to Manchester to meet Professor Eugène Vinaver, who held a chair in Medieval Literature at the University of Manchester. Steinbeck had read Vinaver's books (and he often worked from Vinaver's annotated edition of Malory), and he wanted to talk with him in person about their mutual subject. Vinaver was shy but welcoming; he quickly volunteered to help Steinbeck in any way he could. A day after this cordial meeting, which took place at Vinaver's large Victorian house in Manchester, Steinbeck wrote to thank him:

> I cannot tell you what pleasure and stimulation I had in meeting and talking with you. I carry a glow from it in the mind as well as well-defined gratitude for your hospitality which was princely. Just as Launcelot was always glad and returned to find that a good fighting man was also a king's son, so I am gratified to know that the top of the Arthurian pyramid is royal. Having read you with admiration, I could not have believed it to be otherwise for I have been fortunate in meeting a number of great men and it has been my invariable experience that in addition to eminence, superiority has two other qualities or rather three – simplicity, clarity, and generosity.[25]

There is a deep wisdom in Steinbeck's formulation: simplicity, clarity, generosity. It was these qualities in a person that he admired and cultivated in himself. Though he had plenty of money, he lived in relative simplicity; his houses were not lavishly furnished, nor were they ostentatious. He adored mechanical things, which meant that he liked to have good cars and boats, but they were never purchased for show. Although he enjoyed 'dressing up' for the theatre or going out in New York wearing a top hat, with a satin cape and a cane, he dressed most days in khaki trousers and open shirts. Like Mark Twain, he thought it best to avoid all occasions requiring a change of clothes. Clarity, of course, was the essence of his art, and none of the convolutions or pretentious allusions associated with literary modernism can be found in his books. As so many people who knew him say, generosity was a trademark with him; he never forgot old friends, and he was always willing and eager to help them in periods of emotional or financial crisis.

Steinbeck rented a car in Manchester, and he and Elaine toured the west and north of England, visiting Warwickshire and other places associated with Malory. He devoured everything he saw, and Elaine took masses of photographs. They sailed home on 25 July, on the *Queen Elizabeth*, having stayed in Europe much longer than either of them had intended. 'But it was somehow an important journey for John, this one,' Elaine claims. 'Because of Malory, there was a focus. It was exciting for both of us. It clarified in John's mind the scope of his project, I think.'

Steinbeck wasn't in New York for a single day before he began to regret that he had accepted the invitation to Tokyo to attend the PEN conference, but he could think of no way to avoid going. He wrote to William Faulkner immediately for advice, recalling that he had been to Japan before. Faulkner replied in amusing detail:

> The thing to watch for is their formality, their excessive prolongation of mannerly behavior; I had to watch myself to keep from getting fretted, impatient, or at least from showing it, with the prolonged parade of social behavior, ritual behavior, in even the most unimportant and unscheduled social contacts. They make a ritual of gift-giving – little things, intrinsically nothing. I was always careful to accept each one as if it were a jade Buddha or

ivory fan, and return in kind, I mean with the same formality, giving the same importance not to the gift but to the giving, the act. . . . That's all you need remember. A culture whose surface manners are important to them; a people already sold in our favor; they will know your work by the time you get there much better than you will ever know theirs. They will really make you believe that being a writer, an artist, a literary man, is very important. Probably the nicest gift you can give is an inscribed book of your own.[26]

He flew out on the last day of August on a flight that lasted thirty-eight hours, arriving in 'a barrage of cameras usually reserved for M.M. [Marilyn Monroe]'. Elaine did not go with him, but he was rarely without company. John Hersey accompanied him, as did John Dos Passos. Hersey recalls, 'John was tired. He had just been travelling in Europe for several months, and he didn't want to go to Japan at all, not just then. The reporters drove him wild, begging for interviews. He was the only writer they seemed really eager to meet, and he dutifully talked to the press from dawn till dusk.'[27] At the conference itself, in the presence of the Japanese Prime Minister (who spoke for forty-five minutes) and the Mayor of Tokyo, Steinbeck delivered an impassioned address that lasted all of three minutes. The address was loudly applauded, and the Japanese newspapers published its contents on their front pages. Somewhat facetiously, he wrote home to Elaine, 'It has been compared to Japanese poetry and someone has set it to music.'[28]

Later in the week, he fell ill with an unspecified stomach flu. 'I couldn't keep down things I swear I never ate,' he told Elaine. Doctors flocked around him. Meanwhile, the conference moved on from Tokyo to Kyoto, leaving Steinbeck behind to recover in his hotel room. 'I saw enough of this first Congress to know it is my last,' he wrote home. 'I guess some people just aren't cut out for them.' He signed his letter Tokyo Rose.[29]

A day or so before he was scheduled to fly home, on 10 September, he felt well enough to tour the city of Tokyo and visit the Emperor's palace. (The Emperor had hoped to meet Steinbeck, and vice versa; the meeting, however, did not take place because of scheduling problems.) The weather was abominable: 'It's like swimming in warm blood, humidity 300 per cent,' he wrote home to Elaine. 'You don't breathe, you bubble.' He was acutely aware of the nuclear legacy of World War II: 'The feeling about the bomb is something. It is strange and submerged and always present. It isn't quite anger and not quite sorrow – it is mixed up with a curious shame but not directed shame. It is an uncanny thing – in the air all the time.'[30]

Hersey, who had written at length about Hiroshima and its devastation, comments: 'This was not such a long time after Hiroshima and Nagasaki, after all; just a little over a decade had passed. John was very much aware of the sensitivity of the Japanese people to this devastion, and it preyed on his mind. We sat together on the long flight home, and he kept dwelling on the subject with me. The very idea of the existence of the atomic bomb upset him, and it made him aware of the fragility of the human race and the desperate shortage of compassion in the world. He was particularly upset that Americans had so quickly and easily shrugged off those attacks.'

Steinbeck returned to Sag Harbor for several weeks, then moved back into the townhouse on 72nd Street, where he resumed work on the Malory project, poring over a microfilm of the Caxton edition he had acquired in England. He also began making notes towards a novel that would become *The Winter of Our Discontent*. His life fell back into the familiar pattern. 'He got up early, made a large pot of coffee, and went into his study. He would take regular breaks and take walks or go into the garden out back. There was always something that needed doing,' Elaine says. 'He didn't say a lot to me during the day. I was busy, of course. We didn't really talk until the evening, when we would sit for a pot of tea or a drink, depending on the day. Sometimes in the afternoons John would visit with Frank Loesser or with Elia Kazan. Loesser always cheered him up, but Kazan made him so damned depressed. In the evenings we often had dinner with friends or went to the theatre. John never lost his love of the theatre.'

Burgess Meredith had drifted away from Steinbeck by now. 'It was just one of those inexplicable things,' Meredith says.[31] 'We lived in different parts of the country. We moved in different circles.' But this December, as the year 1958 and icy weather approached, Meredith approached Steinbeck about the possibility of joining an expedition to the Caribbean. A friend of his by the name of Kevin McClory (who later hit the jackpot as a producer of James Bond films) believed he knew where a vast Spanish treasure lay buried off the coast of Nassau in the Bahamas. The idea was that several friends would go in with McClory to finance the expedition. For fun as well as profit, they would personally excavate the wreck and, if successful, make a film of their adventures.

The author of *Cup of Gold* could hardly resist such a larky adventure and signed up eagerly. Each member of the expedition paid his own way to Nassau, and they went in together to pay for the boat and diving equipment. It all proved rather expensive – more so than either Meredith or McClory had guessed – and Steinbeck saw that the entire project was a sham at once; he told Meredith that McClory was making a fool of everyone. 'I disagreed with John about this,' says Meredith. This was the beginning of a falling-out that never really repaired itself.

Steinbeck returned home disgruntled, with no gold in his suitcase. Adding to his troubles, Elaine had to have a fairly serious operation. Fortunately, the Malory research preoccupied him throughout the spring while Elaine went through the operation and recovery period; in March, he wrote to Elizabeth Otis that a 'curious state of suspension has set in, kind of floaty feeling like the drifting in a canoe on a misty lake while ghosts and winkies, figures of fog go past – half recognized, and only partly visible. It would be reasonable to resist this vagueness, but for some reasons which I will set down later, I do not.'[32]

There was a strange unreality about the Malory project. Like Pierre Menard, the character who rewrote *Don Quixote* word for word in a famous short story by Jorge Luis Borges, Steinbeck was trying to become Malory, to acquire every bit of knowledge he had, to enter totally into his world. This was not possible, of course; the project thus remained infinitely open-ended, tempting Steinbeck down any number of roads that led nowhere. 'I don't think any of the research on this project was wasted,' he hastened to add in his letter to Otis, 'because while I may not be able to understand all of Malory's mind, at least I know what he could *not* have thought or felt.'

In early April, when Elaine was fully recovered from her surgery, they moved back to Sag Harbor. 'The great problem with the house there was that John had no place to work if the children were staying,' says Elaine. He decided to build a study on the bluff overlooking the ocean, 'a cute little structure, six-sided, with windows looking in all directions'. It was designed to look like 'a little lighthouse. John had read somewhere that Mark Twain wrote in a six-sided study, and he wanted one just like that. The place wasn't even going to be big enough for a bed. He didn't want to sleep there. Just a desk and a chair, and a place for his manuscripts.' He later christened the workhouse Joyous Garde, after the castle to which Lancelot took Guinevere.

In June, Steinbeck decided to revisit England to make fresh contact with the soil that had nourished Malory. Somehow, the project kept petering out, and he needed something to inspire him. He and Elaine flew to London, where they met

Professor Vinaver. They visited Colchester together, then Winchester. In London, Steinbeck went alone to West-minster Abbey and the Tower of London, where by chance he met the playwright Robert Bolt (author of *A Man for All Seasons*), and they immediately hit it off. In another serendipi-tous meeting, he ran into John Kenneth Galbraith in a hotel lobby. Galbraith, who had been lecturing in Warsaw the week before, told him that he had met a student in Poland who said to him, aphoristically, 'Under Capitalism man exploits man, whereas under Communism it is just the reverse.'

Whenever Steinbeck travelled abroad without his sons, he worried and thought about them almost to excess. The boys were fourteen and twelve now, precarious ages, and Steinbeck sympathized, even identified, with them, recalling the agonies of his own adolescence. On 14 June, he wrote to John O'Hara about Thom and John:

> My boys are moving into the smelly, agonizing glory of
> manhood. I won't know the world they will inhabit. I just
> get glimpses of the life they live now. But the incredible
> gallantry of a child facing the complication of living with no
> equipment except teeth and nails, and accumulated instincts
> and memories that go back to the first activated cell in a
> house of plasm, never fails to astonish me. And I am
> amazed at their beauty, pure unadulterated loveliness. My
> boys have been going through the horror of disintegration
> about them and handling it with more wisdom and integrity
> than I could whistle up.[33]

In a painful moment of truth, he confessed that there was little in the way of direct communication between himself and the boys, although he did posit 'a deep and wordless love' that seemed to creep through from 'both sides of the barricade'. The tension with Gwyn never seemed to slacken, and Steinbeck told O'Hara that he was glad the boys were going away to a boarding school in the fall, to a place where they would be safely out of their mother's clutches.

Back in the States, Alfred Kazin, the critic, had recently struck a blow against Steinbeck that would have important negative ramifications. Kazin, who specialized in pompous sweeping views of the literary scene, had seized the occasion of a review of a critical book about Steinbeck (on the front page of *The New York Times Book Review*) to display his superiority by trumpeting Steinbeck's inferiority.[34] He argued that the writer had done very little of note after publishing *The Grapes of Wrath*, and he wasn't even so sure about that any more; this was followed by an attack on the later works, which he said were characterized by 'cuteness' and 'sentimentality'. He castigated the 'banal propaganda of *The Moon Is Down*'.

Pat Covici and Harold Guinzburg were outraged by Kazin's piece, and they wrote to Steinbeck in Britain about their feelings. Although he had not been especially incensed at first, Steinbeck became agitated. He knew that Kazin had enough power in the culture to make a particular argument stick, however simplistic. Indeed, to this day many critics, especially those within the confines of academe, dismiss Steinbeck rather casually, saying he wrote nothing of consequence after *The Grapes of Wrath*. The truth is that he produced some excellent work in each decade of his writing life, and that *The Wayward Bus*, *Cannery Row*, *Sweet Thursday*, *The Winter of Our Discontent*, and *Travels with Charley* add up to a diverse body of work almost any writer would be proud to own. These books are continuously rediscovered by readers around the world, and they deserve an audience unfettered by tedious and out-of-date arguments such as those put forward by Kazin.

Steinbeck returned to Sag Harbor in July and threw himself into the Malory project once again. He disciplined himself strictly, writing five days a week for a set number of hours and allowing no interruptions. But the project continued to give him trouble; he simply could not find an appropriate mode for the translation. Furthermore, he was restless, feeling cut off from his life as a writer of fiction. After a month of struggling, he gave it up for the time being to work on a novel which he tentatively called 'Don Keehan', a modern version of *Don Quixote*. Briefly, he was enthusiastic about this work-in-progress, trying to interest Elia Kazan in a movie version of the story. He even wrote to his old friend Henry Fonda to say that he was writing the story directly for him!

He worked steadily through the autumn on this book, remaining in Sag Harbor, where he felt extremely comfortable. 'My life is coming back now,' he wrote to Pat Covici on 17 October, waxing elegiac about the landscape. To John O'Hara he said, 'I grow into the countryside with a lichen grip.' And to Shirley Fisher, who worked with McIntosh & Otis, he wrote, 'It is getting lovely and cold out here now. Tonight the bay is smooth as milk and little curls of mist, millions of tiny white pin curls are rising about a foot in the air. It looks a little like a burning stubble field.'[35]

Throughout November he pounded away on 'Don Keehan', although he began to sense that the book was not going well. He felt guilty, too, about having spent so much time researching Malory only to abandon it when it was barely underway. Elaine understood his problem. One night she said to him, 'Are you troubled about not working on Malory?' He replied, 'Of course. Always troubled, even when I have explained it to myself.' She quickly suggested that they get away somewhere, to Majorca or Positano, anywhere. He lit up, and he said in an astonished voice, as if revelation had struck: 'Somerset – where it happened.' And that sealed it. They would go to Somerset in March so that he could sink into the atmosphere and rhythms of the place.

This, he felt sure, would light the necessary fire beneath him and his Malory project.

In December, the day after Christmas, he wrote to Pat Covici to say that he was abandoning 'Don Keehan' altogether:

> It isn't a bad book. It just isn't good enough – not good
> enough for me and consequently not good enough for you.
> It is a nice idea – even a clever idea but that isn't sufficient
> reason for writing it. I don't need it. The danger to me lies
> in the fact that I could finish it, publish it, and even sell it.
> The greater danger is that it might even enjoy a certain
> popularity. But it would be the fourth slight thing in a
> series.
>
> It would bear out the serious suggestion that my time for
> good writing is over. Maybe it is but I don't want that to be
> for lack of trying.
>
> Frankly this is a hack book and I'm not ready for that yet.
> To be a writer implies a kind of promise that one will do the
> best he can without reference to external pressures of any
> kind. In the beginning this is easier because only the best
> one can do is acceptable at all. But once a reputation is
> established a kind of self surgery becomes necessary. And
> only insofar as I can be a more brutal critic than anyone
> around me, can I deserve the rather proud status I have set
> up for myself and have not always maintained.[36]

The attack from Alfred Kazin had stung, and Steinbeck was painfully aware that he must do better. He was, perhaps, even overly self-conscious; 'external pressures' must also mean the pressure from critics like Kazin, who seemed to believe that a writer should always write the same kind of book. Steinbeck's last four productions may have been 'slight' in some ways, but not one of them was unnecessary. They formed a demonstrable part of his growth as a writer, reflecting his genuine concerns of the moment. Few writers in the history of American fiction have written with such self-willed fidelity to their experience – even when that experience was imaginary, as in *Pippin*.

After the New Year, 1959, Steinbeck spent seven weeks wrapping up whatever business was on hand: paying bills, finishing his few remaining journalistic assignments for *Saturday Review* and other magazines, and arranging for the rental of a cottage. Robert Bolt taught school in a village in Somerset, and found the perfect place for them: Discove Cottage, in the village of Bruton. 'It was an unbelievably pretty little house,' Elaine recalls, 'with thick stone walls and a thatched roof. It belonged to a manor house nearby. There wasn't any heat in it, but we had a fireplace and a coal stove for cooking.'

The Steinbecks sailed in late February, arriving in March in Southampton; in nearby Plymouth, they acquired a Hillman station wagon and drove to Bruton. 'At first, there was no refrigerator and no plumbing – these were added while we were there. It was all very primitive, but John loved it. It was just what he wanted, and what he needed.' There were two narrow stairwells at either end of the cottage which led to a sequence of bedrooms with low ceilings and damp walls. 'John bought a card table and set himself up in a small bedroom near the one where we slept.'

'It is a stone cottage,' Steinbeck wrote to Pat Covici.[37] 'It is probable that it was the hut of a religious hermit. It's something to live in a house that has sheltered 60 generations. My little work room on the second floor overlooks hills and meadows and an old manor house, but there is nothing in sight that hasn't been here since the 6th century. If ever there was a place to write the Morte, this is it. Ten miles away is the Roman fort which is the traditional Camelot.' He added, 'The whole thing is dream-like and I like the dream. I've had enough of so-called reality for a while. A few months of this and I will be a new person.'

Steinbeck set to work to make the cottage more habitable.

He bought weather-stripping from an ironmonger in the local village, and he tightened all the windows and doors, 'trying to seal out the creeping English damp'. He chopped wood for the fireplace and began making the ground ready for a garden. Before very long, it felt to him as though he had 'lived there forever', as he told Elizabeth Otis. Not until mid-April did he begin to write, taking long walks in the nearby fields and woods before going to his desk in the morning.

In late March he discovered dandelions in the fields and collected them for dinner several nights in a row. 'They are delicious. Do you ever eat them?' he asked Graham Watson. 'You cut the little plants at the place where the root branches out to a white bundle of stems – wash them and cook them slowly and for a long time with pieces of bacon. Don't taste them while they are cooking because they will be bitter, but when they are done, they are most delicious.' He added, 'Field mushrooms we shall not have until July, but the meadows are filling up with interesting things, many of which I don't know – but I will. I may even try some of the climbing strawberries.'[38] Here was a man in his element, delighted by the natural world at his doorstep, eager to explore and garden.

Steinbeck immersed himself in the life around him, painting the barn, creating garden plots, fixing things. The gardener of the manor house – a hard-bitten, red-faced man in his sixties – became a friendly adviser to Steinbeck on his various projects. (Steinbeck had won him over by proving he knew how to use a scythe.) He spent a certain number of hours each day poring dutifully over Malory. 'My work is going beautifully,' he reported to Graham Watson in March, 'and I didn't expect that for a long time – at least a month.'

Elaine was thrilled by her husband's response to his new surroundings: 'John's enthusiasm and excitement are authentic and wonderful to see,' she wrote to Shirley and Jack Fisher.[39] 'I have never known him to have such a perfect balance of excitement in work and contentment in living in the ten years I have known him.' The alternating black moods and periods of high anxiety passed; Steinbeck wrote to friends about his sense of well-being. He began to see his life in a new perspective, as a letter of 1 April to Elia Kazan suggests: 'You say that success is like a candy – quickly eaten. But the analogy is closer. The first piece is wonderful, the second less so. The fifth has little taste and after the 10th, our mouths long for a pickle to clear the sweet cloy away.'[40] He claimed not even to remember writing his most famous books, and so he could take little credit for them now. In recent years, writing had become a habit, a pattern of activity, and he had lost the 'flavor of trial, of discovery, of excitement'. Life had turned dusty in his mouth, giving him no joy. He said that he had come to Somerset, to Glastonbury, because 'it has been a holy place since people first came to it'.

He described his early morning routine: 'At about six in the morning a bird calls me awake. I don't even know what kind of bird but his voice rises and falls with the insistence of a bugle in the morning so that I want to answer, "I hear and I obey!" Then I get up, shake down the coal in the stove, make coffee and for an hour look out at the meadows and the trees. I hear and smell and see and feel the earth and I think – nothing. This is the most wonderful time. Elaine sleeps later and I am alone – the largest aloneness I have ever known, mystic and wonderful.'

He scolded Kazan rather sharply: 'Lift up your mind to the hills, Gadg. Criticise nothing, evaluate nothing. Just let the Thing come thundering in – accept and enjoy.' 'John was always upset by Kazan's carping. He often said that Gadg wore his talent like a hair shirt,' Elaine comments. Clearly, Steinbeck had come to a deep period of understanding. It was the landscape and history of Somerset that inspired this spiritual knowledge, but it could not have happened by chance. Steinbeck had, throughout his life (like most of us) flickered in and out of what might be described as a knowledge of the Tao, an awareness of a reality that transcends 'success'. As the thirteenth chapter of the *Tao Te Ching* says,

> Success is as dangerous as failure.
> Hope is as hollow as fear.
>
> What does it mean that success is a dangerous failure?
> Whether you go up the ladder or down it,
> your position is shaky.
> When you stand with your feet on the ground,
> you will always keep your balance.

On the last day of April, the Steinbecks visited the ancient mound where King Arthur supposedly held court. He wrote to Professor Vinaver about the experience: 'Yesterday I climbed to Camelot on a golden day. The orchards are in flower and we could see the Bristol Channel and Glastonbury too, and King Alfred's tower and all below. And that wonderful place and structure with layer on layer of work and feeling. I found myself weeping. I shall go up there at night and in all weather, but what a good way to see it first. I walked the circuit of the ramparts and thought very much of you and wished you were with me.'[41] Steinbeck had returned, imaginatively, to the enchanted garden of his California boyhood, where he roamed the hills near Salinas pretending to be King Arthur or Lancelot. The layers of sophistication acquired through more than a decade of living in New York City peeled away, exposing the Romantic core of the man. From across the Atlantic, however, the unromantic aspects of life intruded themselves rudely upon him.

His son John was having trouble in school, and Waverly, Elaine's daughter, had concluded that her marriage was a mistake; she flew to Mexico in late April for a divorce. 'John just wanted to keep these things out of his head so he could work,' Elaine explains. 'But it was always difficult. Things kept cropping up that would upset him.' To promote a sense of calm, visitors to Discove Cottage were kept to a minimum. Mary came for a couple of weeks, as might be expected, taking great pleasure in the English country setting. In July, Robert and Cynthia Wallsten came for a visit. But for the most part, Steinbeck managed to keep the 'real' world at bay.

The extent of his desire to sink into the past is revealed by his use of the quill pen. In a wonderfully idiosyncratic passage he wrote to Professor Vinaver in May:

> I always write by hand and my fingers are very sensitive to shapes and textures. Modern pencils and pens are too thick and ill-balanced, and you will understand that five to eight hours a day, holding the instrument can make this very important. The wing quill of the goose is the best for weight and balance, curve and the texture of quill is not foreign to the touch like metal or plastics. Therefore I mount the best fillers from ball points in the stem of the quill and thus have for me, the best of all writing instruments. When I find particularly fine quills I will send you one.[42]

Despite Steinbeck's fuss over pens, the Malory book was not going well. A few chapters had been sent back to Elizabeth Otis and Pat Covici, and their tepid response chilled him. It seems they had vaguely expected something like T. H. White's *The Sword in the Stone*, a romantic adventure story that might secure a big audience. Instead, Steinbeck offered a translation of Malory which failed to catch the poetry and swing of the original – itself, after all, a translation. Tellingly, Steinbeck's work ground to a halt at the point in the narrative where Lancelot allows his love for Guinevere to move from the platonic to the physical level, thus betraying Arthur, his king and friend. This unchivalric act is the moral crux of the story, of course, but Steinbeck did not feel happy with the option chosen by his favourite knight. He wanted perfection in his hero, the perfection Olive Hamilton Steinbeck had hoped for in her son. He did not, alas, find perfection in Malory, as he had never found it in himself.

He became quietly frantic, and with some trepidation decided in August to shelve the writing to concentrate on imbibing the atmosphere. He would build up a storehouse of impressions that he could draw upon when he returned to New York in the autumn. With the Wallstens and Elaine, he set off for Wales, touring the Wye Valley in search of Arthurian sights and relics. On the way home they stopped at Berkeley Castle to see where King Edward II was murdered. They also made various forays into the Somerset countryside, always in search of history.

In mid-October, very sadly, Steinbeck closed up the cottage in Somerset. He realized only too well that his quest for Arthur had failed: the Malory project was not a good one for him; he couldn't pull it off. Worse, the prospect of returning to the United States depressed him further. What would he do next? The contrast between the rural gleam of Somerset and the urban cacophony of New York City was more than he could bear to think about. 'It was just so hard to leave England that time,' Elaine recalls, 'John had discovered something about himself in Discove Cottage.' The question was, would he be able to put this self-knowledge to good use?

It Must Have Been Good

'Tom Wolfe was right. You can't go home again because
home has ceased to exist except in the mothballs of
memory.'

Steinbeck, *Travels with Charley*

The slope to death begins at birth, but for John Steinbeck the
downhill slant became much steeper on his return to New
York. Late in autumn 1959, Elaine was working in the kitchen
when she smelled something burning. 'I rushed up to the
third floor, where I had left John reading, and there he was
unconscious and smouldering. He had dropped a cigarette in
the bed, and it had set fire to the sheets and his pyjamas. I put
the fire out, woke him, and called an ambulance.' This turned
out to be another of his 'episodes', a small stroke. 'Looking
back, I can see how all of these incidents formed a pattern,'
Elaine says. 'At the time it wasn't so clear.'

The failure to turn the Malory project to account had
depressed Steinbeck mightily throughout the autumn, and it
may (as he believed) have contributed something to this
episode. For weeks afterwards, right up until Christmas, his
speech was uncertain; temporarily he lost the usual nimbleness of his fingers. He wrote to the Vinavers:

> Privately I think my recent illness was largely contributed to
> by the frustration of not being able to do what I wanted to
> do with the book. Such things happen. And nature has a
> way of using shock therapy. I reached a state of confusion
> out of which there was no exit except a dead stop. Perhaps I
> know parts of my theme too well and parts not well
> enough. I have tried to put the whole thing out of mind for

a while, perhaps to get a new start. Arthur is a terrible
master. If you don't give him your best, he wants no part of
you.[1]

Inwardly, he realized that the Malory project was stone dead.
Writing to Elizabeth Otis from Sag Harbor just after
Christmas, he said, 'I'm going to do what people call rest for a
while. I don't quite know what that means – probably
reorganize.' But, of course, rest was never something John
Steinbeck cared to do. He was a compulsive writer, so there
was no possibility of his not writing. Soon after the New Year,
he began working on *The Winter of Our Discontent*, a novel
which grew quite naturally out of his deep unhappiness with
the materialism and moral decay of the United States. The
stark contrast between New York and Somerset had, indeed,
triggered it.

On days when he didn't feel like working on the novel, he
turned to short stories or magazine articles. The arrangement
with *Saturday Review* was still in place, although he delivered
pieces on an entirely ad hoc and sporadic basis. He also
managed to do occasional short pieces for *Holiday* and
Esquire. 'I was so worried about him,' Elaine says. 'He was
suddenly very hesitant about things. He didn't even want to
go out on the boat by himself. But I couldn't stop him from
writing, of course. The work, I think, was part of his
recovery.' In March, he wrote to James S. Pope at the
Louisville *Courier-Journal* that he would like to do 'some Old
Curmudgeon pieces'. The tone of his novel obviously struck
him as one of testiness, and he guessed he might as well take
on the role explicitly. 'I'm in the middle of a book [*The Winter
of Our Discontent*],' he told Pope, 'and it is going swell and I
wouldn't interrupt it for anything, but there is always that
early morning when cantankerousness is the better part of
valor.'[2] The journalism offered a way of warming up before
he turned to the harder work of fiction.

Several universities offered him honorary degrees, but he refused. Rather puritanically, he felt there was no point in accepting a 'fake degree' when he had failed to get a 'real' one from Stanford. Even being offered these degrees appalled him: 'They mean nobody's scared of you any more. You can't bite the hand that sets a mortarboard on your head.' Waves of disgust for American society and the modern world in general coursed through his body, 'My poison glands are still producing a very high test kind of venom and I'll resist being a classic until they plant me at which time I will automatically cease to be one.'[3]

All through spring the novel unfolded, slowly but firmly. And it was good. He explained to Frank Loesser that *Winter* was 'part Kafka and part Booth Tarkington'. He hoped to finish it by summer:

> In the fall – right after Labor Day – I'm going to learn about my own country. I've lost the flavor and taste and sound of it. It's been years since I have seen it. Sooo! I'm buying a pick-up truck with a small apartment on it, kind of like the cabin of a small boat, bed, stove, desk, ice-box, toilet – not a trailer – what's called a coach. I'm going alone, out toward the West by the northern way but zigzagging through the Middle West and the mountain states. I'll avoid cities, small towns and farms and ranches, sit in bars and hamburger stands and on Sunday go to church. I'll go down the coast from Washington and Oregon and then back through the Southwest and South and up the East Coast but always zigzagging. Elaine will join me occasionally but mostly I have to go alone, and I shall go unknown. I just want to look and listen. What I'll get I need badly – a re-knowledge of my own country, of its speeches, its views, its attitudes and its changes. It's long overdue – very long.[4]

Elaine notes: 'This trip was just something John had to do. And he had to go alone. You see, he had been sick, and that had been very disturbing. Now he wanted to prove to himself that he was not an old man. He could take control of his life, could drive himself, and could learn things again.' John Hersey adds, 'That trip – the *Travels with Charley* trip – it was a turning point. One of many turning points in his life. John had spent so much time in Europe in the last few years, and he had been thinking about King Arthur and all of that. I suppose he realized that he had missed something. He wanted to get into touch with an earlier version of himself, the man who really knew America and Americans.'[5]

The idea for the trip had come from Elizabeth Otis, who thought it would put Steinbeck into contact with ordinary people and stimulate another novel, although everybody was worried about the mode of transportation. Meanwhile, he was working on *The Winter of Our Discontent* with a concentration much in contrast to the way he had worked on Malory. 'Usually when we were in Sag Harbor,' Elaine says, 'John got up fairly early and made coffee and walked Charley dog into the village. He would sit and socialize with the fishermen at the diner before strolling back to do some writing. But now he had to prove something to himself. He got up at six, and he went quickly to his workhouse. He talked very little about the novel. This was a very private book.' It was also his first (and only) book to be set in Sag Harbor, although Sag Harbor parallels Monterey in fascinating ways. It was almost as if he were writing about Monterey once again, a transposed east coast version of the town he loved so much.

In his role as Old Curmudgeon, Steinbeck had sent a letter to Adlai Stevenson from Somerset, in which he railed against the 'cynical immorality' of the United States. 'Having too many THINGS,' he said, '[Americans] spend their hours and money on the couch searching for a soul. A strange species we are. We can stand anything God and Nature can throw at us save only plenty. If I wanted to destroy a nation, I would give it too much and I would have it on its knees, miserable, greedy and sick.'[6] Belatedly, Stevenson had leaked this letter to the press; it was, indeed, reprinted in *Newsday*. The result was a mild furore in which people argued on both sides. Among the many voice speaking up for Steinbeck was his old acquaintance, the poet Carl Sandburg, who said, 'Anything John Steinbeck says about this country – about us as a nation – is worth careful reading and study. His record of love for his country and service for it is such that what he says is important.'[7]

Steinbeck did not let the controversy over his Stevenson letter distract him. He was stoking the fires of creativity now as the novel moved rapidly towards conclusion, frequently writing over two thousand words a day. For all this, he remained strangely reticent about this book in his letters, content merely to tell his friends that he was writing a novel and that it proceeded well. By mid-July, a rough draft was done, and he sent it immediately to Elizabeth Otis for comment. 'You won't find it like anything I've ever done,' he told her. Benson wryly notes, *'The Winter of Our Discontent* was indeed a strange novel to be coming from him – but what novel wasn't?'[8] Indeed, few writers have written such a diversity of novels and stories, working in a range of forms and genres from realistic fiction to fantasy to satire to musical comedy. More in the tradition of European than American writers, Steinbeck published novels, plays, essays, stories, screenplays, memoirs, travel articles, and a great deal of political and cultural journalism. As his collection of war reportage, *Once There Was a War*, demonstrated when it was repackaged as a book in 1958, he had also been a war correspondent of the first rank.

'John's mind turned sharply to the American trip that summer of 1960,' Elaine recalls. This was another election year, and – almost reflexively – Americans become more introspective as they move towards the polling booth, egged on by politicians and political journalists, who begin to ask questions about our goals and status as a nation. This trip across America was to be Steinbeck's way of taking the national pulse. On a more personal level, it was a way of proving that he still had it – as a man and a writer. The mode of travel recalled his earlier journey in the 'pie wagon' around California's Central Valley. In the past, his forays into the culture had yielded marvellous ore; this time, his journey would result in one of his most charming books, *Travels with Charley*.

'I remember John showing me his van, which he called Rocinante, after the horse in *Don Quixote*,' recalls John Fearnley. 'He was so proud of that vehicle. It was like a small house on wheels. He was like a boy, so excited by what he was going to do. It was Elaine who seemed frightened. But he knew he had to do this. She couldn't try to stop him.'[9] His departure was delayed by Hurricane Donna, which swept up the Atlantic coast late in summer. He describes this storm at the beginning of *Travels with Charley*: 'The wind struck on the moment we were told it would, and ripped the water like a black sheet. It hammered like a fist. The whole top of an oak tree crashed down, grazing the cottage where we watched.'[10] Steinbeck's boat at the time was a motor launch called the *Fayre Eleyne* – obviously his wife's namesake, and it suddenly broke loose from its moorings: 'She was dragged fighting and protesting downwind and forced against a neighboring pier, and we could hear her hull crying against the oaken piles.' The wind was registering over ninety-five miles an hour.

Steinbeck found himself running towards the bay, fighting the wind. Elaine, in protest, ran after him with a neighbour. 'Stop, John!' she cried, but he couldn't hear her. Helplessly, she watched as her husband (who was still, in her mind, recovering from a stroke) jumped into the water and fought his way through the spindrift towards the boat. He cut it loose and jumped into it. Miraculously, it started at a touch, and he steered it some hundred yards into the bay, where he dropped anchor in safe waters. 'Well, there I was,' writes

Steinbeck, 'a hundred yards offshore with Donna baying over me like a pack of white-whiskered hounds.' No skiff could possibly make it across that roiling sea. Suddenly, he saw a branch go floating by and jumped in after it. The wind was driving towards the coast, which meant he merely had to hang on to the branch and be washed up near shore. Soon Elaine and the neighbour were dragging him, still in his Wellingtons, out of the surf, and before long he was sitting at his kitchen table with a whiskey in hand to steady his nerves.

This little tale, so fetchingly told by Steinbeck, forms a paradigmatic moment: the author is caught in a storm, finds himself diving into the thick of it, bringing things around safely, letting himself go, drifting to safety, returning to Elaine and home having discovered something about himself. It's the classic journey of the hero in miniature, and it's equally a quixotic journey: the knight errant becomes, in effect, Sancho Panza himself – a canny doubling. The hero searches, as usual, for himself. Not surprisingly, Steinbeck christened his journey 'Operation Windmills'.

The storm damage had to be repaired before setting off; this included fixing a broken window and repainting the name ROCINANTE on the side of the truck. Clearing his desk, he sent a flurry of letters to old friends and put a few last touches to *The Winter of Our Discontent*, which he had been rewriting since he finished the first draft in mid-July. He did not want to leave any loose ends untied: his journey was going to last three months, and he would need a certain purity of mind and conscience to do the hard work of observation he planned.

He set off on the morning of 23 September 1960 with Charley to keep him company. 'I remember when he asked to take Charley Dog,' Elaine says. 'He said rather meekly, "This is a big favour I'm going to ask, Elaine. Can I take Charley Dog?" I said, "What a good idea! If you get into any kind of trouble,

Charley can go get help!" John looked at me sternly and said,
"Elaine, Charley isn't Lassie."' He drove north along the coast
into Massachusetts, where he stopped to see his son, John (who
was now fourteen), at the Eaglebrook School in Deerfield. 'The
first boy I saw on arrival was Cat [his son],' he wrote to Elaine.
'Rocinante was in the parking lot and everybody came to it – all
the teachers and Mrs Chase [wife of the headmaster], and I
made them coffee. It was fine. John acted as master of
ceremonies. . . .'[11] This was his first night away from home.

After a brief visit with John, he headed north to St
Johnsbury, Vermont, where he stopped for the night en route
to Maine. 'Deep Maine speech is not unlike Somerset,' he
wrote to Elaine on 27 September.[12] Maine, with its deep
woods and pastures, reminded him of parts of northern
California, and he drove to the northernmost rim of that
immense state: 'I wanted to go to the rooftree of Maine,' he
writes in *Charley*, 'to start my trip before turning west. It
seemed to give the journey a design, and everything in the
world must have design or the human mind rejects it.' This is
the born storyteller speaking, the instinctive shaper of reality,
the mind that naturally wants to scry the world's random
dots and discover a pattern.

Charley was Steinbeck's 'ambassador', drifting towards
people, 'toward the object', and bringing the world back to
the subjective author for inspection and re-imagination. As
Steinbeck weaved his way up and down the enormous state
of Maine, he filled his notebook with tidbits of memory,
historical reflection and philosophical musings. The form of
the journey-narrative was his natural mode, providing a tight
clothesline on which he could hang all manner of observations. *Charley* contains some of Steinbeck's very best nature
writing: 'In the short time since I had passed, the foliage of
the White Mountains had changed and tattered,' he writes.
'The leaves were falling, rolling in dusky clouds, and the
conifers on the slopes were crusted with snow.' (The Maine

chapter recalls Thoreau's beautiful *Maine Woods*, and reminds us that Steinbeck is best read as a far echo of the American Transcendentalist movement.)

By 1 October, his ideas were beginning to cohere, even though he told Elaine that he had 'no thoughts'. He had, instead, 'impressions'. 'One is of our wastes. We can put chemical wastes in the rivers, and dispose of bowel wastes but every town is ringed with automobiles, machines, wrecks of houses. It's exactly like the Christmas Eves I described – opened and thrown away for the next package.'[13] Decades in advance of the mainstream of the environmental movement, Steinbeck understood that we were trashing America; he also understood that this prodigality was part of a larger malaise. He saw that America had become a country of people without access to what might be termed a discourse of genuine spirituality (he did, of course, note and deride the bogus spirituality of charismatic fundamentalism). He observed the moral waste land of people living in the trailer parks, scattered along the roadsides of America like rootless floating pseudo-villages. 'These are Martians,' he told Elaine. 'I wanted to ask them to take me to their leader. They have no humor, no past, and their future is new models.' He added, 'If I ever am looking for a theme – this restless mobility is a good one.'[14]

One oddity is that Steinbeck's letters home, which he later used as notes for writing the book, are much more critical of America than anything that appears in *Charley*. He was not quite willing to become a Jeremiah, the shrill prophet of doom, in this memoir, although a subterranean note of criticism is an important addition to the book's texture and tone. The narrator of *Charley* is more connoisseur of chaos than harsh critic; indeed, he is deeply attracted to idio-syncrasy and irony and *kitsch*, which he finds in abundance along the road. Reading *Charley* one is reminded of *Lolita*, Nabokov's fictional travelogue, where the gaudy details of

American lower-middle-class life are held up to the glare like butterflies caught in the pincers of the cool-headed lepidopterist. *Kitsch*, especially, Steinbeck loved: things like Swiss cheese candy and seashell emporia and Dairy Queen roadside stands with huge bathtubs in front of them.

He took US 90 through Pennsylvania and Michigan, then drove up through Illinois. The symbolic midway point in the journey was Chicago – Carl Sandburg's 'city of big shoulders', a city Steinbeck decided to leave out of the narrative. He abandoned Rocinante for a couple of luxurious nights at the Ambassador East, a midtown hotel, with Elaine, who had flown in to meet him. 'John got awfully lonely on that trip,' Elaine recalls. 'That was the main problem, I think, though it doesn't really come out in the book much. He was homesick most of the time.' The couple planned to reunite again in Seattle.

Resuming his journey, Steinbeck headed west through Wisconsin ('the prettiest state I ever saw') and Minnesota. Everywhere he listened, asked questions, then listened again. Alone in Rocinante at night, he scribbled notes in his journal, and the anecdotes soon piled up. Stopping at a diner for breakfast near the Montana border, for example, he got to talking with a trucker who remarked that women drove the big trucks all by themselves during the war. 'My god, they must have been Amazons,' Steinbeck said. 'I don't know,' the trucker replied, 'I never fought one.'[15]

Steinbeck avoided most national parks and public monuments, preferring to seek out places of private meaning, such as the birthplace of Sinclair Lewis in Sauk Center, Minnesota. Everywhere he stopped he made an attempt to seek out 'the people' and garner their opinions, but he soon found that Americans had very few real opinions. East of the Mississippi, people tended to talk about baseball, west of the Mississippi their minds turned to hunting. America was not, and is not, a nation where rigorous dialogue and disputation find encouragement. Sports are the national distraction, designed to keep the mind of the nation preoccupied and away from dangerous subjects like foreign policy or the economic system. As Steinbeck began to realize this, he became alternately demoralized and angry.

The truth is that he began to lose interest in America and Americans as he moved from east to west. It is perhaps unfortunate that a profound unease does not come into the text itself; Steinbeck was not willing to go this far, preferring a thinly patriotic note: 'From start to finish I found no strangers,' he writes. 'If I had, I might be able to report them more objectively. But these are my people and this my country. If I found matters to criticize and to deplore, they were tendencies equally present in myself.' Turning the point on himself like this, Steinbeck took the sting out of what he had to say (and thereby lost the opportunity to write a truly great book about America).

While in Montana, he made one of his regular phone calls to Elaine. In the course of their conversation she commented on his chatty letters home, which he planned to use as the basis for his book, that they reminded her of Robert Louis Stevenson's *Travels with a Donkey*. 'That's it!' he cried. 'What?' she asked. 'My title! You've just given me my title: *Travels with Charley*.'

Steinbeck drove quickly from Montana to Washington – rather too quickly to soak up the landscape or discover the people; one reason for the haste, as the reader learns, was that Charley had been stricken by prostatitis and Steinbeck wanted him to be seen by a special vet in Spokane. With this accomplished, and the dog mending, he headed to Seattle for the reunion with Elaine, and they turned south together in Rocinante. 'We followed the coastline south, stopping overnight in the big redwood forests of Oregon,' says Elaine. 'It was so lovely. And then into California. John loved coming back home. We spent a few days in San Francisco, then we drove to Watsonville to see Esther and then to Monterey.' Elaine flew on to Texas by herself, but Steinbeck lingered in Monterey. 'I spent a couple of days with him there,' says his sister, Beth. 'He looked very tired. The visit with Esther hadn't gone too well; she had always been the sister least close to him, temperamentally, and they got into an argument about politics, and this upset him. Then one night we ate at a restaurant and we got so awfully sick with food poisoning. John kept saying that everything was different in Monterey, but that the sea never changed, the light never changed over the water.'[16] One of the startling revelations of that visit was a movie house near the old canneries named The John Steinbeck Theater. Steinbeck remarked about his return to California, 'Tom Wolfe was right. You can't go home again because home has ceased to exist except in the mothballs of memory.'

He missed Elaine so badly that he drove at high speed to Texas, meeting his wife in time for Thanksgiving dinner in late November outside Amarillo. They moved on together to Austin to visit her family, then he and Charley continued alone to New Orleans, where there was something Steinbeck had to see:

> When I was still in Texas, late in 1960, the incident most
> reported and pictured in the newspapers was the
> matriculation of a couple of tiny Negro children in a New
> Orleans School. Behind these small dark mites were the
> law's majesty and the law's power to enforce – both the
> scales and the sword were allied with the infants – while
> against them were three hundred years of fear and anger
> and terror of change in a changing world.

A group of women – white 'mothers', if that word may be used in this context – gathered every day to spit and jeer at the black children as they entered or left the school. They were known in the press, ironically, as the Cheerleaders, and

Steinbeck was curious to witness this spectacle for himself. Disguising himself as an Englishman, he told the people that he was from Liverpool, England, and joined the crowd outside the school. One taxi driver explained to him that it was the New York Jews who were causing all this trouble. 'Jews – what?' he asked. The man said, 'Them goddamn New York Jews come in and stir the niggers up.' The man proposed lynching the Jews, to Steinbeck's amazement and disgust.

Later that day, he was asked, 'Are you traveling for pleasure?' He replied, 'I was until today.' The sight of the Cheerleaders, the naked face of racism, left him with a 'weary nausea'. Some days later, in Alabama, he picked up a black hitch-hiker and was called a 'Nigger-lover' by someone in the street. In a poignant conversation with the young man, he discussed Martin Luther King and his 'teaching of passive but unrelenting resistance'. The young man revealed his impatience and frustration, saying, 'It's too slow. It will take too long.'

Steinbeck now dashed home to Sag Harbor, thus completing the entire journey in roughly eleven weeks. Having failed to capture the meaning of knight errantry according to Malory, Steinbeck had hoped to emulate Cervantes's great anti-hero, Quixote, 'who thought it fit and proper, both in order to increase his renown and to serve the state, to turn knight errant and travel through the world with horse and armour in search of adventures, following in every way the practice of the knights errant he had read of, redressing all manner of wrongs, and exposing himself to chances and dangers, by the overcoming of which he might win eternal honour and renown'.[17] But it would be a mistake to imagine that Steinbeck exposed himself to fate or tilted much at windmills.

What he accomplished on this two-month journey was, however, important to him emotionally, and it laid the groundwork for *Travels with Charley*, his last full-length book. This book coincided with Steinbeck's final major effort to rethink America, to come to terms with the soul of a nation which had been his major subject for three decades. His mood is reflected in a letter to Pat Covici:

> In all my travels I saw very little real poverty, I mean the grinding terrifying poorness of the Thirties. That at least was real and tangible. No, it was a sickness, a kind of wasting disease. There were wishes but no wants. And underneath it all the building energy like gases in a corpse. When that explodes, I tremble to think what will be the result. Over and over I thought we lack the pressures that make men strong and the anguish that makes men great. The pressures are debts, the desires are for more material toys and the anguish is boredom. Through time, the nation has become a discontented land.[18]

As Steinbeck pulled into his driveway in Sag Harbor, having circled the nation, he felt exhausted but pleased that he had accomplished the trip with no major problems. He knew that the real work still lay ahead of him: the composition of a travel book from fragmentary notes. But he was buoyant with the sense of personal accomplishment and began, almost immediately, to work on *Charley*.

The New Year began, publicly, for Steinbeck when he attended the inauguration of John F. Kennedy in January 1961. Kennedy liked to be surrounded by intellectuals and artists and made a point of inviting major writers, composers, performers and intellectuals of one kind or another to his festivities. Steinbeck normally avoided such occasions, but the lure of the Presidency was (for him) irresistible. He called his old friend John Kenneth Galbraith to see if they might attend the inauguration together, and Galbraith agreed. It so happened that Galbraith, who had become a kind of cultural guru for the New Frontier, was being tracked aggressively by cameramen, and Steinbeck found himself on-camera most of the day, much to his surprise and discomfort.

A few days after the inauguration he wrote to Kennedy in appreciation, saying he was 'profoundly moved by this ceremony'. He said that, for him, the President's address had 'that magic undertone of truth which cannot be simulated'. Kennedy responded warmly, saying that he only regretted that he hadn't been able to spend any time with Steinbeck personally. He added, in a charming postscript: 'No President was every prayed over with such fervor. Evidently they felt that the country or I needed it – probably both.'[19]

As usual, the Steinbecks flew off to the Caribbean for a winter holiday in February. This time they chose the Sandy Lane Hotel in Barbados, although Steinbeck did not find it much to his liking. The remnants of British colonialism upset him: the disparity between rich and poor, the subservience of the people. He wrote to his friends that he missed Sag Harbor, even in winter. As if to insulate himself from the island culture, he poured himself into *Charley*, beginning work each day at dawn in his hotel room and not breaking until lunch. His afternoons were spent on the beach with Elaine, sunbathing, swimming, and snorkelling. To Adlai Stevenson he wrote, 'The Fayre Eleyne progresses from high yellow to octoroon. I simply slough skins like a snake.'[20]

When they arrived home in New York, on 4 March, they were greeted by a surprise. 'There were Thom and John [Jr] just sitting on our doorstep, like orphans,' Elaine recalls. 'They had run away from Gwyn, and they said they wanted to move in with us. Of course we took them right in and agreed that from now on they could live with us.' Steinbeck had long been anguished by his failure to communicate properly with his sons, and he welcomed this turn of events. Perhaps now he could do the fathering that had eluded him.

Unfortunately, he had to turn around immediately and take another trip, leaving Elaine home alone with the boys in their shaken state. 'John had agreed to act as historian on a geological project,' says Elaine. 'He was supposed to witness a scientific expedition to Mexico called Project Mohole.' The goal of the project, in Steinbeck's words, was 'to take a core off the coast of Mexico at 12,000 feet'. As in the days of the Sea of Cortez expedition, Steinbeck grew animated; it was almost as if Ed Ricketts were alive again, and he was himself still young and ready to learn new things. He flew to San Diego and went out, with his hosts, Willard and Rhoda Bascom, aboard an experimental drilling barge, *Cuss I*. The barge and the preparations for the journey thrilled him, with 'trip-hammers going and pounding on the steel hull with sledge hammers and the engines all running, hundreds of them', he wrote home on 23 March. 'We are supposed to sail at dawn.' He was ecstatic, watching the mechanics and scientists at work, finding himself once again at the centre of purposeful activity. Two days later, he wrote home again: 'We are at sea now since last night, a heavy swell, towed by a tug and heavy weather on us. We are rolling like an old sow pig.'[21] They were ninety miles west of San Diego now, travelling at four knots. The next day they idled up into the buoys, which were already in position, and prepared to drill. Steinbeck took up his position in 'the gyroscope room just under the bridge', taking notes for an article on Project Mohole commissioned by *Life*.

The drilling was difficult, but by 2 April they had a sample of the earth's core for geologists to study. They managed to bring up 'a great core of basalt, stark blue and very hard with extrusions of crystal'. Steinbeck asked for a little piece of the crystal for a memento but was rudely pushed aside. Like a schoolboy, he stole a sample when nobody was looking. Later, to his embarrassment, one of the scientists presented him with a piece of the core. He felt compelled to sneak into the room where the core was kept and replace the bit he had stolen!

Steinbeck returned to Sag Harbor with Elaine in mid-April, the boys having been sent back to their schools. Once again he forged a daily routine conducive to getting his book written, rising at seven, drinking two or three strong cups of coffee, wandering into the village, returning by nine to work on *Charley*, which moved forward in fits and starts. In July, he wrote to Pat Covici without enthusiasm that the book was 'a formless, shapeless, aimless thing', adding ominously, 'it is even pointless.'[22] Then pieces of his travelogue were extracted and published, to considerable acclaim, in *Holiday*, boosting the author's confidence that he was on the right track.

One day in July he got a call from the London *Daily Mail* asking him to comment on the death of Ernest Hemingway. This was how Steinbeck first heard of the suicide. He wrote to Covici that he found it 'shocking', adding that Hemingway 'had only one theme – only one. A man contends with the forces of the world, called fate, and meets them with courage. Surely a man has a right to remove his own life, but you'll find no such possibility in any of H's heroes. The sad thing is that I think he would have hated accident much more than suicide. He was an incredibly vain man. An accident while cleaning a gun would have violated everything he was vain about.'[23]

The Winter of Our Discontent appeared in June, to a range of responses, some perceptive and others – those still in search of *The Grapes of Wrath* – blind to Steinbeck's originality. Carlos Baker, a longtime fan, reviewed the novel in *The New York Times Book Review* (25 June 1961), calling it 'a highly readable novel which bristles with disturbing ideas as a spring garden bristles with growing shoots'. Joan Didion, in the *National Review*, responded to Baker with a wickedly droll aside, '*Nada te turbe*, Carlos.' *Newsweek*, on the other hand, declared without reservation, (26 June), 'This is Steinbeck in his old, rare form,' a consistent strain in the reviews which echoed Saul Bellow's dustjacket blurb: 'In this book John Steinbeck returns to the high standards of *The Grapes of Wrath* and to the social themes that made his early work so impressive, and so powerful. Critics who said of him that he had seen his best days had better tie on their napkins and prepare to eat crow.' Writing to Elizabeth Otis, the writer confessed, 'The reviews of *Winter* have depressed me very much. They always do, even the favorable ones, but this time they have sunk me particularly.'[24] They sunk him for good, as it were; he never wrote another novel.

This novel represents a final attempt by Steinbeck to restate his major themes in a fresh way. The book's firmly drawn hero-narrator, Ethan Allen Hawley, is a man of breeding, education and integrity who feels threatened by the modern world, with its temptations and depredations. He is much younger than Steinbeck, being 'just under forty', but his children are fourteen and thirteen – not very different in age from Thom and John. An ex-army officer and Harvard graduate, Hawley lives with his wife, Mary, and their children in a fictional version of Sag Harbor called New Baytown, a small whaling town on Long Island.

Hawley is a lowly clerk in a store he once owned but lost through mismanagement to Alfio Marullo, a mercenary and untrustworthy Sicilian who now controls the business. The novel opens symbolically on Good Friday 1960, and the Christ theme – a Steinbeckian constant in so many of his novels and stories – is made explicit. There are, however, many other echoes: of *Richard III* (from which the title is taken) and the legend of Ethan Allen, hero of the American Revolution. But the great stage that Shakespeare conjured in his play has shrunken hugely by the mid-twentieth century. The human problem now, as Robert Frost put it, 'is what to make of a diminished thing'. What Americans have inherited, in Steinbeck's view, is a time and place where meanness of spirit and dirty tricks triumph in the marketplace, and where the marketplace is all that matters.

The Sicilian, Marullo, voices the dominant ethos that so disgusts Steinbeck (and his counterpart, Hawley): 'Business is money. Money is not friendly. . . . Money is not nice. Money got no friend but more money.'[25] Although Hawley knows better, he is ultimately tempted by Mammon and embraces Marullo's worldview in the end, however reluctantly. As was typical of Steinbeck, the maker of parables and morality plays, many levels of myth intermingle: Hawley is Christ turned Judas in the end: he is also both the Prodigal Son and Cain: 'I am my brother's keeper and I have not saved him,' he cries out early in the story, referring to his spiritual brother, Danny Taylor, a boyhood friend who was expelled from the Naval Academy and has degenerated into the town drunk. Like Richard III, Hawley's moral decline manifests itself in a plot against his brother, although here, as elsewhere, the comparison shows up Hawley's diminishment. The heroic becomes, over and again, the mock-heroic.

Steinbeck's writing, *per se*, was never better, as in the opening chapter when Ethan leaves his house on Good Friday to go to the store:

> He looked back at the fine old house, his father's house and
> his great-grandfather's, white-painted shiplap with a
> fanlight over the front door, and Adam decorations and a
> widow's walk on the roof. It was deep-set in the greening
> garden among lilacs a hundred years old, thick as your
> waist, and swelling with buds. The elms of Elm Street
> joined their tops and yellowed out in the new-coming leaf.
> The sun had just cleared the bank building and flashed on
> the silvery gas tower, starting the kelp and salt smell from
> the old harbor.

This lyrical, image-centred writing, wherein each detail is luminously clear, occurs on every page of *Winter*. Steinbeck summons what Henry James once called 'the palpable present *intimate* that throbs response' to the immediate moment of the story. The blunt, successive sentences fall, one by one, invoking a world in all its concreteness. The novelist's plotting, however, is slight: a problem with most mythopoetic dramas. Briefly, Ethan is tempted by his 'friends' until he gives in to his baser instincts, financial and sexual; finally, having succumbed and 'succeeded' in winning the store back and improving his finances, he loses all belief in himself and retreats to a cave to commit suicide, his wallet full of money. But he can't do it – at least not yet.

One of several subplots that reinforce the main outlines of the story concerns Ethan's son and namesake, Ethan Allen, Jr, who wins a national essay competition, the 'I Love America' contest. It turns out that Junior has cobbled his essay together from fragments of patriotic writers like Henry Clay, Daniel Webster and Thomas Jefferson. Even Abraham Lincoln's Second Inaugural is quoted without acknowledgement. Though confessing to this plagiarism, Ethan, Jr remains unfazed, claiming that 'everyone does it'. Ethan becomes increasingly aware throughout the novel of the cheating and underhandedness that in his mind characterize American culture in 1960. (At that time, quiz shows, for instance, were shown to be rigged, and this deceit becomes a symbol for Ethan of the country's overall moral debasement.) He decides, at last, to trade an old-fashioned 'habit of conduct' for 'a cushion of security', entering what he calls a 'strange, uncharted country'. But his 'success' comes at a very high price for a man of his standards. He has to sacrifice a sacred inner sense of integrity which was, Steinbeck suggests, his true birthright.

Another key subplot concerns Ethan's desire to rob the town's bank. In this, Steinbeck harks back to his short story, 'How Mr Hogan Robbed a Bank', published five years earlier in *The Atlantic*. In that cautionary tale a middle-class man with no good reason to rob a bank does so for what might be called aesthetic reasons: he commits the perfect crime because it was there. In a move that becomes an important echo in *The*

Winter of Our Discontent, Mr Hogan rewards his children, who have just won a prize in the Hearst 'Why I Like America' contest, with a crisp five-dollar bill each. Hawley has no need to rob the bank and does not share Mr Hogan's aestheticism. He triumphs through other means.

It is interesting that Steinbeck's last novel is told in a first-person voice which seems close to the author's own: grainy, curmudgeonly, poetic. The author was unworried about creating a confusion between himself and the narrator; he seemed not to care if a stray reader should draw untoward parellels. 'John had become incredibly thick-skinned in some ways,' Elaine says. 'But he was thin-skinned in other ways. If anyone asked him if his work was autobiographical, he would just smile.' Without doubt, the novel is nicely centred on the 'palpable present' of the story, and on the moral and physical landscape that Steinbeck evokes with consummate skill. He was writing about something he knew intimately, and this gives a satisfying veracity and authority to the work. As a reviewer in *The Atlantic* noted (July 1961), 'Steinbeck was born to write of the sea coast, and he does so with savor and love.' The dialogue bristles with the sound of real speech; not since *The Grapes of Wrath* had he managed such natural and 'realistic' conversation. The hyper-rhetorical dialogue of *East of Eden* and *Burning Bright* has vanished.

Steinbeck's almost visceral contempt for the current American scene, with its materialistic preoccupations and low regard for such Yankee virtues as honesty and a fidelity to one's honourable instincts, was very much his own. There is always a danger in reading a work of fiction too bio-graphically, but one can hardly resist speculating that Steinbeck may have believed he had been entrapped (like Ethan) in reaching for the Mammon represented by Broad-way or Hollywood. This grasping had almost invariably led to disasters; the money had made him prey to friends and foes alike; the fame had tormented him; the desire for 'success' in terms of critical acclaim had led to nothing but frustration.

The Winter of Our Discontent brought to an end Steinbeck's career as a novelist for many different reasons. Ill health was probably the crucial factor behind the decision not to write more novels: he was just not feeling well, and the little episodes continued to plague him. He found himself less steady on his feet and unwilling to work long hours in his study. There was also the general feeling of disappointment over the critical response to *Winter*; the reviewers had failed to appreciate the risks he had taken or to understand the nature of his achievement. He was bone-tired of having each new book weighed, unfavourably, against *The Grapes of Wrath*, and had lost patience with the inevitable rejoinder: Whatever happened to John Steinbeck? There was also the lure of *Morte D'Arthur*, a project that would not leave his mind.

Despite his fierce depression over the reception of his novel, Steinbeck dragged himself to his workhouse overlooking the sea each morning to finish *Travels with Charley*. He was suffering from what he described to Otis as 'a very painful pleurisy', although Elaine urged that it was 'purely psychological'. As before, he would unconsciously transform a psychological pain into a specific physical ailment, giving it substance and body. As a 'real' ailment, it could be objectified and contained. 'This was just something one expected from John,' Elaine says. 'I didn't take these particular kinds of illness too seriously.'

Thom and John were seventeen and fifteen now respectively, and Steinbeck had an idea one morning at breakfast. Whenever in the last couple of decades he finished a major writing project, he went abroad to counteract the inevitable letdown. Travel was soothing and pulled one out of oneself. He wrote to Dook Sheffield's mother about his plan:

> About a year ago, I . . . began to wonder what I could do
> for my boys that would have surviving meaning and value
> to them. And suddenly it seemed very clear. I would give
> them a large part of the world and fortunately, for the time
> being at least, I can afford it. Early in September we will
> start out and travel slowly around the world taking ten or
> twelve months to do it. A young Irish tutor will go along so
> that their school work can go on.[26]

A plan was made to sail on the *Rotterdam*, leaving on 8 September for England. The family would rent a car and tour the British Isles, then continue south through France and Italy without having to keep to any fixed schedule. Whatever caught their fancy would hold them for as long as it continued to hold their fancy. They would proceed eventually to Greece, Turkey, Israel and Egypt. From there, they would go through the Red Sea and on to India, the East Indies, China, Japan, and then meander through the Pacific Islands via Australia and back to San Francisco. It was a lovely idea: to give his sons the traditional gentleman's 'grand tour' writ large.

The Irish tutor Steinbeck mentioned was a young American by the name of Terrence McNally, today a well-known and acclaimed playwright. McNally was then 'about 22 or 23', he says. 'I remember being told about this job by Molly Kazan, Elia Kazan's wife. It sounded like a great opportunity and very Turgenev-like to go off and be a tutor, and then Molly said the name Steinbeck, John Steinbeck. I was taken aback.'[27] Elaine Steinbeck adds, 'I remember Terrence coming to see us on East 72nd Street. He was very young and handsome, and so lively and yet serious. He seemed extraordinarily learned, too, a remarkable thing in a young man. It made him ideal for the job, and John loved him at once. Everyone loved Terrence.'

Steinbeck suggested that NcNally come to Sag Harbor for a few days to see if they all enjoyed spending time together, and NcNally recalls that Thom and John 'had the usual stresses and strains of older and younger brothers. But there were other strains. I remember saying to myself as we sailed on the *Rotterdam* past the Statue of Liberty, "My God, I hardly know these people." Then I realized that they hardly knew each other. The boys had really not spent that much time with John and Elaine. They were running away from their mother, Gwyn. Now they were finally getting to know each other as a family.' The stress of travel added to the difficulty, 'Travel is always difficult and stressful, so you had to factor in that element, too.'

They docked in Southampton and travelled by train to London, checking into the Dorchester. The Steinbecks – John and Elaine – were now used to travelling together, but this was more like an expedition, with so much luggage and five people, three of them adults. 'John was particularly eager to show the boys around England,' NcNally says. 'He knew a lot of English history, and he had very specific sites in mind for us to visit. It was quite wonderful listening to him talk about these things that he loved. He was a good teacher, full of enthusiasm and a kind of particular knowledge grounded in anecdote that somehow makes the fact digestible.'

McNally took his duties as tutor extremely seriously. 'Terrence was so amazingly confident and really committed to the boys. He knew so much, too. History and music, art and literature. John and I were absolutely delighted. And he made the boys work hard. One time, just as we were about to leave a hotel in England, Terrence said, "Wait a minute. We can't go until Thom gives me the paper he was supposed to write last night." ' This resulted in a screaming fight between Thom and John that Elaine claims to have 'botched rather badly. There were some really horrible days. But we had wonderful days too.'

Steinbeck began to feel the tension generated by the circumstances of family travel; he was also upset by the news that his Swedish friend Dag Hammarskjöld had died. 'My hand is shaking pretty badly,' he wrote to Elizabeth Otis from London just after he got the news. 'Guess Dag's death hit hard. I'm all shaky inside.' From Bruton, their old Somerset haunt, he wrote to Otis again, in a better mood. 'The weather is that fine combination of sun and rain, probably the best time of the year. . . . The whole thing is like coming home.'[28] He also noted that Terrence and Thom were 'locked in mortal combat'. Apparently Thom had shown immense resistance to having daily lessons at all. 'Thom and John thought this was a vacation, but it was much more than that,' Elaine says. 'Terrence was determined to make this year abroad have some educational meaning for them, but it wasn't easy.' They visited all the nearby Arthurian sites during the next week.

They went to Dublin, where both Steinbeck and McNally were keen to visit the famous Abbey Theatre and to walk along the Liffey, the river which had so many literary associations from Swift to Joyce, then they toured some of the nearby Irish counties. Thom and John loved it, 'especially the chance to stop in pubs', and Steinbeck was inspired by the landscape that had been the home of his mother's ancestors. He wrote to Frank Loesser and his wife from Dublin, 'I do hear the low rumble of poetry. The greatest stories are the oldest ones because they didn't fall down.'[29] The group returned to England for a tour of Northumberland, where Steinbeck had some particular medieval sites in mind.

Having toured part of the British Isles to their satisfaction, they crossed the Channel to France, moving through Paris and on down through southern France to Avignon and Nice, which Steinbeck loathed. 'We are staying at the Brice-Benford,' he wrote to Otis, 'a dismal hotel which required great genius to have everything in bad taste.'[30] Elaine says, 'Part of the problem here was that John hadn't realized how expensive Europe was going to be, especially for five people. He began to worry about money. I said, ''There's nothing to worry about," but he wouldn't relax. "I can't afford this!" he said, and suggested that we cut the trip short. There just wasn't enough money to keep going all the way around the world. He became very gloomy when I just refused to go right home.' Once again, money became symbolic for Steinbeck, reifying his fear of over-reaching; the son of John Ernst, who had 'ruined' the family through his lack of fiscal sense, could not believe he was a rich man – rich in resources, spiritual as well as financial. This late in life, he still had difficulty accepting his inner strength and imaginative power.

On 25 November they went on to Milan. 'We checked into a very draughty and damp hotel,' Elaine recalls. 'Everyone hated it, but John insisted that we stay there. And then the boys started fighting again – they didn't want to do some assignment that Terrence had given them. And John grew more and more agitated, and then he just went unconscious. It was the worst thing I could imagine: really frightening. I didn't know what to do, but the boys and Terrence were helpful and several doctors came and we stayed up all night by his bed.' This was another of the episodes that had become a part of his life; the most serious yet. 'The doctors couldn't agree on what exactly had happened to John, whether it was a minor heart attack or a stroke, but he seemed to recover quickly.'

Terrence and Elaine decided that it would be best if he took the boys around northern Italy by himself, to Florence and Venice and various hill towns in Tuscany and Umbria. 'The plan was that we should all meet up in Rome for Christmas,' McNally says. They met as planned, at the Lagazione, a hotel 'presided over by an Ethiopian girl, a serpent of the Nile, an asp, even a half-asp', Steinbeck wrote to Elizabeth Otis a few days before Christmas.[31] Elaine recalls, 'John hated the Lagazione, so we moved to the Hôtel de Ville, which Robert Capa had introduced us to years before. We had a marvellous Christmas and New Year there, in four large rooms with a

Christmas tree and all the trimmings and everything. The hotel was at the top of the Spanish Steps on the Via Sistina.' The weather was cold, clear and sparkling. The sun shone over the city and turned it 'a wonderful pale gold'. Steinbeck was feeling much better, having had a month's rest. His Italian publisher had arranged for them all to have a private audience with Pope John XXIII, on Christmas Eve, followed by a concert of Gregorian chants.

In spite of the good holidays, a string of recent deaths added to Steinbeck's general uneasiness and psychological discomfort. Perhaps the worst of these was the death of his publisher, Harold Guinzburg. 'This was really awful for him,' Elaine says. 'And though he was cheerful and claimed to feel much better, it was very clear that he could not go around the world. We decided to change course. We wouldn't even think about India and Australia and China. For the moment we would rest on Capri. John always liked Capri – ever since the war.' NcNally adds, 'The idea now was that I would go off with the boys to various places in the Mediterranean; we would use Capri as a kind of centre, a base. Italy was really the best part of the whole trip, for me and the boys. We covered every inch of the country, it seemed. We could really afford to take a detour to see one particular fresco somewhere if that seemed like a good thing to do. I wasn't really so much older than Thom, and in fact he looked older than me. Sometimes the waiter would bring him the bill instead of me! It was mildly embarrassing.'

The Steinbacks rented an old villa in Capri with colourful tile floors and a *terrazzo* with a view of the sea. 'John was extremely happy there,' Elaine says. 'The light was extraordinary. He settled into a pattern of reading and a little writing . . . mostly letters to friends. He was correcting the proofs of *Travels with Charley* while we were there, and the publishers were a little resistant to the chapter set in New Orleans. I remember there was some discussion of changes, but John wouldn't hear of it.' On 10 February Steinbeck wrote to Pat Covici:

> We live a life of incredible quiet. Although somewhat
> troubled by vestiges of a Presbyterian conscience, I have
> succeeded in doing nothing whatsoever, and it seems to be
> working because I feel much better. We rise late, take a
> walk, read the papers. Sometimes we have dinner in and at
> others eat at little restaurants deep in the thick and Moorish
> walls of the old buildings.[32]

The temperate winter climate of Capri approximated that of Monterey: brisk winds, lots of sunlight in the middle of the day, icy nights, occasional bouts of driving rain. The sea was grey most days, and choppy. Ferries arrived each morning, bringing handfuls of tourists who dutifully climbed the winding road to the town square for a meal or a round of shopping before returning to Naples or Positano the same afternoon. It was a ghostly place in winter, steeped in history, and Steinbeck was inspired by all of this. Among the many books he was reading were *South Wind*, an evocative account of life on Capri by Norman Douglas, and Rousseau's *Confessions*; he also read Plutarch and Suetonius, the ancient historians of the Roman Empire.

One of the few visitors to Capri was Allen Ludden, the television entertainer, whose wife Margaret had just died. Although Ludden was hardly a close friend, he had met Steinbeck in New York on many occasions and thought him a man with great spiritual resources and moral depths. He flew to Capri on a whim, grief-stricken, and talked all day and all night to Steinbeck, who devoted himself to helping this man through his private agony. This was a very important side to Steinbeck: he was someone who could speak closely to another man about things of great emotional import; he could be tenderly human in difficult situations, and compassionate. It was a noble aspect of the man.

On 27 February he turned sixty. His face was now deeply lined, craggy and rough-skinned; his large eyes had sunk into his cheekbones, creating dark circles. His hair was thinning and grey, and his huge barrel chest tipped his balance forward, so that he stooped slightly when he walked. He looked like an old man. 'I don't know how it happened but there it is,' he wrote to Pat Covici, referring to his age. To Elia Kazan, he observed, 'When this last illness struck me, it was like a moment of truth. All kinds of things got washed away and my eyes became much clearer because the fogs of purpose and ambition blew away. My own past work fell into place in relation to other people's work and none of it with few exceptions was as good as those cave paintings. So I will go on working because I like to, but it won't be like any work I have done before.'[33]

The Steinbecks left Capri and joined the boys and Terrence in Positano in April, touring southern Italy, Greece, and the Greek islands with them. 'I remember going into a little Italian *trattoria* with everyone,' McNally says. 'I don't know how word got around, but soon people were lined up to meet John. A man with a tattered copy of one of his books in translation asked for an autograph. I was really struck by the fact that John's work had travelled so passionately from one culture to another.' In May, they took the ferry to Greece for the last leg of their journey. 'One day that stands out in my memory is when we all toured the Parthenon together,' Elaine recalls. 'Terrence said to the boys, "You remember the Elgin Marbles that we studied in the British Museum, don't you?" The boys nodded their heads. "Well, let's see if you can tell me where they would go." The boys squinted up at the ruins, then pointed. "The horse's head goes over there," Thom said. "And the chariot goes there," Johnny added. John and I actually wept. We realized that everything had fallen into place for them. The trip had somehow worked.'

After a tour of the Greek islands, the Steinbeck entourage

was ready to return to the United States. To Elizabeth Otis, from Mykonos, he wrote a final note on 28 May: 'Now this trip is over technically. Thom will fall in love twice more and on ships' food gain another ten lbs. John will preen and worry about his hair. Terrence will gadfly them with school work. But now an era is over. It must have been good.'

A Time for Recovery

'When it comes right down to it, nothing has changed.
The English sentence is just as difficult to write as it ever
was.'

Steinbeck to Pat Covici, 28 January 1963

The Steinbecks returned to Sag Harbor for the summer, just
in time for the publication of *Travels with Charley* in July 1962.
For the most part, the book was well-received. *The New York
Times* (27 July) called it 'pure delight, a pungent potpourri of
places and people interspersed with bittersweet essays on
everything from the emotional difficulties of growing old to
the reasons why giant Sequoias arouse such awe'. *Newsweek*
(30 July) said it was 'vigorous, affecting, and highly entertaining,' and *The Atlantic* (August) crooned, 'This is a book to be
read slowly for its savor, and one which, like Thoreau, will be
quoted and measured by our own experience.' What few
objections the critics could muster were faint. Indeed,
Steinbeck had not experienced such acclaim since *The Grapes
of Wrath* came out three decades earlier.

The reading public responded warmly, as usual, scooping
up so many copies that Charley was soon lofted into the top
position on most bestseller lists. Soon everyone was reading
and talking about John Steinbeck and his poodle's prostate
trouble. As in the past when he had been praised, Steinbeck
found the acclaim hollow and disingenuous; he wrote to Pat
Covici to say that he felt extremely uncertain about his future
as a writer. It was unclear to him that he would ever write
another book. Covici responded on 2 August:

Of course it is not for you to judge your work, successful or not. I recently came across a quotation from James Baldwin which I copied in my notebook and here it is:

'The effort to become a great novelist simply involves attempting to tell as much of the truth as one can bear, and then a little more. It is an effort which, by its very nature – remembering that men write the books, that time passes and energy flags, and safety beckons – is obviously doomed to failure. Success is a word which cannot conceivably, unless it is defined in an extremely severe, ironical and painful way, have any place in the vocabulary of any artist.'

After middle age most of us experience and suffer a great change, but often we also experience a new birth. As you well know, Sophocles wrote one of his best plays at the age of 80, Anatole France a novel at 79, Goethe finished the second part of *Faust* at the age of 81. The fact that you mean to do some long slow thinking is proof that there are many more fish in your sea.[1]

There were, sadly, few fish left to gather in the net of his prose. 'John was simply exhausted, and he was not well. He seemed fragile, especially after he had a few drinks in him,' says Tom Guinzburg, the son of his publisher.[2] 'His health was really the issue now, though it was not something he liked to discuss.' There must have been within him a nagging feeling that *Travels with Charley* was not the book it might have been. While the descriptive writing is superb, as good in places as anything he had ever done, the shape of the book as a whole is flawed. The twin climaxes of *Charley* are the visit to Monterey which goes badly and the scene in New Orleans with the so-called Cheerleaders. They are good scenes, but they come too close together and stretch the book in different emotional directions, the one private and the other public. One also regrets the lack of a proper denouement: the travelogue ends abruptly, with the reader dumped on the kerbside in Long Island and wishing for a concluding chapter in which Steinbeck meditates on his journey and what it meant. The author was obviously in a hurry to finish the book, and the haste shows.

Steinbeck withdrew to Sag Harbor and his boat, spending long days out on the water. This was the beginning of the period of 'long slow thinking' he intended to accomplish, but the process was soon interrupted in the most severe manner. 'It was on a morning in late October,' Elaine says. 'I was cooking breakfast and John was watching television. He didn't usually watch television, but this was during the Cuban missile crisis, and we were glued to the set like everyone else in the country. Then a news flash came on, saying that John Steinbeck had just been awarded the Nobel Prize for Literature. We stood up and started dancing around the house, and suddenly the phone started ringing. It was the wildest thing that ever happened to us. We called the boys at their schools to tell them, then John called Pat Covici and Elizabeth Otis. Telegrams started arriving. Then Pat Covici said that John should fly into Manhattan immediately to give a proper press conference, so we did – that very afternoon we left. But we drove. On the way into the city, John was eager to listen to the radio: "Maybe they'll announce it again," he said.' It turned out that the letter from the Swedish Academy had been sent to the New York apartment, which is why Steinbeck heard about it first on television.

The next day they were met by seventy-five reporters and cameramen, and this on the worst day of the Cuban missile crisis! Steinbeck was dressed in a blue shirt with a tie, his hair combed straight back like a schoolboy reluctantly dragged into church for a mid-week service. He responded to all questions in a terse, staccato manner, puffing on a small cigar. 'This prize is a monster in some ways,' Steinbeck wrote to Bo Beskow a few days later. 'I have always been afraid of it. Now I must handle it.'[3] Like T. S. Eliot, who called the prize 'a ticket to one's own funeral', he knew that Nobel laureates rarely accomplished much original work after having won it. For Steinbeck, the Nobel would indeed be hard to handle, harder than he imagined.

The next day, 26 October 1962, *The New York Times* ran an editorial about the award that would have a harsh impact on the man and his reputation:

> The award of the Nobel Prize for Literature to John Steinbeck will focus attention once again on a writer who, though still in full career, produced his major work more than two decades ago. The award will bring back the vivid memory of the earlier books: the relaxed gaiety of 'Tortilla Flat'; the stark force of 'In Dubious Battle'; the anger and compassion of 'The Grapes of Wrath', a book that occupies a secure place as a document of protest.
>
> Yet the international character of the award and the weight attached to it raise questions about the mechanics of selection and how close the Nobel committee is to the main currents of American writing. Without detracting in the least from Mr Steinbeck's accomplishments, we think it interesting that the laurel was not awarded to a writer – perhaps a poet or critic or historian – whose significance, influence and sheer body of work had already made a more profound impression on the literature of our age.

Elaine was justifiably horrified when she read this, and she cried, 'Damn! Damn it!' 'It doesn't matter, Elaine,' Steinbeck reassured her, 'It really doesn't.' But it did matter, at least in the short run. *The Times* had stirred the same old pot – Steinbeck's best work was behind him, written long ago. He had failed to live up to the promise – indeed, the achievement – of his earlier novels. 'I think this reaction to the Nobel weighed heavily on John,' Tom Guinzburg says. 'It made the whole thing so difficult. It was so outrageous that Americans weren't rooting for the home team.'

Hemingway was luckier, for complex reasons: he was not savaged when he won the Nobel, even though a good argument could be made that after his first book of stories (*In Our Time*) and his first novel (*The Sun Also Rises*), every single subsequent book represented a diminishment of energy and concentration. It could also be said that William Faulkner in his two decades did not produce work even remotely equal to the novels of his most innovative phases, in the late Twenties and Thirties: *The Sound and the Fury* or *As I Lay Dying* contain work of a different order from, say, *The Town* or *A Fable*. So why was Steinbeck singled out for rebuke? And why was *The Grapes of Wrath* reduced to 'a document of protest', such a slyly belittling phrase? Why avoid the fact that Steinbeck's work had been important to readers throughout the world?

Stupidly, most American periodicals joined in against Steinbeck. *Time*, *Newsweek* and the *Washington Post* all attacked the rationality of giving him the award and decried the Nobel committee for being out of touch with contemporary writing in America. Steinbeck read these pieces with dismay, and explained to Bo Beskow that he had never been liked by the 'cutglass critics, that grey priesthood which defines literature and has little to do with reading'. These critics were 'beside themselves with rage' over his award, he said, perhaps exaggerating their response to make himself feel better. For obvious reasons, Steinbeck felt immense pressure now to write a speech worthy of the Nobel, and he wrote around to friends for any suggestions they might have.

Letters of congratulation poured in, and they were of some comfort. John O'Hara impishly wrote, 'I can think of only one other author I'd rather see get it.' Steinbeck replied that getting the prize wouldn't have been nearly as good without this greeting. He added, 'The thing is meaningless alone. But if my friends like it – suddenly it has some dignity and desirability.'[4] He wrote on 6 November to Professor and Mrs Vinaver: 'The prize is a good prize – good in intent and valuable if properly used. But it can be a dangerous and engulfing thing. To many within my memory it has been an epitaph and to others a muffling cloaklike vestment that smothers and warps.'[5]

Steinbeck answered personally each of the many hundreds of letters from around the world. 'We had to hire a few secretaries on a temporary basis,' Elaine recalls. 'There was so much commotion, and John was working very hard on his speech.' She adds, 'One day, just before we left for Sweden, John said, "Elaine, I have a special favour to ask." I looked up, wondering. "The last American to go to Stockholm sober for this prize was Pearl Buck. I'd like it if we didn't drink anything alcoholic while we're there." ' Elaine agreed at once, aware that the endless round of cocktail parties would be very bad for him if he were drinking.

With Alice Guinzburg – widow of Harold Guinzburg – as companion, the Steinbecks flew to Sweden on 8 December and were duly fêted by the Swedish government, by Steinbeck's Swedish publisher, Albert Bonniers Forlag, and by the US embassy, which held a grand dinner party in his honour. 'You can't imagine the number of parties,' says Elaine. 'The whole thing was a crush of reporters. John was called up to the King of Sweden to get his medal, he bowed to the King, then he bowed to me as he passed me on the way back.' The next night, giving his speech, he began: 'Your Majesty, your Royal Highnesses, Members of the Academy, *mein vakra fru* [my beautiful wife] . . .' Uxoriousness had become a habit!

His speech was simple, dignified, and inspiring. The core of its message, while somewhat self-justifying and defensive, is none the less sound:

> Literature was not promulgated by a pale and emasculated
> critical priesthood singing their litanies in empty churches –
> nor is it a game for the cloistered elect, the tinhorn
> mendicants of low-calorie despair.
> Literature is as old as speech. It grew out of human need

for it, and it has not changed except to become more needed. The skalds, the bards, the writers are not separate and exclusive.

He ended with a plea for understanding and communication in the age of the atom bomb: 'Man himself has become our greatest hazard and our only hope. So that today, Saint John the Apostle may well be paraphrased: In the end is the *word*, and the word is *man*, and the word is *with* man.'[6]

Steinbeck takes his position, *qua* writer, against the 'emasculated critical priesthood', which doubtless included Alfred Kazin and the editorial writers of *The New York Times*. His sympathies lay with the so-called common reader, not with the academic critics who lamented his lack of 'development'. His final remarks, about 'Man himself', point to his essential humanism, his deep belief in the power – destructive and constructive – of the human imagination. His final gesture, towards the word 'is' man as well as 'with' man, invokes a theory of language as old as the *Gospel of John* (or St Augustine, who argued in his *Confessions* for a sanctification of language in which human speech finally becomes the Word itself).

When the Nobel ceremony and the many receptions were over, the Steinbecks retreated with Alice Guinzburg to their hotel suite to have, at last, a drink. 'There were so many gifts and telegrams and all of that,' Elaine says, 'we were rather giddy.' The next day they flew to London to do some Christmas shopping. 'Alice had stuffed some envelopes, odds and ends, into her purse,' Elaine recalls. 'And suddenly before we left she said, "I suppose I can get rid of all these things now." She noticed that one of the envelopes was from the Nobel committee. John took the envelope and, to our amazement, it contained the prize money! He smiled and said to Alice, "I'm glad you found that. It might have been a little embarrassing to have to wire and stop payment." '

They arrived home a few days before Christmas, exhausted but happy. The way he was received in Sweden had certainly helped to counterbalance the reaction of his own countrymen. Writing to thank Bo Beskow for all he had done for him, Steinbeck added, 'Now is coming the time for recovery. As soon as Christmas is over and the boys back in school, I am going to withdraw completely into work to prove to myself that this need not be an epitaph. It is a contract I have made with myself.'[7]

It was not, however, a contract he would keep. The Nobel Prize was a weight, and he had not heard the last of the negative criticism. Indeed, the original harsh editorial in *The New York Times* was followed on the eve of the award ceremony in Stockholm (9 December 1962) by a scornful article entitled 'Does a Moral Vision of the Thirties Deserve a Nobel Prize?' It was written by Arthur Mizener, another of the despised priesthood of academic critics whom Steinbeck had scorned in his Nobel speech. Mizener, with that pose of academic objectivity which often disguises deep-seated and thought-free prejudice, claimed that after *The Grapes of Wrath*, most 'serious readers' had stopped reading Steinbeck altogether. His work was deeply flawed by 'sentimentality'. Mizener swept through the writer's career, stopping at every book from *In Dubious Battle* on to mock and belittle. It was a sorry moment for American literary culture.

'Does he say that there are no relationships between people which he would call sentimental?' Steinbeck asked Pat Covici, open-mouthed with astonishment over Mizener's piece. 'If this is his meaning he is wrong or inexperienced or unobserving.' He continued: 'Mickey Spillane is writing for Mr Mizener much more than I am. Never will he catch a Spillane character in such abominations as humor, love, compassion, or thought. What it boils down to is that everything exists, it is what you pick out of the grab bag of experience that matters.'[8]

'Critics like Mizener and Alfred Kazin', says Gore Vidal, 'are always furious when a writer has voluntary readers. They operate on a late nineteenth-century aesthetic. Essentially, they believe that good literature is written for a small, elect group of people like themselves. They could never forgive Steinbeck for saying things that people wanted, or needed, to hear.'[9] Steinbeck understood this, as his letters to Covici and Otis show, but it was nevertheless hard to bear such criticism, and in such public places. It destroyed much of the satisfaction of getting the Nobel Prize.

Steinbeck moved from the city back to Sag Harbor in January, hoping to begin a new project. Once again, he thought of doing a play, although nothing came of whatever gestures he may have made in this direction. In a long, introspective letter to Pat Covici on 28 January 1963, he meditated on the growing preference among readers for non-fiction over fiction:

> Fiction, it seems to me in its inception was an attempt to put experience in a form and direction so that it could be understood. Not that fiction could be understood but that reality could. Now perhaps that has changed. Perhaps people can no longer find themselves and their neighbors in fiction and so go searching in non-fiction for some likeness of experience.
>
> There is one difficulty in this. Writers of fiction are usually better writers than writers of fact. This was not always true. But perhaps fiction writers are no longer fastened to reality. Maybe their 'schools' have taken them away from their source. Are the Greek myths fiction? Are the Sagas fiction? Not in the sense that is understood today. Ideally – the fiction writer must be much closer to reality because he does not have the corroborations as proof that the non-fiction writer has. You can write anything in the morning paper so long as it happens. The fiction writer wouldn't dare do this. What he writes must . . . not only happen *but continue to happen*.[10]

He said he was relieved to be in Sag Harbor, away from the mail and the 'damned telephone', and he hoped soon to 'get back some balance'. The Nobel experience was something 'capable of confusing anyone'. But this didn't change his relationship to his craft: 'When it comes right down to it, nothing has changed. The English sentence is just as difficult to write as it ever was.' Indeed, the difficulty for him seemed only to increase. Almost daily he found himself sitting at his desk without the impetus to write, a peculiar and unnerving situation for a man who had written compulsively for so many decades.

A succession of public occasions rescued him from this barren phase. As a recent Nobel laureate, he was in great demand. He travelled quite often into New York for events of a kind that years earlier he would have scorned, such as a grand dinner at the Waldorf in honour of Carl Sandburg's eighty-fifth birthday. (Steinbeck was among a dozen famous guests who stood to toast the hoary-headed poet.) Another time-consuming activity was that of moving. The townhouse on East 72nd Street had become burdensome to Steinbeck, with its steep stairs and lack of security, and he 'didn't want to live behind bars'. It so happened that a large and luxurious apartment building had just been erected a block away on the same street. The Steinbecks decided to sell the townhouse and buy an apartment in the new building, which had an elevator and a doorman. This new address would be Steinbeck's last.

In early spring, Steinbeck was asked, at the suggestion of President Kennedy, to visit the Soviet Union as part of a cultural exchange programme designed to help defuse the Cold War. Robert Frost had recently participated in the programme, with great success, and Edward R. Murrow, the broadcaster, had urged the President to invite Steinbeck next. While agreeing in principle, Steinbeck asked that Elaine be included, and he asked that Edward Albee go too. Albee, a close friend of Terrence McNally, had recently made a splash on Broadway with his play, *Who's Afraid of Virginia Woolf?* Wisely, Steinbeck thought that any cultural exchange should include younger writers too.

By early May the Steinbecks had moved to Sag Harbor for the duration of the summer. One morning Steinbeck woke up and discovered that he had lost his vision completely in one eye. 'I'm blind!' he said to Elaine. Elaine recalled that an eye surgeon of some reputation, a Dr Paton, had retired to Southampton, and she called him immediately. Then she drove her husband to the hospital in Southampton, where he was operated on at once for a detached retina. 'It was a tricky operation in those days,' Elaine remembers. Blindfolded and immobilized by sandbags, Steinbeck lay in bed for weeks. Visitors were limited to his family and closest friends. 'John O'Hara came almost every day,' Elaine recalls, 'driving a long way, back and forth, to visit John. He'd read John the newspaper or bits and pieces from books – whatever he thought would interest him. 'O'Hara was a difficult man, hard to keep as a friend, but he loved John, and John loved him. This was a beautiful gift that O'Hara gave him, and it really helped to pull John through this nerve-racking time. When John came home, he had to use blinders – to train his eyes to see again. He walked around with a cane most of the summer. One of the things he missed most, though, was O'Hara's visits.' Steinback himself said that this recovery was much 'like peering through a knothole full of cobwebs'. Gradually, the vision came back. In some ways, since he was having difficulty in writing anyway, this illness came as a relief of sorts, providing an ideal excuse.

Late in September, fully recovered from the eye surgery, the Steinbecks flew to Washington for a briefing at the State Department on their way to Moscow via Helsinki. 'John met with the President,' Elaine remembers, 'and he said, "I hope

you don't mind if I kick up some dirt while I'm there?"
Kennedy laughed and said, "I expect you to." ' Just before
leaving, Steinbeck wrote to Dook Sheffield about the trip, 'I
think maybe I'm too old for this kind of thing.'[11] Indeed,
upon arrival in Finland Steinbeck was besieged. 'Every
minute was filled with things to do,' says Elaine, 'receptions,
meetings, dinners, press conferences.' One morning, for
example, he was introduced to an auditorium filled with nine
hundred booksellers.

Edward Albee joined them in Moscow in mid-October. The
idea was that Albee, being younger and less well-known,
might have a better chance of mingling with dissidents and
outsiders. 'I think that was true,' Albee says.[12] 'John was
such an imposing and important figure that everything he
did was closely watched. I had a bit more leeway. Luckily,
our itineraries didn't exactly coincide. I probably got to meet
more of the writers out of favour. John and I both kept asking
to see this writer or that writer, and we were often told they
were "unavailable". Oddly enough, this "unavailable"
writer would often turn up on the last day of our visit to some
place or, even, at the airport. Word got around – probably
through the underground – that we wanted to talk to
someone, and that someone would appear. It was quite
miraculous.'

He recalls, 'We travelled for a couple of months, often
together. We would meet with large and small groups of
writers. Sometimes we would go into schools. I remember
that once, in Leningrad, we were together before a very large
class in a school. We looked around, and it surprised us that
quite a few of the people in the class were forty or fifty years
old. When they began asking hostile questions, we realized at
once that they were plants – KGB or whatever – put in there to
try to make us look bad. One of them began harassing John
with questions about why he once wrote books that attacked
the capitalist system but caved in later. This made John

furious, and he would scream back at them things like, "You son-of-a-bitch, don't you realize that times change, that America in the Thirties was different from America in the Fifties." And so on.' Albee adds, 'John was always straight with people. He said exactly what he thought. We disagreed on a lot of things, but that didn't come between us.' Elaine comments, 'It struck some people in the Soviet Union as incredible that John and Edward would disagree in public. They didn't speak with one voice. This confounded them.'

'One of the writers John wanted very much to meet was Viktor Nekrasov,' Elaine says. 'He had heard about him, and he understood that Nekrasov was having a hard time with the authorities. He was from Kiev, and he had been pushed aside by the Writers' Union and his books were banned. Well, several times John asked to see him, but he was always told that Nekrasov was unavailable, that he was sick or busy or travelling – there were endless excuses. We were attending a large meeting of writers in Kiev, when suddenly a big door opened and this man in a baggy old suit – a peasantlike man – stormed in. He rushed up to John and slapped his hand down on the table, shouting "Nekrasov!" John loved it. He slapped his hand down hard and yelled, "Steinbeck!" After that, he came back to the hotel with us, and he and John stayed up all night talking.'

The Steinbecks travelled to Georgia, where they were introduced to local writers and journalists by Irakli Abashidze, First Secretary of the Writers' Union in Tbilisi. 'It was again the usual round of dinners and meetings. We felt very comfortable in Georgia. They weren't as tied into the Soviet state, it seems, as they were elsewhere,' Elaine says. They returned by plane to Moscow, where they met Yevgeny Yevtushenko and others. Erskine Caldwell and his wife, Virginia, were in Moscow on a private holiday, staying on the other side of Moscow at the National Hotel on Red Square, and the Steinbecks joined them for dinner in their suite.

Each day Steinbeck was ushered around by someone from the Writers' Union. He met the poets Andrei Voznesensky and Bella Akhmadulina, and a number of unknown or barely known young writers. 'It was rather dizzying,' says Albee, 'meeting so many people in a short time. Of course John's work was well known to the Russians.' Elaine adds, 'Even *The Winter of Our Discontent* had already been published in Russian – without royalties, of course. John complained loudly about the royalties. This was part of the business of kicking up some dirt.' One night the Steinbecks went to see a performance of *The Moon Is Down* in Russian – an odd play for a totalitarian country to let through the censors!

They went to Leningrad with Albee on 8 November, and no sooner had they arrived than Steinbeck collapsed from exhaustion. They had been riding the merry-go-round for weeks, and this was murderous for a man in his weakened condition. A doctor came to the hotel room and ordered Steinbeck to the nearest hospital for tests. 'While John was in the hospital,' Elaine says, 'Edward and I walked around the haunting streets of that city. We were very worried about him.' The Russian doctors determined that he was not seriously ill, gave him glucose shots and vitamins, and recommended two or three weeks of total rest and relaxation; he, of course, would not hear of the latter. He was having a terrific time, and the very next morning he addressed a large group of eager students at Leningrad University.

On 15 November the Steinbecks left for Warsaw (without Albee, who remained in the Soviet Union for a while longer). They toured Poland and met Polish writers and journalists and academics in various cities, large and small. To avoid another collapse from exhaustion, they spent a few quiet days in the Mazurian Lake District, where Steinbeck was taken on a wild boar hunt, much to his delight. In Krakow, he addressed an overflow audience at the university and met privately with students interested in American literature. He also toured a museum of medieval weaponry: just the thing to fire his imagination.

The Steinbecks returned to Warsaw on the fateful day of 22 November 1963. 'That was a day none of us would ever forget,' says Elaine. 'John and I had just gotten back to Warsaw when the news broke on the radio that John Kennedy had been shot in Dallas. The first report was that he was wounded, and we were horrified. Then we heard he was dead. It was so moving what happened: the Poles all surrounded us and hugged us, saying how sorry they were to hear this terrible, terrible news.' Steinbeck decided he must take a break from his tour, that he could not go on. Elaine says, 'We really needed time to mourn. We called the State Department, and they suggested that we go to Vienna for a few days, so we did. There was a funeral service for Kennedy at the cathedral there, and we attended it. It was a memorable and a wrenching day.'

From Vienna they went to Budapest for a few days of complete rest, although wherever Steinbeck travelled he was mobbed. 'We really got to meet the people in these countries,' Elaine says. 'We went into homes, we talked to them, we got to know them. After John's death, it was a surprise to me how many of them wrote personal letters to me from these satellite countries. I never expected this, but John's books had mattered to them.' Hundreds of people in Budapest crowded a book store one morning when it was announced that Steinbeck would appear for autographs – and this was only one of many such occasions. They returned to the United States via Prague and West Germany, having spent two months behind the Iron Curtain. 'In all my time with John, this was about the most important thing we ever did together,' Elaine says. 'We were both aware at the time that this had been a remarkable trip.'

In mid-December, they travelled again to Washington for a debriefing, and while there they were invited to the White

House for dinner with the new President, Lyndon Johnson, whose wife Lady Bird had been a student at the University of Texas with Elaine many years before. 'Lady Bird and I were old acquaintances,' says Elaine. 'But after this dinner, the relationship between us and the Johnsons deepened.' President Johnson made the unusual gesture of walking the Steinbecks back to their hotel, the Hay Adams, just across Lafayette Square. The Secret Service agents scurried about, frantic to protect the President on this unexpected outing. 'Please, don't walk us home,' Elaine said to Johnson, but he insisted. From then on they would stay with the Johnsons at the White House.

The Steinbecks celebrated Christmas in their bright apartment high over 72nd Street with Thom and John, who were home from their schools on vacation. 'It seemed that everything went very well at Christmas,' Elaine remembers. 'After the holidays we saw the boys off to school on the train, but the next day the headmaster called and wondered where they were. We told him we had no idea. It turned out, after frantic searching, that they were both with Gwyn. Once again, they had gone back to live with her. It was all very distressing and confusing.'

Obviously, something had gone wrong. Thom and John were deeply unsettled, and they had not been able to make a satisfactory connection with their father. In later years John Jr would say that his father's drinking and moodiness played a large part in his estrangement. Terrence McNally speculates: 'I think the tensions that normally arise between fathers and sons were all there, and adolescence is a notoriously difficult time. John was not in good health, of course, and this added to the problem. And he was depressive, and he did drink, but these were not the problem. John was a shy man, very sensitive, and he could not relate to his sons very well. He couldn't get as close to them as he would have liked, I think, and this had a lot to do with the problems with their mother, who of course said awful things about John to the boys. It made a very difficult situation that much worse.'

Steinbeck felt that he must get back to work despite the anxieties over Thom and John. Time was passing swiftly, and he felt the burden of his growing silence. But what would he write? The idea for a play had dissolved, and it seemed unlikely that he would make a significant advance in that direction. He had no inclination to begin another novel and had recently turned down a poignant request from Mrs John F. Kennedy to write the official biography of her husband. 'It was such a sad meeting,' Elaine recalls. 'We met with Mrs Kennedy, and she talked so movingly about her husband that I began to cry. She told me quietly but sternly to go into the bathroom if I needed to weep.'

Steinbeck knew himself well enough as a writer to see that a biography of John Kennedy would be impossible for him to do, but he still hoped to write about Camelot – the real Camelot. Once again he took out his Malory notes and began to work. (He even sent Mrs Kennedy a copy of some of his translation-in-progress.) In early March – not long after his sixty-second birthday – he wrote to Dook Sheffield about his recent idea of writing an autobiography: 'I have thought about writing an autobiography but a real one. Since after a passage of time I don't know what happened and what I made up, it would be nearer the truth to set both down. I'm sure this would include persons who never existed. Goethe wrote such an account . . .'[13]

Several letters about a Kennedy biography passed back and forth between Steinbeck and Mrs Kennedy, and years later, when Elaine was collecting letters for an edition of her husband's correspondence, she received a letter from Mrs Kennedy (now Jacqueline Onassis):

I have found the letters of your husband –

I can never express what they meant to me at the time – they
helped me face what was unacceptable to me.

You will never know what it meant to me to talk with your
husband in those days – I read his letters now – and I am as
moved as I was then – All his wisdom, his compassion, his
far-seeing view of things – I can't remember the sort of book
we were discussing then – but I am glad it wasn't written.

His letters say more than a whole book could – I will treasure
them all my life –[14]

In addition to not being able to write and the trouble with
Thom and John, Steinbeck was dealt another blow by Gwyn,
who initiated a lawsuit to make him pay additional child
support. It irked him that Thom and John were going along
with her in this, especially after the long trip abroad. Hadn't
he done a great deal for them? Didn't they realize how much
he cared about them? Was Gwyn able to supply something
emotionally that he could not? 'John could not understand
what the boys were doing,' says Elaine, 'and the fighting with
Gwyn was hard on him just now. He really hated this sort of
wrangling. None of it made any sense. We decided to go to
Rome for Easter to get away from this mess.'

Although they got away, they had a date in court. In mid-
April, Gwyn's case came up in the New York Family Court.
Gwyn testified, the boys testified, and Steinbeck testified.
Then the judge met with each of them separately. Through all
this, Steinbeck remained calm and simply told the judge what
he had tried to do for the boys. The judge finally decided to
award Gwyn a small increase equal to the rise in the cost of
living. 'Just because this man is famous and well-off, I will not
see him abused,' the judge declared in formal session. Gwyn,
hysterical, ran to the window of the courtroom and shouted
to the boys, who were waiting outside, 'Nothing! Nothing!'

The boys explained to their father that summer, after the
dust had settled, that Gwyn had insisted they go along with
her against their better judgement, and he accepted their

reasoning (although he continued to feel that they were old enough to judge these things rationally). 'The boys were a disappointment to him, I'm afraid,' says Elaine. 'He loved them very much, but he could not understand their behaviour.' Terrence McNally says, 'It's never easy to be the son of a famous man. There was a certain pressure on them, but it was not of John's doing. These were natural pressures, but I suppose that did not make it easier for either Thom or John. They were good boys at heart, warm and affec-tionate.'[15] But there can be no doubt that Steinbeck failed his sons on some crucial level, just as his own father, however supportive and loving, failed to connect with him emotionally.

With some relief Steinbeck moved out to Sag Harbor for the summer of 1964. Apart from a brief flurry of phone calls and letters when it was announced on 1 July that he was to receive the Presidential Medal of Freedom at the White House in September, his life moved along quietly. He remained at home, turning again to Malory, reading and writing and thinking about Arthur and his court. His mood is reflected in a letter written on Bastille Day – one of the last he would write to Pat Covici:

> I consider the body of my work and I do not find it good.
> That doesn't mean a thing except that the impulses have
> changed. If I have any more work in me, which I sometimes
> doubt, it will have to be of a kind to match my present age.
> I'm not the young writer of promise anymore. I'm a
> worked-over claim. There may be a few nuggets overlooked
> but the territory has been pretty thoroughly assayed. More
> and more, young people look at me in amazement because
> they thought I was dead.[16]

His next (and last) project fell into his lap unexpectedly. Tom Guinzburg, who now ran Viking, appeared at Sag Harbor one day in August with a collection of photographs representing a cross-section of American life. The original idea had been to put captions to the pictures, but Steinbeck grew interested and the captions became essays; much of the material arose from his recent trip around the country in Rocinante. In effect, *America and Americans* (as the book was eventually called) was an elegant spin-off from *Travels with Charley*. While it hardly counts as one of Steinbeck's major productions, it is a revealing piece of work which in many ways has more 'bite' than *Charley*. Steinbeck was too old and ill now to worry about pleasing his audience. He wrote and said exactly what he thought about his country, and it is still worth reading.

The relationship between Lyndon Johnson and Steinbeck became more complex and, in a sense, deeper. When he appeared at the White House to receive his medal in September, Johnson asked him for help on his acceptance speech at the upcoming Democrative Convention. These men had much in common. They were both tall, rather homely and awkward men. Both were Westerners who liked the outdoors and lived in cities uncomfortably. They were not 'sophisticated' in the Ivy League way of many intellectuals, especially those who had clustered around John Kennedy. John Hersey comments, 'It must also be said that Johnson saw in John a person he could use – a famous author who was admired by Americans generally. And I don't mean to suggest that Johnson was taking advantage of John. He was a politician. Politicians must know how to "use" people for their own ends.'[17]

As ever, Steinbeck enjoyed having the attention of the President of the United States. He had worshipped Roosevelt, had courted Stevenson, the presidential contender, and had loved knowing Kennedy; now he found himself a real friend of Lyndon Johnson. 'We often stayed at the White House,' Elaine says. 'That was a thrill, of course.

We slept in the Queen's Room or the Lincoln Room. We sometimes went to Camp David with them, and I would occasionally do shopping for Lady Bird: she just gave me her credit card and said, "Elaine, go around and buy me things." She couldn't just do that for herself without a lot of fuss, and it was lucky that we were the same size.'

Johnson was curiously fragile in his own way, and aware of the fact that Steinbeck probably admired Adlai Stevenson more than him. 'You really wanted him in this office, didn't you?' he asked one night after dinner over a glass of whiskey. 'Yes, I did,' Steinbeck admitted. For him, Adlai Stevenson was still the archetype of the possible, the sort of person who could have transformed America. For all his grasp of nitty-gritty politics, Johnson was a far cry from the philosopher-king Steinbeck would have preferred.

The low point of 1964 was the death of Pat Covici. Steinbeck's relationship to his editor had been extremely close, although occasional ripples of awkwardness between them were noticeable towards the end. In the Bastille Day letter quoted, for example, Steinbeck chided Covici for his 'school-girl talk and school-girl thinking' about their friendship. Yes, he said, something had changed of late: 'If it hadn't it would be either a lie or an abnormality.' Steinbeck's largeness as a man connected to his ability to accept change, and to modify his approach as the world shifted before his eyes. Since winning the Nobel Prize, he had become reclusive, and he understood this as a need that had to be met. He no longer needed Covici for endless encouragement and advice, but Covici could not swallow this. 'That you were born and in some small way I have been of use to you in bringing your books to light means a great deal to me, possibly infinitely more than you may ever realize,' Covici had written to Steinbeck on his fifty-sixth birthday in 1958.[18] Now old and suffering from a bleeding ulcer and other health problems, he wanted the reassurance of sameness; he also wanted the emotional boost he got from feeling connected to Steinbeck.

In September, Covici attended the White House for the award of the Presidential Medal of Freedom, and he beamed in reflected glory that in part was genuinely his. Unfortunately, this was the last time Steinbeck saw his old friend, who died suddenly on 14 October, only a few weeks later. 'Only the death of Bob Capa hit him so hard,' says Elaine. 'Covici and he had become so close, closer than John seems to have realized.' Writing to Alexander Frere, his British publisher, he said, 'Pat Covici's death was a dreadful shock to us. I can't yet go to Viking offices, not because he is not there but because he is.'[19] The memorial service was held in New York, and the eulogists were Steinbeck, Saul Bellow and Arthur Miller, each of whom owed a huge debt to Covici as literary editor. Steinbeck said,

> Pat Covici was much more than my friend. He was my
> editor. Only a writer can understand how a great editor is
> father, mother, teacher, personal devil and personal god.
> For thirty years Pat was my collaborator and my conscience.
> He demanded of me more than I had and thereby caused
> me to be more than I should have been without him.

Feeling the need to get away in the midst of this sadness, the Steinbecks flew to California to visit Esther in Watsonville. (The rift between Esther and her brother that had marred their last visit had healed, but there was never an easiness in their relationship. Esther, perhaps like Olive, was deeply conservative and suspicious of the glitzy world her brother inhabited. There was always a faint odour of disapproval in her dealings with him, although – as Beth says – 'at the most basic level John got along well with all of us. Family loyalty meant a lot to him.') Steinbeck also called on Dook Sheffield and Toby Street, both of whom he had not seen in several years. It was as if he needed to touch base, to reconnect to the land, and the friendships, from an earlier time. He wanted a sense of continuity. 'But nothing shook the sadness out of him,' Elaine says. 'He just needed time to digest the loss of Pat.'

Work on *America and Americans* ground to a halt that autumn, and Steinbeck knew enough to abandon his desk for a while. As in similar situations before, he decided to go to Europe. Travel had often worked to cheer him up in the past, prick his imagination and get his pen moving again. So he accepted a casual invitation from John Huston to go to Galway, in Ireland, for Christmas. Huston, once described as 'a larger than life character of the sort who eventually gets played in the movies by Anthony Quinn',[20] had renovated in lavish style a Georgian manor house, St Clarens. It was a jewel in the verdant Irish countryside, complete with a Japanese bath in the basement where Steinbeck and Huston sat for hours on end cooking up projects that would never come to pass.

'We loved John Huston,' says Elaine. 'He was a man of such energy and wildness. John just adored being around him; he was so full of stories and projects, and he knew so many people. He was a foxhunter, and we went with him on one of the big hunts – the Galway Hunt. He was Master of Hounds.' Writing from the Dorchester Hotel in London in the New Year, Steinbeck thanked Huston profusely: 'It was the most memorable of all Christmases, the kind that can and will turn to folklore surely. And after a short time I won't be sure what happened and what didn't and that's the real stuff of truth.'[21]

The Steinbecks went to Paris, where sad news came of the death of John's sister, Mary. Steinbeck had 'always felt closest to Mary and rushed home for the funeral'.[22] A few days later, on 2 February 1965, he wrote to Dook Sheffield,

A week ago, Mary Dekker, reading in bed, took off her

glasses, laid down her book and went to sleep. Just that. No struggle, no fear, no intimidation. And with her medical history, she must be considered one of the lucky ones. I think I knew at Thanksgiving that I would not see her again, but that's not really valid because I had that feeling about lots of things when it wasn't true.[23]

Mary was only sixty, but she suffered from the cardio-vascular problems that seem to have been part of her inheritance from the Hamilton side of the family.

Grief-stricken, suffused with nostalgia for the lost world of childhood, Steinbeck flew back to New York for the rest of the winter. Somehow, this rush of feeling loosened his pen, and he began to work again on *America and Americans*. The manuscript grew thick on his desk. 'The same routine he established at Sag Harbor was typical of New York,' Elaine says. 'He would get up before me, make coffee, and go into his study. He had a large room with a bookcase and desk and a chair for reading. He looked out over 72nd Street. He always began by sharpening his pencils. He wrote letters first, then began whatever project was before him. Sometimes he went down into the street. He was always dressed very casually – not like a New Yorker. And he made friends easily and quickly with shopkeepers in the city, with his barber and the waitresses in coffee shops.' Tom Guinzburg adds, 'There wasn't an ounce of pretension in the man. He was straight, absolutely straight with people, and it didn't matter who they were. He could talk easily to anyone.' Within months, the book was finished.

In the meanwhile, he followed Lyndon Johnson's Presidency with a keen eye, and was thrilled by Johnson's advocacy of civil rights. When the President addressed Congress on 15 March 1965, and decried the 'crippling legacy of bigotry and injustice' which had prevented blacks from voting, Steinbeck was roused to admiration. He wrote to Johnson two days later:

In our history there have been not more than five or six
moments when the word and the determination mapped
the course of the future. Such a moment was your speech,
Sir, to the Congress two nights ago. Our people will be
living by phrases from that speech when all the concrete
and steel have long been displaced or destroyed. It was a
time of no turning back, and in my mind as well as in many
others, you have placed your name among the great ones of
history.

A touch of sentimentality creeps into Steinbeck rhetoric.
When writing to a President, in particular, he felt compelled
to raise the level of his diction and formalize his syntax by a
few audible notches; one prefers his salty conversational
letters to Dook Sheffield or Elizabeth Otis. Johnson had, to
some degree, mesmerized him, and this would have sad
consequences in the last years of his life. As the Vietnam War
began to smoulder and burst into flame, Steinbeck watched
apprehensively. He would be sucked into the core of that fire.

XX

'Bright Is the Ring of Words'

'I am trying to regroup as does a military unit that has
been shot to pieces. Trying to determine if and what I have
left to write.'

Steinbeck to Dook Sheffield, 29 January 1968

In late April 1965, President Johnson invited the Steinbecks to
the White House for a spring weekend in Washington. It was,
as Elaine says, a 'low-keyed, informal occasion'. During
dinner in the President's private dining room, Steinbeck got
on especially well with Jack Valenti, Johnson's Press
Secretary, and wrote to him upon his return to New York. In
the course of this letter, in which he poked fun at Johnson's
perpetual confusion of the words 'ingenuous' and 'in-
genious', he raised the subject of Vietnam:

> The Vietnam war is troublesome. Groups have been after
> me to denounce the bombing but I don't sign anything I
> don't write. I wish the bombing weren't necessary, but I
> suspect that our people on the ground know more about
> that than I do. I certainly hope so.
>   But I do have a couple of ideas. People can get used to
> anything if it is regular. Change of pace throws them.
>   But there is another thing I miss in this war. And that is
> North Vietnam dissent.

The fact that nobody in North Vietnam seemed to object
to the Hanoi government was, indeed, 'troublesome', especially for those involved in propaganda of a certain kind.
Steinbeck also raised the issue of 'the thousand years of China
phobia' that was apparently part of Vietnam's legacy of an
endless border war with its vastly larger and more severely

armed neighbour. His instincts were, in retrospect, entirely correct; something was badly wrong with this war. The Johnson Administration kept saying that it must be fought to prevent the Chinese from taking over Vietnam in the guise of the Viet Cong, but the Viet Cong hated the Chinese even more than they hated the Americans who were bombing them.

Steinbeck was caught between the proverbial rock and a hard place. Reason suggested that the Vietnam War was a grave error, one that was likely to rip America apart and cruelly damage a small Third World country, but Steinbeck felt strongly connected to Lyndon Johnson, who had befriended him and his wife. He believed that giving emotional support to one's President in a time of trouble was honourable. Rather oddly, he fell hook, line and sinker for an old-style patriotism which argued that one should support one's country in a time of war, even if that war happened to be immoral and stupid.

In the course of the next year, Steinbeck tried to justify the Vietnam War in various ways, to himself and others. In *America and Americans*, he focused on John Kennedy's famous lines: 'Do not ask what your country can do for you but what you can do for your country.' It seemed to him that part of the trouble with America was its selfishness, which festered within the culture of materialism he so despised. What he admired in Americans of the past – people like his own California grandparents, who struggled with the land to carve out an economic and physical niche for themselves and their families – was their willingness to give something of themselves. He despised the lack of generosity, the self-centredness, that he saw everywhere around him. 'Leisure', he writes, 'came to us before we knew what to do with it.' Rather perversely, he saw the war in Vietnam as an opportunity for young Americans to give something back to their country, to sacrifice something.

There is an argument here, although it is not based on any reality that existed in the late Sixties. The Americans who were drafted to go to Vietnam were, for the most part, disadvantaged people already: blacks, poor-white farm boys, Chicanos. The leisured classes remained in college on deferments of one sort or another. It seems difficult, in retrospect, to argue that it was worth giving even one young life for that particular cause. America was foolishly interfering in a civil war. The widely publicized domino theory, which argued that if Vietnam fell to Communism all of Asia would fall in its wake, was put forward as a leading argument for the war; but it was seen through by an army of commentators.

In an article published in September 1967 in *Ramparts*, Noam Chomsky put the war into fierce perspective:

> Since 1954 there has been one fundamental issue in
> Vietnam: whether the uncertainty and conflict left
> unresolved at Geneva will be settled at a local level, by
> indigenous forces, or raised to an international level and
> settled through great-power involvement. Alone among the
> great powers, the United States has insisted on the latter
> course.[1]

The Saigon government, behind which Lyndon Johnson had thrown the weight of US military power, had little indigenous support. To stand a chance of winning a war in this situation, one would have to increase the number of troops in the field to astonishing numbers, which is exactly what Johnson did. What had been envisaged as a 'limited war' at the outset became a massive military effort. But it was still impossible to win. As President Thieu, America's puppet leader in South Vietnam, said in a widely quoted speech, 'The main reason the Viet Cong remain so strongly entrenched . . . is that the people still believe there is little difference between the French whom they called colonialists and the Americans whom they call imperialists.'[2] It's easy to see why the Vietnamese people believed this.

Steinbeck, however, refused to listen to anti-war arguments, especially after his son, John, decided to enlist. By this time, Steinbeck had met the President on many occasions, at the White House and at Camp David. Hearing of Johnny's impending departure to Vietnam, Johnson invited Steinbeck and his son to the White House in May 1966. Steinbeck wrote to Johnson a couple of days later, 'I am grateful to you for receiving my son and me. It meant a great deal to both of us and I am sure that seeing you reassured him that responsibility is behind him and backing him. He had never been to Washington before. From the plane I took him first to the Lincoln Memorial. He stood for a long time looking up at that huge and quiet figure and then he said, "Oh! Lord! We had better be great."'[3]

In the same letter, he turned to the issue of the war protesters:

> I know that you must be disturbed by the demonstrations against our policy in Vietnam. But please remember that there have always been people who insisted on their right to choose the war in which they would fight to defend their country. There were many who would have no part of Mr Adams' and George Washington's war. We call them Tories. There were many also who called General Jackson a butcher. Some of these showed their disapproval by selling beef to the British. Then there were the very many who denounced and even impeded Mr Lincoln's war. We call them Copperheads. I remind you of these things, Mr President, because sometimes, the shrill squeaking of people who simply do not wish to be disturbed must be saddening to you. I assure you that only mediocrity escapes criticism.

There is a deep wisdom here. Steinbeck knew, I suspect, that this war was wrong in principle; his letters and comments on the subject are always hedged, wary and nervous at the edges. He never threw himself uncritically behind the war in the way Johnson had hoped he might. But having Johnny in the war certainly put it into a more personal perspective, and he tried to see it from the point of view of the ordinary soldier who was doing what he considered his patriotic duty. He saw these men as victims and heroes at once – much like the Joads in *The Grapes of Wrath*. History had put a burden on their shoulders, but they carried it well.

On 14 July, Adlai Stevenson died, and this was yet another blow to Steinbeck. 'Stevenson was a great man and he was my friend,' he wrote to Jack Valenti.[4] His first reaction to the news was 'one of rage that Americans had been too stupid to avail themselves of his complete ability'. There is something touching, however naive, about this belief that Stevenson could have changed the course of American history. That national problems are, for the most part, systemic and do not depend on the individual acting alone for change is something Steinbeck would have understood earlier in his life but seems to have lost sight of near the end.

In this same letter to Valenti, he again brought up Vietnam: 'There is no way to make the Vietnamese war decent. There is no way of justifying sending troops to another man's country. And there is no way to do anything but praise the man who defends his own land.' He ended this letter sternly, 'Unless the President makes some overt move toward peace, more and more Americans as well as Europeans are going to blame him for the mess, particularly since the government we are supporting with our men and treasure is about as smelly as you can get.' This was written in mid-July 1965, when Johnson was beginning to escalate the war in major ways. Nevertheless, Steinbeck refused to come out against the war publicly and remained behind Johnson, even when his son began to write anguished letters from Vietnam saying that the war was a grave error and that the government was systematically lying to the American people. (These letters formed the basis of a book, *In Touch*, which Johnny eventually published.)

That summer, for Elaine's birthday, Steinbeck had a swimming pool built between the house at Sag Harbor and Joyous Garde, his workhouse. He put in a stepping-stone on which he wrote, 'Ladye, I take recorde of God, in thee I have myn erthly joye.' As the world seemed to be going up in flames around him, he grew even closer to Elaine, who had become his comforter and confidante. 'This was a great love affair, one of the great ones,' says Marjorie Benchley. Robert Wallsten concurs, 'I think John really leaned on Elaine in those last years. She was wonderful with him. They were friends above all else.'

On one of Steinbeck's White House visits, Lyndon Johnson suggested tentatively that Steinbeck might want to go to Vietnam and report on the war. What Johnson had in mind, of course, was propaganda. It would have been a powerful arrow in his quiver to have persuaded a Nobel-winning writer to argue from the front line that the US was doing the right thing in South-east Asia. Johnson was hypersensitive to the criticism of intellectuals, and he resented the fact that so many of them had flocked to John Kennedy yet spurned him; Steinbeck was one of his few links to the intellectual community. For the time being, however, Steinbeck cast aside the notion of going to Vietnam, believing he was just too old for such an adventure.

One of Steinbeck's writing projects during these last years was an occasional column for *Newsday*, the Long Island newspaper. He was approached by Harry F. Guggenheim, the publisher whom he had met a few years before in Kentucky, to write for him. Since *America and Americans* was still not quite finished (except in the roughest draft), and since the Malory book had once again stalled, he eagerly took to these informal scribblings. As he so delightfully put it, he 'succumbed to the fatal itch and joined the gaggle of columnists'. These columns bore the title 'Letters to Alicia', and were ostensibly written as epistles to Guggenheim's late wife. In his column, he ruminated freely on anything that preoccupied him at the time. A compulsive writer, he now had a form that was undemanding but, in obvious ways, rewarding: his audience consisted of his neighbours in Long Island, and he could expect a direct response from his readers.

Perhaps the most controversial column he wrote for *Newsday* concerned a medieval manuscript he and Professor Vinaver had uncovered in the library of Alnwick Castle in the Scottish border country. Once again, the Steinbecks had decided to attend John Huston's Christmas festivities in Galway, and they stopped in England for the month of November. The Duke of Northumberland had welcomed Steinbeck and Vinaver to his castle, and they were delighted to find this forty-eight-page manuscript that began with a list of legendary kings and concluded with the death of King Arthur. They were tremendously excited by it, and Steinbeck wrote an enthusiastic column about the discovery in *Newsday*.

After the holiday in Galway, the Steinbecks returned to England to discover that news of the discovery had leaked to the British press, who had mangled Steinbeck's column badly, wildly exaggerating the importance of the manuscript and claiming that it was indeed a genuine manuscript by Malory, when it was no such thing. Professor Vinaver, as might be expected, grew agitated and refused to speak to the press. It also came out that, in fact, the manuscript from Alnwick Castle had been microfilmed two decades earlier by researchers and that copies were on file at both the Library of Congress and the British Museum.

Steinbeck was abject and wrote to Vinaver on 15 January 1966, 'I will get out of the whole field if you think I am an interloper. . . . I am miserable if I have been a cause of unease or unhappiness to you.'[5] Vinaver replied politely, but a chink had opened that widened as time passed with no further communication between them. This incident brought Steinbeck's Arthurian adventure to an abrupt end. (After his death, Elaine was persuaded to let her husband's work on Malory be published. It appeared in 1976 in a volume edited by Chase Horton called *The Acts of King Arthur and His Noble Knights: From the Winchester Manuscript and Other Sources*.)

The Steinbecks travelled on to Israel, at Harry Guggenheim's suggestion, arriving just after the beginning of February 1966. They were given the royal tour – Jerusalem, Tel Aviv, the Dead Sea and Masada. The Israeli government had assigned a driver who happened also to be a history teacher, and the Steinbecks revelled in his rich sense of the past. Elaine recalls, 'Everywhere we went I had a Bible on my lap. It was like a map of the ancient world.' Steinbeck was 'in his element, very relaxed. Everybody was so informal and so full of good talk. John got along very well with the Israelis.' As on the trip to the Soviet Union, he met 'writers, teachers, students, people from the embassy'. They were hosted in Jerusalem by the city's well-known, affable mayor, Teddy Kollek. At one dinner party, Steinbeck recalled that his great-grandfather had come to the Holy Land to convert the Jews, and some erudite guest pointed out to him that in Herman Melville's *Journal of a Visit to Europe and the Levant*, a Deacon Dickson – clearly Steinbeck's ancestor – is mentioned in passing.

In his columns for *Newsday*, Steinbeck wrote about Israel with boyish enthusiasm, praising 'the incredible texture of human endurance and the tough inflexibility of human will power' that was demonstrated by 'this little area of the world'. As ever, he was struck by examples of durability, courage and will power, all traits he increasingly found lacking in America. (One must note, of course, his naiveté in swallowing the Israeli Tourist Board version of Israeli history without even noticing that the Israelis, in their quest for statehood, had displaced millions of Palestinians, many of whom were living in filthy camps along the River Jordan and elsewhere. The Steinbeck of three decades earlier would surely have sniffed out the injustice – or at least the tragic contradictions – inherent in this situation.)

He was perhaps intent upon contrasting Israel's energetic vision of itself with America's loss of vision. The moral decay of his own country became, in effect, the theme of *America and Americans*. He ends that book with the stark suggestion that America has 'no new path to take, no duty to carry out, no purpose to fulfill'. Although Steinbeck believed strongly in the value of myth, he felt that in the twentieth century America had turned away from its founding myths of 'equality and self-reliance'. The country had toppled into a life without meaning or purpose: 'Americans, very many of them, are obsessed with tensions. Nerves are drawn tense and twanging. Emotions boil up and spill over into violence largely in meaningless or unnatural directions.' He locates the source of our national malaise in the excess, the very abundance, created by the hard work of our ancestors. Furthermore, he takes no solace in the power of the land itself to renew American spirituality, arguing that we have so abused our natural resources that the opportunities for renewal appear slight. As in his conversations with John Hersey on the way back from Japan, he takes a final swipe at the atom bomb, 'I did not know about the bomb, and certainly I had nothing to do with its use, but I am horrified and ashamed; and nearly everyone I know feels the same thing. And those who loudly and angrily justify Hiroshima and Nagasaki – why, they must be the most ashamed of all.'

America and Americans was published in 1966, when it was pretty much dismissed as a 'coffee table book'. Richard Peterson, however, has astutely seen in its pages important continuities with the massive body of fiction that precedes it:

From *Cup of Gold* to *East of Eden*, Steinbeck has observed
and studied human nature within the framework of myth.
In *America and Americans* he reiterates his faith in the value
of myth, even if the people have lost their visionary powers.
He is not, however, a Tiresias wandering about the waste
land, admonishing himself to find order in his own soul.
Steinbeck's concern and love is for America. As an observer
of America, he has witnessed the terrible things Americans
do to each other and has faithfully and sorrowfully recorded
them. As an American, however, he still expresses a belief
in those myths and dreams which comprise the spirit of
America, and he insists that the energy remains for America
to rediscover its principles and purpose.[6]

Upon his return from Israel, Steinbeck began to express his
support for Lyndon Johnson and his concern over the
protests against the Vietnam War in his *Newsday* columns. 'A
lot of his friends didn't agree with him,' Edward Albee says,
'but we – I, certainly – never fell out with John over this. He
had his opinions, which were extremely thoughtful and
complex, and he held them forcefully. Unlike some, he also
allowed other people to express their opinions. He was very
open that way, and never dogmatic.' When writing in
Newsday about the Free Speech movement that had been
organized at the University of California at Berkeley,
Steinbeck said, 'I hope when they get it [free speech]
themselves, they will allow it to others.'

Apart from this journalism, Steinbeck wrote very little. He
did attempt several short pieces of fiction, with no success;
nothing would cohere. 'As you may know, I've been having a
bad time – work unacceptable, to me, and a strong feeling
that my time was over,' he wrote on 28 October 1966, to Elia
Kazan.[7] One day Harry Guggenheim suggested that he go to
Vietnam as a correspondent for *Newsday*, and suddenly it
seemed like the right time for this expedition. Elaine notes
'that ever since Johnny went to Vietnam his father wanted to

go there, too. He was dying to go. But he didn't want to go as Lyndon Johnson's emissary or anything. It was important to him that he go independently.' As usual, he would not go without his wife beside him. 'I am not going places any more without Elaine,' he wrote to Willard Bascom. 'Life is too short to be away from her. But I must say one thing. She'll go anywhere and lick the other dog when she gets there.'[8]

Steinbeck had been invited to Washington in December to attend a dinner at the White House for members of the Arts Council, of which he was a member. By now, Lyndon Johnson had virtually no support from within the artistic or intellectual community, and he clung to Steinbeck as his one genuine ally. But Steinbeck had to refuse this invitation because of the upcoming trip to Saigon. He explained to the President that he was just leaving to visit his son, John, in Vietnam, and that he would stop on the way to see his other son, Thom, who was also in the army and doing his basic training at Fort Ord in California. 'We visited Thom,' says Elaine, 'then we flew to Hawaii. We were in Pearl Harbor for the twenty-fifth anniversary of the bombing, and we attended a very powerful ceremony aboard the USS *Arizona*.

'We flew all through the night, and when we woke up we saw land and we knew that when we did it was Vietnam,' she recalls. 'It was a little nerve-racking to land there.' Instead of descending gradually, the plane had to bank steeply and dive into the Tan Sohn Nut Airport in Saigon to avoid sniper fire or rocket attacks. 'Johnny was waiting for us at the airport,' says Elaine. 'It all seemed incredible.' The Steinbecks were taken to the Caravelle Hotel, which had become a kind of informal home-away-from-home to the international press corps.

It was a rickety place, with dim lights and temperamental air-conditioners that hummed loudly all night. The furniture was tacky and old-fashioned, and the Steinbecks occupied two small rooms. 'CBS had its headquarters there,' Elaine remembers, 'so there was a lot going on.' They saw a great deal of Vietnam in a relatively short time. 'I didn't see as much as John, of course,' says Elaine, 'but I would go with him whenever I could. He went right into the fighting, which is something they wouldn't let me do. I think being in Vietnam reminded John of his days as a correspondent in World War II. He just loved it. But it wasn't easy; we were often in danger. I remember we were sleeping out in the jungle in a tent one night, and there was gunfire very close by. I said to John, "I sure hope that's friendly fire." He said, "Just pretend it is and go back to sleep." '

Marine Major Sam M. Gipson Jr was assigned to Steinbeck. The young Texan had read a few of his books and was excited about showing the famous author around Vietnam. He introduced him to many of the hundreds of journalists in Saigon, who ranged from Japanese television reporters to high-powered print journalists like Joseph Alsop. On 4 January 1967, Steinbeck wrote a vivid letter to Harry Guggenheim that gives a sense of his daily life while in the field:

> I've been out in the really hairy boondocks, in the waist-deep paddies where your boots suck in mud that holds like glue. The patrols go on at night now down in the Delta area and are really ambushes set up against the V.C. [Viet Cong]. There are caches of weapons everywhere and very few of them are found. All a running V.C. has to do is to sink his weapons in a ditch or in a flooded paddy and later return and retrieve them.
>
> Yesterday, I was out with a really good bunch of men. We climbed out of ditches, went through houses, questioned people. We came on one cache of weapons and ammunition in the bottom of a ditch. They smear grease on the guns and seal the shells in jugs. Every house in the area is surrounded by water – in fact the raised place where the house and its garden stand are made by dredging up the

mud in baskets and piling it up to dry to a platform. Our
men were moving slowly along in the water feeling for
weapons on the muddy bottom – a slow and very fallible
method.[9]

Steinbeck immersed himself thoroughly in the experience of
daily warfare. He explained to Guggenheim that the Viet
Cong who are captured are 'tough and secret'. When they are
taken, they refuse to talk at all. If only they would talk, they
might tell the US military where landmines were planted,
thus saving thousands of lives. Steinbeck, ever trying to come
up with practical solutions to problems, suggested to his new
friends in Vietnam that they get some scopolamine, a drug
that relaxes inhibitions and turns the person injected with it
into a compulsive talker. (Similar techniques were, in fact,
often used by interrogation teams in Vietnam.)

While Elaine stayed mostly in Saigon, Steinbeck dressed in
field gear and set off, day after day, with Sam Gipson. They
had the use of military helicopters, and this enabled them to
get to far-flung quarters quite easily. For longer trips, they
would beg seats on C–130 aircraft, huge transport planes that
carried troops and equipment to major locations. Steinbeck
did not hide behind the lines but went straight into battle in a
helicopter with the First Cavalry several times; he also
followed closely behind another Marine assault and sat with
an artillery unit outside Saigon that was protecting
approaches to the city. In one of his most daring escapades,
he witnessed B–52 raids in the north from a helicopter, which
hovered near the bombing site and was nearly hit by the Viet
Cong's surface-to-air missiles.

Elaine says that 'one of the first things John wanted when
he arrived in Saigon was a weapon, but they dissuaded him
from this. He did take some kind of course there in firing the
M16 automatic rifle, and he took a course on how to avoid
landmines.' The American press were present on some of
these occasions, and one of the photographs sent by wire to

the US pictured Steinbeck pushing through a swampy jungle in military fatigues and helmet, looking like a lost soldier from the Italian campaign of World War II. This image of the author as a warlike hawk inflamed the American left, who saw him as Lyndon Johnson's patsy, and his stock plunged among the intelligentsia.

Steinbeck's 'Letters to Alicia' in *Newsday* were taken as enthusiastic support for the war itself, although he judiciously avoided discussing the war in any general terms. As when he covered the conflict in Europe three decades earlier, he focused on the daily life of soldiers, describing what he saw in detail, evoking smells and sights and sounds. The human element mattered to him more than geopolitical arguments, and he found significance in the little stories around him, avoiding any master narrative about the nature of the war, its origins or possible outcome. He knew, and said in print many times, that most of the American soldiers he met in Vietnam did not want to be there but felt an obligation to their country.

Elaine did accompany her husband on an exotic mission into Laos, where most journalists did not venture (or were not allowed). 'We were taken into Laos in those STOL planes [Short Takeoff and Landing],' she recalls. 'One time we landed in a rice field at the bottom of Laos, a place where a lot of agrarian reform was happening – John was always interested in agriculture and he wanted to write a story about it. Suddenly a message came through that said, "Get the Steinbecks out of there as fast as you can! The North Vietnamese Army is coming at you and the planes are on their way!" So they started trying to find a plane that could take us out. We were standing out on the runway, rather frantic, when this plane swooped down to examine the field and the pilot realized who we were and landed. "What the hell are you doing here?" he cried. "You're getting out just in time." And we did. We weren't gone a few minutes before the North Vietnamese came rolling through.'

'John realized pretty quickly, you know, that the North Vietnamese were mostly hidden in these underground tunnels, which formed a kind of invisible network for them to use as they liked. He said, "We're never going to win this war. We'd have to get these people into the open to win it, and we can't do that." ' Steinbeck met all the top brass, including General William C. Westmoreland, the officer in charge of all military operations in Vietnam. He soon realized that Westmoreland and the others were lying to the President about the war and determined to tell the President himself what was really going on, then write about it. In the meantime, he remained loyal to the American troops and wrote a patriotic and somewhat inflated letter to President Johnson about his time in Vietnam:

> I know, Mr President, that you get many reports through your official channels of information. But I want to tell you by this completely unofficial means, that we have here the finest, the best trained, the most intelligent and the most dedicated soldiers I have ever seen in any army and I have seen soldiers in my time. These men are the best we have ever had.[10]

Steinbeck was unable then to admit to himself – or to Johnson – the deep ambiguities of the Vietnam War. Partly out of misplaced loyalty to the White House, he could not recognize what was in front of him: a demoralized army largely composed of lower-class kids who wondered where in the hell they were and why they were there. Had he spoken out against the war, his authority, as a major American writer, would have been welcomed by the anti-war movement, most of whom grew up on *The Grapes of Wrath* and *Tortilla Flat*. But this was not to be. 'John certainly felt the pressure from the anti-war groups,' says Edward Albee, 'but he resisted anything like that. He never signed petitions. He just wasn't that sort of man.'

The Steinbecks used Bangkok as their base of operations for the tour of Laos. 'Bangkok was so strange,' Elaine remembers. 'With all of those American boys on their leaves – R & R. The place was teeming with whorehouses and so crowded, the traffic unbelievable. It was a nightmare. The best thing was when we had an audience with the King and Queen of Thailand at their palace.' At the end of their stay in Thailand, in late February, they travelled by train for twenty-seven hours through the Malay Peninsula to Penang. 'Shades of Warren Hastings, Lord Cornwallis, Kipling and Somerset Maugham,' Steinbeck wrote to Elizabeth Otis.[11] In Penang, they stayed in air-conditioned luxury at the Eastern and Oriental Hotel, and suddenly the three months of travel and frenetic activity caught up with Steinbeck and, in his own words, he 'went all to pieces'. He slept for seventy-two hours straight.

He certainly deserved the rest. In three months he had covered a vast amount of territory and had sent fifty-two short columns to *Newsday*. Their plan was to return home via Indonesia, Bali, Hong Kong, and Japan. 'We met Johnny in Japan – he was on his leave. And we went together to Kyoto and spent the night lying in the grass in a fragrant park under the cherry trees,' says Elaine. 'It was such a beautiful place, so peaceful and such a contrast to Vietnam and Thailand. We were very happy there. But in Tokyo John's back went out suddenly, and he could hardly move. It turned out that he had two or three really smashed discs in the spine, and he was in excruciating pain.'

Steinbeck's immediate feelings about his trip to South-east Asia emerged in a letter written from Hong Kong to some friends in Sag Harbor: 'This has been a good trip and in many ways a sad one. I haven't dwelt on the killed and the wounded. I've seen other wars and have hated those too. But every dead GI (and many of them have been my friends) breaks your heart in a way that can never be repaired. If I could shorten this war by one hour by staying here, I would never come home.'[12]

Back in Sag Harbor for the summer, his thinking about the war began to deepen. He wrote to Elizabeth Otis in August,

> I understand your feeling about this war. We seem to be sinking deeper and deeper into the mire. It is true that we are. I am pretty sure by now that the people running the war have neither conception nor control of it. And I think that I do have some conception but I can't write it.
>
> I know we cannot win this war, nor any war for that matter. And it seems to me that the design is for us to sink deeper and deeper into it, more and more of us. When we have put down a firm foundation of our dead and when we have by a slow, losing process been sucked into the texture of Southeast Asia, we will never be able nor will we want to get out.[13]

Depressed about the war and still in pain because of the back injury, Steinbeck found himself unable to write. 'The words will not form or, if they do, there is no flavor nor any joy in them,' he told Otis in despair. In many ways, the Vietnam War had sunk John Steinbeck as a writer. It had sucked him into a vortex, and it would not free him. As autumn came, his back problem seemed only to worsen; the pain was such that he had no choice but to try surgery. He checked into the University Hospital of New York University in mid-October, hoping to be out and about by Christmas.

Johnny, meanwhile, was back from Vietnam and living in Washington DC, where he had a job with the army's Information Office at the Pentagon. He was working quietly on an article about the use of drugs by soldiers in Vietnam, a subject he would write about directly in his book, *In Touch*. One morning, in mid-October 1967 – only days before Steinbeck had his back operation – *Newsweek* called his

apartment to say that his son had been arrested for possession of twenty pounds of marijuana. Elaine took the call and
thought, 'My God, I've got to get to John before the press
does.' But Steinbeck had already heard the story on the radio
in the hospital.

The press swarmed around the Steinbecks, who had to
muscle their way through this one together. Steinbeck stood
by his son, believing his story that the cache did not belong to
him. On 18 December a jury in Washington accepted his
story, acquitting him of all charges. 'This was just a terrible
time for John, and for Johnny,' Elaine says. 'Johnny came to
the hospital to explain what had happened to his father, and
he was in a bad state. This was very hard for them both.'
Steinbeck, like so many parents in the late Sixties, found
himself on the other side of that great divide called the
Generation Gap. It was excruciating for those standing on
either side of the gulf.

'The outcome was a relief,' says Elaine, 'but the whole
affair did not help John's relationship with Johnny, and
Johnny got more and more resentful in later years.' Indeed,
John Steinbeck IV and Thom Steinbeck never quite pulled
themselves together. 'It was sad to watch the boys as they
became men,' says one friend of the family.[14] 'Neither of
them ever really earned a living for themselves. They lived off
their father's inheritance, trying their hand at this and that. It
was sad. They seemed incapable of mature behaviour. John
knew that he had failed them, and it gave him great pain. But
it was never something he understood. He preferred not to
speak of them, or refer to their problems. I think he expected
Johnny to succeed as a writer; Johnny had a lot of talent. But
the family dynamics were such that both boys felt constricted
and angry, and that has never changed. Johnny, in fact, died
in his mid-forties, rather tragically, without ever pulling
himself together. Thom is a would-be film producer, though
one can't say his life has worked out terribly well either.'

Steinbeck's operation, which involved a fusion of discs, lasted five hours; it was a 'really massive job of surgery', as Steinbeck said to John Kenneth Galbraith in mid-November. The recovery, however, lasted many months. 'In a way he never recovered from it,' Elaine says. 'We went out to Sag Harbor after he got out of the hospital, and John could really do nothing but lie in bed and read.' Just before Christmas, they flew to Grenada in the Virgin Islands. 'We had a little cottage on the beach,' says Elaine. 'John was terribly weak, but he would get into his bathing suit and lie on the beach and sometimes go in for a swim. The setting was so beautiful. John was always happiest by the sea, and the warm weather made life easier for him. He was in such a lot of pain.' They spent a whole month there, and Steinbeck soaked himself in a long history of the love affair of Napoleon and Josephine and a number of 'old romantic novels' and mysteries, as he told Elizabeth Otis on 9 January.

They returned to Sag Harbor in the last week of January 1968, and Steinbeck almost immediately sent a note to Dook Sheffield:

> I am gradually coming back or ahead or something. The nervous shock as well as all the sedatives kind of move you into another and rather fuzzy reality. But healing is a slow process except that I know when the process is complete, I will have a stronger back than I ever had. I haven't written because it is only recently that I could sit in a chair with any comfort and I dare you to write lying flat on your back. I tried and it doesn't work. Meanwhile I am trying to regroup as does a military unit that has been shot to pieces. Trying to determine if and what I have left to write. Maybe something, maybe not, but if not, then there was no point in the surgery.

Instead of progressing, Steinbeck seemed only to feel worse each day. He was having frequent 'little episodes', Elaine says. 'He would suddenly lose the nimbleness in his fingers, like in Italy. His speech would slur. He would seem lost. But then he would recover and everything seemed normal again.' In early spring, the Steinbecks returned to their apartment in New York because, however much he preferred Sag Harbor, it was simply easier for Elaine to take care of her husband in the city, where doctors and a good hospital were easily available. Steinbeck's current doctor, who was also a good friend, was Denton Cox. On 5 March, Steinbeck wrote him a long letter that accompanied his medical history, and it contains some extremely revealing passages. In one paragraph, for instance, he explains his view of religion with typical bluntness and rigorous honesty: 'I am not religious so that I have no apprehension of a hereafter, either a hope of reward or a fear of punishment. It is not a matter of belief. It is what I feel to be true from my experience, observation and simple tissue feeling.'[15]

He added that he had 'had a good span of life', and from now on would not feel short-changed if anything happened to him. 'I have had far more than my share of the things men strive for – material things and honors and love,' he said. His letter ended with a touching (if somewhat paternalistic) note about Elaine, 'I love Elaine more than myself. Her well being and comfort and happiness are more important than my own. And I would go to any length to withhold from her any pain or sorrow that is not needful for her own enrichment.'

Steinbeck felt miserable in the city, however, and by April they returned to Sag Harbor, although he was forbidden to garden or go in a boat or fish or lift things. 'It's a bloody bore,' he wrote to Toby Street. In late May, Steinbeck had another of his little episodes, although this time it was more frightening. Elaine says, 'We went to a little restaurant down on the waterfront. I suddenly noticed that John couldn't pick up a fork. He was trying to, but he just couldn't. I said to him, "John, are you having trouble?" He said, "I think so." And I said, "Get in the car." A few friends helped him into the car, and he went unconscious. We took him straight to the hospital in Southampton, where he was put through every kind of test and examination. He recovered quickly, but it seemed obvious that he was not getting any better.'

In July, a huge heat wave hit Long Island, and this only exacerbated Steinbeck's condition. One day he was crossing the living room and he grew faint and simply couldn't breathe. 'John had a little heart attack that time,' says Elaine. 'He was taken to the hospital and put into an oxygen tent. That was when Denton – Dr Cox – decided he should move back to the city, where he could be under close observation. John hated the idea, but he went along with it.' He was taken to the University Hospital in Manhattan, where he remained for several weeks.

At Steinbeck's insistence, he and Elaine moved back to Sag Harbor on 31 August. 'John couldn't stay away from there. He wanted to be near the water,' Elaine says. 'And somewhat to my surprise we had a lovely fall. John was feeling rather better, and he would sit in a deck chair and watch the men who were building a new dock. He would read and write a few letters. One time Toby Street came to visit from California. He wanted John to raise hell with him, to drink and stay up late into the night and tell stories like they used to do, and John tried, but it was very hard on him. He couldn't keep up, and this upset him. He realized then, with Toby, that he was not the same person he had been. His body just wasn't responding to his brain.'

In early November, Steinbeck's breathing became more difficult. He was now suffering from emphysema as well as the more serious problem of hardening of the arteries. His heart was very weak, and he was having mini-strokes at rather frequent intervals. One morning he was in such bad shape that Elaine said, 'I'm calling Denny [his doctor].' Dr Cox drove out to Sag Harbor, examined Steinbeck, and insisted that he return to the city again.

Elaine found it very difficult looking after her husband by herself, so a French-Canadian nurse, Elaine LaTulipe, was hired to spend some hours each day with him. 'John would say to me, "Let's have Tulips spend the night so you can get some rest." She was good company. John just adored her.' Frank Loesser, who lived nearby, would often stop by for chats, as would other old friends, such as Elizabeth Otis and Tom Guinzburg. Dr Cox came by frequently to examine his friend and patient.

'They were just starting to do heart by-passes at University Hospital,' says Elaine, 'and one day John asked Denny Cox to bring some of the heart surgeons over to see him. He wondered if he might have one of those operations. The doctors came, and John was examined. Afterward they told him there was nothing they could do for him. It wasn't just his heart, it was the whole system. John apologized to the doctors for bringing them all the way over to his apartment, but he was very sad. I think he realized then that it was over for him. There was nothing that could be done.'

A light snow was ticking against the big windows of the apartment high over East 72nd Street on the morning of 20 December 1968. It was Friday. Elaine had spent the night in the guest room to get a little rest. She knew instinctively that her husband did not have long to live. 'I don't know how you know these things,' she recalls. 'But you do.'

It was a long day, the last day. After breakfast, Elaine went into his room and found him sitting up in bed with an oxygen mask on his face, fed by tubes through his nostrils. His mind was very clear and calm. Elaine read to him through much of the morning, but at noon Steinbeck began to feel awful and asked to see Dr Cox who came at once and did everything he could to make his patient comfortable.

All afternoon Elaine sat beside him, reading. At one point, Steinbeck said, 'Can I ask you something?'

'Of course,' she answered quickly.

'What would you say was the best time we had together in our twenty years?' He looked at her with a bemused severity, waiting for her reply.

Elaine started to answer but hesitated. Then she said, 'You say first, John.'

'No,' he said. 'I'm dying and you would just agree with me.'

'I'll tell you what I'll do,' she said. 'I'll write it down here on this notepad.' She scribbled something and put it in the palm of his hand.

'Now,' she asked, 'what's the best time we ever had? You say it.'

'The time in Somerset,' he said firmly.

'Open your hand,' she told him.

On the little sheet of notepaper was written one word in caps: SOMERSET. Elaine lay beside him, and they reminisced about the year they had spent at Discove Cottage.

Some time during the afternoon Elizabeth Otis and Shirley Fisher came by. A nurse from the hospital also turned up, having heard from Dr Cox that Steinbeck's condition had worsened. Another old friend, Dr Nancy Kester, also appeared later in the afternoon. Elaine remained alone with her husband while the others talked in the living room. 'I lay beside him a long time,' says Elaine. 'Slowly he slipped into a coma . . . very peacefully and slowly. Then he just stopped breathing.' Steinbeck was pronounced dead by Dr Kester at 5.30 in the afternoon, a few hours before the official beginning of winter.

According to Steinbeck's wishes (and in spite of his atheism), his funeral was performed according to the rites of the Church of England. 'I just don't want a bunch of people getting together to tell yarns about me,' he had said to Elaine. The service, attended by several hundred people, was held at the St James Episcopal Church on Madison Avenue. Henry

Fonda, a friend since the filming of *The Grapes of Wrath*, flew in from Hollywood to read aloud from Petrarch's sonnets to Laura, Tennyson's 'Ulysses', and some lines from a poem by Robert Louis Stevenson that had been one of Steinbeck's favourite passages in English poetry:

> Bright is the ring of words
>   When the right man rings them
> Fair the fall of songs
>   When the singer sings them
> Still they are carolled and said
>   On wings they are carried
> After the singer is dead
>   And the maker buried.

The Order from the Burial of the Dead was read from the English Book of Common Prayer by the rector, as were Psalms 46 and 121.

On Christmas Eve, Elaine and Thom flew to California with Steinbeck's ashes in a Georgian silver box. Elaine recalls, 'We got to the 11th Street house on Christmas Day, and I put the silver box on a little fountain in the garden. John always loved it there.' Steinbeck's ashes were taken a few days later to their permanent resting place beside John Ernst, Olive and Mary in the Garden of Memories Cemetery in Salinas, but the day after Christmas a special memorial service for the family was held at Point Lobos on a cliff overlooking the sea. A young, long-haired priest in a white robe read from the Bible; he picked up a handful of dirt and threw it towards the sea, crying 'Dust to dust, ashes to ashes', as seagulls squawked overhead and the surf crashed loudly on the rocks below.

Epilogue

Steinbeck's death released him, or his reputation, into the wobbly hands of eternity. His work – some twenty-six volumes of fiction and non-fiction – has 'survived in the valley of its making', as Auden once said of Yeats. 'There is never a night when one of John's plays isn't produced somewhere in the world from Peking to Peoria', says Elaine Steinbeck. Hundreds of thousands of copies of his work are sold each year, while virtually every single book that he wrote remains in print: a version of eternal life granted to very few authors.

In most ways, Steinbeck's writing life was a happy one. He found his vocation early, while still in his teens, and he never wavered in its pursuit. With the financial support of his parents, who suppressed their scepticism and paid the bills, Steinbeck could learn his craft in relative peace. His first novel *Cup of Gold*, appeared in his twenty-seventh year: hardly a long wait for a budding novelist to make it into print. By the age of thirty-three, he had a bestseller in *Tortilla Flat*, and from that point on he would never really lack money. Before his fortieth birthday he had won the Drama Critics Circle Award for the play version of his novella, *Of Mice and Men*, and both the Pulitzer Prize and National Book Award for *The Grapes of Wrath*. More importantly, he had by this time written at least four books which would become a permanent part of the story of American literature.

However 'successful' a person's career may look to an

outsider, what matters is what happens daily. Steinbeck was among the lucky ones here too: he took immense pleasure in the routines of life, in making coffee and sharpening pencils, in the process of writing itself, in conversation with his family and friends, in whittling or sailing, or in repairing a broken household object. 'He loved getting up in the morning,' Elaine Steinbeck recalls. 'It was as if he couldn't wait to get going, to get to his work.' His voluminous letters attest to the high quality of his engagement with the world around him, a deeply rooted tie which showed itself in the texture of his prose.

Steinbeck's many close friendships fed his sense of himself in crucial ways. Toby Street, Dook Sheffield, Ed Ricketts, Pat Covici, and Elizabeth Otis – to name only the most obvious – lived in his heart; he talked to them in his letters, on the telephone, over drinks; they came to know and love him deeply. As Sheffield once noted, 'John had a gift for friendship. When he talked to you, you felt as though he were only interested in you. And he *was*, while you were talking with him. He cared, and that was clear.' His most intimate relations, of course, were those with Carol, Gwyn, and Elaine: his three wives. These were all complex relations, as marriages always are. Certainly the early years with Carol and the last twenty years of his life with Elaine were immensely satisfying. But he suffered horribly when his marriage to Carol broke down, aware that the fault was as much (or more) his than hers. With Gwyn, he seems to have had few joyful moments. 'That was a bad match, and the pity of it was that children were involved,' says Marjorie Benchley. Doubtless both Thom and John suffered as a consequence, and their later problems followed from what happened in their early childhood. Their father (and mother) paid a high price in anxiety and disappointment for this ill-considered marriage, which had the single advantage of being short-lived. For all this, one would not even want to deny Steinbeck the pain of his failed marriages. His emotional instrument had many strings, and each of them was plucked in turn.

The darker side of Steinbeck's life owes a good deal to his difficult family background. As we have seen, John Ernst's business failure and his refusal to stand up for himself unnerved his highly sensitive son, who developed a fear of failure that dogged him to the end. Olive's perfectionism only worsened this fear: in adulthood, Steinbeck was forever upbraiding himself, angered by his own inability to perform flawlessly in all things. His anger towards his parents and his own feelings of inadequacy led to bouts of depression which he was never entirely to be free of, although he came to terms with some of these issues in his last two decades.

Whatever his faults and failings, John Steinbeck was a clear-eyed, affectionate man who well understood that he must detach himself from the public side of success to maintain a firmly centred life. Writing to Elia Kazan from Somerset in 1959, he admonished his friend with a wonderful lack of restraint:

> Lift your mind up to the hills, Gadg. Criticize nothing, evaluate nothing. Just let the Thing come thundering in – accept and enjoy. It will be chaos for a while but gradually order will appear and an order you did not know. No one survives in other people more than two weeks after his death unless he leaves something he has much more lasting than himself.

The awsome clarity of spirit reflected here is the essence of Steinbeck, a man who sought that almost Taoistic detachment from the claims of ordinary egotism which makes an inner life possible. This is not to say that Steinbeck was a saint – indeed, he sinned boldly with the best of them. He often ignored his own advice, losing himself in the dark woods of fame and power as he courted movie stars and presidents.

But he moved through and out of these thickets into that clearing where he survives in his work itself.

This book attempts to answer what David R. Noble has called 'the Steinbeck question'.

> The Steinbeck question, as with all problems of this sort, is actually a collection of issues, mysteries and conundrums. For example, when in an average year his contemporaries and fellow Nobel Laureates, Faulkner and Hemingway, are each treated in perhaps 120 or 130 scholarly books and articles, why is Steinbeck the subject of only fifteen or twenty? Why is it that the work of this enormously popular author is disappearing from the pages of anthologies even faster than the work of Hemingway, Faulkner, Fitzgerald and other major figures of the traditional canon? Why has Steinbeck not received the intense academic scrutiny awarded his peers?[1]

Answers spring to mind, some more useful than others. For a start, Steinbeck did not write in the modernist tradition that has been the focus of most academic inquiry; he did, however (rather like Robert Frost) absorb many of the techniques of modernism, diverting them to his own purposes while cultivating an almost childlike simplicity that has discouraged literary critics, who find little in his books to untangle or annotate. There is also the bewildering range of his work: *The Red Pony* must sleep uneasily on the library shelf beside *The Wayward Bus*, for instance. More subtly, Steinbeck's version of the mythopoeic approach in his later career proved rather difficult for critics, who continued to judge this work (from *The Wayward Bus* onwards) by the standards of social realism set up by *In Dubious Battle* and *The Grapes of Wrath*. The achievement of the later fiction went unnoticed by critics, many of whom were simply looking in the wrong direction.

Steinbeck has not been studied much in universities for another, less complicated reason, as Jackson J. Benson, the

Dean of Steinbeck studies, notes in a recent article: 'As *The Grapes of Wrath* became more and more often a part of the high school curriculum, colleges and universities tended to shy away from it, partly for fear of repeating material already studied, but also because they came to believe that such adoptions demonstrated that the novel was not college-level material.'[2] Benson also points out that any writer who ventures into the realm of comedy risks disparagement. 'Frequently discarded or overlooked, Steinbeck's comic trilogy – *Tortilla Flat*, *Cannery Row*, and *Sweet Thursday* – is not even considered as part of the canon by some critics.' Steinbeck was thought by some to be treating poverty and social degradation with an unbecoming flippancy in those books, so they dismissed them as 'slight'. In fact these novels contain some of Steinbeck's finest prose and most inventive narration; their tone is 'light' without being condescending.

John Steinbeck was a uniquely authentic writer who, over nearly four decades, produced two dozen or so books that evoke life in this century with unfailing compassion, wit, and magnanimity. He was, in his own measure and style, a socially conscious writer whose fierce and loving engagement with the world has about it an almost visionary quality. 'Summon a vision and declare it pure,' the poet Theodore Roethke said. Steinbeck did just that. The purity and wholeness of his vision will haunt, inspire, and move readers for years to come.

Bibliography
Works by John Steinbeck

Cup of Gold. New York: Robert M. McBride & Company, 1932.
The Pastures of Heaven. New York: Brewer, Warren & Putnam, 1932.
To a God Unknown. New York: Robert O. Ballou, 1933.
Tortilla Flat. New York: Covici-Friede, 1935.
In Dubious Battle. New York: Covici-Friede, 1936.
Of Mice and Men (separate editions of play and novel). New York: Covici-Friede, 1937.
The Red Pony. New York: Covici-Friede, 1937.
Their Blood Is Strong. San Francisco: Simon J. Lubin Society, 1938.
The Long Valley. New York: Viking, 1938.
The Grapes of Wrath. New York: Viking, 1939.
Sea of Cortez: A Leisurely Journal of Travel and Research with a Scientific Appendix. Co-authored with Edward F. Ricketts. New York: Viking, 1941.
The Forgotten Village. New York: Viking, 1941.
Bombs Away: The Story of a Bomber Team. New York: Viking, 1942.
The Moon Is Down. New York: Viking, 1942.
The Moon Is Down (*Play in Two Parts*). New York: Dramatists' Play Service, 1942.
Cannery Row. New York: Viking, 1945.
The Wayward Bus. New York: Viking, 1947.
The Pearl. New York: Viking, 1947.
A Russian Journal. New York: Viking, 1948.
Burning Bright. New York: Viking, 1950.
The Log from the 'Sea of Cortez'. New York: Viking, 1951.
East of Eden. New York: Viking, 1952.
Sweet Thursday. New York: Viking, 1954.
The Short Reign of Pippin IV. New York: Viking, 1957.
Once There Was a War. New York: Viking, 1958.
The Winter of Our Discontent. New York: Viking, 1961.

Travels with Charley in Search of America. New York: Viking, 1962.
America and Americans. New York: Viking, 1966.
Journal of a Novel: The 'East of Eden' Letters. New York: Viking, 1969.
Viva Zapata! (script of 1952 film). New York: Viking, 1974.
Steinbeck: A Life in Letters. Edited by Elaine Steinbeck and Robert Wallsten. New York: Viking, 1975.
The Acts of King Arthur and His Noble Knights. Edited by Horton Chase. New York: Farrar, Straus & Giroux, 1976.
Working Days: The Journal of 'The Grapes of Wrath'. Edited by Robert DeMott. New York: Viking, 1988.

Notes

Prologue

1 For a study of Ricketts's influence on Steinbeck, see Richard Astro, *John Steinbeck and Edward Ricketts: The Shaping of a Novelist* (Minneapolis: University of Minnesota Press, 1973).
2 Unpublished essay by Edward Ricketts entitled 'Non-Teleological Thinking', dated March 1941.
3 Horst Frend, ed., *Nobel Lectures, Literature, 1901–1967*, 'Acceptance' (New York, 1969), p. 575.
4 Thomas Kiernan, *The Intricate Music: A Biography of John Steinbeck* (Boston: Little, Brown, 1979).
5 Jackson J. Benson, *The True Adventures of John Steinbeck, Writer* (New York: Viking, 1984).

Chapter One

1 I had many interviews with Elaine Steinbeck between September 1990 and September 1993. All quotes are taken from these taped and transcribed interviews.
2 Steinbeck interview.
3 Interview with Elizabeth (Beth) Ainsworth, 28 December 1992. All Ainsworth quotations derive from this interview.
4 ibid.
5 *Steinbeck: A Life in Letters*, eds. Elaine Steinbeck and Robert Wallsten (New York: Viking, 1975), p. 278. Hereafter *LL*.
6 Interview with Margaret Carey, 12 January 1991.
7 My characterization of the relationship between John Ernst and Olive is based on an interview with Mary Graydon (who lived on Central Avenue at the time) in December 1991. Corroborated by Beth Ainsworth and others.
8 Interview with Edgar Reese, 14 June 1990.

9 Carey interview.

10 ibid.

11 Ainsworth interview.

12 Interview with Tom Guinzburg, August 1993.

13 ibid.

14 Quoted by Kiernan, op cit. p. 10.

15 Ainsworth interview.

16 Interview with Morris Scott, Pacific Grove, December 1991.

17 ibid.

18 Quoted by Nelson Valjean, *John Steinbeck: The Errant Knight* (San Francisco: Chronicle Books, 1975), p. 40.

19 Carey interview. The point is also nicely made and elaborated by Benson, op. cit., pp. 27–8.

20 Ainsworth interview.

21 ibid.

22 The yearbook is available for reading at the Salinas Public Library.

Chapter Two

1 Interview with John Hersey, April 1991.

2 Interview with Webster Street. On tape in the Steinbeck Collection of the Stanford University archives. Hereafter Steinbeck/Stanford.

3 ibid.

4 Hersey interview.

5 Interview with Burgess Meredith, 12 October 1992.

6 Street interview.

7 'Mice, Men, and Mr Steinbeck', *The New York Times*, 5 December 1937. Also in Benson, op. cit., p. 364.

8 According to George Mors.

9 Benson, pp. 44–5.

10 Street interview.

11 Meredith interview.

12 From an interview with Robert van Gelder in *Cosmopolitan* (April 1947), reprinted in *Conversations with John Steinbeck*, ed. Thomas Fensch (Jackson: University of Mississippi Press, 1988), p. 46. Hereafter Fensch.

13 Interview with Carlton Sheffield, on tape in Steinbeck/Stanford.

14 Interview with Edward Myers, 12 August 1992.

15 *LL*, p. 8

16 Edith Ronald Mirrielees, *The Story Writer* (Boston: Little, Brown, 1939), p. 4.
17 Interview with Edward Markham, August 1992. He was a student under Professor Mirrielees at Bread Loaf Graduate School of English.
18 *LL*, p. 8.
19 Edmund Wilson, 'The Californians: Storm and Steinbeck', *The New Republic*, 9 December 1940, pp. 785–7.
20 Benson, p. 55.
21 Quoted by Benson, p. 67.
22 Unpublished letter of Sam Waterson to Frederick Barnett, 12 June 1958, courtesy of Ruth Barnett.
23 *LL*, p. 8.
24 Interview on tape in Steinbeck/Stanford.
25 Ainsworth interview.
26 Like many of Steinbeck's early stories, it is preserved at Stanford University in the Steinbeck Collection of the Green Library.
27 Undated, unpublished letter, Steinbeck/Stanford.

Chapter Three

1 Interview with the author, 22 August 1988.
2 Street interview, Steinbeck/Stanford.
3 This trip is described by Steinbeck in a piece he wrote for *The New York Times Magazine* on 1 February 1953, 'The Making of a New Yorker'.
4 Interview with Robert Wallsten, 9 February 1993.
5 *LL*, p. 9.
6 Steinbeck/Stanford: unpublished letter to Katherine Beswick, 27 February 1928.
7 Ainsworth interview.
8 *LL*, p. 9.
9 Ainsworth interview.
10 ibid.
11 Henry David Thoreau, *Walden* (New York: Norton, 1951), pp. 148–9.
12 Ainsworth interview.
13 Boodin, *Cosmic Evolution*, pp. 73–4.
14 Hersey interview.
15 Steinback/Stanford: unpublished letter to Katherine Beswick, 24 March 1928.

16 Steinbeck/Stanford: unpublished letter to Bob Cathcart, early April 1928.
17 Steinbeck/Stanford: Excerpts from unpublished letters to Katherine Beswick, 1927–8.
18 Steinbeck/Stanford: unpublished letter to Bob Cathcart, 14 April 1928.
19 Ainsworth interview.
20 Benson, op. cit., p. 111.
21 Steinbeck/Stanford: unpublished letter to Dook Sheffield, 28 February 1928.
22 Steinbeck/Stanford: unpublished letter to Katherine Beswick, 10 March 1928.
23 Steinbeck/Stanford: unpublished letter to Katherine Beswick, 25 February 1928.
24 Steinbeck/Stanford: unpublished letter to Katherine Beswick, March 1928.
25 ibid., April 1928.
26 ibid., May 1928.
27 ibid.
28 Benson, p. 135.
29 Steinbeck/Stanford: unpublished letter to Katherine Beswick, September 1929.

Chapter Four

1 Benson, op. cit., p. 143.
2 Steinbeck/Stanford: unpublished letter to Katherine Beswick, September 1928.
3 ibid., February 1929.
4 Steinbeck/Stanford: unpublished letter to Robert Cathcart, 13 March 1928.
5 LL, p. 18.
6 ibid., p. 15.
7 Quoted by Benson, p. 160.
8 Meredith interview.
9 LL, p. 18.

Chapter Five

1 LL, p. 21.
2 Steinbeck/Stanford: letter to Ted Miller, January 1930. Quoted by Benson, op. cit., p. 168.

3 Interview with Frank Hills, 29 December 1993. Hills was a friend of the Lovejoys.

4 *LL*, p. 20.

5 Steinbeck/Stanford: unpublished letter to Katherine Beswick, March 1930.

6 *LL*, p. 22.

7 ibid., p. 23.

8 ibid., p. 24.

9 ibid., p. 25.

10 ibid., p. 26.

11 Typescripts of the stories are available in the Steinbeck/ Stanford archive.

12 Ainsworth interview.

13 Steinbeck/Stanford: unpublished letter to Katherine Beswick, March 1930.

14 *LL*, p.27.

15 ibid., p. 29.

16 'The Depression: A Primer on the Thirties', *Esquire*, June 1960, p. 86. Quoted by Benson, pp. 177–8.

17 *LL*, p. 30.

18 ibid., p. 5.

19 Interview with Allen Simmons, 22 August 1992.

20 J. S. Haldane, *Mechanism, Life, and Personality* (New York: Dutton, 1923), p. 80.

21 William Emerson Ritter, *The Natural History of Our Conduct* (New York: Harper, 1927), p. 4.

22 Available in typescript in the Steinbeck/Stanford archive. It was written in 1934.

23 John Steinbeck, 'Some Thoughts on Juvenile Delinquency', *Saturday Review*, XXXVII, 28 May 1955, p. 22. See also Astro op. cit., pp.64–8.

Chapter Six

1 *LL*, p. 36.

2 ibid., p. 37.

3 Recalled by Beth Ainsworth and Allen Simmons.

4 Steinbeck/Stanford: unpublished letter to Katherine Beswick, April 1931.

5 *LL*, p. 38.

6 ibid., p. 39.

7 ibid., pp. 42–3.

8 ibid., p. 48.
9 T. S. Eliot, *The Sacred Wood* (London: Methuen, 1920), pp. 52–3.
10 Steinbeck/Stanford: unpublished letter to Katherine Beswick, January 1932.
11 *LL*, p. 53.
12 ibid., p. 55.
13 ibid., p. 61.
14 Steinbeck/Stanford: unpublished letter to Mavis McIntosh, 25 January 1932.
15 Steinbeck/Stanford: unpublished letter to Katherine Beswick, March 1932.
16 All the quotations from Campbell and most of the information about his relationship with the Steinbecks are from Stephen and Robin Larsen, *A Fire in the Mind: The Life of Joseph Campbell* (New York: Doubleday, 1991), pp. 165–210.
17 Larsen, p. 166. Campbell's journal is called 'the Grampus journal' and remains unpublished, although large extracts appear in the Larsens' biography.
18 Steinbeck/Stanford: unpublished letter to Katherine Beswick, April 1932.
19 Benson, op. cit., p. 254.
20 ibid., p. 256.
21 From the author's introduction to a 1929 edition of *Winesburg, Ohio*.
22 Louis Owens, *John Steinbeck's Re-Vision of America* (Athens, GA: University of Georgia Press, 1985), p. 100.
23 See, for example, 'Steinbeck's Cloistered Women' by Charlotte Hadella in *The Steinbeck Question: New Essays in Criticism* (Troy, NY: Whitston, 1993), ed. Donald R. Noble. (Hereafter *SQ*). See also Mimi Reisel Gladstein, *The Indestructible Woman in Faulkner, Hemingway, and Steinbeck* (Ann Arbor, UMI Research, 1986).
24 *LL*, p. 67.
25 These comments are from a ledger that accompanies the manuscript of the novel in the Stanford archive.
26 John Steinbeck, *Journal of a Novel: the 'East of Eden' Letters* (New York: Viking, 1969), entry for 30 March 1951. Hereafter *JN*.
27 *LL*, p. 73.
28 ibid., p. 79.
29 ibid.
30 ibid., pp. 79–80.

31 ibid., p. 84.
32 ibid., p. 88.

Chapter Seven

1 *LL*, p. 76.
2 ibid., p. 88.
3 ibid., p. 90.
4 Simmons interview.
5 David Prindle, 'The Pretexts of Romance', in *SQ*, p. 31.
6 See J. R. LeMaster, 'Mythological Constructs in John
   Steinbeck's *To a God Unknown*', *Forum* (Houston), 9 (Summer,
   1971), pp. 8–11.
7 *LL*, p. 87.
8 Interview with Emma Torville, 12 August 1992.
9 Benson, op cit., p. 286.
10 *LL*, p. 91.
11 ibid., p. 97.
12 Unpublished journal entry for June 1934, which accompanies
   manuscript of *The Long Valley*, courtesy of San Jose State
   University Library.
13 Steinbeck/Stanford: unpublished letter to Webster Street,
   August 1934.
14 The story of the relationships between Steinbeck and Covici is
   told in detail by Thomas Fensch in *Steinbeck and Covici: The
   Story of a Friendship* (Middlebury: Paul S. Erikkson, VT, 1979).
15 *LL*, pp. 98–101.
16 Steinbeck/Stanford: unpublished letter to Mavis McIntosh, 2
   April 1935.
17 *LL*, p. 107.
18 ibid., p. 110.
19 Sylvia J. Cook, 'Steinbeck's Poor in Prosperity and Adversity',
   in *SQ*, pp. 140–1. For another dimension, see Robert E.
   Mosberger, 'Steinbeck's Happy Hookers', *Steinbeck Quarterly*,
   15 (Summer–Fall, 1976), pp. 101–15.
20 *LL*, p. 117.
21 ibid., p. 119.

Chapter Eight

1 Maxwell Geismar, *Writers in Crisis: The American Novel Between
   Two Wars* (Boston: Houghton Mifflin, 1942), p. 250.

2 Mary Ann McCarthy, 'Minority Report', *The Nation* (March, 1936), pp. 236–7.
3 Willard Stevens interview, September 1992.
4 Fensch, p. 62.
5 Julian N. Hartt, *The Lost Image of Man* (Baton Rouge: LSU Press, 1964), pp. 74–6.
6 For a particularly useful discussion of the politics of *In Dubious Battle*, see John H. Timmerman, *John Steinbeck's Fiction* (Norman: University of Oklahoma Press, 1986); see also Howard Levant, *The Novels of John Steinbeck: A Critical Study* (Columbia: University of Missouri Press, 1974).
7 *LL*, p. 123.
8 Street interview.
9 Benson, op. cit., p. 327.
10 ibid., p. 330.
11 *LL*, p. 133.
12 F. Scott Fitzgerald, *Correspondence of F. Scott Fitzgerald*, ed. Matthew J. Bruccoli and Margaret M. Duggan (New York: Random House, 1980), p. 612.
13 Carey McWilliams, *Factories in the Field* (Boston: Little, Brown, 1939), p. 305.
14 The articles were reprinted in a pamphlet by Steinbeck, *Their Blood Is Strong* (San Francisco: Simon J. Lubin Society, 1938).
15 David Wyatt, *New Essays on* The Grapes of Wrath (Cambridge: Cambridge University Press, 1990) p. 12.
16 From John Steinbeck's 'Foreword' to an unpublished novel manuscript by Thomas. A. Collins. The piece was eventually published in *Journal of Modern Literature*, April 1976, pp. 211–13.
17 Interview with Eleanor Wheeler, 12 September 1991.
18 Interview with George Sterns, June 1991.
19 ibid.
20 For a detailed account of Steinbeck's interest in the folk songs of the period, see H. R. Stoneback, 'Rough People Are the Best Singers: Woody Guthrie, John Steinbeck, and Folksong', in *SQ*, pp. 143–70.
21 Interview with Edward Kastor, 11 September 1991.
22 Benson, op. cit., p. 347.
23 *LL*, p. 132.
24 Benson, p. 348.
25 *LL*, p. 134.
26 Interview with Judson Gregory, December 1992.

27 Mark Van Doren, 'Wrong Number', *The Nation*, 6 March 1937.
28 Antonia Seixas, 'John Steinbeck and the Non-teleological Bus', in *Steinbeck and His Critics*, edited by E. W. Tedlock Jr and C.V. Wicker (Albuquerque: U. of New Mexico Press, 1957), p. 277.
29 Peter Lisca, *The Wide World of John Steinbeck* (New Brunswick: Rutgers University Press, 1958), pp. 138–9.
30 *LL*, p. 136.
31 ibid., p. 137.

Chapter Nine

1 John Steinbeck, *A Russian Journal* (New York: Viking, 1948), p. 19. Hereafter *RJ*.
2 Interview with Alison Harley, 14 July 1991.
3 Benson, op. cit., p. 360.
4 John Steinbeck, *The Grapes of Wrath* (New York: Viking, 1939), pp. 197–8. Hereafter *GW*.
5 Gregory interview.
6 Stark Young, 'Two from the Novel', *The New Republic* (15 December 1937), p. 170.
7 Meredith interview.
8 *LL*, pp. 144–5.
9 ibid., pp. 152–3.
10 ibid., p. 153.
11 ibid., p. 156.
12 Harley interview.
13 *LL*, pp. 161–2.
14 *Working Days: The Journal of* The Grapes of Wrath, ed. Robert De Mott (New York: Viking, 1988), p. 7. Hereafter *WD*.
15 *WD*, p. 13.
16 Gregory interview.
17 Meredith interview.
18 Unpublished letter from Williams to Steinbeck (23 September 1928) in Rare Book and Manuscript Library, Columbia University.
19 Charlotte Hadella, 'Steinbeck's Cloistered Women', in *SQ*, p. 61.
20 Harley interview.
21 The view is summed up by Mary Rohrberger in *The American Short Story: 1900–1945*, ed. Philip Sterick, (Boston: Twayne, 1984). See also R. S. Hughes *John Steinbeck: A Study of the Short*

Fiction (Boston: Twayne, 1989), an excellent overall guide to the stories.

22 Quoted by F. W. Watt in *Steinbeck* (Edinburgh: Oliver and Boyd, 1962).

Chapter Ten

1 *LL*, pp. 174–5.
2 ibid., p. 177.
3 Astro, op cit., p. 129.
4 Frederick L. Carpenter, 'The Philosophical Joads', *College English*, 2 (January 1941), pp. 324–5.
5 Chester E. Eisinger, 'Jeffersonian Agrarianism in *The Grapes of Wrath*', *University of Kansas City Review*, 14 (Winter 1947), p. 150.
6 For an interesting overview of the conflicting philosophical viewpoints presented in *The Grapes of Wrath*, see Michael G. Barry, 'Degrees of Mediation and Their Political Value in Steinbeck's *The Grapes of Wrath*', *SQ*, pp. 108–24. For a comprehensive guide of recent critical views, see Harold Bloom, ed., *John Steinbeck's* The Grapes of Wrath: *Modern Critical Interpretations* (New York: Chelsea House, 1988).
7 Harley interview.
8 ibid.
9 Larsen, op. cit., p. 211.
10 Interview with Gore Vidal, 3 May 1993.
11 Interview with Janet McCall, 14 December 1992.
12 *LL*, p. 186.
13 Interview with William Irwin, 4 September 1993.
14 *LL*, p. 188.
15 Benson, op. cit., p. 407.
16 Burgess interview.
17 Harley interview.
18 Benson, p. 412.
19 Simmons interview.
20 Harley interview.
21 *LL*, p. 189.
22 ibid., p. 194.
23 Interview with Anthony Quinn, September 1992.
24 Quoted by Martin Staples Shockley in 'The Reception of *The Grapes of Wrath* in Oklahoma', *American Literature*, 15 (May 1944), pp. 351–61. Reprinted in *A Companion to 'The Grapes of*

Wrath', ed. Warren French (New York: Viking, 1963), pp. 117–31.
25 *LL*, p. 203.
26 ibid., p. 202.
27 ibid., p. 195.
28 George Bluestone, *Novels into Films* (Baltimore: Johns Hopkins University Press, 1957), pp. 147–69.
29 From *The Boys in the Back Room*, quoted by Bluestone.
30 *LL*, p. 205.

Chapter Eleven

1 *LL*, p. 193.
2 ibid., p. 196.
3 ibid., p. 199.
4 ibid., p. 201.
5 John Steinbeck, *Log from the 'Sea of Cortez'* (New York: Viking, 1951), p. 2. Hereafter *LOG*.
6 *LOG*, p. 98.
7 ibid., p. 270.
8 Steinbeck/Stanford: unpublished, undated letter to Toby Street, 1940.
9 *LL*, p. 206.
10 Harley interview.
11 *LL*, p. 209.
12 ibid., p. 211.
13 ibid., p. 214.
14 Harley interview.
15 *LL*, p. 227.
16 ibid., pp. 228–9.
17 *LOG*, p. 115.
18 *LL*, p. 232.
19 Interview with Elia Kazan, 12 August 1992.
20 Donald V. Coers, *John Steinbeck as Propagandist: 'The Moon Is Down' Goes to War* (Tuscaloosa: University of Alabama Press, 1991), p. 12.
21 John Steinbeck, 'Reflections on a Lunar Eclipse', *New York Herald Tribune* (6 October 1963).
22 *LL*, p. 238.
23 Coers, op. cit., p. 9.
24 See 'Reflections on a Lunar Eclipse'.

Chapter Twelve

1 *LL*, p. 240.
2 ibid., p. 237.
3 Coers, op. cit., p. 13. Coers reviews the critical reaction to *The Moon Is Down* extensively, and my account is taken mostly from his book.
4 Coers, p. 21.
5 John Steinbeck, 'My Short Novels', *Steinbeck and His Novels*, ed E. W. Tedlock, Jr and C. V. Wicker (Albuquerque: U. of New Mexico Press, 1957), p. 39.
6 Coers, p. 23.
7 *LL*, p. 242.
8 Noted by Robert E. Morsberger, 'Steinbeck's War', in *SQ*, p. 188.
9 Quoted by Benson, op. cit., p. 506.
10 Morsberger, op. cit., p. 190.
11 Lisca, op. cit., pp. 184–5.
12 Morsberger, p. 191.
13 *LL*, p. 250.
14 See Benson's excellent account of the 'blacklisting' of Steinbeck, pp. 511–14.
15 Vidal interview.
16 Interview with Lewis Young, 12 March 1993.
17 *LL*, p. 262.
18 Meredith interview.
19 Benson, p. 541.
20 *LL*, p. 266.
21 Ainsworth and Elaine Steinbeck interviews.
22 Interview with John Hersey, 14 August 1992.
23 *LL*, p. 273.
24 Simmons interview.
25 *LL*, p. 279.
26 Cook, in *SQ*.
27 See Mimi Reisel Gladstein, 'Missing Women: The Inexplicable Disparity Between Women in Steinbeck's Life and Those in his Fiction', *SQ*, p. 91.
28 Stanley Alexander, '*Cannery Row*: Steinbeck's Pastoral Poem', *American Literature*, II (1968), pp. 281–95.
29 *LOG*, p. 89.

Chapter Thirteen

1 Fensch, p. 39.
2 Interview with Edna Robertson, August 1991.
3 *LL*, p. 279.
4 ibid., p. 280.
5 ibid., p. 284.
6 Interview with Eileen Wilson, 8 August 1991.
7 *LL*, p. 287.
8 Wilson interview.
9 Interview with Marjorie Benchley, May 1993.
10 Nathaniel Benchley, *Side Street* (New York: Harcourt Brace, 1950), p. 11.
11 Benchley interview.
12 Harley interview.
13 *LL*, p. 295.
14 'Interview with Best-Selling Author: John Steinbeck', in *Cosmopolitan* (April 1947), p. 18.
15 Ainsworth interview.
16 Cf. Robert E. Morsberger, 'Steinbeck's Happy Hookers', in *Steinbeck's Women: Essays in Criticism*, ed. Tetsumaro Hayashi. Steinbeck Monograph Series, No. 9, 1979, pp. 36–48.
17 Meredith interview.
18 Elaine Steinbeck interview.
19 *LL*, p. 301.
20 Meredith interview.

Chapter Fourteen

1 See Roy S. Simmonds, 'Steinbeck's *The Pearl*: Legend, Film, Novel', in *The Short Novels of John Steinbeck*, ed. Jackson J. Benson (Durham: Duke University Press, 1990), p. 173.
2 *LL*, p. 303.
3 ibid., p. 305.
4 ibid., p. 307.
5 ibid.
6 Interview with Ted Munson, 12 August 1992.
7 *LL*, p. 312.
8 Benchley interview.
9 *LL*, pp. 314–15.
10 Kazan interview.
11 Meredith interview.

12 *LL*, p. 319.
13 ibid., p. 321.
14 The independent accounts of people who knew Gwyn and John Steinbeck well seem to match. Meredith, Ainsworth and Benchley all agreed.
15 Harley interview.
16 *LL*, pp. 324–5.
17 ibid., pp. 341–4.
18 ibid., p. 344.
19 ibid., pp. 347–8.
20 Elaine Steinbeck interview, May 1993.
21 *LL*, p. 352.
22 ibid., p. 370.
23 ibid., p. 372.
24 ibid., p. 375.
25 ibid., p. 377.
26 ibid., pp. 380–1.
27 ibid., p. 397.
28 ibid., p. 400.
29 ibid., p. 408.
30 John Ditsky, ' "I'll know It When I Hear It on the Stage": Theatre and Language in Steinbeck's *Burning Bright*', *SQ*, p. 227. See also Ditsky's 'Steinbeck's *Burning Bright*. Homage to Astarte', in *Steinbeck Quarterly* 7, 3–4 (Summer–Fall, 1974), pp. 72–6.
31 Sam Zolotow, '*Burning Bright* Quits Tomorrow', *New York Times*, 27 October, 1950, p. 24.

Chapter Fifteen

1 *LL*, p. 417.
2 *JN*, p. 4.
3 Fensch, p. 146.
4 Fensch, p. 168.
5 Benchley interview.
6 Fensch, p. 151.
7 *LL*, p. 427.
8 ibid., p. 429.
9 ibid., p. 431.
10 ibid., p. 443.
11 Fensch, pp. 184–5.
12 *LL*, pp. 446–7.

13 ibid., p. 450.
14 Fensch, p. 176.
15 *LL*, p. 453.
16 ibid., p. 457.
17 ibid., p. 454.
18 ibid., p. 456.
19 John Timmerman, *John Steinbeck's Fiction: The Aesthetics of the Road Not Taken* (Norman: University of Oklahoma Press, 1986), p. 15. See also Charles L. Etheridge, Jr, 'Changing Attitudes toward Steinbeck's Naturalism and the Changing Reputation of *East of Eden*: a Survey of Criticism since 1974', in *SQ*, pp. 251–9.

Chapter Sixteen

1 *LL*, p. 461.
2 ibid., p. 463.
3 ibid., p. 472.
4 ibid., p. 474.
5 ibid., p. 476.
6 Interview with Graham Greene, 12 August 1989.
7 V. S. Naipaul, *The Overcrowded Barracoon* (London: André Deutsch, 1972), p. 163.
8 Lisca, op. cit., p. 282.
9 *LL*, p. 495.
10 Benson, op. cit., p. 765.
11 *LL*, p. 500.
12 ibid., p. 501.
13 Hersey interview.
14 *LL*, p. 505.
15 ibid., p. 509.
16 ibid., p. 511.
17 ibid., p. 516.
18 Ethan Mordden, *Rodgers and Hammerstein* (New York: Abrams, 1992), p. 174.
19 ibid., p. 173.
20 *LL*, p. 518.

Chapter Seventeen

1 *LL*, p. 519.
2 Interview with John Fearnley, 4 August 1993.

3 *LL*, pp. 524–5.
4 ibid., p. 526.
5 ibid., p. 529.
6 Quoted by Benson, op cit., p. 786.
7 *LL*, p. 533.
8 ibid., p. 535.
9 Interview with Charles Whitaker, 14 September 1992.
10 *LL*, pp. 536–7.
11 Steinbeck/Stanford: unpublished letter to Elizabeth Otis, 18 October 1956.
12 *LL*, p. 541.
13 Ainsworth interview.
14 *LL*, p. 548.
15 ibid., p. 549.
16 ibid., p. 552.
17 ibid., pp. 552–4.
18 Steinbeck/Stanford: unpublished letter to Elizabeth Otis, 16 April 1957.
19 John Steinbeck, *The Short Reign of Pippin IV* (New York: Viking, 1957). All quotations are from this edition.
20 Wallsten interview.
21 John Steinbeck, 'The Trial of Arthur Miller', *Esquire* (June, 1957), p. 86.
22 *LL*, p. 555.
23 Hersey interview.
24 Interview with Alberto Moravia, 14 July 1989.
25 *LL*, p. 557.
26 ibid., pp. 564–5.
27 Hersey interview.
28 *LL*, p. 568.
29 ibid., pp. 568–9.
30 ibid., p. 571.
31 Meredith interview.
32 *LL*, p. 576.
33 ibid., p. 588.
34 Alfred Kazin, 'The Unhappy Man from Unhappy Valley', *The New York Times Book Review* (4 May 1958), 1, p. 29.
35 *LL*, p. 597.
36 ibid., p. 609.
37 ibid., p. 617.
38 ibid., p. 618.
39 ibid., p. 623.

40 ibid., pp. 624–8.
41 ibid., p. 629.
42 ibid., p. 638.

Chapter Eighteen

1 *LL*, p. 656.
2 ibid., pp. 663–4.
3 ibid., p. 664.
4 ibid., pp. 666–7.
5 Hersey interview.
6 *LL*, p. 652.
7 Quoted by Benson, op cit., p. 877.
8 ibid., p. 880.
9 Fearnley interview.
10 John Steinbeck, *Travels with Charley* (New York: Viking, 1962). All quotations from this edition.
11 *LL*, p. 677.
12 ibid., p. 679.
13 ibid., p. 683.
14 ibid., p. 684.
15 ibid., p. 686.
16 Ainsworth interview.
17 Miguel de Cervantes Saavedra, *The Adventures of Don Quixote*, trans J. M. Cohen (Harmondsworth: Penguin Books, 1950), p. 33.
18 *LL*, pp. 702–3.
19 ibid., p. 691.
20 ibid., p. 693.
21 ibid., p. 696.
22 ibid., p. 702.
23 ibid., p. 703.
24 ibid., p. 698.
25 John Steinbeck, *The Winter of Our Discontent* (New York: Viking, 1961). All quotations from this edition.
26 *LL*, p. 709.
27 Interview with Terrence McNally, 20 May 1993.
28 *LL*, p. 717.
29 ibid., p. 719.
30 ibid., p. 724.
31 ibid., pp. 728–9.
32 ibid., pp. 734–50.

33 ibid., p. 740.

Chapter Nineteen

1 Fensch, p. 224.
2 Interview with Tom Guinzburg, 11 August 1993.
3 *LL*, p. 743.
4 ibid., p. 745.
5 ibid., p. 749.
6 ibid., pp. 897–8.
7 ibid., p. 759.
8 Fensch, p. 229.
9 Vidal interview.
10 Fensch, pp. 226–7.
11 *LL*, p. 777.
12 Interview with Edward Albee, August 1993.
13 *LL*, p. 798.
14 ibid., pp. 800–1.
15 McNally interview.
16 *LL*, p. 802.
17 Hersey interview.
18 Benson, op. cit., p. 961.
19 *LL*, p. 803.
20 Relayed to the author in conversation with Seamus Heaney.
21 *LL*, p. 804.
22 Ainsworth interview.
23 *LL*, p. 806.

Chapter Twenty

1 Noam Chomsky, *American Power and the New Mandarins* (New York: Pantheon, 1969), p. 222.
2 Quoted in *The New Republic*, 6 January 1968, p. 29, from an interview with Henry Brandon of the London *Sunday Times*.
3 *LL*, p. 831.
4 ibid., p. 825.
5 Benson, op. cit., p. 977.
6 Richard F. Peterson 'The Mythology of American Life: *America and Americans*', in I. Hayashi, p. 15.
7 *LL*, p. 839.
8 ibid.
9 ibid., pp. 840–1.

Index

Titles of books are to be found under the heading John Steinbeck: writings